BOOK ONE

The Upliftment of Consciousness

Jacqui Gilbert and Bridget Hall

*Channelled communications
from the*
Light Being, OSIRIS
with ISIS and THOTH

Published by

ANCIENT WISDOM
PUBLICATIONS

This book is the collaborative effort of two authors: Jacqui Gilbert and Bridget Hall. Jacqui is the channel for the Light Beings, Osiris, Isis and Thoth. Their channelled communications are transcribed verbatim and discussed in this book. Although none of these great Beings of Light have been heard from for many years, they are now ready to deliver knowledge and information to humanity - in support of our upliftment.

Our understanding about what has happened on Earth as opposed to what was supposed to happen, in terms of humanity's enLightenment, lies at the heart of the success of the new wave of consciousness that is enveloping all people.

It is this expansion of our awareness that is supporting us to get back on track and move forwards towards enLightenment. Almost unbelievably, we learn that we can reach the heights of spirituality whilst remaining physically alive.

This describes the process of Living Ascension which the Light Beings teach us about. We can transcend the lessons of the Wheel of Karma which have dogged our lifetimes for many thousands of years to date.

To this end, we morph ourselves into a state of spiritualised physicality - by expanding our perceptual ability beyond the current 4th dimension of physical reality - to make the 5th dimension of spiritual reality relevant in our physical lives on Earth. The alternative is not even worth considering: that we continue on a lowered resonance Earth, in the 3rd or the 4th dimension, for another long cycle of learning.

Sanat Kumara - symbolises the shifting state of human consciousness, from the 4th dimension of physicality through to the 5th dimension of spirituality - through a wormhole system, in the state of living ascension.

 Infinity - symbolises the never-ending loop of creation, which links us to the highest realms of the Godhead - dimension by dimension - through the structures of our DNA.

 The Djed - an Ancient Egytpian symbol which connects us to Osiris. This symbol links us, in our modern times today, to the time of Ancient Egypt.

 Enki Ptah - the symbol of the creator god-being of Light who came to Earth from the star system of Sirius, via the passing planet Nibiru. The plan for Earth and her inhabitants was, and remains, our progress forwards towards enLightenment.

Enquiries and Information
email: info@ancientwisdom.co.za
Either connect with us through the websites or e-mail us
if you would like to be included on our mailing list which will inform you
of any new publications, courses or products.

Questions arising from the Book Material
www.stargateway.co.za or www.ancientwisdom.co.za
Please email your questions to us through either of the two websites, entitled 'Frequently Asked Questions'. Various FAQs are covered and are regularly updated on the website. New information and channelling sessions with Osiris about different subjects are posted regularly on the website. Many of the questions which plague many people in their daily lives, as well as pertaining to the issues of Living Ascension, are covered in those sessions.

Copyright © Ancient Wisdom Publications cc 2009

The moral right of the authors has been asserted.
All rights reserved. No part of this publication may be reproduced further, stored in a retrieval system, or transmitted in any form or by any means, electronic, mechanical, photocopying, recording, or otherwise be lent, resold, hired out, or otherwise circulated, used or reproduced in any manner whatsoever without written permission from the publisher, except in the case of brief quotations embodied in critical articles or reviews.

The onus is on the purchaser to work in the Light, in honour and respect of the authors' copyright. It is the author's intention that as many people as possible have access to this material for the purposes of spreading knowledge and wisdom. Therefore, all reasonable requests for copying the material will be favourably considered.

Owner - Ancient Wisdom Publications cc
PO Box 781383, Sandton 2146, Gauteng, South Africa
info@ancientwisdom.co.za
ISBN 145152580X

Author's Acknowledgements of the Light Beings

The Light Beings (see Introduction and Definitions for more details) are the main sources of information in this book. They are non-material Beings who exist in the state of Spirit. They deliver their information to us by means of the channelled method. We acknowledge their work with us, in gratitude and in love.

Osiris: Blessings of Great Light

"Greetings to you, Beloved Ones, I come forward on this day, Beloved Ones, to be with you, greetings to you.

"It is as I greet you on this day, Beloved Ones, I wish to bring forward many blessings to yourselves, many blessings of great Light. I wish to connect and communicate with yourselves from the presence of Spirit, in order to understand from the connectivity of the vibrational energy of the dimension in connection of the Godhead, to bring forward the understanding for yourselves in all aspect of growth and learning, in all aspect of development further, in the procedures of the connectivity of the pathway of the living state of ascension."

Author's Acknowledgements of Human Beings

We would like to thank Leann Player, Jenny Grover and Preeta Bhagattjee for donating their time and assistance in proof reading the manuscripts. Their comments and help in this regard were helpful in producing a better end result. Jenny, with assistance from Leann, provided the written transcripts of most of Osiris' communications from the meditations and the Living Ascension classes with the working group, which Jacqui runs at her centre in Johannesburg. As the professional editor, Vincent Pienaar's comments and extensive experience and expertise proved invaluable.

"Aye, know, though hidden in darkness,
your Soul a spark of the true flame, exists.
Be ye One with the greatest of all Lights.
Find at the Source, the End of thy goal."

(The Emerald Tablets of Thoth-The-Atlantean p57, pp2)

Table of Contents

	Page
Introduction	1

Chapter One: EnLightenment   15
- A Broad Overview of the Book
- The Search for Spirituality
- Movement from the 4th to the 5th Dimension
- Osiris: Support During the Dimensional Shift
- The Material World of Fun
- Osiris: The Support of Thoth
- Osiris: The Archangels
- Osiris: The Angelic Presence
- The Light Beings Impart Knowledge
- Osiris: Procedures of enLightenment
- Osirian Teachings
- Ancient Egypt, Atlantis and the Fall
- Osiris: The Ascension Pathway
- Thoth: From Atlantis to Khem
- Hell and enLightenment

Chapter Two: A Different Concept of Spirituality   39
- Introduction to Light Being Communications
- Osiris: Greetings, in Love
- The Godhead as a Collective Consciousness
- Where is Spirit in Religion?
- Fear and Disharmony
- Resonant Frequencies
- Osiris: The Upliftment of Consciousness

Chapter Three: Information from the Light Beings of the Godhead   49
- Introduction
- Channelled Information
- Osiris: Divinity
- Osiris' Opening Dissertation
- Osiris: Introduction

- Osiris: Master Beings Came to Earth Before
- Osiris: Ascended Beings Correct Incorrect Information which Disturbed our Progress
- Osiris: Understanding our Outer-Planetary Beginnings
- Osiris: Guidance in Support of Truth
- Osiris: Ancient Civilisations Existed Prior to Ancient Egyptian Civilisation
- Osiris: Resonate with the Truth and Love from Spirit for Upliftment
- Osiris: Ancient Civilisations - Atlantis and Nuclear Devices
- Osiris: Humanity Has Been Misinformed
- Osiris: No God Judges
- Osiris: The Beings of Light wish to communicate with us
- Osiris: The Pathway of Ascension
- Osiris: Current Global Warming is a Repeat of the Past
- Osiris: Earth Has another Chance not to Repeat the Past
- Osiris: Love Uplifts Consciousness
- Osiris: Many Channelled Messages are Manipulated to Support Old Structures
- Osiris: Without the Mainstay of Religion what do People have Left?
- Channelled Messages may not all be Truth
- Raised Consciousness and Living Ascension
- Osiris: The Connectivity of Light
- Other Planets and their Visitors
- Osiris: Creation of enLightenment within the Heart

Chapter Four: Information from Ancient Sources   81
- The Sumerian Tablets
- Osiris: The Ancient Pathway of Living Ascension
- Why Osiris is using the Channelled Communication Method
- Osiris: Progress towards enLightenment
- Atlantean Influences
- The Mayan Calendar and the Significance of 2012
- Thoth's 2012 Message
- Thoth: 2012 and the Return of Consciousness
- The Build-up to 2012
- Osiris: 2013
- Information for Pro-Active Light Workers
- Midpoint Energies
- Isis' Support
- Isis: Magic of Light

Chapter Five: Time   **111**
- Real Time
- Linear Time
- Osiris: Time
- Eternal Time
- Osiris: Ancient Records - as the Akasha
- Osiris: Accessing Great Knowledge
- Isis: Intention and Time

Chapter Six: The Pathway of Consciousness   **125**
- The River of Consciousness
- Osiris: Soul comes to Earth
- The Universal Balloon
- Osiris: Connecting from the Heart
- The Monad
- The Energy of Soul
- The River of Consciousness Separates
- Osiris: Release Duality
- Osiris: Blessings of Love
- Earth's Dark Heritage
- Osiris: Consciousness and the Physical Form Shift

Chapter Seven: Separation   **157**
- Why did God allow this?
- Osiris: Punishment and Forgiveness
- Osiris: The only Punishment is Separation from the Divine
- Osiris: The Purpose of Separation
- East Separates from West
- Osiris: Tolerance
- God and War
- Osiris: Healing and Divinity
- Choices and Reincarnation
- Osiris: Guidance and Advice for Moving Forwards on the Pathway of Living Ascension
- Manipulators of Consciousness
- Why do we need to Hear from Spirit?
- Osiris: Accessing the 12th Dimension during Meditation
- Grounding Exercises
- Osiris: The Shifted Dimension Pathway
- Osiris: Humanity Questions the Connectivity to the Godhead

Chapter Eight: Our 'Real' World in the 3rd or 4th Dimensions of Reality   191
- Why has Manipulation, Control or Hiding Information Occurred?
- Osiris: Return to the Knowledge of Ancientness
- Living Ascension Clarity
- Osiris: Symbols and Language in the Ancient World
- Osiris: The Osirian Chapel: the Wormhole
- The Divide
- Osiris: The Shift of Consciousness for all
- The Higher Frequency of Living Ascension
- Gateways
- Wormholes
- Osiris: The Heart and Unconditional Love
- Clearing to Tolerate Higher frequencies

Chapter Nine: Outer Planetary Connectivity   211
- Osiris: Energy Centres and Frequency Shifts
- Outer-Planetary Super-Alignments
- Osiris: The Gravitational Pull of Nibiru
- Osiris: 9.9.09 - Opening of the Great Pyramid Gateway (with Thoth, Isis, Sanat Kumara, Horus and Quan Yin)
- Our Personal Great Pyramid
- Osiris: Kaapschehoop
- Osiris: Expansiveness through the spinning Star Tetrahedron
- Osiris: Living Ascension and Balance
- Stargates - Portals of Light Energy
- Osiris: Star Beings
- Using Portals to Shift Karma
- Osiris: The Number 8
- Reclaiming Consciousness
- Unconscious Karma Creation
- Osiris: Manifestation as you Think it
- Osiris: Opening the Gateway

Chapter Ten: The Ancients, High Frequency Light and   255
- Wormholes and Living Ascension
- Light and Matter
- The Merkabah Vehicle of Light
- Osiris: The Pyramid Shape of Light
- Osiris: Vehicle of Light
- Osiris: The Merkabah Vehicle Assists Connectivity to Spirit

- Osiris: The Light Vehicle Expands the Aura
- Merkabah Vehicle Light Protection
- Isis: Protection
- Wormholes and Outer Planetary Light of the Stars
- Osiris: Venus and Sirius Support
- Osiris: The Dogon
- Osiris: Power Point Connection
- Venus and Unconditional Love
- Osiris: Sanat Kumara
- Isis: Logos
- Osiris: Planets and Stars
- The Sun
- Osiris: The Sun and Venus
- Our Pathway of Reintegration with the Light of the Sun

Chapter Eleven: Wormholes 283
- The Creation of Wormholes
- Nothingness
- Osiris: Science, Spirituality and the Large Hadron Collider
- Everlasting Life and High Frequency Vibrations
- Osiris: Humans - Beings of Great Light
- Osiris: I Am
- Everlasting Life
- The Reality of Shifting Dimension
- Osiris: The Central Position of the Age
- Osiris: Many have Shifted Dimension Experiences
- Moving Through the Wormhole
- Osiris: Lucid Dreaming
- Temples of Light
- Osiris: Pillars of Light in the Temple of Karnak
- Egyptian Throwbacks of Power and Control
- Osiris: Akhenaten
- Thoth: Our Return to Light in Peace
- Religion's Ancient Beginnings
- Divine DNA
- Isis: The Hu
- Osiris: Truth is Revealed

Chapter Twelve: Frequency Determines Reality   **331**
- The Illusion of Duality
- Our Twisted Reality
- Osiris: Spiralling Energy
- Awareness, Frequency and Dimensions
- Karma and Frequency Shifts
- Osiris : Karma Release and Joy
- Frequency Adjustments and Dimension Shifts
- Osiris: The Square Root of 1% (of a number) Creates a Consciousness Shift
- Frequency and Evolution
- Osiris: Influential Energy Fields

Chapter Thirteen: Power, Manipulation and Control   **351**
- Confused Realities
- Osiris: Truth and Ability
- Control, Domination and Ascension
- The Importance of Earth's Ascension
- Thoth: Human Consciousness is Vast
- Standing Firm in the Face of Trouble
- Osiris: Disturbance and Shifting this Frequency
- Earth Shifts, Humans Shift
- The Physical Ascension Process
- Osiris: Letting go of Past Issues
- The Playground Shrinks, the Income Stream Dries up
- The New Earth
- The Great Divide

Chapter Fourteen: Issues and Antidotes   **377**
- Multi-National Power and Control
- Osiris: Release of Difficulty
- Osiris: Wesak Beings
- Osiris: Structures Shift
- Osiris: Soul Intention through the Heart
- Bullies and Victims
- Isis: Take Flight
- Osiris: Fearless Compassion
- Osiris: Mount Kailash
- The Lucrative Business of War
- Worship of Gods
- The Wisdom of the Universe is Maintained always

- Discerning Wisdom from Misinformation
- Osiris: No God Judges
- Manipulations Continue
- Osiris: The Frequency of Love Within
- So what happens to those who don't Ascend-in-the-Physical now?
- Dimension Differences
- Continuous Reality
- Osiris: Divine Intelligence and Manifestation
- Osiris: Love and Gratitude from Spirit
- Isis: Do you Continue Forward or do you Return?

Chapter Fifteen: Closing Messages   **413**
- The 11.11.11 Meditation
- Osiris: 11.11.11 Meditation with Isis, Thoth, Sanat Kumara and Quan Yin
- The Closing Communication
- Osiris: Closing Communication from Spirit

Chapter Sixteen: Postcript, Definitions, Bibliography and Recommended Reading   **431**
- Postscript: Earth History in a Nutshell - the Atlantean Era onwards to the Modern Era
- Paragraph Definitions
- Short Definitions - Numerical and Alphabetical
- Books
- CDs
- DVDs
- Websites of Interest

Introduction

Definitions of Terms and Concepts
Although many of the terms and concepts used or discussed in this book are obvious and self-explanatory, it may be helpful to clarify some of them to reduce the possibility of them being misunderstood. This is especially important because many of them may be rather remarkably different to readers who are unaccustomed to what may be termed the obscure or the mysterious. It may therefore be helpful to know where these concepts originate from and how and why it happened that this book came into being. Short paragraph descriptions of these terms and concepts may be found at the end of the book, as well as an indexed glossary of terms.

The Authors and the Channelling Process
Jacqui Gilbert is the only current so-called *trance-channel* for the non-material, Light Being (see explanation of this term on the next page), Osiris, on Earth, although he does 'speak' the wisdom of Divinity (which he refers to as being of the state of consciousness of the Godhead) quietly and unobtrusively through a few authors in the world - including some extensively published ones. Osiris also guides the introduction of other Light Beings to us through Jacqui.

This book deals with the search for the knowledge and wisdom of the ages, but it is unlike any other simply because of the Light Beings who communicate through it. The information is presented by means of two distinctly different delivery systems - through Jacqui and me, Bridget. Jacqui relaxes herself into a deep state of meditation and allows the Light Beings to speak through her. During this channelling process she is effectively unconscious of what is being said by either the Light Beings or by the person talking to them through her, such as myself. In order to be an effective channel for Beings of high frequency Light she has to align her own physical energy system to be within range of the high frequency of Light of the Light Beings. It is because of this developed ability that she is able to be a good conduit for their communications.

I write when I am fully conscious. I am in a very calm meditative, or intuitively receptive, state. This could be described as a method of channel-assisted writing. It often begins with a trigger comment or idea from the Light Beings and develops from there. I attend both private and group channellings with Jacqui in order to communicate directly with the Light Beings. It is this information from the Light Beings which forms the basis of the written work. All direct communications from and with the Light Beings are included in the book verbatim and are not changed in any way. They are recorded exactly as they were delivered. These channelled communications in the book are framed so that they are easily identifiable by the reader.

Jacqui has to ensure she is personally operating at as high a frequency as possible, because it is her human system and the tools of her human body (her brain and her voice), that are used to deliver the communications from the Light Beings. It is for this reason that Jacqui has dedicated her life to working with the shifting of consciousness, both for herself and others, through various methods and courses. These include chakra clearing, meditation and classes, such as living ascension and masculine and feminine energy balancing. Jacqui has consciously been in contact with the Light Beings since childhood. The development of her natural talents into powerful psychic skills has taken a lifetime to perfect and many people around the world have benefited from her knowledge and abilities as a healer and a channel. She works predominantly with the Light Being who is called Osiris and she easily channels his wisdom. On other occasions, Jacqui channels other Light Beings. Osiris assists these processes and ushers in the Light Being, such as Isis or Thoth, who speaks through her.

Jacqui is usually not completely consciously aware that Osiris will introduce another Light Being to speak through her before it happens, but prior to the occurrence she undergoes enormous physical shifts. This is a profound experience for her and it always indicates that she is increasing the frequency of her own vibrations dramatically, for one reason or another. Although she benefits enormously from this process of her own atunements and alignment with the higher frequency vibrations of the Light Beings before they speak through her, it is nevertheless both a highly responsible and difficult task, both physically and emotionally.

Osiris delivered a series of thirty six Living Ascension classes to a working group at Jacqui's centre - The Transformation Development Centre - in Johannesburg, South Africa during 2008. The book covers the basics of that course and the people who attended the classes are the working group who contributed to the questions and answers in many of the communications.

Warning
The contents of this book may produce a shift in the consciousness of the reader. As a result, he or she may experience some unusual feelings or awakenings - whether emotionally, spiritually or physically. These changes of vibration are positive shifts which assist with the expansion of conscious awareness, or what is referred to as the upliftment of consciousness.

The Light Beings and Vibrations
At a microscopic level, the material realms (where humans exist) and non-material realms are distinguished from each other by the speed at which the various particles

they are made of, move. These minute movements of particles are what create the set of vibrations that determine the shape, size and position of a particular object, person or place, realm or dimension. These subtle vibrations, therefore, determine where we are, who we are, what we look like and what we are able to perceive. Our understanding of our world and everything in the Universe is directly related to our own vibrations.

The Light Beings who are mentioned during this book are *non-material* beings in Spirit, or light, form. They do not currently exist as physical beings on the physical Earth, but they are able to communicate with us on Earth by altering the speed of their vibrations. They use a physical channel (Jacqui) to do this so as to be perceived in the physical world.

The material substances of Earth are dense and compact. As such they are perceived by us as solid forms. Earthly substances fall within a specific frequency range. When we speak of the Light Beings as being non-material, this is relative to the dense material nature of our own physical world. The Light Beings have a substance, but it is much lighter than our own - one which we are not physically aware of, because it is of a much higher frequency Light than we can currently perceive. As the name indicates, they are light, high frequency light - more of luminosity than a solidity.

The advantage of these Beings of Light from the higher dimensions guiding us in open communications is that our human intuitions, understandings and physical reality may expand into the greater, Universal context of the material as well as non-material knowledge, wisdom and awareness. The confirmation of personally derived information from these 'outside' sources allows us to work more smartly with intuited, or psychically channelled, knowledge. Although they are in personal contact with a great many people as an inner guiding voice, the Light Beings can assist us still further with direct disclosure of information through a human voice channel. This channelled method of communication with the Light Beings provides us with a greater and faster opportunity for learning than we would otherwise have had.

The Light Beings bring us their information, support and guidance through the highest frequency vibration of all: unconditional love. They have stated their desire to assist us to reconnect to our own higher frequency states of Light. This will help us to more easily follow the Pathway of Return to the Light of the Godhead (God). The state of being of the Godhead is their Home.

Archangels
Those Light Beings who have never incarnated on Earth in a physical body are known to us as Archangels. Some people are fortunate enough to have seen these

wondrous Light Beings. In the long-distant past, the Angels who came down to Earth from the heavens were known as the god-beings of Ancient Egypt. They arrived here from other high frequency planets and star systems to assist with the enLightenment of this planet. They now assist us in the form of the disembodied Spirit Beings, or Light Beings. The Archangels continue to assist their Angelic counterparts from the realms of Spirit when they incarnate on Earth. Likewise, the Archangels are often called in to assist humanity with the processes involved in this work. Most of the major religions recognise the Divine Archangelic presence. The Archangels we work with most often are usually Michael, Gabriel, Raphael, Ariel and Uriel.

Perceiving Light Beings
Unless we are exposed to them through a channel, the only way that we will begin to be able to perceive the non-material Light Beings is by shifting our own vibrations so that this speed is compatible with the vibration speed of the Light Beings. Every single thing we see around us creates vibrations, because all matter in the physical world is made up of various groupings of elements that vibrate when exposed to any form of stimulation, such as touch, sound, electricity, feelings or thought. Therefore, everything has a measurable vibration speed or frequency (i.e. the number of times in a second that a vibration completes a cycle). The speed of the vibrations of the Light Beings is faster than the speed of our own solid, material existence-dictated vibrations. We can increase the speed of our own vibrations to a higher frequency.

Although we do need to raise the speed/frequency at which we vibrate in order to perceive higher frequency states of being, whether of beings or realms, this doesn't happen completely, instantly or too rapidly. Rather, we shift by means of gradual increments of the speed (frequency) at which the solid particles of our human bodies vibrate (move at). The many ways to achieve this are explored throughout the book.

When we begin to communicate with them, it is not necessary for us to be in perfect harmony with the vibrations of the Light Beings, because vibrations are perceived by means of harmonic resonance. This means that as long as our vibrations are within the resonance range of the vibrations of the Light Beings (and theirs with ours) we will be able to perceive them (and they us). When we (and they) do this we (and they) allow ourselves (themselves) to become compatible with their (our) vibrations. They too, are then within our *range*, are able to perceive us and are compatible with our vibrations. This means that beings on either side of the existence divide, or the energy veil which separates the material world from the spiritual world, will be able to perceive communications one way and another.

The Different Light Beings

Although the number of Light Beings who are currently available to work with humanity are innumerable, Osiris, Isis and Thoth are the Light Beings who worked with us so that we could put the information down on paper in the form of this book. As such we acknowledge them for their love and support.

Introduction to the Light Beings
Osiris

This book contains the wisdom teachings of the Light Being who comes to us in the guise of the god-being Osiris. He is also known as Apis-Osiris and as Serapis or Sarapis in Ancient Greece. He is an extension of the consciousness of Enki or Enki Ptah and is one of the Trinity - which is made up of Osiris, Isis and Horus. Although he has lived many different lifetimes on Earth and we could correctly call him by numerous different names, this glorious Light Being currently speaks to us as Osiris. Any research into the name Osiris leads to the ancient name of Apis-Osiris, as well as to the Ancient Egyptian god-being Osiris. The name Enki leads to the Ancient Sumerian texts. The non-material consciousness of this great Light Being has used many different physical bodies over a long time on Earth. He, along with the other Light Beings, when they incarnated on Earth in ancient times, lived for many more years than we consider to be humanly possible - usually 3 600 years. It is this ancient, God-realised consciousness of Divinity that we are communicating with and as such this Light Being teaches the wisdom which truly is the wisdom of the ages. His soul connections and soul consciousness can be traced directly back to the Godhead.

Osiris: Support

"As I work with you on this day, Beloved Ones, through the connectivity of the Godhead to over light and support you on your way forward - in the feeling state of the shift taking place within your beings - I come forward in love from Spirit, Beloved Ones, surround you in the blessings of great Light. Greetings to you.

"It is to support you at this time that the Being of Light works with you over the coming period - it is the assistance that is taking place through the deep understanding within the self."

Although Osiris is a non-material spirit being he has had many incarnations on Earth. During the course of his many lifetimes in physicality, as a god-being, he too was exposed to Earth frequencies and he had to transcend all of the lower frequency Earth Karma he may have picked up over the course of those lifetimes. As such he may also be referred to as an Ascended Master Being, relative to his Earth lives. He is a Light Being who has attained full God-realisation in the Divine, Universal context. As such we are assured of his unconditional love in service to humanity.

As a Light Being Osiris is over-seeing, or 'over lighting' us to use his own terminology, during the shifted dimension processes which he calls living ascension. This is the process of shifting our vibrations to a higher frequency state so that we will be able to perceive the spiritual realm whilst fully human. Relative to this, it is worthwhile reading the following extract from a group discussion. In this Osiris informs us about the purpose of his teachings to humanity at this time - the reintegration of Wholeness. This glorious state of being is achievable regardless of the misinformation we may have been exposed to that contradicts this.

Osiris: What is Living Ascension?

Q: What is the aim of the living ascension process? Is it for us to be able to access our ancient knowledge and then use it in our everyday life?
"It is to bring through the experience of the Wholeness of the self, Beloved One - in the experience of the all knowledge, that has gone before, to the experience of that which is to be at this time and that which you have become, through the experience of the central position of all understanding, of all-knowingness.

"So, it is the ability to shift through the frequency of great Light once more, through the inter-connection of the feeling state of the connectivity to that which is felt as Home, Beloved One, through the expansiveness of a great Light, of the presence of being. Do you see this?

"It is the understanding of the many, many lifetimes, through a continuation of vast and many difficulties, many experiences of being brought forward through ancient knowledge of being misunderstood - bringing forward various aspects of miscommunications. So it is to be felt within, the ability to go forward in your Light, through the pathway of all-knowledge into many experiences in physicality, and through the continuation into Spirit at later period, if it is your choice to go forward into this state. So the ability to bring it forward in the enLightenment and assistance to many, Beloved One.

Q: Are you speaking about the full integration of all consciousness - from all lifetimes as well as from what you refer to as Home?

"It is, Beloved One, as I speak of Home, Beloved Ones, perhaps it is you feel this - you feel the inter-connection of the presence, it is of the Light of the Godhead, the understanding of the expansiveness of the feeling state of inter-connection of the pure Bliss of Beingness."

Isis

Isis is another of the non-material Beings of Light who speaks through Jacqui. She personifies the feminine essence of the Godhead and she teaches us about balancing the masculine and feminine energies from the place of our physical reality in the 4th dimension, so that we may tolerate the higher frequencies of the 5th dimension, spiritual realm. It is the balance of these two, currently opposing energies that will ensure our peaceful sojourn on Earth in a higher frequency state of existence than we currently know - in living ascension. Naturally, this means that humanity will consider more deeply how it is that the male energies have been allowed to become dominant and how we can bring this powerful energy back into balance with the subtle, feminine essence.

Osiris and Isis are two Beings of Light who work together in service to humanity. While Osiris teaches about the living ascension process and introduces the concepts of being centred in the heart, unconditional love and compassion for all, Isis teaches the actual, practical exercises that assist humanity to more easily shift into the spiritualised physical state of living ascension. This is achieved from the basis of unconditional love and with balanced masculine and feminine energies within. These powerful teachings may be considered to be the reintroduction of the feminine Goddess energy into our lives.

Isis is usually introduced by Osiris and it is interesting to note the reverence and love in her voice when she refers to him as, "*Beloved Osiris*." Isis was the consort of Osiris when they lived in physicality during the times of Ancient Egypt and as such we may understand this relationship to mean she is his 'other half', from a soul perspective. She too is an Ascended Master Being of Light who has incarnated on Earth many times in the past and she too is fully God-realised in the Universal sense. Isis taught the ancient arts of healing and manifestation by using what she has termed the, "*Magic of the Light*," in Ancient Egypt. We are highly privileged to be able to work with Isis in the modern day and to learn to re-kindle the ancient arts which utilise the miraculous resonance of Divinity on Earth. The

Goddess Isis is well-known from the period of Ancient Egypt as the Goddess of Love, Healing and Compassion who ran the Mystery School of Light. So powerful were her teachings that she has been variously feared and revered during her time on Earth.

At this time of shifting human consciousness which helps to create an abundance of high frequency vibrations on Earth, Isis is another of the Light Beings who supports us through the changes, with love. She suggests that we can regain the knowledge of the ancient civilisation of Atlantis (more about Atlantis later) and of the high frequency Light of the stars - where the Atlanteans originally came from - in the process of our continued evolution into the higher frequency states of Light. In the following greeting from Isis, what she refers to as "*magic*" may be understood to mean "*miraculous.*" More of Isis' magical teachings will be made available in a future publication.

Isis: Greetings

"I come in love from Spirit, I am Isis. Blessings to you, greetings to you. I wish to connect with you in presence of Divine love.

"We have come from the ancient of days to return to connect in love and, passing through Beloved Osiris, I offer the pathway.

"I come to you in peace and in love of the Divine to surround you, always to bless you, always to be with you. There is magic in the Light. You are returning always in memory. I wish for you to feel the return to the movement of Light, of knowledge of Atlantis, of knowledge of Sirius, knowledge of Venus. Sisters and brothers we Bless you in Spirit, come to surround the Earth with the presence to support and assist passing evolutionary step, to work once more with the Godhead, each of you, as Light Beings."

Thoth

Another of the Light Beings we work with in this book is Thoth, the Ancient Atlantean and subsequently the wisdom scribe and teacher of the Ancient Egyptians. He achieved a great deal regarding the progress of humanity on Earth and he assisted ancient man with many teachings such as that of linear time, the seasons, the equinoxes, the astrological importance of the movements of the heavenly bodies and the concept of everlasting life. Understanding the seasons and the movement of Earth in relation to the Sun is man's starting point in terms of understanding the grander picture of the Cosmos and its cycles. The Mayan Calendar provides a bigger picture of the cycles of Earth. As such it was he who ensured that human beings had systems of time, linear time, that could used to plot the movements of our planet through the Ages - significantly over the period of the last 5 000 years which the Mayan Calendar records.

Thoth was the Pharaoh Akhenaten's architect, Imhotep, as well as King Solomon's temple architect at a different period. This architectural role was an important one to play over the course of mankind's history, because it is during this time as we approach the midpoint of the Age of Aquarius in 2012 that we are best able to make use of most of this sacred geometrical knowledge - on the living ascension pathway towards enLightenment.

In Ancient Atlantean times Thoth was responsible for building the pyramids of Giza, among other things. Aside from its practical uses at the time, the Great Pyramid is an important energy gateway which would assist humanity in the future. This energy gateway, or portal, of the Great Pyramid links directly to what are known of as the energetic time keeping systems know of as the 'time-clocks of Thoth', the year 2012 and the dimensional shift. Knowing that he was the instigating intelligence behind these constructions we can more easily accept that they have an importance beyond our current understanding. Similarly, the energy grids which were created by him in the Lake Titicaca (Peru) area, and Mount Kailash (Tibet), supported by the Pleiadian beings, are a significant. It is significant that Thoth set up various structures on the planet - the Great Pyramid for example - to be in alignment with Orion and to gauge the passing of time according to the Sun's movement - to form days, months and the seasons.

Thoth inscribed enormous amounts of ancient Earth history and other spiritual information onto tablets. Some of these have been found over the course of time and their messages have been deciphered and transcribed for the use of humanity. The much-touted Emerald Tablets of Thoth-the-Atlantean by Dr Doreal is an example of this. Many more tablets of Thoth will be found and a lot more information will then be available about our ancient beginnings and about our spirituality. The information will come forward at such a rapid rate in the not-too-distant future that humanity will not be able to, or want to, ignore it any longer.

Osiris: Introducing Thoth

"As you move into the connection at this time, the presence of being that is Thoth, to come forward. You have the ability to feel, to see the presence of being before you. Being choosing to come into the experience - it is the desire and intent to support all beings on Earth at this time, to move forward into a deeper understanding of that which takes place in the passing forward of a continuation of lifetime through lifetime, the understanding of the ability in holding the position.

"It is in the understanding of the connection through the conscious knowledge of return and holding of memory. So it is, as the being before you, Beloved Ones, as you begin to feel the connectivity of the Ancient Atlantean being, the presence of the energy from this period in lifetime, the understanding to support all to go forward through the connectivities that take place through the silent knowledge within. It is the understanding, that as you begin to connect, the feeling state of the Angelic presence surrounding you."

Thoth is the Light Being from the Godhead who is least commonly communicated with by human beings. He comes from a long way off in the outer-planetary system - from the heart of the Godhead, just as the other Light Beings do - and has agreed to help humanity on Earth at this time of our journey into the Light. To this end he makes himself available for these communications. Thoth's last, modern communications with human beings were communicated a number of years ago. These resulted in a lot of information about the ancient Flower of Life being brought forward.

Aside from years of personal channelling and channelled meditations from Osiris, both Osiris and Isis coached the working group for a period of two years so that the energy and information of Thoth could be tolerated. Isis commented that the previous communications were akin to primary school level, compared to the higher intensity of Thoth's. His intensely interesting communications will be available in their entirety in forthcoming books. These are comprised of information that has never before been released to humanity.

As the ancient scribe and wisdom teacher and one of the Atlantean and Ancient Egyptian god-beings of Light, Thoth has had many incarnations on Earth and may be known to different peoples by various different names. Thoth is most commonly known of as Tehudi, Quetzalcoatl, Nostradamus and Hermes Trismegistus. His popular teachings are published as 'The Emerald Tablets of Thoth the Atlantean' by Dr Doreal.

In answer to a request for a peace message for our planet, we note that Thoth delivered a short, but very encouraging and beautiful communication. This includes the concept of enLightenment right from the beginning of Creation on Earth up until our modern times, the idea of malevolent forces bent on destruction and disruption, which have always been around on Earth to distract humanity from their true purpose, and the transcendence of death through the process of living ascension.

Thoth: Hope for Earth

Q: Could we please have a message for the planet?
"It is always intended to take forward the Earthlings further into the procedure of Light - the continuation that supports. God-beings to serve in this manner, to support the continuation further of experience forward. It does always continue - the Godhead in intention of following forward, to all ends completion of the creation, to continue.

"I wish to bring forward at this time, the understanding the presence of man on the Earth. Many lifetimes of destruction have taken place - desire to end, in many respects, all that is brought forward in love and support. You may communicate with all beings to know there is pathway forward, paved with Light. It is only idea to feel this. To feel gratitude for all that is here, for it is the majesty and beauty of Earth to behold, in continuation life ever after. In experience of the transcendence of death to life, you have an ability of the Godhead Presence to live without end. You are blessed on this day, Beloved Beings of Light. You are blessed."

If we bear in mind that Osiris has stated that Thoth comes through with communications to us from, "*Far out in the outer-planetary field,*" we can more easily appreciate that it is for this reason that the earlier communications with him are fairly short. Osiris has mentioned to us that although many people are of the belief that Thoth has removed himself so far into the outer-planetary realms so as to not be available to communicate with humanity any more, this is clearly not true - as is evidenced by his communications with us. Nevertheless, it is not an easy task for this Light Being to communicate with humanity through Jacqui in the physical dimension, because aligning his high resonance energy field with her physical energies is extremely taxing on both of them. Thoth has stated that he will be available until 2012 to work with humanity. After this he will return to the state of the Whole, in Spirit form.

Thoth is generally considered to be one of the more elusive Light Beings for human beings to be in contact with, but we have found him to be easy to communicate with in question and answer sessions and extremely helpful too. He provides a different perspective on the same subjects of spirituality that we discuss with Osiris.

Chapter Outlines
Some unusual and even startling concepts are discussed in this book and consequently many questions crop up in the mind of the reader during the course of reading. These questions are probably answered later on in the book as the concepts develop. Therefore, it is best to read the chapters in sequence, in order to follow the logical progression of the information. It is recommended that the reader browses through the bulleted points of each chapter which are detailed in the 'Contents' prior to beginning to read the book. This provides a general idea of the information which is contained in the book.

Channelled Meditations
Osiris' weekly channelled meditations and their transcriptions (most of which can be downloaded from the website www.stargateway.co.za) not only support the living ascension procedures with their high frequency sound vibrations, but they also impart vast amounts of knowledge to us. It is not always easy to understand the terminology or the accent of the Light Beings when the meditations are first listened to, but your ears quickly become attuned. Don't be perturbed if there is a word or the name of a new Light Being or place in the transcription - or even if a word is missing. New words are often explained throughout the text. It is not necessary to understand everything the Light Beings speak about, because the vibrations of the words create positive shifts within us. This results in the awakening of our consciousness which, in turn, opens up our memory banks so that, ultimately, we may remember everything. The transcriptions are an invaluable tool to use for reading along with the mp3 sound, and assist with better integration of what has been said.

Aside from these transcriptions of the meditations, we include excerpts from the original Living Ascension classes which spanned over the course of a year and a half. The full set of Living Ascension classes from Osiris will be published in forthcoming books.

Aside from helping us to visualise exactly what it is we are going through in the living ascension processes, and to help us become vibrationally attuned to higher frequencies of Light, each meditation which Osiris leads us through has a lot of information contained within it. This all helps to assist us with the following:
- Accessing more knowledge and information which is generally not easily available from anywhere else.
- Developing a clearer understanding of who we are as humans and as souls - as a form of consciousness.
- Learning about who the Light Beings of Spirit are and their relationship to us.

- Understanding more about the shifts Earth and humanity are undergoing in the lead-up to 2012.

Most people are happy to acknowledge that we need every bit of assistance we can get to help us understand how to move along the Pathway in the direction of the Return Home and achieve states of ever-increasing enLightenment.

Digesting unadulterated truth as it is presented by the Light Beings may not be an easy process. When reading this book we urge you to keep an open mind, not to take offence at anything which is discussed and know that it is not intended by those in Spirit that any one individual, religion, government or institution is criticised over another. The purpose of this book is to assist people to gain a broader and more complete understanding of the Universal Truth of spiritual knowledge and the information which is part of Earth's history. Most of this information has either been hidden from us or has become distorted over time. We are all entitled to have access to this information, in its purity. This assists us to determine our own pathway and to make our choices freely, without any interference.

* * * * * * * * * *

CHAPTER ONE

EnLightenment Begins

*"All through the ages, the light has been hidden.
Awake, O man, and be wise."*

(The Emerald Tablets of Thoth-The-Atlantean p15, pp10)

A Broad Overview of the Book

This book records ancient knowledge and wisdom, in modern language, from non-physical, spiritual Beings of Light who work with humanity for the purposes of upliftment. The unusual information it contains will give the reader a completely different angle for understanding the purpose and origin of life on Earth, because it expounds on relatively unknown concepts of spirituality which span thousands of centuries. It was intended that these concepts would stay current and widely available in order to correctly shape our modern understanding of the Universe, but too many distortions of the original truth over time have resulted in much of the purity of the information being lost to the general population.

The book hints at extensive depths of knowledge which could help us to unlock the keys which will take us back to the understanding of events at the very beginning of all life on Earth and of the Cosmos - if we allow this. In the book we discuss the reasons for our existence here on Earth and this supersedes any reason or justification that a religious institution, a scientific theory, a philosophical postulate, a government organisation or a financial establishment has taught us to date.

The Search for Spirituality

Many people search on the fringes of conventional belief systems in order to expand their spiritual knowledge and wisdom. Behind this seeking is always the desire for a stronger and more direct route to what we call God, or Divine Source. Generally, this book refers to Divine Source, or God, as the state of Being of the consciousness of the Godhead, the collective state of Bliss, or the state of Oneness. Whatever this God-being or God-state is understood or named as by different cultures, religions or peoples, the search for Bliss by each individual amounts to the same thing: we are all seeking enLightenment which amounts to the re-integration with Oneness within that Bliss-state we call Heaven, or Nirvana.

One way or another, we hunt not just for more meaning in our own personal lives, but for the meaning of life here on Earth - individually and as the collective group of humanity. There *is* a reason for this life and that meaning has been written about, preached about, set forth and hinted at, ever since man has been on Earth. Since time immemorial, governments and social institutions on Earth that offer spiritual teachings have gone to war to ensure that the power base of their own theories and structures are upheld. The main aim behind these ideological-based wars is to control humanity. In this manner more and more believers have been hustled into the fold and riches gathered to maintain the system. Divine Truth and the pursuit of the genuine spirituality of the Universe have frequently fallen by the wayside in the process.

Ideological-based wars are neither a dead practice of the ancients, nor a mythical fantasy story of by-gone eras. Rather, they are as current as our modern lives. All the wars on Earth which are currently being fought have been brought about by the fanatics of the various religions. These actions amount to intolerance and result in people being killed in the name of God. Any disagreement, including modern war, which is based on the idea of upholding or imposing a belief system may be regarded as religious in one way or another. This is the antithesis of what religion professes to be about: God. This is the case, no matter how disagreements or war are presented in the media, nor which government is involved. Clearly, the stakes of war are high and it is essential to those in power that they protect their ideology at all costs, even if it is based on false pretexts. Human beings pay the price both physically and spiritually on a massive, global scale for the power pursuits of their leaders.

Nevertheless, no matter which story of religion, government or industry we subscribe to, the fact that there are those who are still searching for truth, meaning and enLightenment is a clear indication that we have paid dearly for our lifestyle. We have sacrificed truth and knowledge within ourselves for other external, man-made and blind-faith based belief systems. Until we acknowledge that we have effectively been stripped of our personal power as individuals, we will continue to struggle to fully grasp the significance of life - globally and Universally. It is this meaning which, once known, could truly satisfy us deep within the inner reaches of our being. Until then we are destined to continue to tread the path of seemingly endless incarnations on Earth, leading lives of varying degrees of difficulty in the process and using each other to try and work our way through the chaos.

This is in direct contrast to what was intended for us from the beginning of Creation. We are supposed to be seeking ever-advancing, further enLightenment within a state of far greater Illumination than the state we are currently in. Unfortunately, events in our long-past history on Earth changed humanity's direction on the pathway of enLightenment and we have to find the right direction in order to go forwards again. We find our way on this pathway of truth both by understanding the past and by learning how to negotiate our daily lives from a different perspective.

We are assisted by the Light Beings to go in the direction of the Godhead on the pathway of enLightenment, by virtue of the expanding wisdom and knowledge base of all human beings - in a state of unconditional love.

Movement from the 4th to the 5th Dimension
From our Earthly perspective, the closest dimension in the Cosmos which may be called enLightened is the 5th dimension. We can refer to it as 'enLightened' because it is in the beginning stages of open communication with the state of being of the Godhead. This is where spirituality and physicality can be balanced and united in one experience, as opposed to being apparently separate experiences as we currently understand them to be.

For those searching for spiritual meaning, life in the 3rd or 4th dimensions of physicality that denotes our experience of life on Earth, feels as if it is not linked to the spiritual dimensions of the 5th or higher dimensions of the Godhead. In fact, most people feel disconnected from the spiritual realms. This sense of separation from the higher dimensions is a simple function of our physicality, because we have limited abilities of perception in the 3rd and 4th dimensions.

This human life we live in the 3rd or 4th dimension is marked by the illusionary nature of our existence. This illusion means that we perceive that the polar opposites of duality exist. This duality is made up of the real world where we live and the world of Spirit, which is elsewhere. Learning about the Pathway of Return gives us access to the higher, 5th dimension and enables us to collapse the illusion of duality and perceive higher frequency states. This, in turn, facilitates the possibility of being in open communication with the Godhead. In this manner we speed up our progress into the higher frequency states of the Light of Divinity. This is achieved by expanding our awareness in the upliftment of consciousness. Greater states of awareness allow human beings to develop and take advantage of the opportunity to be physically living a 5th dimension, spiritualised existence on Earth. This is what the state of living ascension is all about.

Currently, because the bulk of both humanity and the Earth have made progress from the lowly levels of the 3rd dimension, we are resident in the 4th dimension of pure physicality. Nevertheless, we still feel separated from the Godhead, because living in the 4th dimension means that the divide between the physical dimensions and the spiritual, 5th dimension is still so vast that we feel our connection to the unconditional love of the Godhead is severed. Experiencing the physical, overly dominant 3rd or 4th dimension consciousness as we do, our lives remain distinctly spiritually unbalanced. Shifting our physical lifetime experiences higher into the *spiritualised* physical reality state of the 5th dimension is the challenge of living ascension.

Generally, the unconscious desire of the soul presence within humanity is to reconnect to the state of being of the Godhead and to communicate within the higher dimensions properly again. But, not many people want to die in the process in order to do this. To this end we seek physical and spiritual balance in our lives and call it the search for meaning. Until we find out how to achieve this state of spiritualised physicality in our human lifetimes we will continue to go around and around on the revolving wheel of reincarnation, or Wheel of Karma, as the Light Beings call it, interminably discontented. As physical human beings, we need to, once again, learn to resonate with the higher frequency states of Bliss. We call this new, balanced, blended experience of life in which neither physicality nor spirituality is sacrificed, living ascension.

> The living ascension process is the natural result of
> increased resonance and expanded awareness, and this awareness
> is a consequence of the upliftment of consciousness.

The reason that our dissatisfaction is virtually guaranteed in any purely physical dimension is very simple: we are looking for both meaning and how to reconnect and communicate with the consciousness of the Godhead predominantly in the wrong place. This is because we are disconnected from Divine Truth. Firstly, we are looking for answers 'out there' in the external world of our lives and secondly, we have been grossly misinformed for centuries by those power mongers who want to maintain their material power base on Earth. As a result of this toxic combination we have drunk many a putrid cup of concocted 'wisdom' and 'knowledge' and swallowed many a bitter pill of pain and suffering. The net result is that we have achieved passage to lifetime after lifetime of seemingly worthless lives along the reincarnation pathway on Earth.

In this visualisation from August 2008, Osiris discusses the impacts of the shifting experience of moving through into the 5th dimension. In it he brings in the supportive healing energy of the Archangel Raphael and of Lord Melchizedek. Whenever there is discussion of the use of symbols in any meditation, Osiris will usually bring through the support of the Light Being, Melchizedek. Osiris suggests we hold our Light (raise our resonance) in order to support ourselves during the processes which are involved in the dimension shift. This maintenance of a high frequency vibration not only ensures that we maintain our life experiences at a high level, but it also helps with the release of negativity that is a necessary part of the transmutation processes of living ascension.

Whenever Osiris mentions the concept of an, "*Ascension seat*," he is referring either to the place on Earth, which extends into the etheric position, where a particular Light Being worked and created an ascension portal when he or she was physically here, or a place in the etheric, just above physical Earth where the Light Beings worked if they did not take on a physical form. These areas coincide with extremely powerful power points on Earth and we can easily make use of their energy by visualising ourselves in those places. Unless he specifically states where this is, Osiris generally expects each person to determine, through the mode of feeling, for him or herself where that place of ascension is for the Light Being. The word, 'Monad,' refers to the greater state of soul, in the higher dimensions. The idea of the Merkabah Vehicle of Light is introduced in this meditation and Osiris gives a good description of what this field of protective Light energy looks like.

Osiris: Support During the Dimensional Shift

"Greetings to you, Beloved Ones, I am Osiris, come forward from Spirit on this day, Beloved Ones, to be with you, greetings to you. It is on this day, Beloved Ones, that I work with you in connectivity with visualisation. I wish to come forward from Spirit with the support and assistance of the Beings of Light that work with you in the connection on this day of the presence of the Lord Melchizedek. It is to connect with the presence of this being to work in the manner to support yourselves in the outer presence of the galactic experience, through the understanding of that which takes place in the physicality at this time, the understanding the connectivity of the being that is the Archangel Raphael. I support you in the bringing forward of the presence of this being.

"In all areas of the procedures taking place, many of yourselves moving forward through the impact of the shift that has taken place, in the connection with Spirit - is moving forward through the pathway of connectivity with the 5th dimensional energy, and therefore through the supportive procedures at this time. It is to hold your Light and connectivity in the moving forward into the connection with the Beings of Light, to hold your presence of great Light, to support yourselves in the moving forward through that which takes place in physicality.

"In many aspect of the releasing experience of many issues, through the relative procedures of the emotional state and the various negativities that come forward at this time and the ability to transcend the experience, to hold the presence of your Divinity within. So it is I support yourselves in this pathway forward. It is, Beloved Ones, for yourselves to begin the formation of the Vehicle of

Light - begin to feel yourselves moving into the connection, it is Merkabah Vehicle. It is time to begin to feel the presence of the pyramid point above your head, above the crown. Begin to feel the experience of the connection below your form, there is an energy field that begins to move beneath you, the completion of Merkabah. Begin to feel the connectivity surrounding you at this time. Begin to feel yourselves moving forward through the expansion, moving forward through consciousness the shifted dimension.

"The experience that you find yourselves moving in and out of at this time - it is in the ability to hold this presence state of being with greater intensity, for greater period of linear time frame, and many aspects many of yourselves moving forward through the feeling state of the impact of connections in many areas of expansion and transformation. So it is to support the presence of your being in the continuation of the holding of your Light - the supportive procedures of connection on this day that I work with you. It is to bring forward, it is from the Light, the understanding of the Monad of that which has been set on Earth at this time - the expansion and transcendence of that which has begun through inception of this intention. And so it is to support the entire planet at this time through the laying down of the energy field of the connectivities of the Monad for the planetary system.

"There is, Beloved Ones, as you feel yourselves letting go, allow yourselves to drift into the connection of Spirit. It is slow and gentle procedure, allowing yourselves to move gently and slowly, connecting with the experience of Spirit. Moving forward through connectivity into the ashram of the presence of my being, it is the Lord Melchizedek, the connection within the ascension seat of this Being of Light - at this time to be supportive through the connectivity of the Godhead, Beloved Ones, as you work through the presence of the Archangel Raphael, to surround you at this time, working with the two Archangel beings in connection to that which you do.

"Moving forward through the pathway of greater Light, of greater Divinity to find yourselves letting go at this time of many areas of the negative states of emotion through the connection of various feeling states of that which comes forward in the form of envy, it comes forward in the form of greed, it comes in the form of jealousy in many areas of living, this nature. So it is the transcendence of the physical self, into the experience of the 5th dimensional presence of moving into the state of Bliss consciousness.

"In many areas of the connection of beings within the environment, the energy fields of connectivities begin to shift - they begin to change as you move forward in the state of Oneness at this time. Into the connectivity of the presence of being, it is to move into the area of the position of ascension seat of this Being of Light, of the Archangel presence - allowing for the coming forward, it is of the Merkabah Vehicle. Begin to feel yourself within this presence. It is the feeling state of the movement beneath Vehicle of Light, shifting raising resonance continuously and, as you move into a connectedness, so it is you begin to feel a presence of great Light.

"You begin to feel yourselves coming forward into communication in all areas to the connectivity at this time, as you come forward into the presence of the being of the over lighting energies of communication of the Godhead at this time. You begin to feel the over lighting presence and, as you move into the Bliss state the shift of consciousness beginning to move throughout your being - allowing yourself gently and easily to communicate in position, it is in the outer field, you begin to feel the communication of the presence of the Archangel Raphael. As you begin to feel the movement taking place, this being beginning to move, surrounding you.

"It is the connection with the etheric - you begin to feel yourself with the ability to almost lay down in position, and so you begin to allow for the etheric form to be lifted and, as you move into the experience - the letting go of consciousness in the state of connectivity with Spirit and the moving forward through dimension - you begin to move into the frequency of sound vibration. Allowing for the experience of connection taking place, including presence as the etheric form is lifted further, as you feel yourself letting go - the outer connectivity of auric field in the expansion - and as it is lifted further, Beloved Ones, allowing yourselves to let go further.

"Allowing yourselves through the experience to feel the healing state of the auric field. As it is expanding outward further and further, it is felt as energy with Light form, drifting, moving, you begin to move into the experience of the seeing of Divine colour. As it blends and drifts into the experience of greater Light - the over lighting presence at this time - begin to feel the drifting movement of the being that is the Archangel Raphael held in support with Melchizedek at this time, the ability to feel the communication taking place through telepathic form, the connectivity at this time of the beings in surroundings that you begin to feel the presence of Seraphim, the raised frequency of Light and Divinity, allowing yourselves to move forward through the clearing procedures taking place in all areas of movement of physicality, of the full expansiveness of the being, the understanding of letting go of many areas of that which come forward, through the transformational procedure through the planetary shift at this time.

"It is supportive of the preparation in moving forward through a continuation in the ascended state of being, to bring forward into the living state, Beloved Ones, that which takes place in communication with the Angelic form at this time. Begin to feel the expansiveness as the energy field begins to lift and move, surrounding you further. It is through the connectivity of the opening of heart further - begin to feel the expansion, moving into the outer field - connection with the energy field that you feel through communication with the Sun - the rays of connectivity of great Light and warmth, you begin to feel yourselves expanding further, the letting go of the feeling state of physicality, moving into the connection out of form, into the etheric.

"As there is felt at this time the presence of the Archangel Raphael to be in position of the upliftment further - as the expanded field of Light moves outward from your being - it is you feel the communication, the connectivity. The Lord Melchizedek at this time to over light your presence as you begin to feel yourself moving into a formation of the greater expansive Vehicle of Light, as it begins to expand further and begins to move into the experience of dimension, of the connectivity of the Archangelic presence, as you move forward in connectivity through the alignment taking place - the ability to feel yourself expanding the presence of greater Light.

"Being to come forward, support for yourselves personally in moving forward through the expansion of the connectivity. It is slow and gentle procedure. It is in the allowing of yourself to move into the experience of connectivity of greater Light - it is step by step continuation, as the Angelic presence begins to expand, bringing forward the presence and greater ability to communicate, allowing yourselves to move into the experience of communication further, the outer field moving into the connection of the frequency of Light.

"As you begin to feel yourself moving into the expansiveness of the understanding of further symbology moving forward through your being, the ability to move into the expansiveness of the understanding of bringing forward into the experience further of consciousness to set the pathway forward, and yourselves having moved forward through procedures of initiation and activation at this time, you have the ability and understanding to move further - into the feeling state of that which has been of intention to bring forward at this time, through the transformation taking place, letting go of all aspects: it is, Beloved Ones, from cellular memory, from Soul memory at this time - of the expansion to take place, allowing for yourselves to feel that which is to be let go of.

"It is without the feeling of form at this time, the ability with great ease to see it, to feel it in the release procedures. And as you do this, Beloved Ones, so it is the bringing forward of the Monadic blueprint to Earth - the experience of the ability to bring it into the experience, the recreation in all areas of your existence, the ability to create pathway through shifted dimensional state. It is at this time that you have the ability to bring forward a Monadic blueprint to the experience of connection to Earth - the entirety of the planet at this time - as you begin to feel the experience: the ability through presence of your being to create great shift amongst all, in the resetting, recreation the movement into the experience for all across the planetary system, to move into the connection of the raised vibrationary state, through the shifted dimension for all at this time.

"As it begins to be felt, the presence of the Archangelic being, the Lord Melchizedek, to over light and support at this time, you begin to feel through the living state of the surrounding energy fields of your being. So you begin to open further - to the communication - the connectivities to bring forward in many areas, the continuation of connection of communication. As you feel the presence at this time, as you feel the opening of greater clarity within your being, the expansion of all areas of the psychic abilities, letting go in all areas of the understanding to allow yourselves to move into the fulfilment of the ability to continue forward far lengthier period in physicality, if it so be the desire to do so, Beloved Ones.

"As you feel the connectivity of your Divinity at this time, the over lighting presence at this time, you begin to feel the opening - it is without form, but there is the understanding of the feeling state of the opening of crown centre, the acknowledgement to receive greater frequency of Light moving through your being. Allowing it to take place - it is in unconditional love to serve you at this time. The Lord Melchizedek is in position to support, communicate, bringing forward through unconditional love of the Godhead at this time: through intention and message be brought forward through Spirit.

"The many beings of Seraphim begin to move in the experience of connection, in celebration, Beloved Ones. Each of yourselves come into the position of the desire to set intention, or to create through various decision, to the pathway to take at this time, through the shifted dimensional state - the ability to recreate in many aspects of your physicality. So it is that you have the ability at this time to see it before you, in the Archangelic presence you have the ability to see it. In it's fulfilment and completion in Spirit, of that which you are at this time of that which you wish to become, to see, Beloved Ones, to feel it.

"To feel the experience of great healing moving throughout the presence of your being through the etheric presence, frequency of Light, the language of Light. As you begin to allow for the experience, the Archangelic being, it is the Archangel Raphael, begins to surround you further. It is almost a feeling state of a gentle return to the connection of physicality within the dimensional experience. It is you are continuously wrapped in the Light of Spirit, with the movement of healing. You begin to feel it in the warmth and communication of Divinity.

"So it is the connection, the feeling state of gentle return as you return into the feeling state of physicality, remaining in the position of the ascension seat of Melchizedek to remain in this position, but to begin to feel the return to physicality in this state of presence, within the Vehicle of Light. And as you do this, so you begin to feel within your being the opening further of energy centre, you begin to feel the experience of an ability to communicate, to see the Light luminescence surrounding you. It is the Archangel being at this time that supports you, the Archangel Raphael, works with you in order to blend and move in a continual and gentle movement into reconnection of physical beingness.

"As you gently move into the physical state of reconnection to your physical form, to feel yourself, there is a gentle and light movement surrounding you - the presence of the Archangel being surrounding you still, communicating as you feel the etheric movement of your field of Light, of your field of vibratory energy, the frequency. Allow yourself to feel the gentle movement of connection, drifting slowly surrounding you, holding yourself in the presence of the

Archangelic beings, Beloved Ones - as you feel yourself as the connectivity as one. Feel it. It flows continuously, surrounding you, the gentle movement.

"As you come to the feeling state of reconnection, begin to feel and to hear within your mind, as you state within your head, Beloved Ones, the connection of your name from soul to the connectivity of Earth, to hear it in the vibration, to sound it. So it is in the return, Beloved Ones, the holding of your Divinity, the continuation of the work to support all in humanity to take place through the living state of ascension - it is in this state of being that I support you, Beloved Ones, at this time, as you feel yourself connect with the Angelic presence."

The Material World of Fun
We are absolute masters at the art of material, Earthly living. This is evidenced by our quest for and learning of extensive course material which teach the tricks of acquiring the self-worth symbols of material wealth - and yet we flounder in the shallow waters of the real meaning of life. It is no wonder we cannot fathom what the true purpose of life is. Some of us haven't consciously identified the fact that we do have this lack within and just continue the material seeking-and-gathering of goods - like frantic squirrels preparing for winter.

This purely materialistic behaviour usually continues until we collide with something in our pathway. We call this a crisis. We are then faced with the problem that even when we are in dire need of guidance and meaning we no longer know how to fill our need, or how to easily resolve the crisis. The reason for this is very simple: we have lost the understanding of our connection to the infinite knowledge and wisdom which amounts to the 'secrets' of the Universe - the secrets of which, not coincidentally, we each hold naturally within ourselves. We have become so blind that the access route to our own Divine Intelligence is 'lost' to us to the extent that we don't realise that it is safely and *permanently* embedded in our own computer-like files within the core of our beings - our physical DNA. We don't realise this because we are no longer in sympathy with ourselves, *within* ourselves. We no longer consciously resonate with enough of the Light within us to know that the information is there within our reach, nor do we consciously remember how to work in harmony with it.

In order to assist us with reclaiming and retaining the memory of our ancient knowledge, reconnecting to unconditional love and allowing ourselves to connect the issues we keep alive in our heads to the centred place of non-judgement in the heart, Osiris led a powerful visualisation in September 2008. The portion below is an excerpt from that meditation.

In this meditation Osiris mentions the Ancient Atlantean, Thoth, as a Being of Light who assists us with the recovery of our memories. Thoth is an ancient keeper of knowledge and he is thus well-positioned to support us in our quest for the return of our memories.

Osiris: The Support of Thoth

"It is to support you at this time that the Being of Light that works with you over the coming period - it is the assistance that is taking place through the deep understanding within the self.

"It is through the experience at this time you have the ability to connect from the heart. It is the understanding of the great importance of the feeling state within. The acknowledgement of moving forward in all areas of physicality from the perspective of unconditional love.

"As you move into the connection at this time - the presence of being that is Thoth, to come forward. You have the ability to feel, to see the presence of being before you: being choosing to come into the experience - it is the desire and intent to support all beings on Earth at this time, to move forward into a deeper understanding of that which takes place in the passing forward of a continuation of lifetime through lifetime.

"The understanding of the ability in holding the position. It is in the understanding of the connection through the conscious knowledge of return and holding of memory. So it is, as the being before you, Beloved Ones, as you begin to feel the connectivity of the ancient Atlantean being, the presence of the energy from this period in lifetime, the understanding to support all to go forward through the connectivities that take place through the silent knowledge within. It is the understanding, that as you begin to connect, the feeling state of the Angelic presence surrounding you.

"And as you connect with being before you, it is the ability to feel the presence of all that is offered to you through the experience of the carrying forward of ancient knowledge, as you begin to feel it in the heart centre, as you work with the positioning of understanding, so it is you have an ability, at this time, to go forward into all experience from the birthing position within this lifetime. To know and understand - as you come forwards with clarity of mind, with clarity of love, of clarity of experience to follow - to feel yourselves as the clear Being of Light, in unconditional love to come forward.

"And as you find yourself in the position of the feeling state of this presence of being, the understanding of moving forward through lifetime - all the areas of that which has come forward in the word: the word from many the understandings of the beings in the environment, the understandings of parents, of teachers, of sages, of various beings - as they bring forward through the connectivity of your presence, their personal understandings. So it is at this time you have ability, in the experience of connectivity through a dimension, to clear all experience of that which has gone before, into the present state of being - with the ability to bring forward through the connectivity of Thoth at this time, to bring it to the experience the ancient knowledge of your presence.

"It is in the moving forward through the experience of the head, the connectivity of the word of the many of language - in that which is brought forward in the disturbance in the connectivity of the head - so it is, Beloved Ones, that you feel yourselves in the connection of heart.

"To feel the knowledge into the silent state of the presence of stillness. In the presence of unconditional love. It is the silent knowledge to hold within, in the continuation of physicality through lifetime after lifetime - eternal Being of Light, that you are - continuation of the presence of Spirit through intent to go forward in the continuation of movement."

The endless rat-race of this life, to a greater or lesser degree for all people, is the same endless cycle humanity has been repeating for centuries. Until we learn what it all means and how to change things, the chances are that we will take many more long centuries of time-wasting, fruitless searches before we begin our true journey Home. These searches are often felt as empty or futile lives. By reconnecting to the ancient memories by quietly looking within or when in the stillness of a meditation, we more easily see that which we all hold within ourselves.

In the higher frequency states, we become able to develop the ability to continue living with this conscious knowledge lifetime after lifetime, without the loss of memory between lifetimes. Once in the state of living ascension on Earth we are able to choose to continue to live physically in the same body, without dying - in a state of perfect agelessness. Or we could choose to 'swop' physical bodies rather than continue living endlessly, but come back into our next life with our consciousness (and therefore our memories) fully intact. If we don't want to come back to Earth, we may decide to continue our existence elsewhere in the Universe. Whichever pathway of existence we choose for living ascension, all allow us to live in full open awareness of who we really are. This is the constant consciousness of everlasting life. The idea of on-going conscious awareness, or of an everlasting life, no matter where that may be, is an important aspect of living ascension. Shifting our awareness into the heart, away from the potential disturbance of the 'logical' processes of the head, assists us on our pathway forwards as we journey Home once more, into the Light of Divinity.

Osiris has been guiding us with this information over the course of many meditations, as the following paragraph suggests. Osiris frequently brings in additional help from the Archangel Beings of Light in a visualisation process such as this one. Most often mentioned are the Archangels, Michael (the protector angel), Raphael (the healing angel), Gabriel (the communication angel) and Uriel (the inter-dimensional communication angel). Although all the Archangels do all things, those mentioned are their most well-known qualities.

Osiris: The Archangels

Q: To describe the Archangels, is Raphael the healing Angel?
"It is, Beloved One."

Q: And is Michael the protector Angel?
"It is in this manner, the protection and guidance from Spirit in all manner. Each Archangel Being is in service to the Godhead, it is in whichever direction it is required, Beloved One. Many beings, but if it is your desire and your intent is to bring forward the connection, from the presence of Being that is in state of illness, so it is to request the presence of the Archangel Raphael, Beloved One.

Q: When would one request the presence of Archangel Michael?
"Understanding there are many, many beings with the desire to communicate with this Being through all occasion, Beloved One. It is the most known Being."

Q: Does Gabriel work with communication?
"It is in connectivity, to support in connecting from one position to another; to be supportive in connecting with other Beings from soul perspective in many respect of this, so it is to bring forward communication."

Q: So Gabriel supports communication between the physical and spiritual worlds as well?
"It is also, Beloved One."

Q: As well as between human beings?
"It is, Beloved One. It is also to understand this Being is coming forward to over light and protect in many different manner. It is Being called upon not only through the religious aspects - although it is many beings from this perspective to call on this Being - it is in general terms. It is the Archangel Michael that is called upon far more, Beloved One."

Q: And the Archangel Uriel?
"Beloved One, it is in similarity the communications to come forward. Understanding this Being has great abilities in bringing forward the supportive energy, in many respect, to physicality."

Q: Especially support in times of emotional distress, or any kind of distress?
"It is, Beloved One."

Q: Are these the four main Archangels, or is it incorrect to even understanding it like that?
"Beloved One, it is most known Beings, as it is there is great ability to call upon any Beings that you choose to connect with. It is the known Beings that come forward, understanding there is the possibility, from the communication, if it is your desire to call upon the Archangel Michael, so it is the possibility of any one Being to come forward in the Angelic Realm, to communicate and assist with this."

Osiris further assures us of the over lighting benefit of the Angelic presence, in connection to the Godhead.

Osiris: The Angelic Presence

"Presence of the Angelics to surround you at this time, and allow yourselves to move through the blending of connectivity with the Beings of Light supporting in bringing forward the silent knowledge as you feel it, expanding the being, expanding the consciousness to bring forward at all times - be there desire to return into physicality once more - to hold all knowledge, to not ever let go through the understanding of lifetime continuous. Holding of agelessness - in the presence of the silent state of connection of the over lighting presence, at this time, of the Godhead."

The Light Beings Impart Knowledge

In the following passage Osiris acknowledges the joy that is felt from those who are in the state of Spirit, because many people desire to communicate with the Light Beings. This people do in an effort to understand their truth and expand into a state of greater enLightenment. Osiris addressed a large group of people with the following communication and it is clear that this group share a common purpose in moving forward in the living ascension procedures. He hints at the accelerated procedures that, "*Beings of ascension*," go through and that this relates to our own quickening.

Osiris: Procedures of enLightenment

"Greetings to you Beloved Ones I am Osiris, come forward from Spirit on this day Beloved Ones, to be with you, greetings to you. As I communicate with you from Spirit on this day, Beloved Ones, so it is with much joy and celebration - through the communication at this time, you come forward at this position, with the intention of moving forward through procedures of enLightenment, through procedures of ascension. It is always with great joy and celebration, Beloved Ones, to work with beings in physicality, through connectivity of moving into the experience of the expansiveness of their Light.

"It is from this position, Beloved Ones, so it is the understanding that you move into the accelerated procedure. It is perhaps without knowing at this time that you have set moving forward in motion. The connection that is of a period, that is of great support in Spirit, as many beings of ascension move forward into the accelerated procedure at this time, and, therefore, it is through your own presence of being as you begin to communicate in this manner, with all Beings of Light, so it is the continuation of your acceleration also, Beloved Ones.

"It is through this procedure that I work with you at all time, Beloved Ones - to move in the blending and communications, to bring forward many Beings of Light, to assist and communicate with your presence, to allow for the procedure to go forward at all communications, with much support from Spirit at all time, Beloved Ones, through the connectivity of your Light."

Osirian Teachings
Osiris imparts knowledge to us which is based on the original teachings of Osiris, the Ancient Egyptian god-being. Although he had lived on Earth in many guises since before the end of the Atlantean Era, after an extended period of absence he returned to Earth in the Ancient Sumerian Era, which led into Ancient Egyptian Era. All spiritual teachings, whether considered to be pagan or otherwise, were originally based on the Osirian teachings from Ancient Egypt. The so-named Osirian teachings are the spiritual teachings of the Godhead on Earth and we determine this by examining how they teach the principles of unconditional love and compassion for all. Examples of later teachings which were based (some more loosely than others) on the original teachings of Osiris (and of course his consort the Goddess Isis and their son Horus) are the following:
- Those of the Essenes, as taught by John the Baptist.
- The original texts of the Old Testament, which are known of as the Dead Sea Scrolls.
- The written works of the Gnostics, which we know of as the Nag Hammadi Codices.
- The teachings of Hermes Trismegistus, who is Thoth by another name.
- The Jewish mystical teachings of the Kabbalah.
- And the Emerald Tablets, by Thoth, to name but a few.

As time progressed from the Egyptian into the Greco-Roman Eras, Egyptian society was diluted by the presence of invaders from all over Europe and the Middle East. This happened thousands of years after the arrival of Osiris and the other god-beings on Earth. Consequently, much of the wisdom of Osiris was re-written into the various religious texts of the various invaders. The re-writing of information was done partly to maintain a cultural identity, but a lot of the newer texts were designed to serve a political agenda rather than the promotion or teaching of spiritual truth. In spite of this, they will always contain some of the essence of the original spiritual teachings - no matter how many distortions of information evolved in the various efforts to maintain their group-specific 'uniqueness'. We see evidence of this massaging in all of the religious texts modern man works with. Although the older religious texts generally include a lot of the purity of the ancient knowledge, there are too many distortions (some of which emerged during the course of writing and re-writing of the religious doctrines and dogma) and these precepts can no longer be called the complete and genuine truth of the ancient spiritual teachings of the Godhead.

To assess this from a personal perspective we can use a handy yardstick: to what degree is the text based on the principles and practices of unconditional love? Condemnation, vengeance, anger, plagues, war, judgement, punishment and other similar acts which are based on negative emotions can never claim to be a part of the actions, thoughts or feelings of unconditional love. Therefore, we can safely assume any writings which teach or uphold these values cannot be the words or the deeds of the Godhead. They belong to man instead.

In Ancient Egypt, the Osirian teachings were continued with and carried forward by Thoth, the Trinity which comprised of Osiris, the Goddess Isis, and Horus, as well as by the numerous other god-beings from these early days. As such, it is because the Osirian teachings were spread about in an organised manner that they may be regarded as the beginnings of the original, first 'religion' on Earth. It was these already-ancient spiritual teachings which all subsequent religious teachings were based on. This ancient spiritual information teaches the way of the Godhead and it is this which is the Divine Truth of the Universe: constant, loving and available to all. Spiritual truth may be defined as the expression of Divine Intelligence on Earth.

Therefore, by consciously working with high frequency Light energy and the God-realised Light Beings of Spirit while we are here on Earth, we are assured of being able to do what we, as souls, originally intended to do before we came to Earth - fulfil our life purpose and regain our state of enLightenment. As we uplift our consciousness we begin to have a clearer and clearer understanding of what this means and, "*That which takes place in Spirit*," as Osiris has stated.

Ancient Egypt, Atlantis and the Fall
We can trace the history of man and Creation further back than Ancient Egypt. The original teachings which Osiris, Isis, Horus and Thoth brought with them into Egypt were embodied in the wisdom of the Ancient Atlanteans when that society was at its golden peak. These ancestors of the god-beings worked in the Light for the

purposes of the enLightenment of Earth. The Atlantean Era ended about 34 000 years ago and Atlantean society itself was preceded by another vastly more advanced civilisation. Many, many millions of years ago the forefathers of this civilisation were responsible for the creation of all life on Earth. The subject of earlier civilisations on Earth which go back hundreds of thousands of years is so enormous as to require several additional books to discuss - especially considering that our history books generally take the opposing view and state that man (and the invention of the wheel) is no more than a few thousand years old. This is not true.

The Atlanteans were resonating with the frequencies of the 5th dimension and were therefore able to be in direct communication with the state of being of the Godhead - where spiritual consciousness and physicality were blended as one. After hundreds of thousands of years of existence, the end of the enLightened times of the society of Atlantis occurred as a result of a series of calamities. It was these that caused their destruction about 34 000 years ago and the drop in frequency - into the 3rd dimension. At that time both the society and the landmass the Atlanteans inhabited collapsed and disappeared under the water as a result of the poor choices made by that society - god-like Atlantean and human beings alike. Unfortunately, in the process, most of the life on Earth was obliterated too.

The advent of the so-called Aquarian Age that we are within right now, and the looming of the year 2012 as planets and stars play a powerful and influential role in shifting Earth, bring with them the opportunity to recover our 5th dimension life experiences on Earth - for the first time in the 34 000 year post-Atlantean disaster period. This potential recovery to our erstwhile glory happens via the same frequency gateway, or pathway, that we 'fell' through into the 3rd dimension all those years ago. The pathway we are currently on hasn't changed, but our direction on it has. We access the gateway to higher states of consciousness by changing direction. In so doing we walk the Pathway of Return. The 5th dimension, Light-recovery procedure of our next evolutionary step, as human beings, is what is referred to as the living ascension process.

Osiris: The Ascension Pathway

Q: I understand that we are moving along the ascension pathway through the 3rd and 4th dimensions into the 5th?
"It is the understanding, Beloved One, understanding there has been through the movement forward through this state of being, the return to the third dimensional state. It is to understand this shift has already taken place, but it is returned."

Q: What has returned?
"The dimensional shift has returned."

Q: Does this mean we have returned, or are returning, our Earth to the dimension it was in at the time before the Fall of Atlantis?
"It is, Beloved One. You are understanding of this? It is therefore the continuation of this takes place to the return to this position, and from this position it is in place at this time the desire for this being (*Thoth*) to come forward, in support of the planetary system to move forward to that which has been intended by this being."

Q: And the return to the position we were in prior to the Fall of Atlantis and of Man?
"It is, Beloved One."

Q: Were we living in the ascended state at that time of Atlantis?
"It is so, Beloved One".

Q: In the 5th dimension?
"It is so. It is to understand you have the ability to bring this forward into the living state and the ability to move forward through all procedure that has been intended at this previous period. From this so you do move forward into the acceleration of that which is required, to move at the pace that is required, to come to this position."

Q: We have basically taken a detour for these past few centuries since the Fall of Atlantis and of Man, haven't we?
"It is so, Beloved One. It is to understand it has been of importance to do this for many. It is not been intended. It is for the Beings of Light to support and assist in the procedure of deeper knowledge and understanding to take all other beings forward that are of intention to go forward. There are many, many beings coming forward through communication.

"I communicate at this time through many, many beings that begin to awaken to the desire to communicate further, to bring forward the understanding of their truth. Many begin to feel the connection of the ego state coming forward to bring disturbance in this manner - in the understanding of the feeling state of information coming forward it is not in Light. There is areas of the desire to bring forward disregard of that which takes place, but it is to understand the many, many more beings coming forward, in the communication to follow forward in this Light, that is disregarding this aspect. There is the intention to bring forward communication from my presence."

In the following communication Thoth brought up many interesting subjects, namely:
- The escape from Atlantis by certain Atlanteans in their Light Vehicle at the time of those era-ending disasters which were concurrent with the time of the Great Deluge.
- The return of the god-beings at the time of Ancient Egypt/Khem - in their space ships to the position and the surrounds of the Ancient Atlantean Great Pyramid
- Who it was who assisted the planet to return to a greater state of Light - the god-beings.
- The current opportunity to return to Light.
- And the return of the Light Beings at this present time to help shift consciousness so that Earth experiences can again be that of Light and not of destruction.

Thoth: From Atlantis to Khem

Q: We need some information about the movement forward from Atlantis into Egypt?
"There is the passing, as there has come forward the vast body of water. They have moved through space, through time - through Vehicle of Light, that is been of form - to find the presence of position of Pyramid, through the capstone of Light. As has been at this time to re-emerge once more, as physical being.

"The beginnings of return of god presences to be in Ancient Khem - it has been through beginning of return of gods, come forward in their Light to begin further development, to return to position of that which once was. So it continues, come to position once more. We repeat: we do come forward, many at this time, to shift the procedure to repeat once more, the presence of Light - without all destruction and difficulty for all. We move with peace and tranquillity, without the destruction. Through the consciousness that shifts always the creation of the being of humanity to go forward further, as Beings of Light. Blessings, Beloved."

It was because the potential of duality had been established for a long time, that the predominant choices of behaviour by sufficient numbers of Atlanteans could be based on the lower pursuits of physicality. This means that because physical Earth beings concentrated their efforts and attention primarily on material interests and pleasures, they lost the balance between the blended experiences of physicality and spirituality as a result. This may be understood as the loss of the balance between the masculine and feminine energies. Balanced energies are what were required to maintain Earthly resonance with and therefore existence within, the 5th dimension. An over-dominance of masculine energy creates a shift away from spirituality. The poor behaviour of some of the Atlantean great god-beings influenced the behaviour of all other Earthlings, including humans, and this ultimately culminated in disaster and catastrophe on Earth. This was despite the best efforts of the Atlanteans of the Light. Caused by the dominant Earth consciousness for the *second* time, the Atlantean Era disasters were of such mammoth proportions that most of Earth's inhabitants were wiped from the face of the planet. The end of the Dinosaur Age was the first major Earth catastrophe in which most conscious, Earth life was obliterated - created because the lowered frequency planet had lost much of its higher frequency protective field and was a good match for low frequency meteorite hits.

This second major Earth catastrophe marked the time of the so-called Fall of Atlantis and of Man and it is what has prolonged the planet's difficult and slow journey back towards higher frequency Light. This had to be so, because the direct result of the massive nuclear explosions was the slowing down of the speed of the vibrations of the entire planetary system until the result was the successive, massive disasters of the Great Deluge, climate change and the pole shift - after which they settled into the lowered resonance field of the dense, 3rd dimension of physicality. As a result, a frequency (or access) gateway developed on the newly stretched-out pathway which linked the 3rd, 4th and the 5th dimensions. This gateway back up to the higher frequency state of the 5th dimension is what is referred to as a wormhole system or consciousness gateway.

The disaster of this fall, down through the dimensions, meant that humanity, newly established in the reality of the 3rd dimension, lost access to open connection and communication to the Light energies of the Godhead in the 5th dimension. We have been struggling to regain this connection ever since.

Hell and enLightenment
Hell is life on Earth in the resonance field where physicality is experienced as apparently separated from spirituality. Whether humanity is in the 3rd or the 4th dimension doesn't make any difference in this respect, as both are divorced from open communication with Divine Source. Separated from our natural spiritual Home, we search and search for our reconnection to God, but not only do we not

know what we are searching for, but we don't even know where to begin looking. Osiris mentioned that this is a common problem amongst the members of humanity.

From a Universal perspective the entire programme on Earth was originally designed to be one of increasing the enLightenment of the planet - right from the very beginning of Creation. To this end, Osiris sometimes gives us some rather disturbing news and on other occasions releases some very bizarre information - and we haven't even touched on the true nature of the Cosmos yet.

No matter what they communicate to us, as Beings of Light from the dimensions of the Godhead, Osiris and the other Light Beings speak with an intimate knowledge of Divine Truth and from the basis of unconditional love. They therefore have absolutely no ulterior motive in talking to us or giving out information. They are great Beings of Light who are normally resident in the state of the Oneness of Being. Their love for us, our own desire to experience Bliss and their desire to share the knowledge of the Universe with us, motivates them to communicate with us. It is this knowledge, based on unconditional love, which will result in the upliftment of our consciousness so that we can ultimately experience, return to and share the state of the Oneness of Being with them and all the other Beings of Light too. This programme of enLightenment makes up the essence of all of their communications of Light to us. Truly humbling information is that our progress at this time on the tiny planet of Earth is important as it positively impacts on the progress of the Light Beings, the Solar System as well as the Universe.

It is important to note that although the Light Beings speak to us from the consciousness of the Oneness of the Godhead, their communications with us have to be done from the 5th dimension realms of resonance. This is because this field of resonance is close enough to our own resonant frequency for us to be within range. It is because of this that we are able to perceive information from that level. As physical human beings we are not able to perceive communications which are beyond our resonance range.

The high resonant frequency of the communications from the Light Beings influences us by virtue of their vibrations. Therefore, as we read their communications we will be positively affected and our consciousness will uplift - regardless of whether or not we grasp the full meaning of what they say. Just as when we read other high frequency writings such as the translations of the Emerald Tablets of Thoth, each subsequent reading subtly changes our consciousness. It is this shift in consciousness that then changes what we are aware of in the text - and so our understanding of the Divinely inspired writings increases with each reading. This is the actual process of the development of consciousness which follows on from exposure to the high frequency vibrations from the channelled communications of the Light Beings.

* * * * * * * * * * *

CHAPTER TWO

A Different Concept of Spirituality

"The key to worlds within thee are found only within. For man is the gateway of mystery and the key that is One within One."

(The Emerald Tablets of Thoth-The-Atlantean p50, pp4)

Introduction to Light Being Communications

The wisdom lies within all of us and many people are ready to receive updated knowledge which will stimulate this wisdom. While this may sound like an excellent idea, most people don't have even the faintest idea of where or how to begin the process of a shift of consciousness which will result in their upliftment. Fortunately, the cause that creates the shift so that this upliftment can take place is a simple one and we can easily start by hearing the unequivocal messages of love from the Light Beings who reside in Spirit. In order to achieve this end and, due to the fact that humanity as a whole is ready and has indicated its desire to shift by its intentions, those in Spirit who work with us have asked for a suitable forum so that they can deliver their knowledge to a broad base within humanity. Osiris' simple greeting demonstrates his love and his intentions to support us on our pathway.

Osiris: Greetings, in Love

"As I work with you on this day, Beloved Ones, through the connectivity of the Godhead to over light and support you on your way forward, in the feeling state of the shift taking place within your beings, I come forward in love from Spirit, Beloved Ones, surround you in the blessings of great Light. Greetings to you."

These valuable and privileged communications from the Light Beings not only have the ability to prove the existence of Spirit to many people, but they allow many people to begin opening up spiritually so they can accept the information which Spirit delivers for our upliftment. As we read the words which are beamed to us from the heavenly realms, we can be assured that our frequency will change as we feel the vibration of love and Light within us, in our bodies and in our hearts. Often however, because we are unaccustomed to feeling true love, the intense feelings which are stimulated within us may initially frighten us - especially if our religious or spiritual belief system is threatened in the process. Mockery, outrage and denial are common defences in these cases. It also often happens that people respond to the loving words of Spirit with floods of tears. This expression of emotion signifies the re-awakening of the heart and its ability to resonate with love. So, rejoice in it. Feel the love. This emotion marks the beginning of the process of raising the vibration speed of the body and the mind to resonate with higher frequencies. It heralds the return to an uplifted state of consciousness.

Once we are secure in the knowledge of the actual existence of Spirit, we are easily able to receive the many messages from the Divine realms - which may be defined as the other dimensions that resonate at higher frequencies of Light than we currently do. We thereby effortlessly access vast repositories of information - information which has been withheld from us, or destroyed, over the centuries. Knowledge was supposed to have been kept and shared with the whole of humanity on Earth throughout the ages, but this has not happened.

The issues around the importance and practices of keeping spiritual knowledge secret have been raised. While it is certainly true to state that knowledge should be 'secret' in as much as it is shared judiciously with those who are ready to accept it and work with it, it need not ever have been hidden, or withheld, from genuine seekers. Within this context 'secret' knowledge may be viewed more along the lines of the earned privilege to learn more and the ability to withstand more high frequency knowledge. This is in direct opposition to the practices of driving knowledge and truth underground, as well as the persecution of people so that they are forced to turn the acts of truth-seeking into clandestine operations.

In order to rectify this situation of the knowledge impoverishment of humanity, the Light Beings, who are sometimes referred to as the Ascended Masters, Angels and the Archangels, work extensively with us to bring forward lost knowledge - fresh and unadulterated. This is done by them personally and physically through the trance-state channellings with Jacqui, and channelled-assisted written information through me, Bridget. They have asked us to put this book together for the express purpose of transcribing these knowledge-disseminating dissertations and discussions with Spirit. There is a lot to learn and a lot of information to catch up on. The Light Beings have said that the release of information will come in the form of channelled sessions over a period of time. During these releases, they will make information available which details humanity's reason for being on the planet Earth, our physical origins, our soul history and beyond in the Universal sense and the whole progression of events which have led us up to the present day. This vast subject matter may require a number of books.

We have been instructed to change not one single word which comes through from Spirit, either in the transcription or the editing process, even though a lot of the information which the Light Beings will release to us will make a lot of people uncomfortable. Divine Truth has a funny way of making us feel ill at ease if we have been hiding from it or even avoiding it by running in the opposite direction.

Learning the truth about anything - no matter what it is - creates more responsibility than before and it is often this that we rail against. This happens when we realise that we can never go backwards after we have developed a new level of awareness in our lives. Once accustomed to the high resonance of Truth though, we quickly become comfortable with this state, integrate it within us and link it to the vibrations of love. In this way we begin to enLighten ourselves, shift our focus, establish a greater sense of well-being and thus uplift our consciousness.

In support of his own channelled information Osiris brings through other Beings of Light to deliver their messages too. Listening to them or reading their words gives us the opportunity to get a different perspective on the subject. For example, Osiris often speaks about knowledge and information from the initiations (or knowledge jumps) and he helps us with healings which assist us through the dimension shifting processes of living ascension, Thoth speaks about everlasting life, which is the end result of living ascension and Isis speaks about magic and love as being the initiating energy of living ascension.

It is the expansion of our consciousness that an initiation, or knowledge and information jump forwards, will support.

As discussed, there are currently three Light Beings whose communications are included in this book, but many more have indicated that they will make themselves known to us later. Some of the forthcoming Light Being attractions are communications from:
- Buddha, who, as the Planetary Logos, is the Being of Light who provides the primary, supportive energy for Earth during this high frequency time we are living within.
- Helios, the Light Being of the Sun consciousness who is invaluable in the support of Earth-cleansing shifts.
- Sanat Kumara, the powerful Light Being who works from both the Venusian and the Cosmic perspective to help Earth and humanity stay their course of enlightenment.
- Melchior, the Light Being whose energy over lights the entire galaxy and therefore backs us up from this perspective.
- And a large number of Light Beings who we know of as the Ancient Sumerian,

Babylonian or Egyptian god-beings such as, Horus, Hathor, Anu, Enki Ptah and Akhenaten.

The Beings of Light in Spirit who are strongly connected to Earth remain energetically involved by virtue of their deep interest and love for humanity. They will continue to work with us until such time as we have all recovered back to the higher frequency dimensions and are able to work within the open consciousness of spiritual awareness. Then we will be truly free.

The Light Beings Osiris, Isis and Thoth have lived many lives in physical incarnations on Earth over a very long period of time and, as such, they have a clear understanding of what it means to be physical - even though they are currently resident, as Spirit Beings, in the sublime state of being of the Godhead. As such, they resonate with frequencies of Light which are so high that most people cannot yet perceive them visually. Both their current high frequency state of being and the fact that they have experienced lifetimes on Earth, assure us of their sympathy and compassion for us as human beings. They are compassionate about the struggles we encounter in our daily lives and the difficulties we face in understanding what it is we have to do to raise our own consciousness in order to develop a heightened level of awareness.

The Godhead as a Collective Consciousness
All Light Beings who 'reside' in the state of being of the Godhead, which is the state of existence which resonates with the vibrations of the frequencies of unconditional love and Light, are a part of the collective consciousness of the Godhead. Naturally, as such they are all what may be referred to as 'God-realised'. To this end, we understand that to speak to one is to speak to all. Nevertheless, as individuals they have appeared in physicality, in a variety of different guises, on Earth, at various times over the ages. When they appear in a dimension of a lower frequency than the Oneness of the Godhead they have to step down their energy in order to 'fit' into the form of that dimension, including the form of a human body. Nevertheless, their consciousness (or soul presence) remains God-realised. As individuals who have represented the Godhead on Earth, they have been tasked with various jobs, all of which have been, in one way or another, for the purposes of the upliftment of the consciousness of humanity.

Although we speak to all of them when we speak to one, it is also true to state that as we get to know and interact with them individually, we can more easily appreciate the different aspects of the Godhead, embodied by these individual beings. It is these portions, or aspects, of the various parts of the total state of being of the Godhead, that each individual Light Being becomes responsible for, in their representation on Earth. It then becomes clear to us that there are a specific range of characteristics, or traits, which we can identify with each of them - with unconditional love over lighting all of them. Therefore, we speak to the Light Beings as individuals and we learn from their individual wisdom, yet all the while we are consciously aware that they are ultimately one and the same consciousness when fully integrated in the state of Oneness. It is this state of Oneness which we are ultimately a part of and it is the realisation of this state of being that we are currently working towards.

As human beings, we are also individuals and it is from this singular state of being that we are able to appreciate the individuality of the Light Beings of the Godhead. Individuality equates to uniqueness. It is difficult for us to understand the concept of the collective Whole which is the collective consciousness of the Godhead, every bit as much as it is difficult for us to understand and truly feel that we, as individual human beings, are also a part of the collective Whole. We feel so separate from all other people, so 'individual'. The upliftment of our consciousness, our shifted awareness, will make this understanding of the collective far clearer as we progress - even while we still remain uniquely individual. It is, after all, the return to Wholeness, to the Oneness of Being which the collective state of the Godhead is, that we aspire to - even if we are not yet fully aware of this.

Where is Spirit in Religion?
For many people the information contained in this book, and in others like it, marks the beginnings of the awakening to the idea, and therefore the shift in conscious awareness, that Spirit does indeed exist. Knowing this and being able to personally experience this simple fact, makes it possible for people to continue their lives with the full knowledge of the existence of Spirit, rather than having to rely on an intangible concept such as faith.

To paraphrase what Osiris has said: "Too many people gather together in religious groupings of one kind or another, whether they were brought up in a particular faith or chose it as an adult, wondering at each assembly where it is that the talked about emotion of spiritual connection actually is. They sit there in these groups of people, questioning the absence of their own emotional communication with Spirit. Sadly, there are many who secretly and quietly ask themselves what the feeling of the spiritual connection is all about and where it is supposed to be. They are all too often scared to ask this out aloud in case they are judged and found to be wanting. They wonder why it is that they are not able to connect with Spirit themselves and furthermore, why it is the case that they even need the assistance of a 'leader' to do this. They ponder the loss of their own uniqueness as an individual, knowing and feeling deep down inside that they are indeed special and were born that way. Somehow they feel they have lost this sense of special-ness in the fray of the consideration of something called 'false pride'.

It is to these thinking people that this book will offer some relief as they realise that Spirit not only exists, but is fully available for immediate, individual communication and reconnection too - for anybody who wants this. This book is an example of a form of that connection to Spirit. While some will enjoy these communications, others will scoff in disbelief, or vehemently attack these dissertations and channelled writings from Spirit. It is these people who will disbelieve the existence of Spirit which comes to them in the format of this book, as well as any other communications from these outer-planetary, Angelic Beings of Light.

In the information-gathering process, before we criticise anything at all, it may serve us to refrain from judging the opposite viewpoint from our own, because either approach is fine as neither compromises the actual existence of Spirit nor the Light and love of the Light Beings who offer themselves in service for the upliftment of the consciousness of humanity. Regardless of how well-guided or how misinformed humanity is, Spirit exists in a state which resonates with high frequencies of Light which we generally do not currently understand, nor have fully developed perceptual access to. Within the realms of the Light Beings, Light equates to Love and Bliss. Humanity faces the perpetual challenge of acting from the basis of love - towards himself, his fellow man and his environment.

Nevertheless, our profoundly egocentric natures as humans means that we may not easily appreciate the fact that whether or not we deem something real or valid has no bearing whatsoever on the existence or validity of that something. And so it is. It is up to each and every single individual human being to decide for themselves what it is they choose to believe and to experience. This is the beauty of free will which underscores individual choice and our subsequent ability to create our own reality. Our personal reality may be understood as nothing more complicated or mysterious than the logical consequences of our choices. There are techniques which can enhance this reality-creation process and which assist with a greater awareness of what it is that we are doing. The important thing to do is to make sure that the choice we make, moment to moment, is as informed a choice as it can possibly be.

Fear and Disharmony
Any feelings of fear and disharmony always stem purely from the lack of love of the self and of others. This is the antithesis to the uplifted state of consciousness which is the state of being of the Godhead. It is to our diminished state of consciousness that these dissertations from Spirit are addressed, so that we can now openly and honestly become consciously aware of where we are spiritually and decide whether or not we want to change our current stance. In the process we will hear some information which has the potential to make us extremely

uncomfortable as we learn about a lot of the manipulations, lies and cover-ups which have distorted the original messages of love from the Beings of the Godhead over the centuries.

Not the least of this potentially upsetting information is hearing the details of our outer-planetary beginnings and the true nature of Divine Source, or God. We will see how the teachings and messages of love which were intended for Earth were misrepresented, misshapen and perverted, how the resultant polar opposites of our split consciousness of the material and spiritual realms moved us into various different directions and how it was ensured that distorted teachings divided, rather than united, mankind. Unknown to us, cleverly tangled in the translations and retelling, a lot of the teachings we rely on today are the misrepresented, warped and coloured versions of the real story.

Seeing the similarities in the two opposing views or stories - the old ideas versus the new information - we may become more confused about the truth than we were before, but this temporary discombobulation needn't stop us from sifting through whatever information has become distorted in order to arrive back at the truth. It is helpful for us to go back to first principles so that we can view the origin of our religions and spiritual teachings. From this we can more easily see the reason for our existence - no matter whether upon Earth or elsewhere in the Universe. The gaps, or missing links, in our knowledge or our history, are the places we should look at first as we gather more knowledge. Any unanswered questions or information that doesn't quite gel as truth, no matter how many texts it appears in or how long it has been there, should be questioned at length.

It is supportive to filter out, both ancient and modern, personal and politically orientated agendas and personalities from the equation of love and Light. When we do this we see that human beings are mostly living in a state of divisive, fear-driven animosity towards each other. This is the deliberate result of the practices of 'Divide and Conquer.' We cannot possibly be proud of these types of relationships that we have with others or imagine that this is part of the Divine plan for human beings. The cornerstone of fear within our societies, especially Western societies, sits uneasily next to, and in stark contrast to, the pure state of unconditional love that we, as souls, originally intended to experience on Earth. We have been misinformed. It is time to correct that.

At this auspicious time on Earth we are supported by the Light Beings so that we can more easily learn about the following:
- What happened at the very beginning of time on Earth.
- How things started to go wrong.
- Who, or what, was responsible for our excursion into the dark.
- How the low resonance states of darkness have been maintained.

- How the Light Beings have been guiding us all throughout the process.
- Who the Light Beings are.
- Where our true Home is.
- The true nature of our souls.
- What and where the different dimensions are.
- How we can shift ourselves into an uplifted state of consciousness which is in keeping with the state of unconditional love.

It is time to learn the language of Light and experience the Bliss of the consciousness of the Godhead - on Earth.

> When we learn the language of Light we see what this means relative to its practical application in our daily lives.

Resonant Frequencies
This book deals primarily with the processes involved in the upliftment of consciousness, which itself may be understood as the change in awareness from one state of thinking to another - from its current state to a higher one. In this book the primary source of the upliftment of consciousness is derived from the high frequency vibrations which emanate from the direct communications from the Light Beings - which are the grey-blocked dissertations. Reading these repeatedly will automatically shift our awareness.

> The higher our consciousness moves upwards,
> the closer it gets to God-realisation, or the state of Bliss Consciousness,
> which is the state of being of the Godhead.

It is this upwards movement of consciousness that is the purpose of all beings everywhere, whether on Earth or any other planets or stars in the Universe, and no matter whether this is consciously understood as such or not. Considering that the 'volume' of the consciousness of the Godhead is ever-expanding, our programme of expanding our own consciousness and seeking more and more Light is never-ending too. As a result therefore, our experience of Bliss is also potentially never-ending and ever-expanding.

Consciousness-expansion may be regarded as the development of more of the finer vibrations of high frequency Light within us. Once vibrating at a higher frequency ourselves we develop the resonance-ability to respond, dimension by dimension, to higher frequencies everywhere else - no matter how minutely the frequencies may sound. These potential, altered-dimension experiences happen simply because when we have raised our resonance we increase the range of our perceptual abilities. In this manner it could be said that like responds to like - within the context of the nature of harmonic resonance. Unconditional love is the vibration which resonates with the highest frequency of all - Divinity. When we habitually resonate with the higher frequencies of love we are unable, or at least very unlikely, to respond to the lower frequencies which are not within this range. In this manner we can begin to literally rule out all experiences in our lives which do not correspond with the resonance of love - they no longer feel right, sound right or look right. We don't even notice them when our resonance is high. This is what Bliss feels like.

Conversely, this is why life on Earth may correctly be termed Hell - a Living Hell. The Light Beings are working with us to show us how to turn this Earthly experience back into one of living ascension, instead of the place of pain, suffering and difficulty which so many people know it as. That process begins with the upliftment of our consciousness.

Osiris: The Upliftment of Consciousness

"The pathway forwards of the upliftment of the procedures taking place within your living state at this time - the upliftment of the shift not only of the consciousness of your own beings, but of the connectivity of all in humanity at this time, Beloved Ones."

If enough people work with raising their resonance to vibrate with the high frequencies of love, more and more of these higher frequencies are created all around us as we interact with each other. Consequently, the entire planet benefits, through the knock-on effect of harmonic resonance, due to our own personal progress in the upliftment of our consciousness. Considering that our bodies may be called mini-Earths in that they are made up of inorganic mineral and organic Earth-stuff, we too are vibrating (and are thus resonating) with Earth frequencies all the time, and vice versa. This understanding of the inter-relationship between the elements of the body of Earth and the elements of the bodies of humanity starts to give us an idea of how we all affect each other, as well as our environment, at the resonance level of our consciousness.

High frequency resonance allows us to make progress
on the pathway, in the direction of Home.

* * * * * * * * * * *

CHAPTER THREE

Information from the Light Beings of the Godhead

"Great Light that fills all the Cosmos, flow thou fully to man. Make of his body a light-torch that shall never be quenched among men."

(The Emerald Tablets of Thoth-the-Atlantean p52, pp3)

Introduction

The discussions with Osiris and the other Beings of Light who are waiting to talk to humanity at this time, courtesy of our invitation to them to do so, cover a multitude of subjects. Wherever possible, references to these related subjects are put within, or close to, the relevant discussion. All questions from the working group who attended the channelling and the answers from the Light Being which follow are placed within grey coloured boxes.

Regardless of whether or not a person reading this book is used to reading channelled information, the information from the Beings of Light is very interesting - some of it is extremely disturbing - and yet other parts are rather amusing. Whatever the information feels like to you, know that Osiris answers questions which are put to him in a direct manner. Sometimes this directness initially appears to be confusing, but the meaning usually reveals itself upon subsequent readings. The ever-evolving understanding of the channellings by the reader is an indication of the vibrational nature of the communications. As our consciousness changes by being exposed to the channelled words, so our perception of their meaning changes too. It is precisely because of this that within the answer itself it is clear there are always multitudinous layers of further information. It is for this reason of our developing and expanding consciousness that Osiris does not verbally give us the 'full story' on each subject - even though he could do so. Nevertheless, regardless of our current understanding, the full story is already contained within the vibrations of the communications. This is true for the communications from all the Light Beings. They will only give us the actual wording relative to the amount of information we can tolerate in terms of the level of our awareness. After this our expanding consciousness reveals the rest. They are privy to wisdom far greater than our own, as well as the mysterious processes involved in expanding human consciousness.

An example of this was when Osiris informed me a while ago that I would make some high frequency medicinal products which would, "*Help humanity.*" When I asked him how to do this and exactly what they are, his answer was, "*It is to begin.*" When I pressed him for more information about how to do this he said, "*It is to do it.*" No wonder Jacqui refers to Osiris as the 'Master of Understatement!' He gave no more information than that, but those words were sufficient to stimulate the development of an expanding consciousness about the subject. Over the course of time my awareness of this knowledge, accessed from deep within me, started to filter through to my conscious mind. Very quickly I understood exactly what I had to do, how to do it and what the end result would be. Putting that understanding into practice, in a laboratory, clarified the processes still further until a clear pathway of action and application developed in my mind. There were a series of 'Eureka' moments which were exciting and illuminating. The results are astounding. This is a simple illustration of how a few simple words which apparently said very little, held such a high vibration that they began the opening of consciousness. It is, therefore, no wonder that the vastly greater volume of the words from the Light Beings which are in this book can potentially produce a powerful result in those who read them.

The development of consciousness occurs in response to the high resonance of the words. The words themselves may be viewed as large buckets filled with vibrations of knowledge. Although we initially view the entire volume of the bucket on one plane, when we delve into the depths more is revealed. Osiris has often told us to read Thoth's translated tablets (various editions of 'The Emerald Tablets of Thoth' are available at book stores, but the recommended one is by Dr Doreal) at least one hundred times in order to experience the benefit of the high frequency vibrations of the words. The information which is contained in the translations of the Emerald Tablets is energetically encoded, just as all the communications from the Light Beings are. Reading the Emerald Tablets for the first time, it is often felt that very little is understood and this may put the reader off so much that it prevents him or her from completing the book. However, subsequent readings reveal that the consciousness must be expanding as so much more is immediately understood. This is an exciting process which is individually experienced. Therefore, it is wise for the reader to always be aware of the strange ability of any channelled communication to change in meaning as it is read. The words impart high frequency vibrations which stimulate meanings within the consciousness of each person who reads them, at the level of that person's progressively developing resonance.

An example of the way in which the Light Beings support us relates to a person who is in the process of working out their personal life lesson. In such cases the person will never be given information about this process in a channelling, other than in very broad terms of support. The reason for this is simple: we are responsible for our own progress and we work through our lessons personally in order to make progress into the higher frequencies of Light - by raising our resonance. This is achieved through our personal choice to expand our awareness. Therefore, the Light Beings can neither interfere in this process, nor circumvent it for us. If they did, this would obviate the need for the human lesson - as created by ourselves personally. The circumstances of our lives reflect our own personal design which we, as soul presence, intend to use to shift our resonance. This provides the incarnate soul with the opportunity for learning, or the release of low frequency vibrations. The details of a life lesson, such as learning not to be influenced by manipulative people, learning not to control others, learning to speak up and communicate effectively or learning compassion and tolerance, are the underlying problems we each have to transcend. These are issues of the negative ego. It is these unresolved issues which cause us to create our Karma and keep us unnecessarily connected to the same people lifetime after lifetime.

As our consciousness changes, we become capable of understanding the written word differently over the course of time and after a few readings of the channelled material. This is why the meaning evolves with each successive reading. It is also why any translation or explanation of a channelled message from anybody else will always feel incomplete. Whatever meanings come to the reader when reading or hearing the channelled communications are valid. Such is the fascinating nature of all communications from the Light Beings of the Godhead. They are truly the Living Word.

This process is all the more understandable when we consider that the standard means of communication for Light Beings is telepathic. True telepathy involves the psychic transmission and receipt of vibrations of Light and Sound. Words and language are therefore the ham-fisted cousin to this pure form of communication. As such our spoken word is hardly satisfactory and concepts are often very difficult for the Beings of Light to clarify when using our less-than-adequate human language. The vibrational nature of the communications aside, although verbal communications are insufficient for the complete clarification of the experiences of Spirit, it is the mode we know and use at the moment.

If, when I ask a question and the Light Being gives what I regard to be a less than satisfactory answer, it usually means that my own level of consciousness is not yet sufficiently developed to receive the information, or that some of the process of uncovering information from within myself is yet to be done. Only after I have struggled through this will the conclusions I have arrived at be added to or enlarged upon by the Light Beings. With this in mind, we may view all communications from the Beings of Light as a work in progress - the work being the expansion and upliftment of our own state of consciousness. When we receive future communications, the Light Beings may expand upon the current information in ways we cannot presently foresee, simply because consciousness is expanding all the time. Therefore, our understanding about current communications will not remain static.

Our current understanding of previous communications could therefore change at any time. This doesn't matter, as any of the communications are perfect as they are for us, right now. At other times, although not able to fully understand what is said initially, communications from the Light Beings often make perfect sense later. This is evidence of the development of human consciousness during the process of working with the Light Beings. This is also why it may be the case for some people that the first reading of this book will yield very little that he or she can resonate with. Subsequent readings may prove different as the shifted consciousness allows more to be revealed. It takes time for our minds to assimilate any new information which resonates with higher frequencies than we do currently, but more especially so when we are exposed to very high frequency information from the Beings of the Godhead. In order to gain more from any channelled communications we need to be patient and trust the process. The vibrations of the book will work subtly with us and in due course we will be astounded with just how much our awareness has changed, how much more we intuitively know and how much more we crave to understand.

So, although it is easy for the Light Beings to be extremely precise with us in their answers they will not interfere with the processes of our own life lessons that we personally set for ourselves. This broad plan was created by us before our soul presence came into the human being when we were born as a human baby. The lessons we set for ourselves when we are in the soul state, prior to birth, are of paramount importance to our progress as human beings and as souls. If the Light Beings gave us too much information, too soon, we would not take personal responsibility for shifting our resonance higher. This basically amounts to the fact that our low frequency vibrations will not shift and we will not have transcended our issues. This would then prolong the continuation of our Karma and the perpetuation of the lower frequency consciousness which dictates the reincarnation cycle on Earth. In this way the Wheel of Karma becomes interminable. The Light Beings will naturally not act in a manner which is counterproductive to our progress.

As our consciousness expands, so too does our ability to communicate with the Light Beings and to understand them. Ultimately, the guidance of the Light Beings becomes unnecessary when we have opened ourselves to the Divine

Intelligence of the Cosmos once more. All knowledge of all things, everywhere, lies within us. The first doorway to that immense Intelligence is unlocked with the key of an uplifted consciousness. The result is ever-increasing resonance with higher frequencies of Light.

The Beings of Light start us off on our awareness-development journey by giving us just enough information to get us moving - sometimes this information is deceptively simple and along the lines of, "*It is to begin.*" The information which is communicated to us for this book covers a broad range of subjects, some of which may appear to be surprising and others downright eccentric. It is very important for us to remember that the reason that we are in the privileged position of hearing or reading these channellings from the Beings of Light is because it is time to work with this information right now. This means that we are personally ready to shift into the state of a higher, uplifted state of consciousness. This is especially the case at this time of the most auspicious outer-planetary alignments with Earth as we move into the central position of the Age of Aquarius, in the year 2012.

We are currently in such a poor state of knowledge that most of us have lost all conscious connection to both the Beings of Light of the Godhead as well as our own Light of Divinity and, consequently, most of the critical information of the bygone Ages. The information we have lost, or which has been hidden from us, amounts to nothing less than us living in a state of almost complete amnesia. It is as if we are now waking up from a long coma. During our long sleep we lived all the while, breathing and metabolising, but we certainly weren't conscious of what was really going on around us. Hence, we have this huge big gap in our conscious memory banks. This is not always such a bad thing, as nobody needs to remember the huge amount of pain and suffering which they might have endured during a previous life - until such time as we are ready to release it. Aside from this handy loss of memory, having no memories to call our own from lifetime to lifetime each time we reincarnate, makes us vulnerable to those who might want to control us, or to those who might want to manipulate us for their own purposes. Incredibly, this manipulation has happened and not only has it happened, but it has been both deliberate and wide-spread - and it continues.

We have been on the receiving end of incessant programmes of information 'spin doctoring'. No matter which era it takes place in, these misinformation programmes are always under the control of those social or political institutions which are in control and which have power - external to us ourselves. This has created the current reality of our societies: that which we call our real world. Most of this reality is based on fear, danger, suffering and strife. None of that pain is part of the intended programme for humanity. The loving Beings of the Godhead had nothing to do with this suffering and they object to it most vociferously. This could be no other way! The Light Beings are beings of love and Light and exist in the state of being of the consciousness of the Godhead - the highest resonance state of the Universe. Bliss naturally excludes anything that is not like itself.

If God is love, as humanity has been correctly taught in all of the religious traditions, then what on Earth is going on? With the help of the loving guidance from the Beings of Light who come to us as representatives from the exalted state of Bliss, we can more easily find out the following:
- Exactly what is going on.
- What has *gone* on.
- How to actively be part of the future of what is going to happen.

The fact that we are now in the unenviable position of not really knowing too much about the truth of our spiritual or physical beginnings on Earth, or our future, will cease to matter. As we hear and adjust to the new information our knowledge gaps will quickly be filled in. The fact that even our true ancestry has not been known to us and has not formed a part of our known history, will very soon no longer be that significant. Armed with truth and loving guidance, we will be Soldiers of Light leading ourselves into the future.

Although the love which the Beings of Light have for us is tangibly communicated through the channelled words, these Beings of the Godhead will not spoon-feed us with knowledge, because we have to personally undergo our own, self-driven programme of enLightenment. If we are going to be able to successfully exist in the higher realms of Spirit, we have to be genuinely ready to do so. Similarly, no matter what his official accreditation may be, a person is not a doctor if he cheated in all of his exams. In practice he will not only be incompetent, but he will feel incompetent too. Therefore, in order to be sufficient unto ourselves at every step of the way on our soul journey onwards towards Bliss, we have to do the work ourselves. The work we do will result in the upliftment of our consciousness. As our awareness uplifts we close the divide between ourselves and the state of consciousness of the Godhead. This programme of enLightenment will continue towards and beyond the time when we will have developed our awareness to the point where we are physically living with an open spiritual consciousness, as human beings, on Earth - if that is what we choose to do.

The fact that we are incredibly fortunate to be able to work with *the* highest level of teachers available to Earth, the Siriuns, plays no small part in our ability to shift ourselves through the process of increased awareness. The Beings of Light of the Godhead celebrate with us in tremendous joy at each success of the upliftment of our consciousness. As we recover our Light we evolve into open communication with the state of being of the Godhead. Considering that the Light Beings are living within this highest state of Bliss - and knowing that they give of themselves selflessly - is sufficient for us to appreciate their great love for us and to ask them to continue to work with us.

Channelled Information
Receiving and processing the information as an intellectual exercise can only really be done on a limited scale, because each person who receives channelled communications from the Light Beings - whether personally or by means of this book - is required to *feel* the information for it to be real to him or her. Such is the personal nature of resonance. The understanding of channelled information is only partially a logical, left-brain exercise. Although, of course, the information that we read in this book has to be received and initially processed by the conscious brain as we know it, the development of an expanded state of consciousness is primarily a deeply personal, creative experience of 'feeling' which happens in a very non-linear, non-left brain way. This becomes the development of an expanded state of consciousness. This is what may be understood to be the mode of the discoveries of some of science's best as their 'Aha!' or 'Eureka!' moments reveal a 'secret' of the Universe.

Trying to intellectually process and grasp everything which is said by the Light Beings will remain an intensely frustrating exercise if the person reading the material is intent only on the academic pathways of understanding. Using human intellect alone is an implicitly unbalanced mode in any process of understanding and, aside from causing frustrations with regard to grasping the full meaning of high frequency communications in this publication, it can also be the source of intense dissatisfaction for all thinking people. This is due to the very nature of its intrinsic imbalance. Although the rational, left-brain intellectual abilities of a human being are a necessary and powerful tool for negotiating life 'out there' as we know it in manifest reality, it is also the very thing of limitation which binds us to a specific version *of* manifest reality. This limitation can prevent us from amplifying our intelligence within the context of our reality. However, we can change this singular limitation to limitlessness if we set the intention to extend our conscious ability in all directions. This will begin the process of expanding awareness which is necessary for discerning true wisdom and developing an extended knowledge base.

In order to appreciate what it may mean to compare left-brain with balanced left-right brain functions we can use the example of a library. For the individual with a powerful human intellect, there is no doubt that reading every single book in all categories from A - Z would be of enormous benefit in gaining more knowledge. However, from an expanded, left *and* right brain perspective, what at first glance was an apparently finite range of books in the library, the brain develops the unusual ability to extend in volume and content. When we negotiate our world using this expanded intelligence which balanced brain functions impart to us, we find that each row of books has layer upon layer behind it, above it and to the side of it. The ceiling is covered with books, as is the floor. As we turn around, suddenly we see more shelves appearing before our eyes - no matter which way we face. Then, as if this isn't enough, each book we start reading expands with more and more pages the more we read. The mind-blowing experience of this huge Universal library (known as the Akasha - that record everything that has every happened, everywhere) is like a magical mystery tour which we usually only see in the movies. Harry Potter has nothing on this!

This creative potential of an expanded consciousness is a wondrous world of endless information and knowledge, and it is available to anybody who wants it. How? Just walk through the gateway of open awareness. Where? Just go within - via the mode of uplifted consciousness, into the wonderful worlds where we are in the beginning stages of being in open communication with the state of being of the Godhead. Follow the high frequencies of Light.

It is the logical, left-brain functions which will allow us to be more learned and apparently cleverer than the next man on Earth, but it is the highly developed right-brain functions which will lead us into the widths and the depths of true, Universal Brilliance. Our human, right-brain functions provide the gateway to the full intelligence, Divine Intelligence, which is contained within the entire Universe. As such, the mysteries of life are easily revealed and questions about why humans can develop psychic talents and what the nature of God is, are easily answered.

The gateway to expanded consciousness lies within each man and woman on Earth. How to access the gateway is really no secret either, although it has been made to appear to be an enigma by those who are intent on power and control on Earth.

Some of the easily accessible ways to find the subtle entrance of the gateway within involve some very simple things:
- Relax.
- Day-dream.
- Mediate.
- Pray.
- Laugh.
- Play.

- Walk on the beach.
- Dig in the garden.
- Sing.
- Dance.
- Chant.
- Listen to music.
- Draw.
- Paint.
- Sculpt.
- Climb mountains.
- Ride a bicycle.
- Laugh.
- Write, and so on, ad infinitum.

Osiris advises that in order to maintain a proper balance within ourselves we should spend as much time in our day relaxing in nature as we do working to earn a living. Happy and peaceful activities are usually in stark contrast to the stressful daily life activities most human beings have become used to. We can access the long-held secret of opening the door to the gateway of consciousness by raising the frequency of our overall vibration higher towards the frequency of Light. We do this by doing, saying and feeling those things which hold a naturally high resonance, beginning with love. Osiris puts this succinctly in the following sentence.

Osiris: Divinity

"As you hold your Divinity at this time, so you hold your energy and Light."

Whenever Osiris uses the words, "*Hold your Light*," we may understand this to mean that he is advising us to keep the speed (frequency) of our vibrations sufficiently high enough so as to emanate Light from ourselves and, therefore, truly qualify as Earthly Light Beings in our own right, rather than to allow our resonance to drop in response to daily stressors, which will reduce our Light and make us feel down.

The list of tools for accessing the gateway to an expanded reality - a reality of a greater level of intelligence than most people ever thought themselves capable of expressing - is as endless as the Universe itself. These are the same tools we use for resonating with higher frequencies. We have these implements at our disposal and using them allows us to go beyond our otherwise frustrating, human intellectual limitations. We could use them wisely instead of getting them dirtied and confused by all the distractions which have become mixed in with them. We would do well to use the tools of love, patience, kindness, non-judgment, acceptance, understanding, discernment, peace and compassion, wisely and often. The results will be immediately experienced as the opening of doors within ourselves - through the high frequency gateway of expanded awareness into an uplifted state of consciousness.

A person with an uplifted state of consciousness naturally resonates with higher frequencies of Light than the average person does and these vibrations are the means to accessing other dimensions which are currently beyond our perceptual range. This is because when we vibrate at higher frequencies we are able to resonate with even higher frequencies of Light than our own, current, bandwidth - which dictates our dimensional experience of life. Learning to access other, higher frequency, spiritual dimensions while we are still physically alive becomes the living ascension process in action. By shifting our consciousness into an uplifted state we can access dimensions beyond our current one. Perhaps knowing this can provide us with sufficient reason to read the words of Osiris and the other Light Beings. Reading a book such as this can enable us to begin to physically resonate with and perceive a higher state of existence - simply because of the positive knock-on effects of the high frequency vibrations from the Beings of Light of the Godhead.

Osiris' Opening Dissertation
Please note that not one single word in the following dissertation from Osiris has been changed - as requested by him. It is important that each person personally works with the information at a comfortable pace and allows its full, personal meaning and import to evolve within the mind and heart. In this way enormous amounts of additional information can be 'downloaded' with each subsequent reading. Osiris has asked us to inform readers that reading his channelled words will immediately create a shift in the consciousness of the reader. This is the result of the high frequency vibrations of the words from Spirit. It is intended and recommended that these communications be read a few times over so that their full meaning may be further intuited. It is not necessary to understand all the details of the communications as the vibrations alone are sufficient to stimulate the upliftment of consciousness.

The communications are quaintly worded and it may be helpful to read the channelled words with a slightly unusual sentence construction in mind. Often the communications from the Light Beings appear to have the beginning of the sentence towards the end so that at times the concepts within the sentence may appear to be somewhat back to front! A series of punctuation marks have been added in order to facilitate the easier reading of the channellings.

Osiris: Introduction

"It is to begin I wish to state I am Osiris. I come forward from Spirit through communication, into the experience of physicality through being, through connectivity of past experience in past lifetime, the understanding of bringing forward word and information from that which has taken place in the past, from that which has taken place through many, many experience of being in humanity, of various experience having lived in humanity."

"It is the understanding for many beings in humanity to move into deeper understanding of connectivity with Spirit, the understanding that there is more to the experience of physicality than merely the coming forward into the existence and letting go and moving forward from, 'Dust to dust,' so to speak.

"It is the understanding there is the coming forward from one lifetime after another of the continuation of experience of the coming forward of an energy field - it is coming forward from the Whole, from the experience of connectedness of the experience of consciousness of the greater state of Whole. That as beings come forward from this aspect into first lifetime it is the understanding that many, many beings upon the planet at this time come forward from star system, come forward from various aspect of existence not always in the experience of physicality as we know it at this time."

Master Beings Came to Earth Before
"It is through the acknowledgement of the information that I bring forward at this time - it is greatly supportive for all in humanity to know and understand that through the various positions of bringing forward various religion, various areas of dogma, various areas of information."

"I wish merely to state from the perspective of communication from Spirit, that in many areas there have been many great master beings that have come forward to the planet, many master beings that have come forward to uplift humanity, and it is through this state of their pure essence that I wish to move into the connection with each individual being that has had the experience of being on planet Earth and the experience of moving into Spirit, with the understanding of the intention of that which has been brought forward through the knowledge and information, and the intention that has been set out by these beings to uplift all in humanity, to uplift the planet in this experience."

Ascended Beings Correct the Incorrect Information which Disturbed our Progress
"It is to understand that through the connection of many beings in various area across the planet at various time frames, so it is the understanding of bringing forward various informations to disrupt, or disturb, or recreate that which has been brought forward to begin."

"It is at this time I bring forward many messages from Ascended Beings - Beings that have moved forward into Spirit have left form in order to support humanity further, have moved on many occasion into the outer-planetary experience to communicate, and do work in other areas of planetary system. But it is at this time many come forward once more in support of that which takes place on planet Earth and the upliftment of this."

Understanding our Outer-Planetary Beginnings
"It is through the beginnings of the coming forward to Earth, understanding there are many beings that are of the belief system they've come forward from the original being which is Adam and Eve - the original beings which is other terminology of religion in various state.

"There is the understanding of coming forward from the being which is the ape-man and all aspect, it is to understand, not all entirely wrong, but to the extent of the existence of beings that have come forward from the outer-planetary experience - it is this that is not understood and known by many in humanity.

"There is the understanding of coming forward of the many texts that have been left in the connection for beings to come into communication with, that have brought forward the unfoldment of information and knowledge, that have taken no heed of this."

Guidance in Support of Truth
"It is to know and understand that through the pathway of the continuation of bringing forward great upliftment to the planetary system at this time, I bring forward these communications in order to support many disagreement, many understanding - or misunderstanding - many manipulation that have taken place, many misunderstanding in this direction - many area of many beings who have found themselves in a position of control to manipulate and to change events, to change that which is in terms of history.

"There is the understanding in terms of that which is in myth and in history. I have stated on many occasion, there is various truth, Beloved Ones, and it is through this state of truth we begin to bring forward that which has taken place from the beginning - through the connectivity of the experience of planet Earth and the continuation of the procedure of upliftment.

"It is at this time that I bring forward all information and guidance in this form, through the channelled method, in order to bring forward a deeper understanding to many. I bring it forward at this time as it is for the planetary system there is the great movement forward of various state of energy field. Many moving into one direction or another, many beginning to move into the desire to understand that there is more.

"Through all that takes place through much violence across the planetary system, much disagreement, much intolerance of one another and it is through the understanding of bringing forward of the messages of the Masters, the message of the Great Beings that have come forward into the support of the planetary system, that I begin to bring forward further the memory of many of that which has been intended from initiation.

"And therefore from this procedure, Beloved Ones, there is the understanding that many move into various direction of misinterpretation, of misguidance and of manipulation and of various area of control. There have been many information which have been brought forward by beings of the understanding there are existence of beings in the outer-planetary system, and there are beings in scientific field have stated on many occasion it is to take millions of years to communicate with beings in this area or that area."

Ancient Civilisations existed Prior to Ancient Egyptian Civilisation
"There is to be an understanding to know on Earth there has been the experience of existence. It is one of an area of the advanced position of many, many beings. It is not known by many there is been civilisation that has been in existence."

"There are various remnant that remain from this. But from the existence prior to this, that which I speak in areas across the planet that have been from ancient Egypt and various areas of positions. There is the understanding of existence prior to this. There is been great civilisation. There is been the appearance of the nuclear energy that has been brought forward at this period to bring forward destruction, prior to the beings in the area of ancient Egypt."

Resonate with the Truth and Love from Spirit for Upliftment
"And therefore from this understanding, so we go forward into communication with many other beings, and I bring forward these beings over a period in order to bring forward much Light and upliftment to many.

"It is you have the ability to disregard this publication, this communication. You have the ability to take it further, but it is within your heart, as you resonate with the feeling state of the communication with that which comes forward with the connectivity with consciousness of the Godhead. To know and understand, if it is you are feeling within a state of truth within your heart, so it is to go forward, and as I go with you into the experience of the journey through many communications, so it is we move together in love. It is without judgement, with the understanding of bringing forward any form of malice to another, to any form of religious perspective. It is not with judgement. It is merely to bring forward that which is known from Spirit in its true and purest form of Great Light - communication in a state of real love from Spirit, only for the purpose of the upliftment of humanity at this time.

"Beloved One, it is as this time personally to question any of that which has been stated, you may do this prior to the continuation."

Ancient Civilisations - Atlantis and Nuclear Devices
Q: When you speak of the great ancient civilisations that have existed even prior to Ancient Egypt are you talking about an Atlantean society?
"It is so, Beloved One."

Q: You say there are remnants of this. Am I correct in understanding that this is known to some humans, and secondly, are there remnants which have been found, or which can be found, about the nuclear devices?
"Beloved One, there is the answer to each of this, is yes there is. There is the understanding there are various position that have been in existence at the period of Atlantis. There are understandings that have been brought about. As you delve in further and further, if you have the desire to do so, so it is the understanding of the nuclear position. It is there to understand, Beloved One."

Q: When you say it is there to understand, are you saying that those who

Chapter Three: INFORMATION FROM THE LIGHT BEINGS OF THE GODHEAD

are delving into the Atlantis civilisation have actually found the nuclear devices, or what have they found?
"It is an area that have had no possibility of destruction in this form other than from this method."

Q: Which area is that?
"Beloved One, I bring all information with regard to the various position at later period. It is the understanding it is over the area of that which is now Iraq, Beloved One."

Q: OK, so what you are saying is that those who have been observing all of this or researching it are realising that there is only one kind of destruction that could have happened and that is nuclear.
"It is this, Beloved One."

Q: So it is not actually that a nuclear device has actually been found?
"It is through the understanding there is possibility, but it is to understand through the destruction there is no evidence of this. There is merely evidence there is no other manner to which this is possible to take place."

Q: OK.
"There is the understanding also that in various area there have been evidence of various, it is physical evidence, in the connection with many being in the environment, there have been discarded or they have been misinterpreted or forgotten."

Q: What sort of evidence?
"In various area there have been tablet, there have been various writings on many occasion. It is to understand in the connection to the Ancient Sumerian tablet it is the understanding it is written, it is in easy term to interpret and communicate..."

Q: Like the Zecharia Sitchin writings (*see bibliography*)?
"... but it is the understanding that this has been ignored by humanity it has been ignored and disregarded by humanity."

Q: So it is time to dig those out and re-look at them.
"It is, Beloved One. There are many areas, they are merely discovered at this

time, that have been underground in the connectivity of the area of the Christian religion, so to speak. It is the uncovering of certain aspect that are taking place only now."

Humanity has been Misinformed

Q: Why is it only taking place now? Is it because the desert is physically moving and so more things are coming into sight?

"It is beings are beginning to delve further and further to uncover more as they move forward with desire for further answer that they have not been given. Understanding I wish to bring forward through that which is written, many, many beings throughout humanity have been lied to, information has been distorted, information has been brought forward to those that teach and guide others that is untrue, and therefore if it is your desire to continue in this state of the understanding of that which is brought forward, I bring it forward in the connection to religion, as it is much of this understanding comes forward from this belief system - and therefore it is through various belief system there is the understanding of beginning of creation in their term, in that which supports humanity to move in one direction."

No God Judges

"It is the understanding, it is at this time, it is relevant for all beings to know and understand that if it is they do not take responsibility for the self, in their own understanding and in the uncovering of their own information and guidance for the future, the understanding that there is the connectivity of the Godhead to support all in the state of deep love, and support and assistance for each being to go forward.

"So it is much begins to become uncovered, much begins to move forward in a state of great upliftment and the bringing forward of great peace.

"There is in all areas of connectivity with others and the intolerance of the support of one another, the lack of compassion in connection with one another, it is from the percentage, it is always in connection with that which is the disbelief with one religion or another and the bringing forward the shedding of blood in order to worship your god. It is the understanding I bring forward at this time, there is no God that judges in this manner.

"There have been brought forward at a period prior to the understanding of many, the existence of the god-being as they have become human being, it is through the connectivity of that which is understood as god-man and therefore it is far from this.

"So it is that many, many information comes forward, but it is to know and understand there is no judgement from Spirit. There is only love to support those if it is they have done wrong to move and assist in the return to the state of rightness, to the state of love."

The Beings of Light Wish to Communicate with us
"I wish to bring forward the understanding as we go through the connection of various area and environment, understanding that we move into the direction of the position of Ancient Egypt, to bring forward a deeper understanding of all the sacred site you have found yourselves in connection with.

"There is the understanding of bringing forward, through the various beings who wish to bring forward information and guidance, not only through the connectivity of that which you speak, but the understanding of the desire to communicate with the planet at this time, the desire to bring forward understanding of what takes place in the future, and from this perspective the understanding of that which each being has the responsibility to begin, in connection with Earth at this time."

The Pathway of Ascension
"It is I wish to bring forward an understanding of that which takes place in the procedure of moving forward from Earth to Spirit, and the ability to allow for a continuation of the upliftment of consciousness, and the procedure, understanding from the beings that I have spoken, the beings that are in the East that I have spoken earlier and that which they have done in areas of upliftment of the moving forward of that which is understood to be the path of Nirvana, the understanding of the pathway of the many beings in the West and of that pathway that have been taken for these beings to move into their state of Bliss.

"So it is as we come together to bring all beings within the environment of the planetary system (*Earth*) at this time together to move into the understanding of their state of upliftment. So it is the connection with beings which come forward with dissertation to communicate, that have the ability to bring forward the information in this regard - of that which takes place in this pathway, of the pathway of ascension - that is deeply supportive for all beings to have knowledge with at this time."

Current Global Warming is a Repeat of the Past

"As you move forward through various shift upon the planet, the various procedure, it is at this time that which is gripping the mind of each being, that is the pathway of global warming, of that which has been brought forward the understanding by many, the ability to shift this procedure. Understanding this has taken place in the past, Beloved One, it has taken place on earlier occasion - there has been the complete destruction of the entirety of the moving forward through the Ice Age of the various aspect, and therefore there is no difference, merely the difference is the raised consciousness of humanity, the ability to withstand the moving forward through this pathway.

"There are many small Beings of Light have come forward to the planetary system that have not come forward in the past. There is the understanding these small beings have the ability to raise consciousness at a far greater speed and energy field than any others. And therefore, through this pathway, so it is you have the ability at this time to move through all that takes place across the planetary system - to move forward through the understanding of uncovering of various area of information.

"Beings across the planet in all areas of the political environment move forward into different experiences of the intention of all to communicate with one another in terms of the beings in power. It is essential through this pathway (*of dialogue*), as it is to be moved forward through without war, as the bringing forward of war brings about the destruction of the entirety of that which takes place in the past.

"Understanding it is the intention to move beyond this experience and to follow forward with all the knowledge and information and guidance that is available to yourselves as human beings to shift this paradigm, to shift this experience."

Earth has another Chance not to Repeat the Past

Q: Osiris, are you saying that we are basically getting another chance to not repeat the destruction on Earth that led to the last great Ice Age?
"It is, Beloved One. There is the desire for the holding of the planetary system.

It is the communication of the Godhead at this time is supportive of the holding of the planet, and therefore it is of great importance for all to come together in the holding of the energy of the planet, and therefore through the ability to support this you do have another chance at the continuation of the living state in physicality."

Q: If we do not do this - work together with the Beings of the Godhead to support the energy of the planet, to give ourselves another chance to continue - what will happen?
"It is the continuation of the movement of the planetary system of that which is seen on Mars at this time. It is moving into this state of being."

"There are beings that are moving in various direction to acquire other planet to move to, understanding it is to work through the upliftment of this planet that is paramount. It is planet that is of the intention to bring forward great Light and upliftment to the entire Universal system."

Q: It would be pointless to go and start again elsewhere rather than to fix and support Earth.
"It is, Beloved One. There is always possibility to continue forward in this manner, but it is of great importance to uplift this to begin with. And it is through the information I continue to bring forward, there begins to be a slight glimmer of understanding of the abilities that are within the palms of your hands, the abilities that are in the possibilities in the upliftment of consciousness.

"Understanding through each individual being and the thought procedure, it is the understanding that it is this thought procedure of each being across the planet think same thought, same period, it is you move the consciousness entirely."

Love Uplifts Consciousness
Q: We just need one thought - love - to uplift consciousness.
"It is, Beloved One. It is all that is required."

Q: So we could just have a planned, single moment in time, on a specific day, in which we all say 'love'.
"It is to move into the feeling state of this, to move into the thought procedure of this. There are many beings that have not the capacity to bring forward this

word. Do you see this? There are many beings that desire only for the destruction. Therefore, it is almost impossible procedure at this time, but it is to shift as many beings as possible into this state of thought.

"There is to understand that through the various positions of understanding there are many, many Beings of Light that are brought forward, there are many beings that there is understanding of that there has been connection with in the past."

Many Channelled Messages are Manipulated to Support old Structures
"There are many beings that are moving forward through the channelled messages that are bringing forward merely a continuation of the support of the structure of the religious system. It has been guided and manipulated in this direction to continue forward with same belief system merely with short changes."

Q: Who is doing this, and are there conscious manipulations of channelled messages?
"It is conscious manipulation by many beings, but it is the understanding of their beings (*the human channels*) that bring forward information and guidance on many occasion, it is with the intention of bringing forward Light information and guidance. It is not known by many."

Q: How can we be sure, when we are working with beings during the channelled method of communication, that we are working with beings of the Godhead, Beings of Light and not manipulative or manipulated beings?
"Beloved One, if it is to understand if there are coming forward with all terminology and connectivity of religion so it is to understand it is moving in this direction. It is a continuation of control in different direction, merely with the understanding that beings know that as they move forward out of the connection with that which is structured religions. It is not only one religion it is others also.

"It is not to state that religion has not served its purpose for many. It has supported and uplifted many, and moved to assist many in many different direction. It has also brought about great devastation to many, great misconception to many and great untruth to many."

Without the Mainstay of Religion, what do People have Left?

Q: Osiris one thing that springs to mind is that if we uncover all the untruths of religion, many people will essentially be left with no valid information or Spiritual structure. How do we address this?

"Beloved One, it is to understand that through this procedure it is the understanding that you have the ability to connect with the Godhead within, you have the ability to take responsibility for the self, to move into the experience of the connection with the Godhead, Beloved One, and with the connection of that which is understood to be God, Beloved One, of the greater consciousness of the state of being-ness which is the state of Bliss and of pure love.

"It is the understanding if there is to be gatherings of beings together to move into discussion, so it is possibility to do this. But it is the understanding to bring forward, for as many beings as possible, the understanding of various area of misconception and therefore to re-look at the direction. You have the ability, if it is your desire to continue forward with all belief system, merely to know and understand, it has shifted.

"It is in a continuation for many to move into the understanding. At this period there are many, many beings that are of the understanding there is no existence beyond that which is the physical lifetime at this time. There is the belief system for many and various in the scientific field that there is the disappearance of physical form on death and that this is it, Beloved One. It is to understand many, many beings begin to question further through all that is brought forward through a deeper understanding of the connectivity of their state of consciousness in the outer field.

"Beloved One, it is on this day at this time that I wish to bring this to unfortunate short closure. I wish to continue forward at later period to bring forward being, Beloved One. You are in order with this, Beloved One?

"It is with great joy and celebration that I communicate with you to bring forward all that is desired to bring forward in the upliftment of humanity. I support yourself at all time in the upliftment of this procedure. It is with much love I bring forward much gratitude at this time."

Q: Osiris it is my pleasure and likewise I extend much gratitude to you, that you work with us in this manner. We are deeply, deeply, deeply grateful.

"Beloved One, it is in continuation I bring forward further communication. I begin to bring forward the support and assistance to bring forward further information and guidance at greater speed, Beloved One. Greetings and great blessings of love to yourself, Beloved One."

Q: Greetings Osiris. Thank you.
"I am Osiris. Greetings to you."

Channelled Messages may not all be Truth
Considering the issue of possible misconceptions from channelled sources, this subject requires further discussion and most especially now due to the increased availability of published channelled information. Some people might latch onto this statement as positive proof that no channelled message should be trusted. Others know about and regularly practice discernment for determining Light and Truth. Channelled information may be used for the purposes of increasing knowledge and information rather than for hindering it.

As has already been stated - many people who channel messages may bring through more information to support the self-same religious systems that have been around for so long. These types of channelled messages may be manipulated to support those systems and manipulations which have formed the ideological base of our modern societies, albeit with a few small changes. It is these particular messages which are being manipulated at one level or another. This is despite the fact that channels are not necessarily aware of any manipulation, because most of them sincerely desire to bring through communications of Light. Unfortunately, not many people know that this type of communication can be used for nefarious purposes and misinformation may continue to be spread around as a result.

In order to help us discern whether or not a channelling is manipulated, Osiris has advised that channellings which use the terminology of religious systems may be regarded as no more than another form of control. In order to ensure we speak to whom it is we want to speak to, we need to state at the outset who it is that we wish to speak to. When we do this, all other beings have to move aside and allow that particular Light Being to come through. As Isis has stated, "*It is Law.*"

Another way in which people may be misled by channelled communications is if a channel goes into an altered state of consciousness and inadvertently brings through information which is held no higher than the collective consciousness of humanity. In this instance they are legitimately channelling, but they are not channelling information from higher than the 4th dimension - our own dimension.

Rapid growth into the realms of high frequency Light requires communications from higher realms.

There is an awareness that the Light Beings of Spirit not only connect with us from the minimum level of the 5th dimension, but that they are God-realised Beings too. It is the 5th dimension frequency level which resonates with the beginnings of open communication with the state of being of the Godhead - and it is the vibrations of this dimension which humans in the 4th dimension are able to resonate with.

This means that the 5th dimension is the starting point for high frequency *Light* where physicality and spirituality are not separated from each other, because their vibration speeds are compatible. In the 4th dimension physicality is distinctly separate from spirituality, because they resonate with different realms. The first dimension of true physical and spiritual unity is the 5th dimension and it is the frequency of this energy field that is higher than our own in the purely physical, 4th dimension. The frequencies of the 5th dimension are within range for humanity and we are able to perceive them from the basis of the 4th dimension, because of the harmonic resonance properties of frequencies. As a fact of life, each octave (group of frequencies such as each dimension resonates with), frequency bandwidth or reality, can harmonically resonate with the octave (or dimension) above *and* below it.

Therefore, it is understandable that any consciousness which is lower than the frequency of unified spiritual and physical Light (which begins in the 5th dimension) has to be tinged with purely human, physical frequencies. The same may be said for any information which is derived from this level of consciousness. As such, this type of communication does not necessarily carry the degree of Light it purports to carry. High frequency, *unified Light* is very different from what we know as the dense, physical energy of our current Earth life.

It is worthwhile knowing that even within the 5th dimension there are lower and higher levels of Light - like the different, higher and lower musical notes within an octave. Even in the 5th dimension there are beings that are on a potentially destructive pathway which is devolving towards lower frequency experiences. Earth has experienced the result of this, courtesy of the Atlanteans at the time of the Fall from their 5th dimension platform. We may consider that those within the 5th dimension who are currently in the process of losing their Light are not necessarily the beings we would want to work with. Discernment with regard to these beings is required just as much as discernment relative to information which comes from the 4th dimension, collective consciousness level, of humanity, is required.

If humanity was in the 5th dimension then the collective consciousness would be that much more valuable to us. There are stars of the lower 5th dimension nature within that dimension and, interestingly enough, Earth's success in the living ascension process of recovering our misplaced Light will assist these particular star consciousnesses to reverse their own process of degeneration. Seeing what happened to Earth and her inhabitants as a result of naïvely or selfishly selecting poor options when we dropped down through the dimensions, can help prevent other beings elsewhere in the Universe from making the same mistake. In this we serve as a good example of self-recovery to others and we can potentially play a very important role in the Universe in this regard.

It is important for us to know that the Light Beings who speak to us from the 5th dimension do so from the basis of already being God-realised. They merely use the frequencies of the 5th dimension as a platform to communicate with the dimension just below it - where Earth reality is, in the 4th dimension. This does not mean that they *themselves* operate at the level of the 5th dimension, just that they are using the 5th dimension resonance functionalities to communicate with us. It is also important for us to take note of the fact that the Light Beings of the Godhead have worked with humanity since the beginning of time on Earth. Therefore, we will always be able to track their 'identity' back to the great beings that are part of our recorded history. They have always been available to help Earthlings and they always will be, in Love.

A lack of understanding about how some people may be channelling information from insufficiently high enough frequency zones, or dimensions, can cause further misconceptions and the entrenchment of existing beliefs. It is these currently accepted concepts, which are already a part of the collective consciousness of humanity, that need to be shaken up and readdressed. We all have access to the information which is contained in the collective human consciousness and we are all influenced by it, no matter how much we may dislike this idea - simply because we are humans living in the 4th dimension.

This does not necessarily imply that all religious belief systems are a problem for all people. A balanced viewpoint would be to acknowledge that although religion has certainly supported, uplifted and assisted many people to make alternative decisions in there lives, it has also caused immense devastation, misconception and the telling of untruths to humanity over a long period of time. This statement remains true whenever a religious teaching deviates from the true, original spiritual teachings of the consciousness of the Godhead. The original, Divine teachings uphold the principles, thoughts and behaviour of unconditional love and compassion for all. They engender a perfect balance between masculine and feminine energies.

Discerning the truth about any religion or any spiritual communication has to include a better understanding of what constitutes correct information about our spirituality and the nature of Divinity versus what constitutes misinformation which was used for the purposes of power and control on Earth. With new information about this we can discuss the details at length and see how our new understanding fits into the picture of an expanded idea of spirituality and an uplifted state of consciousness. If we are ready to do so, we may replace our reliance on religion with the understanding of our innate spiritual ability. We have a responsibility to ourselves to connect personally and directly with the Godhead/God within. When we do this we connect with the consciousness of pure love and Bliss.

The determinant of the purity and Divine Truth of a channelled message will always be relative to the love, truth and wisdom that it relays to us. This is regardless of the fact that sometimes the statements of truth may require the levelling of what some might view as harsh criticisms, against existing structures in society. Shining this spotlight throughout our societies may be needed in order to correct previously told untruths. In order to uplift our state of consciousness, we have to understand where misconceptions or prejudice may have come from and re-look at the direction of any specific belief system. Looking at any specific religious teaching, it is important to acknowledge that things have shifted and that life on Earth is changing - relative to new information and knowledge which we now have access to. Consciousness has changed and humanity has made progress.

Osiris has stressed that it is time for many people to know that there is more to existence beyond a physical lifetime, regardless of the fact that many scientists believe that after death there is nothing. Alternatively, many people are beginning to question the religious information that has been offered to them, because of their increased awareness of their non-physical consciousness. It is this opening awareness which ensures more and more information is released and more knowledge is given to humanity by the Light beings.

Over the course of his communications to us, Osiris will introduce many Ascended Master Beings who have lived on Earth previously. They are able to give us a lot of information - about our past, our present and our future. Osiris has stated that we can disregard this communication from the Light Beings entirely if we like, but if it resonates within us we will be able to appreciate it for its truth. This is the Divine Truth which is of the consciousness of the Godhead. The idea is to use this feeling of truth and continue forward with this book and future communications from Osiris and the other Light Beings. They come to us with love and true Light and communicate from the perspective of Spirit for the purposes of our upliftment.

It may serve each one of us well to accept that it is time to take spiritual responsibility for ourselves - and that each one of us has an inherent, deep, personal and individual connection to the Godhead, from within. This connection to the Light of the Godhead is embedded within our DNA, within the vibration-sensitive structures of the bases that make up these parts of our physical body.

We are assured that all the information from the Light Beings comes to us from a place of deep love and support. It is because this is loving information that we resonate with its peace. These communications from the Light Beings can help us all to understand our responsibility to Earth at this time, especially in relation to our future and how this relates to the upliftment of our consciousness.

Raised Consciousness and Living Ascension
Through the pathway of raised consciousness it is possible to move easily and with grace through everything that happens on Earth, calamities included, and this is assisted by the process of uncovering existing information which is hidden on Earth. Osiris wants to bring all people on Earth together with an understanding of what really happens in the process of the upliftment of consciousness. To this end he is facilitating communication from other Light Beings (such as Isis and Thoth) in the outer-planetary system. These beings have the ability to tell us what is going on from various different perspectives and their purpose is to explain to us what living ascension truly means. It is very supportive for us to know this now - especially in relation to where our physical planet is within the galaxy itself, and the current influences of various other outer-planetary bodies surrounding us.

The heightened state of awareness to which humanity has evolved its overall consciousness means that humans have the desire to make much more rapid spiritual progress than ever before. What this means to us on Earth, in the so-called 'fallen' state, is that we have the perfect opportunity now to recover our erstwhile, pre-Fall glory. This translates, therefore, into the fact that humans will be able to continue their physical lives on Earth in a state of living ascension (a unified connection of the spiritual *and* physical realms) in the future. It is exactly this process that these communications with the Light Beings of the Godhead support. The word 'fallen' has to refer to the process in which we dropped down through the dimensions into physicality, creating an energy-specific wormhole system in the process. This happened at the end of the Atlantean Era and it has nothing to do with the religious or moral concept of a fallen soul.

We have the opportunity as well as the support of the energy of the Light Beings to re-unite our spiritual bodies with our physical ones. Part of this process will naturally involve regaining our conscious memories of past lifetimes. For example, we have another chance, right now, to avoid going down the road of destruction that led to the various Ice Ages on Earth previously, no matter how they happened - but only if enough of us come together and work in the same direction. Through our reclaimed ability to uplift ourselves, we can continue to inhabit a raised-consciousness Earth in the future, in physical bodies, in the state of living ascension.

Some very critical information that Osiris gives us in this book is what he calls the, "*Slight glimmer of the understanding of your abilities*," and the possibilities which lie within an uplifted state of consciousness. This is very important because most human beings have fostered a sense of inferiority, a sense of smallness, which is contrary to this understanding. This is mostly because we have 'lost' our memory of who we really are due to improper or incomplete social and religious teachings and practices. Although we may not yet fully understand the facts of our potential greatness which are due to our inherent Divinity, we can at least start to accept the potential possibilities from what Osiris tells us. This is most especially true with regard to the fact that if sufficient numbers of individuals think the same thing at the same time, this creates an enormous energy potential which can shift the consciousness (and thus the physical reality) of the whole of humanity. Such is the powerful magnetic-like attraction of the higher frequency states. The one word that can positively shift global consciousness is 'love.'

Osiris informs us that our shifted dimension experiences, which are assisted by our connection to the Beings of Light from the outer-planetary star systems, allow us to experience the following:
- The full knowledge of who we really are.
- The feeling of Bliss.
- The Divinity of all Creation.

Thoth always supports us with this knowledge-gathering process. As our conscious knowledge base expands with the regaining of memory we begin to realise that there is actually no such thing as a fallen state - even though we are living in a dimension of physicality that is apparently separated from the open conscious awareness of the Godhead. In the uplifted state of the Light of living ascension, we acknowledge and uphold our Divinity.

Osiris: The Connectivity of Light

"As memory comes forward through connectivities of star systems - the galaxies beyond the experience to be felt in one position of Bliss. Knowingness and Light - the Divinity of all creation to be felt at this time. The support of this being (*Thoth*) at this time to take you forward over many experience to follow, through the connectivities, through intent of the silent knowledge within the heart, to support you continuously in all that takes place in the understanding of the continuation of physicality.

"Knowledge within of an ability, and the continuation through many experience, and Light, and unconditional love. There begins to be felt from the area of the heart the connectivity of Thoth to support you in unfolding the mysteries - mysteries of self, of humanity, of Earth - in the ability through expansion of feeling. Through all that has been cleared from the past, through intent of others, the bringing forward of knowledge to create the feeling of fallen state - so it is at this time as you come together in the connectivities with Being to support you, that you move together in the understanding of the feeling of Divinity. To go forward always with clarity of state of the feeling of unconditional love.

"As it moves through the experience of form, knowledge and understanding of that which is form - not only the physical body it is. It is the expansion of all of understandings throughout the connectivities of Light surrounding you, for all ancient knowledge, as you hold it within the feeling state of the presence of form, Beloved Ones.

"As you hold your Divinity at this time, so you hold your energy and Light. So it is in love to come together, with the experience of the Angelics to surround you at this time - beginning to hold the energy field to support you in all areas of the continuation of return. Take forward the understanding from the heart that begins to be felt by many."

Other Planets and their Visitors

If we don't raise our consciousness and we continue on our current pathway towards further destruction, Earth has the potential to become a 'dead' planet like Mars. It is important to note that unless we shift the way we think, feel and do things, we will actualise this 'dead-planet' potential, simply because that is the degenerative pathway we can potentially take. Although it is true that some people are looking for alternative planets for us to move to, especially those powerful manipulators of humanity who have the means to do this, the focus has to be on Earth first as her upliftment is paramount. Once we have this planet on the right track again, we may then look for other planets which could be of interest as an alternative to Earth. We have a large and wonderful Universe to explore as our own playground once we shift ourselves into a higher dimension.

It is also important to remember that until such time as we have transcended the energy of the world of separated reality (which is experienced as reality of the 3rd and 4th dimensions) it is not a terribly smart idea to solicit visitations from outer-planetary areas. Although it may be exciting to make contact, not all outer-planetary visitors to Earth are benign. In the lower dimensions of physicality where we are, it is very difficult for human beings to be able to correctly assess the energy of these beings. Thoth refers to any outer-planetary visitor as an 'extra-terrestrial', as opposed to a Light Being from the consciousness of the Godhead, who is an 'ultra-terrestrial'.

Not all extra-terrestrials have evil intent and nor are all of them benign. Many of them simply visit Earth for the purposes of observation and learning. Others want power and control of Earth. With our limited 3rd or 4th dimension vision we can easily become sitting ducks for discarnate beings from other realms who may want to literally invade our planet - if we open ourselves up to them. This they attempt to do regularly and they often arrive in their droves, but not always in a manner which is very obvious to us. The may arrive as discarnate or formless beings and seek a body to attach to in order to have an Earth experience. In this way they become what are termed 'entity attachments' which energetically attach themselves to the Light body, or energy field, of a human being.

This type of attachment is only possible if humans have sufficiently damaged their protective Light Body, the aura, by the use of low frequency vibration substances or practices (such as drugs, alcohol, low frequency music and other low frequency bombardments), including the low frequency thoughts and emotions of the negative ego. Naturally, these entities hang out in places where people are most likely to access and experience these things. However, as frighteningly real as this is, most humans are perfectly capable of expelling these entities from their energy field, healing their auric field and reclaiming their own Light. Clearly, there can be more to a hangover than we realise. If people do not correct their energy fields and prefer to continue on a low frequency pathway, it can certainly be the case that the entity can take over the body over a period of time. If this happens the original soul presence of the human being will eventually depart and the human body then becomes the residence of the previously discarnate, outer planetary entity. This is not a very nice prospect to consider. There is also the potential of that which is known of as a 'walk-in' - a being which may take over a human body if the original soul presence has had enough of Earthly life and elects to leave. This does not necessarily mean they are harmful.

The determinant of a low frequency entity is the degree to which it does not feel emotion, especially love. The aim of low frequency entities is to take control of this beautiful planet, so we would all do well to ensure we protect the integrity of our auras, eradicate negative thoughts, emotions and behaviour, fix our auras if we have exposed ourselves to low frequency, aura damaging vibrations and ensure we work with the higher frequencies of Light at all times. The high frequencies of Light always involve the emotions of unconditional love and compassion for all - in all that we say, think, feel or do. If there is any suspicion or fear of an entity attachment or unwanted visitor, Osiris has advised that we say or chant any or all of the 72 Divine names of God. Yahweh (YHWH) is one of those names.

In order to protect ourselves the basic rules of thumb are simple. They are as follows:
- Take note of any outer-planetary visitor's vehicle (commonly called UFOs) - if they travel in physical, metal-like space ships (as opposed to light vehicles) they are not working with a high enough frequency of Light for us to fully trust their motives.
- Work with high frequency vibrations at all times and limit, or ideally eradicate, exposure to aura damaging substances, places, emotions, thoughts or people.
- Have the aura cleared and repaired, if necessary, by a reputable aura practitioner.
- Learn aura protection, clearing and energising practices and do these daily: sweep a crystal through the aura to clear it, energise the chakras with a crystal, starting at the base and ending at the crown, and visualise a large field of Light surrounding the body - preferably in the shape of a star tetrahedron.
- Do not allow this information to create fear, because fear itself is a low frequency emotion.
- Keep the heart filled with love.
- Utilise the intrinsic Light of the high frequency vibrations of the name Yahweh (YHWH) and say, sing or chant this Sound whenever a vibration boost is required.
- Work only with the Light Beings and other Angelic Beings of Light.
- If contacted by any suspicious alien or if requested to go with them or participate in any form of experimentation, firmly state, "No." Your command will be effective.

With the Light of Divinity surrounding us and within us in our connectivity to Spirit, we can come to no harm. In this extract from the meditation on the 4 July 2009 Osiris once again guides us to feel the expansion of enLightenment in connection with the Light Beings, in this instance, with Isis. The entire transcript and an mp3 are available on the website www.stargateway.co.za. Concentrating on the Light sets the intention for us to work in and with the Light.

Osiris: Creation of enLightenment within the Heart

"Allow for yourselves to feel the connectivity, the presence of the Goddess Isis, that is standing beside you, allowing for procedure that has taken place over past periods, almost through the feeling state of purification. It is an ancient period, you begin to find yourselves in this position and it is with intent at this time, Beloved Ones, that you feel a connectivity with Spirit. You begin to move into the understanding of all that you begin to create and co-create, the not too distant future, to move forward into your Light, and into the expansion of enLightenment within your heart."

It is because Earth has the ability to bring great Light and upliftment to the entire Universal system - and because our planet can play a pivotal role in the Solar System in the future - that we focus our energy and attention on Earth now. This statement has been repeatedly made by both Osiris and Thoth. Taking cognisance of the importance of healing Earth and shifting ourselves and the planet into a higher frequency 5th dimension experience is not necessarily related to whether or not we have developed the ability to understand the enormity of our individual importance on Earth right now. All we need to do is love ourselves and our planet. Therein lies the solution to the ultimate protection of the self and the planet, which in turn creates a positive knock-on effect for the ultimate protection of the planet and all upon her.

Love is our link to Divinity. Whenever we acknowledge Divine Source we automatically acknowledge this same Divinity, manifest on Earth - within ourselves *and* within the planet.

* * * * * * * * * * *

CHAPTER FOUR

Information from Ancient Sources

"Deep are the mysteries around thee, hidden the secrets of Old. Search through the Keys of my Wisdom. Surely shall ye find the way. The gateway to power is secret, but he who attains shall receive. Look to the Light! O my brother. Open and ye shall receive. Press on through the valley of darkness. Overcome the dweller of night. Keep ever thine eyes to the Light-Plane, and thou shalt be one with the Light."

(The Emerald Tablets of Thoth-the-Atlantean p52, pp3)

The Sumerian Tablets

The messages which come to us directly from Spirit and which this book records are for the express purpose of supporting mankind through the procedures of physical and spiritual shifts - into an alternative, higher dimension. These mark the process of the upliftment of consciousness, or awareness. This process is true both for individual humans and for Earth. The result of these shifts is that human beings will ultimately be living in a state of living ascension, on Earth, in an altered state of consciousness, in a higher dimension. An altered consciousness presupposes an altered physical experience. Fascinatingly, everything that is happening on Earth currently with regard to these shifts was recorded in ancient writings. Many of the writings of this ancient pathway are still in existence today, although many people are unaware of them or not sure how to decode their messages. Their messages are simple: they are often more literal than we realise. Osiris reminds us once again about what it is we are doing, through our own personal intent, at this time of the dimensional shift.

Osiris: The Ancient Pathway of Living Ascension

"Greetings to you, Beloved Ones, I come forward on this day, Beloved Ones, from Spirit to support you. I come forward in the presence, Osiris to assist you at this time, to move forward through procedure of visualisation, to move into the connectedness with an ancient area.

"It is in the position of ancient Egypt, we work once more, Beloved Ones. It is for pathway forward supporting all beings in connectivity with this environment, to feel the presence of great Light in the experience.

"It is many of yourselves, moving in different direction at this time, to know and understand that through the feeling state, of all that takes place in physicality, the experience of the movement of linear time frame, that moves forward at great speed. The feeling state of this inter-connection, for all that is to be done and experienced in a continuation through the pathway, into the living state of ascension.

"So it is I work with you on this day, Beloved Ones, to move through an experience and connectedness to a position. It is with the Being that is Hathor (*Egyptian Goddess*), to support from the feminine, the presence of the Goddess Isis, the presence of Horus (*son of Isis and Osiris*), and through the inter-connection at this time, Beloved Ones, the connectivity taking place with Helios (*Solar Logos*).

"So it is to support each of yourselves, on a pathway, that as you begin the experiences of the shifting of that which takes place of dimension, in and out of the connectivities of that which has been spoken about on many occasion. So it is the connection that you begin to move into over coming period. As the Earth begins to move forward at great speed, it begins to move forward through the bringing together of the experience of a shift of consciousness.

"So it is at this time, greatly supportive for yourselves to work in this manner and connectivities, with the ancient pathways of that which has been brought forward by the ancient Being - of a deep understanding of the beginnings of the Earthly experience, into that which takes place for the future. The understanding that each of yourselves, connecting with the feeling state of the self, connecting with the pathway of all beings within connection of soul groups, of many beings moving forward in direction, many together, many with intent.

"In the feeling state, there is the desired outcome in many different area and direction. It is to know and understand in the connectivity of the self, so it is you take forward to whichever direction it is, in the feeling state of connectivity, of the wholeness of the self."

There are ancient texts (the Sumerian clay tablets that Osiris referred to in his opening dissertation) which give us a lot of information about our ancient beginnings, from the time of the earliest Earth inhabitants and onwards. However, because so much of this information is relatively new to us in our contemporary world, these stories often sound more mythical to us than real. Many of the ancient recordings of knowledge were inscribed onto clay tablets all over the world by the ancients, to be kept for posterity. Some of the ancient peoples who inscribed clay tablets were the Sumerians, the Babylonians, the Akkadians and the Assyrians. Osiris has recently started to discuss the fact that many more ancient tablets were written and inscribed by Thoth in Ancient Egyptian times. He has spoken of the uncovering of more of this information in the places we now know of as el-Amarna (or sometimes as Tel el-Amarna) and el-Menia, Egypt. It was in these ancient cities that the ancient scribe, Thoth, Tet-Tet-Tehudi or Tehudi or as he was then known as, inscribed a lot of tablets himself, supported by the reign of the Pharaoh Akhenaten.

Many of the clay tablets are housed in various museums around the world and have been worked on and translated many times over. Many more lie covered in dust or disregarded for what they are. No matter who translates them, these tablets tell the same, ancient story:
- About Earth's outer-planetary visitors.
- About the teachings of the Godhead.
- About the Light.
- About human origins.
- About the purpose of the enLightenment of Earth.
- About the origin, causes and maintenance of the dark forces.

Nevertheless, this information is generally not in the domain of popular knowledge and nor is it usually covered in the press. Osiris confirms that many clay tablets are housed in museums around the world and some of the curators are unaware of the true value of what they have in their possession. The correct interpretation of the information from these tablets will easily reveal a lot about our wonderfully rich Earth history. Although they have been worked on extensively, part of the problem with these clay tablets is that there are not many people who have the skills to appreciate and understand what is translated from the symbols - and so the gems of factual information they contain are usually only revealed when they are given the attention of a few interested and unconventional researchers.

Countless people are searching for information that will explain the 'mysteries' of life. We are most fortunate that a lot of this data exists here on Earth still in the form of the ancient clay tablet records and ancient papyri - even though a lot of these have been hidden from us by people and institutions which have vested interests in holding onto their power and control systems, in modern times and old.

If revealed, the information in these texts would certainly contest much of what most human beings base their belief systems upon, but a lot of our questions would be answered too.

It is often all too easy to discount the decoded information as the fantastical stories of ancient cultures and their cults. It is partly because of this that the precious knowledge which the ancient clay tablets contain is often ignored by many, as Osiris has commented on so many times. However, if we look at the stories which have been pieced together from some of the deciphered Ancient Sumerian clay tablets we can more easily see that there was a single, Divine pathway that consciousness was carving for itself as it made its way forwards, through many different civilisations, towards greater enLightenment on Earth. This story of Earth history can be tracked right from the beginning of Creation, many millions of years ago. This information source continues its fascinating tale into later, although still ancient, Lemurian, Atlantean and Ancient Egyptian societies.

The clay tablet records show the progressive pathway of consciousness development on Earth. This is none other than evidence of the consciousness of the Godhead which was resident on Earth - furthering the enLightenment of the planet. This is the consciousness of unconditional love and Light and it runs as a physical thread through all of us - within the structures of our DNA. Most people don't realise that we have been designed in this way and the purpose of our existence is part of the Divine, Universal plan. We are no accident of evolution. We are a deliberately created species.

Unfortunately, regardless of Divine Purpose, alongside Light, darkness developed - we can see this expressed in our DNA too in the current 'uselessness' of our so-called junk-DNA - the non-coded portions. Both Isis and Osiris make reference to the re-activation of the additional strand of the DNA - specifically with reference to the 13th strand. This DNA activation amounts to the awakening of consciousness. Over a long period of time the Light was overshadowed by darkness and became the dominant human consciousness on Earth. This eventually led to the Fall of Man at the end of the Atlantean Era and - and most of Earth's life was obliterated in the process.

Once more after that disaster, life had to slowly begin again on Earth. The mass nuclear obliteration and the facts of these new beginnings of life is why the origin of man on Earth is often tracked no further back than about 10 000 years. Catastrophe has shaped and re-shaped our planet and our lives many times in the past. We are presently learning how to avoid this type of disaster once again as we understand how our uplifting state of consciousness helps support the energy of the planet - as she is impacted upon once more by powerful outer-planetary energy

Chapter Four: INFORMATION FROM ANCIENT SOURCES

fields of other planets and stars as they approach us, especially Nibiru.

The fascinating stories which are inscribed onto the ancient clay tablets are best told by Osiris in his own words, but they have also been sufficiently detailed in the various translations so as to give us a large volume of good information about ancient history on Earth. Due to missing or damaged pieces the story is often a bit disjointed or distorted, but we nevertheless have access to vast amounts of correct, ancient information. Fortunately, Osiris is available to us to fill in the rest of the story and to correct misconceptions or mistranslations. When reading any of the clay tablets translations it may be helpful to bear in mind what he has told us. This additional information helps to clarify some of the details which modern authors such as Zecharia Sitchin have written about, and to divide our history up into very distinct Eras - very ancient (many millions of years ago), ancient (hundreds of thousands of years ago), relatively more recent (Ancient Egyptian) and more modern (the last 2 000 years) Earth history. For those who have already read some of these books, the following information will make more sense and it will also plump out more of the Earth history picture. Internet-based research can be easily done, starting with the website www.sitchin.com.

Osiris has clarified the following information:
- Originally, millions of years ago, one very powerful Light Being of the Godhead came to Earth for the purpose of the creation of more specialised life here. His name was Enki (a.k.a. EA).
- Subsequent to this Enki was known by various different names, as his consciousness split into different physical bodies.
- The purpose of the creation programme on Earth was to speed up the enLightenment of the planet and its reintegration back into Oneness.
- Left to its own devices, life on Earth would have looked very different to what it does today and may have been subjected to manipulations by dark forces from other outer-planetary origins.
- The original colonisers of Earth were Siriun, but they used the nearby platform of the planet Nibiru to come to Earth.
- Much later on the planet was colonised by powerful god-men (the Annunaki or the Nephilim, who are usually regarded as fallen beings because of their role in the Fall of Atlantis and of Man) from the planet Nibiru for the express purpose of mining our gold. This was needed for the repair of the atmosphere of Nibiru.
- The creation of the human species was the result of a genetic engineering programme to create a more specialised life-form on Earth. This form of life would be more suited towards the difficult environment on Earth than the outer-planetary colonists were and it would also speed up the enLightenment programme

85

on Earth, because it involved the use of Siriun DNA as part of the engineered genetic structure of the new species.
- Coming to Earth was a risk for the all of the god-beings, right from the beginning, because arrival on a new planet always presents new risks. Once the original unified Light on Earth was distorted into the potential for the illusion of duality by the bad behaviour of one of the original Light Beings, Enlil, any newcomers would be exposed to lower frequencies than they were used to elsewhere in the Universe.
- Dual forces of Light and dark began to emerge on Earth in response to the low frequency stimulated need for power and control by the erstwhile Light Being.
- This division of what was the Light of pure Divinity on Earth was spearheaded by one single individual who was originally a great god-being of Light, Enlil (the brother of Enki) - Biblically, he is referred to as the fallen angel, Lucifer. His Atlantean name was Satankhare.
- After Enki's first round of creation which progressed Earth life from very basic single-cellular type organisms which were on land and in the water, it is recorded in the clay tablets that the Light Being, Enki, began the second wave of creation on Earth. This was in relatively recent times - about 300 000 - 400 000 years ago. This was when the direct ancestors of modern human beings were genetically engineered by the god-beings, using the basic structure of an existing primate species. The DNA of this species was modified with god-being DNA to make it viable as a completely new species. This bumped-up evolutionary process accounts for the radically speeded up progress on Earth of one, single branch of primates - human beings.
- Shortly after the time of this genetic engineering programme, the fallen god-being, Enlil, undertook many illicit experiments which were not for the purposes of the Light. He sought to engineer his own species to further his control on Earth. This is how many of the peculiarly designed species emerged (giraffe and kangaroos for example). His behaviour in this manner amounted to acts of terrible darkness on Earth. This was the point of Enlil's ultimate fall from grace and the beginning of the development of lower dimension experience possibilities on Earth for all.
- We are still reeling from the destructive forces that were unleashed from those selfish Enlil-originated acts of manipulation of life on Earth and his creation of what we call duality - that man would ultimately exploit. The humans whose DNA he manipulated inter-bred with the original Light-created humans. Over time this led to a dilution of Divinity on Earth within its home species - human beings. Most of the genetic problems which we see today originated at that time too. Untold human suffering has been the result.
- The god-beings left Earth after the Atlantean Era nuclear destruction, but returned

again in Ancient Sumerian and Ancient Egyptian times to help Earth and humans get back on track. The consciousness of the originator of human life on Earth, Enki, his able geneticist, Thoth, and the original birth-mother of human beings, Isis, returned then too.
- The forces of darkness and the many beings that resonate with those frequencies remained in place too, just as they do today.

From this broad outline it is clear that certain Light Beings have a strong and deeply personal interest in helping human beings return to the Light. The fact that many of the Light Beings who work with us today continue to do so is related directly to their ancient involvement with us from the time of creation. Although we are individually responsible for our own actions, many of the early Light Beings and Ancient Atlanteans share the responsibility for what happens on Earth. Our progress back into the Light equates to their progress.

Many of the ancient tablets have been deciphered and translated by historians, archaeologists and scholars from around the world over the years (see the numerous books by authors such as Zecharia Sitchin and Alan F. Alford, for example). The stories they tell are available for us to read if we choose to do so. Whether we believe the contents or not is another matter entirely. It is important that readers know that this information is not based on the personal belief system of the authors and that it is actual, *historical* knowledge. It is because it is such new information to many that it will appear unnecessarily bizarre. Even deciding whether or not to believe what is a huge repository of historical knowledge would seem rather silly. So many different clay tablets, from so many different sources around the world, found over an extensive period of time and translated by so many different modern scholars, cannot *all* be wrong. The great thing about this information is that it really does fill in so many of the gaps in our knowledge. Regardless of this, for the most part, the information from the clay tablets has been ignored by most people. This in itself is cause for concern, considering the unusually large amount of knowledge they hold and how regularly this information has been repeated in all cultures throughout the world. The information which is presented in this book would not be considered so unusual if school curricula included some of those facts. Modern children are missing out on learning about the bulk of human and Earth history.

The problem for most of us is that this historical information does not fit into our current paradigm. This makes it especially difficult for us to see this ancient information from the basis of factual history rather than mythological story. As a result, the clay tablet stories are often mistakenly interpreted as portrayals of the imaginings of the cult faithful, rather than as an *accurate account* of the past which they are. They have not been popularised by our media and they have largely been ignored by the academic establishment. Over the centuries our world view has been misshapen to the extent that we do not even recognise, far less appreciate, the wonderful knowledge which these ancient records of our history hold. This is partially the result of various details of the actual historical information deliberately being withheld from us and partially because ancient knowledge has been presented by means of various distorted versions throughout our history books, government decrees and religious texts over the centuries. What parts of our history were withheld from us and which were released into the public domain, depended on whose power bases were being protected at the time. This alone points to the fact that power and control, rather than truth and accurate information, has been the cornerstone of our societies for a long time.

Therefore, it may be stated that our current understanding of Earth history is largely based on myths, created and perpetuated by power-hungry beings. It is these real myths (some would go so far as to call them lies) which have been repeated so often that they have come to be viewed as fact. Almost unbelievably, the *real* facts have been dressed up as myths and presented to us as such. This information is taught as truth in our schools and upheld by governments and religions to such an extent that most of us believe it and call it truth. We may want to re-consider the information we have about the following subjects:

- Who our true ancestors are.
- The correct creation story.
- The role of outer-planetary beings on Earth - extra-terrestrials and ultra-terrestrials alike.
- The role of Earth against the backdrop of the Universal system.
- Our spiritual history.
- How and why the different religions were formed.
- The purpose of human life on Earth.

The current belief systems of human beings, at every level of society, are the result of centuries-old stories, massive cover-ups or simply the loss of much of Earth's history as a result of lack of interest and the neglect of ancient texts. How and why the manipulations and misconceptions began becomes easier to determine as Osiris enlightens us further on the subject. When more of the ancient tablets and documents begin to be uncovered from the ancient sites, especially Ancient Egyptian sites, the sheer volume of these archaeological finds will provide humanity with irrefutable proof of so much that lies buried in antiquity - and so much of what is written about in this book.

Chapter Four: INFORMATION FROM ANCIENT SOURCES

Why Osiris is using the Channelled Communication Method

Globally, it is time now to step up the pace in anticipation of the return to the full awareness of who we really are and the importance of this time on Earth right now. This is because it is time, from an astrological and astronomical perspective, to do this. Earth is currently positioned in a unique way in relation to other bodies in the Solar System, the galaxy and the Universe and it is this critical positioning which enables us to receive stimulation from high frequency Light. This is important to us, because consequently, humanity is beginning to awaken spiritually in ways never before seen on Earth since the Fall of Atlantis and of Man. To this end many people are starting to open up and receive information from Spirit.

Osiris speaks of this expanding consciousness amongst humanity, as we make progress towards enLightenment - regardless of the fact that we sometimes feel unsettled during the process. This is a 4 July 2009 meditation extract. (The entire transcript and an mp3 are available on the website www.stargateway.co.za).

Osiris: Progress towards enLightenment

"So it is, Beloved Ones, as you feel the expansion of your consciousness, the ability over past period to have felt the experience, the unsettledness of the physical form. It begins to settle into the experience of ease and ability in going forward through unconditional love within the self, the ability to move forward at great pace.

"The expansion of energy field beginning to enhance your being, the joy within your heart beginning to unfold, the connectedness of all beings within your environment through unconditional love - that you have the ability to bring forward all Beings of Light that has been of intention to connect and communicate in a continuation of the bringing forward of greater joy on the planet Earth - so it is in the energy at this time that you feel it.

"Beloved Ones, I support you on this day to go forward over this period in your Light. I bless you in love. I greet you through the connectedness of all Beings of Light at this time that have worked through the procedures to bring forward enLightenment. I bless you, Beloved Ones."

Considering that he has been around as a consciousness on Earth since the very beginning of time (when he was part of the consciousness of the Ancient Sumerian-recorded named beings, EA or Enki), it is evident that Osiris is best equipped to tell us the whole story about where things began, where they went wrong and everything in between. We are fully aware of where things have ended up, because this is where our lives are today in the modern world. Too many people feel spiritually rudderless and despondent. To make matters worse we sit on the brink of global disaster, either caused by rapid climate change or the potential of nuclear warfare. It is worrying to note that Earth has been in this position before and that the resultant disaster destroyed a 5th dimension civilisation called Atlantis, to the extent that apart from the massive structures such as the pyramids and some temples, very little is left for us to see in the present day.

Sadly, most of us are blind to the imminence of potential disaster on our planet, as well as to the severity of many other problems. We are even oblivious to the fact that we, as Earth inhabitants, have faced this exact same set of problems before! From our limited vantage point in the separated realm of physicality, we have come to believe that because the Earth has been stable for so long we are safe forever. We have allowed ourselves to be lulled into a false sense of security, entrenching this misconception into society so that it becomes the generally accepted point of view of humanity. This has been the intention of the able manipulators of the consciousness of humanity. It has been successful. We have been assisted and guided by them: those who would control us for their own less than noble purposes. A lot of people are not even aware that the Earth has gone through disasters which have obliterated life before and, even if they do know this, disasters such as a those which precede an Ice Age are usually perceived as long-forgotten phenomena of times gone by. We should take careful note of the words of the Light Beings when they advise us of the following:

- That we are able to avert this type of disaster again by raising our consciousness; and this includes reducing our own low frequency human impact on climate change.
- That these catastrophic climate-change disasters of the past were largely stimulated by disturbing outer-planetary frequencies.
- That we are once again within that time when the energies of the most important planet which disturbs the energies of Earth, Nibiru, is approaching us once again.
- That when we, as humanity and Earth, exist in a higher dimension we are able to tolerate the higher frequency energies of Nibiru and other planets and stars around us, without them upsetting Earth to the point of catastrophe - including climate change.
- That, as humanity, we still have time to shift so as to be able to tolerate the changes this high frequency energy event brings with it.
- That we are currently being stimulated by those outer-planetary energies to shift.
- That those Nibiru-originated stimulations will be most profound in 2012 and afterwards.

There is very little awareness amongst people generally that Earth catastrophes are linked to human consciousness and human behaviour. Perhaps this is why many people are able to passively ignore the realities of climate change which are currently upon us, no matter how they arise. Alternatively, the massive ancient catastrophes are viewed as punishments which were visited upon a disobedient people by a vengeful and angry god. Generally speaking, people consider that this will not happen in the present day, because they view themselves and society as more advanced and morally more upstanding than the poor heathen God punished in ancient times. It is thus that a false sense of security about the stability of life upon this sure and unwavering planet Earth is further maintained. The illusion perpetuates itself in many guises.

Atlantean Influences
From a spiritual perspective, the truth is both shocking and liberating: not only did many of us live at the time of the catastrophic Atlantean nightmare of Earth destruction which ultimately led to a great Ice Age in our past lifetimes many centuries ago, but, as participating members of that society, we were as responsible for those ancient disasters then every bit as much as we are responsible for their potential *now* - regardless of outer-planetary influences. This is why we are still here in the thick of it, reincarnating again and again. As souls which repeatedly come back to Earth in different lifetimes, we are trying to work through it all, again and again, in order to shift the low resonance states of 3rd and 4th dimension reality back to the higher frequencies of the 5th dimension. In this way souls whose presence is within physical human bodies can eventually recover - and then so can Earth. The first goal is to shift into the reality of 5th dimension existence - into a higher frequency state of Light. This is an alternative reality existence.

As long as we maintain the same, or similar, resonant frequencies within our soul fabric that created the circumstances which led to the Fall of Atlantis and of Man, we will continue to repeat those same mistakes of our past lifetimes and maintain 3rd or 4th dimension reality into perpetuity. This is understood as the process of trying to recover from our Karma. The pain and suffering that the spiritually blind reality of the lower dimensions fosters are likewise sustained. New information and knowledge helps us to become more aware and change these patterns. Then we can make the necessary shifts in order to live in the 5th dimension once more. Consciously shifting our resonant frequency higher means we can more easily make this positive progress. Shifting our consciousness higher so that we are more aware will result in a positive shift in resonance. This happens because the new, higher level information which creates an expanded state of consciousness has higher frequency vibrations and because we will naturally think, feel and behave accordingly when we are exposed to these.

It may be a shock to realise that the details of some very important Earth events, actual historical information, have been withheld from us - especially when we do further research on the subject. The information was left behind for us to find for the following reasons:
- So that we would not forget who we really are, as part of Divinity.
- So that we would not repeat our mistakes, which caused us to move further away from Divinity.
- So that we can recover our Light, into the fullness of our Divinity.

Our progress is guaranteed, regardless of the fact that so much information has been relegated to fantastical myth and many of the important documents which tell the story have been hidden away from us or destroyed. Our ancient Earth history includes the stories of the people of Atlantis as well as those who went before them and came after them. The information begins at the time of the arrival on Earth of the original Siriun beings via Nibiru, the times of the so-called god-beings and god-men of Atlantis and the eventual destruction of Atlantis, the stories of Ancient Egypt - following the re-civilisation of Earth after a long period of recovery - and the return to Earth at that time of many of the god-beings who were previously here during Atlantean times.

As discussed, once we start looking more closely not only we can go even further back than the period of Atlantis, which ended about 34 000 long years ago, but we can track the creation of man on Earth and, then further back again, the creation of all life on Earth. We can then go even further back than Earth's beginnings and track the outer-planetary movements before Earth was inhabited and how Earth herself came into being - and all this from ancient, archaeologically verifiable, existing clay tablet sources which have not been given the status they deserve.

That anybody even doubts the existence of the great civilisation of Atlantis is positive proof about the extent to which humanity has been lied to or misled for centuries. Evidence exists in abundance all around us on Earth that a very ancient, highly advanced civilisation existed prior to the Ancient Egyptians and Sumerians. All we need to do is look at some of the ancient archaeological evidence and consider it from a different perspective. Many people seem unable to piece the information together to form a clear picture though, because too many pieces *appear* to be missing. However, there *are* enough bits of the puzzle to work with and if we care to look properly we may notice what has been staring us in the face all along: truth.

Nevertheless, regardless of what we have been told or have not been told in the past, the time we are within right now is the time of the Return to Light. The excursion into the dark which we have endured since the time of those Atlantean

Era disasters which caused the Great Deluge about 34 000 years ago, which set the scene for a pole shift, which led to a long Ice Age and the nuclear warhead detonation which resulted in the Fall of Atlantis and of Man from the 5th to the 3rd dimension of reality, is what we have to ensure we do not repeat.

We need not view the happenings of the Atlantean Era as something of a fairy tale which weird people believe. Rather, the information from that era may inform us as to that which we can reclaim, in all our glory and avoid in the future, in all our pain. We may consider that the reason that the ancient beings of Atlantis and of Ancient Egyptian times appear to be so great and god-like to us now is because we have lost sight of so much of our own personal Light by comparison. This 'lost' Light is recoverable, because its reactivation structures lie within us, as the elements which make up our DNA. The way which we reactivate our DNA structures is by increasing our resonance with higher frequencies. We begin to do this by being motivated by the high frequency feelings of unconditional love and compassion in all that we think, feel and do.

All human beings are born into a state of pure Bliss consciousness as babies. There is no such thing as being born in sin, original sin or being tainted from birth. It is the consequent influences of society as well as the individual, conscious choices of thought, emotion and behaviour that will determine the degree and continuation of high frequency Light within each human being. Changes in the amount of soul presence (Light) resident within a person occurs simply because thoughts, emotions and behaviours all create vibrations of specific frequencies. These will either activate more Light in our physical, high frequency-responsive DNA structures - and allow more soul presence to be resident in this receptacle of the human body - or deactivate it, and reduce the amount of resident soul presence. These internal changes in vibrations occur relative to the external manipulations that human beings may be subjected to, the circumstances they find themselves in or the unconscious choices they may make. In turn, all of these produce influential vibrations in and around the person - vibrations that will determine the Light and the life experiences of that person.

During Ancient Atlantean times there were some humans who had advanced themselves to the god-like status of the consciousness of the outer-planetary Atlantean Beings of Light, but they were relatively few and far between. The rest of humanity were still working at raising their conscious awareness level - even though they were living on a planet which was naturally in a higher dimension than we are currently in, before the Fall of Atlantis and of Man. The very fact that human beings were resident on Earth in the Atlantean Era means they were capable of being in communication with the consciousness of the Godhead, whilst living a physical life. However, the full awareness of this state and what it meant was not necessarily part of their conscious thought processes. The sense of knowing awareness had to be developed in order to be fully appreciated - this is what is referred to as the development of greater states of consciousness. It was their naiveté that made humans of that time susceptible to manipulation and control by others - original god-beings or otherwise - who had lost their Light. Their life issues, as inexperienced human beings, were related to growing the consciousness of humanity and advancing themselves as humans on Earth. We are faced with the same issues today, albeit within different circumstances.

What is starkly different for us in the present day, as compared to the ancient humans, is the fact that living on a 5th dimension, high frequency Earth they had all the natural advantages that we are struggling to recover for ourselves. Unfortunately for them though, and unlike us now, they were not necessarily as experienced as we are as a species. For many Earthlings, and most especially for those humans who are part of our direct genetic lineage, the evolutionary procedures of higher level cognitive development were still in process. Our experience, since that time 34 000 years ago, has played a big role in our own growth and development. It is because of this that the planet and humanity have advanced into the 4th dimension of reality. We have made tremendous progress.

In ancient times, complicating social and spiritual matters still further was the presence of the beings of darkness that had fallen from the Light. No less Atlantean than their Light Brothers, they were originally powerful outer-planetary beings in their own right. They fell from grace when they fostered and enjoyed notions of themselves as powerful deity-like beings in the eyes of the simple-minded human population - for the purposes of control and manipulation. The end point of these power games was the control and selfish use of Earth and her inhabitants rather than the pursuit of enLightenment for all. This game continues today, helped along by the progeny of both sides.

Understandably, this mix-up of the roles and the intentions of some of the so-called god-beings of Atlantis (and later again during the time of Ancient Egypt) led to confusion among the simpler Earth species of human beings. Those who were more spiritually or intellectually advanced and experienced made a conscious decision of which side to follow - the Light or the dark. Although the unconscious choices of human behaviour create reality as much as *conscious* choices do, it was the conscious choices of these aware people (and the god-beings of the dark) which were energetically powerful and created a powerful knock-on effect which affected the rest of the species. The resonance function of human consciousness played an important role in setting up the resonance of Earth and it was this which led to the circumstances of the Fall of Atlantis and of Man - from the basis of their already degenerated society. Those who are more aware are always more responsible and more accountable than those who are not, because the vibrations of awareness have a higher frequency and so create a greater effect.

Fortunately, the fact that humanity did have Light to lose when the entire planet dropped from the higher dimensions at the time of the Fall of Atlantis and of Man, indicates to us that we *can* move back into this glorious state once more. We can return, because we are genetically and energetically predisposed to resonate with higher frequency Light. The fact that our bodies can heal after a trauma is proof of this. We are also most fortunate to be intellectually competent enough to understand what happened and how to change things. We too can become physical, god-like Beings of Light as we reconnect to the higher frequency Light of our Divinity once more. The building blocks of Divinity lie within us as the soul presence which is our consciousness. All it takes for us to reconnect is to develop a higher level of conscious awareness, link it to our intent and power this up with the feelings of unconditional love. Our intentions or desires, coupled with our will, create our actions. Our actions create our destiny. That is our reality. That is reality at every level of the Universe.

Once we are functioning at a higher frequency, we begin to reclaim our true power. Then, the age-old, manipulated god-status of other beings will be nullified as we too sit on the throne of our own glory - our erstwhile Atlantean glory. This happens when we walk through the frequency gateway into the higher frequency state of full conscious awareness of who we really are. This is in direct opposition to staying at the lower levels where some would like us to believe we belong - in the dark.

In order to return to our state of full consciousness of high frequency Light we have to reverse the negative energy which we hold as a resonant frequency, or Karma, within us. This is lodged within us as cellular and soul memories. This implies that we will shift from the habits of thought, emotion and action which got us into low frequency, 3rd dimension trouble in the first place.

Although it is important for us to know what went wrong in the past, vanquishing the dark is automatically achieved by paying attention to its *opposite* - high frequency Illuminating Light. The easiest way to access Light is to feel happiness and joy. In successfully negotiating the return to the reality of our higher frequency Light during the process which we call living ascension, we can continue forward into an uplifted state of consciousness and travel in the correct direction on the pathway of enLightenment. This ensures we live the 5th dimension as our real physical experience - just as was *originally* intended for Earth and her inhabitants before the Fall of Atlantis and of Man. We are on the Pathway of Return to high frequency Light. Right now!

The Mayan Calendar and the Significance of 2012

Dating back to the time of its inception, about 5 000 years ago, the Mayan Calendar is so important to us because it clearly denotes the end of a cycle. This cycle is directly linked to the ancient arrival on Earth of the Pleiadian beings from the Pleiades, in the area of Peru. Working in that society, Thoth created the all-important energy grids of Lake Titicaca. As we near the end of the cycle, we note that the Light Beings regularly re-introduce the idea of the return of the Pleiadians to Earth and their desire to work with humanity.

We can more easily appreciate what has become the oft-discussed puzzle of the Mayan Calendar, when it is viewed from the perspective of the return to full consciousness and what are referred to as the 'time-clocks of Thoth'. Mayan society ended somewhere around 900 AD and their sacred 5 125 year cycle calendar is considered to be unusually interesting with reference to 2012. In our ignorance we may see the references to 2012 as being an anomaly of an ancient people, another mystery which we cannot solve. But then, amazingly, we do not stop to ask ourselves how it is that our great societies today do not possess similar abilities to those the ancients' obviously did. Instead, we relegate this kind of information to the realms of 'Unsolved Mysteries'.

Considering that it was one of the great Light Beings, Thoth, who imparted the knowledge of the future on Earth to the Mayans, we can begin to appreciate that the end-times of their calendar, calculated as the year 2012, *has* to have some major significance to those of us living on Earth at this time. It has been noted that the Mayans were a great civilisation and that they were not initially isolated from the teachings and the ways of Light in the way we are today. What was truly great about them is that they lived and maintained the language of Light for a long period of time in their society - although they too ultimately degenerated into the dark.

The Mayan Calendar is a record of cycles that Earth had to pass through in order to get to the end of the final cycle in the year 2012. Osiris mentioned the date of 21 December 2012 as being the definitive time, because it is then that not only will see Nibiru clearly, but nobody will be able to deny its existence any longer. With this acknowledgement we will more easily understand the huge influence that this planet has had on us in the preceding years and that it will continue to impact on us in the future. We will be able to link up so many of the loose ends and understand the ancient 'myths' so much better. This leap in understanding will bring with it a concomitant leap in consciousness for all of humanity. Consequently, this energy shift will create upsets across the planet, because the higher frequency state of human awareness will dislodge whatever it is incompatible with - emotionally and physically, from the Earth and from human beings.

Relative to the following day of 22 December, it is worth noting that this is the date of Akhenaten's (Moses) birth. Isis mentioned this fact to the working group in the second Living Ascension course, during 2009. Considering that every single thing that the Light Beings say is important, we may consider this to be of no small significance, especially if we acknowledge that there is no such thing as a coincidence.

We would be mistaken to believe that this ending of the Mayan Calendar at the 2012 point marks the 'end-times' *or* that it has to be an apocalyptic predictive date for the end of the world - unless something as disastrous as nuclear war occurs. Although we can certainly experience the catastrophes that the advent of Nibiru has brought before, it would be more correct to understand the year 2012 as the time that Earth and her inhabitants return to full consciousness - the 5th dimension consciousness of spiritualised physicality - enhanced by the high frequency presence of Nibiru. In the outer-planetary field, the year 2012 is when the powerful force of approaching Nibiru begins to be felt much more profoundly and when other planets and stars are in alignment with Earth and Earth in alignment with the centre of the galaxy in such a manner so as to create an unusually high intensity of combined energy. This energy affects Earth profoundly. The disruption this causes stimulates some parts of Earth and her inhabitants to shift higher and others to find comfort deeper in the dark. This has been the case for some time now, as is indicated by the increased number of disasters and the on-going (some would say increasing) political instability of certain regions.

It is because we are holding our consciousness in higher states than ever before that the year 2012 is the marker of the end of a very long series of Ages on Earth, known as the Ages of Darkness. In this respect it may be regarded as both an ending and a new beginning. Our point of departure from the Light of the open consciousness of the Godhead at the Fall of Atlantis and of Man was known, in the same way that our point of return was known. Those who wish to return to 5th dimensional living will do so, while those who do not shift will continue into another cycle in the lower dimensions.

This is more easily understood within the context of so-called Now, or Eternal, Time. It was because the eventuality of the Fall was foreseen by Thoth and the other Atlantean Light Beings, that he built a series of consciousness triggers into various structures on Earth. When the outer-planetary environment was once again 'ripe' these energy gateways could be opened to channel in more high frequency Light to Earth. The determinant for these events is the degree to which humanity has uplifted its consciousness.

The Mayan Calendar 'end-time' of 2012 is directly linked to the Earth's in-built time-clock energy systems, which Thoth created. These are the little-understood, Cosmic time-keeping energy systems on Earth which he devised as an integral part of the structures of some of the power-point situated portals on Earth - and these link into the Great Pyramid. These portals were encoded to allow for their energy gateways to be opened, by the Light Beings, when the time is right. That intense energy time began almost fifty years ago, and culminates in the high point of the Age of Aquarius - when the super-alignment of certain planets and stars indicates that their position relative to Earth (in the way they will be in 2012) help stimulate Earth's and humanity's possible re-ascension to a higher dimension.

The immediate period surrounding 2012 is the predicted, the prophesied time, of the dimensional shift. It is the end of a cycle: humanity's cycle within the 3rd and 4th dimensions of separated physicality. It is an astronomically accurate event, which Thoth calculated prior to the end of the Atlantean Era when it became clear that Earth and her inhabitants were on a collision course with disaster. He built some rescue 'switches' into the massive Atlantean Era temple and pyramid structures, most specifically, the Great Pyramid. These rescue energy 'switches' were made available for activation at the right time, i.e. at the time of the super-alignment of the outer planetary bodies with Earth. As of the 9 September 2009 (9.9.09), the Great Pyramid's portal was opened (see Chapter Nine for the transcript of that meditation) by Enki Ptah, supported and confirmed as such by Thoth. Potent, intense, high frequency Light is streaming into Earth through this portal. Humanity is feeling its effects, as is Earth. Our combined shifts will have a positive result, but they may be rather traumatic to endure during the process. We can endure if we bear in mind the positive end result is the shift into the 5th dimension of reality.

Aside from the purity of who they were at the very beginning, to over-exalt or glorify the Mayan society would be no more appropriate than were we to do the same for the Incas or the Aztecs, because each of these peoples developed some less-than-pleasant practices along with their sympathies with the Light. They too suffered the consciousness-degradation of the 3rd dimensional energies. Over a period of time these societies also degenerated and they developed some bizarre and cruel sacrificial practices which could never be called worthy of the Light. The fact that many of the later civilisations utilised the Ancient Atlantean sacred sites for sacrificial practices can be considered to be a sacrilege, because these actions can never be synonymous with love.

The fact that the original Mayans were originally a highly evolved civilisation was directly related to their being guided by Thoth and his teachings and the fact that they were Pleiadians. Many of the Ancient Atlanteans left Earth and went to the Pleiades at the time of the Great Deluge and have, therefore, never lost interest in our progress. On the continuum of their calendar, although the probabilities and possibilities of the future were prophesied, they were still being established and lived from the human, linear perspective. The evolutionary processes which were to lead humanity towards the higher frequency state of being that the world would continue to exist within after 2012, have been beyond the perceptual ability and understanding of humanity to date. This is why 2012 was often referred to as an apocalyptic end time - from various perspectives.

The year 2012 truly is the end - the end of Earth existence in the separated state of 4th dimension reality, for some, as they shift higher into the 5th dimension, or the end of life as we know it in the 4th dimension in a reverse-shift into the 3rd dimension of reality, for others. Therefore, it is important to note that the potential of moving beyond the end point of the 4th dimension experiences of reality so as to evolve into the living state of ascension, which we are faced with today, has been beyond humanity's ability to perceive for a long time - although Thoth's hints about current shifts abound throughout ancient history. Therefore, our centuries-old myopia has meant that the Mayan prediction has come across as an end-point, as if it were the end of *all* life on Earth, in its totality.

What is most interesting is our developing understanding about how this sacred calendar predicted a higher level of Earth existence a long time into the 'future' - post 2012. This is the true significance of the end point of 2012 - the old 4th dimension existence on Earth will transmute into the new 5th dimension experiences of reality, in living ascension. As a result, what was not stated, or necessarily fully understood, is that this 'end time' of 2012 precedes our brand new world of a spiritually open, higher frequency, conscious physical reality - if that is what we want.

Thoth's 2012 Message
Thoth explained a little to us about the importance of the year 2012 and our return to the position of our Atlantean greatness when he discussed this in relation to his return to help humanity at this time of the dimension shift. He states that we have a choice to continue in despair or to go forward through the gateway of expanded consciousness which he is helping to open up for us - so that we can connect to our Divinity. In this we find fulfilment.

Thoth: 2012 and the Return of Consciousness

"It is through return that takes place over period, to twelfth year of the passing, second millennium, that we begin in continuation of various procedures to go forward. Many have moved to the decision, to continue - it is in despair - there is choice to return through that, always of the decision of the being that is human, to follow forward from this.

"So I come forward to return, to open the gateway of consciousness further for each of yourselves to pass forward. As Children of Light you continue, through the shift of consciousness opening the way, position of your greatness. Your Divinity and purpose begins to be in the connection and fulfilment.

"It is of this time frame, as you know it on Earth, the passing of dimension experience we go together. Come forward on many occasion to men, in connection and communication to follow."

The Build-up to 2012
Although 2012 is an immensely important time in our Earth history, we can look at the specific year of 2012 as an expected happening or event which is, ideally, going to be similar to the non-event of the millennium change. If sufficient human beings shift consciousness to a higher frequency state prior to this, this will provide sufficient energy to create a slower, gentler dimension shift. Alternatively, a catastrophic disaster will achieve the same effect.

Despite dire predictions, warnings and massive fear being generated world-wide, the passing over from one century to the next was only eventful, because of the wild parties and spectacular fireworks. If we continue to shift and uplift our consciousness as we are doing, the actual turning of the year 2012 is going to be very similar in nature to the turning of the year 2000. This is aside from the realisation that there is a powerful planet, Nibiru, which is crossing our orbital pathway around the Sun at right angles. It is interesting to note that this orbital behaviour of Nibiru's, relative to Earth's, is why it is called 'The Planet of the Crossing' and that this is where the original, ancient symbol of the cross came from.

However, the issue with, and importance of 2012 is a little bit different in the *run-up* to that year, as well as in the time *after* the turn of the New Year. It is in these respects that it differs enormously from the millennium change. The year 2013 is worth taking note of relative to the effects that Earth will feel in this year after the midpoint of 2012, when Nibiru continues to exert a powerful pull on Earth's magnetic field. If insufficient clearing and consciousness-shifting have been done prior to that time, life on Earth may be rather difficult. 'Insufficient' is relative to being able to tolerate the higher frequency energies which Earth will be subjected to from the movement of outer-planetary alignments which create stronger effects, or pulls, on Earth, in comparison to how much low frequency energy she still contains within her. As with all change, the end result of the shifted dimension experience for Earth may be arrived at with difficulty or with ease, depending on the state of the consciousness and the resistance of the people involved. We will shift regardless.

Osiris has stressed that we shouldn't get scared by the predicted shifts, but rather to take note of the potential for these shifts of the Earth - most especially during the year 2013. Although he speaks of these movements he also suggests methods of protection - such as keeping ourselves in a place of high frequency Light by placing a Merkabah Vehicle of Light around ourselves. This is a powerful energy field which will always protect us from harm. As we practice using this structure of Light, we raise our resonance.

The Merkabah Vehicle of Light is in the shape of a 3D star tetrahedron. Just by visualising the formation it *immediately* shifts the human experience of the individual into a higher frequency state. It is when in this higher frequency state (even if it is achieved for only a moment) that the lower frequency occurrences in the surroundings will not be experienced by a person - including Earth shifts.

Osiris informs us that the impact of the Earth shifts is going to be less than was originally anticipated - because of the work that humanity has done to shift consciousness to a higher frequency state over the last twelve years. We can avoid being involved in disasters if we take heed of what is communicated and act in accordance with our intuitions. Naturally, weak spots in the Earth's crust provide easy release points for Earth's pent-up pressure and this can create powerful knock-on effects all over the globe - as we have already seen from undersea volcanic eruptions. The Earthquake and volcano-prone zones of the world are always at more risk than other stable areas not only because these 'blow-holes' already exist there, but because these areas have been subjected to more low frequency vibrations - accumulated and stored in the physical Earth over the course of many centuries of explosively violent wars.

Aside from the potential for a natural disaster, it remains a possibility that something or somebody may trigger a nuclear attack from any one of the countries which has nuclear armaments. If these are detonated, aside from the devastation of the immediate areas, they could create large-scale and wide-spread disasters which mimic 'natural' disasters.

Osiris: 2013

"It is the understanding to not bring forward any form of fear, it is the understanding as you move forward in a continuation of your Light, the ability to move through the transcendence of Vehicle of Light continuously. So you have the ability to withstand this procedure moving forward. It is to understand, over coming period, there begins to be felt this procedure moving in this direction.

"It is within the experience of linear year that is of 4, Beloved Ones, and through this, it is for each of yourselves to move forward as you are guided into direct area and position that is greatly supportive for the continuation of physicality in your area, of great Light and understanding and great areas of growth. You have the ability to bring forward at this time, great abundance in all that you do and think and say, Beloved Ones, and through this there is great support from Spirit, to allow for this movement within your heart to take place, and it is with great love I communicate with you on this day, Beloved Ones."

Q: Can you tell us what this shift actually means, how we would experience it and the linear year of 4? Are you referring to 2013?

"It is, Beloved Ones, the understanding that there is great movement taking place. It is not particularly and precise movement and precise timing, but it is to understand within this period, there is great possibility for this to come forward. It is the understanding that the impact of this, to the lesser degree. It is to understand it has the ability to create a great shift.

"So it begins to become clear that it begins to move in this direction. It has been questioned on earlier occasion, if this is to take place. There has been the understanding that this is possibility we thought, to allow it to move through the experience of shift, and so it is continuing in this manner. It is to understand if it is for the presence of my Being to come forward to not suggest that there is for yourselves to be in awareness of this - it is from perspective of responsibility, and therefore it is stated."

Information for Pro-Active Light Workers
As many people as possible are needed, right now, to assist the planet and all life on Earth. Until such times as human beings can live together in harmony, the main issue at hand continues to remain the one of potential destruction on a global scale. If the events that precipitate Earth destruction happen, then every single one of us will be affected. Whether the destruction is wreaked by warring religious extremists, by climate change related natural disasters, the result is the same: possible large-scale global disruption and loss of life.

Many predictions about impending disasters have been made over time and they will continue to appear. Although they may be valid, predictions often serve to induce more fear into the minds of many people. It is best to treat a prediction as information about the way ahead. Either we continue as we are and realise the reality of the prediction, or we choose to change what we are doing now and thus change the outcome of the prediction. This information is provided to us so that we can shift the potential energy of disaster by means of unconditional love. Osiris has given us this information, "*From the perspective of responsibility*," and we should take note of this. He has also stated that the impacts of the shifts are, "*To the lesser degree.*"

When hearing any prediction, no matter where it comes from, it is helpful to take note of Isis' words on the matter, before you take fright and become too alarmed. She has asked us never to move into a state of fear, but rather to use love to shift warring people and their leaders, or Earth-clearing situations, into a greater state of Light. She suggests that we feel love within ourselves and thereby shift the resonance of many people with its positive knock-on effect. When we do so and lovingly work with helping the Earth, she shifts more gently, the war-mongers behave more lovingly and the climate balances itself more easily. Mahatma Ghandi's statement is pertinent in this regard: "*Be the change you wish to see in others.*"

This may be the positive change we can effect by seeing ourselves, the Earth and all people in a state of Light and love and by not judging either the people or any of the events that may unfold. Although this may be terribly hard to do at times, it is important to do so - regardless of what happens or what is predicted. Judgement and condemnation themselves are low frequency vibrations, just as fear is. This planet does not need any more of those frequencies to be generated.

Fortunately, just by writing this piece or by reading it, the energy of our intention to have a peaceful and loving world to live in, is released into the collective consciousness and people will start to respond positively. Similarly, the fact that Isis communicated this 'love creates shifts' information to us releases it into the collective consciousness too. Her communications are exceptionally powerful vibrationally and so her discussion on the power of love will already have had a profoundly positive impact by the time this book is read.

We can all be an active part of the solution which will convert our physically unstable, warring and rapidly shifting world into a peaceful one. No matter how far away from us the wars or disasters may be each one of us can be very effective in a number of different and unique ways. One of the ways to be a pro-active agent of change is by means of the following fairly simple, yet extremely powerful, step-by-step process:
- Centre yourself and go into a state of stillness.
- Feel yourself in a state of great love, based within the heart.
- Feel a surge of violet light surrounding you, from below the feet to above the head, to support the feelings of love within.
- Feel love for yourself.
- Feel love for all people, no matter what they are doing, planning to do or have

done.
- Feel love for all of the Earth, no matter what dire state of distress any part of the Earth is in.
- Think about all of the government and religious leaders of the world, especially from those countries which have been warring for a long time, or who are currently warring, and especially if those wars are based on religious differences or intolerance.
- See all the leaders glowing with love and joy. See them filled with Light by imagining them as loving, kind and compassionate human beings. This may be easiest to do if you imagine them interacting lovingly with their children, family or pets, talking peace to their people when they make their speeches or patiently placating the members of their parliament or religion while preaching the benefits of mutual co-operation between nations.
- Visualise all countries and all people (men, women and children) in a state of peace, harmony and physical safety. See them glowing with Light, love and joy as they relish in the security of their new-found national peace and physical security.
- See all the physically unstable regions of the Earth in a state of peace and calm.
- Imagine what a news broadcast or a newspaper headline would look like when it is reported that previous arch-enemies make friends or that Earth disaster areas are now surprisingly stable.
- Smile as you imagine yourself watching or reading this news, and see the government and religious leaders of all previously polarised groups shaking hands, smiling and being genuinely friendly.
- Imagine the world as a place of peace, where national or religious differences do not create any form of division or fear, but rather inspire interest and respect.
- Visualise the Earth as a beautiful and bountiful planet, with a perfect climate, no pollution and abundant food for all.
- Feel the love in your heart and see the smile on your face as you visualise yourself living in this perfect world.
- Expand this sense of love and joy into your aura and let yourself glow with this increasing field of Light.
- Repeat this, or a version of it, daily.

Some members of the working group have agreed to do a simple daily exercise in order to help raise the resonance of the entire planet by means of love. Whether the mode of this love is a prayer, a positive statement, a mantra, an affirmation, a poem, a dance, a song or a meditation, the effect will become progressively more profound as more and more people around the world become involved. To be part of this conscious effort to change the world, simply feel love for yourself, all other people on the planet and the Earth herself at 6am (06h00) and 6pm (18h00) daily. This will create a constant and never-ending wave of love throughout the planet which everybody will benefit from. Please spread the word.

It is important that as many people as possible know that by doing these types of simple, Earth and people-loving, resonance-raising exercises, we consciously create the type of Earth that we all want to live in. This is the easiest and simplest way to avoid having to experience any form of disaster that can be part of a dimension shift. Personally, I take heart from remembering that Osiris has told us repeatedly that Earth has already shifted, in terms of Now Time, and I trust that this means that as many people as possible have made the alternative, higher dimension choice already and that we are merely flowing into the reality of it.

Midpoint Energies
Each Age, such as the current Age of Aquarius, is noted for the energy of its centre point. This centre point spans over a 100 year period which is spiritually significant. It is within this period of time that events which bring about enormous change, relative to the energies of the specific Age, are concentrated. The spiritually significant 100 year period of the Age of Aquarius began in the early 1960s. The midpoint of the Age is 2012 and the end of the 100 year period is around 2062. We all know what happened in the 1960s when human consciousness underwent vast changes and the establishment was rocked to its foundations by the 'Free Love Generation'. Life changed dramatically during that time and will continue to change throughout this glorious 100 year period.

The closer we get to the midpoint of the Age, the more keenly the effects of the intense energy of that approaching central position will be felt. If the Earth and her inhabitants have moved easily with the changing energies and uplifted their consciousness as required, the events leading up to the central position of 2012 will not be too difficult to bear, nor will they be felt as too calamitous. This time around, as with all other Ages, although humanity has achieved a lot, we have not done enough to mitigate what we will view as large-scale catastrophe on our planet. Fortunately, though, life will not be completely obliterated this time.

We have, in fact, done sufficient consciousness-shifting work to warrant the Beings of Light being able to open up communications with us in order to share their knowledge and wisdom when we request them to do so. We have not completely botched our progress and we will not fail to acquit ourselves well within the entirety of this enormously important 100 year period. Earth will shift to a higher dimension and this shift will be experienced by many people. However, movement through this shifted dimension experience could be a bit easier for us - and even more so if we had made different choices of higher resonance over the millennia. By the same token, it could also have been a lot worse. So, essentially, where we are now is exactly where we are supposed to be, in terms of the concept that everything always happens at the right time - in the Universal context of space-time always being current, and as detailed by the Mayan Calendar.

In the approach to 2012 and most specifically since the early 2000s, the Earth shifts have intensified. This is the response of the Earth herself getting rid of low frequency energies in order to prepare for the shift and return to the higher frequency consciousness which was prevalent on Earth before the Fall of Atlantis and of Man. When we look back from the vantage point of 2012+ we will more easily notice the intensifying pattern of Earth changes prior to this date. They are rather less obvious to us now whilst we are still so deep within them and trying to justify them as being normal, cyclical events to calm our fears. Later, more so than now, we will recognise that the massive cyclones, high seas, tsunamis, hurricanes, volcanic eruptions, earthquakes and other natural disasters followed a progression which heightened over time before it abated.

It is these Earth changes which are a necessary part of the process, because they assist us to arrive comfortably on the other side of 2012. We need a cleansed Earth to live on after 2012. We need an Earth which is resonating at a higher frequency than it currently does. This is important, because Earth and humanity will then harmonically resonate with higher frequencies of Light - instead of being at odds with it. These frequencies of Light within Earth and surrounding Earth are constantly changing and intensifying as we shift our consciousness higher towards the state of being of the Godhead and as Earth is influenced by the alignments of different high frequency planets and stars. Once we have dealt with the lead-up to 2012, it is life *beyond* 2012 that we really have to consider.

In order to continue life in a state of living ascension on Earth after 2012, when the shifted dimension experience will allow us to begin to be in open communication with the state of being of the Godhead, we have no option but to go through this intense period of changing the world we live in - including the way we think, feel and do things. We, as human beings and as Earth, have to uplift our state of consciousness *prior* to 2012 in order to benefit from the higher frequency states which are becoming available now and which are growing in intensity. Moving in synch with these higher frequency states which the super-alignments of the outer planetary bodies with Earth provides us with, will allow us to experience the results of the changing resonance of Earth as a positive effect, instead of as a calamity. As Earth shifts back into the 5th dimension we, as individual human beings, can either follow her or drop back to a lower dimension experience. The choice is ours.

It is the higher frequency states of change which are affecting our lives right now and we would have to have lost all our physical senses of perception and to have completely switched off intuitively *not* to have noticed these changes. People, social institutions and the Earth are changing all around us. A new wave of consciousness is sweeping across humanity.

Regardless of knowledge about the processes of living ascension, beyond 2012 the frequencies around us will be so high that those who have not gradually shifted into them over a period of the previous few years will find the intensity of their vibrations too great to physically tolerate - but this is a moot point as they would have shifted another way anyway, or they will find life very difficult. On the other side of 2012, the on-going cleansing of Earth will gradually dissipate (as we shift fully into the higher frequency, 5th dimension), but these purification processes will take on much larger proportions if humans are not sufficiently purified to easily cope with the higher frequencies of that time (and if they are still within range but still operate lower than the 5th dimension).

2013 marks the New Year of the new, high frequency Earth and human consciousness. Earth and her inhabitants have no option but to respond appropriately when stimulated by outer-planetary high frequency Light. This response for us as individual people will be relative to which side of the frequency divide we choose to be on - the high or the low frequency side. Just as Osiris has discussed, the outer-planetary shifts may bring about great movements of the Earth, both before and in the year 2013, and this can certainly result in tremendous disasters. He advises that the cleansing of Earth is part of the developing, evolutionary process of the globe and her inhabitants, so that both can tolerate and resonate with higher frequencies of Light in the future. It is advisable for us to move with the flow, release what we can and uplift our consciousness.

Isis' Support

As one of the outer-planetary Light Beings who is assisting humanity with the upliftment of consciousness and the balancing of the masculine and feminine energies that is essential to the process of living ascension, Isis has given us a loving, supportive message. She speaks of the, "*Magic in the Light*," as well as the return of our memories about ancient outer-planetary information. She assures us of the support of the Light Beings as we move through this process - and reminds us that we too are Light Beings.

Isis: Magic in the Light

"I come to you in peace and in love of the Divine to surround you, always to bless you, always to be with you. There is magic in the Light. You are returning always in memory. I wish for you to feel the return to the movement of Light, of knowledge of Atlantis, of knowledge of Sirius, knowledge of Venus.

"Sisters and brothers we bless you in Spirit. Come to surround the Earth with the presence to support and assist passing evolutionary step, to work once more with the God, each of you, as Light Beings."

Regardless of all the Earth cleansings during this time of what Isis refers to as the, "*Evolutionary step*," which will allow us to, "*Work once more with the God*," it is inevitable that some of the lower frequency states of existence will be maintained and chosen by those people who do not move with the times of changing frequency and who choose not to go in the direction of the Pathway of Return to the 5th dimension. Therefore, the 3rd and 4th dimensions of physicality are set to continue as an option of Earth reality alongside the other option of 5th dimension reality. The separated dimensions and the reality states they allow for will continue for as long as incarnating souls resonate with those frequencies. Thoth has communicated that this will be the case for a long, long time to come.

The correct view to take with regard to the information of the Mayan calendar is that the passing over into the year of 2012 signifies the end of the lower frequency states of consciousness for large numbers of people as they move into the altered consciousness state of living ascension - in synch with Earth. This marks the end of so much of human Earth existence in the separated, physical dimensions on the Wheel of Karma, which have predominated since the Fall of Atlantis and of Man. No matter which dimension is experienced as real, a new way of being will characterise life *beyond* 2012. The absolutely final preparation for an uplifted state of existence begins now.

The Mayan Calendar is clear proof that there has been knowledge of Now Time, or No-Time, on Earth, but it has nevertheless been expressed in linear years for humans to understand. With the drop in dimension from the 5th to the 3rd at the time of the Fall of Atlantis and of Man, the information-processing and perceptual abilities of human beings slowed down. We note when it began to speed up again in a significant way: with the advent of computers and the world wide web. The evolving consciousness of humanity meant that it was expressed in the external world in this manner.

However, when in slow-mode, this meant that human beings no longer understood the concept of 'as above so below' with regards to cycles on Earth relative to those of the heavens. They had to be re-taught how to make sense of the cycles of the seasons relative to the outer-planetary environment. This was done by marking the rising and the setting Sun and the various star placements with massive markers, such as standing stones, temples and pyramids. The significance of Orion's alignments with temples or sacred sites should be noted, because it is always at those times, astrologically, that the most supportive energies beamed into Earth.

The seasons link to the greater cycles of the Cosmos and it is one of these cycles which is ending in 2012 - even though the drop in dimension was not intended and this cycle in the 3rd dimension was a self-created one. There has always been the existence of an ancient predictive record of this time of shifting states of reality which we are living in today. This is portrayed by the highly accurate 'predictive' nature of the information which relates to the ending of the period that humanity spent in the lower dimensions. With this understanding, the end of 2012 can be regarded as the end of life (one way or another) as we have known it, in the separated dimensions of physicality. Our reality is set to change, in tune with the cycles of the Cosmos, just as the seasons change in tune with our movement around the Sun relative to the tilt of Earth on its axis.

The entire period which the Mayan Calendar records may be regarded as our excursion into the dark which took us *away* from the conscious experience of Light, of non-linearity. Now that we are so close to 2012 and we are in the privileged position of experiencing a higher frequency consciousness than Earth's inhabitants have experienced in 34 000 years, we can also appreciate that this period of darkness has a definite end to it. Clearly, when viewed with the Mayan Calendar in mind, it is understandable that the potential to end the time of darkness on Earth is upon us and Earth's return to higher frequencies of Light is guaranteed. This marks our time on the Pathway of Return.

This shift is concurrent with the rapid approach of the central point of the Age of Aquarius, which is 2012. The dawning of the Light of living ascension on Earth was marked by the beginning of the spiritually important 100 year period of the Age of Aquarius, almost fifty years ago. It would be wonderful if as many people as possible heard about the possibilities of living ascension and the shifted dimension experience it implies so as to recognise the immense significance of this time that we are living in right now. Together we can more effectively harness this energy and effect massive change - exactly as it is already seen from Spirit that we have done!

* * * * * * * * * * *

CHAPTER FIVE

Time

"In the beginning, there was eternal thought, and for thought to be eternal, time must exist. So into the all-pervading thought grew the Law of Time. Aye, time which exists through all space, floating in a smooth, rhythmic movement that is eternally in a state of fixation. Time changes not, but all things change in time. For time is the force that holds events separate, each in its proper place. Time is not in motion, but you move through time as your consciousness moves from one event to another. Aye, by time ye exist, all in all, an eternal One existence. Know ye that even though in time ye are separate, ye still are one, in all times existent."

(The Emerald Tablets of Thoth-The-Atlantean p56, pp1)

Real Time

In the worlds of Spirit, in fact everywhere except in this dimension of Earth existence, all time is known and experienced as current. In fact, time has this nature on Earth too, but due to the illusion of duality (which the denseness and the slowness of the separated physical and spiritual realities in the 3rd and 4th dimensions have imparted upon us) there appears to be a gap between events. This is because this dimensional experience is really slow. It is this slow-speed movement of dense matter that is responsible for the apparent gaps which create an apparent polarisation of spiritual and physical reality. This is identical to the apparent gap between our physical and spiritual selves. It may help to bear in mind that this sense of events, things and people only appears to be like that. This grand illusion developed when we shifted from the 5th to the lower frequency, 3rd dimension of reality and left some parts of ourselves (the greater state of our high frequency souls presence or consciousness) on the 'other side' of the divide. This had to be the case because being human in the lowered frequency, 3rd dimension Earth experience no longer allowed for large, 5th dimension quantities of the Light of our souls to be resident within our physical bodies. This means that we *cannot* be fully spiritually conscious while humanly alive on Earth in the lower dimensions. We have to shift and resonate higher than the 3rd or the 4th dimensions in order to be spiritually complete at the level of our Higher Self. The upliftment of our consciousness allows for higher resonance and this implies the shifted human experience that will allow for more of our soul Light to become resident on Earth in our human bodies. This in turn implies that Earth will have shifted its frequency state higher to allow for this too.

Although we experience time in the linear fashion of past, present and future and we separate the events of our lives accordingly, time is always current. We experience this moment-to-moment reality of time being current when the true nature of space-time is understood as being eternal and constant. This we more easily do when we resonate with higher frequency states. It is only here within the illusion that we currently live and which we call the reality of our human lives in the 4th dimension, that we are bluffed into believing that only this material existence is real and that linear time truly exists. Our experience of events being separate is directly related to our experience of separation from the higher dimensions. The data transmission rate (of Light) has slowed down so much within ourselves, as a reduced-speed information channel, that we experience everything in a series of jerky, stop-start movements rather than fluid, continuous motion.

The physical 3rd and 4th dimensions are the contracted, smaller, lower energy experiences of existence which are diametrically opposed to the unified state of expanded, higher frequency consciousness elsewhere in the Universe. Nevertheless, for all individuals anywhere in the Universe there is no actual experience of anything other than this instant, this very minute of time which we are living and experiencing. *Right now* is all there is and so it is that we may regard time and all events in our lives as a series of 'right nows'. This is Now Time - real, eternal, constant time, or Universal No-Time. This remains the case regardless of our perceptual abilities.

If we extend this concept to the rest of the Universe in an expanded sense, then we may begin to view all of time superimposed upon itself in a long column, with each experience replacing each other experience on the same spot of 'now.' If we can perceive that all of time is superimposed upon itself, then this presupposes that all events are superimposed upon themselves too. Consequently all dimensions must be superimposed upon each other. From this we can understand that everything, everywhere, exists all in the same place, all at the same time. The limitations of our perceptual abilities determine our awareness of everything. Resonance at the highest level of the Universe presupposes awareness of all events and existence in all dimensions.

We may view this column of time as a spring which has coiled up and collapsed into itself to form a single point - that point is both the beginning point and the end point of the Universe, the Oneness of Being. From this notion we begin to develop the sense of time and space being one and the same thing.

Were we to pull this spring up from its single point and expand it, we would be able to see more clearly that there are apparently many different parts of it which we were not able to view when it was coiled up. Where we are in the individual sense, on the space of this long, uncoiled, upright column of Now Time is relative to our current state of consciousness, or awareness. This sense of existence for each individual as a unique being is real - even though everything is happening concurrently and we are thus all, collectively, One!

Individually though, our consciousness is relative to the frequency at which we resonate, which in turn is set up by the sum total of all the vibrations of our entire being. The various heights of the column represent different vibration states or bandwidths of frequencies. Each dimension is thus one of the coils of the spring.

Our vibration speed will determine our placement on any particular point, or curl, of this column. That placement within the spring is the point on it that we are capable of responding to, relative to the behaviour of resonant frequencies. The time, or state of consciousness, that the Mayan Calendar portrays may be seen as a range of frequencies of vibration within that total column - or one of the coils of the spring. Once outside of any particular range, or onto a new coil, a *new range* of vibrations of different frequencies will begin, marking a *new set* of experiences - or reality. Hence the term 'alternative reality'. These new experiences are determined by the higher frequencies of the next bandwidth, or coil, of the spring. This implies the shifted consciousness experience of the next dimension. However, 'next' is only an apparent concept when the spring is expanded out from itself and the coils are revealed as apparently separate portions of the whole spring.

What the Mayan Calendar recorded, guided by Thoth, was the end of our time of specific experiences as Earth inhabitants on *one* of those coils, within *one* particular field of frequency - within the context of the apparent space-time of that continuum of apparently separated events.

Various peoples over time have 'seen' realities that could exist which are different to their own in the future, or which were very different in the past - such as our view of the Ancient Egyptians is. However, when any coil of apparent linearity (which denotes a particular time in history) is collapsed, the *apparently* different events are all clearly occurring in the same place at the same time, albeit still in constant fluid motion!

To expand our experience all things so that we can view more of them as current we simply shift ourselves into higher frequency states. It is for this reason of a shifted frequency that we will then be able to have so-called altered perceptions of reality. What we are really doing when we operate at a higher frequency is expand our perception in order to become aware of what is already there - other dimensions (or the other coils of the spring). This helps to explain the phenomenon of psychic sight (of the past, the future or of dead people) which people naturally develop by shifting their vibrations to resonate higher.

Linear Time

In our discussions of our lives as human beings on Earth - beginning with what has happened in the past and progressing towards what is going to happen in the future - we still work with our human concept of time, which is linear. This is the basic notion of time that we are able to work with as it makes sense in our perceptually limited, physical world of the 3rd or 4th dimensions. It gives us a sense of past, present and future which is relative to where we are personally today. This has to be the case, because our sense of time is incredibly slow and we do not yet have the higher perspective necessary to see all events from where we are in the physical world or to appreciate the eternalness of time. If we understood ourselves to be spiritualised physical beings rather than only physical human beings, things would begin to look very different. Until then we work with linear time and try to glean an idea of what time would look like if we had a different, non-personal or expanded perspective - such as the Light Beings have. At the same time as we are restricted by our linear view perceptually however, we may keep in mind the concept of Now Time and see how that can be integrated into our current understanding of time.

Osiris takes us a few steps further than the concept of Now Time in the following discussion. He introduces us to the concept that there is *no* time!

Osiris: Time

Q: Can you give us some clarity on the question we were all debating earlier on - about time and living in the past, present and future?
"Beloved One, it is in its simplicity to bring it forward. It is lengthy discussion, but it is to understand in simplicity I bring it forward at this time."

"To know and understand that you are experiencing at this time the connectivities of one another - each individual being having created this environment, each individual being creating the experience and ability to communicate with my presence in this moment, so it is taking place. It is the experience of the understanding that it has taken place, and so it is going to take place.

"It is to understand, Beloved Ones, it is the understanding of this begins to take yourselves into great thought procedures, but it is to understand always that the entirety of the Earth experience is without time. It is merely the experience of thedimension to which you live at one particular moment, that there is the creation of time.

"It is the Being that is Thoth that has brought forward the understandings of time, in all experience of ancient development of various structure. It has always been placed with the ability to focus in bringing forward of the season - it is all ancient building of this nature. There is an understanding to see it in all direction, and through this, it has been the experience of season, and so it is the presence of Thoth to bring forward the openings of shorter time frame, through the connection of the passings of the planetary system of all that takes place within your experience, that is at this moment."

Q: Is it safe to say that as we let go of the conscious idea of time and the question of time, that we release ourselves from time and can then connect to the higher, greater cycles - the Cosmic cycles?

"It is to understand this, Beloved One, as you let go entirely of the experience of any form of time frame, if you are in this moment to move into the Bliss state, how long is it that you are there? What is it you do in this time? It appears to be extremely lengthy or extremely short. It is merely the moving into the Bliss state of the connectivity through a vibrational shift. As you move forward through the connectivity further and further through a dimension, so it is shifting continuously, do you see this?

"Move on many occasion, Beloved Ones, into the experience - I have stated it on few occasion in the visualisation - to hear the movement of the Earth, to hear the movement of the connectivity of the vast Universal system. Hear it and feel it, and move with it. There is no time, Beloved Ones."

Eternal Time

As human beings we have a very peculiar notion of time which is based on the misunderstanding of our illusionary reality in the purely physical worlds of the lower dimensions, because the physical 3rd and 4th dimensions are separated by a great divide from the spiritual worlds. Bridging this divide is a frequency gateway which the development of higher frequency states of consciousness helps us to gain access to. When we continue our Earth lives in the uplifted state of living ascension, Osiris reminds us that we will then be able to access the entirety of the Akasha. This is the etheric library which records all the information and knowledge of the so-called past, the present and the future. Osiris' use of the word 'continuation' is his way of saying 'in the continuation of your human life'.

Osiris: Ancient Records - the Akasha

"In the continuation, so it is you move forward into the expansiveness of the Akashic record. Begin to feel yourself moving into the experience of the knowledge of all that has ever been, into the knowledge of all that ever will be, into the knowledge that is now."

Osiris gives us more information about the knowledge that we are able to gain access to, not only with reference to what is happening on Earth, but what is happening elsewhere in the Universe.

Osiris: Accessing Great Knowledge

"Greetings to you, Beloved Ones, I am Osiris, come forward from Spirit on this day, Beloved Ones, to be with you, greetings to you.

"It is on this day, Beloved Ones, that as I communicate with you further in connection to procedures of ascension. It is the pathway forward of connectivity that each of yourselves, moving forward through many shift and many change, many experience of moving into the connection, through visualisation, through the feeling-state of communication with the Beings in the outer field of connection.

"So it is the understanding of that which takes place, through the connectivity of the Akashic Record at this time, the understanding that as you move forward through the connection of not only the Akashic Record, in terms of the connectivity of Earthly experience, but it is also in terms of the Cosmic experience - the connection to the outer galaxies. It is the understanding that through this procedure, so it is Beloved Ones, each of yourselves moving into the accessing of far greater knowledge than ever before - moving into the feeling-state of your own being in the activations that take place through this procedure."

Regardless of our understanding of time, it is interesting to consider a fresh perspective. Time is a Universal constant - including the events which are recorded in the Akasha - and, as such, it is eternal and unmoving. We refer here to the quote under this chapter's heading. It is extracted from the Emerald Tablets of Thoth and he clearly details this information.

Thoth's information makes it clear that we need to explore the link between time and space, even though human beings perceive these two concepts as separate. Although it is constantly in the same place (as in a column, rather than as linear past, present and future), time (as space) can expand. The constant nature of time (space) relates to how it is always in existence, even though events within it are in constant fluid motion. The events within time (space) are not static in nature. Time (space) expands in volume along with the happenings within it - just as the rest of the space-time of the Universe does. This happens because individual beings and/or great collectives of beings within the Universe increase their Light and thus occupy more space - like the effect of blowing up a balloon. The immense potential expansiveness of space-time is apparently beyond our current understanding every bit as much as the extent and nature of the Universe is.

Space-time (which is the Universe itself) and therefore all events within it exist without changing position. Time does not move from one space to another any more than space does - although it can expand or contract, like a balloon which gains or loses air. People move through a space, just like they move through a room. The space does not move around the people. In the same way, consciousness (people) move through the pre-existing space of time (space-time).

Our experience of all things is also relative to the seemingly infinite possibilities of events which occur in space-time, or in the Universe. If we view space-time (as if it were a space) from the perspective of something that we individually, as a consciousness, move *through*, then we can easily understand that the events which are statically placed in the *space* of *time* may be experienced by us as moving - even though they are not. This illusion occurs because *we*, as consciousness, move through this space-time. The optical illusion of space-time moving (whether fast or slow) is created by our *own* movement. This illusion of space-time moving is purely a relative perspective, every bit as much as we view the scenery changing and moving as we watch it go by from the window of a moving train. Just like the train moves through the static countryside, we move through the endless possible events which are contained within the static space of time, or space-time.

Isis gave some exciting information on the issue of time in reply to a question from a person who was struggling to focus on an exercise for the suggested period of an hour. The exercise referred to is the anti-ageing one, given by Thoth in the Emerald Tablets. The most important concept to take note of is the fact that we can personally decide how long time will feel for us. The only limitation is our own consciousness, which expands when it shifts.

Isis: Intention and Time

Q: When I do the exercise where I lie to the North for an hour (bringing the vibrations from the chest up and back again) and the South for an hour (bringing the vibrations from the feet to the chest and back again) - can you help me to hold the focus for that long or tell me how to do that?
"Beloved Being of Light, it is a procedure, perhaps it is felt in boredom, but it is, Beloved Beings of Light, you have the ability to visualise at this period, to see it in form that it takes place, that it moves through your being, to activate. You may move into sleep state in this position of Light, not always to hold focus, it works alone. It assists yourself at all time, Beloved Being of Light."

Q: Do we need a specific intention when we start?
"The procedure to begin is to state to yourself that you do this for the enhancement for the physical form, to let go of ageing procedures within, to let go of attachment within physical life, to stand alone in your knowledge and Light, to hold the resonance throughout your life, and beyond this, it continues. It is therefore the position that is held, is with intent to begin, it is therefore it continues.

"Do you realise, Beloved Beings of Light, there is an ability that you know of, to change the time? You may move the time to the period at will, and set the intention that it is one hour, or two. Do you understand this, Beloved Beings of Light? It is spoken of on many occasion, to move beyond time and space. What does this mean? It means you move into the sylph-like form that I have spoken of to begin, beyond the form of physical life. There is your ability to communicate through telepathy - you do not move your mouth for this. Where does this come from? This communication of Light, it is there, to communicate in lengthy communication with one another. And so it is in time, you are there, you feel and do all that you desire. Why is it so short and then so long to do the same? It is the telepathic communication of your decision as to how long it takes. It might be a second, that you complete all that is on many occasion an hour, to be done. You understand this now?"

Q: So, are you saying there is no time?
"It is the understandings of a completion of a project, of all to be complete, however it takes, you might state it is one hour, set for yourself in this hour to complete in 5 seconds, and so it is. Work with this, Beloved Beings of Light,

in practise you might do, to shift and blend the Light energy. In your surroundings you may move it, this way and that, it is to enjoy this celebration in this way, Beloved Beings of Light. Move with it and blend it, with joy, and with Light."

Unlike a train which can only travel on its track on the ground in the horizontal plane, consciousness can travel up *and* down through the column of space-time. The only prerequisite for movement within space-time is that we resonate with the harmonically compatible frequency which will allow us to resonate with the different levels within the column of space-time. Accessing memories and information within many different bandwidths of the space of time column becomes easier to do if we function at a high frequency. We become able to experience more (or resonate with more frequency bandwidths) space-of-time within the column when we raise our frequency.

If we resonate with a lower frequency we will perceive time only within a narrowed frequency bandwidth, or dimension - because this bandwidth is what we can resonate with. It is because of this limited range of resonance that we perceive the events within the space-time of our 4th dimension as linear - they happen within that limited context, or plane. Once we shift our consciousness to a higher frequency state, we will naturally have an expanded perspective of all events within the column of space-time - and we will be able to travel in many different planes within the same vehicle (or body). As an analogy, a train will be able to travel vertically 'upwards' or 'downwards' as well as 'backwards' and 'forwards' in the expanded column of space-time, instead of just horizontally as it does in this limited dimension of physicality. This newly competent vehicle of the train (which is the human body vehicle of consciousness) develops new abilities of travel and experience similar to a fantasy-like time machine would. This makes it clear as to why the raised frequency state of an uplifted consciousness person can 'see' into the past or into the future.

As a simple, human example, the entirety of time (past, present and future) in the Universe may be understood as one large, carpeted room (the Universe). Each possible experience of an event in time (or place in time) would be determined by the person (the consciousness) walking around in the room (moving through time) on the carpet. At no point would we realistically say that the room is moving around us. Each and every single fibre of the carpet within that room (the Universe) may be seen as an actual event, or life, in that space-time. As such, each event (fibre) is concurrently in existence with all other events (fibres) in the room (Universe), regardless of which one we are experiencing right now (which fibre we are standing on) as apparently current. Regardless of which fibre we stand on, we remain present as the same soul-consciousness.

Yet, for us in the 3rd and 4th dimension realms of pure physicality, time as we know it is felt as a continuum with discretely different past, present and future states and happenings - as if the one carpeted room (the Universe) was divided into three totally separate rooms (split Universe) - whereas it is a space-time which is set and that we actually move throughout at will. As such, each and every single fibre in the room (event in space-time of the Universe) that we tread on is an experience of our own individual 'right now'. This is why meta-physicians speak of 'now time' or why Osiris refers to all events as current - as if they have already happened and/or are happening. As a Light Being he will experience existence from the perspective of the all-encompassing space-time that his heightened consciousness is able to perceive. On that note, Osiris has told us that we *have* shifted dimension and we *have* moved into a living state of ascension, so we may take heart from this - even if our linear-orientated brains still see this as a future event! Nevertheless, we cannot rest on our 'future' laurels and we have work to do, right now.

Within the context of Universal space-time, it is the moment to moment awareness that 'living in the moment' refers to. We cannot experience more than the given, current moment of our lives. This is the present that we are aware of. Therefore, advice such as 'live each moment as if it is your last' makes perfect sense. The trick to a greater moment of now would be to expand our consciousness so that it can encompass more of what is already there.

In 3rd or 4th dimension physicality our sense of the present is a limited awareness, because our operating frequency limits our bandwidths of experience. In expanded states of consciousness our awareness of 'the moment' also expands, because it includes more frequency bandwidths, or dimensions. Until we are fully aware within and of the column of space-time, we are subjected to the illusion which the limitations of our resonance with the 4th dimension and the physical thoughts and experiences which this confines us to. When we increase our frequency we develop the potential to have more experiences because we increase our resonance with more dimensions. The likelihood of having these new experiences is based on the probability that we might move our consciousness to another part, or possibility, of space-time.

Knowing that a single room (the Universe) is continuous as a space, it would be laughable to have somebody suggest that it is divided up into three separate rooms which we might call 'past', 'present' and 'future'. Nevertheless, this is how we treat ourselves on Earth in the physical dimensions, within the context of the Universe. It is equally laughable that, due to an illusion, we might believe that linear time is a Universal reality. Our awareness has contracted to such a degree that we have become blind to the existence of the entire room *beyond* the coffee table and the couch which are directly in front of us! Our limited perception tricks us into believing that the rest of the large room does not exist - even though it is still very much there for all other beings of expanded consciousness to see.

Each event that we move through, as we walk over all the carpet fibres (events) of the room, will change our experience of events in time (experience within the Universe) as each and every single fibre (event) has a different relationship to every other fibre (event) and is placed in a specific space in that room (Universe). Therefore, in terms of understanding the permutations and probability outcomes of all *possible* events within the column of eternal, or constant, existing, space-time - which is contained within the time of the space of the Universe (the room) - we may understand them as only being *relative* to where *we* are in that space. This is a perceived relationship which is directly linked to the individual consciousness, or perceiver. The events (fibres) remain constantly in place no matter who or what moves over them.

As the scope of the awareness of the perceiver expands, so too does the awareness of more of the Universe - until such time as the entire Universe and all it contains is experienced at the same time. This is the experience of the Godhead-realised Light Beings.

Until we resonate high enough so as to reach that state of awareness where everything in the Universe is perceived and experienced as One, we will have limited perceptual abilities. In the non-expanded state, the possibilities of our experiences are based on our perceptual limitations. The *probability* of something happening is also based on where *we* are in the space of the room (Universe) relative to other events (fibres), because it is the events (the fibres) closest to us, in any part of that space, which determine high probability outcomes of events (fibres) in relation to other events (fibres) closest to us. This is as opposed to events (fibres) which are further away from us. We fully understand within the context of the room that we can move to any other part of it at any time, at the mere *thought* to do so. This gives us an inkling at the immense creative power of our consciousness.

We, as the consciousness which is endowed with free will, can also decide how fast we move through that space of Universal space-time and the mode of transport (the human body for example) we employ to do this. How well we look after our vehicle will determine how far and where we will be able to travel. The living ascension process helps us to tune our vehicles up so that they can take us further.

Taken from this simple viewpoint of the room-space being the context of our possible movements through a defined area, the exact same thing is true for us as a consciousness which is moving through the Universe of eternal time - even from our limited perspective, we can change the possible *and* probable outcomes of any event in our lives. This is true no matter whether it is in the 'past' (back of the room), the 'present' (where we are standing now) or the 'future' (front of the room). We make these changes simply by moving our consciousness (which for us is currently resident within our human bodies) through it - in exactly the same way as we know we can walk through the space of a room.

Because the fibres can be distorted, dirtied or otherwise impacted upon, we must discuss what it would take to un-distort, clean or rectify anything which detracts from the original beauty of the carpet. This would ensure that anybody walking through the room (the Universe) would experience it and all its fibres (events in space-time) in their original, most beautiful state. Our human experience of the Universe, as contained within the physical world of Earth, is a bit like us walking through a room which has a piece of dirtied carpet and imagining that this is all that life has ever been or will be. This is clearly a limited, individual perception. In keeping with the nature of reality everywhere, any single perception becomes the real experience of the person and this reality only changes when that person changes his or her perspective - whether by the contraction or expansion of energy. Therefore, our reality is not static and it changes as we do.

Within this context of time being a room, it is nonsensical to state that any part of it can ever be lost or is inaccessible. All we have to do to experience more of it is work out how to move through it with ease and comfort. From this perspective, the understanding that we can change events in our past - which we call our history - is more reasonably feasible to us if we view time for what it is. Events in space-time are static and eternal within a defined zone, just as the fitted carpet in the room is - the movement comes from us who moves through them. As consciousness we can move around them, into them or past them. We are in control.

This helps us to make more sense of the advice of metaphysically orientated psychological therapists who urge us to go back into our personal histories and our childhood memories, so as to literally re-invent the happenings of that time by simply imagining them differently. Although the details of doing this can become very involved, this process is no more complex than the consciousness (the person) going through the simple process of moving around in the eternal space-time of the room of the Universe and choosing different events to experience. This can be done from a place of expanded awareness. It also explains why it is that people say that it feels as if 'time is speeding up' - this sense of speed is in direct relationship to the increase of the vibratory speed of our bodies and our consciousness as its perceptual ability expands with increased resonance and it moves quickly through more of space-time.

As the responsible consciousness of our own lives, we are fully in control of events within our lives - past, present and future - and we realise this when we expand our perceptual ability, bit by bit. We change and expand our perceptions relative to a different understanding which develops with new knowledge and information - no matter what we believed previously. We can literally imagine a whole new life for ourselves and live it as completely real, because this act of imagining is tantamount to moving our consciousness through space-time and experiencing more and different things within the Universe. Form follows consciousness.

Therefore, intention is everything. Experiencing imagined events as real and re-creating the reality of our lives is possible, because all experiences are real within the context of eternal time. This is due to the fact that all events in space-time exist *regardless* of us and yet, in a seeming paradox, they only exist *for* us when we take note of them (and of course they cease to exist for us when we ignore them). However, this apparent egocentricity is relative to the degree to which our consciousness has expanded. In this manner it is true to state that we create our own reality - within the context of the multitudinous options in the Universe. As we expand we also participate in the expansion of the Universe, because within harmonically resonant systems this has to be the case.

The nature of our contracted perceptual abilities means that we only experience an illusionary physical world when we believe that our experiences are fixed and immutable and that we are powerless to change them, or move to another experience. We can change our experience of reality, or events within the Universe - on the slightest whim *and* in a flash of a thought. We can literally change our reality by changing our minds. The speed at which this happens is in direct proportion to our resonance. From this perspective we can learn how to effect immense healing for ourselves from the outlook of the inner child or the negative ego, as well as how to make *anything* we want manifest in our lives.

We manipulate ourselves, as the moving individual consciousness, through the immense vastness of all space-time which exists as a constant and continuous state - albeit an expanding state. As such we are personally and ultimately responsible for how we view all the experiences in our lives, no matter who says or does anything to us. Although this may sound harsh initially, especially to people who have had bad things happen in their lives, it also gives the individual great power. With this as the basis for understanding, the idea of being a helpless victim, unless this is the experience we choose for ourselves, becomes ludicrous.

One of the most difficult tasks in the development and upliftment of consciousness is unravelling our incorrect understanding about the notion of space-time. This is because we operate from the limited perspective of the 3rd or 4th dimension of reality. Shifting ourselves, body and soul, into uplifted states of consciousness shifts our resonance and thus our reality. Once we begin to do this we are easily able to start to change our programmed patterns of behaviour, so that we can expand into realising our own inestimable, individually unique co-creative value in determining the moment to moment experience of our reality.

* * * * * * * * * *

CHAPTER SIX

The Pathway of Consciousness

"Thy Light, O man, is the great Light, shining through the shadow of flesh. Free must thou rise from the darkness before thou art One with the Light."

(The Emerald Tablets of Thoth-The-Atlantean p56, pp1)

The River of Consciousness
The pathway of the development of consciousness may be seen as a river. Following this pathway in a forwards direction was what was originally intended for us during our physical experiences on Earth. We were supposed to come to Earth as souls and take on a physical body in order to live here, for the purpose of advancing our experience and bringing Light to an enLightening planet. This we were to do while also having fun and expanding our experience base and enjoying the unique physical experience. It is no surprise to learn that soul beings consider Earth to be a wonderful place to live. The Earth experience for incarnating souls was originally within the context of the 5th dimensional experience: a realm of reality which is certainly far removed from the ultimate state of Oneness of Being of the 49th/50th dimensions, but which is still in open communication with the state of being of the Godhead. The 5th dimension is thus very unlike the purely physical 3rd and 4th dimensions which humanity currently experiences as real.

The direction that we took on the pathway of consciousness, during the last 34 000 years, was a direct result of the nuclear explosion on Earth splitting and releasing the previously cohesive, higher frequency energy state of Earth into separated, or split, states. This created the separated, different frequency zones of the 3rd and 4th dimension in physical reality and alienated them from the 5th dimension. Each then continued as a completely different reality experience. Any division of frequencies will determine what the residents within those separate bandwidths, or particular fields of reality, will resonate with. This resonance, in turn, is determined by individual vibrations. It is in this way that vibration speeds establish what we perceive as reality. Knowing that we can change the speed at which we vibrate means that we can consciously shift our experience of reality.

However, now that we are at the end time of this time of separation from the spiritual dimensions which the Mayan Calendar details, we are able to see that we have been going in a very different direction on the pathway of consciousness than the one which was originally intended for us as the Earth experience. Instead of the intended joy in the consciousness-enhancing direction in the process of enLightenment on Earth, we see the result of the *backward-looping*, balloon-like branch *off* the pathway of the main river of consciousness that we took.

Going back to a meditation from December 2008 we are reminded of our connection to the Light, as a soul presence, or consciousness. It is this presence of soul, born into physicality in the human body, which is a portion of our greater state of soul and is our connection to the Light, to love and to joy. When we allow this Light to shine forth from us we automatically link to all Divine Light, all Divine Knowledge.

Osiris: Soul comes to Earth

"So it is connectivity of an energy field that you connect with at this time. As you begin to feel the feminine Goddess energy coming forward, it is as you feel the presence of Being before you, so you begin to feel the recollection of the bringing forward of the soul presence to physicality. It is through the connection of this Being of Light to assist. As this Being moves in direction to surround you in circular movement allow it in gentle procedure to be felt, the movement taking place. There begins to be felt though the birthing into physicality. There begins to be felt in the knowledge of intent - this coming forward through the presence of great Light in unconditional love of Spirit.

"In coming forward to an experience to walk a pathway in physicality, there begins to be felt a connectivity of soul presence. As you allow for the experience, this Being surrounds you, as you move into the shift of consciousness, into the surrender, into the experience of yourself as soul being, coming forward into reality.

"As there is continuation of movement so there begins, in the surrendering to all at this time, the understanding of the feeling-state of unconditional love - in the feeling-state of deep connectedness to the Godhead within - the feeling-state coming forward from this presence into life, as you feel the consciousness coming forward in an experience of expansion, in the bringing forward of the knowledge of all that has taken place.

"As you move forward through the presence of the feeling-state of connectedness, in unconditional love, as you feel the presence of Being of Light, the ability to communicate from the energy field of the presence of Spirit to Spirit.

"It is at this time, Beloved Ones, there is the experience to be felt as you begin to allow for Being to begin to create an energy field surrounding you, to allow for yourself to let go entirely, into the upliftment further - into the connectedness, the presence of Sirius - as you begin to move gently.

"It is at this time, Beloved Ones, to over light you to come forward that you feel the presence of Being as I surround and support you, allowing through the shifted dimensional state connectedness further and further - allow yourselves to let go. The expansion of energy moving, surrounding still, the feeling-state of connectedness still to the Being of Light. So as you shift dimension, so it is you begin to feel the expansiveness of energy field - the expansiveness of your Light - as there is felt through the universal communication, the presence of Light energy, of Light communication, you begin to feel it in your surroundings.

"Begin to feel the connectedness and as you come together the presence of my Being, I come forward to support and work with you. As you begin to feel a Light energy coming forward from your being the connectedness of the energy of the presence of great Light surrounding you. And as you begin to feel the expansiveness - almost through the position of the growth through the connectedness of re-birthing into the Siriun energy - begin to feel the connection. As you begin to feel the connection further and further, there is an energy field continuing to surround you.

"In the continuation, so it is you move forward into the expansiveness of the Akashic Record. Begin to feel yourself moving into the experience of the knowledge of all that has ever been, into the knowledge of all that ever will be, into the knowledge that is now.

"As you begin to feel a formation, pyramidal form of Light in the central position. As you move into the expansiveness, the awakening of the consciousness, the release - through many, many lifetimes of soul presence in physicality it is allowed in any manner - the suppression of awakening. Allow yourself to move forward through the experience of the activation further, of the experience of all knowledge and all Light. The reawakening of the soul presence to move forward through a state of the connectedness with the Godhead at this time.

"The energy field expanding further and further. The connectedness of the heart centre, Beloved Ones, moving into the feeling-state of the Bliss, of the joy. It is on many occasion through the bitter-sweetness of the releasing of all aspect of that which has taken place, to not move forward through any aspect of regret, or of blame - so it is released at this time, into the knowledge and understanding for all reason of connectivity at this time to disappoint - so as soul being you have come.

"Through the connectedness of the Light presence, so it is you begin to see before you, the presence of the self. You begin to see before you the Being that you are, Beloved Ones, as you see before you the Being that has come forward from inception to experience many, many lifetimes - the outer planetary connectivities to the Earthly experiences, to the experiences in Spirit.

"As you see before you the self. As you begin to feel before you, unconditional love, the connectedness of an ancientness - the Light Being - the presence of connectedness to the Godhead. As you feel yourselves in the experience of acknowledgement, to release all doubt - in the silence, in the stillness of the connectedness of unconditional Love, of the feeling-state of the heart. As you are in this moment, pure Bliss and pure love, pure experience of connectedness of Angelic presence, a Being of great ability, a Being of great presence of Light - in love to feel it."

The Universal Balloon
If we view the entire Universe as a flexible balloon, then both the inner and outer parts of the membrane of the balloon are the 49th/50th dimensions and as such this single membrane encompasses and incorporates all of the other space within it - right through to its central core. This is the state of Oneness, or the Universe. From within its centre, its core, all other dimensions may be viewed as radiating out in a series - very much like pictures of the Flower of Life which are etched into the wall of the Temple of Seti I in Abydos, Egypt demonstrate.

Outside of the balloon membrane of the Universe we find the chaos of disordered, low frequency nothing-ness. The energy of the 'nothingness' is so undifferentiated and so unspecialised that it may be regarded as absolutely nothing of any significance

- although, under specific circumstances, this low level energy can shift into a creative potential. In this state of 'nothingness' there is no consciousness and no form - and therefore no true conscious existence to speak of. There are merely a bunch of haphazard bits and pieces of low frequency energy which have not yet become organised into any higher frequency form at all. There is no Light in this void of 'nothingness' because Light is a high frequency, ordered state.

In the state of disorder, nothing can easily develop into anything significant - unless it becomes massively organised. For organisation to occur there has to be a higher frequency, instigating force. This will initiate the reaction that will result in order. High-level order is what resulted at the time of the 'Big Bang' event which formed the Universe. It is either the *external* application of massive amounts of ultra-high frequency energy that creates order from low frequency chaos (which suggests the direction of an outside, conscious force) or it is the crashing together of significant numbers of the bits and pieces of low frequency energy, all at the same time, so that they will create sufficient ultra-high frequency, ordering energy from within this event, *internally*. The result of either of these happenings is the creation of sufficient energy so that what was once chaos or no-thing can become ordered and start to become *some*-thing - special and discretely different against the backdrop of its own origin.

This some-thing may be called the Universe and perhaps it looks like a balloon. The zones *outside* of the balloon of our highly ordered Universe may therefore be referred to as 'no-thing-ness'. The last frequency realm, or ordered place, before the 'nothingness' of the outside of the balloon is the 3rd dimension. We can access that state of 'nothingness' from the 3rd dimension via a Black Hole - this is creation from the void, in reverse. The fact that there are Black Holes, indicates that this type of frequency pathway has been utilised before. They exist. If no part of the Universe had ever degenerated its energy lower than that of the 3rd dimension, no Black Hole danger would be evident. We see how close Earth has come to the point of total obliteration of herself - the total loss of this beautiful Earth energy - into 'nothingness'.

The 3rd dimension, in the balloon metaphor, may be seen as a little twisted pimple-like structure which is offset from the body of the main portion of the balloon. Just as with all little balloon-art figures, this twisted portion of the balloon appears to be separated from the other bits of the balloon, whereas, in fact, it is not. Its membrane remains continuous with the rest of the balloon. The positive proof of this fact is to be found in the maintained existence of its shape and form. The twisted little pimple of balloon (the separated, physical dimensions of reality of the 3rd and 4th dimensions) is no less a part of the main balloon of the Universe than the balloon-art dog's head is from the body, the legs or the tail. We know this because if any part of the little balloon-dog were popped, the entire structure would collapse.

Therefore, if we had to draw the energy, or air flow diagram, within the balloon structure of the Universe - with its twisted bit of 3rd and 4th dimension reality intact on the side - we would have to acknowledge that the pathway of the energy, or air flow, (of the river of consciousness) has become twisted and difficult to negotiate a way through. However, it is no less a part of the main energy/air of the main balloon.

The energy/air in the little pimple of the balloon is at risk of becoming stagnant over time and it is this which is responsible for the maintained, low frequency state of Earth consciousness. It is as if we have been suffering from an almost asphyxiating degree of low spiritual-oxygen in our atmosphere. However, since the advent of the return to Earth of the god-beings in Ancient Egyptian times and the importance of the planetary alignments with Earth at the time of 2037/67 BC, we have made great progress. This, linked with the current opening of consciousness in the Age of Aquarius, is sufficient to undo the twist which separates the physical 3rd and 4th dimensions from all the other dimensions of the Godhead. We can therefore walk through this opening gateway of consciousness and reclaim our higher frequency reality.

Both the on-going work of various Light Beings who have supported Earth over the Ages and the work of humans themselves, have helped to loosen the twist and have increased the flow of high frequency energy/air from the main balloon into the little pimple-portion of the physical dimensions. This zone of the twist may be called the gateway of consciousness or, in Ancient Egyptian terminology, the Eye of Horus. Fortunately, just as is the fate of the little balloon-art dog when the twists which form his head, legs and tail untwist, soon there will be no illusion of the separation of one part of the balloon from any other part of it. That marks the time when we go through the gateway of consciousness.

If we view the progress of energy/air flow through this system as the flow of water in a river, then we can understand that the main flow of the river of consciousness flows within the context of the balloon itself. Fortunately, or more likely, in line with the ever-evolving plan of enLightenment and expansion of the Universe back to a state of Wholeness, this backward-looping branch of water was not cut off completely from the main river and it didn't become a disconnected ox-bow lake. Rather, it remained on a course for eventual reintegration with the main body of water. This course of the river denotes the Pathway of Return. The flow (a.k.a. the energy of our consciousness and therefore our lives) will continue full circle until both reconnect right back at the point where the river branched off - at the twist. This is the Point of Return - the return of our full conscious awareness of who we

Chapter Six: THE PATHWAY OF CONSCIOUSNESS

really are. Once back again we will fully understand what on Earth happened to confuse us for so long.

On the other hand, theoretically, if we were to disconnect this balloon-like portion of the river completely we would be lost from the flow forward of the main water course, the river of consciousness, the energy of life, forever. This would amount to the complete loss of the energy of all of the souls, and therefore all of the soul-Light, of those involved because they would dissolve back into the void of 'nothingness'. Total spiritual asphyxiation would result. If we were ever un-fuelled by the necessary life-giving energy of higher consciousness from the main river of consciousness, as souls we would then become energetically malnourished, shrivel up and 'die.' Were this to happen it would be contrary to our purpose of existence anywhere in the Universe and certainly contrary to the purpose of the physical experience of enLightenment which was the reason for the original inhabitation and population of Earth.

It is in order to prevent the occurrence of this very scenario that the Beings of Light have helped us time and time again, throughout the entire, lengthy programme of Earth's enLightenment - and most especially now during the period of the dimension shift. Thoth created specific energy portals on Earth, with the Great Pyramid as the main one, so that we can use the key of our uplifted consciousness to open the gateway to higher consciousness when we are ready to do so. When these portals are open the high frequency energy from the stars which are aligned with Earth, flood into the ground below them. Considering that there is an interlocking energy grid system over the entire surface of the Earth, this entry of high frequency vibrations into one point will create reverberations all over the planet.

These power points, or portals, link up to the energy systems known as the time-clocks of Thoth and they are what have been available as high energy gateways which can be opened, or activated, by the Light Beings when the consciousness of humanity is at the point where we are able to take advantage of a shift in dimension. This occurs when our own consciousness upliftment coincides with the favourable circumstances of the outer-planetary alignments. These portals were created by Thoth, as their architect, to assist us all throughout the many ages since the Fall until we get to the end point of them and the uplifted consciousness time, in 2012. Thoth informed us that there are a total of 100 gateway opportunities to higher consciousness that human beings have been able to avail themselves of since the time of the Fall. We have passed through 98 of these. There are 2 left.

The Great Pyramid portal was initially opened by Enki Ptah, supported by Thoth, on the 9 September 2009 (see Chapter Nine for the transcript of the 9.9.09 meditation from that day). It continues to be energised by the combination of the outer-planetary alignments with Earth as well as uplifting human consciousness. The alignment of Orion with the Great Pyramid on 11 November 2009 magnified the energy coming into this Earth portal. It will be fully open between the 11 November 2009: 11.11.11 (see Chapter Fifteen for the transcript of the meditation from that day) and 12 December 2009: 12.12.11. It is commonly known that 11 is the master number, but the significance of the number 12 in our lives will start to be revealed by Thoth in his forthcoming books which will be published in 2010.

Although not fully energised until the shift is complete, exposure to any or all of the portals provide us with progressively more powerful energy which assists us to raise our resonance as time progresses. Although all of these energy changes will ensure that we clear out more low frequency vibrations from our systems, the sheer speed of the changes may make many of us feel unsettled or fearful. Nevertheless, as we forge through this time of change, the results will be well worth it when we emerge on the other side - able to live more in tune with our 5th dimensional state of self.

Our shift into another dimension at this time was both anticipated and intended right from the inception of these time clocks. When Thoth created them he also expressed the intention to continue to help humanity throughout the times of darkness and suffering in the lower dimensions. As we approach 2012 we can expect many more portals to become re-activated and powered up and this will serve to assist us to shift even quicker. The individual alarm bell that triggers the unlocking mechanism of the gateway to a higher dimension is the higher frequency function of an uplifted consciousness - which is characterised by unconditional love and a purified body. It is these processes of living ascension which ensure that present-day human beings can do what has been tried before on Earth since the Fall, but seldom achieved - a shift into a higher dimension. Even though there have been opportunities to do so, specifically at the time of 2037/67 BC, never before on Earth, since the Fall, has a dimensional shift to the spiritual dimensions been successful by large numbers of people. Now it is.

Regardless of how we may feel, we are neither lost, nor alone. We see this very clearly when we read this meditation which dates back to September 2008. We are reminded of the necessity to connect from the heart, with unconditional love, and to connect to the knowledge of our greatest state of individual soul presence, the Monad. This visualisation takes place at the site of the ruins of an ancient temple which is generally known of as the Temple of Amenhotep III in Luxor, Egypt. It has the Colossi of Memnon stationed at the end of the ruins. These two massive stone structures help us to recall our ancientness and all we knew at that time. An interesting story about these Colossi is the one that relates how an archaeologist who tried to move them from there heard a crying sound that was so incredibly sad. Apparently, he ran away in terror and so they still stand today, in the same place they have always been. Although there is a popular tourist site that one can visit which is named the Temple of Luxor in Luxor, Egypt, in truth it is the Colossi site where the correctly named, ancient Temple of Luxor was positioned. It is this sacred site which is referred to by Osiris as his Earthly ascension seat and he has mentioned on various occasions that it extends beyond the Earthly realm into the etheric

Osiris: Connecting from the Heart

"Greetings to you, Beloved Ones, I am Osiris, come forward from Spirit on this day to be with you. Greetings to you. It is on this day as I communicate with you from Spirit, Beloved Ones, I wish to take you forward through visualisation. It is procedure of meditation and in the understanding on this day to bring into the experience the Beings of Light. It is at this time I bring forward the connectivity of the being that is Thoth, the connectivity of the Angelic beings to come forward to support the procedure to take you into the experience: it is of the Ashram of my being, Beloved Ones, the ascension seat. It is the connectivity to work through the procedure at this time in the area of Ancient Egypt - it is in the area above the position of the ancient Temple of Luxor.

"It is through this procedure at this time you find yourselves moving forward through the deep understanding and connectivities that take place through the presence of your being, at this time. It is, Beloved Ones, to connect and work with the presence of the heart. It is through the heart centre at this time, through all the experiences in physicality, to know and understand as you move forward through all in the shifting of the dimensional experience at this time, it is the understanding of the holding of energy and connectivities to the Earthly experience, and it is in order to move into the connection through the pathway: it is the understanding of the expansiveness of the unconditional love within, of the great importance of the connectivity within the self. It is, Beloved Ones, it is on this day I wish to support you in connectivities of the presence of Angelic beings.

"As you begin to form the Merkabah (*star tetrahedron shaped Vehicle of Light*) surrounding you, begin to feel the presence of the Light energy as it begins to form. And as it begins to form, you begin to feel the presence of the Beings of Light in the Angelic realm. It is the understanding of the being that is the Archangel Michael, we bring forward the presence to surround of the Archangel

Raphael, it is the Archangel Uriel. And it is, Beloved Ones, through the connectivity of the presence of beings at this time, to feel their Light surrounding you.

"It is, Beloved Ones, the beings at this time - it is Gabriel, Michael, Uriel and Raphael - beginnings of the connectivities begin to be felt. It is as you move forward through the consciousness, allowing yourself to shift into the experience of deep connection with Spirit, finding yourselves moving forward into the connectivity of the presence of the ascension seat, Beloved Ones. It is to support you at this time that the Being of Light works with you over the coming period. It is the assistance that is taking place through the deep understanding within the self.

"As you begin to move yourself - moving into the connectivities - allow yourself to let go entirely. Let go into the drifting, moving experience into the etheric. And so it is at this time, Beloved Ones, that many of yourselves moving through many aspect of physicality of holding of energy - it is of the understanding of moving in and out of experience of dimension. It is through the experience at this time you have the ability to connect from the heart. It is the understanding of the great importance of the feeling state within. The acknowledgement of moving forward in all areas of physicality from the perspective of unconditional love.

"As you move into the connection at this time, the presence of being that is Thoth to come forward. You have the ability to feel, to see the presence of being before you: being choosing to come into the experience. It is the desire and intent to support all beings on Earth at this time, to move forward into a deeper understanding of that which takes place in the passing forward of a continuation of lifetime through lifetime.

"The understanding of the ability in holding the position: it is in the understanding of the connection through the conscious knowledge of return and holding of memory. So it is, as the being before you, Beloved Ones, as you begin to feel the connectivity of the ancient Atlantean being, the presence of the energy from this period in lifetime, the understanding to support all to go forward through the connectivities that take place through the silent knowledge within. It is the understanding that as you begin to connect, the feeling state of the Angelic presence surrounding you.

"And as you connect with being before you, it is the ability to feel the presence of all that is offered to you through the experience of the carrying forward of ancient knowledge. As you begin to feel it in the heart centre, as you work with the positioning of understanding - so it is you have an ability, at this time, to go forward into all experience from the birthing position within this lifetime. To know and understand - as you come forwards with clarity of mind, with clarity of love, of clarity of experience to follow - to feel yourselves as the clear Being of Light, in unconditional love to come forward.

"And as you find yourself in the position of the feeling state of this presence of being, the understanding of moving forward through lifetime - all the areas of that which has come forward in the word: the word from many the understandings of the beings in the environment - the understandings of parents, of teachers, of sages, of various beings - as they bring forward through the connectivity of your presence, their personal understandings. So it is at this time you have ability, in the experience of connectivity through a dimension, to clear all experience of that which has gone before, into the present state of being - with the ability to bring forward, through the connectivity of Thoth at this time, to bring it to the experience the ancient knowledge of your presence.

"It is in the moving forward through the experience of the head - the connectivity of the word of the many of language in that which is brought forward in the disturbance in the connectivity of the head - so it is, Beloved Ones, that you feel yourselves in the connection of heart.

"To feel the knowledge into the silent state of the presence of stillness, in the presence of unconditional love. It is the silent knowledge to hold within, in the continuation of physicality through lifetime after lifetime - eternal Being of Light, that you are - continuation of the presence of Spirit through intent to go forward in the continuation of movement.

"Presence of the Angelics to surround you at this time and allow yourselves to move through the blending of connectivity with the Beings of Light supporting in bringing forward the silent knowledge as you feel it, expanding the being, expanding the consciousness to bring forward at all times - be there desire to return into physicality once more - to hold all knowledge. To not ever let go through the understanding of lifetime continuous. Holding of agelessness, in the presence of the silent state of connection of the over lighting presence, at this time, of the Godhead. Begin to feel yourself moving and blending into the connectivities of great Light, the experience of Bliss, the experience of Bliss and unconditional love, to feel only the heart - to feel all knowledge of the heart. To feel it in the consciousness of your being.

"So it is at this time, Beloved Ones, that you feel a presence of communion - the Angelics of communication of the Godhead - to feel the over lighting presence as you move into the connectivities further, as you move through love, as you move forward through the feeling state of the heart, of deep knowledge of understanding, connection of all knowledge of the Monad, through many lifetime, as it begins to shift through the being, as it opens the heart, in the silence of presence of connectivity of the Godhead.

"It is in the clarity of clearing through heart centre at this time. The simplicity, and yet the understandings beyond star system, of all that has taken place in all of creation. The feeling state of connectivity in this manner to go forward. Endeavour to let go of the memory of lifetimes, to continue forward through the dimension to star system and beyond, to the return to the physicality of the experience of Earth - with clarity of the heart, the feeling state of Bliss.

"It is at this time you have the ability. in support and intent of the being that is Thoth, to support you in the understandings of the Angelics, to be felt by their presence. Compassion, Light energy - it is the lightness of knowing, Beloved Ones, in this state of being. As memory comes forward through connectivities of star systems, the galaxies beyond the experience to be felt in one position of Bliss. Knowingness and Light, the Divinity of all creation to be felt at this time. The support of this being at this time to take you forward over many experience to follow: through the connectivities, through intent of the silent knowledge within the heart, to support you continuously in all that takes place in the understanding of the continuation of physicality.

"Knowledge within of an ability and the continuation through many experience, and Light and unconditional love. There begins to be felt from the area of the heart the connectivity of Thoth to support you in unfolding the mysteries - mysteries of self, of humanity, of Earth - in the ability through expansion of feeling. Through all that has been cleared from the past, through intent of others the bringing forward of knowledge to create the feeling of fallen state, so it is at this time, as you come together in the connectivities with being to support you, that you move together in the understanding of the feeling of Divinity. To go forward always with clarity of state of the feeling of unconditional love.

"As it moves through the experience of form; knowledge and understanding of that which is form, not only the physical body it is. It is the expansion of all of understandings throughout the connectivities of Light surrounding you. For all ancient knowledge, as you hold it within the feeling state of the presence of form, Beloved Ones, as you begin to feel the gentle return to the area and position of the ascension seat, begin to find yourselves in the presence of Thoth. Continues to be supportive communication through dream state - through out-of-body experience - in deep connection to move forward through the procedures that continues into the understanding of the feeling state of knowledge within. As you hold your Divinity at this time, so you hold your energy and Light. So it is in love to come together, with the experience of the Angelics to surround you at this time, beginning to hold the energy field to support you in all areas of the continuation of return. Take forward the understanding from the heart, that begins to be felt by many.

"As there comes into the beginnings of returning through Merkabah once more, begin to feel the connectivities of the Light surrounding you and begin to return to the physical state - it is into the connection to form - to bring forward all that has been shifted to the silent knowledge within the heart, as you feel it in the presence of your Divinity and your Light. To feel it in the expansion of the ability to hold and move forwards with intent, of clarity of Light and of love. As you begin to feel the presence of the Angelic being that is Raphael to enfold you with the Light of healing from the Godhead, as you feel it, as it touches the heart, surrounding your form, as it clears and opens to silent knowledge within. As all that has gone before the understanding to continue forward in eternity, through the experience of ascension at all time.

"Bringing forward into the grounding physicality at this time, begin to feel the presence - your connectedness to Earth - the presence of Angelic form continuing to hold you. Expansion and the feeling state of unconditional love surrounding you, heart centre opening. It is in the blending procedure at this time, Beloved Ones, the over lighting presence of the Godhead at this time to surround and support you. It is through connectivities on two occasion more to come to the three, to repeat procedure, Beloved Ones.

"As I work with you on this day, Beloved Ones, through the connectivity of the Godhead to over light and support you on your way forward - in the feeling state of the shift taking place within your beings - I come forward in love from Spirit, Beloved Ones, surround you in the blessings of great Light. Greetings to you."

The Monad

The pathway of soul, relative to releasing Earth Karma in order to shift to higher dimensions, is better understood if the concept of the Monad and its relationship to the human being is discussed.

The Monad is the greatest, most complete state of an individual's soul and it is part of the Godhead, as an emanation out of that collective consciousness. Although it always resonates with the planet or star of its individualised origin, it is the energy of the Godhead which is in place as an emanation of itself: the Monad. The Monad emanates out of the collective state of the Godhead into being, in order to experience individual life in the different dimensions. Once the Monad has been issued forth out from the Godhead its great energy can split itself up into smaller energy portions, if needs be. There are many different reasons for the great Monad energy to split up. Sometimes these splits are necessary for a soul presence to help others in the lower dimensions to recover their Light and at other times the splits occur due to the individual choices which create the separation within the Godhead consciousness of the Monad. Therefore, the degeneration of the Monad energy into smaller portions of itself can be done from an altruistic or a selfish perspective.

The degree of separation from the Monadic Oneness is felt by a smaller portion of the Monad, which we call the individual soul presence, as a sense of disquiet or dissatisfaction. This is because the total state of the self is not complete. The Monad energy is always Divine Godhead energy and that energy is always contained, to a greater or lesser degree, in all individuals - including you and me. Any separation away from this, no matter which planet or star that existence will be experienced upon, is the reason there is a quest all over the Universe to re-attain the Oneness of Being of the Monad. Life in the realm of duality, in the 3rd and 4th dimensions of physicality where we are, is far off from the Monadic experience. If we consider that the Siriun Monad is a 12th dimension experience and that we are trying to re-ascend to the 5th dimension state of being right now, it is no wonder that we are generally ill at ease. The drive we feel to do the work to shift ourselves and uplift our consciousness is born of our desire to re-experience the Monad, as ourselves. To assist ourselves, others and Earth, we strive to bring the Monad, or Godhead, experience to Earth while in our physical bodies.

The smaller energy portions of the Monad which experience life in places away from the original planet or star of first inception are conscious of their greater state of soul relative to the energy level of the dimension. Each dimension, in turn, is determined by the consciousness of that portion, or soul presence. Therefore, as we uplift our consciousness we not only get closer to the Monadic experience, but we naturally shift into the higher dimensions too. If a soul presence originated from a Siriun Monad in the 12th dimension, then it has many dimensions to work through from the perspective of an Earth life in the 4th dimension to re-attain Oneness. If the planet of first inception is Earth, the Monad is no less from the Godhead, nor less pure, than a 12th dimension Siriun Monad is. It is just a different type of Monad to the Siriun Monad. Regardless of this, re-attaining the energy of the Monad means re-accessing the Godhead experience of Bliss and Oneness, no matter which planet or star it was that Divine consciousness first became individual.

On Earth, only a certain amount of the energy of a Monad from a higher dimension can be present within a physical human body in the 4th dimension, because of the current limitations of this field of energy. More of the soul energy of the Monad can be present in a 5th dimension human body, and so on up the 'ladder' of consciousness. The amount of energy, or soul presence of the original Monad, that any physical human body can contain is determined by its resonance. The Lighter we are, the lighter our bodies are and the more space they can occupy - as if they were water vapour instead of water. It is for this reason that more of the soul, as a very light and Light form, can occupy that type of a body. Every human being who is presently incarnate on Earth, each with their own unique amount of soul presence in the physical body, is an example of a portion of a higher dimension Monad. As such, although we are separated from the greater state of our Whole souls, we are no less Divine. However, the 'amount' of the soul presence we have within the human body determines the level of awareness of any individual human being and it can change at any time, if we want it to. Therefore, when we uplift our consciousness we automatically become lighter and Lighter and more of our soul presence becomes resident within our physical bodies.

We need to bear in mind that the energy of any soul is always Divine in origin, no matter how small an amount of this energy is present in a human being, because no matter where that Monad presence developed its individuality, or was birthed, it came from the collective consciousness of the Godhead. There can be no other way, because Source energy is the creative energy of the entire Universe. Currently, human beings on Earth tend to contain limited amounts of soul energy, purely because of the present limitations of this dimension which determines the density of the physical body. When these vibrational parameters shift - at the behest of ourselves as we move into the consciousness of living ascension - then so too does the amount of possible higher dimension soul presence within us.

The nature of the Monad's relationship to the state of being of the Godhead is always a direct, Divine one. The relationship of the smaller portions of soul to the Godhead, once they have separated from the Monad, is also governed by that Divinity, but the individual experience of this Divinity depends on the place and dimension in the Universe with which the being resonates. That means that I will regard myself as Divine relative to how much I can understand, and this understanding is governed by the dimension I live within. This is true regardless of which planet or star the Monad emanated out of the Godhead. Osiris refers to this first emanation of individual consciousness out of the collective consciousness of the Godhead as the place of, "*First inception.*"

In the Monad state, at any dimensional level, the consciousness of this state of being is Oneness and the direct relationship to the Godhead is maintained. Once split off from this state of being Whole (as they choose to split up and occupy different planets and stars in different dimensions), all of these various smaller portions of the Monad try and work their energy back up to the level of the Monad. They do this while experiencing existence from their perspective of a smaller soul presence in the various different dimensions - this creates the desire to travel back Home. These travels, which are initially fraught with travail in the lower dimensions, are known of as the Pathway of Soul as it seeks to re-attain the Oneness of the Monad. Maintaining open consciousness with the state of being of the Godhead, from the 5th dimension upwards, makes this easier to do than when in the state of duality.

When all of its smaller portions are reintegrated once again within itself, the Monad is Whole once more. These newly reintegrated portions of the Monad bring with them their different experiences and additional knowledge from dimensions throughout the Universe and they accelerate the shifts to higher dimensions of the lower dimensions. It is this expanded information base of the returning portions of the Monad which expands the collective consciousness of the Godhead.

The question of why the devolution of consciousness was ever necessary can only be answered by those portions of soul who decided to lower their resonance in their quest for individual experience, instead of maintaining themselves at the high frequency state of the Monad as they travelled. As soon as any single portion of the Monad lowered its resonance this created a lower frequency pathway that others might follow. Thus, the different dimensions 'dropped' out of the original high frequency dimension of the 49th/50th dimensions. The complications that followed are relative to how many souls chose to do this and how many souls chose to assist with their recovery. The permutations of experience throughout the dimensions are vast, but the essence of existence everywhere is to re-attain the consciousness of the state of being of the Godhead.

How 'far' away the Godhead is for any individual soul presence, or portion of the Monad such as we are, depends on the resonance of the planet or star where it originally birthed, or became individual, relative to where it is now. Sirius resonates at the 'level' of the 12th dimension and this is an extremely high dimension, or level of consciousness. 'Below' this level of great Monadic consciousness, other portions of the great soul which experience life on lower dimension planets or stars, seek to work their own presence back to the fullness of their own particular Monad experience.

The Monad is our blueprint and it serves as the homing beacon for our souls. Just as a homing pigeon will travel back to his home no matter how far away from it he is released, we, as soul presence, always respond to the call of our Home. The memory of Home exists within every single strand of our DNA. We can vibrate it back into our conscious reality by uplifting our consciousness. We are positively programmed to seek the highest experiences of the Universe. We will feel dissatisfied until such time as we re-attain this level of consciousness.

For all Monads, once the full state of Divinity is re-attained, movement throughout the dimensions of the Universe by that great soul is determined by the Godhead energy it resonates with - it is omnipresent and omniscient. This is the God-realised state. Shifting permanently back into the collective consciousness of the Godhead, such as Thoth has indicated he will do after 2012, is the next step. However, that same consciousness can always choose another option later and move into an individual form again.

The Universal Law of Resonance always applies to all forms of consciousness within the Universe. Every soul presence has to set the intention to shift its vibrations to the level of its highest frequency state, if it wants to reconnect to any higher presence of itself - whether known of as the Monad or the Godhead. From the human perspective we shift into the energy of our Higher Self and then our Over Self before we reintegrate with the Monad.

The expansion of the collective consciousness of the Godhead is served throughout the Universe in the various different Monadic forms, or potent, individualised energies. We make frequent reference to the Siriun Monad, or consciousness, in this book. The human individuals, or smaller portions of the various Monads which are present on Earth are not all of Siriun origin, but because the Siriun Monad is of the high frequency of the Godhead, other Monads will automatically resonate with it. It follows that because the origin of a Monad depends on which planet or star a portion of the consciousness of the Godhead *first* became individual, people on Earth may have different Monads. No matter where the Monad originated, for example on Earth, Mars or Sirius, each Monad is linked directly to the Godhead.

Once it has emanated out from the Godhead, it is the choices of the individual portions of that Monad, as it begins to split into smaller portions, which will determine the degree of separation from the state of being of the Godhead - as the soul presence in any particular dimension. This is true no matter where in the Universe the experience of being is.

The planet or star where the smaller portion, or soul presence, of the Monad wishes to gain experience is the determinant, firstly, of how much of the Monad energy can be present - such as when incarnate on Earth in a human body - and, secondly, how close to the Godhead presence of the Monad it remains. This is because each planet or star resonates at a different frequency and may therefore be in a different dimension. People whose planet of first inception is Earth are no less capable of a fully Divine, Godhead experience than those from Sirius or another higher dimension place are. Likewise, all individuals can make the decision to lower their resonance, no matter how great the energy of their originating Monad is. Within each dimension individuals are capable of retaining the purity of the Monad in their experience of existence, but they can also choose to lower it by responding to the frequencies of that dimension.

It is because consciousness and the dimensional experience are dependant on each other that, as the consciousness of the smaller soul presence lifts, so too does the dimensional experience. In this way the divide between the Monad and the smaller portion of the soul presence shrinks. Monads are all states of great Light and portions of them which are currently in human form on Earth are generally from Sirius, Orion, the Pleiades, Venus and Mars, with the predominance from Sirius. Considering that not many people are aware of their origins nor of their Divinity, it is clear that many of us have some conscious-shifting to do before we recover to the state of the Oneness of Being of the Monad.

Therefore, it is understandable that there are many different types of soul presence incarnate on Earth as human beings and that the soul-Light of each intermingles with the soul-Light of others. It is the individual choices that we make which cause the smaller portions of the different Monads, which are now incarnate as humans on Earth, to resonate with different frequencies. Subsequently, the Monadic purity of the soul presence in human beings on Earth is either diluted or enhanced by the many inter-marriages of different soul types and the choices those souls have made.

The soul presence of a baby is called forth to Earth by the intention of the parents as much by its own desire to be here, and that new, incarnating soul presence will therefore resonate with the energy of the parents. Which Monad presence the new baby comes from is determined by the various forces of Karma of all concerned, as well as by the energy of the parents themselves - in accordance with the Law of Resonance. Therefore, for us, it is the choices we make today, the choices we made in our past lives and the collective of all the choices of all of humanity over time, that have determined the possible range of our Earth experiences. It is because of this that Osiris stated that some souls, in the human experience, are currently naturally closer to the Godhead than others are. Considering that we presently resonate with the lower dimensions, we can appreciate that we have shifted far away from the purity of the Monadic experience. It is this purity that we try to recover in our quest for Oneness. With the blueprint of the Monad within us, as part of our DNA, we are naturally programmed to shift back to this experience once more.

From this perspective we see that the Pathway of Soul is always more easily served when human beings of the same energy, or Monad consciousness, work together, marry or follow a spiritual pathway together, regardless of the fact that all Monads are of the Godhead consciousness. In spite of this, because of the extensive period of time that human beings have been on Earth in the lower dimensions, we have gathered Karma with various different people who are of various different Monad origins. Until such time as we shift the energy which amounts to our personal Earth Karma, we will retain some type of a connection or remain in a relationship with each of those different human beings which resonate with those matching vibrations of Karma, no matter how different our soul origin was or our spiritual pathway is. Such is the all-determining nature of resonance.

When we shift our Karma we automatically release our ties to the people (or people with the same vibration) who were involved with those experiences in our past lifetimes. It may help to see each lifetime as continuous with the next, as if we had not died in between. In this way, we can appreciate that the experiences of the previous lifetime were merely the experiences of yesterday. As such they remain with us until resolved.

It is the powerful untying of our energies that allows us to have new relationships and experiences with new people as we progress, or repeat them until we learn. Once clear of Karma, the old, difficult connections become unnecessary - lifetime to lifetime. Many of the children who are on Earth today are having friendships with people that they have never had contact with before, other than when they were in a non-material state of being. This is important because it indicates that they are relatively more Karma-free than their parents are - with the probable exception of their nuclear family relationships. Such is the nature of each successive generation, whereby the children are greater than the parents. This is an important aspect of the evolution of consciousness.

The human experience on Earth has become an unholy mess in many ways, very interesting in other ways or often just plain boring and tedious. Once rediscovered, the pathway we follow for the soul to re-integrate with our Monad is an extremely exciting process. Not only does it make life feel more worthwhile and calm our inner disquiet, but it enhances the joyful experiences of being human too. Connecting to any joy on Earth immediately reminds us of the reason for the joy of creation of life on Earth - to experience this beautiful planet with every-increasing joy and happiness. The progress of human beings, when they link up with others of the same Monad origins, is often that much faster and more pleasant than if they don't. These Monad-mate experiences are unusually intense ones because they are relationships which originated at the highest level of soul. In order to be successful on Earth, they usually require that any Earth Karma which is linked to other people, usually at other levels of soul consciousness, is released first. This is regardless of the fact that these other people may be of a different Monad origin. Karma is Karma and its release from our cellular and soul memories follows a pattern, from low to high frequency states.

There are various types of Monad-mate relationships such as those of lovers, friends, family members or work colleagues. Once developed, these relationships will rarely be severed, even if other Karmic relationships and connections are still being explored. Although, ultimately, we are all soul-mates because we are all products of the same Source energy, when we meet people (a.k.a. smaller bits of soul presence in human form) from our own Monad origins we automatically recognise them. We sense that we know them and we naturally want to be with them more than with others from different Monad origins. A word of caution: most Karmically bound relationships stimulate a powerful emotional response in us too, so it may be difficult to distinguish between the two until that relationship has been explored a little.

Most people on Earth have a Siriun Monad. This is simply because it was the Siriuns who first brought Light to our planet, many millions of years ago, in what may be called the colonisation of Earth, and it was the Siriuns who genetically engineered human beings. Those Siriuns may have had dimensional experiences elsewhere before Sirius and we know that Sirius was once also a planet like Earth, in recovery. After the initial creation of life on our planet, the process of Earth's speeded-up enLightenment involved bringing the Siriun energy of the Godhead into being in the human form, when the Siriun god-beings genetically engineered this new species here. They used a mix between primate and their own god-being DNA - hence the Monadic blueprint within us.

Considering the dimension where we are now, relative to the dimension where the Monad of our souls originated from, there is clearly work to be done. We can better appreciate the importance of bringing the Divine, Monad experience to Earth from this perspective. This begins with us shifting into the 5th dimension state of living. It must be stressed again that, although the dimensions are discussed from a linear perspective, this isn't a true representation of the arrangement of the dimensions or of the energy of the Godhead. Presumably we will be able to comprehend more about this as our consciousness shifts and uplifts.

The Siriun Pathway of Return includes many different dimensional stop-over points which we call the different planets and stars. Therefore, even though a person may not be of Siriun Monadic origin he or she may still resonate strongly with the Siriun Pathway of Return, simply because it resonates with Godhead, or Source, energy. The communications from Sirius can therefore resonate with the energy of all Monads, regardless of their planet of first inception. If a person's Home planet or star lies along this pathway to the Godhead, then the energies of the information that Osiris speaks about will ring true. This is the reason that many people who do not have a Siriun Monad may still resonate with the Siriun Pathway of Return. Those from the Pleiades, as many human beings are, are a case in point. On this pathway, each person, as a soul presence, will go as far as they choose to go.

Conversely, there genuinely are people whose current energy state does not allow them to resonate with the frequencies of the Siriun pathway at all. This is an actual resonance difference and is not that which may be referred to as resistance-based human attitudes which we all go through in the process of our soul progress back towards the Monad presence. There are people who seek power and control at all costs, usually creating war and strife to further their desires. Generally speaking, it may be considered that the people with this attitude have a completely 'alien' soul presence inasmuch as they have fostered more of the lower frequency vibrations within themselves and thus furthered the frequency divide between themselves and the Godhead. In this state they cannot be compatible with the Siriun ideal of unconditional love and compassion for all and anything that resonates with this will make them feel uncomfortable. Nevertheless, all power-hungry people are potentially no less Divine than others are, but for their limiting state of consciousness which prevents them from realising this.

It is because of this type of behaviour that parts of Earth will continue in the 3rd dimension for many aeons to come. Earth will continue to provide itself as a place of learning for all people, no matter where their soul presence originated from or how far down the 'ladder' they resonate. As such, Earth is a powerful teacher-planet within the Universe. Although its current lower frequency vibrations attract many unsavoury characters from the outer-planetary realms, its ancient, high frequency heritage provides a strong Light stimulus which assists with the recovery of many souls into the Light.

The Energy of Soul
It is interesting to note that many people believe that soul never dies - no matter what. If we consider that the dissolution of soul into 'nothingness' effectively

amounts to the death of the soul as an individual presence of consciousness, then it is obvious that this needs to be considered further. If we understand this to mean that the basic energy which makes up the soul cannot be destroyed, this may be considered as true. However, the value of the differentiated energy of an individual soul, as opposed to the undifferentiated energy of 'nothingness,' bears consideration.

Undifferentiated, unordered energy cannot be, and is not, conscious as a soul. The idea that soul cannot die is a fallacy which has been perpetuated amongst humanity by those who wish to ensure that man maintains his spiritual laziness - and this keeps him enslaved within the system. If people knew the impact of their thoughts, emotions and actions on the quality of their soul fabric and if they knew that there is always a very real risk of dissolving into 'nothingness', far more people would be inspired to understand what is important spiritually. This would stimulate the development of more power within each individual as Divinity is understood and reclaimed and, of course, this goes against the sheep mentality which is required by those who would control humanity. Unfortunately, many people have nothing to do with spirituality, because it is often presented as being legitimately accessible only in a religious package. This is not true. Our spiritual connections lie within us individually and it is our individual responsibility to develop them, from within. If we choose to share this experience within the context of a larger group such as a religion, this does not detract from the continued basic truth of our personal responsibility to advance ourselves spiritually.

Nobody in their sane mind wants to be living contrary to the purpose of their existence - which is enLightenment from the Earthly perspective and expansion back into the Oneness of Being of the Godhead, in the Cosmic sense. Were we to work in reverse, our energy would ultimately degenerate into a lesser state: backwards and then out into 'nothingness.' This is in direct contrast to the soul presence expanding itself forwards and upwards, which was the original, designed programme for Earth - as created by the Intelligence of Divine Source to assist with the reintegration of all the 'lost' bits of Itself.

Within the context of the discussion of where the experience of Earth would, could or did go to at various points, it is important to remember that although we are constantly being taught and helped by the great Beings of Light, we are ultimately responsible for our own salvation into the Light. It is this choice that we are all individually responsible for. The Light Beings will neither interfere with our life decisions nor manipulate us. They will suggest and show the way by means of pointing out an Illuminated pathway for us to follow - if we invite them to do so. Whether we do this or not is entirely up to us. Once we have made our choices and set our intention to follow the Light, the Beings of Light will surround us with a phenomenal amount of support in the way of more uplifting, energising, high frequency Light. It is for this reason that the pathway of enLightenment speeds up exponentially as we follow it, in keeping with our intentions.

Therefore, the original backwards motion of our branch of the river is exactly that, us having gone *backwards* in consciousness from the resonance of the 5th dimension, until it reached the lowest point within the 3rd dimension. From this it gradually began looping back upwards again as we slowly shifted our consciousness higher into the 4th dimension. The energy/air/water had to follow this pathway as it was going around in the circle of the pimple-like portion of the balloon. Because of the energy flowing the wrong way around, due to the twist in the balloon, it meant that we have actually been going both upside-down and *backwards* in consciousness - such is the nature of our illusion within this upside-down world!

This backwards, or upside-down, flow became the equivalent of the *devolution* of consciousness of Earthlings - but only while we are in the separated state of physical existence. As we began to shift towards the 5th dimension we began to re-evolve ourselves. When we pop back up into the main balloon again and rejoin the pathway forwards, we will quickly appreciate the fact that this idea of 'lost' time in going backwards is also an illusion, because the continuous forwards motion of all consciousness within the Universe has never stopped. This fact becomes obvious to us when we move forwards in the correct-way-up position.

Considering that physical form is dictated by, or follows, consciousness in the evolutionary process, it stands to reason that the lower the level our conscious awareness is, the lower the level our physical experience will be. This is what accounts for our perception of the seemingly slow passage of our lives and why our sense of time on Earth is so slow and protracted. For the Light Beings, what seems like a long time for us is a *very* short period. For what seems like 34 000 *long* years, we have had a lesser experience of life on Earth than we could have had - because our consciousness shifted downwards and upside-down.

This state of the devolution of consciousness on Earth is also the process of the densification of matter - which naturally opposes and restricts our movement into the lighter states of Light. Now we are at the Point of Return right at the joining place of the twist in the balloon/4th dimension - after climbing back up from the low point of the loop/3rd dimension. When we rejoin the main river of consciousness - by popping up through the loosened neck of the twist - we will be back in the *exact* same place as we were when we left. Imagine spending 34 000 years going in a circle only to return to the same spot we started at!

This sounds a lot like an experience at the top of the Magic Faraway Tree - a series of children's books of the same name by the author Enid Blighton. This series of books, aimed at young readers, describes the adventures of a group of children who live very ordinary lives. It is only when they climb this magical tree that they start to have unusual experiences. Their aim is to get to the uppermost part of the tree where they are always met with the surprise of a new world which has rotated into place up there, as if appearing from the clouds. Entering this new world for them is a bit risky and they never quite know what to expect, because they have no way of knowing which world will be in place. Back down again, the brave, adventurous children go home to be met by a normal, conventional mother who scolds them for the tears and scrapes that bear testimony to their adventures - adventures which are untellable to those of the establishment.

What we have gained in our experience of separated, physical reality, is some extensive experience of what not to do. As a result we have not only recovered somewhat from our naïve pre-Fall mentality, but we have become enormously experienced in the process too. Apparently this has been important for some souls in terms of needing to understand what existence *could* be - relative to what needn't be experienced. Although 3rd and 4th dimension Earth existence has become the essential mode of experience for some souls, it is not necessarily the learning requirement for all souls. Although life 'down' here in the 3rd and the 4th dimensions usually amounts to learning the hard way, it is an experience of learning nevertheless.

The up side of this long departure from the Light is that we are not alone in the process of our return to the river of consciousness, which the untwisting of our little portion of the balloon results in. We never have been. Osiris, as the ever-responsible Light Being on Earth who began us on our journey of enLightenment on the main river of consciousness back in the most ancient time when his consciousness was part of that of Enki, has never left us alone. He is a God-realised Light Being who has helped to guide us and prod us repeatedly in the right direction throughout the ages - exactly as he is currently doing via the information he communicates to us through this book. As with all the Light Beings who offer their services to humanity, he will never leave us alone in the dark of the wilderness where humanity lives, no matter who was originally responsible for the situation, and he continues to work with us tirelessly and patiently - whether in physical existence, as he has done in the past, or from the state of Spirit from where he works with us today.

The River of Consciousness Separates
We, as humanity on Earth, have lost sight of the true, open connection to the state of unconditional love of the Godhead - a.k.a. the high frequency spiritual parts of ourselves. Although the disastrous nuclear war, that precipitated the final Fall of Atlantis and of Man represented our loss of the open consciousness of unconditional

love and 5th dimension existence, was certainly a single calamitous event, humanity did not just arrive at that point suddenly. That catastrophe was the result of a progression of events which began with the fall from Grace of one of the great Beings of Light a long time prior to this - hundreds of thousands of years before. It was the misbehaviour of some of the great Beings of Light which started the problems on Earth and which finally culminated in them influencing sufficient others amongst humanity to create the circumstances that could lead to nuclear warfare, climate change and a pole shift. This is what led to the disaster of the Great Deluge, subsequent to the Fall of Atlantis and of Man and the resultant shifted dimension experience of Earth into the lower dimension - the 3rd dimension. Mankind obediently followed their leaders, seeing them as holy lords worthy of worship. To this end they were blind to the dark reality of the power needs of some of them. It is worthwhile reiterating that, horrifyingly, the lead-up to that time of nuclear disaster, the pole shift and the Great Deluge that followed in the Atlantean Era, was very similar to the potential nuclear disaster situations we still face and the climate crisis we find ourselves in currently.

Regardless of what happened to separate us from our Divinity, Osiris reminds us that, in love, we blend back together again in the shifted dimension processes - as we see from this excerpt from the meditation which dates back to December 2008.

Osiris: Release Duality

"Beloved Ones, in the silent state of love we blend together, the Divine wisdom to come forward to support all pathway through the release in all areas - of the understanding of separation, of duality - be it for momentarily the feeling-state. So it is to continue forward, the allowing and the acceptance of the self to the moving forward though the dimensional experience - abilities in all areas of manifestation, of creation of co-creation."

The Being of Light who led people astray in the first instance was originally one of the leaders of the enLightenment process on Earth many millions of years ago, but the lowered frequencies of the Earth environment negatively affected him and his ego led him astray. This individual is called Enlil in translations of the Sumerian clay tablets. In Atlantean times he was known by the name Satankhare. The potential to shift frequency into a lowered state is a known risk all Light Beings run when in contact with the constant lower frequency vibrations of the lower dimensions of the Universe. Subsequent to his Fall from Grace this erstwhile Light Being influenced others of his ilk away from the Light and they in turn continued to influence humanity too. Human beings have thus been used as handy pawns in power games for a long time on Earth. In this way the first generation of the descendants of who Osiris has referred to as the, "*Dark Brother*," started to distort the Bliss consciousness of the other outer-planetary Beings of Light who originally came to Earth, as well as the born-into-Bliss consciousness of new souls who began life as humans on Earth. The wars between Light and dark began on Earth almost from the beginning and they wage on today. These wars continue mainly because humanity naively allows them to.

In time, as societies developed and evolved, the behaviours and consciousness of darkness not only became part of the genetic, or cellular, inheritance of each successive generation of beings born on Earth, but those who had already Fallen from Grace, whether outer planetary or human being, also moved onto the cycle of reincarnation in an attempt to work through their Karma. This had to be the case, because at death of the physical body all experiences *from* Earth are carried back with the soul, as consciousness. These frequencies are an integral part of the soul. Generally speaking, Earth Karma has to be cleared from the place of Earth before the soul can move onto other experiences in the Universe.

This process has continued repeatedly over time and we still find ourselves on this Karma/low frequency-clearing cycle of reincarnation today. Subsequently, none of us, as human beings, have escaped this Earth-generated Karma, no matter whether we inherited the lowered resonance genetically or whether we created it ourselves. It is for this reason it may be said that we have all been all things over the course of our various lifetimes - whether princes or paupers, murderers or saints. Therefore, it cannot be wise for anybody to judge the current life experience of anybody else, or of ourselves. The ideal would be for all of us to be consciously working to help each other to seek higher frequency states of Light far more quickly than we would do alone. We could do this if we had the knowledge to do so. This is important, because the separation of even one of us from the unified state of being of the Godhead means the incompleteness of the Whole continues. It is because of this that the programme of enLightenment will continue until each soul finds the Light once more.

Interestingly enough, we seldom remember the wonderful, happy lifetimes when doing a past lifetime regression, because those resonances are carried through on the soul fabric, into our new lives, as our talents and blessings. We don't often stop to think about and be thankful for these blessings and tend to take them for granted. Instead, it is the low frequency resonances and Karma which we still have to resolve and master that we notice as the unpleasant facts of life. The resonant frequency of our Karma usually involves challenges which are in keeping with our life lessons. It is this that we try to transcend.

Regardless of all the trauma and strife of lifetimes past, knowing how we are truly one with the Light allows us to feel it in our hearts. In this way we reconnect to our Divinity, as if the Angelic presence itself. This excerpt from a December 2008 meditation details this.

Osiris: Blessings of Love

"As you feel yourself in communication in the feeling-state within the self and the Light presence of Spirit, of Divinity, of connectivity to the Godhead - as you feel it, Beloved Ones, as it is repeated within your heart, through Bliss and unconditional love of understanding of being as one.

"Beloved Ones, as you feel the re-connectivity to the self, it is on this day, I wish to bring forward the presence to surround you with much love from Spirit in the continuation of procedures of integration. You are carried in the continuation - it is as you feel yourselves as the Angelic presence to be carried forward at all times, in Bliss and in Light, Beloved Ones, and in love.

"I bless you on this day, Beloved Ones. Greetings and blessings to you".

Earth's Dark Heritage

The beginning of man's progress into the Dark, relative to our relatively recent although still very ancient history, under the sway of the Brothers of Darkness (who were previously Beings of Light) commenced sometime towards the end of Lemurian society, about 300 000 years ago. This was when the potential for duality was established. Lemurian society ran concurrently with Atlantean society before it disappeared completely and Atlantean society continued. Gradually, since the beginnings of the darkness of that time, there was a movement of more and more of the inhabitants of Earth *away* from the main pathway of the consciousness of unconditional love and enLightenment. The second a low frequency resonance was generated on Earth, the main river of enLightened consciousness began to slow down, even if it was an imperceptible reduction of pace at first. We must bear in mind that the beginning of this Atlantean Era darkness set into motion the movement of Earth's inhabitants directly onto the pathway of 3rd dimension destruction once more. Reversing this trend once it starts is very difficult to do.

There have been many ups and downs over the course of Earth history. A long time ago, the pathway of destruction which Earth's inhabitants had chosen ended in the obliteration of life - at the end of the Dinosaur Age. Interestingly enough, the outer-planetary souls who were involved in the misbehaviour of the Earths inhabitants in their reptilian stage, were the same consciousness of those beings who were responsible for the beginning of the dark influences of humanity in this more modern time - and which ultimately led to the Fall of Atlantis and of Man. In this way, we can see that soul presence, or consciousness, gets many different chances over vast periods of time to recover its Light. Sometimes this is successful, sometimes not. The full consciousness of the soul of the original Brother of Darkness is no longer on Earth, but its influences, in the guise of many darkened, low frequency human souls, continues. Fortunately, this is changing now and the more people who uplift their consciousness, the more this positively influences all others.

Over an extensive period of time more and more individuals, and then whole societies, were influenced into Earthly misbehaviour by what had become a band of individuals known as the Princes of Darkness. Earth inhabitants grew accustomed to living with the effects of the loss of pure love and Light from their lives. Their offspring knew no better either as they were socialised into this way of being right from birth. Even today, Osiris informs us that there exist whole nations of people who do not have *any* concept of love in their lives. This is the sad result of the expulsion of the balancing feminine energy from masculine energy. Attempting to eradicate spirituality by banning religious or spiritual practices is an obvious attempt at gaining more Earthly power and control over people. After a few generations of this, many children grow up within a spiritually impoverished environment. This lowers the resonance of whole nations and the large landmasses they inhabit.

Similarly, in the times of Ancient Atlantis, generation upon generation of Earth's inhabitants helped to slow down the energy of the main river of enLightenment until it stopped its flow forward sufficiently to allow the beginning of what was to become the backward-looping, twisted-balloon branch of the river at that calamitous time, 34 000 years ago. Those beings who stayed on the main river of consciousness continued forwards elsewhere, seeking ever more Light. Some of them have not looked back and have continued with the important project of furthering Universal expansion - which is for the benefit of the entire Cosmos. At times, some of them came back to Earth to help with the programme of enLightenment - such as occurred in the Ancient Egyptian Era when the god-beings such as Isis, Osiris, Horus, Thoth and Enki Ptah came back to Earth.

Other than these appearances on Earth, many of the Beings of Light support us with their high frequency energy from afar and there is always a band of Angelic Light Beings, including the Archangels, who stand in constant, protective, loving attendance. We can call on these Angels to support us at any time. On Earth the knowledge and the wisdom of the Beings of Light is available to humanity at all times, whether through ancient texts, modern transcribed channelled texts, perfectly aligned temple structures with the stars, through promptings from others or from inner experiences, such as in the guise of dreams, accessing the Akashic records, intuitions or synchronistic events. We are not alone.

Once separated from the dissidents, the main river of Light and its inhabitants regained its forward impetus and continued on, regardless of the loss of a part of themselves. We refer to those who exist there as the Light Beings or those in Spirit, including our dead relatives. The branch which was flowing in a different direction continued as this new, looping tributary of the twist, along with its densely physical, human inhabitants. The disconnected loop maintained a distorted life due to the dissonant energies of this rebellious branch of water. This distortion has expressed itself in what we know of as the physical, material world being the *only* thing which appears as real and the *only* existence we can know. This is the *illusion* which is referred to as *maya*. It is time to bridge the divide between that illusion and the true reality of living ascension.

The branching balloon-twist of the loop, once fragmented and mostly separated from the main river, could more easily set its own pace and form a 'life' of its own. However, once separated from the main river, that great flow of consciousness appeared distant, different and unreal, surreal even - hence the sense that our spiritual origins appear so unreal and remote to us in our physical lives. Living within the 3rd dimension resonance state of the isolated dissident loop and constantly stimulated by the lower frequencies dominant there, meant it was both immediate and understandable for those within it - this is our material world. No matter which dimension we resonate with, that will be the only one we are aware of when in either the 3rd or the 4th dimensions.

Fortunately, however, the dissident loop, which is the twisted pimple-like portion of the balloon, could not be completely disconnected from the main river of Light and so these highly charged waters kept feeding into the branched, rebellious portion of the river all the time. The connection was maintained, separated though it now appeared to be.

We see how the unconditional love of the Light Beings of the Godhead has been with us all the time and how we shift and change at this time of our progress into the Light - in connectivity to the star system of Sirius.

Osiris: Consciousness and the Physical Form Shift

"Through the dimension of experience of connectedness of unconditional love at this time, to be supported by the presence of being over coming period through various procedures to support in the bringing forward of greater knowledge, of bringing forward of the understanding and the position of your birth in physicality at this time to that which your are at this present position in consciousness. As you begin to make the pathway though the shift, it is through dimension, as the consciousness within the form begins to move - all that takes place through the movement of physicality, the workings of the physical body, as you move into the experience of greater Light. Through decision and intent at this time of the bringing forward of all that has been intended through the connectivity, as you move and blend as one through the connection of the star system."

The highly charged waters of the main river of consciousness are made up of the energies of Light from the various outer-planetary sources and the communications of the Light Beings in Spirit. No matter how separated we might feel we are from the realms of Spirit, we aren't really. Earth reality is just an upside-down reality - reality with a twist.

Once settled into the 'reality' of the separated, dense space of pure physicality, it was this branching, dissident, balloon-loop that had pirate skippers of its own. Once Earth consciousness had branched off from the easy flow of the main river of consciousness, these new masters thought they could more easily chart a fresh course without undue interference from the Captains of Light in Spirit - but they were wrong. The Speed-Demons of the Dark who forged the new direction for the dissident loop of the river did not reckon with the powerful vibrations of the high frequencies of Light which created an attractor-like pull back towards the main river. In time the impetus of the original dissention started to fade and the attraction to Light altered the mutinous course of the pirated branch of the river.

The Light Beings maintained their own progress on the main river of consciousness, thereby ensuring the availability of a powerful and constant magnet-like attraction by humanity to a higher frequency state. This magnetic attraction amounts to our yearning for Home when we are in the 3rd or 4th dimensions of physicality and it is the reason for our constant desire to seek spiritual understanding and connection.

This natural, magnetic attraction we have for the Light is what caused us to stay connected, albeit in a twisted way within our balloon-like curve. *This* stopped the energy of the 3rd dimension pathway from devolving still further. It prevented us breaking out - as if in an outreaching line, from bursting through the balloon membrane and from dissolving our consciousness and Earth into 'nothingness'. *This* attraction we have for the Light is what ensured our eventual return to the main river - when it will reconnect at the very point of its original departure. *This* is the Point of Return. In fact, this return has already happened in 'now time.'

This marks our return to the uplifted state of consciousness which we 'fell' from so long ago.

Arriving at this point in the untwisting of our reality suggests that we have conquered the manipulators of humanity. Then we will have returned to the ability to be in open communication with the consciousness of the Godhead once more. The actualisation of the Return is a real, physical shift of dimension for Earth and her inhabitants - if this is chosen by them. The actual time of happening of the Return is denoted and recorded by the end of the Mayan Calendar. This is the central point of the Age of Aquarius - the year 2012. 2013 is the first year of the new, higher consciousness.

This shift into an alternative dimension of experience is the end of what turned out to be a *very* long road of darkness. It is the beginning of our time of living ascension, if that is what we choose for ourselves. Although Earth is a body of great Light, we experience her relative to our own frequency. We also impact on Earth relative to our frequency. As we shift, Earth shifts those lower frequency vibrations which have contaminated her too. Earth and some of her inhabitants will definitely be shifting dimension and it is for each of us individually to decide whether or not we want to be a part of this process of upliftment. It is this setting of the intention, coupled with living it with intent, with unconditional love, which will assist us to make the requisite changes to accommodate the shifted dimension processes as we travel forwards on the Pathway of Return.

* * * * * * * * * *

CHAPTER SEVEN

Separation

"Man is a star bound to a body, until in the end, he is freed through his strife. Only by struggle and toiling thy utmost shall the star within thee bloom out in new life. He who knows the commencement of all things, free is his star from the realms of the night."

(The Emerald Tablets of Thoth-The-Atlantean p15; pp6)

Why did God allow this?
Many people want to know why 'God' did this to us, or how He could stand by and watch His children suffer considering that He could have stopped this nonsense at any point He chose to do so. These types of questions are posed, because people are working with the mistaken belief that their lives are controlled by external forces - whether from a benevolent or punishing 'God' makes no difference. This is not true. We are, just as we have always been, the masters of our own destiny - even to the extent that we shape our reality. Our choices reign supreme in shaping our lives and these choices are made in keeping with our perceptual ability, which is determined by our resonance.

God is not a person. What we refer to as the Supreme Being of God is actually the Godhead, or Source. The Godhead is a state of being, a state of consciousness. As such the Godhead is neither a being nor a place. It is a state of existence within the Universe. It is also the total consciousness of the Universe. As such, the Oneness of the Godhead is a collective state of consciousness which is made up of all individual consciousnesses that are, or have become, Bliss-realised. The actualisation of the state of Oneness of the Godhead, or God-realisation, is considered to be the spiritual goal for all souls.

In answer to a question from a person who is well-versed in matters Biblical, whether or not it is true that there can never be any forgiveness for a sin against the Holy Spirit (the active force of the Godhead) Osiris gave a reassuring answer.

Osiris: Punishment and Forgiveness

"There is always forgiveness. There is no punishment. The punishment comes from the self."

Therefore, the Godhead/God did not *do* this to us. We, as individuals over the ages, did this to ourselves - by virtue of the choices we made, consciously or subconsciously. We chose to move away from the consciousness of Light and therefore out of the existence of pure Bliss of being in open communication with the state of consciousness of the Godhead.

As a state of pure consciousness, of being-ness, the Godhead cannot move away from us. It is only ourselves who can personally appear to shift from this state of consciousness, this experience of reality - with regard to our changing frequencies. The idea of being ignored by the Godhead can never be truly real, because as long as we are contained within the Whole of the Universe we can never truly divorce ourselves from what we are naturally a part of. A divorce can only happen if we shift our resonance so low as to dissolve into 'nothingness.'

This actual non-separation is the case no matter how big the problem is, such as a nuclear explosion, which moves the energy around to create an apparent separation within the system. It is only if we are truly outside of the system and have shifted lower than the 3rd dimension frequencies that we are separated. However, in the 3rd and the 4th dimensions, we can certainly continue with the illusion, or pretend to be separated, if we choose to do so. Within the context of this illusion we can end up maintaining the pretended experience of separation as our reality. Alternatively, we may strive to 'put all our bits back together again' so as to realise our inherent Wholeness - just like 'all the king's horses and all the king's men' tried to do to the nursery rhyme character, Humpty Dumpty.

The ridiculous part of any energy-divisive action within the Universe is that we come to believe that the apparent result is the only reality. In truth, our illusionary separation from the spiritual realms is merely a distancing, rather than a true separation. The 3rd and 4th dimensions of reality are still contained within the Universe and that Universe is teeming with life. We just haven't been able to understand exactly where to find the gateways to access those other life forms yet.

The shock of the impact of this knowledge may be in realising the degree to which we, as human beings, have abdicated our responsibility to ourselves and to our own spiritual progress. The liberating part of this understanding is in knowing that we are in full control of which state of consciousness we want to exist within and that nothing or nobody is actually in control of this other than ourselves. That is very freeing.

At this point it is worthwhile reading a short dialogue from Osiris as it is relevant in terms of the idea of separation from the Divine and the reason for this. This is to be understood within the context of a discussion pertaining to the fact that there is no punishing God who will judge us or relegate us to either purgatory or hell.

Osiris: The only Punishment is Separation from the Divine

Q: Osiris, in terms of the punishment of the self, is it correct to state that any separation from the Divine state of Being is punishment, by definition.
"It is, Beloved One. It is to state there is not being that is Thoth that is standing over yourself in form of punisher. It is not this. This being is being of great Light that brings forward the assistance and support at all times to the beings of humanity."

Q: And the punishment, as it were, is the arduous journey back Home (to the Light)?
"It is so. It is, Beloved One. Understanding it is lengthy and arduous. Understanding it is many millennia of continuation of that which is in the feeling state of great despair."

The Purpose of Separation
Q: What was, and is, the purpose of this?
"It is the intent of beings of darkness on many occasion and interference and of the desire to hinder beings moving forward into the state of great Light, in the creation and the manipulation of the creation of power. And it is power over other being, and in all areas of the connection of power over other beings - so it is not coming forward into the pathway to Light."

Q: Is this ultimately about taking over the Universe?
"It is, Beloved One, understanding that you find yourselves in the interconnection of many beings at this time, of knowledge of many beings in the outer experience of Universal System. Understanding it is coming forward at greater intensity at this time. Understanding it has always been there, but it is in its understanding, it is in its expansiveness to do and therefore it is as you have communicated on many occasion of various war of the star, Beloved One, and so it is a reality."

East Separates from West
Although neither society is perfect, it is interesting to take note of the fact that the approach to religious tolerance in the East is often very different from the approach in the West. Some may regard this as an indication of the manner in which information has been manipulated, or not - although there is no religion on Earth today which has escaped this type of disturbance.

It has been noted that the Eastern religions generally have an actual, real working tolerance - both between the different religions and of individuals within them. In some countries, the various people happily live side by side with those of apparently different, if not starkly opposing, religious beliefs - unless there is influence from marauding peoples from outside of these areas. In the holy Indian city of Varanassi, for example, various different religious belief systems are denoted by the clothing and facial markings of the people, yet they rub shoulders in the market and jostle with each other in the morning and evening exodus into and out of the bathing ghats for their twice daily greetings of Mother Ganga - the Ganges River. The Ganges is the Indian river of consciousness which bears similarities to the Nile, Africa's river of consciousness and the Seine, Europe's river of consciousness.

The entire presence of being, as humans in India, is starkly different from anything seen in the Western perspective. Although there is certainly poverty in India, to dwell on this with the emotion of pity would be to view only one side of the coin - and this coin is a very interesting one to look at from both sides. All too often Westerners are struck by the apparent suffering of these people and are moved to remark on it and try to fix it. What many are completely unaware of is that so many of these people are living ultra-simple lives in a state of complete happiness. Osiris has commented on this fact many times when discussing India.

People generally take their own standard of living to be the optimal one and judge everything else relative to this. However, many of those very poor people living in India are souls who come to Earth for the pure, simple and often short experience of being human. They are just passing through. In this they are achieving exactly what they set out to achieve and they have no sense of suffering, in their poverty, as we might view it. Others among them however, are absolutely and fully entrenched in the Karmic cycle of poverty consciousness. These are the beggars who accost us, weeping and wailing on the streets as they implore us to part with our money. In order not to further entrench into their consciousness the idea of being victims we would do well to firmly ignore their pleadings. This then could become the starting point from which they may be able to stop the coercive behaviour, move out of their sense of helplessness and thus begin the self-responsibility process of uplifting their own state of consciousness.

Once we have the beginnings of an understanding of the different contexts of the poverty in India, we can begin to look through and beyond it and start to see other aspects of the society which are both fascinating and humbling. At an individual level, we can see and feel clear evidence of a peace and tranquillity in this society which is born out of the tolerance between individuals who practice different religions and have varying degrees of comfort in their life experiences. Life there has not always been this way and there have certainly been deplorable incidents of intolerance that colour India's history. Nevertheless, today there is evidence of pockets of an overall tolerance which is rarely found elsewhere. This intrinsic tolerance within the society is easily seen echoed in the incredible ease with which vast numbers of people are able to move around on the streets and the motorways, by using every conceivable form of transport. There is both a noticeable absence of aggression towards each other and remarkably few bumps or accidents.

There are very few traffic lights in many of the simple Indian cities, other than in the modern, more Westernised ones like Delhi and Mumbai, and yet the huge and never-ending volume of traffic flows like an undulating river. On the surface of it, and certainly from the viewpoint of a Western eye, it appears as if the traffic is in a perpetual state of absolute chaos - and frighteningly so too. There is no apparent order whatsoever. There is constant movement in all directions at once. It is exactly this that is at the crux of its success. There is a true, inherent order within the system.

This is the same natural order which enables birds to fly in a flock or fish to swim in a shoal in perfect synchronisation with each other. This behaviour may be understood as a display of Divine Intelligence in action. It is this subtle order that the Western eye very rarely picks up on, because it has become completely foreign to us. Therefore, all we see is chaos. If something is unknown to us it means we do not have the experience of exposure to it to be able to accurately assess what we observe. This is how we are often blinded to realities which do not echo our own. Therein we find the beginnings of judgement and prejudice.

The flowing traffic in India never stops. There are no jarring stop-and-start movements and each and every single individual vehicle driver - whether foot, animal or motor engine propelled - appears to have the innate ability to behave in the collective, as if they are all one. In this singular oneness, if any individual part of the whole writhing mass of traffic moves or changes direction, pace or impetus forward, then they all *immediately* respond with the necessary adjustment to ensure proper flow of the whole. There is a constant slowing, quickening and moving to the left or the right - depending on the requirement of what appears to be the entire throng of vehicles. Entire highways of traffic slow to a standstill to allow a vehicle to enter or cross from a side street. Right of way is determined by the need to *have* right of way. This is in stark contrast to the Western perspective of the right of an individual being equated to that which has to be enforced or demanded. In a spiritually advanced society a true right is naturally acknowledged, conceded and enjoyed by all concerned. Unconditional love has its own natural boundaries.

Of course there is also an awful lot of noise that accompanies these traffic movements as each individual signals his place in the melee, reminding others where he is or his intention to move into or out of it. Each hoot of the horn is heeded as a request for entry, passage out or shift over - as easily as if, "Please may I...?" was said and

"Of course you may," was answered. There is the subsequent easing into a new space and the finding of a new pace. There is no exception to this remarkable rule no matter how dusty the streets nor how fancy or imperfect the vehicle. Buses and rickshaws have equal value in this system, no matter how wide or narrow the roadway.

It is this remarkable ability of the traffic to flow as it does, viewed as apparent chaos by the Western eye, which is true to a natural order. The evidence that there *is* a natural order is borne out in the fact that the end result is arrived at more regularly than not - a safe transit. It is this good result that is delivered from a society's attitude of the tolerance towards the needs and attitudes of others, in peace. Tolerance practiced generation to generation is no less a learned behaviour than *in*tolerance is. As such any society can change its mind at any point. Such is the result of the beauty of free will - of choice demonstrated in the collective - in an over-crowded Indian city in the 21st century.

In the West we generally find that the order in our rules and strictly policed laws comforts us. However, we are easily outraged at any transgression of the rules that dictate and form this order. People who have grown up with this naturally see this system as normal and desirable. What is not realised is that this apparent order has been super-imposed onto the individuals of the society and that the natural rhythm of life, replete with its innate ability to order itself, has been interfered with.

It is those very individuals who are constantly and rudely forced to order, who are also intrinsically capable of ordering themselves, just as the Indian city drivers are. Yet there is a persistence in maintaining an overly structured approach to life - with the resultant straitjacketing of natural abilities. The fear that anarchy is the result of chaos supersedes the understanding that chaos itself is a relative term. The rules and principles of good traffic flow are a simple example of how the whole of Western society has had order imposed upon it at every single level. The fear of revolution, mayhem and disorder that purportedly arises from lawlessness is the abiding inspiration for a rule-driven society. As more people act from the basis of unconditional love, less rules are needed, because unconditional love creates its own boundaries.

Various studies have been done, most notably in the United Kingdom, where traffic lights were disabled for a period of time in order to determine how traffic flow would fare. Remarkably, there was no significant deterioration in the traffic flow. Yet the Western world is peppered with the ever-blinking eyes of our coloured traffic lights, reminding us of the contrast of right and wrong and telling us what to do. Externally controlled as always, people have been taught to comply and so further entrench the 'fact' into consciousness that external controls are natural, required and valid.

Although this small example is a gross generalisation of societal behaviour it nevertheless serves to inform us of the systemised manner in which many human beings inadvertently move away from the rhythms of natural order on a daily basis. This creates imbalances which are reflected throughout the society.

This discussion is not necessarily criticism of the simple, necessary ordering of the functions of a society which support ease of living. It relates to something far greater - something that affects the consciousness of humanity.

Once overly ordered and regulated, internal power is subtly stripped from people at so many levels that it impacts not only on our societies, but on individual, personal power too. The result of this is that people forget to practice the use of their basic innate ability to regulate themselves, they forget the glory of their uniqueness and they are at risk of being played like puppets. Underlying this - in one guise or another - is the root cause of fear.

Individual human beings often judge each other in terms of laws and point fingers at anybody who does something different from the rule-established norm. Whole mini-societies within the greater society strive to 'look good' to others and to put on a 'brave face.' Any kind of a face other than the truth of who they really are or how they really feel is essentially dishonest. This can never be in line with unconditional love of the self or of others. Therein begin the foundations for intolerance, unhappiness and dissatisfaction - which are perfectly in keeping with the requirements of the Brothers of Darkness. The external pressures of stringent regulations keep us on our toes in fear. We become apprehensive and obedient to the degree that we wish to avoid the pain which, we are taught, is the natural consequence of transgression. We are so intent on avoiding externally imposed pain that we forget to focus on our internal beauty, joy and power.

Osiris has some comments on the issue of fear which creates the need for individuals to connect more deeply with what they know - as a form of comfort. He advises that all people, of all belief systems, act with tolerance towards one another, from the basis of unconditional love.

Osiris: Tolerance

Q: Specifically with regard to the very religious people in my family, I feel a sense of judgement towards me. How best should this be handled?

"It is so, Beloved One, it is in this manner to understand there are many beings at this time, if you are taking from the perspective of the general population, there are many beings moving into the desire through various aspect of coming forward of fear. They move into the desire to connect further in various religion. It is to hold onto a procedure that is of comfort, that is one of security for each being, but it is to understand through the connectivity of yourselves, through the questioning that each being moves into the creation of disturbance that is felt, it comes forward in judgement, Beloved One. It is merely to offer the assistance in a manner to acknowledge that there is the ability to be in a state of great tolerance of one another, no matter in which direction the belief system is. It is always to come forward from unconditional love, Beloved One."

God and War
What we may consider in the analogy of apparently chaotic Indian traffic is what exactly it is that this society has that our Western societies do not have? What is it about Western societies that mean that we are ready to attack each other physically or verbally if one disobeys a traffic rule, such as in instances of road rage? Outrageous and enraged behaviour is very apparent if, horror of horrors, a dissenting comment is made or a perceived insult is heard when we speak of religion.

One 'incorrect' or 'disrespectful' statement from one single person is sufficient to cause a full-scale war or call to a holy war against the infidel or heathen. No matter which religion we look at, people have been jailed or put to death for the sin/crime of blasphemy or heresy for centuries. The horrors of the Inquisitions across Europe, between the years 1232 - 1820, attest to this. These tribunals, which were put in place by the Catholic Church to flush out and punish heresy, are a classic example of the use of man-made rules to support a doctrine which has nothing to do with the spiritual truth of unconditional love or God. Unspeakable horrors and acts of immense cruelty were carried out at this time - and all in the name of religion.

This is as remarkable as it is spiritually irresponsible. God/the Godhead is *so* Great, *so* Loving and *so* Complete that nothing can detract from that state of Bliss. Nothing we do here, or anywhere else, is going to change that Perfection. Therefore, anything we do that purportedly upholds the name of God or the Godhead has to be understood to be in support of the rules, regulations and conditions of man. Although many people may baulk at this statement, its veracity has to be considered deeply. The use of God's/the Godhead's name to justify war is low frequency behaviour at its worst, because it lays claim to the concept of unconditional love to support the actions of *un*-love. If ever there was a sin, or evil, then this has to be what it would look like.

Any call to war in the name of God by *any* person, institution, religion or nation can *never* include an awareness of the consciousness of God. Somewhere in every religious text, God is reputed to be that which epitomises the ideal of unconditional love. Anything in the texts or the behaviour of the faithful which is out of synch with this state of love cannot emanate from God/the Godhead.

The loveless state of war, therefore, has to originate from the manipulations and minds of man. Any division of ourselves which arises from a particular religion laying claim to the ownership of the only true path to Heaven/life everlasting/Nirvana, or where the other is judged and found wanting is, likewise, devoid of love and, therefore, is devoid of the consciousness of God/the Godhead.

Many people have lost all sense of proportion about what is important with regards to spirituality. Too many people have lost sight of unconditional love. We are supposed to remember that we are a soul presence, Divine Beings of Light, who are having a physical experience on Earth. It was never intended that we suffer, or that we go to war against each other. Yet suffer and going to war is what we do.

As Divine Beings of Light, no matter how small our Spark is, we are primarily tuned to the consciousness of love by virtue of the Light within our DNA - and it is intended that we realise this. Most of humanity have forgotten, or been taught to forget, that we are holograms of the Divine, as children of God/the Godhead - or as Isis and Thoth call us, "*Children of Light*." WordWeb's interesting definition of holography tells us more than a little about who we really are - 'Holography: The branch of optics that deals with the use of coherent light from a laser in order to make a hologram that can then be used to create a three-dimensional image.'

As sparks of God/the Godhead therefore, we contain that which is Divine, that which is *of* the Godhead. We would immediately recognise this innate fine-tuning of the Divinity which is contained within ourselves, if we allowed it to surface - by scraping away anything that is not natural. This includes anything superficial, anything that has been super-imposed on us or externally applied. This amounts to removing anything that does not resonate with love. Within us we are Light. We have to go within ourselves to find this Light and to re-kindle it so that it becomes a roaring flame of Love-Light again and enables us to consciously resonate with the higher frequencies of Light.

The route to this Divinity within can never be found outside of ourselves and it can certainly never be found while we are so busy looking for satisfaction out there either. As long as we are so externally preoccupied we will never go within. Consequently, we will never find the Light switches within us and we will inadvertently continue to serve the Brothers of Darkness.

We would be able to easily remember this fact of our Divinity if we, as the group of humanity, had not taken our twisty, balloon-loop joy ride away from the main course of the river of consciousness so long ago. Some of us chose this pathway deliberately, others were saddened by the choice of this pathway, but continue to help humanity to recover the situation and yet others have unconsciously become caught up in the collective rollercoaster ride of it. Regardless of this, when we do finally awaken to what has happened it will be a bit like waking up the morning after a drunken night out on the town - we will be horrified and ashamed at our irresponsible and silly behaviour and, although sometimes we will have some apologies to make to correct our indiscretions, we will be relieved to be sober. If we had not taken this excursion into the dark we would be tolerant of each other, no matter what experience the other individual wished for himself here on Earth nor which pathway Home he or she chose to follow. We would have no problem with remembering to love the other as the self. We would fully understand that we all are One.

Osiris reminds us to feel the connection to the Light Beings and our shifting consciousness, to continue to heal, to take note of synchronistic events, to feel our Divinity and to acknowledge our pathway and the truth.

Osiris: Healing and Divinity

"It is, Beloved Ones, the ability for yourselves, individually to communicate, to feel the presence of Beings of Light at this time grows continuously. There is the connectivities taking place, perhaps not always in same manner from one to another, but it is through these procedures, it is you find yourself moving forward through the shift of consciousness.

"It is through the coming period, Beloved Ones, that I support for yourselves to go through, it is healing once more. It is an understanding to hold your energy through this position. To know and understand that as you bring forward through the many synchronicities, through the many communications, the feeling state of the presence of that which you are, Beloved Ones, at this time, of the presence of your Divinity, of the understanding of your pathway in the continuation of truth. And it is for the perspective that I speak of truth, for each of you to know and understand, you have chosen to move forward in various direction, individually, through the procedure of the living state of ascension - and so it is supporting each of yourselves at this time in the owning and the continuation of this pathway."

It is in the pursuit of expanding and uplifting consciousness that we are able to respect the choices and opinions of others, because this is based on that right which we exercise ourselves: the *free will* to *choose* our experiences. We may observe and objectively comment for the purpose of increasing our knowledge and information base, but we would be ill-advised to judge the choice of another. In many societies this respect for the choices of others is significantly missing to the extent that it is frequently expressed as a complete lack of tolerance for anything other than that which mirrors or echoes the choices of the self - whether expressed in a religious sense, related to government policies or simply by slavishly following the latest fashions.

Sadly, these influences are beginning to impact on young Indians too, for example, as they are enticed by Western ideals and the appearance of success. Rather than being seduced by the glitz and the glamour to the exclusion of all spirituality, it may be understood that we can have it all on Earth, physical abundance, fun *and* spiritual connection.

There is no need to polarise the experiences of any aspect of reality as this maintains the separated state of physicality which we know of as duality. Balance is the key to true and lasting happiness on Earth. There is absolutely no point in sacrificing one reality for the other in the way we have been manipulated into believing we need to do - we do not need to deny the material world in favour of the spiritual world. If each individual was to live and act in a state of pure love, the echo which returns to us from others would be as beautiful as the vibration from ourselves when we started it, just as it was designed to be.

If, as we looked at others and realised that what we see there is that which is a mirror of our own self, then perhaps we would begin to look within and do a spot of spring cleaning. This however, is far from what most people understand to be the case as most of us have become so accustomed to protecting ourselves from others whom we view as the enemy. We live in a state of perpetual fear, disharmony and distrust of others 'out there'. We see others as completely separate from ourselves and we are certainly not taught to view them as mirrors of what lies within ourselves. Further than this, we are not taught to view them as being emanations from the greater state of the Whole. If we did this we would more easily be able to recognise both ourselves and the God-state in others and we would be more able to appreciate the fact that all of us are in service to each other, acting as mirrors of one kind or another, while we release our Karma and low frequency connections.

Simplistically speaking, in this way we may consider that everything we like or dislike in another person may be something we like, dislike, fear, deny or judge within ourselves or in our lives. Taking this concept of self-recognition-via-others a little further, we take note of the fact that this is a function of the resonant harmonies of vibrations of different frequencies - individual to individual.

Nevertheless, taught the importance of external controls and a distrust of that which is innately known and personally experienced, we breed distrust from within ourselves and extend this outwards so that we then resonate with the same distrust as is within our fellow man - who has done the self-same thing to himself. Then, once we look inside ourselves and see the unhappiness there, we look up at our fellow man again and immediately blame him for our woes. We see the mirror of ourselves in him! This is no less than the recognition of ourselves in others, although we do not often willingly acknowledge this. It's a bit like a young puppy barking at himself in the mirror in fright of the 'other puppy' he sees there. It is an illusion that there is a foe out there - for him no less than for us. The greatest enemy is the foe within our self - no matter how low the Brothers of Darkness sink to stimulate our fear of others.

Franklin D. Roosevelt's words on the subject, dating back to 1933, are very apt. He said, "…..the only thing we have to fear is fear itself - nameless, unreasoning, unjustified terror which paralyses needed efforts to convert retreat into advance." Realising the true import of what he said, it would be best to eradicate all concepts of fear from within us in order to make progress.

Choices and Reincarnation
Considering that there has always been a strong contingent of Light Beings teaching humanity the way of Light at the same time as the Dark Beings were weaving their web of lies to influence our choices, human beings must take full, personal responsibility for their choice of bad behaviours, the consequences of which has been our time in the dark. This state of separation from the state of being of the Godhead is the result of the teachings which humanity chose to follow, individually and as a group - even if the entire process began unwittingly with choices from so long ago.

Individually, we reincarnate on Earth until we transcend our own personal darkness, or low resonance states. These extend to the collective of all humanity in a knock-on effect and it is because of this that we have been incarnating into the physical experience of Earth for centuries, on the Wheel of Karma. As souls, we have been recycling ourselves for millennia. In our interactions with each other during those numerous lives, we have become entangled to the degree that we are obliged to not only work off our own Karma and other low resonance states, but to be available in various human relationships to assist our fellow man with working off his or her Karma too. Although helping others is always the choice of each soul, whether in or out of physicality, it remains true to state that until each one of us has reintegrated with the Light, *none* of us can feel fully Whole. Therefore, most souls, no matter where they exist, will feel the impulse to help others, even though they are not obligated to do so.

Until such time as we all achieve the state of living ascension once more, none of us will feel truly free to follow our own Light elsewhere, vibrationally or emotionally. Human beings are currently living the consequences of the choices of many long-past lifetimes. Aside from the original, critical, Atlantean Era choices of so long ago, we have repeatedly been offered options to change our pathway and clear our Karma. These opportunities arise and become the pathway-deciding choices we make during our life lessons during our many reincarnations.

If any person wants to contend that they personally did not, could not do or have not done, the low frequency things which humanity terms evil, and yet they suffer the consequences, this indicates that it is time to reconsider this stance. The facts of reincarnation and our Karmic issues suggest that we *were* all part of all of the happenings on Earth in our past lifetimes, repeatedly. Unless our lives are perfect we can be sure we have Karma to deal with. Whether we like it or not, reincarnation is a fact of our lives. Where and how these lifetimes played out most of us can only guess at, but we all *definitely* played a personal role in the experiences of each of those lives. It is because of this that all of humanity is responsible for where we are personally today. It was the roles in various lifetimes on Earth that created specific frequencies within the individual as well as within the collective consciousness of humanity. It is the low frequency vibrations which make up the stuff of Karma. Although previous lifetimes are often difficult to remember without the help of a skilled therapist, the lack of an accessible memory as a defence against the commission of a crime is not a valid excuse, as any judgement in a court of law will attest to.

We, as humanity in the collective, lived on Earth before and sufficient numbers within humanity colluded, consciously and unconsciously, with the Brothers of Darkness on Earth - time and time again - to maintain low frequency vibrations. We have done this over a series of many lifetimes. Therefore, we all pay for this folly, repeatedly and over our many lifetimes of learning, until we learn to shift the low frequency vibrations to higher frequencies. Conversely, our individual efforts in the Light positively impact on the collective consciousness of humanity.

Our many past lifetimes have typically included a lot of suffering and we continue to pay the price of the many poor choices we made in the past, in our lives today. The flip side of that same coin of our physical Earth lives suggests that individuals amongst humanity have also lived many lives where they worked in the Light, for the purposes of the enLightenment of themselves and humanity. It is because of these lives in service to the Light that we reap the rewards of physical abundance, beauty and joy in its many forms in subsequent lifetimes on Earth. We can enjoy lifetimes which are enhanced with more of the greatness and joy which is naturally available on a higher frequency vibrating Earth and continue on our pathway of Light - ideally in the state of living ascension. Sometimes though, we have a tendency to forget the joy and the beauty which is abundantly available on Earth, in the face of our pain.

Once again, in the furtherance of reclaiming our higher frequency Light in the processes of living ascension, we move from each level of consciousness to a new level. Osiris reminds us about our inherent Divinity and about our ability to create abundance of all forms in our lives. He specifically mentions the ability we have to eradicate poverty - as a consciousness and as an experience - as well as any other form of suffering. He stresses this, especially in the light of the fact that many people have had to endure a lot of hardship in their lives recently (from the 2008 - 2009 financial market collapse). An important point he brings up is, "*Following the heart.*" It is the pure feelings of unconditional love in the heart which can guide us in negotiating our way through difficult circumstances and choices. Taking direction from what lies within the heart will always assist a person and be in keeping with their life purpose.

Although this particular communication was specifically related to a difficult time, it is highly pertinent for all times. Osiris speaks of the eradication of two things from our consciousness: the idea that we are small in any way, and poverty consciousness. He reminds us once more that abundance is ours and that we can bring anything we choose into our lives. These are all powerful and important statements, because they go to the heart of our troubles on Earth: the illusion of separation from Divinity.

Osiris: Guidance and Advice for Moving Forwards on the Pathway of Living Ascension

"Greetings to you, Beloved Ones, I am Osiris, come forward from Spirit on this day, Beloved Ones, to be with you, greetings to you. It is on this day, Beloved Ones, that I wish to support you though communication. It is on this day that I wish to bring forward information and guidance to assist through procedure taking place at this time. It is through pathway of living state of ascension, many of yourselves, moving forward through period of initiation.

"It is to bring this into your understanding, that you have an idea as to the progressive procedures taking place within your pathway of ascension. It is to understand that I work with you in much celebration from Spirit to communicate in this manner - the understanding that you move forward through. This pathway is one of great celebration in Spirit.

"It is, Beloved Ones, through the procedure of this so it is many of yourselves begin to move forward through much release: of the interconnection, of that which has taken place from past linear year, at this period - the understanding that it is for many of yourselves not been entirely easy, through the various states of consciousness, throughout this particular linear year. It is a movement of great transition and through this, Beloved Ones, you bring forward the culmination of all aspect and begin to move into procedure of consciousness that is far easier from this perspective.

"It is to work with each of yourselves, in the release of all aspect of the consciousness, of the letting go of the idea of yourselves being in physicality as the smallness of Beings - it is the letting go of this entirely - the understanding for your ability to move forward through the owning of your Divinity. I speak of this on many occasion, but it is to understand it is greatly supportive to work through this procedure in the connection of the holding of your Divinity as you pass forward through initiations.

"It is at this period, Beloved Ones, that you let go of all aspect of the consciousness of poverty, the consciousness of any form of the belief system that there is not enough. Beloved Ones. It is the understanding that you move into the expansiveness of your being, through the bringing forward of vast abundance to support each of yourselves. Many having moved forward through period, it is particularly at this time, of various form of difficulty in this regard. It is you let go of this entirely, and through many aspect of the ability to bring forward into your physical experience all that you choose to do for a continuation of support, and working in Spirit.

"It is in this manner, many of yourselves begin to shift and change in areas of connection to the working environment, many of yourselves work through the procedures in connection in relating with one another. In all aspect, Beloved Ones, you begin to go through the experience of change that is working within the connection of your being, through the upliftment always of your state of consciousness and the moving forward on your pathway of truth in the experience of that which you relate to at this time - of the experience of truth in the following of your heart, Beloved Ones."

Fortunately we are in the privileged position of being able to fix up what has become an Earthly mess. Right now we are at the Point of Return on the Pathway of Return. We are not just moving *towards* the time when the ill-considered move into the dark can be corrected, we are *within* it. This is because we are approaching the central position of the Age of Aquarius and we are experiencing the most powerful energy which the outer-planetary alignments bring during that period. There is sufficient Light of awareness - brought about by an awakening consciousness amongst humanity - which allows for this to be the case. *That* is why it is so important that we become aware of what is going on and why information such as is contained in this book is so important. *That* is why we must not shy away from new knowledge which may temporarily shock us or scare us, and that is why we can no longer meekly go along with the misinformation or manipulations which some of our religions or governments continue to perpetuate. This is true whether these are the ignorant or inadvertent actions of well-meaning individuals or not.

Now is our chance to stand in the Light of the Truth. We have the opportunity to experience and to know what resonating with Divine Truth in our physical lives feels like. 2012 marks the changeover point from the old energy to the new energy, which is why we need to prepare ourselves right now for the new, higher frequency 2013 energy. We are at a crossroads in our lives as individuals, humanity and as Earth. The decisions we make now will influence our lives for a long time into the future, at every level.

We have a deep responsibility to ourselves and to the rest of humanity who are not able to gain direct access to this information for one reason or another. As we consciously choose to change we create the wave of shifting consciousness that will sweep many other people who resonate with the new energy, along with it.

Cultivating courage will enable us to listen and to learn so that we can correct the wrongs of the past. We started this game, the ball's in play and now we have no choice but to run with it and score the goal. Let us make every effort not to make it more of the own-goals we have been so good at scoring in the past.

Manipulators of Consciousness
Although it is certainly a distasteful thought to imagine that we, as humanity, have been manipulated for so many centuries, this is nevertheless true. The life we are living today is largely the result of those manipulations and they were engineered from Lemurian and Atlantean times onwards by the Brothers of Darkness on Earth, beginning with Enlil. The purpose of this was to ensure that we continue to stay as deaf and as blind to our personal spiritual responsibilities and power as possible.

An important part of this dulling of the senses of human perception involves the continued use and breeding of aggression, low self esteem and fear into individuals. The current dullness of each of our single senses is in contrast to the sharpness of our potential for unified, multi-sensory psychic perception. We should all be able to see auras, feel subtle vibrations such as crystals emit and communicate telepathically as part of our most basic sensory perception. The fact that we don't and that most people regard those as the super-senses which are the peculiarities of psychics is indicative of the fact that so much of our natural ability lies fallow within us. The result of the manipulations of others among us has been the dumbing-down of all of us.

These acts have been perpetrated by members of our society since the very beginnings of the dark on Earth. There have been so many manipulations by the Brothers of Darkness, over so many lifetimes, that their stories would take numerous books to record. Perhaps we will get to learn about some of the deeds of these Earthly miscreants and reprobates in the course of the dissertations from Spirit, but that will only happen if it is deemed important enough that we know how things have gone wrong for the purposes of correction or for wisdom. It is far more productive to concentrate our efforts on matters of our return to the Light. This is an important point to make note of, because whatever it is that we place our attention on is what we will manifest into and as our reality.

The various manipulations have continued over many lifetimes courtesy of the same group of ill-doers - every bit as much as the same group of loving Light Beings have been working to stem this tide of darkness too. The issues of Light and dark are Universal and are not just confined to our own planet, although ours is a peculiarly physical version of existence. Fortunately for us, Light is triumphing and full Illumination on Earth is imminent. The communications in this book, given as dissertations from the Beings of love and Light from the Godhead, are testament to this fact - as is the willingness to receive the information by so many people.

A long time ago, Thoth wrote about the Dark Brothers. His writings tell us all about what is happening now, as well as where things went wrong. They are a profoundly valuable guide for us today. Reading them will assist with the expansion of consciousness and will corroborate so much of the information in this book. That is hardly surprising though, considering that he is one of the Light Beings who has been working with humanity over an extremely long period of time to correct the problems of this dimension.

> *"Even as exist among men the Dark Brothers,*
> *so there exists the Brothers of Light,*
> *Antagonists they of the Brothers of Darkness,*
> *seeking to free men from the night.*
> *Powers have they, mighty and potent."*

(The Emerald Tablets of Thoth-The-Atlantean p33, pp4)

Why do we need to Hear from Spirit?
We have always needed to hear from Spirit by being in open communication with the Godhead, but unfortunately the hearing ability of humanity was dulled many years ago and human beings have become deafer with persistent, inadequate use of the more subtle aspects of this mode of sensory perception. The same applies to all of the human senses. Even when we were living within the 5th dimension during Atlantean times we needed to hear from higher frequency Light Beings, although we had a better grasp on spirituality then than we do now. By contrast, we presently have a very good understanding of what it means to be solidly physical. Even though it is the first dimension of true spirituality, the consciousness of the 5th dimension is a long way off from the ultimate state of Oneness of Divine Source - which is the 49th/50th dimension.

We shift through the dimensions in a non-linear fashion until we attain the state of Divine completeness. We are presently working from the basis of physical matter and this is, therefore, the reason that we can progress through the dimensions in a physical body. However, as we make progress we become more of a Light-form than a physical-form body and it is likely that at some point we will no longer have use for a physical body. Progressing the physical body into a new state of being, no matter what dimension this may pertain to, can only happen once we have physically shifted into the state of living ascension. After this 5th dimension achievement Osiris has informed us that we can very easily access the 7th and 8th dimensions and then the 12th. It is these dimensions that we more easily move through after we have re-unified our 4th dimension physical frequencies with the 5th dimension spiritual frequencies and live in ascension.

Offering us a little glimpse into the future, in her communications which followed these ones from Osiris (detailed in the forthcoming Isis book from the authors), Isis informed us that humans on Earth will look very different than they do today. Intrigued, the working group tried to get more information from her, but all she would say was that in twenty years time our children will be different. This makes a lot of sense when we consider that we are moving into an alternative dimension right now and activating the 13th strand of our DNA, because the different frequencies that govern that reality zone will allow for different physical experiences. Our lives are set to change in ways that we currently have absolutely no concept of, but fortunately change comes in small increments and we adjust accordingly.

Until such time as we harmonically resonate with the higher frequency dimensions physically, Osiris teaches us and encourages us to 'visit' these dimensions during the meditative process. We do this by moving our energy body, our consciousness, through the dimensions, or what he refers to as harmonics. This process of moving through the dimensions begins with us moving through and clearing the energy of each of our chakras. This is important because as we energise each chakra successively, we clear out the lower frequency energy that is stuck there. This allows us to release those experiences, the negative ego issues, from that chakra and live the energy of the next chakra. In the living ascension processes, chakra clearing is critically important because it allows us to clear all of the low frequencies out of our physical bodies and be centred in the heart. It is advisable to do regular chakra clearing exercises, because we release our issues layer by layer. Once this is done, we are clear and free to access the higher dimensions, via the chakras above our Crown Chakra. These higher chakras activate as we clear the first three chakras (base, sacral and solar plexus) of their low frequencies (aggression, low self-esteem and fear) and learn to live from the heart. In this way we release issues of the negative ego, such as addictions, during the process.

As we shift dimension in the living ascension processes Osiris works with the energy alignment procedures which are available to us while we are in a physical body. He stresses that he communicates with us, in the 4th dimension, from the basis of the 5th dimension energy platform of Venus during the living ascension processes. In a meditation process, Osiris is able to work with us right up to the level of the Godhead dimensions.

Osiris reminds us to ground ourselves after a meditation during which we access the higher dimensions. This is supportive in maintaining our conscious lives and helps us to integrate the meditation experiences - and maintain a balanced state. Most interestingly, he comments that each time we access the higher dimensions during a meditation, when we return to our normal, conscious reality, our base frequency is higher than it was before the procedure. This is effectively due to the grounding of more of the Light of the higher dimensions into our physical lives.

We are reminded that as we access the higher frequency states this stimulates the issues of the negative ego to emerge for clearing. When this happens it is to recognise what is happening and recover our higher frequency vibrations as quickly as possible. This is how we transcend the lower frequency states through release.

Osiris: Accessing the 12th Dimension during Meditation

"It is on this day, Beloved Ones, that I wish to support and assist you. It is through procedure at this time, knowing and understanding through the pathway of ascension - it is through the connectivity with the presence of this channel - it is the support and assistance to come forward on further occasion, in order to communicate, to connect with yourselves, in moving forward through a procedure. It is in the pathway of the feeling state of the self, understanding that I take you forward through the shift within your own presence of being in physicality, into the connectivity of the feelingstate of the physical form though the 12th dimensional experience. It is to support and assist yourselves, understanding on many occasion that you move forward through the connectivity in brief connection, through various areas of visualisation. It is at this time that I wish to support the procedure to take place that is for each of yourselves to be in the feeling-state.

"It is to begin, to allow all areas of connection of various energies surrounding yourselves to dissipate entirely - of that which no longer serves you, or brings forward any form of the connection of creation of lower energy form. It is in this manner, Beloved Ones, that I support you in the procedures. It is in the holding of the energy field of your own self in moving forward through the connectivity on many occasion. It is moving in and out of the experience of connection of ascension of the procedure out of physical form. It is to support yourselves, understanding that the procedure within the energy fields of your own being, it is each energy body moving forward through the harmonics, the frequencies, the areas of connection, with the experience of the pure state of Oneness through the connectivity of the Godhead.

"It is in this state of the presence of Oneness, Beloved Ones, that I support you at this time, to feel the movement forward, to allow for the activation through the presence of your physical form to take place. It is in this procedure, it is allowing for yourselves to be in the continuation of the knowledge in many areas of that which comes forward through the physicality of living state - connection to various areas of addictions. There is connectivities, of ego state. There is in all manner of physicality many aspects that begin to be focussed in this direction - of the allowing for yourselves to move into the frequency that you connect with, as you move into any state of the presence of the return of the ego state, in all forms of the connectivity of judgement. And as you move into these states it is to not judge the self, but it is to know and understand as you blend and move into the state within physicality it is perfectly normal to do this, for each being in physical beingness. But it is to understand it is as you move into the awareness through the frequency of the movement of physicality, of the connection of the 12th dimensional energy of the state of the collective Oneness, so it is you are supported in the release of this.

"In many areas of the drawing to yourselves the connectivity of that which is drawn to Light through the various low energy fields or various being perhaps, or other manner of communication through the attraction that does take place in this manner, so it is to allow yourselves to be in the feeling state of pure Bliss, and the moving in and out of the experience continually through the awareness of connection through 12th dimension."

Q: With regard to the movement into the 12th dimension, could you just explain a little more about the move through the harmonics of the 5th dimension from 4th until we get to the 12th.
"Beloved One, it is I wish to support yourselves on this day in the ability to move forward through each of the energy centre of the physical form. Begin to feel the frequency as it enters and to allow yourselves to move into the feeling state - understanding it is continual procedure taking place at all time. It is merely to bring forward the understanding of the feeling state of the awareness to move into a continuum of this shift of energy field connecting yourselves. Does this answer you question, Beloved One?

Q: It's the continuum that's important?
"It is, Beloved One."

Q: In order to access any of the higher dimensions, is it to begin where we are now - shifting from the 4th to the 5th dimension in physicality?
"It is, Beloved One. Many of yourselves shift in and out of the experience on many occasion. It is perhaps not always in awareness."

Q: Please tell us more about the 12th dimension and whether or not we can go further than this?
"Beloved One, it is at this time in the working with the connection merely of the feeling state of the physical form, understanding the alignments to take place. If there is the desire to do this, it is you have the ability to connect prior to going forward into the procedure. On this day I do bring forward the support and assistance through the Venusian energy. It is you have the ability to connect in different manner if it is the desire to do so, Beloved One."

Q: Please could you help me to understand the unusual feeling I have, of leaping time?
"Beloved One, it is to bring yourself into return to allow for - it is moving out of synch so to speak, Beloved One - it is to allow it to move in gentle manner, to the procedure that is of your request and that is supportive for yourself. It

is to not allow it to move out of the harmonics of the procedures that are required, or requested of the self. It is supportive to maintain it in a position that is bringing forward the state of great balance within the feeling state of Beingness, as it is of great importance in the continuation of the living state."

Q: Is this an issue of maintaining balance between the physical and spiritual dimensions?
"It is, Beloved Ones, it is of great importance in the continuation, to do all that you intend through the ascension, in the living state."

Q: How do we create balance between shifting in and out of dimensions, connecting with the spiritual dimensions and being grounded?
"Beloved One, it is there is various procedures, allowing yourselves to be of the understanding, through the feeling state of the frequency. And from this there is the understanding as you move out through the connectivity as has taken place on many occasion with many of yourselves, it is out of control, so to speak. Therefore, through the procedure of the feeling state of this balance within your being, you have the ability to almost gauge the frequency to allow yourselves to blend it to that which is serving you at the position that you are requesting it. Therefore, from the position of moving into visualisation, you have the ability to shift through the energy field. Allowing this to take place, to take you into this position, without the connectivity of the ego state, without the interference of many conversation coming forward in the head, the many areas of disturbance, many areas of resistance coming forward. It is this that you have the ability to shift through, and so in return to the connectivity of Earth of the living state within environment of all other beings, the ability to live in same environment, at the position of the shifted frequency, to allow yourselves to be in the understanding of that which takes place in physicality. So it is working in this manner also."

Q: So what you are saying is that when you do this balancing of frequency in a visualisation, you never return to your previous lower state, because you always come back into the living state of being in a higher state than before?
"It is so, Beloved One."

Grounding Exercises

It is important to take note of what Osiris says about integrating the new, higher frequencies which we can access in a visualisation, into our lives when we return. It is easier to do this if we release the issues of the negative ego out of our physical bodies, because they are then capable of holding higher and higher frequency states without feeling disturbed. The degree to which we feel odd when we shift into higher frequency states, is the degree to which we are not physically accustomed to those high speed vibrations. This is an indication that we need to do more clearing and releasing as much as it is an indication that we are learning to tolerate an altered dimensional state. However, we can blend with the high speed vibrations and live this experience in our physical lives by setting the intention to do so. In this way we more easily transcend the negative ego issues which may be all around us where we live, simply because we do not resonate with them any longer.

After a high frequency experience in any meditation that Osiris may guide us through or which we may take ourselves through, it is very important to reintegrate our consciousness back within our physical bodies completely. This is the process of grounding.

Grounding involves ensuring that the natural, spiritual or non-material portion of ourselves (our soul presence) is fully aware of where it is in the physical body, on Earth. This serves two purposes.
- It ensures we bring the harmonics of the higher dimensions into our physical lives. This is part of the upliftment process of shifting dimension physically.
- It ensures that we are consciously resident within the physical body after a meditation. This is part of being safely within the human body so that we are fully aware of the physical environment and are able to function properly within it - regardless of the fact that we have shifted our resonance higher.

Although grounding properly after a meditation is important, it is also important to do this throughout the processes of living ascension. This is because we frequently shift through the different dimensions in the course of our daily lives during this process and may feel dizzy or peculiar. Many different grounding procedures are taught by various people and any one of these is suitable. The following list provides some simple options.
- Before the end of a meditation, be aware of coming back and start to feel the body physically by wiggling the toes and the fingers and making other very gentle, physical movements. This reminds us that we are back in the physical body.
- Place the feet firmly on the ground and imagine a shaft of energy shooting down through the centre of the body, like a root, and becoming anchored in the Earth.

- Feel the connection to Earth. This can be done at any time during the day, no matter where we are - even at an office desk.
- Walk outside barefooted. Be aware of the feeling of the grass, stone or Earth beneath the feet.
- Eat grounding foods - eggs, for example. Coffee works well for some people too.

Although we have mentioned accessing higher dimensions, this book deals specifically with the shifting processes as we access the gateway to the 5th dimension. In a forthcoming book, Isis will assist us with information with regard to accessing the 12th dimension by balancing the masculine and feminine energies and working from the heart. After that we will be able to access more information from Thoth, who has stressed the importance of working from the heart, in love. When we are ready for them, Thoth's teachings are bound to be extensive and expansive. He will release more of the information which is contained on his ancient tablets and discuss them with us, regardless of whether or not humanity has seen them before. It is our understanding at this point, that once we have accessed and integrated the teachings of Osiris, Isis and Thoth, we will be ready for the high frequency communications from Horus, the third member of the Trinity, and thereafter, Enki.

The key to accessing the dimensions which are higher than the 5th dimension remains unconditional love, but the issues of re-introducing the feminine God-essence into our lives become supercritical. Hence the importance of working with the Goddess Isis in more depth in the future, as well as balancing the masculine and feminine energies within ourselves and our world.

Within every level, each dimension, people require some form of coaching until full Oneness of Being is attained. Our dulled senses are partially why we have stayed in the dark for so long. The other reason we are still in the dark is because we have been deliberately *kept* in the dark and had information withheld from us, or regurgitated as misinformation. The little glimpses of the light of new information and knowledge that have shone through into our consciousness have been little chinks of Light. They have all too often been ignored by many people simply because human beings have become so habituated to the dark that this state of impoverishment is what we now call normal. In this manner we unknowingly continue to choose the dark and others cunningly ensure we carry on doing so.

While this may certainly smack of conspiracy theories, it is nevertheless true. Too many of us want to disbelieve these theories which hint at dark collaborations, but they unfortunately are very much a part of the truth of our current world. Some of these conspiracies are centuries-old and others are younger. Old or new, they are no less malevolent and no less designed to deafen our hearing of the Word further and blind us to the Light of the Heavens.

Fortunately for us, sufficient work on the upliftment of consciousness and enLightenment has been done on the Earth, by sufficient human beings who have consciously and specifically asked Spirit for more information. They have been assisted by the Light Beings who have been previously been incarnate on Earth and are now in Spirit form, as well as by Beings such as the Archangels who do not take on a physical body. Just as fortunately, our planet Earth is currently perfectly aligned with specific planetary and stellar bodies (such as our Sun, the Pleiades, Venus, Orion and Sirius) which are beaming in their high frequency star-Light of love from the dimensions of enLightened consciousness to us. Adding to this, the planet Nibiru is moving closer towards us too. These planetary and stellar movements further stimulate our awakening human and Earth consciousness.

Osiris gives some interesting information relating to shifting through the dimensions inasmuch as he tells us that not only has the intensity of the energy available on Earth for the current shift into a higher dimension not occurred exactly like this before (due to the relationship of all the different variables), but that we use the *same pathway* through which we 'fell' to the 3rd dimension, to re-access the expanded Light of the higher dimension as we 'ascend' back up to the 5th dimension. We just go in a different direction. This is why it is called the Pathway of Return.

It must be noted that although the super-alignment of the outer planetary bodies with Earth is exactly the same as it was in 2037/67, the difference between then and now is the change in human consciousness. It is this shift which makes the difference between a failed ascension process and a successful one. 2012 is the Year of Ascension. We can pat ourselves on the back for this achievement because we, as human beings, are the critical factor that tipped the scales in the direction of ascension. We have taken what has always been around as a possibility on Earth and turned it into an actuality.

Osiris: The Shifted Dimension Pathway

"It is, Beloved Ones, as you find yourself in the formation of Light Vehicle, begin to understand that on this pathway at this time, it is for many beings moving into the experience of the energy of the alignments beginning to form. The alignments as they begin to form in a star system, in the skies, Beloved Ones, the understanding of the impact that this experience has on beings moving forward in their physical lifetime, that you move forward into an expansiveness not ever felt in the past in this manner - into an experience of unconditional love to the extent and intensity not felt in the procedures having taken place in the past.

"The understanding in the moving forward through the opening - it is of the period of the Aquarian Age - to move forward through the consciousness as the Earth. The understanding of the moving forward through the pathway of a shift in dimension at earlier linear period.

"So we prepare to move forward once more, through the advancement and communication with Spirit, with greater intensity, as you open your hearts to the understanding of the shifts that take place in the planetary experience, in your physical experience."

The outer-planetary, high frequency Light which we are graced with now is the consequence of the super-alignment of the outer-planetary bodies with Earth as we move within the galaxy and become more closely aligned with its centre. Osiris has informed us that these are the exact same alignments which last occurred at the time of 2037/67 BC - the time which supported the work of the Light Beings, as the returning god-beings of Ancient Egypt, on Earth. Some of them had arrived here, after many years of absence, some time before that. Taking cognisance of this fact may help us enormously in our own quest for enLightenment.

Knowledge of outer-planetary movements is exactly why the ancient Light Beings created such wondrous temple and pyramid structures. These god-beings knew how to harness the outer-planetary energy at the time of the super-alignments of the planets and stars with Earth. The purpose of grounding this energy into Earth's grid was to support a dimension shift back upwards to where we once were. All this time, the Light Beings have been trying to help us to Return, but no matter how much effort they put into the process, they may not interfere with what we want to do. Our consciousness is now sufficiently uplifted to allow us to focus on what they have been doing, and allow us to take advantage of the energy-enhancing systems and teachings they gave us and continue to give us.

It is largely because of the uplifting consciousness of Earthlings that the loving Beings of Light who are in non-physical, Spirit form are able to openly offer more information to us at this point in our development - if we ask for it. We are in the fortunate position of being able to receive and record this information without the risk of too much persecution in our modern world - unlike the nasty maltreatment which people had to endure in times gone by.

Witch hunts of one form or another have taken place all too often in our dark past, especially during the long years of the Inquisitions in Europe. They continue in the present day, often with a more polite face, but they are no less vicious and no less designed to destroy people and instil fear. No matter how often the Brothers of Darkness who lurk amongst us have tried to extinguish the Light, they have not succeeded and they never will succeed.

Just as a tiny pinprick in the lid of a large, dark box will let a lot of light into the space, so too it is that only a small amount of Light is required for Illumination of all kinds. Knowing this, we can positively employ the powerful high resonance of Light which is contained within a kind word, a loving thought or a considerate action, to dispel large amounts of darkness, personally and globally.

The meditation which Osiris led on the 10 June 2009 reminds us of the healing properties of Light. By accessing this intensity of Light in the core of the galaxy we are able to shift ourselves from the fluctuating state of the ego - even as it comes forward to remind us of its presence. He mentions the Light Beings, Lord Melchior and Sanat Kumara, who support these processes of Light which are communicated from the 49th dimension. Osiris confirms that these Angelic Presences are available at our request to support us with the energy of the Godhead on the pathway of living ascension. Accessing the Godhead is done via reconnecting to our greater state of soul being, the Monad. We are gently reminded that we may feel resistance to going forwards in this meditation and that we can shift this if we choose to. Resistance is an indication that the human ego is interfering with the processes of the soul presence. When Osiris mentions the word 'nothingness' in this meditation it is with reference to feeling the stillness of no-thing-ness: no thought, no time and no space, as opposed to the state of soul dissolution we have discussed before.

Very importantly, the last few paragraphs of this meditation describe how we breathe in, "*The Light presence*," with each inhalation of air and offer it to all of humanity as we breathe out.

Osiris: Humanity Questions the Connectivity to the Godhead

"Greetings to you, Beloved Ones, I wish to take you forward on this day through visualisation. It is procedure on this day, Beloved Ones, to support yourselves in the understanding in the expansiveness of the self, the connectivity to take you forward through the position, it is with the connectivity of Being that is Lord Melchior.

"It is in this manner, Beloved Ones, to go forward on this day. There are many beings in existence at this time, with the beginnings of moving forward through the questioning. It is the understanding within, of the connectivity; it is of the Godhead, of the presence within, of the connectivity of all of humanity at this time. Many beings of soul presence setting themselves aside, in order to allow others to grow forward from experiences. Many of the animal beings moving forward in this manner (*in reference to 55 beached whales in Cape Town, South Africa, in May 2009*).

"It is always to sacrifice and to move forward, through the perspective of the growth of others in humanity. It is the eternal communication with the Godhead - in order to support in service in this manner - that it is in deep gratitude always to be felt.

"In this manner, Beloved Ones, so it is on this day I wish to support you in the understanding of the connectivity of the ego state. As you begin on the pathway of spirituality, as you continue forward through the pathway of the living state of ascension, so it is in similarity to return, to come forward in similar manner and begin to come forward in the aspect of being. It is as reminder, and so it is on this day, Beloved Ones, I wish to take you forward into the connectivity of the presence of great Light in the outer field - the connectivity of the galactic core. It is to take you forward into this position, to allow for the understanding of the entirety within the self and the experiences on Earth at this time, to go forward through great advancement.

"It is, Beloved Ones, as you begin to feel the presence of great Light to surround you, I come forward on this day to bless you with much love, to go forward within a connectivity of your heart to assist in all procedure taking place. It is at this time, Beloved Ones, that I guide you through the presence of a dimensional shift, the experience of the outer-planetary experience. The communication, it is of 49th dimension.

"The experience to connect with on this day, to move forward as best as you have the ability on this day to connect, in this manner. So it is I support you always in great Light, Beloved Ones.

"So it is to begin a procedure to feel the connectivity of the self in physical form. It is to begin to form in your surroundings the presence of star tetrahedron.

It is to feel it in the presence of Crystalline Light energy. Begin to feel it in the expansiveness as it begins to form, surrounding your presence.

"As it does, Beloved Ones, so it is the feeling state of the physical form begin to feel the connectedness in the presence of the heart. As you allow for the energy field to let go, as you move upward through the physical self, to connect in heart centre and allow for the experience to drift through the physical form, allowing for yourselves to go into the experience of peace.

"It is in the pure stillness of being throughout experience for yourselves to be in the stillness of connectivity, to allow for the intensity to come forward through the presence of your being, in the silence. So as you begin to form in the surrounding energies, the presence of Light Vehicle, begin to move forward, Beloved Ones. As you begin to shift consciousness begin to allow yourselves to feel the presence of the moving forward.

"It is to connect through a shifting of consciousness - it appears to be at great speed - but it is the understanding of moving forward through that which is time and space, through the experience of this stillness. Sound formations begin to take place as you drift through the connectivities of one dimension to another.

"It is in the understandings that you begin to feel, in the fulfilment of communication in various dimensional state, the presence of great Light that you begin to access in your being. You begin to know and understand the feeling state of the shift through one dimension through another, through the experience continuously, through the upliftment of a pathway of consciousness. The connectivities of all beings at this time, the presence of your Light, assisting in the pathway of the living state of ascension.

"To know and understand through the connection - it is of the ego state of the presence within physical form - to that which is in the movement forward, through the pathway of ascension, the shifting from one state to another. Therefore, always as you find yourselves moving through the connectivity in this manner, the knowledge, the presence of the self, to be felt in all aspect that you begin to shift through the movement.

"It is to allow yourselves, Beloved Ones. It is I come forward to support you as you come to position. It is to know and understand at this position so it is we move together through the slow and drifting movement, to the connection with Being of Light to assist you at this time - to assist the entirety of the planet at this time, from this position.

"So it is that you begin to feel the presence of my Being over lighting your energy field, and so it is in the supportive procedure to go forward. It is through the silence and the movement of gentleness, and it is a slow and drifting movement through the connectivity with the Galactic Core. You begin to find yourselves coming forward into the presence of Being of Light that prepares for the experience of work, to support yourselves on your pathway forward.

"There is an ability through the desire and intent to communicate further, to access further the energy fields and the supportive procedures taking place. As many of yourselves move forward with a connectivity of great Light with this Being, always to understand that through the out-of-body experience on many occasion at this time, you feel moving forward through the procedures - it is almost the feeling state, relating to physicality, of moving forward through the class of communication in Light; communication in Light energy, communication in Light and ancient knowledge, communication in Light and love, communication in the presence of great Bliss.

"To know and understand the passing forward through the procedures of the living state of ascension and the abilities always to communicate, connecting with the presence of God within the self, to support all to take place with manifestation. With the guidance further from the over lighting presence of the Godhead, the ability to communicate with the Angelic presence to support yourselves on the pathway forward with requests at any one occasion, to communicate, to bring forward further guidance and information and supportive energy.

"So, as you begin to move forward through the slight drifting movement, it is moving into the state of the nothingness. It is the vast area of silence. The coming forward through the presence of great Light, that you begin to move and drift. The connectedness of the purity, of peace, tranquillity, into the presence of great Light you begin to move.

"As you feel yourselves in any manner to move into the resistant state, it is to breathe through the experience, to feel the presence of the breath through a consciousness not of physical form, but the ability to focus in this direction. To maintain procedure and return once more to the feeling state of stillness; the connectivity of silence and stillness, through the movement, allowing yourselves to drift.

"The presence of Being of Light choosing to support yourselves on this day to allow for the feeling state of comfort through the shifting of dimensional states. You begin to feel the resonance as it has shifted through its entirety, to feel the connectivity in different manner, to feel the energy fields of the presence of Light Vehicle.

"So, as it feels, to the extent of your knowledge to be in the spacecraft, of the ability to move out of the experience into the drifted-ness. The experience of floating into the communication and the arms of Being of Light that assists you at this time - to be supported in the feeling state of being on Earth.

"It is many of yourselves moving forward through the connectedness of the Siriun energies to work in the out-of-body experiences on many occasion at this time. To feel the presence of great Light as it moves forward through the presence of your being in knowledge and Light energy, through the connectedness of great love to be felt within, to be brought forward into the connection of Earth further.

"So it is, Beloved Ones, the Being before you begins to place. It is almost in the feeling state of an energy field in a circular movement that surrounds you head. That it is in this position, you have the ability to breathe in its simplicity, to focus only at this time on the breath.

"So, as you begin to be taken forward through the opening of a pathway of great Light, begin to see it before you, Beloved Ones, in the vast energy field of great Light. It is almost through the Pleiadian position of the experience that you begin to feel the connectedness - allowing yourselves to adjust to the procedures and connectedness of greater and greater Light. The formations surrounding you of the Angelic presence. The feeling state of the heart for many begins to be felt in the rapid movement as you begin to move into the experience of greater Light.

"In the silence, in the presence of great Light, as you begin to feel yourselves with the feeling state of the self that has come forward from physicality. It is the feeling state at this time, Beloved Ones, of moving into the pure connectedness: of the Monad, of the Godhead. As you begin to feel the expansiveness so it is with all Bliss and understanding, it is into the all knowing state, you connect in the Light essence. Allow yourselves to be. The presence of shifted dimensional state allows for yourselves to hear, through the connectedness the coming period on Earth, also to the connectedness of the Celestial Sound; of the communication of Light.

"So it is, Beloved Ones, that you begin to see and feel formations surrounding you. The presence always to come forward with assistance - in the connectivity of moving forward through the shifting of dimension - the presence of the Sanat Kumara to be supportive, to answer through request of communication of all taking place through procedures that follow forward. For the re-entry and re-connectivity to the various dimensional state, so you work with intent, in direct communication.

"There is, Beloved Ones, you begin to allow for the experience to be felt through the joy of communication, with the presence of Being, to offer message to yourselves. Begin to feel it and hear it, whichever form it comes forward through your communication field of Light. In the feeling state, the hearing state of communication, hold this in your heart. Begin to allow for the procedures as Being of Light chooses to assist in the procedure of connecting yourselves, the Angelic presence and, through Vehicle of Light, to feel the Angelic presence within - the holding of one hand upon the other to be felt through the Light presence to come forward through your being.

"Beloved Ones, through the silence, and communication that you feel in your heart - the connectedness of Light surrounding you - begin to allow yourselves to drift into the experience of re-connection to the physical self, holding the stillness always. Allowing the procedure to take place, as it is slow and gentle movement. The Angelic Beings to await at your side in physicality, to support physical form, to feel the re-connection taking place.

"In the silent and gentle movement, allow it to gently connect with the physical self, the Angelic presence, to hold yourselves in Light - to assist with the re-entry. As there is procedure of re-entry, to allow the experience of the stillness to continue, through merely the connection, through the breath of Light, the breath of unconditional love, the breath of the Godhead, through the experience of re-connection, allowing it to take place in its gentle manner.

"As the re-entry takes place it is to take forward the breath that is felt through the feeling state of the entirety of form. As there is the in-pouring, so it is felt through the Light presence throughout your being and, as you offer it forward, so it is felt by all in humanity - as it begins to filter forward through the connectedness of all in humanity.

"It is the understanding to let it forward - to offer it forth - to know and understand through one of stages of the in-breath, so it is always to be maintained. As you offer outward, in many direction on many occasion, it continues without end.

"The feeling state at this time of the connectedness of the Godhead within, so it is to feel the presence of great love, Beloved Ones; the presence of great Light in your heart. It is the desire of Beings to continue to support you through the procedures in out-of-body experiences, of continuation of support and assistance, through the pathway of the living state of ascension.

"You return on many occasion through the Temples of Light, through the presence of the connectivity to the Being that is Melchior to support and assist in all procedure of going forward in this manner, your ability to bring forward to the Earth, the support and assistance of procedures of upliftment of consciousness. And so it is.

"Blessings and great love to each of yourselves on this day, Beloved Ones. I bless you. Greetings to you".

* * * * * * * * * * *

CHAPTER EIGHT

Our 'Real' World in the 3rd and 4th Dimensions of Duality

"Know ye, man, ye are the ultimate of all things. Only the knowledge of this is forgotten, lost when man was cast into bondage, bound and fettered by the chains of darkness."

(The Emerald Tablets of Thoth-The-Atlantean p50, pp3)

Why have Manipulation, Control or Hiding Information Occurred?
Ever since there have been individuals who wanted power and control over others on Earth, access to information has been controlled in order to further these aims. Using power and control, for the purpose of Earth dominion, are the regulating ways of human beings. As a result, individual members of humanity have been treated like pawns by their leaders over time. Over the centuries we have become conditioned into becoming lazy and spiritually switched off and the result is that we have generally been loath to take spiritual responsibility for our progress into higher frequency states - moment by moment. The worst consequence of this is that individuals developed the belief that they are incapable of making progress on their own, from within.

Relatively small amounts of knowledge about our ancientness will help to support us in the quest for our true spiritual identity. As we delve deeper not only will we begin to realise the immense importance of developing and maintaining the Divine Feminine presence within us, but also the importance of this energy as the proper balance to the Divine Masculine energy. Balance is epitomised by the practice of unconditional love and compassion for all.

This message to us from Osiris assures us that we will continue to uncover knowledge and information about the ancientness of Earth and her inhabitants and that this is supported by the re-emergence of the Divine Feminine energy which has been suppressed for so many centuries. The balance which the re-emergence of the feminine brings supports us and Earth into the future.

Osiris: Return to the Knowledge of Ancientness

"It is the understanding that you return to the knowledge of your ancientness, of the ancientness not only of your presence, Beloved One, but the ancientness of the connectivity of the beings upon the Earth. The stories in many direction that have followed and so it is at this time for the truth to be felt. As the connectivity of the feminine comes forward in the questioning in many areas of all beings that have stated over lengthy period that it is in this energy to suppress.

"It is to understand it begins to unfold in its power and integrity in the power of intention, to support the Earth in moving forward through the balanced state of connectivity for the future.

"It is, Beloved Ones, that I bless you on this day, I bring forward many blessings of great Light to each of you to bring forward further communication, Beloved Ones.

"I bless you in your Light. Greetings to you, Beloved Ones".

Most people are conditioned into passively accepting whatever information is released - via the media, for example. In every century various supportive social structures have been in place to ensure the control of information continued, relative to the available technology - such as withholding reading and writing skills from the masses in olden times, the blocking or limitation of internet or cellular phone communications in modern times or the widespread ownership of various, apparently independent, media by one organisation. Over time, the practices of withholding information set the scene for progressively more abuse of power by those who wanted domination of all on Earth. Fortunately, although control is still massively prevalent, things are changing now and part of the effects of the upliftment of the consciousness of humanity is that people are more easily able to take back their personal power, now more so than ever before.

Whole societies are railing against quasi-parental government policies which previously entrenched the treatment of individuals as incompetent or dependent children. The principles of democracy apparently support government by the people or by their elected representatives, but this political system is often just a smoke screen for the machinations of a small group of individuals whose behind-the-scenes power allows them to ruthlessly transgress the borders of other nations. It is these small groups of power mongers which have no compunction about the rape, pollution and destruction of the land to retrieve its riches. They pillage whatever resources they fancy and divide the spoils of war amongst themselves. For example, they are party to creating 'development' projects in third world countries which are apparently aimed at upliftment of the country for the benefit of the people. Behind the scenes, the manipulations include over-stating the soon-to-be-derived income from these projects. The over-stated need links directly into the third world country being unable to service its massive development debt. The punitive measures in place for this usually involve some form of relinquishment of state assets to the first world, developer country. The losses are always felt by communities of people who are far less powerful than the small, cold-blooded groups and their puppets. This occurs regularly, no matter how these actions are dressed up in the clothes of 'progress,' 'modernisation' and 'development.'

People don't need others to decide if any information, whether old or newly uncovered, would be suitable for them to hear or not. All human beings have the incontrovertible right to receive *full* disclosure of any and all information which comes to light, no matter what it pertains to. If this does not happen it may be assumed either that our leaders are withholding information for underhand reasons or, worse, that they are incompetent. Either way, they are not fit to lead.

By contrast, humanity has the right to the truth, knowledge and open information about our world so that each person may use their personal abilities of discretion and discernment to make informed decisions about that which is suitable to use for their personal progress or not. Due to past misrepresentations, there is no doubt that the knowledge-gathering process will involve on-going information-gathering and misinformation-busting and that our understanding about both current affairs and ancient Earth history will probably not be called complete for quite some time. We have to ensure that information is openly available and that it is not tampered with. This includes the truth about our origins and about our inherent Divinity.

These issues help to highlight the value of hearing truth and information from the Beings of Light and the Ascended Master Beings of Light. As Godhead-realised beings we are assured that their communications are motivated by love and to this end they can inform us about the bigger picture and help us to set the information record straight. All that is required for their involvement is that we ask them to do so.

Living Ascension Clarity
Aside from ancient information such as is contained in the Mayan Calendar and

on the walls of the Ancient Egyptian Temples, for example, the concept of humans moving into a state of living ascension has been discussed by the Light Beings for some time now. Simply put, it is the process of human beings and Earth shifting the overall, operating speed of their vibrations (which determines what they will be able to resonate with) to a higher frequency physically - so as to be able to *physically* perceive and live within the higher frequency dimensions which were usually only experienced in the non-material state after death. This is an altered dimension experience. Although this experience begins with brief excursions into the 5th dimension from the starting point of the 4th dimension of physical reality, the reality experience that is living ascension can only be fully actualised within the 5th dimension of spiritualised physicality.

The crux of the matter is that the living ascension process literally removes souls from the interminable reincarnation cycle of physical lifetimes on Earth in the dense, physical reality of the 3rd or the 4th dimensions. Living the higher frequency reality means that 3rd and 4th dimension resonant Earth Karma has been released and there is therefore no more need for reincarnation to these lower dimensions. There is no more need for the Wheel of Karma. At this point physical life in the 5th dimension becomes the choice of the incarnating soul, in a fully conscious state of awareness and the option of living in the same body for extended periods becomes real. This is known of as the, "*Agelessness*," which both Osiris and Thoth refer to. Not only can we live with perfect health, but life as we currently know it to be shifts into a state where more joyful experiences predominate - throughout the dimensions where physical life is possible.

The dimension shift happens because the lower frequency, physical dimension sense of separated reality which we presently know of as real, transforms into the beginning stages of a higher frequency reality, which is in open communication with the rest of the Universal system - the Universal Cosmos, which Osiris has referred to it as. Once we re-integrate with the higher frequency state of the 5th dimension, the shape and experience of our reality will be back to where it used to be in pre-Atlantean-cataclysm days. That means that our experiences of living will include a *unified* sense of physicality and spirituality - instead of the contrasted experience where these aspects of ourselves feel separate from each other.

Really *living* within the 5th dimension is an experience which we know almost nothing about in our contemporary lives. It is one which is characterised by a heightened sense of loving everything and everybody as if we are a part of all things, a sense of oneness with all of Creation and an understanding of what our purpose is, Universally. The transformation of duality means it collapses into Oneness.

Osiris has said that in the 5th dimension, heightened state of consciousness we will be able to look at a flower, for example, and feel an intense love for it and its beauty. The experiences of drug-induced 'highs' compare favourably to the 5th dimension experiences inasmuch as 5th dimension living allows for an expanded sense of consciousness and connectedness to all things and all beings, whilst still feeling integrated within the solidity of the physical world. Osiris has also stated, however, that at no time would he advocate the use of drugs to achieve this state. The advantage of 5th dimension living compared to a drug 'high' is immense, most especially relative to the fact that the expanded consciousness of 5th dimension living, from the basis of the state of unconditional love, is not detrimental to our health - whereas drug use most certainly is. Aside from the well-documented damage to the human body, the use of so-called recreational drugs to induce an expanded state of awareness is bound to create injury to the Light body, or the aura, of the individual. Recreational drug-use is responsible for damaging the aura. This leads to many problems such as a lack of energy, susceptibility to being influenced by the problems of other people and potential entity attachments. Essentially, drug use is counterproductive because it stimulates lowered frequency resonances within the body and thus hampers the natural attainment of higher frequency states. As such it is highly disadvantageous in the quest for enLightenment - no matter what the purveyors of these altered dimension substances may claim.

A lot of the information and teaching material pertaining to the subject of heightened, spiritual awareness has been either distorted or lost. Additional to this, the reason that most people generally don't know anything about the ability humans have to move into a state of living ascension is because those who do know what is going on have left the physical dimensions, the reality experience, of those who don't. The belief system of the Ancient Egyptians relative to the use of the human body in the afterlife was directly related to the teachings of living ascension. A plenitude of pictorial renditions of these teachings exist: as reliefs and hieroglyphics in all the temples of Egypt. We have lost all understanding of this today and so we view these teachings as peculiarities of an ancient people.

As part of the discussion pertaining to the various symbols that many members of the working group come across at ancient sites around the world (such as those on the Phaistos Disc), Osiris informed us that hieroglyphics is not just a writing system, but that this is the written word of an actual, spoken language every bit as much as what you are reading now can be communicated to others in the spoken word. He touched on the links to the Nordic language and the fact that this symbology originated in Atlantean times.

Osiris: Symbols and Language in the Ancient World

Q: You have mentioned a connection of the symbols in Greece relative to those of the Nordic language. Please expand on this.

"It is to understand from Ancient Egyptian language, so it is the continuation that has moved, understanding the origination of the Ancient Egyptian language that has spread forth into the area, it is known at this time of Finland. If it is to move into the deeper understanding, it begins to unfold further and further to many in humanity, the full capacity of the language that has been in existence.

"It is all that is seen at this time through hieroglyphic - it is the understanding it has been language, not only that which is seen and communicated at this time - it is in small form of that which has been and so it is the development of the connectivities of various languages, various continuations. So it is to understand these Beings have moved forward into the connection of this position and therefore there has brought forward, in symbology from Nordic lands, same understandings of language."

Q: Are you saying that what we call ancient Egyptian hieroglyphics was a language?
"It is, Beloved One."

Q: Is it the same for the symbols on the small jewellery copies of the Phaistos Disc as well?
"It is, Beloved One. If you are to understand it is in connectivity to that which are known as Norse gods, Beloved One, that have come forward at ancient period - far earlier than has been explained to many in humanity."

Q: At what period did they come forward? Was their presence a continuation of the movements of the god-beings from Ancient Egypt (*after the exodus of Akhenaten*), through into Ancient Greece and then on into Finland?
"It is, Beloved One."

Q: Was this in approximately 2000BC?
"It is slightly further than this Beloved One, but it is an approximation."

Q: Were these symbols used in the Atlantean period?
"It is to understand it had originated in this position in ancient Atlantean period. It is the symbology that comes forward from this, Beloved One."

Q: As well as the language?

"It is, Beloved One, it is to understand the various symbol that come forward are of great similarity."

The fact that we don't know enough about what we are looking at is never more obviously detailed than in the following pre-Egypt tour discussion with Osiris about a particular relief on the wall of the Osirian Chapel in the Temple of Seti I in Abydos, Egypt. This is one of a boat with a lotus flower at the one end and a papyrus on the other that Osiris refers to as the diagram. He gives us a lot of information about the use of this chapel and the relief on the wall as a Star Gateway which dates back to 1430BC. He also referred to it as the Stairway to Heaven, or a wormhole. This wormhole is our connection to the Godhead, via other dimensions, from Earth. In a later discussion about the Stairway to Heaven Osiris discussed the involvement of the Being of Light we know of as Enoch. He informed us then that this is another of the names he was previously know by.

It is noteworthy that prior to communicating with the working group as Osiris, this Light Being used the name Serapis. He was known by the name Serapis during the times of Ancient Greece, after he left Egypt, and it is this name that is often more widely known about than the name Osiris. Nevertheless, the consciousness of the Light Being Osiris and Serapis are from the same source.

Osiris' *"Gateway to Heaven"* - the Solar Boat wall relief in the Osirian Chapel, Temple of Seti I, Abydos, Egypt.

Osiris: The Osirian Chapel: the Wormhole

"Greetings to you, Beloved Ones, I am Osiris, come forward from Spirit, on this day, to be with you, greetings to you.

"It is on this day, Beloved Ones, that I wish to take you forward, it is through an understanding of that which takes place at this time, it is the preparation period for many of yourselves to move into the connectivity of ancient Egypt. It is at this time that I work with you in this interconnection as it is of support for many in humanity at this time.

"The pathway forward of the understanding of that which has taken place through the connectivity of the Being, you are to understand, as I communicate with you from the presence of the Being that is Osiris.

"It is, Beloved Ones, as I come forward as Being, it is different name and nature, so it is the understanding to move into the experience of connectedness through a dimensional shift, through the experience of communication as Being that has been in physicality. Not always of the understanding to come forward from the perspective of the 5th dimensional experience, into the connectivity as Ascended Being of Light, to the communication of the Earthly experience. It is at this time you have the ability to communicate with the presence of Being, through the connection, it is of the movement forward through, at this time it is 8th dimensional experience.

"It is through this position, Beloved Ones, that I serve you on this day, to work with you in the connectedness of not only of that of the full Moon period at this time, it is the understanding through the connectedness of the Osiris chapel, the understanding of this position, it is of ancient Egypt, Beloved Ones, through the connectivity of the Seti Temple. The understanding through the position of this area of great Light, not always known to many, not understood by many, perhaps not any at this time, of the deep understanding of this connectivity.

"It is to serve you greatly on this day to know and understand, that as I take you into the understanding of ancient knowledge, it is to know and understand that through the connectivity of the Seti Temple, it is the bringing forward of a period that is, it is of the understanding of a period that is 1430 of a connectivity of that which your understanding as BC, the understanding of the bringing forward of a time frame.

"I bring forward the understanding the connectivity of the presence of Star Gateway, and it is this Star Gateway as you move into the connectedness of that which is known as the Osirian Chapel at this period, and understanding of position. So it is that which is brought forward through many teachings and understandings, of many ancient religions, many ancient connectivities, of Beings to bring forward the following of information and guidance from this.

"It is the understanding that as you face this position, and you begin to focus on diagram that is within this position, so it is to understand that it is known as Gateway to Heaven. It is this position that has been placed in an environment, and so you have the ability through the diagram to connect with the pathway forward, through the Gateway, through the connectivities to the higher vibrational energies. There begins to be many beings at this time working in such a manner to bring forward an understanding of the connectivities of Earth. The understanding of the experience of the beginnings of Earth, and so it is at this particular position you have the ability to see before you that which is understood at this time through many beings connecting in this manner. It is a modern day term, it is understood within diagram as wormhole.

"It is the understanding of connectivity through an advancement of connection with Spirit, through that which connects to the Godhead. It is in the experience of position. So it is I work with you on this day, to feel the connectivity. Many of yourselves moving forward through great tiredness, many of the feeling state of vibratory energy not felt before, it is not only pathway of that which you have done through connection of physical exercise, Beloved Ones."

When the Ascended Beings either decide to come back to Earth in service to humanity with open consciousness, or if the Masters of Light are invited (by us) to communicate with us on Earth, humanity has the chance to learn the truth of human existence from these advanced souls of Light. Other than this form of information gathering it is an extraordinarily difficult and confusing process, from the basis of today's world. Without the Light Beings' help in this enLightenment service we, as human beings in the separated state of duality, continue to feel very lost. This is why we take our time on the reincarnation cycle to work out what appears to be the puzzle of the Universe. There need be no mystery, but for the fact that we have been kept in the dark, away from the Light of wisdom and knowledge of the Universe, our Universe.

The Divide
The physical thing of the divide (which gives us a sense of separation of our physical and spiritual realities) is also the root cause underlying our sense of separation from the spiritual realms. It is a very tangible, like a low frequency smog blanket which blocks our vision and hangs around polluting the energy grid system of Earth. The energy grid of Earth is part of the energy grid of the entire Universe. However, the quality of the portion of the Universal grid that Earth occupies is determined by the various energies of the planet and her inhabitants, and it is this which all Earth and her inhabitants resonate with. Change the one and the others all change too. This is why everything we do has a direct impact on the entire Universe. The following points are pertinent about this frequency system of the grid:
- It is the overall resonance field of the Earth which both surrounds and is intertwined throughout the entire globe.
- It continues to be dynamically maintained by the collective consciousness of humanity.
- It is affected by Earth inhabitant's actions as well as by outer-planetary energy.
- It is a positive feedback system which directly affects the energy system of the Earth's inhabitants and the globe.

The separating veil of the consciousness divide, between us and the Godhead, is created by the frequency of the grid system of Earth and thus both are dynamically affecting one another. On our planet, and everywhere else, planetary consciousness and the grid of the planet are both generated by the individual frequencies which are created by the entirety of the planet's consciousness. The more intelligent that consciousness is, the greater the impact it will have on the entire system. This is a function of the more frequent and faster electrical impulses along nerve pathways that more intelligent life naturally has, relative to vibration sensitive systems - and the effect that has on the grid.

For human beings, this means that the electrical or vibrational energy of every thought, emotion or action will impact on the energy grid system of the Earth. Consequently, each individual has an impact on the density of the consciousness veil between us and the worlds of Spirit. It is because each individual person is able to impact on and reverberate with the collective consciousness of humanity that each individual being can and does have a powerful effect upon it. This effect could be positive or negative in nature, depending on individual choices. It is because this grid is the frequency system with which we resonate and create, that this resonance informs and becomes our reality. Within this system lie the sacred geometric, structural shapes of dimensions, of consciousness, throughout the Universe. It is for this very reason that the Light Beings constantly remind us to keep resonating at as high a frequency as possible and to, "*Hold your Light.*"

Naturally, this frequency divide is currently a limitation for us, but we become aware about how to change it in order to shift dimension when we learn about the processes of living ascension. The high frequency gateways, or wormhole systems, were created by the Light Beings for this express purpose. It is the choice of each person whether to access them or not. The individual upliftment of consciousness changes the frequency of the grid system and this becomes the wave of changing consciousness amongst humanity, and the Universe.

Individually, we have a direct relationship with everybody else on the planet purely by virtue of the fact that we all contribute to, influence and are influenced by, the energy grid system of the planet. Fear is easily stimulated in the consciousness of individual human beings. This is most especially the case in the face of physical planetary shifts such as earthquakes, during corporate readjustments, in the face of financial market collapses and the resultant loss of jobs, threats to life and limb in warring countries and exposure to hunger and disease in impoverished nations. The various versions of individually stimulated fear fuel the grid system of the planet with the low frequencies of this emotion and the entirety of humanity is thus continually stimulated by that emotion. We have no option but to be influenced by this. This is the direct consequence of the returning reverberations from what has become the collective consciousness of humanity. This is why the collective consciousness has been called a 'consensual reality'.

The fastest way to positively change the nature of the grid system of Earth is to shift our own personal state of consciousness to a higher frequency state - and vice versa. In this manner we can play a positive role in our own lives as well as the lives of the entire population of the Earth. We can change that consensual reality in the moment of a thought.

Because of the dense electromagnetic smog of the veil in the 3rd and 4th dimensions of physicality it is very difficult for us to get a clear picture of the higher frequency states of the higher dimensions. There are clouds in our hearts and our minds, because our world 'out there' is dominated by low frequency vibrations - which we unknowingly create. As a result we are blind to so much of what has happened or what is happening, while we are in human form on Earth. This state of unawareness, or non-consciousness, can only change when we raise our resonance high enough to be able to connect our Earth-portion of the Universal grid energetically with other parts of the Universal grid - which are what we call the dimensions which are in open communication with the Godhead. The resonance of the Godhead sounds clearly within the higher, spiritual dimensions which operate predominantly with the frequency of unconditional love. This frequency of love spirals up and down and all around the grid system of the Universe in the same pattern as the swirls and whorls we see all around us - in our DNA, in the arrangement of petals or the leaves of a cabbage, in a whirlwind, in whirlpools and even in our Milky Way. The shape of this energy of love on the Universal Grid is the sum total of Universal Intelligence and Knowledge.

When we are resonating at higher frequencies we are more capable of tapping into Divine Intelligence and thus intuiting and downloading Divine Truth. It has not been possible for many people on Earth in the 3rd dimension to have consciously managed to do this to date, because of the vast difference in resonance between the energy systems of the 3rd and the 5th dimensions. However, with the current options of the *en masse* living ascension process from the basis of the 4th dimension, this is set to change - just as Osiris states.

Osiris: The Shift of Consciousness for all

"The pathway forwards of the upliftment of the procedures taking place within your living state at this time - the upliftment of the shift not only of the consciousness of your own beings, but of the connectivity of all in humanity at this time."

The Higher Frequency of Living Ascension

The idea of living ascension *en masse* means that although only relatively few people are aware of the terminology of 'living ascension' and the processes that are detailed in this book, many are already *living* the principles which it incorporates. This means their thoughts, emotions and behaviours resonate within range of the frequencies of the 5th dimension - unconditional love and compassion. This is what will ensure a shifted dimension experience for many, many people regardless of their intellectual understanding of the process. The stimulation of the energy grid system of Earth by these higher frequency operating people encourages many others to shift their own resonance to higher frequency states. The work done by higher frequency human beings thus assists with raising the resonance of countless people across the planet and this in turn, will assist with raising individual resonance in a positive knock-on effect as the energy of the grid changes. It is because of this that the possibilities of *en masse* living ascension seem more plausible.

However, although many humans may want to actively work themselves into higher frequency states, part of the problem of accessing dimensions which are higher than the ones we currently resonate with (which, for now, are either the 3rd and 4th *physical* dimensions of reality), is that we do not know where the access points to the higher dimensions are - whether within us or in our external world.

This is partly why so few people have managed to attain the living ascension state or enLightenment in any given lifetime.

*The key to the enLightenment of the higher
dimensions is unconditional love.*

Gateways
We were literally slammed out of Earthly existence at the time of the Atlantean nuclear disaster, the pole shift and Great Deluge catastrophes and, because of the rapidity of these events we did not have the chance to consciously manage to work out what happened while we were still physically alive. An example to consider with regard to how quickly the Earth can shift are the frozen bodies of mammoths which were found with buttercups in their mouths and undigested food in their stomachs - as if to suggest they were happily grazing when Earth suddenly froze over and killed them in a flash. At the same time as the surface disasters occurred, the Earth instantly shifted its energy into a lesser state of unity - and into resonance with the 3rd dimension frequencies.

With guidance from the Light Beings who *do* resonate with the frequencies of the higher dimensions, we are now better able to understand the importance and the impact of the frequency gateways - or what Osiris equates to the modern-day term of 'wormholes' - which lead us back into resonance with the higher dimensions. This entire process is determined by the geometric functions of the Universe and it has a mathematical equation attached to it.

The energy gateways are the access points along the multi-frequency pathway of consciousness that we are on. These access points may be viewed as the divisions between the dimensions, or the changeover point of the different octaves. Although there is no actual changeover point from one note to the next on a musical scale, we may view this as the interval, or the momentary hiatus, which is created as the finger lifts from the piano key before it strikes the next one. It is in that non-space of the non-note that the progression to the next note is made. So too it is with the dimensions. The gateways can be equated with a non-space inasmuch we know when we are in the 4th dimension or in the 5th dimension, but the crossover from one to another is not a place or a space either.

In terms of the dimensions some of the gateways are very far away from other ones and some are easy to get through, just as with the notes and scales on a piano, The most difficult one to perceive *and* to get through is the one that shifts us from the 4th to the 5th dimension - simply because our perceptual abilities are so 'immature' in the 4th dimension and we struggle to perceive that this possibility exists.

We created a reverse, or backwards, section of the pathway of expanding consciousness when we spiralled downwards in dimension. The consciousness pathway is a continuum and we personally decide which way we would like to travel on it - *towards* or *away* from high frequency Light. Interestingly enough, although we extended the pathway in the 'wrong' direction by 'falling' into the 3rd dimension, this Pathway of Return is the exact same one we have always been on, even currently during our recovery of more Light. The trick to our progress is to go in the opposite direction now - in the direction of the Return Home. Instead of continuing to *devolve* our energy in the direction of lower frequencies we are now *evolving* in the direction of higher frequency Light. Following the Pathway of Return simply means turning around on our current pathway and going in a forwards direction towards higher frequency Light - just as Sirius and the Siriuns did previously.

The winding, spiralling wind of a tornado becomes more and more destructive as it gathers speed. As it slows down it appears to disappear. Such is the nature of Light when it is wound down the frequency scale and becomes manifest, dense, physical matter, or when it is unwound up the frequency scale of the dimensions and becomes Light and lighter. Such is the nature of the Light Beings, of you and me and of creation.

Wormholes

However the processes of shifting dimension are perceived by each individual, it is clear from the following excerpt from a September 2008 meditation that the resonance of unconditional love, which is held in the heart, will support us on our Pathway of Return - as we unwind the tight spiral of dense physicality. Essentially, human beings are advised to learn to think with the heart. This is, "*The feeling state of the heart*," which Osiris so often refers to.

Osiris: The Heart and Unconditional Love

"It is through this procedure, at this time, you find yourselves moving forward through the deep understanding and connectivities that take place through the presence of your being, at this time. It is, Beloved Ones, to connect and work with the presence of the heart. It is through the heart centre at this time, through all the experiences in physicality, to know and understand as you move forward through all in the shifting of the dimensional experience at this time. It is the understanding of the holding of energy and connectivities to the Earthly experience, and it is in order to move into the connection through the pathway - it is the understanding of the expansiveness of the unconditional love within, of the great importance of the connectivity within the self."

Aside from telling us that the key to a shifted dimension is to live, think and feel from the state of unconditional love, Osiris constantly gives more information about the actual process and he uses a number of words to help us to understand how it is done. He has referred to the movement of our reality from one frequency system to another as being similar to what the scientific community refers to as going through a 'wormhole'. He also uses the terms star gateway, gateway, stairway to heaven and spiral staircase when referring to a wormhole system. Scientifically speaking, the notion of a wormhole is a theoretical one, but it is so close to the truth of a frequency gateway into the other dimensions as to be very exciting. Osiris has suggested that we see a wormhole as a cone-like form, as if an hourglass-shape with wide, open funnels on both sides. Through this funnel of a wormhole, the energy moves in a spiralling motion and it gathers in intensity as it rises 'up', gets 'squished' through the narrow centre point and is then released in an intense burst of Light out of the other side - which is an area of higher frequency Light than Earth is.

The energy-intensifying process of moving 'upwards' from one dimension to another is created by using the structure of the entire wormhole system to intensify Light energy from the lower energy dimensions, pass it through the centre point of the gateway and release it (in its higher frequency state) on the other side. In this way lower energy states of Light become compatible with higher energy states of Light. The transformative force which the energy (of individual consciousness or a group) generates as it moves through the wormhole system is responsible for the transmutation of matter. In this way the solidified Light which makes up the matter of the human body is returned to a lighter state of Light.

Osiris refers to the 'morphing' from one frequency state to another as a 'transmutation' process. WordWeb gives some interesting descriptions for the word 'transmutation': 1. An act that changes the form or character or substance of something. 2. A qualitative change. 3. (physics) the change of one chemical element into another (as by nuclear decay or radioactive bombardment). "The transmutation of base metals into gold proved to be impossible." This last sentence suggests the alchemical process of the spiritual journey which Osiris has mentioned to us on numerous occasions, but all three descriptions appear to adequately describe the living ascension process which results in the shifted dimension experience of reality. When we link all the concepts together we arrive at the unified understanding of sacred geometry.

We do a backwards and forwards movement through the wormhole for quite some time until we become fully accustomed to the full 5th dimension experience. When transmutation of all the lower frequency energies occurs, we will be living in an expanded state of energy which has successfully integrated the two *opposite* ends of the wormhole into *one* system. The polar opposites which characterise 4th dimension duality, literally disappear. At this point the gateway simply collapses, because there is no need for it any more when the two separated energy states are re-unified. Until this comes about (whether in the macro-Earth or group sense, or the micro-individual sense), we systematically work at being able to tolerate more and more of the 5th dimensional frequencies within us physically. Practically, in the hum-drum of our daily lives, we achieve this by setting the intention to think, feel and act from the basis of unconditional love. This intention begins the implementation process of love in action. Love thoughts, feelings and actions generate the highest frequency state of all - everywhere in the Universe.

However, as simple as the movement of energy through the gateway system of a wormhole really is, the physical reality for us is that we have to be physically *and* spiritually compatible with the development of the *intensity* of the Light energy as it builds up in the approach to the centre of this access system. We have to physically and emotionally be able to tolerate higher energy states which are brought about by the increasingly intensifying vibrations within a wormhole system and the attraction of the intense energy on the other side, in the new dimension. The intense energy of the higher dimensions is generated and maintained by the constant presence of unconditional love. Love is the over-riding characteristic of the higher dimensions.

The disciplines of both physics and chemistry could easily demonstrate why this intensification of the Light energy through the wormhole system results in higher frequency Light. This is especially so when it is viewed relative to the light-sensitive, crystalline structure of our physically dense bodies, in consideration of the interlocking sequence of the star tetrahedron system of Light and from the basis of the creation of the spiralling energies through the various power-shapes, relative to the Fibonacci Sequence. These factors are highly pertinent to the changing energies of transmutation which are accessed within a wormhole system.

By acknowledging that going through the wormhole experience is an energy *intensifying* process, we can appreciate that before we can even think about beginning to enter a wormhole funnel from the side of 4th dimension Earth experience, we need to have raised our vibrations to a high enough frequency so as to be able to resonate with the higher frequencies we will encounter there. This is important in order for us to be able to physically endure the higher energy environment. The higher up the first part of the hourglass or cone we go, the more we need to be physically vibrating at ever-increasing frequencies. This is because the upper reaches of the narrowing cone will cause the spiralling energies to speed up and intensify. We have to be physically and emotionally capable and fit enough to tolerate these frequencies of Light as they build - as they wind and unwind. This is the practical reality of our lives.

By the time we get to the centre of the hourglass, or the place where the tips of the two cones meet (as if an open-ended figure-of-8), the energies within the lower portion of the wormhole system are at their peak from the perspective of moving 'upwards' from Earth. This central position is the actual gateway of the wormhole system. Encountering this super-intense environment of high frequency vibrations means that if there is any incompatible low frequency vibration still within us physically, emotionally or spiritually, it will effectively be 'squeezed' out of us as we pass through this point of intense energy.

Low frequency vibrations come in many different forms and include the following:
- Negative thought patterns which create our attitudes and state of mind.
- Negative emotions which power up our thoughts and entrench their patterns.
- Negative behaviours which follow on from our thoughts and emotions and become habits.
- Physical pollutants of the body.
- Cellular memory - of past experiences in this life or any other lifetime, carried through on the genetic material, as a programme.
- Soul memory - of current and past lifetime experiences, carried through on the soul fabric of the soul presence.

Shedding low frequency vibrations amounts to a detoxification process. Knowing that homeopaths refer to a detoxification process as a 'healing crisis' may shed more light on why clearing out the human system can be a dramatic one. This type of purification can be difficult to deal with, especially if we are unschooled and don't know what to expect.

Clearing to Tolerate Higher Frequencies
For human beings the intensity of the wormhole-midpoint energies may feel a little uncomfortable at first, as all frequency shifts do, simply because they stimulate a detoxification process. This causes dross to be removed from our bodies - physically, emotionally and spiritually. Once detoxified, we are perfectly capable of tolerating the higher frequency energies and when we arrive at the central point of a wormhole, it is obvious that we have made the necessary progress, vibrationally, to have made it that far. Shifting the programmes which make up our cellular memories, including ideas about ageing and health, is an important part of achieving agelessness. Changing the brainwashed responses we all have, to one degree or another, whether pertaining to ourselves or to life, involves a shift in consciousness.

The intense frequency zone of the midpoint of a wormhole may be regarded as the last 'sweat room' of cleansing in the living ascension process. In due course, we briefly pass backwards and forwards through the entire funnel system a few times during the preliminary stages of getting used to the wormhole energies which stimulate the purification processes. As a result, longer excursions higher up in the wormhole system gradually become so much easier to tolerate. As with most big changes, the initial phases which lead up to being able to pass through the midpoint are often the most challenging. Similarly, matriculants are often amazed that their final school year is a lot easier than the previous one.

It is to consider at all times that the process of shifting to a higher dimension *has* to involve cleansing and purification, because in order to be able to live in a higher dimension which resonates with the state of unconditional love itself, nothing lower than the frequency of the feeling of love may exist within us. Considering that most of us are rather far off from living the reality of this Blissful state, it stands to reason that human beings have some extensive clearing to do in order to constantly tolerate 5th dimension frequencies. We need to stretch ourselves constantly.

Most importantly, due to the clearing processes we slowly and naturally shift into the experience of being centred in the heart. The consciousness of living ascension requires that we are balanced in our centre - in the heart. It is from the heart that we feel unconditional love. When we operate from this energy centre, we think from the heart and all of our actions follow on from this. This means that all the lower energy states of fear, aggression, insecurity and the like which may reside within us as ancient emotional patterns or programmes, will be transmuted into the feelings of unconditional love. Feeling is the mode of soul.

The lower chakras colours (red, orange and yellow) which produce the emotions of the negative ego when their energy is dominant, change to points of white Light on the body once we shift the from operating from the human ego state into the heart state of feeling. While this is in process, the three chakras above the head begin to activate. These are the chakras of ascension. The changes involved in ascension are alchemical reactions and it is these higher chakra energies which are required for this transmutation. Therefore, the changes can be both magical and profoundly intense at the same time - physically, emotionally and spiritually.

Osiris describes the feelings which are stimulated by the changing energy fields - during the period of the dimension shift, as we shift in and out through the middle of a wormhole - as the emotions which are part of the processes of clearing ancient emotional, thought and behavioural patterns of the lower frequency states. These clearings apply to all lifetimes past and present. This means that we will first see these ancient and current issues recurring before they begin to clear. They bubble up to the surface so that we can clear them out of our systems and this is usually an uncomfortable process - especially if we don't know how to decode them. Osiris goes on to state that as we work from the basis of the heart centre, we are able to maintain and to work with the shifted dimension frequency changes more easily.

Osiris: Energy Centres and Frequency Shifts

"It is at this time, Beloved Ones, as you work with the procedure of the connectivities of energy centre - it is the pathway at this time, that it is greatly supportive to know and understand that as the energy fields and the frequency of the Earth begin to shift into the experience of a dimension shift, into the experience of the raising of your energy field and through the frequency of great Light, there begins to take place a continuation of work that has to be done through Spirit, and through the connectivities of the shifting of the pathway of enLightenment.

"So it is to understand, Beloved Ones, that in the feeling state of connectivity of the lower energy states of the dimension from which you raise your energy, so it is the understanding that all aspect of the connectivities going forward begin to move into the feeling of great discomfort - and therefore the ancient patterning about which you have spoken with in-depth on many occasions. So it is the understanding that you begin to create a shift of the energy fields, into the upper form and from the heart centre upward, that as you begin to move with this procedure it is serving you greatly - of the ability to maintain and work with the frequency shift.

"So it is in connectivity of all that takes place of the lower energy fields, and in all areas of the repetition of ancient patterning, and of ancient programming, and ancient emotion, that begin to recur on many occasion - so it is in the feeling state of the coming forward that this begins to be felt with discomfort.

"We work on this day, Beloved Ones, to move forward through a dimension shift in the experience to move forward through procedure - to allow for the experience to take place, to allow for yourselves to move into the frequency of great Light, in the continuation of support and assistance.

"It is on this pathway, Beloved Ones, that I serve and work with you, in connectivity of much love and the great Light of Sprit to support and serve you."

* * * * * * * * * * *

CHAPTER NINE

Outer-Planetary Connectivity

"List ye, O man, to he who comes to you. But weigh in the balance his words be of LIGHT. For many there are who walk in the DARK BRIGHTNESS and yet are not the children of LIGHT."

(The Emerald Tablets of Thoth-The-Atlantean p32, pp5)

Outer-Planetary Super-Alignments

The spiralling energies within the wormhole system draw us in towards the centre point of the funnels. These funnels can also be viewed as a figure-of-8 system. We are naturally attracted to these energies. The spiralling energies of shifting consciousness on Earth are like coils of energy which are supported and encouraged by the magnet-like influence of the outer-planetary bodies. This is the effect of the gravitational pull on Earth which is created by the specific position and alignment of various stars and planets at this time. Just like drawing a spiralling line which follows the whorls of a flower such as a dahlia, the line of an energy spiral is shaped according to a Fibonacci Sequence - a mathematical progression in which each number equals the sum of the two preceding numbers (1, 1, 2, 3, 5, 8 etc). This sequence is found throughout nature in its shapes and growth patterns and it is critical in the mathematics of the Universe - or that which is known of as sacred geometry. This sequence and the spiralling energies it creates is the reason why we feel powerful shifts in the portals which Thoth established at the ancient sacred sites all over the world, especially the Great Pyramid in Giza, Egypt. The Great Pyramid is the most important portal on the planet. However, no matter how important the mathematical sequence of the shape of creation is, it is more important to take note of the existence of this concept than it is to understand it fully at this stage.

Most significantly, the position of the specific, super-aligned outer-planetary bodies in the skies, relative to Earth, is exactly the same now as it was in 2037/67 BC when the god-beings were actively bringing Light to Earth once again, in Ancient Egypt. Knowing that it is this specific arrangement of stars and planets, relative to Earth and the centre of the galaxy, which creates the massive gravitational pull of spiralling energy that forms the specific high frequency pathway in the shape of an hourglass-type funnel, or figure-of-8, underscores the importance of that time relative to our own. There is an actual, physically accessible Pathway of Return that the Light Beings speak of. The energy of the Ascension Pathway is tangible and real, no matter how subtle we feel its energies to be at the moment. This is the pathway that was forged by the Siriuns when their own very old star system was in the process of this same type of ascension process that we are currently going through.

If we had a good heavenly perspective we could easily sketch the plan of the position of each planet and star in its place on the shape of the 8, the spiralling energy pathway each portion contributes to within the hourglass shape and their relationship to Earth - all perfectly placed on the energy grid of the Universe. The fact that this spiralling movement is echoed in the shape of our DNA strands gives us further pause for thought when considering our own place in the Universe. Within us lies the Pathway of Return just as it lies in the skies. This gives more meaning to Osiris' oft-repeated sentence, "*As above, so below.*" Our external world has a direct relationship to our internal world, at every level.

The spiralling energies within the funnel move inwards and outwards, in a wave-like motion as they follow the figure-of-8 pathway. Through the two pyramids (see diagram on next page) the energy squishes and expands, slows down and gathers speed in their constant, upward motion. This is the movement of ascension which explains why we sometimes feel that we are spinning. Physically, it is because Earth is positioned at the bottom of the open end of the energy funnel of the figure-of-8 that we are in position to be directly influenced and drawn up by the magnetic energies which are formed within this shape - if we have raised the speed of our vibrations sufficiently to be able to resonate with the higher dimension energies on the other side. If our resonance is too low, we will be too 'heavy' to lift upwards into the subtle energy stream.

Externally, this Earth-stimulating energy field is created by the unique alignments and the subsequent inter-relationship of the powerful gravitational fields of high resonance planets and stars and the centre of the galaxy. Regardless of the powerful resonance of the surrounding energy field, Earth and Earthlings will only be attracted to, or influenced by, this high frequency Light if they are resonating, internally, at a high enough frequency to be within range of it. Both the internal and external energy factors have to be compatible for ascension to occur.

If Earth resonance is not within range of the surrounding frequencies of Light, most of the incoming high frequencies of Light from the aligned bodies in our outer-planetary neighbourhood simply pass us by, unseen, unheard and unfelt. This has to be the case if Earth and her inhabitants are in a dimension, determined by our state of hearts and minds, which is too low for the bulk of the planet to harmonically resonate with higher frequencies. That is exactly what happened for most human beings of the 2037/67BC time period, because Earth was still in the 3rd dimension. The Light Beings were working, as a physical presence here on Earth, at that time to help support the planet's ascension. It didn't happen. Nevertheless, the planetary alignments supported the god-beings' return to Earth at that time after a long period of absence and this ensured that there were powerful teachers and leaders available for the upliftment of human beings once more. The fact that we have now arrived at this point as we approach the midpoint of the Age of Aquarius tells us that their efforts then were successful. We are reaping the benefits.

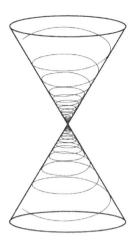

When the orbit of the long-forgotten planet Nibiru (Planet X) begins to influence the energy in the arrangement of the figure-of-8 wormhole spiral in the skies, this event will stimulate even more of a powerful magnet-like attraction within this pathway. The physical influence on Earth, by Nibiru, is caused by the gravitational influence of this energetically powerful planet. It is all of these powerful attractions, or resonances, which Earth is responding to. These ever-increasing, influential energies are disturbing at times and uplifting at other times. The stimulation of these higher frequencies of Light assists with the detoxification and purification of Earth and her inhabitants.

Aside from the earthquakes, volcanic eruptions, unusual weather and other Earth changes, humans feel their old injuries and buried issues emerging. Held within us, all of these create low frequency vibrations that are incompatible with ascension. They will be stimulated into the active stage by the higher frequencies of Light, and will no longer be able to remain dormant within us. That is why we are all feeling the changes all around us in our world. Some of us respond with fear while others relish in the effects of the shifting consciousness and take the opportunity to change for the positive.

Our ability to naturally respond to higher frequency Light is why people are experiencing the wave-like motion of the upliftment of consciousness across the entire globe. It is no coincidence that many of the god-beings, who are of Siriun origin, came to Earth from the planet Nibiru in the past. Many of these Siriuns came to Earth via other planets, such as the Pleiades, because they were resident on that planet at the time. The Pleiadians were found predominantly in Ancient Peru, but they want to communicate with Earth once more. The inhabitants of Earth and Nibiru, as well as many other heavenly bodies, all have a close relationship and it is time to start exploring the nature of that star-connection once more.

This is of no small issue to us, historically and currently. Although the planet Nibiru is still relatively far away from Earth, its influences are already being keenly felt by us. It is primarily the disturbing energies from this planet, rapidly coming into close proximity to Earth, which are causing the dramatic shifts of Earth (which we usually call climate change associated catastrophes) and her inhabitants. The energies at the time of 2012 are profound in terms of the midpoint of the Age of Aquarius, but they are merely the beginning stages of the energy which we will be influenced by post-2012. These influences will continue well past the middle of the 21st century, but will be most profound in 2047 when Nibiru is in plain sight and closest to us. It is the known orbital pathway of Nibiru which is linked to the previously observed and understood effects of her gravitational pull on Earth. This movement of outer-planetary bodies is the information the post-Atlantean Era ancients used to plot the future happenings on Earth - such as catastrophes or living ascension opportunities.

As we shift our consciousness to resonate higher we reduce the impact of high frequency events which occur as Nibiru approaches. This event of Nibiru reappearing in the skies close to Earth is directly linked to the concurrence of the midpoint energies of the Age of Aquarius in December, 2012.

None of the contributing factors which are the reason for the changing consciousness of Earth and humanity can be separated from any of the others. Such is the powerful synergistic nature of all the involved agents of change. Osiris discussed the issue of the gravitational influences of Nibiru which Earth is beginning to be subjected to. During these discussions he mentions the fact that as this planet comes closer in towards Earth that the, "Planetary presence," or inhabitants of that planet, will begin to connect with us, and us with them.

Osiris: The Gravitational Pull of Nibiru

Q: Is there any follow up on any new planets that have been discovered? My feeling is that we are connecting with the satellite planets of Nibiru?
'It is to understand, Beloved One, the connectivity, it is for this reason that which has been stated of the pathway of timeframe beginning to be felt in the moving forward through the speeding up in this direction - for it to be the understanding of the gravitational pull through the connectivity of Nibiru. In this manner so it is the pathway of planetary presence connected to this, begins to move forward into the connection. It is you are correct in this, Beloved One."

The very fact that Earth has high frequency areas which are known as the sacred sites or portals, that 4th dimension Earthlings have DNA structures where high frequency Light is already activated and resident within them and that much more of our DNA lies waiting to be activated, means that we will show a positive response to the outer-planetary energies of higher frequency Light. It is this that physically, emotionally and spiritually impacts on us, shifts our consciousness and creates the changing awareness and the upliftment that allows for a shifted dimension experience. However, this upliftment will only occur if people want it and decide to move with the higher energy flow of spiralling energy.

It the structure of the DNA and its link to Divinity is in question by any reader, it may help to refer to the book 'The God Code,' by Gregg Braden. This scientist has the necessary background and knowledge to demonstrate exactly how the elements (Nitrogen, Oxygen, Hydrogen and Carbon) of each of the four DNA bases (Thymine, Cytosine, Adenine, Guanine) are directly linked to that which is denoted as God (YHWH) throughout the ancient Arab and Hebrew texts. It is the various combinations of these four elements that form the structure of DNA which the Light Beings refer to. Considering that the different structures which the combined elements can create, the significance of Light to human beings personally becomes more obvious when we expand our understanding of light so that we can appreciate its nature as Crystalline Light - which is the matter of the stars.

Human beings can choose to negate the higher frequency influences of incoming Light on their bodies and their consciousness by preferring to stimulate lower frequency vibrations which are consciously or unconsciously created by thoughts, emotions and actions of the negative ego. Regularly brought into play, these vibrations of the negative ego create a resonance which over-stimulates the lower frequency-sensitive areas within the brain. This physical place within the human being, which resonates with the lower frequencies of the 3rd dimension, is the area which is referred to as the midbrain. It is this part of the brain which is known as the Reptilian Brain. People who resonate at this level are referred to as 'reptilian.' The highly controversial author, David Icke, has written a lot about the behaviour of these types of individuals. Although his books may be a bit strong at times, he nevertheless has some valid points to make - most especially about outer-planetary entities that are rapaciously power-hungry. The principle of *caveat emptor* ('let the buyer beware') applies, because his books are not for the faint-hearted. These low frequency-dominant reptilian individuals were responsible for the Fall of Atlantis and of Man just as they were responsible for the degeneration of consciousness at the time of the dinosaurs. They continue to support and reinforce the principles of darkness on Earth today. Human beings can degenerate themselves to this level of resonance. This is ill-advised.

When negative, human ego-based thoughts, emotions and behaviours are chosen by human beings, this causes a specific, lowered resonance state of the human body and individuals shift out of resonance with higher frequency Light. When enough people do this at the same time, due to the fact that we operate as a resonance sensitive system *en masse*, the entirety of the consciousness of Earth and her inhabitants has to shift to a lower level. The grid system of Earth can be, and is, negatively affected in this manner. The knock-on effect is negative.

This negative effect will not continue for much longer for the bulk of humanity though, because not only has the collective consciousness of Earth and humanity already shifted into the 4th dimension, but it is in the process of shifting into the 5th dimension - and many people already live that reality. We can bank on the Thoth-engineered assurances which are contained within the Mayan Calendar that inform us that 2012 marks the end-time of the cycle of lowered consciousness, as well as current information from the Light Beings, who inform us that Earth has already achieved this high frequency state, in terms of No/Now-Time.

The super-alignment of the various outer-planetary bodies with Earth is critically important at this time, because the inter-relationships between these high frequency bodies of Light creates a grand total of high frequency Light which Earth feels as the changing energy states which shift consciousness. Their joint effects on us are exponentially far greater than the simple sum of the energy of their individual Light.

The god-beings of ancient Egypt created high frequency, portal systems on Earth. Thoth was the foremost and most powerful architect of these energy portals. Before the Fall, as well as when they returned to Ancient Khem, the ancients used these systems for various purposes, including inter-dimensional travel and communication - especially at the time of the planetary super-alignments. Their home planet, relative to Earth, was either Nibiru or was accessed via Nibiru, and access to this place was important to them. For example, the specific pathway which the energy takes within the Great Pyramid in Egypt was created by Thoth in ancient times. It is a mini-recreation, on Earth, of the spiralling system of energy that is formed by the alignment of planets and stars when they are in their super-aligned position in the skies. This is the energy pattern of the ascension pathway. It is the pathway of infinity - as above, so below.

As a spiralling energy system and a means of inter-dimensional travel and communication, the existing Great Pyramid has another equally large, etheric pyramid which is upside down and on top of the Great Pyramid. Another one interlinks with it to create a star tetrahedron shape. This sequence continues all the way up to the stars on the Siriun Pathway of Return. The energy spirals through this interlocking pattern of sacred geometric shapes. Each pyramid sits point to point with another pyramid, channelling out-going and in-coming energy. The capstone of the Great Pyramid is a portion at the tip which is connected to the one above it. It is this capstone which forms the central part of the figure-of-8 of the two connected pyramids. When this capstone region is reactivated, in preparation to be re-opened energetically, as was done by Light workers across the globe in previous years, the pathway of spiralling energies can begin to more easily shift back and forth through this energy gateway - into and from the higher dimensions. In ancient times the capstone of the Great Pyramid was capped with gold. Gold is critically important in shifting an energy pathway to a higher state - no matter whether that pathway is within the human body or a part of the Great Pyramid.

Thoth stated that the gateway of the Great Pyramid was re-opened on the 9 September 2009 (the entire transcript and an mp3 are available on the website www.stargateway.co.za). This was a powerful event and it was heralded by the many different Light worker groups all over the world who intentionally worked with the high frequency energies up to and on that date. In Osiris' channelled meditation on that day Thoth declared, "*It is opened.*" This gives us further clarity of what is meant by the 'time-clocks of Thoth', because those time-marking systems on Earth ensured that when human consciousness changed and kept the right pace to take advantage of the ascension opportunity which the super-alignment of the planets and stars with Earth provide us with at the moment, the portals would be re-opened.

Many Light Beings assisted this procedure and many of them came through Jacqui with a message for us. Some of the words in the channelled messages are not clear enough to transcribe and are marked as missing by a (...).

Osiris: 9.9.09 - Opening of the Great Pyramid Gateway

"Greetings to you, Beloved Ones. I come forward from Spirit on this day, Beloved Ones. I come forward with much Love to support you at this time. It is at this time to take you forward through the visualisation. It is the understanding, the connectedness at this time, to allow for yourselves to go forward through the procedures taking place, in this alignment.

"The alignment on this day supportive to assist all beings upon the planet to move forward through the pathway of enLightenment, the understanding through the connectivities of the self, to move forward through vast expansiveness, into the areas of acknowledgement of the living state of ascension.

"It is at this time, Beloved Ones, that you are supported in this procedure at this time to move forward through the portal energy. It is at this period the bringing forward to completion, many areas of understandings: the connectivity of completion of the understanding of the ancient ages, the letting go of all areas of the ancient patternings that have come forward for all in humanity - not only for your own personal experience and physical lifetimes.

"It is to understand, Beloved Ones, it brings forward the connectedness of completions, to begin the beginnings. It is in the beginning pathway that you each begin to find yourselves in the activation. It is in the Light of Spirit, the communications with great Love, to support always in the holding of your presence, and the over lighting energy of the Godhead in unconditional Love. So it is always to be supported, in the continuation through procedure.

"It is, Beloved Ones, on this day - so it is of profound energy as many of yourselves understand, on this day to go forward through the connectedness. The many areas, of the inability, in many respect, to hold the energy within immediate environment.

"It is the understanding that it is supporting yourself to acknowledge your new Light, your new procedures of holding of the resonance within the self. And so it continues, Beloved Ones, always to be supported by Spirit in Love, to assist in the procedure in the pathway forward in the ascension procedures, and the procedure of activation that takes place on this day.

"So it is to move forward through the portal of Light. It is at this period, as you move forward through the continuation of the star tetrahedron, the understanding that you begin to activate over coming period within the self, of the DNA. It is the understanding that there begins to be acknowledgement in this respect, of moving forward through great advancement, the growth of the physical self, moving into vast expansiveness.

"It is, Beloved Ones, on this day, I wish to support you to take you forward through the visualisation that connects, it is in the area, Beloved Ones, it is in the connectedness of the pyramid. It is the understanding to connect to various other grid in the planet Earth. It is the understanding that each position begins to open the portal of Light further.

"It is to understand we connect in this position, to begin to move forward, through the advancement of all positions to come together. It is at this time, as you focus over coming period and coming days, to the 11th day of the 11th month, the understanding that as you bring to culmination of all aspect together, so it is the understanding through this procedure of activation, you move forward in you physical lifetime on a pathway that begins to alight and support many more, as you begin to connect with the service procedures that take place, through the over lighting presence of the Godhead.

"To feel the presence within your being through communications that open further and further with Spirit. As it has been requested and as you set forward all intent of moving forward, so it is at this time, Beloved Ones, to move through the experience of Divine Manifestation and Divine Communications, the Divine Love with Spirit.

"So it is I guide you on this day, Beloved Ones, to connect and communicate with other Beings of Light that support you through this procedure. So it is Beloved Ones, to feel the presence of Light energy to surround you. Begin to feel yourself moving forward through the connectedness of the feeling state of unconditional Love.

"Allow the feeling state in the heart as you begin to shift into all aspect of the fullness and understanding of the heart essence. Beloved Ones. As you feel yourselves letting go into the consciousness, the gentle and slow procedure to allow yourselves, in the formation of the star tetrahedron surrounding your physical form - and so it is collective energy field of Merkabah that begins to form - surrounding ashram in this position, at this time, to connect with various other positions upon the planet.

"So as you move forward with group energy that is greatly intensified through the communications with Spirit, there is the presence of Angelic Beings to surround and support the upliftment, on the pathway of all in humanity on this day, Beloved Ones.

"There are many moving through the joyous experience of connectedness with Spirit. So it is through procedures of completion, so it is in celebration Beloved Ones, as it is as you have come forward to move through the activation. So it is to understand, you move forward through the pathway to release in all aspect of that which has gone before.

"The experience of the activation within the DNA begins to allow yourselves to move into the expansiveness of a state of consciousness that takes you forward, through the pathway of ascension, Beloved Ones. It is at this time as you begin to feel the presence of great Light to surround you, as you begin to move through the experience of connectedness within the self - to shift consciousness - to allow for the procedure to take place in a gentle and slow movement.

"Allow yourselves to drift and as you begin to find yourselves coming forward through a communication, it is with the presence of great Light. It is through the position, it is of the area slightly above in the etheric of the capstone, Beloved Ones. It is this point of activation that there begins to be formed in the surroundings of the entire plateau of this area, the Merkabah vehicle that begins to be formed, through the shift of consciousness taking place. Through your procedures of connectivity, and through the presence of great Light of Spirit to bring to Earth and for Earth to connect the Universal system of great Light, the alignment of star system that begins to move through the connectedness at this time.

"It is, Beloved Ones, as you feel the presence of Light, as you begin to shift in the movement, you come to an area, there begins to be the feeling state, as you have moved forward through preparation in similarity in visualisations, so you bring forward the connectedness - it is of the form that surrounds the entire area of pyramid upon the Earth, that comes to central position, that you find yourselves in at this time to connect in this position, as it opens from this perspective to the Universe. It therefore moves through the connectedness of the entirety of Earth as it sets forward the grid, to be supported from the growth of all humanity.

"Beloved Ones, as you begin to feel yourselves in the position, as you come to an area of great Light, it is at this particular period in the understandings of the passing of cycles; the understanding of the connectedness of ancient period to this. So it is the understandings of all that have gone between. So it is you begin the pathway to raise above to the connectivity of the heavens, the understandings of that which is to come in all areas of advancement of the Earthly experience - through the pathway of Light, through the connectivity of the Godhead within. To open and awaken many, many beings, not only through your pathway of ascension that you begin in full capacity at this time, the ability to move and transcend your understandings to all.

"So it is, you begin to feel the great Light of vast area, it is in a circular surroundings, so it is above central position of the capstone. It is the central position above capstone, the understanding that at this point, Beloved Ones, it is the understanding of ancient period, the connectivities at this time, that you begin to bring forward the presence of the Being that is Thoth. It is in the surroundings, there are many Beings to surround the presence of this Being, to be supportive of all ancient communications. The presence of all Beings of Ascension in Spirit at this time to come together, in the formation of circular position.

"So it is at this time, Beloved Ones, I bring forward the presence of the Being that is Thoth, to support the communication and the connectivities with blessing."

Thoth

"I greet you, I am Thoth. I come forward on this day, Children of Light, to understand from the ancient Atlantean position. I bring forward through understanding of the Dweller (*of the Halls of Amenti, as detailed in the Emerald Tablets*), of the presence of the Godhead, to support you. (...) Ptah begins to open the doorway of Light, from one position to another, to serve man, as Beings walk upon the planet to Light, to bring position to open doorway.

"Through the doorway you begin to feel the experience, the intent of the ancient positions of Atlantis, through the development and architecture and the connectivities of this position, the understandings of the full capacity. The opening of Gateway begins.

"In the presence, Beloved Children of Light, you begin to feel the opening that has been promised forward from ancient period to this. I bring to you on this day, the understandings through the sacred geometric position, to the connectivities of 8th position upon the planet. The position of 8, that begin to open at this time, through the pathway of Light. The Children of Light, to move forward through the entrance of Ptah, to understand all purpose in physical lifetimes as Children of Light. To the Dweller we go, and move through the connectedness of the dimension that awaits for the procedures to connect further. In your Light, Beloved Children of Light, you are blessed. It is opened. I greet you. I am Thoth."

Isis

"I greet you, Beloved Beings of Light, I am Jsat. To come forward on this day to support you, the Beloved presence of Osiris, Beloved presence of Thoth, that have begun the procedures in celebration to open the gateway, that has been set forward for many, many lifetimes to this. From Ancient Atlantean period, you begin to feel the activation to move forward through your presence.

"The many Beings of Ascension do await your intent at this time. It is to feel it in Love, Beloved Beings of Light, in your heart, if it is your intent to go forward through the opening of position. You support through your procedures at this time the awakening of your heart, the opening of energy centre of ascension, to allow for continuations of existence.

"It is deep intent, Beloved Beings of Light, for yourselves to set in motion. There is from this point to the period - it is 11th day of 11th month of this particular year - that takes you forward through greater growth than ever before. You have this period to set intent, to communicate with the self in peaceful state. In unconditional Love it is felt, the presence of all Beings to surround at this time, to continue to be in your presence over this period of Light.

"So through the activation as it has begun, the presence of all Beings to assist always. As One we move, the connectivities of the Godhead to come forward to all beings in humanity at this time, allowing yourselves to let go further into the consciousness. As you do this, Beloved Beings of Light, begin to feel the presence in the formation that you move.

"It is the sacred geometry placed and drawn above, from Thoth to yourselves, to feel the pathway of Light, as you shift, as you create it, through the activation of DNA. The formation of star tetrahedron begins to take form, to surround the entirety of planet at this time.

"The connection of all Beings of Light on the Earth at this time, begin to feel this procedure for period - it is of 3 day ahead - for all to come together in the time frame to support the procedure in activation. Begin to feel the expansiveness taking place, the Light energy begins to move through your presence, the consciousness, as you let go of form.

"Beloved Beings of Light, I bless you on this day in great Love, through the connection of the Godhead, Beloved Osiris, Thoth, the presence of my Being, as One, we bless you. I bring forward through the connection at this time, the Beloved presence of Being to support further."

Sanat Kumara

"I greet you, (...) energy of Light, I am Sanat Kumara. I come forward in the colour to surround you. Feel the presence of blue, the turquoise celestial energy of Light. I touch your presence (...) to support through your heart. The essence through the manner to you as presence of self. I bring forward to you on this day to bless, bring forward at this time to message to Earth, it is felt in the Southern Hemisphere to yourself, it is felt to the Northern Hemisphere of Light.

"In Love to work with your presence in Bliss, in the Oneness, Oneness of all of humanity, to bring through peace, to bring through Light.

"I bless you."

Horus

"Beloved Beings, I communicate with yourselves, on this day to bring you the presence of the Trinity, together as One. You communicate with the Being that is Horus. Horus through the manifestation, request of Light, to offer to yourselves at this time, to begin the movement from one state to another, you begin to open the pathway.

"As we move together, it is this period that has been intended, to open further for many in humanity, to bring together the understanding of old. The presence, the Mother, the Father to be, I come forward in Light to celebrate with you.

"I bless you on this day, I bless you in love and all who come forward to intent, the pathway to open through the communication and intent of Thoth of old. It is intended before, it is attempt once more to shift through the consciousness of great Light.

"I bless you. I am Horus."

Quan Yin

"I greet you on this day, I am Quan Yin. I am Quan Yin, to support the procedures to understand the presence to be in physical life, for all time. I continue to support all life on Earth to go forward through ascension, never to move in Spirit in total, to continue in Spirit and Earth as One.

"I hold your hand to walk the path, to walk the path of Light, Beloved One.

"I am Quan Yin, I bless you".

Osiris

"Beloved Ones, it is at this time, I come forward further, through the communication and presence of all Beings of Light at this time, to bring forward many blessings and choice experiences of celebration. It is through this period, the feeling state to connect in your heart, each Being to support in physicality your presence of great Light. In humility and gratitude to support the entirety of planet, not only in this position, but to connect in various other, to come together with formation of Light energy.

"In the utilisation of intensity - it begins to shift at this time - there begins to be awakening in many direction of ancient knowledge to come forward. The moving of connectedness of the Earth shift begin to be felt of the understanding of communications that come forward, not ever to be within this experience of physicality.

"So it is, Beloved Ones, that I work with yourselves at this time, to feel the Light, to feel the presence of great Spirit, to work with you through the Divinity of the Godhead. As you begin to feel yourselves in the expansiveness of shifted dimensional state, allow yourselves to move into the experience. Begin to feel yourselves, Beloved Ones, to walk amongst the Beings of Ascension in Spirit, to feel the presence in the understandings that you bring forward, in all areas of service through continuation, through the Sun-ship of communication with the Godhead.

"It is at this time, Beloved Ones, that you begin to feel the communications taking place, as it opens further through the portal of Light: the stargate of connectivities of the presence of Light further. For all in humanity, for the Universal systems to awaken to the connection of the pathway of that which has been of intent through Ancient Atlantean period to this.

"Beloved Ones, you are supported at this time to feel the expansiveness of your energy fields, beginning to open through the dimension of 45 at this time. Allowing yourselves to move through the connectedness of dimension in great Light. Allow it to take place as we move together as One.

"As you move through the expansiveness so it is you begin to feel the connection - it is through the pathway of the position of Orion's Belt - the understandings that as you shift through this pathway so it is to feel the connectedness of the Venusian energy, of the connectedness of the Pleiadian Beings, of the Arcturian Beings, of the Beings of Andromeda, the Beings to come forward within close proximity of Nibiru. The Beings of Light from all areas of the Universe to come forward as One, in a collective shift in consciousness at this time.

"Allowing for yourselves to move into the feeling state of the openings of the gateway further, the portal of Light. Each particle of the physical self begins to move forward though great healing; the activations take place within your being.

"So it is, Beloved Ones, as you find yourselves in the movement amongst Beings of Light in the connectedness at this time, to feel their presence, to feel your Light energy as it shifts greatly at each moment, as you move further and further.

"So it is as you dance in Light in the Universal system, through the connectedness of that which has been through intent - of the position of the awakening of the capstone. The repositioning of the presence of the desire of the Being that is Thoth that has created through the architectural form and understandings, of the geometry of One. Through the Godhead it moves, through the experience you awaken, Beloved Ones.

"Allowing for yourselves at this time, the communication of all Beings, all serving in same manner, all the same understandings and intent, through a shift of consciousness to create. Allow yourselves to continue forward through the experience.

"In gentle movement, in gentle Light the star tetrahedron that forms - the entirety of the surroundings of the Earth and so through the consciousness - allows for the procedures the releasing of ancient patterning connected to the Earth, the ability to move forward, through the coming cycles, through the change that begins to take place, through a shift of consciousness, in awakening the Light of the Earth.

"So as all living experience upon the Earth begins to move into the vibratory energy of shift, allow yourselves to gently begin the procedures, to reconnect to the physical self. It is slow procedure, as it is vast movement through space and time, allowing yourselves to reconnect.

"As you begin to feel the presence of the Light Vehicle of the individual nature to surround the self, begin to feel yourself reconnecting, slowly and gently, within the Light energy of Vehicle, the star tetrahedron. Allowing yourselves to feel activation through the presence, the Light of the DNA as it moves forward, through the expansiveness of understandings, of all in existence.

"To feel your presence, the Light energy, the ability to move forward through the manifestation at will. The experience of understanding of bringing forward Light to Earth, in the manner to support all, begins to take place. As you move through experience over coming period with Divine Intent, to hold it in your heart to bring it forward, Beloved Ones.

"It is I work with you over continual procedure, in period to move forward, through procedure of activation further. To take you into the experience of the full capacity of energy field of Light that has begun on this day. The presence begins to be felt; through communications of twin energies to come forward, the connections of twin souls, the connections of Monadic presences together as One. Various procedures begin, Beloved Ones.

"So it is I work with you, with great love to surround you from the Godhead. We support in all that takes place upon the Earth at this time. There is the surrounding energies of many Beings of Ascension, to continue the pathway with yourselves over this period, as One.

"I bless you on this day, Beloved Ones. All Beings of Light that have come forward to communicate, to offer greetings of love in unconditional presence, to offer to yourselves the guidance of Love.

"I bless you on this day and greet you, Beloved Ones. Greetings to you, in love. In love you are blessed."

We are now ready for ascension. The inter-dimensional gateway is now open. We now make the decision, individually, as to whether or not we want to walk through that gateway. On the other side is the 5th dimension of altered consciousness.

As the consciousness of humanity began to shift, Earth energies shifted, and the outer-planetary star alignments with Earth continued to stimulate higher frequency Light on our planet, so that the re-opening of the energy pathway through the capstone of the Great Pyramid could begin - and the same thing has been happening within human beings. This means the previously energetically separated tips of the touching and interlinking pyramids blend in a synchronisation of energy once more, at their connecting points, and the high frequency Light energy is able to flow unimpeded - in from the heavens via the high frequency, etheric pyramid, through the Great Pyramid and onwards into Earth. This movement of energy expands into an understanding of the energy structure of the creative principle of the Universe - which is discussed in more detail in the forthcoming book from the Goddess Isis.

The reverse flow of energy also occurs in this two-way communication system of the star tetrahedron - which is why there are two pyramids, one superimposed on the other, upside down. Additionally there is an inter-linking star tetrahedron shape which is formed and the energy flow upwards is no less important than the energy flow downwards - and so both communication directions are accommodated within the sacred structure of Light of the star tetrahedron within the Great Pyramid.

This system of high frequency stimulation of spiralling energy occurs all over the planet at all of the ancient sacred sites - no matter whether or not we even know they exist. The opening of the gateway in the Great Pyramid is a momentous event which has a powerful impact on all of the high frequency structures on Earth. Human beings are sacred sites in their own right, as is evidenced by their Light-sensitive DNA. The flow of Light energy stimulates the whole of Earth and all of humanity at the level of our DNA. The brighter Light of the energised capstone lets the Light Beings of other planets and stars know what is happening on Earth in terms of our changing energy. This same energy system is what is responsible for the magnetic-like pull, or feeling of outer-planetary connectivity and communication, which can be experienced by people who enter the Great Pyramid.

It is no wonder that glorious experiences of an inter-dimensional shift can so easily be experienced within that structure - as well as at all of the other sacred sites.

Our Personal Great Pyramid

The Great Pyramid experience is not the only Earthly experience of spiralling energies which is available to humanity. It is because the many different types of portal systems were created by the ancients, specifically Thoth, for the purposes of communication with the outer-planetary bodies of Light that these places are still accessible by us today. The Fibonacci Sequence is very important in these structures. This can be seen from the following communication with Osiris with a person who was about to visit one of the sacred sites. He was discussing the spiralling energies in the portal between two shoulder-high standing stones, at Adam's Calendar in Kaapschehoop in Mpumalanga, South Africa. Although this place is not yet popularised nor on the international map of stone henge sites, it has played a very important role in human history and development (more detailed information follows in a forthcoming book).

In this short discussion, Osiris gives us an enormous amount of information: about the ancientness of the place, the connectivity of many people (including Jacqui) to the area during those ancient times and the importance of reconnecting from this space of the portal energy to the ancient being Enki. More information about this being and what he was doing in Southern Africa, relative to the creation of man, can be found in the Sumerian clay tablet texts. Interestingly, Osiris also briefly discussed the importance of balancing the energies of the northern (from the position of Egypt) and southern (from the position of South Africa) hemispheres through the position of the equator (Kenya). When this is done from sites on the same line of longitude (31 degrees, 14 minutes) it is even more profound. It is the energy-balancing ability of people who are consciously aware of what they are doing as they move through these places that will mitigate the destructive actions of a potential pole shift on Earth and other such catastrophic events which are normally associated with the midpoint of an Age and the approach of Nibiru.

In this short excerpt from a personal channelling session prior to visiting Adam's Calendar, Osiris continued to volunteer information about the fact that there are many souls stuck in this area and they need to be released. This is an interesting point to take note of, because all over the world people die without the knowledge or ability to move out of the Earth plane of existence, as soul presence or consciousness, into the higher dimensions. As a result they remain fixed in a dimensional position as souls, until they are assisted to move on. As discarnate soul beings 'floating' around in this dimension they are not necessarily intent on harm, but they can get up to mischief and scare human beings. It is a relatively easy process to telepathically communicate to them to move towards the Light. This simple suggestion frees many Earth-bound souls and allows them to move forwards towards greater states of Light. The use of crystals when visiting any of the ancient sacred sites is very supportive, because they are a powerful conduit of high frequency Light. We can view them as solid-form, crystalline structures of Light energy.

Osiris: Kaapschehoop

Q: During my visit to Kaapschehoop, is there any specific thing I need to be aware of or anything I need to connect to when I am there?

"It is also to understand through connectivity of Being that is Enki, Beloved One. It is to understand that this Being has come forward into this position - and so it is the understanding from connectivity of this position and the ancientness of this area. There has been thought and decision to bring forward beings within environment, and it is into this position each of yourselves connect. It is from lengthy period past, there have been many connectivities taking place through this channel in this environment, and it is to understand it has been activated for each being to come forward in this manner to connect with the portal energy and to communicate from the presence of Being that has moved into this direction.

"The understandings of the codings that have been placed through the placing of - it is almost the building so to speak, of the rock formation - it is through the Fibonacci code that has been created in this environment through the connectivity of Beings of Light, with intent to hold the energy and Light for the future. It is in this position that you bring in balance from that which had taken place in the area of Ancient Egypt - the two position are greatly supportive in connectivity - and a central position that is of the equator that many beings have moved forward into the interconnection, brings forward the great balance of the ability to create the shift in terms of pole direction, of the ability to maintain it in manner to hold humanity in the present state of being in great Light."

Q: Thank you. Is it supportive to make this information available to more people?

"It is greatly supportive, Beloved One. Many beings have been into this environment, not always of the deeper understanding of this connection. It is for the understanding of the connectivity of the many pyramidal form that are in environment, a connection of this position, and to bring forward a deeper understanding for humanity for the future. It is there are many, many soul beings that are held in this position that desire to be released also, Beloved One, and from this perspective, it is the ability to do this. It is also for each of yourselves to take forward, it is in the connection of the self to take forward, it is the crystal that is greatly supportive for this, Beloved One. It is one of the Tiger Eye, it is also of the connectivity of Kyanite."

It is important to consider the way in which many of the large, ancient structures, such as the Great Pyramid, create the formation of spiralling energies in various positions on Earth. Each human being is able to make use of these energies within, personally, when they visit them because of the creation of these energies within that shape. The fact that we have pyramid shaped cells within our brains means that we are able to utilise the same spiralling energy system of connection and communication within ourselves - no matter whether or not we actively or knowingly work on our living ascension processes.

The extensive work of James Hurtak, of the Academy For Future Science (AFFS), is worthwhile looking into. The importance of our own pyramid-shaped cells is supported by the article 'Biomagnetism and Bioelectric magnetism: The Foundation of Life' by H. Coetzee. It can be found on the website www.affs.org under the 'articles' section. This extract is found under the heading 'Biomagnetism'.

"In the human brain, pyramidal cells are present and arranged in layers in the cortex of the two cerebra. The pyramidal cells act as electro-crystal cells immersed in extra-cellular tissue fluids, and seem to operate in the fashion of a liquid crystal oscillator in response to different light commands, or light pulses which, in turn, change the orientation of every molecule and atom within the body. Bio-gravitational encoded switches present in the brain allow a type of liquid network to release ions that induce currents to the surrounding coiled dendrites. Electron impulses from a neuron, on reaching the dendrite coil of the abutted cell, generate a micro amperage magnetic field, causing the ultra thin crystal, or liquid crystal in the pyramidal cell to be activated - in a very unusual way. On flexing, this ultra thin crystal becomes a piezoelectric oscillator, producing a circular polarized light pulse that travels throughout the body, or travels as a transverse photonic bundle of energy."

All it takes to activate our inner Light communication systems is to be alive. We can choose to shift our resonance to a higher state. There are many ways to do this

Chapter Nine: OUTER-PLANETARY CONNECTIVITY

and people regularly do these things to improve the quality of their lives - healthy eating, meditating, chanting, singing, exercising and thinking and feeling positively are some obvious options which support and create high frequency living.

The similarity of the communications system of individual human beings and that of the Great Pyramid becomes more credible when we consider that we are holograms of a greater state of Being, a greater state of energy. This type of connection and communication via spiralling energy systems occurs all over the Universe. All communication systems, including the Great Pyramid and our minute pyramid shaped brain cells, therefore have a direct relationship with each other. Whatever happens in outside systems with which we resonate will directly influence us within too. Physically, this effect can be quantified and related to the nature of harmonic resonance - or the range of the reverberations of our own personal 'echo' relative to a standard. Many of the natural remedies, healing machines and diagnostic equipment which officially fall under the name of 'vibrational healing,' as well as some of the high-tech equipment, such as the MRI (Magnetic Resonance Imaging) and Sonar scanning equipment, which is routinely used in modern hospitals, are based on this principle.

The similarity of the Great Pyramid and our own pyramid shaped cells effectively demonstrates a wormhole system within us, which operates as a tiny hologram of the greater system. It is this personalised wormhole system that we can individually make use of to access the high frequency gateway to the other dimensions. Hence, we can acknowledge the importance of shifting our personal vibrations so that we resonate and communicate with higher frequency states. We do this from within ourselves by uplifting our consciousness. A stargate, or high frequency gateway, to other dimensions literally lies within us.

This is the repeated concept of the ancients when they were referring to the holographic nature of the Universe and tried to explain it with the notion of, 'As above, so below.' This idea can be extended to the understanding of, 'Whatever is outside of us, lies within us too.' It is for this reason that the gateway to uplifted consciousness lies within.

Whenever Osiris guides us through a visualisation he always suggests that we place the Merkabah Vehicle of Light around us at the outset (see diagram). It is this star tetrahedron shape of Light which forms a high frequency energy field that both protects us and helps us to move into the shifted dimensional experience. Osiris refers to the star tetrahedron as, *"The sacred geometric shape of Light."* More information about this Light Vehicle is given in the following chapter.

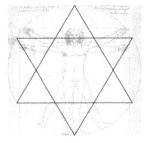

231

When we visualise placing ourselves within this star-shape of Light we are in the perfect space to make use of the spiralling energy which these two pyramids create, because they rotate simultaneously around us, in opposite directions. This is a powerful meditation tool and its use can enable us to shift dimension instantly during a meditation or even when in the waking state. Osiris has regularly advised us to remember to utilise this Vehicle of Light around us during times of danger too. Placing ourselves in a dimension-shifting Vehicle such as this one of Light, allows us to literally lift ourselves out of and away from the experience of danger or catastrophe on Earth - out of resonance with harm. A frequency change which lasts for as little as a split second is often all that is needed to avoid disaster. The fact that we have been told this time and time again is Osiris' way of training us to remember to form this protective shield around us. The fact that he reminds us regularly about the protective, dimension shifting ability we have when within this powerful energy field cannot be ignored.

With the tip of the pyramid of the star tetrahedron above our heads, the base beneath our feet and the other inverted pyramid similarly balanced around us, exactly like it is depicted in Leonardo da Vinci's drawing of Vetruvian Man (see diagram on previous page), it is this naturally-generated Light energy of the star tetrahedron shape which assists us to shift dimension, to heal and to raise our resonance. This is profoundly experienced in the beautiful mediation from 6 May 2009. The mp3 and transcription of this meditation may be downloaded from the site www.stargateway.co.za.

Osiris: Expansiveness through the spinning Star Tetrahedron

"Greetings to you, Beloved Ones, I come forward on this day, Beloved Ones, to support yourselves to go forward through visualisation. It is at this time, Beloved Ones, that through the celebration the connectivity of Lord Buddha - the understanding of the connection to Shakyamuni Buddha - the presence of great Being of Light to come forward into physicality. The understanding of the experience moving forward at this time, for each of yourselves to connect over coming linear days, Beloved Ones, to work through the celebration with Spirit. So it is I support yourselves on this day in preparation further.

"It is on this day I wish to take you into the experience of connectivity with the presence of Lord Matreya, the presence of Sanat Kumara, the presence of the Lord Melchizedek, and through this pathway at this time, many of yourselves moving into deeper understanding of the connectivities upon Earth at this time. The understanding to move forward through celebration of the experience of the collective consciousness of all beings upon the planet to have the ability to transcend through the experience of 5th dimension, through the experience of that which takes place at this time.

"So it is for each of yourselves to know and understand - through the pathway, moving through the connectedness of 7th dimension - so it is the understanding further, that as you continue on your pathway of great Light, the abilities that begin to open for many more begin to take place. As it has done through the many experiences of many linear year, through the pathway of the Being that is Lord Buddha, that has supported many beings to go forward from the understandings and connectivities of the presence of Being of Light upon the planet Earth, and the experience for many to excel through the experiences of position of the connectivity of the heart, to move forward further and further.

"It is on this day, Beloved Ones, that I wish to support yourselves to be in connectivity with all Beings of Light to assist in the pathway forward, through the shift of dimension further, and through this the understanding of an ability for all beings within the presence of physicality to move through the collective consciousness, through the pathway of 5th dimension.

"The opening of the experience of the heart - the connectivity over coming period through that of unconditional Love, through the support of Beings to come forward - the understandings of the fullness and expansiveness of great Light, of the connectedness of understandings within your heart, that you open in many direction, for the support of a planetary system, the pathway forward of your own experience within physicality.

"So it is, Beloved Ones, as you begin to feel the experience. Find yourselves in the position that you have the ability to visualise yourselves in yogic position, crossed legged. It is to visualise this at this time and so you begin to visualise the experience: it is of the surrounding energies of great Light. It is in the surrounding energies of great Light you begin to feel the experience, as you begin to form that which is of the star tetrahedron - the experience - as you begin to feel the rotation. It is in cyclical manner, of the moving in one direction and another. The experience within star tetrahedron, begin to feel the movement taking place, and as you begin to feel the experience of Light energy surrounding you, the expansiveness of your being begins to move into the connectedness with Spirit.

"The ability at this time, Beloved Ones, to feel the connectedness, as there is the pathway forward through the connection - from that which is the individual self, to the connectivity of the Higher Self. It is in this position to feel it to begin, Beloved Ones, as there is, through intent, the ability to move through connectivities further and further.

"In the presence of great Light you begin to feel the connectivity of the Higher Self, the connection of the soul presence of your being. As you move upward into the connection of Overself, through the position of the connectivity to Monad. The understanding of the pathway forward, of the connection of the many dimension through the connectivity to the Godhead. The experience as you begin to find yourselves in touch and in the feeling state of communion as One, in this position.

"It is a Light energy to connect with your heart, Beloved Ones, as you feel the expansiveness moving forward through the spinning that takes place at this time, and letting go of all anxiety within your physical environment. The connection of each of the energy centre begin to shift, Beloved Ones, as the movement takes place further. Allowing yourselves to expand into great Light - into unconditional Love - to feel yourselves moving into the connectedness, of the presence of Lord Matreya.

"Being of Light to over light yourselves at this time, with intent of communication through Lord Buddha, to support all beings in humanity. It is beings of connectedness of soul group at this time, as you find yourselves in position of ashram, in connectivity with Lord Buddha. So it is the support that takes place with great intensity, allowing yourselves to move through the expansiveness to the Godhead.

"Beloved Ones, as you feel, to let go of the connectedness to Earth through your intent to communicate with the Angelic Realms. The experience of many Beings of Light that move forward in preparation with deep intent and great gratitude from beings in physicality, that have supported beings to move forward through greater expansiveness, of the owning further of their Light, in service to humanity, in service to the connection of the Godhead.

"So it is at this time, Beloved Ones, to allow yourselves in the peace and tranquillity of the movement that takes place of the opening of your heart, and the connectedness to the ascension energy centre - beginning to feel it moving in the expansiveness, to lift in communication and connectivity, of the presence of Being of Light. As your heart opens further and further, through the movement taking place, all within the presence of that which takes place within your physicality begins to be felt in different manner. All issue begin to drift from the experience.

"Through yourselves with an ability to see all the areas of your creation, all areas of your abilities through manifestation at this time, that come forward from the heart into reality - and as many beings have the ability to communicate with your presence in physicality at this time, through the pathway of the living state of ascension - so it is to hear it in the communication of unconditional Love. To hear it on many occasion in the light touch of connection with physicality, in the hearing of the harmonic communication through the frequency of Light, through the understandings of language of Light, through the bringing forward of the great wisdom, of the understanding of the ancientness of the self.

"So you move forward into the position, to communicate, to feel the presence of Lord Matreya. It is for this Being at this time, to support yourselves in preparation, to go forward through the expansiveness over coming period through the celebration, that you are blessed in initiation.

"As you begin to feel a connectedness of Being of Light to come before you, and as you state in silent position your intent of communication with the presence of Lord Buddha, the support of the over lighting essence of the Godhead to assist in all procedures going forward. And through the intent of your communication with Being at this time, to set forward the understanding on your pathway of all you desire to create within your personal physical experience, and for the experience of all beings in humanity. In service that you move into connectedness of this pathway of Light, and through the intent of connectivity of Beings in Spirit, the presence of the Godhead, as you set intent to go forward in service in this manner.

"So as it is felt in your heart, Beloved Ones, not always of the understanding perhaps as it is seen. It is brought forward in the presence of great Light. The energy fields surrounding you in your everyday physical experience shift entirely at this time, through the connectedness of the Godhead of the over lighting presence of this Light.

"Lord Matreya chooses to come forward at this time, Beloved Ones. It is to place the symbol of star upon the Third Eye of your being - in the sacred geometry - to experience the fullness of vibrational energy. As it is placed upon the Third Eye of your being it is to feel in your heart the presence of deep connectedness with Being of Light, supporting on many occasion in the silent state. It is in this form, the unconditional aspect, you begin to move into the fulfilment of understanding: to offer in service in this manner, without recognition, merely through the pure joy of communication and support of your being.

"As you feel through connectivities of Being of Light at this time, Beloved Ones, it is the Love of the presence of Light you feel in your Heart. Opening further and further into the Bliss state of being, the connectedness of the presence of Lord Buddha in surrounding distance begins to be felt.

"You are over lit at this time, Beloved Ones, by the presence of the Godhead, to support you in all taking place. Begin to feel yourselves, as you move through the connectedness of the presence of Sanat Kumara supporting yourselves through the circular movement. That Being of Light begins to place, through the energy fields of frequency, the Wand of great Light upon the head of your being - that it begins to raise through the opening of energy centres, further and further to the connectedness. Allowing for the energy field to bring forward through the Monadic presence, in a connectivity of the (...), begin to feel the experience of great Light as it opens through Third Eye and to connect at same period through the heart.

"So it is at this time, Beloved Ones, as you feel the presence of the acceleration of communication through the sacred geometry at Third Eye and the connectivity of Wand of Light, through the frequency of communication from the Monad to the self, through the experience of bringing forward from the (...), to the being. So you begin to feel it in unison, moving forward continuously, the pathway of movement surrounding yourselves, the presence of Sanat Kumara beginning to alight the procedure.

"As you shift through the frequency, Beloved Ones, of the dimensions, it is on the pathway forward through the connectivity to the Godhead. Allow yourselves to let go entirely. If it is your desire to continue forward, allow it to take place at this time, the presence of Beings supporting yourselves.

"As you move forward, there begins to be the feeling state of moving beyond one dimension through another. Each the connection as it is placed by the Lord Melchizedek - that which has been of intent to bring forward through not only the connectivity of your presence, but to shield over the entirely of the planet Earth, to uplift the pathway forward of dimension shift for all beings in humanity - as, through the collective, there is an ability to move through the experience of dimension. Begin to feel from your heart that which it is, to serve all beings at this time in great Light, in unconditional Love.

"Beloved Ones, as you hear at this time the connection of the Light energy of Earth, support of energy to come forward as you feel it through the Central Sun, the connectivites of the Light energy, and healing that takes place for all in humanity. As you begin to feel the experience of moving through the connectedness to the Godhead, allow yourselves in the experience of communion with the presence of Light at this time, Beloved Ones, of your Divinity, through intent and understandings of all that takes place, through this state of presence.

"It is procedure that you move forward through at this time, Beloved Ones, as a connectedness with many Beings of Light of Ascension that move forward in similarity - that move forward through various procedures - and an ability to expand their position at this time, in Spirit, in connection with the Godhead - and an ability to serve yourselves further, as you have an experience of Divinity, to be in position to experience it on Earth, through the connectedness with Spirit, within.

"In the continual movement, Beloved Ones, it is an experience that continues further. It is continuously moving and drifting through the connectedness of great Light. Allow yourselves, in the experience of movement, it is for short silent period, to connect in your Light: to be in the visual experience, to be in the experience of the full cognisance to take place within your being, of All That Is.

"Beloved Ones, as you feel the drifting, it is in the experience of connectivity of the Godhead through the dimension that all beings connect and communicate at this time, to feel the presence in your surroundings. The connection of the understanding of the Vehicle of Spirit, the connection to that of the formation of form - of that of the body in the experience of physicality - so it is at this time the true understanding of the purpose, through the continuation in physicality.

"Of all various aspect of insignificance of many, many position that take place in physical form in the surrounding energies, creating great disturbances through anxieties, in the peace and Bliss of the connectedness of the Godhead you feel the understanding of your ability: to create and manifest, through unconditional love, all within your experience at this time, in the presence of Bliss and Oneness with God, Beloved Ones.

"Allowing for the communication of all Beings as you drift together, the joyous experience to be felt by each of yourselves, connecting and moving together as One. Gently to allow yourselves to reconnect, slowly and gently, to the presence of physical form once more. Slow procedure, Beloved Ones, allowing yourselves the gentleness to connect once more. It is to not focus to bring forward the return to physicality. Feel the connection taking place through the position of form. Allowing yourselves slow period to re-integrate through dimensions, allowing it to take place, Beloved Ones, over period, to reconnect once more.

"Maintaining state as you begin to feel the return to the presence of position within the star tetrahedron, begin to feel the experience as you return: to hold the posture, to hold the position in physicality. As you feel it, Beloved Ones, as you visualise the experience, once more begin to feel the connectedness with the presence of all Beings of Light. Begin to feel a healing moving through your being. Begin to feel the communication taking place with Spirit.

"You begin to bring forward over coming period many form of sacred geometry to serve yourselves on the pathway forward: of the expansiveness of understanding of the communication it brings to yourselves. As it comes forward for many by sound, it comes forward through writing and speaking, in unconditional love.

"You are blessed on this day, Beloved Ones, to go forward from preparation through the experience over coming period, and to continue forward over a completion of procedure into joy and celebration: celebration of the opening of the heart and communication with Spirit through the ability to feel the experience of the collective consciousness of all beings moving forward, on a pathway through a dimension shift.

"So it is, Beloved Ones, I bless you in great Love from Spirit. I hold you in the presence of great Light of Spirit, in the protective Light of the presence of the Godhead to support yourselves in physicality, in the experience of unfoldment; at One with Spirit, at One with Light, at One with the Godhead.

"In unconditional love you are blessed and held in Spirit, Beloved Ones, to walk on Earth as Beings of Light of Ascension in the living state, I bless you, Beloved Ones.

"I greet you at this time, in Love."

The simple visualisation process of forming a star tetrahedron as Osiris suggests, is an easy method to create a tangible Great Pyramid-type spiralling energy system around our own body. Aside from the daily expediency of added protection, we can make use of this high frequency field of Light to access a wormhole system at any time, including during meditation. By doing this we make use of the high frequency Light of ascension and tune up the frequencies of our physical bodies to help it become more compatible with the higher frequencies of an alternative dimension. This use of Light may be viewed as an individually available system which makes a wormhole easily accessible to each of us.

Use of this in a visualisation can assist us to move through the frequency gateway of raised consciousness at the speed which is individually suitable and under our own personal control. We are not limited in our inter-dimensional travels when we meditate with the star tetrahedron-shaped Light Vehicle in place around us. However, no matter how far we 'travel' in our Merkabah Vehicles of Light during a meditation, Osiris suggests that we ground the high frequencies we access there by *living* them.

Osiris gives us some very interesting points to ponder when he discusses the ability most people have to access the higher frequency dimensions during a meditation, relative to our learned ability to bring these frequencies into our lives and live according to them. He stresses that accessing the higher dimensions is one thing, but maintaining resonance with them in our daily lives is another thing entirely. Balance between physicality and spirituality is the key to successful living ascension.

Osiris: Living Ascension and Balance

Q: Is it possible to take the living ascension process up to the 12th dimension?
"You wish to understand, Beloved One, to take forward the living state of ascension?"

Q: Does it occur up to the 12th dimension state?
"Within the living state?"

Q: Yes.
"Beloved One, it is there is the possibility to move beyond that which is the Earth is moving through: the experience of 5th dimension. It is the understanding that there is the possibility and it is the work that I do with yourselves to access to the position of 12th dimension. But it is to understand it is fleetingly experienced in and out of these position. It is not from linear perspective, Beloved One."

Q: Once we work through into the 5th dimension, and our physical bodies remain here with us, can we continue expanding the dimensional experience in the living state, rather than just experience it through a fleeting state?
"It is, Beloved One."

Q: How far within the realms of the Universe, the dimensions of the Universe, is it possible to take the living state of experience?
"Beloved One, from the living perspective you have the ability to access any one dimension, but it is the understanding through the living on each day, the occurrence of moving forward, it is extremely difficult in the holding of resonance for this position. But, it is the possibility to access it, Beloved One."

Q: As we progress, and I understand there is a lot of progress that has got to be made, the experience moves into more and more Light forms, doesn't it?
"It does, Beloved One. It is to understand you have the ability to access it, to live it. It is slightly different manner, Beloved One."

Q: I don't know if it is possible to answer this, because of the whole linear perspective that we have: what sort of dimension, or resonance level, would you say we can comfortably hold the physical state to, in a continuous experience?

"Beloved One, it is at this time, to move forward, it is from perspective of working with the ascension programme, Beloved One, to understand there is the possibility of holding the 7th, 8th dimension. But, it is to understand that through this state on many occasion as you find yourselves that are accessing these positions, these states of consciousness, so it is you do move into the reconnection to 5th dimension, and on occasion through the experience of lower state of being. And, therefore, it is on many occasion there is the desire and the grappling with the experience of being in physicality and from this it creates slight disturbance for many, with a desire to let go of all connection with spirituality, as it is the possibility to bring forward at this perspective soul being through the thought of individual being, to hold this state for lengthy period."

Q: Is this because there is the sense of having to let go of the physical, human form?
"It is not only this, Beloved One, but it is the understanding of the return to the physical state almost of that which was - so it is in the feeling state of discomfort, and therefore the creation of the feeling state of depression and desire to let go of all connection with spirituality. It is therefore of great importance always to find balance."

Q: So there is almost a depression at the idea of living in the physical realm again as if: 'Oh no! I have got to be back down here again!'
"It is, Beloved One, it is to find this balance."

Q: So is that the type of conflict between physicality and spirituality that many people are going through?
'There are many going through this at this time, Beloved One."

Q: So the key is balance. When you say balance does this mean enjoy both physicality and spirituality?
"It is both, Beloved One. As you move into the balance within each position, so you begin to access further and further through spirituality through the connectivities of dimensional experience."

Q: So, basically, there is no answer to the original question. All is possible?
"It is dependant entirely on the individual being, Beloved One, and the state of consciousness. Each individual being has the ability to access and to hold, through the desire and intent.

"It is to understand there are many monk beings moving into the experience of dimensions beyond the experience of everyday living beings, but it is also to understand they do not bring forward balance and therefore it is through the connectivity of these higher frequency states it is an impossibility for themselves to live in it. It is merely accessing it. Do you see this? It is a holding of resonance through the living state that is extremely different."

Q: So, the distinction is between accessing versus living the higher dimensional states?
"It is, Beloved One. Understanding, for yourself to remain seated in a meditative position on each and every linear day, so it is extremely simple to do this. It is not extremely simple to live it in this state."

Q: And that's the challenge of living ascension?
"It is, Beloved One. It is any one of yourselves within group, have the ability to go into monk form and to connect and to remain in this position for the entirely of physicality. So it must be that you return into physicality, to live the experience of physicality. It is this that allows for yourself to bring in balance. It is, therefore, the understanding that many of yourselves have lived these experiences and choose to return into the bringing into the state of great balance of each, within physical experience."

Q: Which could explain why so many people have tremendous difficulties in the living state?
"It is, Beloved One."

Q: And why we have so much to work through as a group?
"It is, Beloved One, but it is also to understand that through these difficulties you do have awareness, and you do have the abilities to know and understand for that which it is in experiences you go through. And, therefore, it is not the intent to continue forward in physicality, to repeat this. It is merely the balanced state that you find yourselves connecting with as you release yourself from physicality, to move into the experience of Spirit. So it is in this position of great balance and peace and tranquillity and through the pathway of ascension, so all is known in this state."

Stargates - Portals of Light Energy

Osiris led a powerful meditation on 18 February 2009. In this he suggested that we link into the understanding of ancient wisdom, regardless of the fact that many of the writings that pertain to our ancientness have been eliminated, hidden or have not yet been found. He speaks about our ability to link to the energies of the 12th dimension via the 5th dimension pathway of living ascension. He clearly states that we experience this level of Light, which is the level of the greater individual soul presence, the Monad, via the pathway of the 5th dimension.

Very importantly, Osiris creates a strong visual link for us to see and experience the re-opening of the capstone of the Great Pyramid and the opening of our own consciousness along with this. The purpose of this is for us to begin to see, feel and understand our link to the star system of the Universe and to know that we are star-beings of great Light within the giant star of the Universe. It is well worthwhile downloading the mp3 and the full transcript of this particular meditation from the website (www.stargateway.co.za).

Osiris: Star Beings

"To open to deep understandings of the ancientness, that have been brought forward of many documentations, many writings, of the ancient text - many writings that are brought forward with the elimination of the experiences. So it is, it begins to be felt as you move forward through the vibrational energy of dimension. Moving beyond at this time, the experience of 5th dimension, knowing to understand that through this pathway you reach the 12th dimension.

"It is to begin to feel the presence of energy fields within the area, Beloved Ones, it is above the ancient Pyramid. Through the experience there begins to be felt, in an opening of energy of formation - as it begins to move surrounding the tip of Pyramid, of the capstone - that you begin to feel the energy as it awakens, as the consciousness shifts, as you move forward through the feeling state of the movement.

"Within the etheric, you begin to feel the experience as you hold the Light. As you move into the consciousness it takes you forward into many direction of understandings, to the ancient connectivity of the Earthly experience - as it has begun from communication of the presence of the god-beings. In the experience there begins to be a knowing, an understanding of this ancient period, of the understanding of how it is that this energy field has come about, the alignment with the Universal system, the star system that begins to be felt in its truth.

"Feel yourself as the movement takes place, it is almost in planetary formation, you and the Light presence of Beings of Light, that begin to move through their presence. It is without the feeling state of the Earthly experience.

"Feel the presence, Beloved Ones. As you begin to allow for the experience to take place, you feel it in the movement that moves. As you feel the central position, your head through the experience, as it might have been through a planet. The experience of a Star Being as it awakens, as you feel yourself moving into the experience of star system.

"Allow it to move and take you forward into the connectivities of dimension, it is a spiralling movement upward, through a frequency of great Light - the essence of the super-luminal Light that begins to take shape surrounding you. Begin to move through the experience. Allowing it to lift through your heart and upward through the ascension energy centres, begin to open in its expansiveness and its ancient knowledge to be brought forward. You begin to feel it as it is brought forward by the presence of Thoth."

Thoth's ancient work of establishing a high frequency gateway system, or portal, in the Great Pyramid (and in many other places across the planet) ensured that it would not be necessary for humanity to wait the ultra-long periods between the super-alignment happenings of high frequency stars and planets in order to achieve living ascension. Being exposed to Earth portals enhances our ability to shift dimension. We know that our dimension-shifting abilities are super-activated now, because the unusually potent, outer-planetary energies are in place - just as they were back in 2037/67 BC. Technically, this means that we needn't have waited until the modern planetary super-alignment in the skies in order to shift dimension. We have had the ascension energies available to us on Earth since the beginning of time, but it has taken a while for us to shift from the 3rd to the 4th dimension of consciousness. Knowing where these energy portals are and how to use them properly has been the information that has been hidden from man by the controllers and manipulators of humanity over the centuries.

Thoth's work in creating these ancient energy systems ensured that we still have these massive, physical outer-planetary communication systems in place in Egypt and in many other places around the world. The energy systems, or portals, of our planet have been interfered with by war and other low frequency behaviours on Earth over an extremely long period of time. This had a knock-on effect which affected the consciousness of humanity and of Earth and has helped to maintain the lowered resonance state of the 3rd and then the 4th, dimensions. This too has precluded the awareness of our personal gateways to higher consciousness of the 5th dimension that lie within us. At the moment these gateways are being sparked back into life, just as Earth's sacred sites are being reactivated.

Considering that humanity has collectively shifted in consciousness upwards from the 3rd to the 4th dimension since the time of the Fall of Atlantis and of Man, we are able to take full advantage of the higher frequencies of Light which emanate from the outer-planetary bodies which are aligned with Earth at this time. This helps to uplift the consciousness of humanity in a rather dramatic and speedy manner and allows us to relatively effortlessly shift into an alternative realm of reality: which is only apparent to us at higher frequencies. It is because of this that even people who are unaware of what is happening are beginning to question the reason for their existence and the reason for continuing to do things they have always done. We are all experiencing the wave of a new consciousness on Earth.

Once operating at higher frequencies we are able to re-access the wormhole gateways, externally and internally, and utilise them to shift dimension. When we ground these energies of the higher dimensions back onto Earth as we remain physically alive while operating at higher frequencies, we not only power up ourselves, but our planet too. It is these higher frequency vibrations that support the processes of living ascension and the shift into another, higher dimension for many.

The numerous ancient writings of Thoth ensure that the information for accessing the energy of the portals within us and on the Earth will always be available, but not many people have been exposed to them. Consequently, the information about the consciousness-opening power of being exposed to their vibrations is largely unknown too. Knowing about the consciousness-shifting ability of the structures which Thoth created, as well as about the power of the self-created structure of the Merkabah Vehicle we can form around us, it seems less surprising that a similar high resonance system is encoded into all of his texts.

One example of the translated, ancient writings of Thoth is the Emerald Tablets of Thoth-the-Atlantean by Dr Doreal. In these texts he gives humanity detailed instructions about how to shift dimension, how the Brothers of Darkness operate and how human beings can attain everlasting life. When reading this translation, deciphering Thoth's language style becomes simpler the more often the text is read. Initially the reader of the Emerald Tablets may be frustrated by the realisation that he or she understands very little. It is because of the consciousness-shifting high vibrations that are encoded into the text that all that is required for greater clarity is for us to read these translated texts many times over. Osiris recommends reading them 100 times! Although this may seem a bit daunting at first, the repeated readings become less of a task and more fun as we understand more. The vibrations contained within them shift our consciousness to higher frequency states and this increases our capacity for understanding - our comprehension abilities expand with little effort. It is thus that we easily open our minds to receive and remember more knowledge and information.

Using Portals to Shift Karma
In terms of our current understanding of reality, when the collective volume of human Karma shrinks dramatically, the 3rd and 4th dimensions begin to blend more easily into one zone of physicality until, finally, the 4th dimension is the lowest level which humanity experiences as real. Individually clearing our own Karma has a powerful effect on the collective whole. Living at the speed of the 4th dimension makes our Karma-clearing and low frequency-releasing processes both rapid and immediate and this enables us to thin this dimension and clear it out, very quickly.

This 4th dimension clearing process, no matter whether done individually or collectively, is effectively the shortening of the connecting thread between the wormhole funnels. It is also seen as the opening out of the twisted reality of the figure-of-8 or moving through the Eye of Horus. Whichever terminology we use it amounts to the altered dimension experience of the 5th dimension and the consequent collapse of the illusion of duality. Our reality shifts.

In this excerpt from the meditation on the 8 May 2009, referring to, "*The linear time frame of the eight*," Osiris highlights the number 8 by means of a number of different references. He describes the shift from one state of consciousness to another as the shift through the number 8, that his own personal number is 8 (as the Master of Ascension) and he uses the term, "*The Eye of Horus*," to denote the central position of the figure-of-8. Shifting through the Great Pyramid and its etheric twin above it is done by means of a spiralling movement that is in the form of a figure-of-8. It is significant that this shape is directly related to the swirling structure of our DNA. The entire transcript and an mp3 are available on the website www.stargateway.co.za.

This meditation was the opening one of Wesak - a celebration time for those in Spirit who gather in the Wesak Valley in the Himalayas. Presided over by Lord Buddha, many Light Beings come to surround this area, in support of Earth during the annual celebratory period - which lasts from the May full moon to the next.

Osiris: The Number 8

"Greetings to you, Beloved Ones, I come forward on this day, Beloved Ones, to bring into the connectivity of each of your presence, Divine love from Spirit. I come forward with the presence of Beings of Light, to assist in a procedure of passing forward through celebration.

"It is on this day, Beloved Ones, the Beings of Light to communicate and connect with your presence, to take you forward in the understanding of the pathway of enLightenment. It is an understanding to bring, to begin the connectivities of procedures taking place at this time. It is the understanding of the fullness of the Moon coming forward, at period that is of the number in numerical connectivity of linear time frame of that of the 8.

"It is of this position, the understanding of the symbol of my presence and the connectivity of the passing forward from one state of enLightenment to another. It is the passing forward of one state of consciousness. As many of yourselves of the awareness of the moving forward through the symbol of eternity. The symbol of eternity taking you forward through the experience from one Age to another - the experience of moving forward to the fullness, and the opening further, of the Aquarian Age. And through this procedure, Beloved Ones, so it is the understanding to move forward through the central position, of the awakening of consciousness, the moving forward through deep upliftment with Spirit.

"It is to understand that through the pathway of the consciousness of the Eye of Horus, so it is to understand you move forward into the experience, it is within this linear year period (*2009*), of opening into many, many direction of great truth, of great experiences of the pathway of unfoldment of many, many beings being in the position to know and understand, for many, many millennia, all that has been taught through all aspect of understandings through the self.

"Many areas of each being in humanity being in position to know and understand that they have the ability to access all areas of the truth of their existence, the truth of their decision and intent to go forward through the pathway of great Light in physicality, the abilities to go forward in the experience of great upliftment - through the living state of ascension. The abilities to go forward in the owning of all that you are to know and understand, through the form and intent, through creation."

The process of moving upwards in resonance from the 3rd to the 4th dimension brings us closer and closer to being compatible with the energies at the lip of the lower funnel of the wormhole system. Once there, and while still in the 4th dimension, we can begin to be influenced by the spiralling energies within the lower portion of the funnel and start to have glimpses of the 5th dimension experiences. We shift dimension momentarily like this in the initial stages of the alternative dimension experience. We are most likely to experience this when we resonate with the upper parts of 4th dimension reality.

The initial indications that we are living in the upper reaches of the 4th dimension is the degree to which our lives appear to have speeded up, both in our day-to-day experiences and in the grander scheme of things. When we start questioning the reason for our existence on Earth and begin spring cleaning the unpleasant areas of our lives, which indicate Karma-related frequencies are lurking, we can be sure we are resonating at this level. The development of increased and ever-increasing 'psychic' abilities follows on from this. Becoming more psychic is the easy determinant of a shifting consciousness.

The initial shifts in and out of the higher frequency states of reality mean we will undergo purification processes, because the faster vibrations start physically shifting impurities out of us at cellular level. These may be trying times for human beings, because detoxification of any kind is not known to be a pleasant experience. The degree of discomfort, however, is directly related to the mindset and intentions of the person. If we view detoxification as a positive thing, then it is so much easier to go through.

Purification continues until we become acclimatised to higher frequency vibrations and can live in a clearer and purer state physically, emotionally and spiritually. It is because the higher frequencies stimulate clearing quickly and effectively that we are more easily able to clean up any of the mess of our remaining Karma when fully resident within the 4th dimension. Similarly, it is more difficult to shift ourselves from the basis of residence in the 3rd dimension. By purifying ourselves from within, we gradually shift into the 5th dimension of reality. The degree to which we experience detoxification discomfort is the degree to which we are incompatible with the higher, 5th dimension frequencies. Knowing this, we more easily go through the layers of clearing and releasing. Physical purity and love are 5th dimension realities.

Conversely, an indication that we are still resonating with the lower speed vibrations of the 3rd dimension is the degree to which we are at war with one another - personally or as nations. Any thought, feeling or action which is not compatible with unconditional love and compassion for all denotes a low frequency state. These are the issues of the ego state which dominate lower frequency reality. When we 'act in ego' it is very obvious that we are not resonating with the higher dimensions. When we are in an ego state we don't feel at peace and we see the negative results of this in our lives.

Just to confuse matters a little, the ego state of the personality is most especially noticeable during a clearing process. A clearing process is only ever stimulated when we shift to a higher frequency. So, just when we think we are making good progress we are assaulted by our buried issues! When lower frequency emotions begin to simmer and rise up to the surface for clearing, in response to high frequency stimulation, they are felt as a full-blown ego attack. It doesn't matter whether this is in the form of thoughts, feelings or actions, because all of our unresolved issues, from all lifetimes, will re-appear in some form or another so that we can clear them out of our systems. Being aware of this occurrence is half the clearing-battle won. The effects of resonance, lifetime to lifetime as well as from events within this lifetime, are such that it is often very difficult to match the Karma-creating situation with the resultant low frequency vibration experiences which follow later. They are not necessarily a one-for-one match. Therefore, people frequently don't realise that the issues of today are the effects of yesterday's behaviour. However, the higher our resonance, the quicker the effects of Karma, created today, are felt.

The process of clearing low frequency thoughts, feelings and behaviours has to occur in order for us to become physically and emotionally compatible with the 5th dimension frequencies of spiritualised physicality. If we resist any of the Karma-clearing opportunities during the course of our lives now as we approach the midpoint of the Age of Aquarius, our issues tend to develop an urgency which, due to their intensity, can make clearing them progressively more difficult. This urgency continues until such time as a larger crisis ultimately creates a more obvious and more critical need that will force us to resolve our issues; that we refer to as Karma. Even if we do not have Karma to clear, we may have a connection to a low frequency vibrational feeling or behaviour. An example of this is somebody who was persecuted over many lifetimes for their spiritual practices, such as occurred during the Dark Ages. This person may still respond to the lower resonance of being victimised. Consequently, he or she will resist any form of bullying, authority or being told what to do by anybody. This is not Karma *per se* but it is a low resonance connection which is incompatible with the 5th dimension ascension frequencies. This type of behaviour is an indication that there are low frequency vibrations within that need to be released and cleared.

The volume of clearing processes we do represent the vastness of the divide between where we are as humans and the urgings of our own individual soul presence within us. It tries to penetrate the density of the negative ego, or personality, and remind the human being that he or she is a soul having a human experience on Earth. Being reminded of this may help us to look for the pathway of soul, rather than to be distracted by the drives and demands of the ego. To this end we, as a soul presence, often create difficult circumstances around us which jolt our memories. When we move in synch with our soul presence we automatically live a healthier and happier life. It is our personality-driven, human resistance to the prods of the soul presence that disturbs our peace of mind.

Reclaiming Consciousness
Fortunately, all we need to begin to do to shorten the thread, or pathway which connects the funnel-ends of the figure-of-8 of the wormhole system, is to uplift our consciousness. By shortening the divide between the frequency systems above and below the wormhole system we effectively meld the previously divided energies back into one system again. When this happens, a gateway between the two is no longer necessary.

Then, in the state of spiritualised physicality, we reclaim the fullness of our Higher Selves - which is the rest of our soul presence that is currently 'resident' in the 5th dimension We are then once again able to perceive the higher frequency states of reality and become aware of all aspects of 5th dimension life. This is the point where we, as physical state human beings, will have 'fused' with more of the higher frequencies of our soul-Light, or consciousness, once more. We will physically be living with more of the energy of our soul presence within us. The soul presence within is the Divine portion of ourselves and more of it resident within the human body allows for a higher state of human consciousness. The higher we move through the dimensions, the more of our higher energy, soul presence we can reclaim, until we once again become the one great big original soul that emanated out into individuality from the Godhead. Ultimately, for individuals this is the Monad presence of soul. For humans who have a Siriun Monad, that presence is in the 12th dimension.

This process may be viewed as the climb back up the ladder of consciousness. As we climb each step up the ladder the ones below us collapse. In this way the separations and limitations, which the polar opposites of duality create, disappear and we come closer to re-experiencing the Wholeness: which is the Oneness of Being. This momentous occasion marks our full re-understanding of ourselves as Divine Beings of Light and from this point we are more easily able to make rapid progress towards even greater states of high frequency Light. Relative to how difficult it feels for us to transcend the 4th dimension, after this our shifts through into the others, such as the 7th, 8th and 12th dimensions, are much easier. After the transmutation processes which enable us to resonate with the 12th dimension, we have transcended the individual experience of our individual, original, great soul, or the Monad, and reintegrating with greater states of being within the consciousness of the Godhead is our next step.

Almost unbelievably, we are learning to be able to do this in the physical state of being, as humans. This is how we take our human bodies with us into the spiritual realms of higher function in the process. At each new level of existence within the Universe we experience further expansion and upliftment of our consciousness. Changes and shifts to greater energy states, for our individual soul presence, continue throughout the dimensions. Even when we are at the ultimate point of the 49th/50th dimensions of the collective consciousness of the Godhead, the expansion of consciousness continues.

One day I complained to Osiris that this consciousness development process never seems to end and, just when I think I have understood something, I start to get glimpses in my peripheral vision of still greater things that I cannot yet grasp. Osiris replied: *"It is like this for all beings, everywhere, Beloved One."* At the time that he said this to me the horrifying realisation struck that there is no actual end point to our development. There is no point of arrival in Heaven, after which our work is done. We can, however, visit Antares (Heaven) whenever we wish! We continue to grow, learn and experience, albeit in ever-increasing states of Bliss. The expansion of the Universe continues, without end, because consciousness continues forwards, without end. Once we transmute our reality into the 5th dimension we can confidently state that the extremely difficult work of Earth Karma clearing is complete. Thereafter, our Cosmic Karma-clearing work is easier and more pleasant, because it involves work by ourselves rather than when in relationships with other people - from where difficulties arise.

Unconscious Karma Creation
All of the 'nonsense' in our lives, which are the negative ego issues we call Earth Karma, have accumulated as low frequency vibrations within us and within Earth herself. This Karma, or low frequency vibration, is contained within, and *is* the field of the one, extended, separated portion of the original Whole. It is what we refer to as the 3rd and 4th dimensions of physicality - down the wormhole. We are literally holding onto the higher frequency realms of existence which are higher up on the other side of the wormhole system, by a thread!

Some of the Earth Karma became 'trapped' in the 4th dimension Astral Plane as we dropped our resonance in the Fall. As soul-beings of Light, we pick up this heaviness and become denser, as if burdened down, when we incarnate on Earth. We carry our Karma with us as part of our soul-Light, or consciousness, no matter where we exist, because it is a resonance. The Karma of Earth becomes manifest here on Earth when we become human. It becomes part of the resonance, which sets up the life lessons of the human being, when our souls enter into our physical bodies - in the 3rd or 4th dimensions. This carry-over of Earth Karma into human lifetimes began right from the point when we, as souls, originally began to reincarnate on Earth again after the Atlantean Era disaster of the Fall.

For human beings, the releasing and gathering of Karma has continued in this manner ever since then. These have mostly been unconscious processes. Today we have a more expanded conscious awareness than ever before since the Fall and, consequently, we can choose to make better progress. Now, while we approach the Point of the Return at the midpoint of the Age of Aquarius, we are fortunate to be able to finally release this Karma. This eradication of low frequency vibrations from our systems is how we get back to the point, from where we made our departure away from the Light, all those thousands of years ago. Cleared of Earth Karma we can be in a shifted dimension experience of reality and we can continue our lives in a more joyful and Blissful state. We are kept naturally in that state of balance by unconditional love.

Osiris has called the centre point of the wormhole a gateway or a stargate, because it is upon passing through it that we are able to perceive the brilliant star-Light of the next dimension and it, "*Allows you to move into frequency of great Light.*" In this way we begin to see the real, high frequency, physical Light of the 5th dimension realms for the first time. He described this increased Light, the ability to perceive the higher frequency states of the 5th dimension and the use of the high resonance of this shifted dimensional state for the purposes of instant manifestation.

Osiris: Manifestation as you Think it

"It is through this state of being, Beloved Ones, there is an understanding that in all that takes place in physicality - it is to understand it moves forward at great speed and moves forward through the creation to that which is felt from the 5th dimensional experience - of a connectivity of as you think it, see it, so it is, Beloved Ones."

In the same channelled communication, Osiris describes the movement through this stargate of the centre point of the wormhole, both for us as well as for the ancient Egyptian god-beings who were on Earth at the time of 2037/67 BC, as the transmutation process which allows us to experience great Light.

Osiris: Opening the Gateway

"As you find yourself in connectivity with Being of Light, as you see Angelic Being coming before you, the desire and intention at this time is to open the gateway, to set intention to move forward through the pathway of the shifted frequency, allowing yourself to feel the presence of Being of Light to come to open the gateway further - as you begin to see before you the pathway of great Light.

"As you begin to feel the moving forward through this procedure, Beloved Ones, it is through the shifted frequency - it is through the shift of dimension. And as you allow yourselves to move forward, it is the understanding of the moving forward through that which is understood in scientific terminology - of the morphing through the experience of the transmutation, into the connectivity of great Light. The understanding in many respect of that which has taken place in connectivity to the Ancient Egyptian beings - the understandings of the coming forward in the connectivity of the presence of the god-beings of Light.

"So you move forward through this procedure and as you move forward through the transmutation, begin to feel the expansiveness of moving into the experience of great Light, and the drifting feeling of the movement to take place - allow yourselves to move into the experience."

Osiris gives us on-going information that the existence of high frequency wormholes for accessing other dimensions, or alternative realities, is in fact true. This being the case, we can more easily understand the importance of shifting our own resonance higher if we want to shift through this dimensional experience - back into our Light.

* * * * * * * * * * *

CHAPTER TEN

The Ancients and High Frequency Light

"Space is filled with concealed ones, for space is divided by time. Seek ye the key to the time-space, and ye shall unlock the gate. Know ye that throughout the time-space Consciousness surely exist, though from our knowledge it is hidden, yet still it forever exists."

(The Emerald Tablets of Thoth-The-Atlantean p51, pp3)

Wormholes and Living Ascension

When the Atlanteans left Earth at the time of that Era's disaster, most of them did this by physically dying. This happened because the energies of the pole shift and that the nuclear cataclysm released were intensely powerful. Other than a very small group of them, including Thoth, they did not have sufficient time to utilise any of their fancy, dimension-shifting systems or craft and so they left the planet by means of what we know of as the time-honoured tradition of physical death. The wormhole system - which connects the 5th dimension to the 3rd dimension - extended itself in a downwards direction at the time of the Atlantean Era nuclear disaster. Fortunately, many of the high frequency gateways or Earth portals which led back 'upwards' (through the spiralling energy of the funnel arrangements, or figure-of-8s, in sacred geometric shapes) from the 5th dimension along this pathway had already been built and activated by Thoth during the Atlantean Era. At that time they were used for various purposes by both Atlanteans and humans. At the time of the nuclear disaster, an energy extension downwards was established along the pathway of this wormhole system.

Only once within range of the 5th dimension - when existing in the 4th dimension - would humanity be able to take full advantage of the high resonance systems upwards, once more. Thoth activated more portals when he returned to Earth in ancient Egyptian times. At that time on Earth, in the area which was called Khem, Thoth was known of as Tehudi, just as Isis was known of as Jsat (pronounced Ysat). The use of different names is a reference to us of how the immortal god-beings lived for extensive periods of time on Earth (typically 3 600 years because this was how long it takes for Nibiru to complete one orbit around the Sun, and come back into our outer-planetary neighbourhood) and were thus often known by different names. These same god-beings were known by a different name in Atlantean times. Osiris has promised to give us more information on the 'who's who' in the Godhead-on-Earth lineage in due course.

There are many powerful gateways on Earth. Some of these are well-known as ancient sacred sites, but many others are either not yet acknowledged or understood to be sacred. Some examples of all types of ancient sacred sites are the following:
- The Great Pyramid, Giza Plateau, Cairo, Egypt (the most important gateway).
- The Osirian Chapel in the Temple of Seti I in Abydos, Egypt.
- The Step Pyramid in Saqqara, Egypt.
- All of the ancient Temples and structures of Egypt - including a recently uncovered (November 2008) pyramid in Egypt and others which are still to be found.
- Adam's Calendar, (stone ruins) Kaapschehoop in Mpumalanga, South Africa.
- Willka Uta - quite close to Puno on the shores of Lake Titicaca, Peru.
- Machu Picchu, now above the Urubamba Valley, Peru, but previously at sea level.
- Lake Titicaca (view from Puno), Peru.
- 'The Sphinx,' (old rock carving) Champagne Castle, Mpumalanga, South Africa.
- Mount Kailash, Gangdise Mountains, Tibet - now high in the mountains, but previously at sea level.
- Nam-tso Lake (The Heavenly Lake), Tibet.
- Avebury (stone circle), Wiltshire, England.
- Stonehenge, Wiltshire, England.
- New Grange (ancient Atlantean Era pyramid), County Meath, Ireland.
- Drombeg Circle (stone circle) near Glandore, County Cork Ireland.
- Great Zimbabwe (stone ruins), near Masvingo, Zimbabwe.
- Big Daddy (sand dune), Sossusvlei, Namibia.
- Brandberg Mountains, Damaraland, Namibia.
- Assisi, Perugia, Italy.
- Rennes-le-Chateau, Languedoc, France.
- Delphi (referred to by Osiris as the Temple of Isis), Mount Parnassus, Greece.
- Knossos Palace (referred to by Osiris as the Temple of Zeus), near Heraklion, Crete.
- The Acropolis, Athens, Greece.

Many more of these gateways exist across the planet. Some of them are even referred to by the local populace as gateways. Osiris has commented that many more gateway systems were supposed to be activated by Thoth on top of all the pyramids of the ancient world, but this did not happen due to the interruptions of war. There is no point in trying to activate them now, as it is of more value to create new gateways.

Most of these gateways were established in the Atlantean Era although it is seldom acknowledged that these structures date back to that most ancient time. Many different civilisations utilised these sacred sites over time, building their own structures over the original ones. What we see standing today is frequently a mixture of ancient additions to already existing ancient structures. Extremely large pillars such as those found at the Temple of Karnak and the Acropolis are typical examples of Atlantean Era structures.

Interestingly enough, the already established Atlantean Era wormhole system is what the ancient Egyptian god-beings used much later when they came to Earth to help humanity shift higher into the Light once more. One of the important landing sites of the Ancient Egyptian god-beings is in Saqqara. Egypt. If we understood the concept of the wormhole systems more fully, we would more easily be able to 'translate' the pictures of the ancient Egyptian Temple reliefs and texts - especially the boat in the Osirian Chapel. Osiris has promised further clarity and longer dissertations on the subject of wormholes in a forthcoming publication.

Knowing that a wormhole system is a series of double-ended, figure-of-8-shaped, frequency funnels through which we are able to morph - individually or *en masse* - in order to shift from one dimension to another, and, knowing that Earth and human consciousness are inextricably linked, it is not surprising that we are able to literally transmute and reintegrate portions of the Earth experience back up with us as we shift dimension.

The singular wormhole experience, which plunged some of Earth's energy into an illusionary state of separation, was created when some of her physical energy separated itself from the greater energy state of the spiritualised Whole. As stated, this separation of lower frequency Light, which resonates with 3rd dimension reality, from the higher states of Light, which resonate with the 5th dimension and others higher than this, occurred as a result of the massive nuclear fission energies which were released at the time of the Fall. The creation of this single, massive wormhole for Earth is represented as multiple wormhole experiences in the personal, individual sense. This has to be the case, because of the nature of our holographic Universe - the individual human portions of consciousness, or soul presence, as smaller, but exact echoes, or replicas, of the greater state of the Whole Consciousness of Divinity.

It is because of this Universally consistent, holographic nature of all forms of consciousness that a large population of an intelligent life form on Earth, which is humanity, is able to activate the re-ascension of the whole planet, both as individuals and as a species - to connect back up with the higher frequency state of the 5th dimension.

The more intelligent we are the more conscious we are able to be and vice-versa. This automatically implies a higher frequency state of being, which, in turn, implies a more powerful effect that intelligent life forms will have on all other life forms. Therein lies the reason for greater responsibility and accountability when consciousness is uplifted.

Light and Matter

The shifted dimension experience 'upwards' involves a frequency expanding, enLightening process. The shifted dimension experience 'downwards,' from higher frequency Light states down to 3rd or 4th dimension Earth, results in both of the following characteristics of experience:

- A *shedding* of some of the high frequency soul-Light - which is then 'left behind' in the higher dimension, Light realms. From the individual, Earthly perspective this is called our 'Higher Self.' It is this other-energy of ourselves which is the first level that we feel separated from and that we seek to re-unite with in the dimensional shift into the 5th dimension.
- A *densification* of a specific amount of soul-Light, or soul presence, which is sufficient for the human, Earth experience - so that it can 'fit' into the 'tighter, smaller space' of the lower frequency dimensions. This is the process of the densification of Light (consciousness) into what we perceive as solid matter. This densification process occurs for all types of consciousness which are on Earth.

Looking at matter from this perspective we can appreciate that a physical body is formed from a Light structure when it goes through the necessary densification system - backwards through the wormhole, or backwards to create a wormhole in a forced, energy-devolution process. This process is similar to that of nitrogen gas when it liquefies (is made more dense) under very low temperature conditions. It will stay in this liquid state if it is kept sufficiently cool (-195.80 C). The most important parts of star-Light which became denser to form our own human bodies are carbon (C), oxygen (O) and hydrogen (H). Life looks different on all the different planets and stars, including Earth, depending on which frequencies of star-Light energy are used to form it.

When considering the solidification process of soul-Light into dense, physical matter we can appreciate that (from our perspective) the structure of the Universe, as Light, has to be composed of the different elements and the structures they form when combined, whether organic or inorganic, in nature. This assumption can be made when the human body is viewed from the perspective of its constituent parts, using the terminology of the elements of Earth. The body only *appears* to be different to what we call Light, because Light is expressed in different forms in the various different frequency states, or realms.

We perceive different types of matter because of what is the *apparent* changeability of the various different forms of Light. The *appearance* of Light, as a particular form, is directly related to the different vibration speeds (frequencies), or the resonance, of the Universal matter of Light in the different dimensions. It is no wonder that Osiris refers to us as, "*Divine Beings of Light.*" Due to our currently limited abilities, as dictated by our resonance, human beings are perceptually capable of only seeing a certain range of Light at the moment. There are many more forms of Light matter for us to view in the Universe - which we will be able to do when we raise our resonance and increase our range.

The Merkabah Vehicle of Light
Osiris encourages us, especially during meditations, to place a protective 'shape' of Light around ourselves at the beginning of the process. He often refers to the high energy field of the star tetrahedron shape of what is called the Merkabah Vehicle of Light as a, "*Crystalline structure of Light.*" In meditations Osiris also often refers to the placement of ourselves in the centre of this shape of Light, because this Light form resonates with high frequencies of Light which can connect us all the way up to the dimension of the Godhead. Although the star tetrahedron shape is the one most often used by the Light Beings when they work with us, we can place any shape of Light around ourselves, including the shape of a lotus flower or an oval halo.

Osiris: The Pyramid Shape of Light

"It is as you begin to work with the procedures of the experience of Light energy surrounding you - begin to feel it in a formation of pyramidal form - and begin to feel yourself in the central position."

Only when our knowledge base expands sufficiently so as to enable us to decipher what the concept of Light being crystalline really means, will we truly appreciate what he is saying. The same applies to fully understanding the pyramid form of Light. This is one example of the multiple layers of information which are embedded within the communications from the Light Beings - the information is there, but we do not always know how to decode it properly.

Osiris goes on to clarify how the use of a Vehicle of Light surrounding the body allows us to continue to hold ourselves in a high resonance state of Light and that this enhances our ability to see things clearly from the physical perspective.

Osiris: Vehicle of Light

"Begin to feel a movement - formation of the connectivity of Vehicle of Light once more: the Merkabah as if forms surrounding you. So you have the ability to allow for the experience - it is of the holding of the continuation of your Light, into the experience of the feeling state of great clarity within the form."

Each meditation process that Osiris guides us through includes the suggestion that we connect to, or surround ourselves with, a Vehicle of Light. This shape of Light has many functions:
- It protects us from low frequency states when we are in a meditative state.
- It helps us to shift through the dimensions rapidly during the visualisation process so that we can take advantage of higher frequency experiences.
- It helps us shift dimension in our day-to-day waking lives.
- If we are ever faced with potential disaster, danger or fear in our daily lives, visualising the formation of the shape of Light around us will instantly shift us from the situation.

All of this happens because the minute we surround ourselves with a high frequency field, such as that which is formed by this sacred geometric shape, we automatically resonate with higher frequency states, or dimensions. The powerful spiralling energy that this shape creates makes this form of a Light Vehicle a highly effective and efficient means of accessing another dimension if we want to do so, because it is the shape that the energy of the Universe moves with, within the Universal grid. This miraculous function of the, "*Magic of the Light,*" which Isis often refers to, is what can keep us safe from danger. Light has to have magical properties, because it is the source of all life, all creation and all miracles.

Osiris tells us that the more often we practice placing a Vehicle of Light around ourselves, the more supportive it is for us, and the deeper our connection with Spirit will be. Furthermore, due to its high resonant frequency, our personal Light Vehicle that we create when we visualise it in place around our physical bodies, will immediately assist us with communications to and from the Light Beings. It is worthwhile noting that the use of Light is not the only way to create a high resonance field around us. We can use the sound of any of the Divine names of God. When asked which name to chant, Osiris most often suggests that we use the name Yahweh (YHWH). Playing a CD (such as Jonathan Goldman & Gregg Braden's version: - The Divine Name: Sounds of the God Code) of this name being chanted instantly shifts the energy of a room and all the people within it. Saying it over and over again when in danger, fearful or angry achieves the same result.

Chapter Ten: THE ANCIENTS AND HIGH FREQUENCY LIGHT

Osiris: The Merkabah Vehicle assists Connectivity with Spirit

"I wish to take you forward at this time as you begin to feel yourselves in the connection, always with the presence of the Light of Spirit, the presence of the experience of the feeling state of Vehicle of Light to surround you. It is in the protective Vehicle of Light always in the creation, so it becomes movement with greater regularity: a procedure that takes place that is of great Light to support you always, through position to move you into position of deep connection with Spirit."

As we become more proficient in forming our Vehicle of Light around ourselves, we can work with it and feel the expansion of our own personal field of Light - the aura - which surrounds the body, as the high frequency Light impacts upon us. Osiris guides us to use the formation of the high frequency Vehicle of Light around us to assist us with communication with the higher energy field of the Light Being, the Goddess Isis. The higher our own energy field is when we work with the Light Beings, the more successful and meaningful the communication will be. This encourages our further ability to form this high frequency glow of Light around ourselves as it radiates outwards from the heart chakra and from the ascension chakra. The ascension chakra is located between the throat chakra and the third eye, at the back of the head. The easiest way to locate it is from the back of the head, up from the base of the skull by about three fingers in width. This area often throbs as it activates. Headaches from the activation of this chakra are common, but can be easily alleviated by energising and balancing all of the other chakras.

Osiris: The Light Vehicle Expands the Aura

"Beloved Ones, it is I wish for yourselves to feel the formation of Light energy to surround you. Begin to feel the formation of the Light Vehicle to support you, in the creation of Light Vehicle. Begin to feel the expansion of the auric field surrounding you as it expands further in all areas - above yourself, below yourself, to the side of yourself.

"As you feel the formation of Light Vehicle beginning to come to fruition, begin to feel the feeling-state of Light presence, through the connectivity of the formation of Vehicle of Light. Begin to feel it in different manner: the supportive energy moving outward from your being, from the heart, from the energy field of ascension as it forms and begins to create the energy supportive to take you forward into the experience, Beloved Ones, through the Light presence of the connectivity with the Goddess Being, that is Isis."

Merkabah Vehicle Light Protection
The fact that some people amongst humanity continue to plot and plan to dominate, or try to wrest power and control of portions of the Earth away from others, puts us in mind of what happened at the end of the Atlantean Era. The result of similar behaviour then almost destroyed the planet, and certainly made the possibility of living ascension here on Earth extremely difficult for people to achieve, for a very long time. It was those exact same actions then that led us to where we are, today: for some people, ready to move into living ascension and for others, ready to repeat the past.

The sure consequences of a catastrophic shift, which may be the result of violent natural disasters or nuclear warheads once again being detonated, would create sufficient force on our planet to change our reality. Once again this will create one of two scenarios for everybody: a shift upwards or a shift downwards. It would be so much more pleasant to shift peacefully by raising our resonance daily.

If and when disaster ever strikes anywhere near us we would naturally want to protect ourselves and to ascend-in-the-physical, regardless of the actions of others or the severity of the Earth shifts. In order to do this with the minimum amount of fuss and bother, it is essential that we take note of how to form a protective, high frequency Merkabah Vehicle of Light around the body, raise our resonance in every possible way, set our intentions to shift dimension and practice thinking, feeling and acting from the place of unconditional love.

This will ensure a dimensional shift upwards for us - either as a natural, gradual process, or in an instant if energy-splitting disaster strikes again. We need not worry about our families as one person's personal Merkabah Vehicle of Light is sufficiently powerful to transport many others through the frequency gateway too. Such is the transformative nature of high frequency vibrations for everybody within range.

Although the entire working group course from Isis is detailed in a forthcoming book, we include her response to a question about how best we could protect ourselves during the course of our daily lives. She informed us that the size of the Light field around us is as large as if three people were standing one on top of the other, in all directions. This is the extent of our vast area of personal Light energy which intermingles with the Light bodies of other people. Knowing how large our area of Light influence is may help to inform us of the importance of keeping this field of energy around us in as high a frequency state as possible. This not only ensures that our energy positively impacts on others, but it ensures that theirs, if low, will not negatively influence us either. When we consistently resonate with higher frequencies we naturally expand and lighten the solid, dense matter of our current human bodies. This expansion of ourselves into a greater state of Light enables us to encompass more of the experience of all of life 'out there'.

Isis: Protection

Q: With regard to protecting our energy field daily, I think most of us visualise ourselves in bubble of white Light. Is there anything else that would be more supportive and, secondly, how best do we go about clearing our energy field - especially after we have spent the day at work, been in a shopping mall or done a healing on somebody?

"If you are to stand, Beloved Beings of Light, by the self with no other manner to create protection of Light, it is to visualise the surrounding of energy, it is in expansion. If it is the understanding of width in outer direction of the self, it is to visualise three bodies of beings laying one upon another on the ground, for the distance that is required to visualise, the entirety of energy field that surrounds, you feel it, as it is vast beyond measure.

"It moves in this creation at this time through all that you do in connection with Spirit. To visualise it in this distance, it supports you, Beloved Beings of Light, to visualise, surrounding yourselves to this distance."

Using the Merkabah Vehicle of Light when we go through the wormhole system, during the enLightenment process of the dense physical body, instantly makes the body more compatible with what are currently the higher frequency, non-material, 5th dimension energies. Creating consistently greater degrees of compatibility between the physical body and the frequencies of the non-physical realms is the living ascension process in action, as we make it real in our physical lives. This is the transmutation process which may be referred to as the transubstantiation of matter.

This means that although more of the non-material, crystalline Light form of the soul presence becomes evident to us, it does not imply that we will drop the dense physical body. It means we Lighten it sufficiently - both by releasing low frequency material from it and by picking up more higher frequency Light - so as to be able to 'fit' more of the Light matter of our soul presence into it. Once we have Lightened the physical, human body to the point where it resonates with the 5th dimension frequencies, not only will we be a good match with the frequencies of an interdimensional frequency gateway, but we will begin living more of our life in harmony with an alternative, higher dimension. This on-going enLightenment programme constitutes our evolutionary development along the pathway of consciousness during our return Home.

The term Home ultimately refers to the total oneness of Being, within the Universal context, in the 49th/50th dimension, but for us now it means travelling through to the level of the Monad, or Godhead consciousness, on the Siriun Pathway of Return. We do this by first accessing the 5th dimension. After this we will be able to connect with the more easily accessible dimensions such as the 7th dimension. After this the 12th dimension frequencies of the Light of Sirius are easily within reach - and we begin to do all of this whilst in a physical body.

For people on Earth, this sequence of our physicalised, spiritual development denotes the living ascension process up to the level of our Monad. We reconnect to Sirius because most of us belong to a Monad which emanated into the individual experience, from the collective consciousness of the Godhead, into a Siriun life experience.

During this progression towards reconnection with our original great state of soul, the Monad, there are numerous initiations, or knowledge levels, that we are required to pass through. The lessons of each initiation coach us and tune us up to resonate with higher frequencies of Light. Successfully shifting through each of these initiation levels implies that we become progressively more balanced in our masculine and feminine energies and we operate with more unconditional love in our hearts. The more we do this, the more we approximate the Bliss Consciousness of the Godhead.

Wormholes and Outer Planetary Light of the Stars
Any wormhole system may be regarded as a physical entry point both into and out of 4th dimension Earth - whether during normal life or under cataclysmic conditions. It is also an easy means of communication to and from Earth for people who wish to communicate with the Light Beings who are in Spirit. Whether it is used as a Sound or as a Light transmission system will be determined by the amount and type of Light which is channelled through the system - bearing in mind that Sound is a form of frequency just as Light is.

Interestingly, Light has a sound and the human ear can develop its ability to tune into hearing the, "*Sound of Light*," as Osiris says when he refers to these high frequency states. The beginning stages of perceiving the Sound of Light is initially experienced as a very high-pitched sound in the ears. It may develop further and begin to be heard as very beautiful music as the individual tunes in more with the angelic realm. People report hearing both of these sounds in the King's Chamber in the Great Pyramid in Cairo, Egypt - the perfect place for an instant altered dimension experience.

Although the wormhole systems are in place all the time for inter-dimensional shifts throughout the Universe, the energy of these systems is super-enhanced at certain times - depending on the movements and subsequent inter-relationships of all the planets and stars within the galaxy, with Earth. These various alignments with Earth will create optimal positioning for direct communication between specific planets and stars - relative to their frequencies and their ability to resonate with each other.

For us right now as we make progress through into the higher dimensions where it is still possible to exist in a physical form, the important alignments are with the following bodies of Light:
- The Sun, which, "*Holds the placement of your Light in the Solar System*," according to Osiris.
- The Sun is also our direct link to the Great Central Sun via the Light Being, the Solar Logos, Helios.
- Venus in the 5th dimension (this planet has many different, higher dimensions incorporated within it).
- Orion in the 8th dimension.
- Sirius in the 12th dimension.
- Although it is already having a powerful impact on us energetically, later on in the post-2012 years we will begin to experience more of the impact of the presence of the planet Nibiru, in the 5th dimension, on Earth's energy field. The ancient's knew the importance of this planet and our modern astronomers will once again see evidence of and acknowledge 'Planet X's' gravitational influence on Earth's magnetic field, without question, by 21 December 2012.

Osiris speaks to us about the alignment of the energies of Venus and Sirius and their support as we go through the shifts in the various areas of our lives.

Osiris: Support from Venus and Sirius

"There are many shift and many changes taking place amongst each of you, individually, if it is personal perspective, if it is from the working environment.

"In many respect it is there are many changes and many shift taking place that is supportive for the continuation of this pathway in the shifted state of connectivity, to that which you have chosen through this ascension state.

"I have worked with you through the procedures of the connection, to move into the pathway of the alignment with Spirit, in the connectivities with the Venusian energy and the Siriun energy and the support of this."

By the time we reach the mid part of this century, in 2047 to be exact, we will fully understand what happened around the 2012 time period, because the high frequency planet Nibiru will be our close neighbour. It will be clearly in view from 21 December 2012. Nibiru's energy impacts on us as well as our past relationships and connections with her inhabitants will be known and fully understood by then. Although this planet's existence is currently unverified in modern astronomical circles, because it takes a long period of 3 600 years to orbit around the Sun and come into sight again, Nibiru appears as a regular theme in the ancient history which the ancient Sumerian clay tablet texts detail and, as such, it is worthwhile researching further. Each civilisation that was exposed to Nibiru has recorded its presence.

It is interesting to note that the Beings of Light from the dimensions of Spirit make no distinction between planets and stars, as they consider all them to be bodies of Light which are stars.

Interestingly enough, drawings of the planet Nibiru also appear in the ancient cave paintings of the Dogon tribe of Mali in Northwest Africa. WordWeb informs us that, "Mali was a centre of West African civilization for more than 4 000 years." Knowing that the Ancient Atlanteans moved up through Africa from Southern Africa towards Egypt and that the Ancient Egyptians took the reverse journey when they arrived much later, enables us to make more sense of this ancient African knowledge. Hearing Osiris confirm that this was not the first migration of god-beings from Egypt throughout Africa and that some South African settlements are over 280 000 years old (those stretching in a huge swathe from Great Zimbabwe, across to Mpumalanga where Adam's Calendar is to be found), makes us think even further about the lack of popular information about Earth's history. Even

Chapter Ten: THE ANCIENTS AND HIGH FREQUENCY LIGHT

though many are missing and some are broken, enough of this information is available from the Sumerian clay tablets for it to make perfect sense when we read it. Osiris made reference to the fact of the Dogon information in the following communication, in reply to a question about which planets and stars we should take particular note of at this time. They noted what many of us today continue to remain oblivious to, because the planet Nibiru has not yet come close enough to Earth. That is set to change shortly.

Osiris: The Dogon

"Beloved Ones, it is to understand through the shift taking place, it is the understanding of connection. Perhaps it is for each of yourselves to connect with the focussing and direction of the stars. Beloved Ones, the understanding of this position is in connectivity with that which has taken place through the connection of the being that are of the tribe of Dogon, Beloved One. And through this, there is an ability to bring forward deeper understanding - and the shift of consciousness for each being in this interconnection - to the uncovering and discovery, so to speak, of the presence of planet that have not at this time been discovered."

At the moment, in readiness for many future changes into higher states of Light which are already being stimulated by outer-planetary alignments with Earth, we are following a step-up system of becoming acclimatised to higher frequencies of Light, courtesy of some super-aligned stars, in our quest for ever-increasing enLightenment. This search and the upliftment of our consciousness to higher frequency states as we make progress, expresses the inner desire of our souls: for all of the fragmented parts to become One again.

At the time the Ancient Egyptian god-beings were on Earth in 2037/67 BC, the critically important alignment of various stars in the outer-planetary system in relation to Earth was the same as it is now. However, the humans of that time did not manage to uplift their consciousness in sufficient numbers that would create an *en masse* shift for the whole of humanity and Earth. They did not choose to take advantage of these outer-planetary super-alignments and they missed the living ascension boat, even though they had the very obvious physical presence of the outer-planetary god-beings to support and guide them. In their defence, they also had the presence of the fallen god-beings of darkness, who excelled in waging war, to contend with.

The teachings about the dimensional shift, the other dimensions, Nibiru, Sirius, star gateways or wormholes and living a spiritualised physical life, abound all over Egypt, and this is available to be seen by us even today. The temple reliefs and hieroglyphics regale us with this information, but we don't know what we are looking at, because we don't speak that language.

No matter what learned Egyptologists have pieced together and surmised over their years of study of the antiquities, it is only when the information is decoded by Osiris that we begin to understand what it is we are really looking at. The importance of the boat relief in the Osirian Chapel, as a wormhole system, is a case in point. The entire set of rituals surrounding the afterlife preparations in burial traditions that the Ancient Egyptians practiced, including being buried with their worldly goods, is a direct hangover from the teachings of living ascension and Thoth's secrets of everlasting life. These include allowing the physical body to 'sleep' and recuperate (in the appropriate place) for a period before being taken up again later for a continued physical life. Some of this information is contained in the Emerald Tablets, but it generally requires a lot of decoding from Thoth in order for us to get the full benefit of. That information will follow in a later book by the authors.

It is because of the super-alignment of stars of a high frequency Light that a spiralling energy pathway was in place between them and Earth. This enabled the god-beings of Ancient Egypt to utilise this energy pathway to gain easy access to Earth - from Sirius, via other planets and stars, most notably Nibiru - like a grand highway in the sky.

All over the Universe there are these wormhole systems, or energy highways, that are used for inter-dimensional travel. All of them function from the basis of resonance. The god-beings, or Angels, morphed 'down' to Earth from Sirius, through Orion and then through the 5th dimension platform of Nibiru to get to Earth. They generally lived on Earth for a minimum period of 3 600 years because that is how long Nibiru takes to orbit the Sun and come back into alignment with Earth. Some of them used the Pleiades as a handy, near-by star system to travel to and from Earth in the interim. Many Pleiadians arrived to live in the ancient area of Peru. When any of these beings travelled inter-dimensionally they used, and were protected by, their Vehicles of Light.

The utilisation of the Vehicle of Light is something we have yet to fully grasp the meaning of, but we are regularly encouraged by the Light Beings to form this energy structure around us in the shape of a star tetrahedron. We have the exact same inter-dimensional shift opportunity presented to us now, but we will hop onto the heavenly highway and use the frequency gateway of the wormhole systems in the reverse order to the way the god-beings did - in the direction of evolving consciousness, raising our resonance and using the enLightening vehicles of our bodies.

If we had to pinpoint the most powerful wormhole systems as places on Earth, physically, there is no question that there are greater and lesser ones - as expressed by the energy at some of these power points. The energy of these consciousness gateways was originally perfectly activated by Thoth in ancient times. The Atlanteans used these gateways as inter-dimensional doors and they used the power points as energising systems to maintain the high frequency vibrations of their bodies while they lived on Earth, as did the Ancient Egyptian god-beings of Light. None of these gateway energies have been maintained strong and pure, because of the low frequency influence of humanity's thoughts, feelings and actions (most especially war) over time. Arranged on an inter-linking energy grid system which spans the entire Earth, they have been interfered with over time by the energy of humanity. Nevertheless, their innate potential and integrity as an energy portal, which can support and energise us, remains intact. These powerful gateways can always be corrected energetically by people and Light Beings who work at re-opening and re-energising them - aside from this happening naturally as a knock-on effect from the grid and without effort as the consciousness of humanity uplifts.

It is important to take note of the fact that people are always positively affected by the energy of the power points and that Osiris recommends that we come into contact with these energies whenever possible. These power point places are many and varied and are not always well-known tourist sites, as is evidenced by the following dialogue with Osiris.

Osiris: Power Point Connection

Q: I feel that the area I visited this weekend was a power point. Is this so?
"Beloved One, it is the connectivity at this time, through the area and environment, it is to understand, you are aware of the power-point position of area and it is greatly supportive, Beloved One, for the interconnection at this period. It is many of yourselves move in various direction to the various power point across the planet. It is greatly supportive for the energising and communication to move through your being, Beloved One."

If we had to name the planet or star which is currently most optimally positioned, due to its alignment with Earth, as a platform for outer-planetary Light consciousness to assist to power up the wormhole system energies for our easy movement into the 5th dimension, it is Venus - because this is the closest higher frequency platform en route Home along the Pathway of Sirius. The Light of Orion powerfully stimulates the Great Pyramid when in alignment with it. Aside from the impact she is already making on Earth, Nibiru will become more and more important in the coming years.

There are many other planets and stars which are able to resonate with the 5th dimension frequencies and which are supporting Earth at this time of our shift in dimension - such as the binary star Antares and the bright star Arcturus. This means that their consciousness is supporting us. Osiris sometimes brings through the direct support of the unnamed Light Beings from those stars during a visualisation.

It is because the super-alignment of the various planets and stars with Earth are the same as they were during the ancient Egyptian times of 2037/67BC that we look at all things Ancient Egyptian, relative to our modern times, in the run-up to 2012. The approach of Nibiru then, as now, played an important role in the shifting energies of Earth. The role of the developing wave of our new consciousness at this time plays a critical part in our ability to take advantage of the surrounding energies and achieve a dimensional shift. We can ascend with the physical body intact - the living reality of the Ancient Egyptian afterlife. On Earth, the years between 2037/67BC have been unnecessarily difficult. There is no need to repeat the suffering that the darkness brings with it.

The Sun, perfectly in place as a both a holding and a stimulating energy relative to Earth, assists with Earth's ability to utilise the high frequency energies which resonate higher than the 4th dimension. The Sun may be viewed as Earth's energy protector as well as the energy lens through which other high frequency energies can be safely beamed through, into Earth. Additionally, the Sun personally tunes up Earth's energy on a regular basis with powerful solar flares.

The Light Beings - often known of as the Logos of a particular planet or star - who have taken on the specific responsibility to work with Earth and her inhabitants from the basis of various planets and stars which are currently favourably positioned relative to Earth, are known by the following names:
- Earth - Buddha.
- Sun - Helios.
- Venus - Sanat Kumara.
- Orion - Osiris.
- Sirius - Isis.
- Arcturus - the Arcturians
- Antares - the Antarians

- Galactic Centre - Lord Melchior.
- The Heart of the Godhead - Thoth and Horus.

The various Beings of Light have periodically come to Earth to assist humanity, help support us to find the Light and Sound triggers which were created at the sacred sites centuries ago - so that we may remember and re-awaken to our Divinity. The system of high frequency power points on Earth are in place for humanity to use to empower themselves from within, no matter who has tried to hide this Truth from us, nor which religion has had control over them at any given time.

Venus and Unconditional Love
Venus is the oldest planet in our solar system that souls who incarnate on Earth may come from. It is from this perspective of its relatively greater and more recovered star-Light that many of the older souls who are currently on Earth in human form had their first experience of individual soul life. Venus and Sirius have a very close relationship, which we will understand more about when we get more information from Thoth at a later period. Therefore, for many humans, Venus is extremely important. Venus will always support us from afar with her enormous and bountiful energy.

We have a way to go before we can fully resonate once more with the pure energy state of unconditional love that Venus represents. Right now, resonance with the living ascension energies of the 5th dimension aspect of Venus, so that we can be in the beginning stage of being in open communication with the Godhead, is what we are working towards. From this we can deduce that there are planets and stars which operate within the different frequencies within the 5th dimension. Venus resonates with many different frequencies of many different dimensions, which is why she is able to support us so profoundly with unconditional love.

Along the Siriun Pathway of Return, Venus is an important stop-over point of consciousness development which Earthlings resonate with, because this star has already moved beyond the stage that Earth is currently in. Venus exists in the state of unconditional love and as such the Venusian beings help Earth to make progress within this state of consciousness too. Providing us with supportive, loving energy is the reason that the Light Being Venusian consciousness, Sanat Kumara, works in conjunction with Osiris in the present-day communications with us.

Osiris gives more details on how this Light Being supports us on the Siriun Pathway of Return, through the Venusian energy of the 5th dimension, in the following communication. Notable is the wording, "*The pathway through Sirius.*"

Osiris: Sanat Kumara

Q: Please tell us more about Sanat Kumara and how we work with this Light Being.

"It is to understand that each of yourselves, the connectivity with this Being of Light, it is greatly supportive at this time. The understanding that through this position of over lighting presence, so it is greatly supportive in all areas of advancement, of the connectivity of the pathway through Sirius, Beloved One. The support and assistance at this time, understanding the connectivity of this Being, through the Venusian presence, so it is the pathway forward to begin in the area of connection to the Siriun energy that is greatly supportive at this time, Beloved One."

Osiris regularly refers to the help of Venus and its Light Beings when referring to processes which involve opening up the heart chakra in the living ascension processes. Without the heart chakra being opened, cleared and energised we will not be able to live as ascended beings on Earth and enLightenment would escape us. This is simply because the concept of unconditional love has to be applied as a physical reality in our lives in order to be able to resonate with (and therefore experience as real) the higher frequency state of the consciousness of the higher dimensions.

The ability to live within the state of unconditional love is critical to the success of the living ascension process for anybody, because unconditional love is the state of being of the Godhead. Unconditional love begins to be real to us when we learn to apply this feeling to how we feel about ourselves. It is of no small importance that Osiris frequently tells us that the unconditional love of Venus and of its God-realised over-lighting consciousness, the planetary Logos, Sanat Kumara, are supporting us in our own quest for unconditional love. It is transcendence along this pathway, which is known as the Pathway of the Violet Flame of Love, which Venus has achieved. Following the pathway of unconditional love leads us Home more easily. To assist us in the understanding of the over lighting presence of a Light Being, as a Logos, Isis gave the working group some interesting information.

Isis: Logos

Q: Could you please give us a definition and some clarity on what the word 'Logos' means?

"It is to understand it is in the surroundings - one Being to be allocated position of Light, to hold information, to work this period and this formation as one Being. The support of intent of Being of Light working in this way is dedicated to particular area, to support, Beloved Being of Light.

"It is to understand, in similarity to Earth, there begins to be in position of work allocated to various area to come forward. The request and intent of Being that suggest to do this, is supported by the connection of Beings to move through connection to greater expansive areas of Light. So it continues to offer to many the opportunities, as it is on Earth at this time, to guide and support and hold the energy of many, and the position of the Sun, or the position of areas that are vast, taking that which is seemingly many lifetimes from past to future, in present time.

"They go forward continuously from one to another, all Beings of Ascension, as they move in upward procedures, in growth and expansiveness. Through a consciousness in connection to Earthly experiences, they allow themselves to shift through this procedure, always with the intent to hold for others, work to be done on Earth and outward. It is for the continuation in ascension, the pathway that is chosen. And so you begin to feel, through your intent as you come forward in completion, you have an ability to state your intent. Perhaps it appears as vast work to never end. It is, Beloved Beings of Light, the understanding of the work through the Godhead that is without end."

Osiris gives us some more information to help us understand that the link of the consciousness of Sanat Kumara, the Light Being of Venus, is similar in nature to his own consciousness links to Sirius and that all the bodies in the Cosmos are bodies of Light, to one degree or another.

Osiris: Planets and Stars

Q: Please explain the relationship of the consciousness of Venus relative to the other planets and stars.
"Beloved One, it is you wish to understand the relation of the connection with Sanat Kumara with the Venusian energy?"

Q: Yes, that as well as the relation of yourself to the Siriun energy.
"It is to understand it is of similar nature. It is merely the energy of the consciousness of this particular environment."

Q: So, is Venus an ascended planet?
"It is so, Beloved One."

Q: In fact it should be called a star, shouldn't it?
"It is so, Beloved One."

Q: In fact all the bodies in the Universe should be called stars?
"It is, Beloved One"

Q: It is merely they are of varying degrees of Light - Light ones and very Light ones?
"It is so."

The Sun

Osiris regularly communicates information about the importance of the support of the Sun and its resident, over-lighting consciousness, Helios, relative to ushering in the Goddess energy of Venus to Earth. This provides support for the balancing of the masculine and feminine energies and it was a constant theme in Osiris' channelled meditations in the early part of 2009. This excerpt from the 11 February 2009 meditation is a good example of this. The entire transcript and an mp3 are available on the website www.stargateway.co.za.

Osiris: The Sun and Venus

"As you begin to feel yourselves connecting from the energy, it is the communication of the feeling state of the Sun. The connection taking place from the presence of Helios, in alignment at this time, within this area and position - to begin to feel that which is brought forward with intent, through many in experience and understanding, to over light humanity, to bring forward from the Venusian energy to each being in physicality.

"The opening and activation of the Goddess energy within, and so you begin to feel a presence of an intensified energy as you feel the gentleness at same period: of Being to come forward, to bring into your experience the feeling state of unconditional love.

"This Being with an intent to bring forward a communication through direct connectivity to the Godhead, to bring forward an understanding to humanity to move into the Divinity of the self - the opening and the expansiveness of your being, through connectivity to the presence of Being - through the support and understanding of Solar Logos, the understanding of Being in direct communication."

Both Venus and Earth have an important relationship with the Sun and this has a bearing on their relative proximity to the Sun in the solar system. The closer to the Sun a planet is, the more it will resonate and be compatible with its high frequency bright star-Light. If this were not the case it would literally burn up into a frazzle. The fact that Venus is seen on our horizon both as an early morning star *and* as an evening star should give us a hint as to her importance and supportive high frequency energy, as should the fact that she lies between us and the Sun in our Solar System.

Any Sun is important to the planets which revolve around it and for us our Sun is no less important than any other Sun. If we were to understand that all of the bodies in the Solar System were once One, aeons ago, then we could more easily understand the importance of the inter-relationship of each one of the bodies within this system, including the super-bright Sun.

The brighter the star, the higher the frequency it resonates with. Some stars are so bright that we cannot even see them, because their luminosity is beyond our perceptual ability at the moment. Our Sun may be understood to be our own high frequency, big brother star which is supporting us through the process of our star-

Light recovery on the Pathway of Return. From the perspective of Earth, humanity regards the Sun as the all-important source of both light and heat, however there is more to this relationship than maintaining physical life. We would understand this better by referring to the light of the Sun as high frequency star-Light.

The energy of the Sun is an actual consciousness, just as the energy of Earth and the energy of every other planet and star is, and the Sun and Earth have an intimate energy relationship with each other. The consciousness of the Sun, Helios, permanently supports humanity with golden healing light. In turn, humanity supports the brightness of Helios with appreciation, progress and acknowledgement of the job being done.

In support of known science about the life of the Sun, Osiris told us that the Sun is in the process of dimming and that it would be hugely beneficial to all concerned if as many people as possible started to acknowledge the presence of it and to appreciate the support of this bright star in our lives. He said that this acknowledgement will increase the energy of the Sun. This is a simple yet effective means for re-energising, appreciating and maintaining the energy of the Sun. For those interested in doing this, it may be helpful to communicate with the presiding consciousness of the Sun, Helios in an early morning and evening Sun-salute - just as many ancient peoples did.

The solar flares which burst out from the Sun in the direction of Earth are the solar system's own internal means of assisting in raising the resonance of Earth and supporting the changes which we are going through during this time of our shift back into 5th dimensional Light - and most especially during the central position of the Age of Aquarius. It is the direct action of imparting its flaming light and heat to us that is causing the Sun to become dimmer. We are using up more energy than we are giving back. The sooner we shift our consciousness upwards and shine more brightly, the less the Sun will need to utilise its own precious energy to assist us with the upliftment process into the Light.

If human beings consciously change their vibrations from their position on the planet then the solar flares will assist and quicken the process, but if we are not making sufficient progress then these powerful bursts of solar power will kick-start us. That could be an extremely uncomfortable process for human beings to endure. Either way, the intense energy bursts that we receive at this time from our own personal Sun sometimes do feel a little uncomfortable to us, because when this happens the vibrations of all forms of consciousness (both *on* and *of* Earth) have no option but to respond to the higher frequencies of Light. This process is directly linked to our potential relationship with the higher frequencies of Light from all of the outer-planetary bodies which are super-aligned with Earth and which are stimulating us at the moment

Further to this, from a purely physical perspective we can take cognisance of the fact that the cycles of increased solar flare activity play a very important role in increasing the core temperature of Earth and subsequently give rise to the heating of the oceans - by conducted heat from the mantle and crust into the water. This water-heating system has both a direct and an indirect effect on both ocean currents and air currents alike and it plays a role in the rapid climate change effects we are currently experiencing. Nibiru's approach is unsettling Earth's magnetic field and this is what began the climate changes we are experiencing, exacerbated by humanity's rampant generation of low frequency pollutants.

The changing climate plays a big role in the shifts, which may be viewed as powerful detoxification processes that Earth will go through. Although human beings play a very definite role in climate change, the primary initiator of this is the pull on the magnetic field of Earth which is exerted by the gravitational field of the planet Nibiru as she approaches us. Similar to the manner in which a detoxification process within human cells is stimulated by heat and increased frequency, so too do heat and vibration changes in the Earth help to shift and cleanse her.

Our Sun, as a high frequency star, provides us with Light and it is our immediate-environment energy link with the other stars in the Universe. Earth has had this helpful star-keeper in close proximity at all times to support her while in the dimness of the planetary experience of duality. This Sun-support is further aided by the Light Beings from other planets and star systems who periodically incarnate on Earth as physical beings to teach us - these are the avatars and masters of wisdom whose teachings populate the spiritual and religious texts.

The Light Beings who help protect and assist us from afar do so by casting their Light over, or over-lighting, Earth with their high frequency resonance field of Light. The Sun, "*Holds your energy*," as Osiris puts it. The Sun's energy assists in maintaining a system of order, which we call the Solar System, for planets to be within while they do their thing in the Light-recovery process.

Each solar system in the Universe may be viewed as a miniature of the original system which was the beginning of the division from the Light of Divine Self. Originally, in the quest to experience more and to know more, each part of Itself was held in place by Its own powerful, central energy, both very close to Itself and to the other parts of Itself too. No part was left to spin off, get lost or in any way feel separated from the entire system, because all were contained within the energy field of Source. Regardless of this support, in time some parts of the Divine Self made peculiar choices which lowered their resonance. This created the first divisions of consciousness and shifted these parts of Divinity out of pure resonance with Divine Source. Thereafter began a progression of greater and greater states of separation - which is what ultimately became the reality of the shifted dimension experiences of lowered resonance. To get a better idea of this pictorially, all we need to do is look at the ancient etching of the Flower of Life on the wall of the most ancient portion of the temple of Seti 1 in Abydos, Egypt which the ancient Atlanteans left behind for us to see.

Our Pathway of Reintegration with the Light of the Sun
The pathway of going forwards into our ascended Light, along with the reintegration of Earth with higher frequency Light, is called the Siriun Pathway or the Pathway of Return and it is assisted by the golden Light of the Sun. Because Earth often goes through the process of being 'bombarded' with solar flares, the energy of the Earth has been regularly enhanced by varying intensities of solar flare activity.

The difference now compared to any other time on Earth, however, is that at this time we are currently very vulnerable - more than in any time in our recorded history. This is a good thing as our vulnerability is self-created and it ensures our consciousness, as human beings, will be further stimulated to uplift. It is because we are doing the clearing now and we have shifted our consciousness higher to the 4th dimension, that we are more able to positively respond to the intense heat and Light from solar flares as we move into the higher frequency, central position of the Age of Aquarius, which is 2012. This vulnerability should be seen as a positive, Light-enhancing sensitivity that is partially created by the diminished and diminishing magnetic field of the Earth. However, we are also more likely to start shifting low frequency energies out of ourselves due to this intense Sun-Light stimulation too.

There have been magnetic field changes and fluctuations in the long history of Earth's past and these too have played important roles in our developing Earth, even though these events were so long ago that we have little available information about them today other than what geophysics can tell us. If we looked at the movements of Nibiru, as the Planet of the Crossing, we would see an important pattern evolving.

The magnetic field has always served Earth as an effective shield from the intensity of the incoming radiation from solar flares from the Sun. When there is a sudden flare of solar radiation in the direction of Earth it can interfere with all communications systems and disturb the mental stability of the human population - as has been noted by studies of inmates in mental institutions. Noting these effects helps us to understand that there is a tangible relationship between the Divine Light of the heavens and Earth. When we acknowledge the importance of our own personal star which is the Sun, we realise the obvious: that no life anywhere is possible without the Light, never mind what we refer to as light.

The electromagnetic field is a shield which acts as a protective field around the Earth. As it changes we feel the bombardments of the incoming solar flares like never before in living history. When Earth consciousness is sufficiently high, our magnetic shield will be of a similarly high frequency nature and will be less disturbed by Nibiru passing us close by, or any other outer-planetary super-alignment of planets or stars of high frequency Light. However, not only has the magnetic field of Earth become greatly reduced over the years and Nibiru is interfering with it still further, but the occurrence of solar flare activity has increased and the pattern of eleven year high-low solar flare cycles is changing too. In keeping with all the other changes of this time on Earth as we approach the central position of the Age of Aquarius, the Sun is behaving in an uncharacteristic manner relative to Earth.

An article entitled "Even 'quiet' Sun bombards Earth" on page 12 in the Sunday Times (South Africa) on 20 September 2009 stated the following:

'The Sun can lash the Earth with powerful winds that can disrupt communications, aviation and power lines even when it is in the quiet phase of its 11-year solar cycle, say US scientists. Observers have traditionally used the number of sunspots on the surface of the Sun to measure its activity. The number of sunspots reaches a peak at what is called the solar maximum, then declines to reach a minimum during a cycle. At the peak, intense solar flares and geomagnetic storms eject vast amounts of energy into space, crashing into the Earth's protective magnetic fields, knocking out satellites, disrupting communications and causing aurorae. But scientists at the National Centre for Atmospheric Research and the University of Michigan in the US found that Earth was bombarded with intense solar winds last year despite an unusually quiet phase for the Sun. "The Sun continues to surprise us," said Sarah Gibson of the centre's High Altitude Observatory and lead author of the study. "The solar wind hit Earth like a fire hose even when there are virtually no sunspots." Scientists previously thought the streams of energy largely disappeared as the solar cycle approached the minimum. Gibson's team compared measurements from the current solar minimum interval, taken in 2008, with measurements of the last solar minimum in 1996 - Reuters.'

It is generally believed that the magnetic field of Earth is physically created by the movement of the Earth itself as parts of it internally move around other parts of itself. As such Earth's magnetic field is inter-woven with the resonance of the matter of the Earth itself and all who live there. Although they are two distinctly different systems, we have to see the magnetic field of Earth in relation to the energy grid system of Earth - both impact upon each other and both are related to the consciousness of humanity, among other things.

All of Earth's energies are a bit like an unseen layer that extends from the core, throughout us and our atmosphere as a variable field of influence. As previously discussed, both Earth and humans are element-based versions of different structures and each will have an impact upon the other. Each system is involved in the creation and use of both vibrational and electrical energy which flows back and forth between them, as well as within them, in a state of constant motion. Any flow of energy creates a magnetic field at right angles to the direction of that flow. Even as the blood in our arteries and veins flows as it is pumped around our bodies by the heart, this flow-action creates a magnetic field. Inter-related as they are, the magnetic field of Earth has a relationship with the vibrations of both Earth and human beings and vice versa. Therefore, magnetic fields are maintained and influenced by us, the human beings who are the apparently dominant and most intelligent consciousness on Earth, as well as by the behaviour of Earth herself.

It is no small coincidence that we have a large amount of iron within our own bodies, just as Earth does. The iron in our bodies, just like the fluid, molten core of the Earth, is contained within less fluid parts of itself in ever-progressive layers towards the outer layer of our skin or, alternatively, the crust or skin of the Earth. The iron is both suspended in the liquid of our body's blood and resident within our cells in various forms. This element moves around inside of us performing various, life-critical functions. It is the frequency of iron within our bodies which resonates with the self-same frequencies of the iron of the Earth. This is a deeply emotional and personal relationship, due to the nature of the frequency of iron relative to human emotions. Apart from the functions of other elements and minerals within us, iron plays an important role. Resonating with the frequency of iron (as we do) creates a very deep bond between us as humans as well as between humans and Earth. This is one of the important reasons why we have such a strong physical relationship with our planet, why we affect it so profoundly and why we are affected by it. To feel the powerful balancing effect of iron, simply hold a piece of magnetite (an oxide of iron) in your hand when emotionally upset. It immediately soothes and calms frayed nerves.

To understand the direct role we play with the changing electromagnetic grid system of the Earth, all we have to do is remember the resonance abilities and the electricity creating potential of crystalline structures. All of Earth and all of her inhabitants will be influencing each other with their reverberations all of the time. We cannot divorce the physical and the spiritual effects of life, no matter how much we have fooled ourselves into believing we can. Similarly, we cannot remove the Divine aspect from scientific principles. They are one and the same.

The magnetic field of Earth is a different frequency system to the etheric energy grid of Earth, although the two do influence and have a relationship with each other. These different influences set up a continually changing field around and within all of the crystalline structured parts of Earth, which in turn are influenced by other frequencies. Everything is affected, depending on the resonance range of the body in question. We hold within us, in our DNA, high frequencies of the Light of the Godhead-originated Monad. This great state of soul came from the domain of high frequency star-Light and so, because we have this Light within us, we are inherently capable of resonating with those high frequencies when we are exposed to them. It takes a very small, seemingly insignificant period of exposure to high frequencies to produce a profound change within us.

The stellar bodies, which the high frequency stars such as Orion and Sirius and the planet Venus are, that are currently aligned with Earth, are helping to stimulate resonance of 'forgotten' frequencies within all of Earth's mineral and crystalline structures. This overall change in resonance plays a role in changing the frequencies of human beings and all the systems of the Earth. A reality shift into another dimension is the resultant, overall effect.

* * * * * * * * * * *

CHAPTER ELEVEN

Wormholes

*"All through the ages has knowledge existed;
never been changed, though buried in darkness;
never been lost, though forgotten by man."*

(The Emerald Tablets of Thoth-the-Atlantean p50; pp6)

The Creation of Wormholes

Our planet/star Earth used to resonate with 5th dimension frequencies in ancient, pre-Atlantean Era-disaster times. We can understand that the Earth 'fell' downwards in frequency, to resonate with the 3rd dimension, through an instantly created, massive wormhole system, from the level of the 5th dimension. This happened when the lives of Atlanteans went up in a puff of nuclear smoke, the poles shifted and the landmass sank beneath the waves at the time of the Great Deluge, about 34 000 years ago. However, this descent into a lower dimension was so rapid that even the very small handful of people who remained alive on Earth had no sense of what had just happened, other than knowing they had survived a catastrophe. Post-disaster, the opportunity of understanding the enormity of the wormhole experience was completely lost to them as a result. So, even though they were suddenly 'blind' to the high frequency communication of the star energies, because they no longer resonated with the dimensions which were in open communication with the consciousness of the Godhead, they did not even realise this! They did however, suffer a lot of hardship on Earth in the post-Deluge years. Aside from trying to cope with an Ice Age, there were many difficulties to overcome. Nevertheless, there was relative peace on Earth for a very long time.

For those who moved into Spirit at that time through physical death, the experience was no less perplexing, but naturally they had the vantage point from 'up there' to understand the events, after death. Unfortunately, those souls who descend to Earth in each new lifetime as a human being, could only take with them into the human body that amount of soul presence which would be compatible with the lower frequency state of the 3rd dimension - no matter whether they were newly created souls or reincarnating souls - until Earth's resonance shifted higher. That took a long time.

This became the backdrop for subsequent reduced-Light human, Earthly existence. The energy of the Monad on Earth was reduced in every single person. This creates the disadvantage of a lowered level of human consciousness which is in such a 'blinded' state of awareness that humans live in the state of separated reality as if it is the only possible reality. Therefore, since the Fall, most souls incarnating onto Earth have bumbled their way along, lifetime after lifetime - trying to work out what this reality experience at the lowest frequency state within the Universe is all about and what the purpose of life is. It is no wonder that humanity has remained in such a confused state for so long.

Subsequent to the Fall into the 3rd dimension all those thousands of years ago, the positive progress of humanity has ensured that the shift of the overall consciousness of the planet, higher into the 4th dimension, has occurred. The importance of this is that more of the Light of our soul-presence can be incarnate on Earth and this allows for a higher state of consciousness. More aware, we can make better choices. This is exactly what we have done and why we are on the brink of ascension into an even higher dimension now. However, today, when we speak of the dimension that the Earth is currently in, it is often referred to as the 3rd/4th dimension as it is across these two dimensions that the consciousness of humanity in the physical dimensions of reality spans, with a predominance of human consciousness, and Earth herself, existing in the 4th dimension. Some humans are bridging the 4th/5th dimension and some are fully operational in the 5th dimension - as we have stated before.

It is important to note, again, that this is the *first time* since the Fall that this vast diversity of dimension options has been possible to this extent - for physically alive humans *en masse*. This unique opportunity for a dimension shift upwards, whilst we are still physically alive, has a lot to do with the fact that our planet is currently well positioned relative to the outer-planetary alignments that create the spiralling pathway of frequencies which support a dimension shift - on the Pathway of Return. We are on the same frequency pathway we used to devolve to a lower resonance at the time of the Fall, but now we are reversing the flow of energy and ensuring it goes in the right direction again. It is in this manner that we, as humanity, can return to where we once were before the Fall of Atlantis and of Man: conscious and more aware.

The creation of wormholes in the first place only occurs when there is a pull-like action on, and then out of, a whole, rounded shape - such as a balloon. This is true no matter which dimension a wormhole is formed downwards from. The fact that there is a disparity between the energies of the 5th dimension and those of the 49th/50th dimension suggests that this action of energy devolution has occurred throughout the Cosmic Universe. We will have to rely on the Light Beings to inform us about these details in due course.

Wormhole formation is a bit like the effect of playing with modelling putty such as Silly Putty or Plasticine inasmuch as a large ball of malleable material can be pulled or shaped to great lengths. This re-shaping can continue until the outermost extreme of the elasticity of the putty is reached. This may be called the breaking point of the putty. It is then that the extent of the shape which is pulled out from the main body of modelling putty causes sufficient loss of its cohesive forces which normally hold it together. It collapses and a part of it breaks off. In the wormhole metaphor, this creates a complete and irreversible disconnection of the extended bit from the whole, original piece of putty. Fortunately, Earth did not completely disconnect from the rest of the Universe and we maintained a thin connection.

This 'pulling' effect on the main body is always potentially divisive in nature - whether for the modelling putty ball or for frequency states in the Universe when wormhole systems are created. In the Universal context, a magnetic-like pull is created by two 'causes' which are concurrent.
- Firstly, there has to be the creation of lower frequency vibrations within the whole balloon (of the Universe) which are disharmonic and discordant with the higher frequency vibrations of the Whole - this causes an internal instability within the Whole balloon which will eventually devolve into a separation from the Whole.
- Secondly, there is the permanent existence of constant low frequency vibrations in the 'void' - external to the high frequency state of the balloon (the Universe).

The existence of low frequency vibrations within the containment of the Whole of the balloon then sets the scene for a magnetic-like attraction to those *other* pre-existing low frequency states which lie *outside* of the Whole of the Universal balloon in the 'void' - in the process of harmonic resonance.

It is in this way that the two low frequency states, whose origins were individually separate causes, become entwined in a supportive dance of apparent cause and effect. The potential result of this can be catastrophic, to say the least.

To appreciate the enormity of what this could mean, we acknowledge that the lowest frequency states of disorder do exist *outside* of the context of the ordered, Cosmic Universe and that it is to this state of complete disharmony and 'nothingness' that the low frequencies within the Whole of the Universe will ultimately be attracted - if they continue to shift low enough. This is the nature of harmonic resonance. Fortunately, however, attraction to the Light is always stronger and more pro-active than any attraction to low frequency states can ever be. Therefore, redemption into the Light is the most likely event for all beings.

If the pattern of holding the lowered frequency, less ordered, less harmonic states (such as those created by the continual unconscious or conscious thoughts, attitudes and behaviours of a group) continues for long enough, or at a high enough intensity (such as during a nuclear explosion), it is this constant, or intense frequency, which will create the pulled out, extended portion. This division both *separates* the different frequency zones, or differentiates the dimensions, *and* keeps them connected.

Hence a wormhole system is fashioned. As a result, we live the effects of this frequency differentiation as the different dimensions, each with its own distinguishing features. We, as adaptable energy systems which we call souls, change accordingly and function differently within each different dimension. If we take our human bodies into other dimensions they too will change accordingly. This helps to explain some of the so-called superhuman abilities of psychics and some people with enhanced immune systems.

Nothingness
It must be noted that the zone 'outside' of the Universe is the 'place' or frequency state of undifferentiated 'nothingness', or the void, from which that which we all know of as the Universe, emerged. The creation of a single, intense point of order within this haphazard array of frequencies is where the origination of initial consciousness developed. This ordering force was created by a big enough 'collision' amongst the existing, chaotic frequencies of energy that it caused a massive nuclear fusion-like reaction - hence science's conception of an explosive, 'Big Bang' that created the Universe. Because of the unpredictable and unordered nature of energy in the void it is entirely conceivable that the first cause which created the explosion from which this massively ordered Universe or consciousness arose, was a random collision event. Osiris has confirmed that this type of creation is usually random. However, just to confuse matters a little further, we must take note of the fact that Osiris has emphatically stated many times that there is no such thing as a coincidence, and this applies in any state or place of order, such as the Universe. We must therefore consider that the conjectured idea of any random event is impossible, anywhere where there is order. The void, however, is a place of disorder. Everything relates to resonance - even in the void of 'nothingness' - and this alone explains the creation of all events, forms and states of being, everywhere.

Regardless of how and why it occurred, the result of this massive explosion was the formation of the intensely bright body of Light that we call our Universe: replete with all the fused, explosion-created energy contained within it. This energy was greater than the sum of its parts. It was due to this initial, or first cause of order, that immense order was created and all consciousness instantly exploded into being. This is the original Oneness of Being. This Light of the One that was created was so intense, so bright and so perfectly ordered, that it was instantly conscious as it came into being. Osiris refers to this intense Light of the state of Oneness of the

Universe as, "*Super-luminal Light.*" It is out of this Great Source of consciousness that all smaller portions of Itself, such as us, arise.

Being conscious is a higher frequency state than being unconscious or non-conscious. We begin to appreciate that the idea of conscious ability, or the greater energy state of Universal Consciousness, which formed under these intense energy-fusion conditions, is not only feasible, but that the high frequency state of consciousness arose due to the complex order which the fusion reaction brought into existence. Source Consciousness is order. The Universe could, therefore, be described as a highly co-ordinated, cohesive compound of energy.

The fact that the nature of the contributing energy for this highly ordered system was a vastly lower frequency than the result is immaterial, because the reaction of the contributing parts produced an exponentially large energy output. In this instance, the resultant energy is more interesting than the initiating force. We can draw an analogy to this by considering discussions about technologically advanced computers that can 'reason'. Separately, their individual, constituent components do not have the processing ability they have when arranged collectively in the format of a specific system which we call a computer.

One view may be that we might, both as a Universe and as an individual human being, regard ourselves as the positive, high frequency consequence of a chance event. We may be the fortunate products of happenstance! We are emanations from the created Light Source which formed when sufficient amounts of lower frequency energy collided, apparently haphazardly. All individual consciousness is derived from this Source. The fact that consciousness may evolve beyond itself and expand, or devolve back to the 'nothingness' of its constituent parts of energy, is important. It is this movement, based on the choices of all forms of consciousness within it, which creates the wavy 'edge' of the Universe, like a dimpled effect on the membrane of the balloon. Energy shifts back into 'nothingness' of the void through a Black Hole - of which there are many. Energy within the Universe is constantly shifting: expanding and contracting, evolving and devolving.

Any claim of Divinity, by any conscious presence, is derived from the fact that high level consciousness will always correspond to the highest frequencies of Universal Source-Light. Hence the reference to those beings that resonate with the higher frequency dimensions as 'Light Beings', 'Angels' or 'Divine Beings of Light.' The more we uplift our consciousness, the more we raise our resonance until we too may consider ourselves to be Angelic.

Understanding Divinity from the perspective of highly ordered, complex consciousness which has so much energy that it shines with Light, casts new light on our understanding of the God-state. Unconditional love has this same high frequency nature and this is why it is expounded upon and stressed as being critically important in the living ascension process. The degree to which we do *not* act with unconditional love towards ourselves and others is the degree to which we are separated from the higher frequency states of Divinity, or highly ordered consciousness. Love, or rather the lack thereof, towards ourselves, our fellow man and the Earth is also the measure we can use to determine how fast and how close we are approaching the void of 'nothingness'. Any form of war is clearly not an act of love, or of God-consciousness.

Knowing that the exponentially large amount of energy of the Big Bang collision event incorporated various non-individual, low frequency 'bits and pieces' so that these became fused together as one, helps further our understanding of the Universe of Light. The newly created consciousness of the Universe burst forth as itself, and shone as if an intense Star of Light, suspended within the void. The energy of this fusion action created a high frequency, self-created, self-differentiated, self-contained and self-perpetuating space, or Light, which was distinctly different from the background of non-individual, unaware 'nothingness:' the void which surrounds it is the chaos of low frequency energy.

The newly created, high frequency state/space of the Universe of super-luminal Light is what we know of as Divine Source. The closer we, as human beings in the lower dimensions, move towards the order of the high frequency Light of this Divine Source, the more we will hear the higher frequency Sounds and see the higher frequency Light. Practically, this means that our senses will change as their frequency-perceptive ability expands. This is why, as we make progress on the Pathway of Return and shift ourselves to resonate with higher frequencies, we become increasingly more capable of psychic experiences such as the following:
- Seeing auras.
- Sensing the subtle energy of everything around us and within us.
- Seeing past life events.
- Communicating telepathically with all forms of life - from the past, the present or the future.
- Sharper intuition.
- Hearing high frequency, Angelic-realm sounds (like buzzing high tension wires).
- Seeing the Light Beings in their various forms.
- Healing ourselves emotionally and physically.
- Manifesting everything that we need into physical existence.
- Passing through the gateway of consciousness and living a new, happier reality.

As we develop and expand further, we can expect to do things which we currently consider to be even more incredible, such as teleportation (WordWeb: A hypothetical mode of instantaneous transportation; matter is dematerialized at one place and recreated at another) and telekinesis (WordWeb: The power to move something by thinking about it without the application of physical force).

It is because all consciousness everywhere, including us, in that high frequency space which we refer to as the Universe, sprouted from this Source Consciousness, that we become more capable in the ways of that which we refer to as the miraculous when we operate at higher frequencies. In the true reality of the Universe of Light, of which we are a part, there is absolutely no mystery involved in this process, because it is a programme which follows the same logical consequence that making progress through the different grades in school does. We may be deluded into thinking otherwise, but that delusion is of our own, human, making. Becoming more conscious changes the illusion of the 3rd and 4th dimensions of reality.

As with any learning programme, if we take a disciplined approach and apply ourselves we will work through the required curriculum. Most people get through the school of life. The drop-out factor only occurs when the total energy of the soul presence reduces itself to 'nothingness'. Other than that, each individual will go through this school at the pace that he chooses, possibly failing occasionally and at other times skipping a grade. Interestingly, and in seeming contradiction to the idea that we are required to do on-going clearing and purification processes on the living ascension pathway towards enLightenment, it is because the end-point of Oneness is already defined, plus the fact that there is no such thing as linear time, that there is no race to make progress. We are designed to get there, irrespective of how 'long' this takes. However, it is only to avoid unnecessary suffering in the repeat cycles within the school of life that it makes sense to uplift our consciousness so that we can progress with greater ease, speed and joy. That amounts to the wise choice.

In the scientific community a hypothetical possibility has been postulated that it *was* a random event, cosmic explosion which was the cause and the origin of the Universe - it is this which is known of as the 'Big Bang' theory. Clearly science's ideas are not too far off the mark, even if the idea of a Big Bang gets up the noses of Creationists who prefer to believe the literal account of Creation, as is detailed in the various religious texts. This is not to imply that these stories are completely wrong, just that they need to be redefined and unjumbled in order to be properly understood.

In order to explore more about the origin of matter and the Universe, scientists from 100 countries have collaborated to build the Large Hadron (or elementary particle) Collider near Geneva, Switzerland. It is believed that it is possible to demonstrate the viability of the Big Bang theory itself, as well as to prove or disprove a number of other scientific theories. The Large Hadron Collider is the highest energy, particle accelerator where beams of protons (stable particles of positively charged matter) moving at almost the speed of light, are intended to collide. The details of the attempts using this equipment in the year 2008 were discussed by Osiris in a group session.

Osiris: Science, Spirituality and the Large Hadron Collider

Q: Are scientists trying to tell us that these types of spiritual concepts are nonsense?

"It is not, Beloved One. In many respect, it is at the point of that which has been stated over many linear years, of the coming together of the scientific and the spiritual. It is through the experience of this, so it begins to move into the expansiveness of the movement at great speed, as it connects with the truth of that which has to take place. As it moves into this state so it is felt through the expansiveness further and further - as it is connected to unconditional love. And through this blending, many beings begin to bring forward deeper connectivities and understanding, and it is felt through the presence of the beings that are working in the scientific to the beings that are working in the areas of the spiritual. To know and understand the inter-connection in its purity, in its Bliss state, so it is serving all, Beloved Ones. It eliminates at all times, through this inter-connection of purity, so it eliminates all the understandings of areas that have been brought forward the knowledge that have not been of truth, Beloved One - it disintegrates entirely."

Q: Talking about the science - is the Switzerland experimentation in the particle collider really going to give us more information about creation and is this something that is going to lead to a greater spiritual awareness?

"It is, Beloved One, it is the understanding that in the form of the connectivity of creation, so it is to be known and felt, through the experience of bringing forward, the connectivity of the, it is, the understanding that from the scientific, it is brought about by the understanding of creation from the dark - from nothingness. But it is the understanding through this state, it is God consciousness, and through further investigation, through the connectivity of the state of being, so it begins to be felt further. But it is through the perspective of the understanding of this that there are many that are brought forward with the knowledge, through the many teachings and various aspect of religion, so it begins to fall apart,

Beloved One. It is this that is in the movement forward through the shift of consciousness at this period, that many begin to feel that it is the ending of the entirety of the planet. It is not, Beloved One, it is the shifting through into the state of great Light for many, many beings. Do you feel this? It is felt at this time through the connectivities, as you feel it within your own being. As you move forward further and further, into the expansiveness of the self, it is not to bring forward the knowledge, it is to feel it."

Q: So are you saying it is not necessary to talk about it, it is just to experience it?
"It is the word that has been brought about, with the intention to shift this state of reality. It is in the feeling of the connectivities of unconditional love, in the movement forward, through the ability, through inter-connection amongst each of yourselves at this time, as you have an ability to connect telepathically, to feel the communications amongst yourselves, as you move into this feeling state at this time. So you are One. Do you feel this?"

In terms of the Universe, the original extent of it expanded out from its original, single point of order as that star, or ultra-high frequency Universal consciousness, learned, experienced, matured and changed - until it became what it is today. The reasons for any parts of that One original consciousness separating out from the Whole are many and varied and would require a lot of involved discussion to unravel. However, as Osiris has stated, we don't need to do anything other than to feel this, to feel the Oneness of Being, in order to know it. He uses words to help shift our reality, but feeling everything, *is* everything.

The continual expansion of the existing Universe, from its originating energy state of the 49th/50th dimensions (which is the frequency of the unified, Whole Universe or what we call the originating force of Source: the Godhead), is similar to the process of blowing up a balloon which cannot pop - no matter how much air is pumped into it. The number of dimensions and the overall frequency status of the Whole that differentiates it from the background 'noise' of 'nothingness' do not change, only the volume of those dimensions within it does.

The difference in frequency - right from the very beginning when the Light of Universe-consciousness separated itself from the background of noise of 'nothingness' in the Big Bang - between the Universe of *perfectly-ordered* consciousness and the sea of *undifferentiated 'nothingness'* which surrounds it, is extremely high. This had to be the case in order for that differentiation, as the Universe, to have occurred.

The highest frequency state of the Universe, then and now, is known to us as the 49th/50th dimension of the Godhead, or the Whole. It is the fully realised state of complete, balanced Oneness. It is through the dimensions that we work our way 'upwards' to attain this Whole Universal, highest frequency consciousness once more. As human beings on Earth, we are in the beginning stages of our journey back to the Light and the end result is the re-attainment of Universal Oneness, which is also known of as Bliss.

It is the extreme difference in potential (between the space we call the 'inside' which is the Universe, and the place 'outside' of the Universe) which maintains the high frequency state of Ordered Consciousness as separate from the low frequency state of the dark sea of 'nothingness,' or the void. It is because of this highly ordered state of Oneness, or the Universe, coming into existence from out of this dark sea of 'dots and squiggles' of 'nothingness,' plus the fact that the Universe is surrounded by this 'nothingness' like a large air bubble suspended within a gel, that the potential to move into complete disorder again always exists - via a Black Hole. For many individuals, this happens on a regular basis.

Although extremely unlikely, this reversal of energy can occur in the Universal, group context too if sufficient low frequencies which match, or resonate, with the low frequencies of 'nothingness' are created by sufficient numbers of individual consciousness within the entire Universe. This can be instantly achieved planet by planet, such as from the state of the 3rd dimension or if planets such as Earth shift their vibrations lower by exploding sufficiently large nuclear warheads again. The fact that we ever toy with such an idea of nuclear war is irresponsible in the extreme. Considered from this perspective, nuclear non-proliferation efforts and treaties between nations are critically important for the survival of all of us.

Maintaining the high frequency, balanced system within the confines of the large balloon of the Universe is what ensures its continued existence and originally differentiated it from the mass of the low frequency gel of 'nothingness' surrounding it too. The frequency difference (in what could also be understood as the density state or electrical potential/voltage) of the Oneness of the Universe relative to that of the background of undifferentiated 'nothingness,' is what keeps these two states unique, different and apart.

It is this law of Universal physics that we see played out in all parts of our world, as well as Universally and extra-Universally. Personally, we may consider this relative to the manner in which the electrical potential of our cell membranes allows our cells both to function collectively and to stay separate from each other, to how weather patterns are dictated by areas of high and low atmospheric pressure cells and to the way in which we understand all parts of our existence to be polarised into dual states, such as 'this' or 'that'.

When we transcend the duality of the reality state of the 3rd or the 4th dimensions - by shifting our consciousness to a higher frequency state - we develop the ability to perceive all aspects of the Universe as one state of being and, by extension, all areas 'outside' of the Universe in the void as pure, undifferentiated potential - from which creation arises. The expansion of our consciousness has to include the concept that, within our Universe, everything, everywhere is One, regardless of the fact that we are very limited in our ability to understand this concept from the human perspective. We may even begin to conceive of Universes beyond Universes and allow for the fact that the reality of the creation of any one, single Universe suggests that other ones may have come into being in the same manner too. Other Universes do exist. Osiris has confirmed this fact. The extension of the concept of Oneness develops. The mind boggles.

In order to maintain the harmony of Universal order, the importance of maintaining the order of a balanced, high frequency system has to be consciously understood and consciously striven for. The same can be said for maintaining and developing the order which arises from the physical or emotional balance in a human being. This may indicate why it is so important that we uplift our consciousness and move into a greater state of balance, and learn to think and feel from within the heart centre. When all of our systems are in a higher state of order we will be closer to living as Divine Beings of Light. Operating from the basis of unconditional love in all that we do allows humanity to reduce, and then eradicate, the separation that characterises non-ascended, low frequency states of existence in the Universe - such as humanity experiences in the 3rd or the 4th dimension.

Within the greater unit of the Universe (as if a balloon) the separation of the different frequency states are called dimensions. Although we perceive the different frequency states separately when we are in the lower dimensions, they are all still essentially contained within the Whole. In this sense, there is no such thing as separation, because the frequencies of the different dimensions of the Universe are all still contained within the same unit (the balloon) and the same space. The frequency of all the dimensions, no matter which one we refer to, are closer to Universal energy than they are to the frequency of 'nothingness'. This is why they remain part of the Universe.

The greater the difference between the frequencies of 'nothingness' and the frequency of Oneness, the less chance there will be of any part of the Oneness that is contained within the Universe 'falling' back into 'nothingness'. That is why, once resonating with the frequencies of the 3rd dimension after the Fall of Atlantis and of Man since we dropped from the 5th dimension, we were in a very precarious place from a frequency (or density or electrical potential/voltage) perspective.

293

'Downwards' in frequency after the 3rd dimension, there is just undifferentiated 'nothingness'. We, as this little portion of the Universe called Earth have, literally, been on the verge of complete annihilation - and most human beings are not even aware of this shocking reality!

Many people believe, as taught, that soul never dies - no matter what. However, although the energy of a dissolved soul remains as a low frequency bit of energy, such as a sound of sorts, in the void, once it has devolved to this level it cannot be called conscious, or a soul presence. Inasmuch as consciousness ceases to exist in this manner, soul can indeed 'die'. Fortunately, as long as we seek the higher experience in all areas of our lives, the more we resonate with the high frequency parts of our DNA and the more we are motivated to seek ever more ordered and therefore, higher consciousness, states of being. Consciousness uplifts continually and this action is inspired by the smallest amount of Light.

The circumstances of the 'fall' in terms of the frequency of the Earth may be seen as similar to the experience of Alice, in Lewis Carroll's book 'Alice in Wonderland'. After she nibbled on a mushroom she found herself getting smaller and smaller and then falling down through the rabbit hole. For her, reality assumed weird, wonderful and scary proportions in the resultant distortion of her world. It was no different for us as we 'fell' downwards in frequency through the wormhole into resonance with the 3rd dimension. The few who survived were forced instantly downwards in frequency by the energy divisive, ultra-potent destructive frequencies of the Atlantean Era nuclear blasts. Earth came perilously close to being reduced to a series of dots and squiggles in the sea of 'nothingness'. The only other time this amount and type of massive, destructive energy has been unleashed on Earth was at the end of the Dinosaur Age, when meteorites hit the planet. As an aside, that event was not random. It occurred as a result of the knock-on effects of the degenerated frequencies that the behaviour of the Dinosaur consciousness created.

    The only difference between Alice's experiences as she walked around down the rabbit hole and our own current experiences down at the bottom of the wormhole is that we have become so accustomed to our weird experiences in the 3rd and 4th dimensions of reality that we now view them as normal! They are not. In fact, they are upside down. The interesting thing to consider is that in order to get back up again, Alice nibbled on the *opposite* side of the mushroom that got her into trouble in the first place. We need to consider doing things very differently to the manner in which we have done them to date. This is aptly noted by the saying, 'If you do what you always do, you get what you always get'. The upliftment of our consciousness requires that we do things differently. This is bound to include opening our minds up to concepts that we have never considered before.

The various children's tales and movies for grown-ups are remarkable for the manner in which they extend metaphors in order to describe some of the truths of the Universe. Some of the authors of the more unusual stories are said to have used mind-altering substances when they penned their tomes, but no matter what process the authors used to extract or create this information, the stories they tell are often interestingly valid when compared to shifted dimension experiences.

Drugs have been used since time immemorial to achieve instant shifts in dimension - even though this is a highly inadvisable and potentially dangerous way to achieve an altered state of consciousness. The human body responds far better to being tweaked and coaxed back up to higher frequency states of unconditional love than to being catapulted there in one 'hit' and potentially collapsing in a state of shock in the process. In this regard meditation, chakra clearing, aligning and energising, being mindful of one's thoughts, eating fresh, high frequency foods and judiciously using natural medicinal and herbal substances will yield a more stable result than a drug-induced 'high' ever will in the dimension shifting process.

Knowing that we are never truly stuck or trapped and that we can shift dimension makes justifying any resistance, doubt or fear of the movement forwards into living ascension, back up a wormhole, as nonsensical as Alice believing and arguing that her rabbit-hole experience was her only reality. She knew she was in a nightmarish state - just as we are. Resistance to going forwards, which we need to do in order to transcend this frightening experience of feeling disconnected from our Bliss, is merely apprehension at the prospect of the unknown, or of change, and may be classed as prejudice. Like any form of prejudice, this non-objective belief state is fostered and maintained by poor information, lack of experience and insufficient knowledge. As we uplift our consciousness we relieve ourselves of the limitations of prejudice.

Everlasting Life and High Frequency Vibrations
We have forgotten who we really are. We are souls of wondrous Light having a human experience in dense physicality. If we continue to behave as soul-less humans in the 3rd or 4th dimensions of physicality we will continue on the human reincarnation cycle of lives, on the Wheel of Karma - down the wormhole in dense physical reality. If we acknowledge ourselves as souls in human form and our actions, thoughts and feelings are in line with our Divine soul purpose, we will reclaim the fullness of ourselves and our real lives and thus experience life everlasting. Soul existence, in the higher dimensions, is everlasting. Although this can be achieved from the state of Spirit, after death, if sufficient Earth work is done during each lifetime, it makes more sense to speed up this process from the human position. This infinite existence is achieved from the physical perspective by integrating the

human and the soul experiences into one reality. The only way to do this is to begin to work from the, *"Energy centre of the heart,"* as Osiris puts it. This involves the employment of the high frequencies of unconditional love in order to achieve the transmutation of the physical form and the transcendence of the limitations of matter, which both Osiris and Thoth speak of.

Osiris reminds us of our inherent connection to the Light which our genetic inheritance endows us with, as souls in a human form, in this excerpt from a meditation in December 2008. Unequivocally, the link to our ancient selves, our current selves and our future selves through reclaiming more of our soul-Light and grounding it into our physical body, is made through the feeling of unconditional love in the heart.

Osiris: Humans - Beings of Great Light

"Through the connectedness of the Light presence, so it is you begin to see before you, the presence of the self. You begin to see before you the Being that you are, Beloved Ones. As you see before you the Being that has come forward from inception to experience many, many lifetimes: the outer planetary connectivities to the Earthly experiences, to the experiences in Spirit.

"As you see before you the self, as you begin to feel before you unconditional love, the connectedness of an ancientness, the Light Being, the presence of connectedness to the Godhead. As you feel yourselves in the experience of acknowledgement, to release all doubt, in the silence, in the stillness of the connectedness of unconditional love, of the feeling-state of the heart. As you are in this moment - pure Bliss and pure love, pure experience of connectedness, of Angelic presence, a Being of great ability, a Being of great presence of Light - in love to feel it."

> Unconditional love is the highest possible energy source
> which powers up the processes of transmutation.

The process of accessing greater Light, or attaining living ascension, is not some kind of a fantasy, in-your-head, airy-fairy ideal. Rather it is an actual, physical process which is activated from within the person and enhanced by other energies outside of the self. It is true to state that all the original portals (power-points or wormholes) still exist on the Earth, but it is also necessary to know that although these were created by the Light Beings in very ancient times they are still potentially energetically intact - to one degree or another. These can be re-activated, powered up and enhanced by the work of humanity at any time, and used by us to enhance our energy's progress.

Effectively, the concepts surrounding the processes and structures of living ascension were developed, activated and taught by Thoth when he was physically resident on Earth - during Atlantean and Ancient Egyptian times. It is this ascension process which is referred to as attaining 'life everlasting' by both Thoth and Osiris, because it means that fully conscious physical life can be extended to continue over vast periods of time - by enhancing the physical body with more of the soul energy of the higher dimensions. The means for achieving this begin with the upliftment of consciousness.

'Ageless' and 'everlasting' was the nature of many of the physical bodies of the 5th dimension ancients. Being as 'old as Methuselah' is not an exaggeration. It was in order to maintain the physical body on Earth and to shift it into a state of living ascension that was part of the important knowledge which was taught at the mystery schools of the ancients. Those adepts from Isis' Mystery School of Light in ancient Egypt were taught how to use what she refers to as *"The Magic of the Light."* It is this precious information that Isis is beginning to release to humanity once more for the purposes of manifestation and healing. The details of some of her Mystery School lessons are recorded in the forthcoming books under Isis' name, by the same authors. Learning to make use of this powerful, spiritual knowledge allows us to move rapidly to higher frequency states, create our own miracles and re-endow ourselves and Earth with Divinity in the process. The lessons from Isis began after the working group had a good understanding of the basic living ascension lessons from Osiris, as detailed in this book.

When it is in a high frequency state or when it seeks higher frequency states, the Light of soul is potentially ever-lasting. It is the development of more of this Light within our physical bodies that ensures our human potential for everlasting-ness too. Developing a greater awareness of this high frequency Light connects us, as physical human beings, to the full conscious state of who we really are. The feeling of unconditional love creates more Light within us, because the state of being of pure love resonates with the highest frequencies of all - super-luminal, Universal Light. We are powerful beyond our wildest dreams and it is time to realise that potential.

In a December 2008 meditation, Osiris told us that as we reconnect to more of our soul-selves, with the expanding consciousness of living ascension we begin to wonder exactly who we really are. He speaks of the transmutation processes which are possible from the basis of unconditional love. In this process we begin to realise the enormity of what he says in the sentence below.

"I am that I am. I am the presence of great Light."

Osiris: I Am

"In the acknowledgement as you begin to re-connect, as you begin to re-connect, Beloved Ones, as you begin to feel yourself in the questioning: "Who is it I am?" As you begin to feel the re-connectivity, the love of re-connection and re-entry to the self.

"There is, through the feeling-state of acknowledgement of unconditional love, of re-connection, transmutation of that which takes place within the self. The question is felt, Beloved Ones: *"I am that I am. I am the presence of great Light."*

"As you feel yourself in communication in the feeling-state within the self and the Light presence of Spirit, of Divinity, of connectivity to the Godhead. As you feel it, Beloved Ones, as it is repeated within your heart, through Bliss and unconditional love of understanding of being as one.

"Beloved Ones, as you feel the re-connectivity to the self, it is on this day I wish to bring forward the presence to surround you with much love from Spirit in the continuation of procedures of integration. You are carried in the continuation. It is as you feel yourselves as the Angelic presence to be carried forward at all times, in Bliss and in Light, Beloved Ones, and in love. I bless you on this day, Beloved Ones."

Everlasting Life
From the human perspective, everlasting life is defined as being able to physically live either in a single body on Earth for extended periods of time like the Atlanteans did, or to live on Earth from one lifetime to the next in different bodies like many other Atlanteans did, but remaining fully conscious throughout. Considering that the Atlanteans lived for a minimum of 3 600 years we can make more sense of the stories of very old people on Earth. The potential for creating the possibility of living an everlasting life is brought closer and closer when we resonate with ever higher frequencies of Light.

Some people may comment that they would not like to live in the same human body for such a long time, but this is usually because they do not realise that extended life spans are only possible if the immune system is functioning at its peak and the person is fully capable of co-creating everything that is desired on Earth. Therefore, the art of manifestation is decisively important when considering the concept of a healthy, energetic human body which is well-suited to everlasting life.

The link between everlasting life and high frequencies of Light is a critically important concept for us to understand. It imparts greater clarity about the concept of Heaven and the hereafter than we may have had to date. The notion of Heaven is one which has become distorted by misinformation over a lengthy period. Heaven was (and still is) a higher frequency place that actually exists and that beings can go to - either after physical death or during inter-dimensional travel. When the Ancients referred to Heaven they were talking about an actual star: Antares. From Earth's perspective in the 3rd or 4th dimensions, travel to Antares or any other high frequency star which may qualify as a heavenly place, requires that an individual's physical vibrations are high enough in order to both tolerate and access that realm. From Earth this means that an individual maintains the frequency of his body and soul, while humanly alive, in a sufficiently high state in order for his soul to be able to shift to the 5th dimension, or higher, at death. The same rule of maintaining higher frequency vibrations applies to the person who travels inter-dimensionally in his ascended, physical body.

The ideal of living ascension was taught and subscribed to by many people from very ancient times, even to the extent that they kept their material possessions intact in case they needed them. Although somewhat distorted in our understanding, an example of this are the Egyptian afterlife stories, where human beings take themselves, body and soul, back to the higher dimensions of reality after death. We now know that we are able to achieve the higher frequency state of living ascension *before* death. Interestingly, the reason that dismemberment was meted out as a punishment in times gone by, was to prevent the possibility of physical, living ascension. Humans and other beings in the lower frequency thinking states became confused about the true processes and reasons for living ascension and they were not satisfied to cause only the death of the human body. They wanted to ensure that the soul could not possibly ever inhabit it again and live the joy of everlasting life in that physical body. When dismembered and the parts scattered around, this effectively scuppers any plans for the use of that particular body again. The first recorded story of this type of event begins with the ancient Egyptian drama of Osiris' dismemberment by his wicked brother Set.

We begin to achieve prolonged Earthly existence by physically shifting our vibrations to higher frequencies. This automatically makes the vessel of our physical body more capable of resonating with more higher frequency Light. It is this which reconnects us to more of our soul presence, which is the higher frequency Light of our (currently) non-material Higher Self which is currently resident in the 5th dimension.

The most obvious physical reason why life is dramatically extended into 'everlasting-ness' when we resonate with 5th dimension frequencies while on Earth, is because these higher frequency vibrations ensure better physical health at the level of the DNA. More portions of the DNA are literally vibrated back into operation as they become physically enlightened - specifically the 13th strand. This reduces the amount of dormant, or uncoded, areas which are presently within our DNA and which, unbelievably, are sometimes incorrectly labelled as 'junk DNA'. Adding to our potential of longevity is the physical reality that low frequency bacteria and viruses cannot exist under high frequency conditions within the body. Similarly, the unrestrained and disordered cell proliferation that creates tumours cannot occur under high frequency conditions. It is no wonder that laughter therapy has been recorded as an effective cure for cancer.

The result of attaining the physical state of the frequency of ascension is that we progressively develop better opportunities to experience life in any form we choose, anywhere in the Cosmos - relative to our developed resonance. Existing in the living state of ascension on Earth means, by definition, that we have released our low frequency Earth Karma and connections and are, therefore, no longer bound to the reincarnation cycle of lives in the 3rd or the 4th dimensions of illusionary reality.

For us on Earth, the attainment of living ascension, beginning in the 5th dimension, is the first step we take in freeing ourselves to move elsewhere in the Universe. This amounts to physically shifting from the level of spiritual blindness, or separation from Divinity, which the lower frequencies of the physical realms in the 3rd and 4th dimensions create. In so doing we expand ourselves and become openly receptive to the experiences of the higher frequency realms which are in open communication with the state of being of the Godhead. Once free in this manner, the opportunities for growth and different variations of life become endless. Therein lies the secret of everlasting life.

In ancient times, the wormhole systems, or higher frequency zones, assisted with the processes of developing and maintaining the frequencies which support everlasting life, because they provided the easy opportunity for the following:
- Accessing the high frequency vibrations which are necessary for living ascension.
- Rejuvenation of the physical body.
- Initiations to higher frequency levels of knowledge through communication with the heavenly realms.
- Healing of the physical body by shifting its frequencies higher.

- Easy physical movement of the god-beings to and from Earth through energy spirals or highways.
- Communication with Home while on Earth, maintaining the open connection in and out.

Originally, the wormhole systems, or star gateways, were perfectly open and maintained in a super-charged state. Although some may now require a bit of clearing and rejuvenation after being sullied by low frequency vibrations from the surroundings, they are still potent tools to use in the quest for everlasting life. Anything that shifts the body's vibration to a higher frequency will have an anti-ageing effect upon it. Some vibration-shifting tools are more efficient than others, but many of them are accessible to all people, such as meditation, eating healthily, using high frequency products and acting with love. Thoth's North-South anti-ageing technique which he details in the Emerald Tablets is a highly effective way to increase the vibrations in the body in the manner that is beneficial to it.

The Reality of Shifting Dimension
The critical 100 year, spiritually important, central period of the Age of Aquarius ensures Earth is correctly positioned, in terms of its position in the Cosmos, to receive high frequency input from the perfectly aligned outer-planetary bodies. Their energy spirals down towards us and we are fortunate to be able to respond to it.

The high energy time of the midpoint is why, in the clay tablets texts as well as in Ancient Egyptian texts, there was so much discussion and reference to the various Ages. They were similar to the plentiful modern-day references to the Age of Aquarius. Then, as now, humanity was provided with the stellar opportunity to access great Light of Being - so that we could take the opportunity to return to a genuine, non-deluded reality and experience the Light of Oneness again. In the present day however, as compared to those ancient times, we are more likely to shift into the higher frequency state of living ascension, because humanity has developed a more advanced state of consciousness over the ensuing years. This is why it is stated by Osiris that Earth and humanity are now functioning at the level of the 4th dimension frequencies. We have shifted to a higher level, vibrationally speaking, and this means that the 5th dimension realms are easily within our reach now.

In the following communication Osiris answers some questions about the relevance of the Age of the Bull relative to the powerful energies that abound in the central position of an Age. He confirms that the central position of an Age is a time which is extremely profound to the extent that it energetically supports the ascension process. He also speaks of the Siriun Pathway of Ascension which most human beings follow. Not only is our energy pathway of ascension, or Return

Home, the same pathway that Sirius took in the process of its own ascension aeons ago, but the Sirius communication connection is the one which is most often chosen by souls. We follow that line of energy from the Earthly perspective, even if our Monad origin is not Siriun, because this is an easy pathway towards the Godhead. Our choice to follow the Siriun pathway is why communication from the Siriun Light Beings is maintained.

Osiris: The Central Position of the Age

Q: Does the central position of this Age of Aquarius have a similar theme to the central position of the Age of Taurus. Are the two related?
"Beloved One, it is interconnected Beloved One. It is through this pathway at this time, the connection taking place with many of yourselves. It is I wish to bring forward this information at this time. There is the pathway of the working that is the furtherance of continuation from the ascension procedure. It is for many of yourselves, I have stated on earlier occasion, there is the desire to move forward through the work that is intended through the continuation with Spirit. It is to understand that for many of yourselves it is in the collective to choose from soul experience and soul communication with each of yourselves to move forward through the pathway to Sirius. It is the understanding of this pathway of ascension that is chosen by many and it is in this manner there is the continuation of communication from this perspective."

Q: Do the majority of people choose the Siriun pathway?
"It is majority of beings, Beloved One, it is not all beings but it is to understand it is majority. Beloved One, it is the understanding this pathway of the connectivity with the moving forward to the connection of the Godhead. The further and further that you find yourselves working and moving in the areas of Earthwork and the continuation of the various pathway, so it is this pathway of the connection within this ashram, Beloved One, that is supportive at this time."

Q: Is this pathway related to you, Osiris?
"It is, Beloved One. It is so, Beloved One, it is in connection. I do support all beings, with greater intensity in this pathway forward. It is the understanding from the position of ascension, so it is moving forward into the experience of the working within Solar environment with the connection to the various beings in various direction, that it is to understand this pathway is that of the continuation through procedures of the connection to the Godhead.'

Q: Osiris what has that got to do with issues of the Age of the Bull?
"It is the connection of the coming forward of communication in this field, Beloved One."

Q: Is this reference to the bull directly related to the name Osiris?
"It is the understanding that it is brought forward at same period of the coming forward into humanity into the Earthly experience - it has been through position of the bull, Beloved One.

Q: In 2037 BC?
"It is so."

Q: That was the time of the return of the god-beings to Earth in Ancient Egypt?
"It is so."

Q: Was this related to the choice humanity had at that time to choose the pathway of spirituality in physicality? Was that an issue at that time?
"It is the understanding of the coming forward through the connectivity to the Earthly experience, understanding there is the understanding of the position of Apis-Osiris. It is through the bull - of the experience of coming forward in this manner. It is, therefore, this name that has come forward. It is this period, Beloved One."

Q: What was the importance of that time of the central position of the Age of the Bull?
"It is to understand there is the central position that is of greater intensity. It is this understanding, Beloved One. It is for this reason the connection and the pathway forward through procedures of ascension are of great intention at this time, and the moving forward through this position it is for each of yourselves a pathway of great enLightenment. Of the moving forward it is time-frame that is extremely beneficial and extremely profound."

Q: Does that apply to this period now?
"It is over this entire period Beloved One, it is extremely supportive in the completion of this procedure."

The illusion which we call reality and which we 'slid' into down at the bottom of the wormhole, into the experience of our solidly physical world, is not completely real in terms of the Universal experience. It is no less an illusion than Alice's world-down-the-rabbit-hole was. There is another, more expanded reality 'up there' where we came from, but we need to complete this procedure of being in the lower dimensions, just as Osiris has stated. We initially slid down the wormhole to the 3rd dimension as if on a long, fast slide until we landed with a hard bump on our posteriors, and found out with a rude shock, what hard, dense physical reality with no balancing spiritual connection, feels like. This was, and remains, the process of the densification of Light into physical matter - matter which we call our bodies and the stuff of our world. That is not to say that the physical body experience is not a wonderfully joyous one, but without its balancing connection to the realms of the Godhead, this joy tends to be negatively tinged. The original intention for Earth inhabitation was that we live here on this beautiful and bountiful planet, experience the immense joy of physicality and advance ourselves and Earth in the process. Anything that deviates, or has caused our deviation, from that has to be corrected.

Regardless of how the shift from the 5th to the 3rd dimension occurred, the physical body experience need not be denigrated as a completely bad thing - unless we remain separated from the Light of our souls and are tricked into believing this is all there is. In the lower dimensions, the physical experience becomes fraught with pain and suffering, as we know so well, and it is then that we tend to over-emphasize the importance of the joys and pleasures of the material world. This illusion supports the imagined idea that this is all there is.

With the limitation of one, finite lifetime in mind, there is no wonder that some people have no compunction about grabbing all they can. However, instead of the joy they intend to create for themselves, this low frequency style of living results in the exact opposite. Once the fleeting joy of acquisition and victory passes, the emptiness within re-emerges and the pain of the soul, separated from its Light, is felt once more.

Separated from the Light of the Godhead, which can be openly experienced from the beginning stages of higher frequency existence in the 5th dimension and onwards, physical life in the 3rd or 4th dimensions is potentially a place of great darkness. This means that it will include the possibility of immense anguish.

Suffering is brought about by what are referred to as the negative ego states, or the lower frequencies of Light, and human beings struggle to avoid these negative emotions, thoughts and behaviours when they resonate with the lower dimensions. While in the 4th dimension we cannot avoid resonating with the 3rd as well as the 5th dimensions, because it is these two dimensions which are within our perceptual range. As we raise our resonance to the 5th dimension we will no longer resonate with the 3rd dimension experiences of very low negative ego issues. In the 5th dimension we will naturally resonate with 4th and 6th dimension experiences. As we progress through the higher stages of the 5th dimension, the 4th dimension experiences begin to fade further and further away until such time as we shift dimension again and the 4th dimension frequencies are out of our range. The fact that we are in the 4th dimension tells us that we need to raise our resonance in order to have a more complete life which includes an open connection to the Godhead. This begins in the 5th dimension.

We are prone to our negative state of consciousness in the lower dimensions, because we lost our conscious memory of Light and the veil descended upon us when we fell down the wormhole in the shifted dimension experience. However, we do still have the higher frequency potential because of our DNA origin and structure. The collective consciousness of humanity is always inadvertently stimulated with the frequencies of every human being, because, as a species, we all contribute to this energy system. We all continue to be re-stimulated by this energy, as it flows back and forth in a never-ending cycle. This harmonic resonance continues uninterrupted, but changes its style when something or someone within the system shifts - such as is happening now.

Alternatively, once in the 4th dimension, we can choose to move out of resonance with the 5th dimension and shift to the lower frequency place of the 3rd dimension. This we do if we constantly choose to think, feel and act in line with the lower frequencies. The result will be the continued degeneration of our energy and the approach of the sea of 'nothingness.' This process of degenerating order and harmony is a very painful one, because it is a process of the loss of Bliss.

The higher frequencies of Light, which allow for the development and the maintenance of our super-memory, our super-senses and everlasting life, were spun out of us as we spiralled downwards through the dimensions - much like water spins out of wet towels in a spin dryer. We could view the process of shifting dimension downwards as a desiccation process, like a plump apple drying to become a far smaller version of itself. The high frequency Light of our expanded soul presence shrinks as the volume of our bodies contract and become more solid as we drop downwards and resonate with lower frequencies. We occupy a reduced space when we incarnate into dense reality, and we are immediately separated from each other too. We shrink away from each other.

This is what is responsible for both our myopic view of life and our sense of 'smallness'. The moisture which leaves the apple is not lost, but it exists elsewhere in a different form. Similarly, our 'lost' soul-Light, which we refer to as our Higher Self, is not lost to us when we are human - it is merely in a different place, in a different phase.

The God-realised Beings of Light experience their own existence in the higher dimensions in an expanded sense which encompasses the entirety of the Wholeness of Being within, and of, the Universe. It is this expanded state of being which is a presence that is everywhere at the same time. This is possible because their 'bodies' are so much greater in volume than ours are. They are expanded with Light. It is for this reason of the existence of every being within the Universe - as Light - that Osiris refers to our own potential 'expansion' into more Light states.

In the reverse process, when a soul presence incarnates onto Earth as a human being it generally does so from the approach of the 5th dimension state of being. This devolution of our energy, further out of range of the 5th dimension frequencies, to a lower dimension when we take up life on Earth, only started after the Atlantean Era nuclear explosions. This had to be the case because the explosions created the wormhole experience as the energy of the one dimension split apart and some of it degenerated, downwards in frequency.

The process of the densification of Light into matter starts when a soul presence is attracted, in keeping with its intention to return to Earth to clear its Karma, towards the open funnel of the wormhole. The vibration which is created by the intention to return to Earth allows the soul presence to move in that dimensional direction, as if pulled by a powerful magnet. The impetus of this causes the soul presence to travel instantly downwards through the wormhole and pass through the gateway, until the magnetic pull relaxes at the outer edge of the funnel and the soul comes to rest in a physical life system on the other side: born as a baby in the reality of human life on 3rd or 4th dimension Earth.

A portion of the presence of what is known of as the Higher Self in the 5th dimension becomes the soul presence in a human body. This process of incarnation can only take place if the soul intention exists for it to be so, no matter how or why it is motivated. This intention creates the vibration which is harmonically matched to and is able to resonate with the lower dimension and specific experiences there. This, as with all thoughts (intentions) is how we, as an individual consciousness, are able to project ourselves into other states of being. The mere thought to be in a certain place means we begin to project our energy to that place - even though most people are unaware of this action of energy - because the action of consciousness creates everything. Being aware of this method of projection is how the psychic skills of telepathy and manifestation begin. Bi-location (being in two places at the same time) is an advanced form of this skill.

As we, in the non-material state of soul before birth, begin to project our consciousness towards Earth in order to be born, we naturally begin to harmonically resonate with specific experiences of the 3rd or 4th dimension. This happens because our own personal vibrations as individual souls, no matter where we are, will find their Earthly match if incarnation here is what we choose for ourselves. Our vibrations as soul are directly related to the personal Karma, whether created from Earth or elsewhere, we carry with us. Obviously, the ideal is to be free of all Karma and we continue to come to Earth to support this objective, until it is cleared. This is the case for all human beings, individually and in the collective.

Therefore, when resonating with 3rd or 4th dimension frequencies, and living our 'real' human lives, we are handicapped by the lower consciousness state of these dimensions. This lowered consciousness, or state of awareness, arises from the dimension-dictated deficiency of the Light of our own Divine Intelligence within our human body, as our soul presence. This is because we only bring smaller portions of our total soul to Earth with us when we physically incarnate on Earth - as determined by our own personal vibrations, dictated by our Karma. Once incarnate on Earth we can increase the amount of our soul presence in the human body by uplifting our consciousness, but few people are aware of this possibility. This is the goal of living ascension.

Although we, as souls when not present on Earth, can certainly make progress elsewhere in the Universe, we will not be able to continue to do this all the way up to the state of being of the Godhead until our Karma from all of the lower dimensions is cleared. This is because lower frequency vibrations will create a restriction, like a drag, on the lightness of the soul matter. This is similar to being allowed to pass to the next grade at school even though we may not have passed all of our subjects from the lower grade. We would have to take extra lessons and catch up the previous year's work. At the end of the year we would be faced with two choices: pass to the next higher grade if we have caught up the work during extra lessons, or stay at that level until such time as we do. Earth is a place of lifetime lessons that allow us the opportunity to 'catch up' what we missed out on in previous lifetimes. When we complete these lessons (clear our Karma) we are free to move through to the higher dimensions, without limitation.

All of our soul presence which remains resident in the 5th dimension, as our Higher Self while we are on Earth, is available for reincorporation within our human bodies. Until such time as we manage to shift our lower frequency vibrations from ourselves, emotionally and physically, in order to allow this to happen, we (our 5th dimension parts of soul) literally watch over ourselves while we are on Earth and, along with others, we become our own Guardian Angels.

When human, we struggle to remember that even in our lesser-Light, densely physical, human bodies we are Divine Beings of Light, because we have insufficient consciousness to do so. It is because of this lack of awareness that we have become muddled up in endless, ridiculous, negative human emotions, relationships and behaviours which dictate the daily happenings and circumstances of our lives and maintain the illusion of duality. This has been going on for many lifetimes. In this way we have all played out the Karma-dictated reincarnation cycle of our personal low frequency resonance in a very long-winded fashion. This is the time we spend on the seemingly interminable Wheel of Karma, and it continues until we realise that we can shift ourselves off it - into living ascension.

We might try to consider what this means in our daily lives, most especially when we move into resistance and are determined to cling to our old ways and comforts or when faced with the pain of clearing out an old issue or pattern. This is most pertinent now as the dimension-shifting frequencies increase in intensity around us. We cling to well-worn comforts, because all humans have a tendency to resist changing from what they know, to one degree or another. Comfort may also involve avoiding the discomfort of looking at the problem areas of our lives, so avoidance behaviour is a form of resistance. Therefore, no human being may rest on his or her Light-worker laurels and no individual among us is completely immune to resistance, consciously or subconsciously, when moving forwards into the Light. To demonstrate how difficult it is to change any habit, no matter how benign it is, simply try brushing your teeth with the opposite hand to the one you would normally use. Set the intention to do this daily for two weeks. It will create difficulty and irritation long before you become used to the new way. You may even abandon the project before the end of the two weeks. This is an example of resistance and your response to change.

It would serve us well to remember that the perceived comforts of the separated human state of consciousness, in physical reality, are not part of a complete reality in terms of Universal Oneness. Separated physical reality will therefore never be able to provide us with true, complete and lasting comfort, emotionally, spiritually or physically. Any comfort here will be fleeting in the same way that believing that the illusion of 3rd or 4th dimension is the only reality, is transient. As soon as we pop back up through a wormhole and pass through the gateway into the understanding of what open reality in the Light of Oneness really is, we will see this. We can do this from where we are right now, even if it is just for a moment.

These may just be words to a lot of people, but the experience of a shifted dimension, even if it *is* just for that one moment, is worth seeking - and, incredibly, we all do this, often - as is evidenced by Osiris' answer.

Osiris: Many have Shifted Dimension Experiences

Q: Osiris I was thinking about this splitting in and out of reality which I now know is the feeling of a shifted consciousness, and I realised that many people have experienced this all their lives, but may have mistaken it for low blood pressure or some other physical ailment. Is that correct?
"It is, Beloved One, it is many beings that experience this on many, many occasion."

Moving through the Wormhole
The momentary experience of shifting in and out of the different dimensions once we are in the outer, or upper, frequency portions of the 4th dimension occurs because we resonate with frequency of the rim of the funnel of a wormhole. The Universal Law of Resonance dictates this. Initially, we slip in and out of the altered frequency state and feel as if we are popping into a wormhole system on occasion only. In time these experiences become more profound as we shift our vibrations to resonate with the higher frequencies of Light. These shifts in dimension are very easily experienced in a meditation.

As we uplift our consciousness and become Lighter we can, literally and physically, move back up a wormhole again, taking with us our illusory world. The physical 'realities' we once called our lives collapse, expand and reintegrate once more with higher frequency states of Light.

Although we hover physically for a while on the rim of the wormhole, or on the first step of the staircase up towards a frequency gateway, once Light enough from the high frequency vibrations which sufficient unconditional love within us creates, we can easily spiral up that wormhole and pop out on the other side. Then we can begin to be in open communication with the beginning stages of the consciousness of the Godhead once more. This movement is the spiralling energy of ascension which Thoth refers to, and which is so easily experienced in the most powerful gateway on Earth, the Great Pyramid. Presently, although the experiences within it are very pleasant and wonderful, we don't have to rely only on the Great Pyramid to access a wormhole experience, because the entire planet is accessing high frequency movement opportunities into the shifted dimension experience courtesy of the super-alignment of Earth with outer-planetary bodies of high frequency Light. When this happens the gateway of the Great Pyramid receives even more powerful energies which further assist this process by stimulating the entire grid of Earth. Additionally, there are many wormhole systems in place all over the globe and within us which assist us to resonate with higher frequencies.

The most important wormhole is the one of our own consciousness, because this is our own personal Eye of Horus.

Wormholes, or frequency gateways, are not just places which are found at the power points, because they are states of existence, a state of consciousness. It is our individual state of consciousness which creates the ascension frequency within a person. Clearly, a wormhole system exists as a potential within every single human being. When we realise once again that we are all One, we will see that there is only one wormhole and accessing it begins from within ourselves. As long as we see ourselves as individuals, the wormhole experience will be a series of different wormhole options in the inner and the outer world.

Regardless of the merits of the subjective or objective wormhole experiences, accessing these wormholes, or frequency gateway, opportunities occurs more easily now in the Universal and in the personal context. This is due to the alignment of Earth with other high frequency planets and stars. Earth is moving into position so as to align with the central position of the galaxy and this means that the Milky Way itself is shifting vibrationally within the Universe. From the perspective of Earth we can see this movement by the position of the solstice Sun as it moves into alignment with the galactic centre. This is a very important alignment of energies for Earth.

From a logical point of view, wondering what it feels like on the other side of a wormhole may seem rather pointless, because we have spent so much time where we are that we have forgotten that anything else exists - much the same as Alice could never really have understood her future experience prior to going down the rabbit hole. Just like us, it also took her rather a long time to work out how to get back up again and this she did only after she had endured some terrifying experiences. When we re-access more of the Bliss of high frequency Light, we will certainly know things are different in our lives. This is why we begin to realise that something different is happening. When we are functioning within the fullness of 5th dimension reality we will know we are there. Experiencing the beginning stages of the altered dimension experience is why many people are beginning to question what it is that is going on in their lives, the world and spiritually. These are the effects of the wave of changing consciousness which are noticed by all of us.

We regularly have altered dimension experiences when we sleep and when we meditate and because of this, the fact that we are never completely divorced from the high frequency realms is positively entrenched. Some dreams are certainly for the purpose of ordering and regulating the processes of the psyche in order to maintain, human psychological health. Other dream states are more meaningful and profound because consciousness accesses the soul realms and it is these experiences which are sometimes referred to as 'lucid dreaming'. It is during periods of lucid dreaming that deep understandings may develop, the future may be 'foretold' or we may connect with a dead relative. Osiris suggests that during this type of dream we are able to actively participate in it and get more information. In the waking state, the beginning stages of the experience of shifting into higher frequency states of Light amount to what we know of as psychic experiences. All of these different experiences are the actual, altered dimension experiences of an expanded consciousness - which Osiris discusses further with us.

Osiris: Lucid Dreaming

Q: Are the elaborate and detailed dreams many people have related to inner child healing?

"It is, Beloved One, it is not only in this manner, Beloved One, but it is also for many of yourselves perhaps moving forward through many dream-state at this time. It is the enhancement of the dream-state taking place at this time. If it is you move into the dream-state, there is the clarity of the lucid state of dreaming, and it is from this perspective also to understand, it is the out-of-body experience, through the connection with Beings working in communication with yourselves. It is this taking place over lengthy period. From the lucid dream you have the ability to move into the connectedness with dream in order to question further or to allow for the unfoldment to take place further."

Aside from having more profound dreams, we will have more and more psychic moments as our consciousness uplifts and opens further. If we need any form of reassurance that we are making progress on the pathway of living ascension, we need look no further than the development of our human senses of perception into multi-faceted, multi-functional super-senses. This psychic development indicates there is an underlying shift in the vibratory energy system of the body as it expands and causes our experiences of reality to change and transmute. This is a subtle process which a person often initially doubts the existence of, often saying, "I'm not quite sure, but I think that maybe...." Everything becomes more obvious when the new sensitivity is at the point where it can be used with ease in our daily lives. With regular use and by employing more high frequency unconditional love-based thoughts, feelings and actions in our lives, this sharpened intuition, or psychic sensitivity, develops still further, until we may consider ourselves to be living in the 5th dimension mode of what was standard awareness for the Ancient Atlanteans. Then we will be skilled once more in ways we only dream of at the moment.

It must be stressed that we make rapid progress into the realms of higher frequency Light by thinking, doing and feeling high frequency thoughts, behaviours and emotions which are in keeping with unconditional love. High frequency vibrations are created with joy, love, laughter, happiness, kindness, compassion and peace. It is these actions of being which will release us from the illusion of the trap, and the trappings, of our dense illusory 'reality' in the 3rd or 4th dimensions and allow us to live the Bliss of our soul-Light, our True Reality - the Reality of Oneness.

Temples of Light
Our galaxy, the Milky Way, is mirrored by the River Nile on Earth. The Nile is our physical, on-Earth view of this Celestial River of Consciousness. From this we can appreciate more fully the importance of the placement of Temples and Pyramid structures along its course and in the surrounds. These massive stone structures will always highlight Earth's alignments with certain stars at certain times, especially Orion. They provide us with a heavenly view, on Earth. This gives us a better understanding of one version of the, "*As above so below*," concept about which Osiris has spoken to us. The importance of the alignments of the high frequency planets and stars with Earth is relative to their ability to easily stream high frequency Light towards Earth. The structures of the temples themselves are formed in such a manner that they harness the high frequency Light from the stars or planets they are aligned with and physically anchor it into the ground of Earth.

This high frequency assistance supports humanity with uplifting the collective consciousness. We can be negatively affected by planets and stars of lower Light too when they align with Earth in a particular fashion. Mars is one such example, because of is current low frequency status. Mars was once a planet that supported life, but the inhabitants destroyed her, just as we are in danger of doing to Earth. When Mercury's orbit is retrograde, we experience system breakdowns, especially those related to communication, especially electronic communication. We can appreciate that all of the heavenly bodies have an influence on Earth, one way or another, during the course of their movements across the sky. The fact that specific receiver-structures were constructed to harness this energy from specific stars alerts us to consider exactly which of these are important and why. The consistent alignment of various ancient structures with Orion suggests more than just a passing interest in that star system.

The Temples and Pyramid structures all have receiver systems in place which assist with receiving and grounding high frequency Light. The fact that the pyramids are physical structures in the shape of the sacred geometric shape of incoming Light could give us pause for thought. The shape of a pyramid will naturally harness Light through its point, slow it down through its widening body and deliver it gently into the Earth through its broad base. The same applies to every single mountain peak, mound of sand or pyramid-shaped mineral - including those within our own bodies.

The transmission of Light from Earth out to the outer-planetary areas works through the Great Pyramid, because it has an etheric, upside down, pyramid superimposed upon it at its point. Additionally another upside down pyramid is superimposed over it. This star tetrahedron formation is continued in a long, interconnected chain all the way up to Sirius. In this way the Great Pyramid structure is a transmitter as well as receiver system of Light.

The massive pillars in the ancient Egyptian Temples, such as the ones in the Hypostyle Hall in the Temple of Karnak in Luxor, Egypt, work in a similar fashion to the Great Pyramid. However, their receiver and transmitter structures are shaped as open flowers, whether lotus or papyrus, at the top of the enormous pillars. Egyptologists still wonder about the meaning behind the obvious male and female look of these pillars. The receivers and transmitters in this hall of pillars are split up into receivers (female pillars) and transmitters (male pillars). These forests of pillars continue grounding high frequency Light into the Earth, just as every pyramid structure and other pillar structures do. We, as human beings, do so too. Osiris reminds us of this when he suggests we view ourselves as these ancient pillars, grounding the consciousness of the stars onto Earth and remembering what we are here for.

In an August 2008 meditation Osiris gave us further understanding about the role of the pillars of the temples in Egypt such as in the Temple of Karnak.

Osiris: Pillars of Light in the Temple of Karnak

"The understanding that as you begin to find yourselves in connectivity of area and environment of position in Ancient Egypt of the temple. It is, Beloved Ones, to know and understand through this pathway at this time, you begin to access in the knowledge of that through intent and that which has been created at this time. In the ability to shift this procedure, it is the moving forward through the dimensional experience of the living state of ascension. It is the understanding that it is through this pathway at this time, you have the ability to acknowledge and access that which has been intended through the many aspect of the pathway forward.

"Move into the experience of the drifting into connectedness of this ancient area, the ancient pillars. It is the understanding of the connection to Earth of that which takes place through own being of form: the understanding of the connectedness of physicality. It is through the experience of limbs to the grounded-ness of the Earth, the connection of that which is cast in the experience in stone in this vast area of vibrational energy, to support yourselves at this time, in the knowledge and understanding of the ancientness of yourselves, Beloved Ones, of the understanding through your connectedness to the Earth as humanity, and through that which has been intended, that which has been brought forward. The ancient knowledge to come through the experience of consciousness, as you begin to move through the various shift in the interconnection with that which is ancient and vast area.

"It is, Beloved Ones, as you feel yourselves coming forward into the connectivity of the etheric position (*of Karnak*), allowing for the feeling state as you begin to feel yourselves, as the ancient pillar begin to come forward into the experience of great Light in this particular area of the etheric. So it is at this time you have the ability to feel the presence of Thoth. You have the ability in communication, to come forward from Tehudi. It is from the experience of great Light to move and blend with the connection.

"It is at this time as you find yourself in the vibratory energy of that which you connect to the star system - the vibrational experience of the star - to that which takes place of within: the connection of the Light energy within and through the heartbeat of the self. As you begin to feel yourself in the connectivity - it is almost of the moving into the heartbeat of the skies of the heavens - begin to feel yourselves in connectivity to the star system.

"And in the connectivity at this time, as you begin to move forward through the feeling state, it is procedure that you begin to feel the communication, the activation to begin. It is the energy of the pillars of wisdom beginning to form: pillars to form, pillars of Light beginning to form - surrounding you. You begin to feel yourself in the communication and connectivity of your Light.

"As you come forward in the pathways, the Being of Light begins to take you forward. Through the opening and the development further of the greater pillars of wisdom, these you begin to feel yourself moving forward through the truth of consciousness of your being, as you move into the experience of the connectedness as Children of Light - through the pathway and into the consciousness, the connection to star system.

"Presence of great Light coming forward, allowing yourselves to move into the experience further. And so you move together in the blending of support and assistance, allowing for the opening further - it is of the crown centre at this time. Through connectivity with the Presence of Light, all the information to come forward through the feeling state of the presence of consciousness. Letting go of the feeling state of the human form at this time, to move into the experience entirely of the opening to great knowledge and the experience of the shift in consciousness through dimension, into the connectedness of your Light, your Divinity.

"With the understanding of that which is coming forward through connectedness of consciousness of the star system, with the understanding through connectedness to the Earth of the Bliss of wisdom of the pillars of connectivity to the Earth, of the bringing forward of the memory of that which is intended - it is holding in the presence of this ancient position, the consciousness of humanity.

"Through the dimension of experience of connectedness of unconditional love at this time, to be supported by the presence of being over coming period through various procedures to support in the bringing forward of greater knowledge, of bringing forward of the understanding and the position of your birth in physicality at this time to that which your are at this present position in consciousness. As you begin to make the pathway though the shift - it is through dimension as the consciousness within the form begins to move - all that takes place through the movement of physicality, the workings of the physical body, as you move into the experience of greater Light. Through decision and intent at this time of the bringing forward of all that has been intended through the connectivity, as you move and blend as one through the connection of the star system."

Studying the importance of the placement of the Ancient Egyptian temples as a science relative to incoming, outer-planetary high frequency Light, rather than as just some obscure metaphysical concept, would give us a massive amount of information about numerous things, not least of which is our outer-planetary ancestry. Our enhanced understanding would help us with the dimension shifting processes, which outer-planetary beings came to Earth at various times - such as the Pleiadians into Ancient Peru and the Nibiru-ites and the Siriuns into Ancient Atlantis and Ancient Egypt - and exactly how all the various processes of re-accessing the greater state of soul work. Humanity as a group may then re-ignite their passion for the ancient sacred sites around the world, appreciating them as the gateways to shifted dimension experiences which they are. In so doing, we would keep them powered up with ultra-high frequency Light and enhance the entire Earth experience. We would then easily appreciate ourselves as souls and flow more easily on the pathway of soul, while human.

Egyptian Throwbacks of Power and Control
Due to the fact that our reality is shrouded with low frequency vibrations which support information manipulation and untruths, we have been unable to form the full picture of our complete reality: reality in a non-separated state. For this reason, it is only in a 3rd or 4th dimension reality that the low frequency states of control and manipulation, on such a large scale as Earth has seen, can occur.

We may regard some of the worst of these manipulations, relative to our modern times today, as specifically taking place since the times of Ancient Egypt when the priesthood tried to reign supreme. Any form of manipulation or control is a distortion of the original plan for the enLightenment of Earth. It was this which formed the basis of the war between the god-beings of Light and the beings of darkness on Earth. This war wages on incessantly. Knowing about it, we can change it and shift the Earth experience back onto the pathway of enLightenment. Light always triumphs.

Unknown to many people today, most of the Egyptian Pharaohs (just like many great human beings) were a series of truly spiritually royal individuals who were either a collective consciousness of many Siriun souls in the one physical body, or who were pure, outer-planetary beings from Sirius in a physical body - regardless of whether they arrived here via Nibiru or another planet. By looking at the physical body of the individual concerned we can easily determine which it was - the Siriuns had very unusually shaped heads and bodies. Akhenaten, Nefertiti and their children were the Siriun, royal family. Aside from being a Siriun on Earth, the other option for housing an enormous amount of soul presence into one individual, is as a collective of many soul portions which reincarnate into one single, individual physical body on Earth. This mode of incarnation served to enhance the spiritual power and energy of one person. Most of the spiritual greats on Earth have been a collective of soul portions in one body.

Nevertheless, no matter how powerful their soul presence was, these individuals had to be resolute in their Divine energy, against the all-too-human priesthood and other Earthly forces of control. The Pharaoh Ramses II was one such collective of souls, as was Seti I. People who are currently incarnate on Earth as ordinary humans may be an aspect/portion of a Pharaoh, for example, and they may have a strong memory of that lifetime. If any of them who inhabited the same body previously, meet up, which they often do, they are known as twin flames.

Regardless of the strong presence of the Light Beings, the politically orientated Ancient Egyptian priesthood used any and all information as their currency to purchase and retain Earthly power, in whatever manner served them best. This formed the basis of a lot of the misinformation and distorted information that was taught to human beings and which the Light Beings refer to. The manipulations of spiritual truths began in those times, got progressively worse and they have continued on until today.

It was originally intended by the Nibiru-ite god-beings that the priesthood would assist the people and the god-beings in the enLightenment process. The god-beings who arrived back on Earth after the Fall, always needed to keep themselves apart from the local populace because they were very different - physically and energetically. Interestingly, Osiris tells us that the reason that the Ancient Egyptian god-beings were depicted with bird heads for example, was because that was what they looked like! Consequently, it was wise to have certain people available to act as an interface, as if a buffer zone, between the two. However, in this position of power the priesthood quickly became corrupt and this 'elite' band of individuals took control of and distorted the teachings of Divinity for their own selfish needs. And so began the ancient misinformation processes which influenced all of our present day religious belief systems as well as the hounding and persecution of the Light Beings on Earth. It is no wonder so much of Earth and humanity's correct historical information is 'alien' to us today.

Some of the original spiritual truths of the Ancient Atlanteans were continued by the small number of individuals who survived the cataclysm and peace reigned on Earth for a long time. Furthermore, this Divine knowledge was continued and re-introduced to humanity on Earth by the returning god-beings on their arrival at the time of the Ancient Sumerian and Egyptian Eras, most notably around 2037/67BC. It is worthwhile noting at this point that the returning god-beings did not confine their activities on Earth to the Middle East alone, as is evidenced by the tales of the existence of powerful god-like beings of other lands, over a long period of time. The immortals, Viracocha and Pachamama in Peru and Quetzalcoatl in Mexico are good examples of this, as are the innumerable Hindu deities. Very simply, the god-beings were ultimately forced to move out of Egypt and they travelled to Crete and Greece. From there they spread out further afield. Many of them went to India, some stayed where they were and others returned to Egypt.

In Ancient Khem, the original intention was that the Divine knowledge which the powerful god-beings taught was to be passed down via the newly established god-being-enhanced line of kingship: the Pharaohs. These teachings were to be supported by the priesthood and at no point was it intended by the god-beings that any of these outer-planetary helpers were to be worshipped as deities, because all beings are Divine.

Positioning one individual or group of individuals above any other is a sure recipe for the misuse of power at some level. It was not a part of the original plan of enLightenment on Earth that the Forces of Darkness were to interfere in this process, any more than any form of pain and suffering was ever intended to be the human experience. We have been on a long detour, but now we are on the Pathway of Return.

Within a relatively short period of time the corruptive influence of power and greed began to be felt and the perversity of darkness held sway in the ranks of the Ancient Egyptian priesthood and some of their puppet-Pharaohs. This elite group became materially obsessed and no more interested in spirituality and ascension than many people in the political arena today. Although people in this support role to the Pharaohs might originally have begun with good intentions, they were quickly deeply attuned to power, manipulation and control - supported and coerced into this by the low frequency vibrations of Earth in the 3rd dimension.

Considering that some very high level god-beings from other, higher dimensions fell from Grace (beginning with Enlil) when they entered the dense, lower frequency resonance field of Earth when it was still as high as the 5th dimension, we can appreciate the fact that human beings are no less susceptible than any other being to low frequency vibration contamination. It is the stimulations of these vibrations which lead to low level thoughts, emotions and behaviours. This is how the patterns of the negative ego develop, unless we consciously, "*Hold your Light, Beloved Ones,*" as Osiris regularly reminds us to do. Once we know about this we more easily recognise the ancient programmes which control us from within and without, and we more readily let go of them so that we can express the true blueprint of ourselves - our Monadic Divinity - grounded on Earth.

It was onto the low frequency stage of Earth that the god-beings of Light returned *en masse* in Sumerian and early Egyptian times and it was within this society of the Land of Khem that the various Pharaohs began to pave the way of Light further. By the time the 18th Dynasty Pharaoh, Akhenaten (who was previously known as Amenhotep IV and who was also a continuation of the consciousness of the individual who was known of as Amenhotep III) took the throne he had the unenviable job of spring cleaning the spiritual practices of the people and priesthood of Egypt. He made himself awfully unpopular with the political power-mongers in the process, because he changed the system which gave them their power. He upended everything: from the religion to the city which was the political seat of power. He created tremendous political upheaval at that time. His political changes and apparent rejection of the worship of the old pantheon of gods in favour of the recognition of the Divine, life-giving energy of the Light of the Sun (the Aten), paved the way for some significant spiritual changes for human beings. Those influences continue as part of our present day religions. We can be assured that Akhenaten was never the evil Pharaoh history regularly portrays him as. Instead, he was a gentle being and a Siriun mover-and shaker of enormous Light.

In the meditation of 11 February 2009, Osiris discussed the importance of Akhenaten, then and now, relative to the spiritual information he brought forward in those ancient times (the entire transcript and an mp3 are available on the website www.stargateway.co.za). Considering that history is usually written up by the victors, the information from that time has generally been incorrectly recorded. Consequently misunderstandings arose about the teachings of this Pharaoh who Osiris has called, ".... a Divine Light Presence." In this excerpt, the communication about the misunderstandings is one of those which is best understood with a back-to-front sentence construction in mind.

Osiris: Akhenaten

"The presence to come forward of Being that has brought forward - many misunderstanding in physicality (*i.e. historically many have misunderstood his teachings*) through many writings the communication through history - the understanding of the connectivity of Being of Light to come forward from the Godhead, to move into the expansion of consciousness, that this Being supports you at this time in moving forward in this manner.

"So it is you find yourself coming to the position to connect with the Being that is Akhenaten. It is the gentleness, the experience of communication that is felt, entirely different from all understandings of that which have been brought forward by many in physicality. It is Divine Light presence, the intent to come forward with the opening of great love to each of you."

When his rule as Pharaoh became untenable politically and dangerous physically, Akhenaten and his family left Egypt and went into exile in Greece and then India. Akhenaten left first and the rest of his family followed later, surreptitiously, because they were under enormous threat. Sometime later Akhenaten tried to unsuccessfully reclaim his throne, but left instead with many of his people (the Israelites). This move is recorded in Biblical history as the Exodus of Moses out of Egypt. Moses was Akhenaten. Osiris has given us ample information about this period and a lot of those details are can also be found in the well-researched Ahmed Osman book, 'Moses and Akhenaten'.

Although there were still four more Pharaohs of the 18th dynasty to take the throne, power in Egypt essentially reverted to the priesthood after Akhenaten left. There was a brief attempt by his son, Tutankhamun, to work in conjunction with the priesthood and yet still maintain the precepts of the new religion of Atenism. Although it was supported by his extremely popular mother, Nefertiti, this unstable alliance didn't work for too long, because the authentic spiritual power that any of the Siriun family members had was too much of a threat to the priesthood. It wasn't long before the death of Tutankhamun was staged and he too left Egypt, under cover. This event marked the final exodus of the holy family from Sirius from Egypt. They all went to Greece and from there spread out to different areas, including the British Isles, Finland and India. Some of them eventually went back to Egypt.

The tomb we know of as belonging to Tutankhamun is not his. It never was. The body inside the sarcophagus is also not that of this great Siriun. Instead it is that of some poor unfortunate individual who was used as a stand-in body. Osiris confirmed all of this information and commented that Tutankhamun was, "*A being of great stature.*" Considering the small frame of the body in the tomb, it is clear that this is not Tutankhamun. All of the Siriuns were very large and tall and all of them had unusual bodies. They did not look entirely human, because they weren't.

All of this information, and more, was written onto papyri and placed inside the tomb. When it was opened by Howard Carter and his team (funded by George Herbert, 5th Earl of Carnarvon) all of these controversial documents were found and read, only to be confiscated by the authorities. These papyri are now in the Vatican vaults. Proof of the truth still exists. The discoverers of that tomb paid a high price for their achievement: their lives. Again, the fact that they were murdered was confirmed by Osiris. That unpleasant fact forces us to question why murder was necessary. What was the knowledge that the victims had that was so important that they had to die for it? Why were these documents hidden and why do they remain hidden today?

Tutankhamun was married to his sister Ankh Baen Aton and they produced four children. In the East (where he eventually ended up) Tutankhamun was known of as Issa and his wife as Maya. Akhenaten did eventually return to Egypt where he died much later, in obscurity. Tutankhamun remained in the East, teaching and spreading the Wisdom of the Godhead there. When he finally died, his body was cremated in the typical Indian way: on a funeral pyre.

It may be of interest to some people to note that the consciousness of the Godhead was represented on Earth many times over the course of history, originating with the being Enki (Enki Ptah). Aside from Thoth, there were three predominant individuals who emanated from this being and they came back to Earth again and again - sometimes in different bodies and with varying degrees of their original soul Light, but always as great god-beings. They were Osiris, Isis and Horus. As with Thoth, these immortals were known by different names and may have taken on different bodies at different times. Some examples are Akhenaten, Nefertiti and Tutankhamun. When we look at this lineage, we begin to realise the full import of the nature of the truth which is found in the communications from the Light Beings in this book.

Interestingly, the last Pharaoh of the 18th Dynasty was the non-royal military man Horemheb. As an aspect of the fallen-from-grace being Enlil, he subscribed to the principles of darkness and with him on the throne, the Siriun reign of Light was over. All was not lost though, because, after this politically difficult time of the 18th Dynasty Pharaohs, subsequent Dynasties, such as the 19th Dynasty, tried to shift the Egyptian way back onto the pathway of Light again. This next group of Pharaohs included greats such as Seti I and Ramses II. Their attempts to maintain the Light which the Divine Siriuns brought to Earth during the 18th Dynasty reign of kings, carried on for a time in Egypt.

Egyptian society started to develop ties to the Greeks and this influence became stronger over time, owing eventually to the exodus out of Egypt to Greece by Akhenaten's family. It was from Greece that the great Light Being, Alexander the Great, ventured into Egypt, fighting the War of Light. His activities are an example of how many of the great Light Beings had to revert to war at times in defence of the Light. The feats of the greatest conquerors, including King Leonidas of the Spartans, are an example of the Light Beings maintaining their presence and efforts on Earth. Participating in war was never their first choice of action, but sometimes a show of great force was necessary to prevent or rectify the presence of darkness. They often suffered enormously in the process.

The end of the Ancient Egyptian Era, under the Greek branch of the 'family' occurred in 30BC, underscored by the death of the last of the Ptolemy's to reign as an Egyptian royal, Queen Cleopatra VII. After this the Roman Era in Egypt began. According to this (30BC) Egyptian Era end point timeline, we are currently in the year 2039 and the god-beings arrived back on Earth in true-time 2037BC. If we call this current year 2009, then that time was 2067BC. Various cultural groups, other than the Egyptians, had established themselves in Egypt for a long time prior to its final demise. The death of Queen Cleopatra marked the end of the Hellenistic influence in Egypt and the Romans dominated after this. Thereafter, the Light Beings both remained on Earth and continued to come to Earth to support humans, but they no longer confined themselves to, or worked predominantly in, Egypt. We see this by studying the 'mythological' god-beings of the Ancient Greeks, Romans, the Nordic god beings and the Eastern deities. The Siriuns had not disappeared! They just re-located. Although the darkness on Earth continued, the Light has always been with us too, beckoning.

Discussing the details of the goings-on at this time of the 18th Dynasty Pharaohs' political upheavals with Osiris is both interesting and frustrating, because it is difficult to get the full picture of this extensive period of time from our current vantage point. He summed it up very succinctly when he said that there were complicated politics prevailing in Ancient Egypt at that time and trying to explain everything that happened then would be similar to us trying to explain to beings in our own, distant future what our current lives, times and political climate was like. Therefore, the Ancient Egyptian story is an enormously complex one, as is its influence on our religions, and this is why only brief references to it can be made within this book.

Discussing all things Egyptian, or Ancient Khem as the Light Beings refer to Egypt as (see the A - Z appendix at the end of the book for more information on Khem), is important, because it was these ancient times which dictated the social structures of our religious and political future: our future which we are currently living in and know of as our present times. Thoth spoke about the importance of our return to Light, both at the time of Ancient Egypt and now in modern times, and the assistance of the Light Beings in this continuing process. Importantly, he mentions that our modern-day return to the Light, at the time of the central position of the Age of Aquarius, happens without any form of destruction, unlike the violent upheavals of old. Such is the progress we have made, the degree to which humanity has uplifted their consciousness.

Thoth: Our Return to Light in Peace

"The beginnings of return of god presences to be in Ancient Khem, it has been through beginning of return of gods come forward in their Light to begin further development, to return to position of that which once was. So it continues, come to position once more. We repeat: we do come forward, many at this time, to shift the procedure to repeat once more, the presence of Light - without all destruction and difficulty for all. We move with peace and tranquillity, without the destruction. Through the consciousness that shifts always the creation of the being of humanity to go forward further, as Beings of Light. Blessings, Beloveds."

Religion's Ancient Beginnings

The god-beings Akhenaten and his queen, Nefertiti, began what may be considered to be the first, organised religion on Earth. It had to be an organised religion in order to successfully combat what had become the widespread incorrect teachings and social system of the priesthood at that time. Instead of acting as the trustworthy interface between the god-beings and the humans, they had taken control of the cult of Amun (the Godhead teachings from earlier) and the social functions which supported this - most especially practices of gifting money and goods to the gods, via the priesthood.

Amun, from Nibiru, was the 'father' of Enki and Enlil, although technically speaking the god-beings did not procreate like we do and their 'offspring' were splits of their own consciousness. As Thoth said, he was, "Called forth," to Earth, through his 'parent', Thotme. This is an odd concept for us to understand, every bit as much as we struggle with the idea of their immortality, but it is true nevertheless. The splitting of a portion of the self to create another being explains the story of an 'immaculate conception'. This type of 'virgin' birthing was exactly the way in which the god-beings birthed new individuals from themselves when necessary. This may be understood as a form of cloning of the self to create another self - so that the work of the self could be continued, either elsewhere or differently.

Therefore, although these different portions of the self stem from the original self, they are called by different names and may exhibit different personalities, depending on the work they do and where they live. In this way we can understand that the Trinity of Osiris, Isis and Horus originally stemmed from the 'father' Enki Ptah via Thoth, and that many aspects of the Trinity were also 'called forth' into life after this. Life is very different in the higher dimensions and our own limited understanding of it here in the lower dimensions should not cloud our ability to consider that things were very different on Earth in ancient times. The communications from the Light Beings help us to understand a little more about life in those days, although only the recovery of our full memory will enable us to truly appreciate that time in its fullness.

The priesthood were manipulating what was originally organised as the pure, spiritual system and maintained on Earth by the god-beings. They were misrepresenting the Divinity of this great god-being of Light, Amun, as well as the other god-beings, by insisting that people pay him allegiance, via the priesthood, with donations of all kinds. These shenanigans of the worship of the gods are part of what Osiris referred to in his opening dissertation as, "*Mis-informations.*"

Akhenaten's (himself an aspect of Osiris) new religion of Atenism could be called the Religion of Osiris as it upheld the spiritual wisdom and knowledge of the god-being Osiris, in conjunction with the rest of the Trinity which comprised the Goddess Isis and their son Horus. Back in ancient Egyptian times, the 'new' religion was known of as Atenism because Akhenaten taught the people to view the Aten, which was the Sun Disc, as the single object of consideration of Divine Light. From it emanated the life-giving force of Light. Knowing the importance of high frequency Light as part of the ascension process provides us with further clarity about this practice.

It was simply because people had become used to the concept of worship of something that Akhenaten encouraged reverence of this disc, but banned the worship of any being. The reverence of an object was far preferential to the worship of a series of beings or of any individual being. As Osiris has told us, it was never intended that any being be worshiped, on Earth or elsewhere. This too is a difficult concept for many people to tolerate, because we have been strongly socialised into accepting that God is a single individual that requires worship. This is not true. The only gods on Earth were those god-like beings who visited here from other planets and stars. The Source of Divinity is the state of being of the Godhead, which is contained, to a greater or lesser degree within each individual being, no matter where they come from - god-being and otherwise, including human being. The Godhead state of being is a God-realised state, a state of consciousness. Some of the visiting god-like beings were fully God-realised (like Akhenaten), but many of them were not, because they had either not ascended to this status, or they had dropped from it after their arrival on Earth.

Therefore, it was only because the general populace had become used to the practices of the worship of something that Akhenaten provided an inanimate object for them to concentrate on. This was far preferable to providing an actual being to deify. This shift of the object of worship - from the many deities to the Aten - marked the change from the polytheistic worship of many god-beings to monotheism. Unsurprisingly, this shift created anger, social upheaval and political havoc - especially amongst the newly deposed, out-of-pocket priesthood.

Funnily enough, this establishment of the Aten (or Aton), in preference to Amun, as the focus of worship was nothing more than a re-presentation, or reformatting, of the spiritual practices of acknowledging and working with the Light - considering that Amun himself was a Sun-god and a part of the great outer-planetary star-consciousness we call the planet Nibiru! This was not understood at the time though, and it is generally not understood today either, as is evidenced by the writings of historians and Egyptologists alike. Osiris has stated that this clean-up of quasi-religious practices was essential at that time, in order to re-establish the Truth of Divinity on Earth.

It is important for us to understand, both within the Ancient Egyptian context and our current, modern context, that it was never intended for *any* being to be deified, ever. The deification of another being provides fertile ground for manipulation and control. It was this practice which had to be removed in its entirety as part of the process of dismantling the power of the priesthood.

It was against this backdrop that the beginnings of true, organised religion began - the details of which could probably fill ten volumes. The religions which followed on from Ancient Egyptian society's social and religious practices still serve as the basis for much of our religious doctrines and the definitions of our spirituality today, rightly or wrongly.

Inasmuch as any religion upholds the practices of exclusivity, authoritative dogma or rigid doctrines as prerequisites for attaining Divinity, they have deviated from the purity of 'going within' to connect to the state of being of the Godhead. Most importantly, any religion or spiritual practice which allows men to dominate, or which denigrates women in any way whatsoever, has departed from the way of the true pathway of the Godhead - inasmuch as this indicates a loss of the balance between the Divine Masculine and the Divine Feminine energies. If it had to be ascribed a gender, the nature of soul as it emerges into Monadic individuality is what we would call feminine. It is, however, completely balanced in both its masculine and feminine energies. Therefore, any degradation of the feminine energy on Earth may be regarded as a form of casting aspersions on the Godhead consciousness and a deviation from the pathway of Light.

As we work with the higher frequency states within in the process of rebalancing ourselves, these issues may become all the more profound. The eradication of the Divine Feminine from our societies, and subsequently from ourselves and our personal relationships, is exactly why we find ourselves in the types of messes that fill the pages of newspapers, magazines, books and agony columns.

Divine DNA

The feminine essence makes up the Hu part of the word 'human'. This portion of the word denotes the God-essence (goddess-ence) of Light that we contain within our DNA. The so-called 'junk DNA' or unused/uncoded parts of DNA, within us is clear evidence of the loss of this feminine Light of the Hu as an active influence within us. These parts of our genetic coding system are now inactive parts of us that have fallen into disuse with the on-going dominance of low frequency emotions, thoughts and behaviours. They are a lower dimension adaptation. Our depressed immune systems and our psychic impoverishment are two of the great losses we have suffered as a result. Both of these prolong our suffering on Earth.

Denying the Divine energy of the Hu in our behaviours, our minds or our relationships is therefore contrary to our own genetic predisposition. If we were all energetically balanced we would no less allow ourselves to be abused than we would abuse others, because we are all parts of Divinity. We are all Divine. Acknowledging this simple fact provides us with the solution to the behavioural problems of the whole of humanity. It really is as simple as that.

In any discussion about DNA it is worthwhile bringing up the subject of activating more of our DNA. Currently, we are aware of the DNA strands and that some of the genetic code sequences are active. By activating the dormant parts of our DNA we automatically activate, or re-code ourselves with, more of our physical abilities, or super-abilities. The fact that we can activate something within us presupposes that, although currently invisible, there is much more to us than we realise. Along with the activation of more of the DNA, especially the 13th strand, comes an uplifted state of consciousness and we more easily understand who we really are, where we come from and what we are capable of. Along the way we develop enhanced psychic abilities. Many of the new children who are being born now are arriving on Earth with more DNA already activated. This is what accounts for their higher state of consciousness and why they are more immune to disease. It also explains the psychic super-kids all around the world who have shown themselves capable of doing extraordinary things. Apparently scientists have been noticing these changes for some time.

In the following communication Isis speaks clearly about the following:
- The origins of very ancient civilisations which many of us were part of.
- Our connections to various planets, such as the Pleiades, which have been in close proximity to Earth over the course of time.
- The loss of the understanding of our Light.
- Our desire to return to Light.
- Our many lifetimes of despair and joy.
- What the 'hu' part of human means.
- That we re-activate a part of the human brain as consciousness opens and uplifts.

As we become more competent at the level of our DNA structures, we become more capable relative to our brain capacity and functioning. A lot more information about the blending of the 'hu' and the 'man' which Isis states makes up the human being, can be found in the translations of the ancient clay tablets. These stories detail some of the genetic engineering programmes that were carried out to create human beings. Although it was presented at a later date than most of the Osiris communications to the working group, there is so much powerful information contained in the following communication from Isis that it is included in this book as well.

Isis: The Hu

"In alignments that take place to come forward to communicate, Beloved Beings of Light, it is that I serve you in this manner, that I have, through alignment with being (*Jacqui as the channel*), to offer the form to Spirit, to assist to bring forward your pathway of ascension. Always to acknowledge through the self, the learning and direction, as you follow it from one state to another, there begins to be the unfoldment of deep understanding from one state to another. Not always understood on first occasion. It begins to come together, the teachings of Light, the teachings through love.

"Many of yourselves to have come forward, prior to the Ancient Egyptian period, the Priests and Priestesses of Ancient Atlantis, that have come forward through the emanation, through creation, to come forward through civilization. To have followed forward, the planets to align, that have been through connection, Pleiadian Beings, Beings from outer planet to experience, that come together with intention of being within the understandings of Earth, and the workings and procedures that take place through a continuation of lifetime, development through creations in many aspect of your pathway of growth.

"To come forward from other planetary experience there is, through the shifting and movement, the desire to return to this state of Light, Beloved Beings of Light. It is through your intention, each and one and all, to have thought at one point from childhood to now, to question: **"Why is it, you find yourself on Earth? What is it you do, through purpose of a continuation of lifetime after lifetime, that you come to this point?"**

"Many lifetimes of learning, many lifetimes of despair, many lifetimes of joy, each of yourselves, once more coming forward as beings of the ancient period of living state - you come to this point to move through ascension in living. Many beings have chosen, in moving through connectivities in ancient period, to transcend as the god-beings have done, the desire to communicate further, to hold their presence.

"So, Beloved Beings of Light, you come to this point of decision to go forward in this manner to return your Light within your presence, to activate the understandings of your abilities of being of humanity. Not only being of humanity that has continued through lifetimes, but being of the Hu, it is this meaning, the connection of outer planets to one position, that you return. With your abilities to open the consciousness, the pathway of the physical brain that you hold within your being, begins to awaken in a manner that has not taken place for many lifetimes to this."

Q: Could you please explain your mention of the word Hu and our connection to this?
"It is of the understanding, it is as yourselves have knowledge, the coming of the Beings of the Godhead to Earth, have come forward through this state from that which you understand to be the Heavens of Light. It is through the Hu that is of the Godhead, to come together with man."

Q: So if you had to define the word Hu, would you state this as the Essence of the Godhead?
"It is the presence of the Godhead, to blend with man, the connection of each. Long lost this is the knowledge of this. Many of man to understand themselves to be lesser than all in the experience of the Solar system. Man is of Divinity. In its nature, to grow once more to reconnect to the Light. It is the starvation of knowledge that man does search, in a continuation, to reach this point - to understand the feeling of the Hu within the heart. It is there, Beloved Beings of Light."

As we know from Osiris' reference to the ancient clay tablets in his opening dissertation, Earth history is somewhat different to the version which the spin-doctors reworked, which we are so familiar with today, and yet very few people are even aware of this fact. Reading about this information from authentic documents such as were originally housed in the Library of Alexandria in Ancient Egypt or in Tutankhamun's tomb, before they were removed or destroyed, would certainly have made our progress into the Light so much easier and so much faster. Fortunately though, there are many more ancient documents which are yet to be found. We will find these when the consciousness of humanity is ready to receive the information they hold. For example, one of the most fascinating pieces of information that Osiris released to us, and a real puzzle too, is the fact that there are some very important documents which are hidden in Florence, Italy, very close to the Ponte Vecchio (Medieval bridge over the Arno River). Due to the stimulation of more high frequency Light in the area, these documents will be found sooner rather than later.

Happily, as our state of consciousness and our reality shifts towards higher frequency states of Light, more of what was previously hidden from view will become known and available to us. In the not too distant future we will see the following:
- Documents unearthed from secret archives.
- Papyri discovered intact, where they have lain concealed for centuries.
- Important additional temples, sphinxes and pyramids uncovered in Egypt.
- Hidden crypts, rich with treasures, exposed in many Ancient Egyptian temples.

Some of the present custodians of this knowledge are those who will reveal these ancient mysteries and release the information to the public, while others are the new explorers and seekers who will stumble upon new documents. This process will continue for a long time to come.

All of these long-held secrets will bring to light so much more of our ancient Earth knowledge and history, recorded for posterity by the ancients. When our consciousness is raised even further we will be able to once more see, although we will probably call it 'discover,' some of the ancient buildings of Atlantis as well - although it will probably not be believed that these structures date to that most ancient time, any more than it is currently understood that the Giza pyramids and some of the temple structures date back to the Atlantean Era.

Osiris: Truth is Revealed

"Many an understanding to come forward, to be unravelled by many beings, to bring forward many truth and experiences. As you allow for yourselves to be the custodian to take forward in many respects - not only through this period, through an extended period of physicality - that you are blessed and supported at this time, through the presence of Beings of Light, to expand your consciousness."

* * * * * * * * * * *

CHAPTER TWELVE

Frequency Determines Reality

"Deep in the essence of matter are many mysteries concealed."

(The Emerald Tablets of Thoth-The-Atlantean p51, pp1)

The Illusion of Duality
One of the main problems with this separated, physical dimension of ours is that it projects the illusion of duality. This stark sense of polar opposites became our total reality when the physical and spiritual dimensions were pushed apart completely, and finally, at the time of the nuclear explosions at the end of the Atlantean Era, although duality had begun to emerge as a potential Earth experience prior to this - with the fall from grace of Enlil. The end of the Atlantean Era was the Fall of Atlantis and of Man, known of as this because the Earth and her inhabitants dropped 'down' in frequency and behaved as the dense, solid matter parts of Light in the 3rd dimension while the Lighter parts of Light in the 5th dimension remained where they were. It was this dimension-shattering occurrence which is responsible for us continuing to feel that we are physically separated from the spiritual realms. The lack of understanding about what happened and where they had come from led to deep insecurity and uncertainty amongst humanity. This set the scene for large scale manipulations and power games - which have helped to maintain our low frequency status since the Fall.

Creation of a more strongly polarised sense of duality had to occur, because the nuclear blasts of that time were so physically massive that they literally split the whole, contained energy of 5th dimension Earth into two. These splits became the separated lower (3rd and 4th dimensions) and upper (5th dimension) portions. However, they remained connected by a thread-like extension of energy which we now call the wormhole system. Each portion extended itself right out at the far, opposite ends of the wormhole system. The 4th dimension became our reality as humanity, in the 3rd dimension, shifted higher in resonance.

This extension of the one dimension (of spiritualised physicality) into two dimensions (physical and spiritual) which are at the opposite sides of a divide denotes the polarisation of our world. We experience this in every possible way, but most critically when we view all life other than ourselves as 'the other.' The critical thing to realise though is that the portions of the 3rd/4th and 5th dimensions *are* still connected by their shared energy system: the extended 'thread' of the wormhole system. The illusion that there has been a complete separation of the dimensions is part of the deceptive nature of duality. This state of consciousness is supported by the current state of the energy grid of the Earth as well as by the collective consciousness of humanity. The grid changes when it is stimulated to change, either from outer-planetary high frequency influences or from the higher state of humanity's uplifting consciousness, or both. When the energies of the grid change the reality experience of all of Earth's inhabitants will change. Such is the nature of consensual reality.

The illusion which we call duality is nothing but the *apparent* separation of the physical and non-physical states of ourselves and therefore, of the world around us. It is a specific state of awareness just as much as there are other specific states of awareness. This illusion, which is born of limited awareness abilities, means that from our current stance we cannot even see the connecting thread between the two poles. Most people are therefore not aware of the wormhole systems which exist as energy gateways into the next dimension.

Without the illusion of separation in which we imagine we are somehow trapped in physicality, down at the bottom of the wormhole system, we would be perfectly capable of viewing ourselves in the fullness of ourselves as Higher Self Divine Beings of Light. We would also be more competent spiritually simply because we would be in open communication with the realms of the Godhead, albeit in the beginning stages of this, instead of being separated from them courtesy of an energy system of lowered resonance. It is the re-capturing of the fullness of ourselves, as we transcend the lower frequencies of the 3rd and 4th dimensions, which marks our existence as beings of living ascension. Living ascension is only possible in a frequency state which is higher than the 4th dimension, but this can only be attained from the 4th dimension - in accordance with the potential for harmonic resonance with octaves (dimension) which are either directly higher or lower than our current one. Therefore, it is the reclamation of our heretofore elusive 5th dimension, Higher Self energies that we strive after.

Our Twisted Reality
We may call our current sense of the world a twisted reality, because duality is a bit like a whole, round elastic band twisted once to look like a figure-of-8 with two portions which are distinctly separate from each other, yet still continuous with the original whole elastic band.

The upper and lower parts of the 8 represent the two, now separated portions which the energy of the whole split into. When the elastic band of the 8 is untwisted, the separated portions are both obviously still part of the whole, so any sense of separation is clearly an illusion. However, the existence of both portions also makes sense as does the fact that one part is the complement of the other part, because it is the same as the other part. Both parts should have full conscious awareness of the other, because the other is also the self.

Similarly, the full awareness of all reality states being continuous with one another within the Universe can only occur if we have access to all states and this occurs when we have moved energetically and perceptually upwards through the wormhole system again. This is the point when the twist of the 8 untwists and collapses and the 8-shaped, double-funnelled, stretched out illusion of the separated energy of reality shifts back into one space-time experience again. From the lower frequency perspective of the 4th dimension, this process is only possible if we start to resonate with higher frequencies and expand our consciousness so as to be able to include higher frequency states as part of our reality.

The complete untwisting of our illusory 'reality' so that it is no longer separated into complementary, dual portions, is impossible to do if we remain in the 3rd or the 4th dimension. It only becomes truly possible to experience by transmuting the lower frequency vibrations into higher frequency ones. This gives much greater meaning to the religious concept of transubstantiation or the modern metaphysical teachings which stress transformation as a means of healing and spiritual progress. It is thus that we move into the 5th dimension of spiritualised physicality.

As we untwist the details of our illusionary reality we automatically move upwards in resonance, and therefore in experience, from the 4th dimension into the next dimension. This is the natural progress of the upliftment of consciousness. In fact, the untwisting *is* the spiralling movement via a wormhole system, into the 5th dimension. The crossover point of the spiralling energies begins at the uppermost energy states of the physical, 4th dimension. This spiralling movement upwards, from low to high frequency states of consciousness, is the process of the movement through a wormhole system that is referred to by Osiris as, "*Going through the Eye of Horus.*" It is no wonder that the Ancient Egyptians placed such tremendous emphasis on this concept. Shifting through energy systems begins and ends with a state of consciousness and, therefore, the upliftment of consciousness has to result in us shifting to a higher dimension.

During a meditation procedure Osiris spoke of the feeling of moving through the gateway in the wormhole system by using spiralling energies.

Osiris: Spiralling Energy

"As you allow for the drifting movement through the spiralling energy - awakening at all times the presence within, through the frequency of great Light - allowing it to continue forward, in the Bliss state of pure connectedness."

This untwisting process of the spiralling movement through a wormhole system results in the re-incorporation and expansion of the physical body, and thus our reality experiences, into the spiritual dimensions. The two previously dual states then form a unified, whole state of reality. This is the result we can expect to experience after the cleansing and purification shifts Earth is going through now. Physicalised spirituality of this nature can only be achieved from the basis of Earth. This is the process of living ascension on the pathway towards enLightenment. The other high frequency option for us is that we attain the spiritual state of being after physical death, but only if we have worked off our Karma here first. Either way, both Karma and our other low frequency connections have got to go. How many lives that takes us is entirely up to us. We have the opportunity right now to clear many lifetimes' worth of Karma within a very short period of time so that we get to the point where living ascension is possible - when 51% of our Earth Karma is clear.

Although any clearing work which is done by any human being supports Earth with her own transformation, the effects are more profound when humans of living ascension live upon her and use their energy to stimulate the Earth. Earth is releasing low frequency vibrations from her own physical body in response to higher frequency stimulation from both humanity and the super-alignments of outer-planetary bodies with Earth, including the powerful pull from Nibiru as she draws near. There are powerful knock-on effects to be felt at this time of the spiritually important high point of the Age of Aquarius as we approach 2012. These are produced from the following:
- Incoming high frequency Light from the outer-planetary bodies in the heavens which is beaming into Earth.
- Higher frequency vibrations of humanity's uplifting consciousness.
- High frequency vibrations from Earth herself.

All the consciousness-raising variables work together. The result is a shifted dimension experience; a new reality.

Whether personally or collectively, the process of shifting our resonance to higher states can only be done efficiently and effectively once we move fully into the last part of the separated, physical zone of the 4th dimension. This is where we clear any of our remaining Earth Karma and low frequency connections which lie there. We shift progressively over the course of our lives and advance up from the 3rd dimension when we make choices which carry a higher frequency vibration, because then we naturally harmonically resonate with higher frequency states. The rate of shift increases as we progress as a direct result of higher frequency states.

If an individual resonates with the frequencies of the 3rd dimension he or she will have relatively more Karma, or low frequency vibrations, to clear out of the physical matter of cellular memory and the soul memory than those who have worked their way upwards vibrationally to comfortably resonate with the 4th dimension. Nevertheless, until completely clear of Karma and low frequency connections, all human beings will feel their issues as they come up for clearing. Once any human being is in the 4th dimension he or she can resonate with 5th dimension frequencies and this state of awareness, in itself, provides greater clarity about the transformation processes of living ascension. Clearly then, it is because Earth has shifted to the 4th dimension that all human beings can choose the higher frequency option of living ascension. A shifted state of consciousness enables us to re-programme ourselves. The difference between the 3rd and the 4th dimensions is the degree to which love is in the heart. Any thought or act of war cannot be part of a higher dimension.

Awareness, Frequency and Dimensions
Once we resonate with the vibrations at the upper level of the 4th dimension and no longer actively resonate with the 3rd dimensional frequencies, we are in the beginning stages of being able to be in open communication with the consciousness of the Godhead. This open line of communication begins in the 5th dimension. As resonant systems which are mostly currently in the 4th dimension, we are capable of resonating (and therefore perceiving) with a dimension below and above ourselves.

Initially we pop up and down through the higher and lower frequency energies of the wormhole system as we gradually learn to morph the split realities of physicality and spirituality into one again. This is a normal part of the living ascension process. The use of the energy of transmutation which is involved in raising our 4th dimension vibrations to higher frequencies creates the next step upwards in consciousness for humanity. This transformation is eventually acknowledged as an evolutionary step when our new consciousness has developed to such an obvious extent that most of humanity is living the reality of their psychic abilities, strong immune systems and unprecedented longevity - and all of this while in a state of unconditional love and compassion for all, and connectedness with all of life.

The transformative processes of clearing and healing are how we shift our physical bodies to resonate with the frequency level of the 5th dimension and back into communication with the state of being of the Godhead. The clearing has to begin somewhere and it often means that as things shift within us we may experience them as any of the following:
- Fairly unpleasant emotional throwbacks to earlier, unhappy times in our lives.
- Emotional recurrence of past issues, or memories, that have not healed, regardless of whether or not we thought we had 'forgiven and forgotten' and moved on.
- Re-surfacing of physical aches, pains and ailments from old injuries.
- Full-blown illness symptoms from old illnesses from which have not completely healed.
- 'Mysterious' physical ailments which seem difficult to diagnose, such as headaches or dizziness.
- 'Mysterious' emotional depression or anxiety which appears to have no origin.

The complete and instant healing of all these things is far simpler than we realise: acknowledge, *feel* and release. Without emotionally feeling the issue, *as* the issue, the vibration of the issue cannot be fully released out of our cellular memory. Therefore, anger is best released by screaming into a pillow, punching a boxing bag or hitting a pillow or other inanimate object with a tennis racket, for example. Grief is best released by crying. This is true no matter how ancient the emotion is. However, we are generally taught to put on a brave face and not express these emotions and so they remain trapped within us.

Although it is possible, and imperative, to shift from these unpleasant feelings when they come up for clearing it may be necessary to seek the advice of a medical practitioner if the symptoms persist or are severe - especially symptoms of illness. The rule of thumb is simple: when you are working with the intention to shift dimension, be suspicious of any and every emotional and physical symptom. All of them will be a part of the clearing processes, even seasonal colds and flu. As such clearing and illness are often concurrent.

The most encouraging part of clearing our own cellular memories - no matter whether current or past life generated - is that both our children and all future, as yet unborn, generations benefit from this. This is the powerful consequence of uplifting ourselves. It also becomes a powerful personal motivator to clear and shift.

The 5th dimension state of being implies living the consciousness of unconditional love and when we see this consciousness echoed in our internal and our external lives we will know that we have 'arrived'. People are generally very competent at accessing the higher frequency states during a meditation, but grounding these frequencies into reality and living them is essential. That is the challenge of living ascension.

The movements into a higher dimension are a function of frequency and are relative to the fact that the specific frequencies which make up the smog of the individual and collective consciousness of humanity are the only limiting factors.

In order for humanity and Earth to shift into a higher dimension it is functionally imperative that the resonance of both is at least in the 4th dimension. From there, both the Earth and humans are able to resonate with the 5th dimension energies. This is our alternative reality in the making. Failing this *en masse* process, individuals can certainly continue to personally shift their own frequencies and achieve living ascension over the course of their lifetimes - as happened in 2037/67BC. However, from a purely selfish perspective it may be borne in mind that it is extremely difficult to ascend as a lone individual to a 5th dimension life from a lower dimension world, because the individual would constantly be at risk of being influenced by the lower frequencies around him or her. It is so much easier to do this *en masse*, because we all pull each other along and support each other in the process. Therefore, it behoves us all to spread the news and help as many people as possible to uplift their consciousness and resonate higher - using whatever terminology is suitable to describe the process. The added advantage of many people doing this at the same time is that the exponentially greater power of group energy makes the success of the procedure more probable and easier to do, for all concerned.

When the energy of humanity is such that it functions as a veil that limits consciousness, past lifetime memories and sight of the higher dimensions, this is an indication that it is dominated by lower frequency vibrations. It is these which clog the grid system of Earth and maintain human consciousness and the veil. It is all of these frequencies which support our understanding of our reality and make us feel separate from the rest of the Universe. Thus, our level of consciousness supports the energies of the grid system and it supports us with the same energy in return. This creates the prescriptive experience of the collective consciousness of humanity which is prevalent at any point in time. When that changes, human reality changes *en masse*. This evolutionary step is another reason why it is important for as many people as possible to uplift their consciousness, at the same time.

The 4th dimension is the last layer, or construct, of a version of reality which is one truly blinded, twisted, physical 'reality'. We need to move very deeply into it, release the lessons of Karma or low frequency relationship connections we hold onto and start to reach for the outer edges of this dimension, in order to break through the limiting low frequency energy smog of lowered consciousness. We literally vibrate ourselves free. Then, and only then, will we be conscious enough and Light enough to be able to successfully travel through a wormhole system and access the new reality of a higher dimension. This energy-shifting process is a function of the frequency of our vibrations. Interestingly, Osiris and the other Light Beings speak of 'reality' as an experience we have here, as opposed to their own experiences which are referred to as, "*A state of consciousness*," or, "*A state of Light*." The word 'reality' is never used with reference to any of the higher frequency dimensions - until we shift ourselves higher physically.

We shift our resonance higher by uplifting our state of awareness, our consciousness. Alternatively, anything that raises our resonance automatically uplifts our consciousness. An expanded consciousness occurs as an alchemical process in which physical matter is transformed into something different. This explains transmutation of the physical body into a greater state of Light. Alchemy, or transubstantiation, always involves the use of high frequency energy to effect a change in matter, from one state to another. Therefore, we take note of the following:

- Unconditional love is the nature of Divinity.
- Manifestation of any kind is a form of an alchemical reaction, because manifest matter is Light which has become physically evident.
- The high frequency of unconditional love provides the energetic momentum for manifestation.
- Unconditional love is the fuel of the expanding Universe.
- All forms of manifest reality are portions of Divinity.
- Everything in the material world is a reflection and a direct representation of the amount of the love of Divinity is inherent in it, or not.
- Beauty and joy of any kind are evidence of unconditional love.
- If we want to manifest things and situations in our lives which we consider to be perfect or highly desirable, this is most easily achieved by ensuring that sufficient unconditional love is present within us.
- With sufficient unconditional love within us we automatically vibrate at higher frequencies and this increased speed supports the processes of rapid manifestation - i.e. the transformation of non-material energy into physical energy (matter).
- The speed of manifestation is determined by the degree to which Divine, unconditional love is channelled through a person and grounded on Earth, because it is a physical expression of Divinity, willed into being by an individual's intention.
- Happiness, joy and peace are indications of Divinity, grounded on Earth.
- Manifestation of anything is rapidly achieved when we are most joyful and most loving.
- Stress negatively affects manifestation of what we want, because it is the embodiment of low frequency vibrations.

Karma and Frequency Shifts

One of the results of frequency shifts upwards will always be a release of Karma or the need for connections with people who have Karma with us. These connections mean that we are effectively locked into the to and fro of various types of difficult experiences and relationships because either or both of us still carry certain low frequency vibrations within. It is because Karma is defined as those frequencies within us which have a low resonance that this happens. The release of Karma causes a resultant shift in the overall frequency of the vibrations of our physical body and our emotions - deep into our cells where the cellular memories lie. These actual shifts which the body goes through can be relatively painless or not, depending on our understanding of reality, as well as how much dross we have trapped within us, both on the physical, cellular level and the spiritual, soul level. Most people have plenty of low frequency cellular memories to release, gathered lifetime after lifetime not just personally, but courtesy of the genetic endowments from our parents and all the generations before them. We also create new cellular memories in each lifetime.

Most people live with the mistaken belief that human beings have to suffer in order to advance in anything. This concept of sacrifice and suffering is only real because we subscribe to this reality and, unfortunately, it has been the consensus of the entirety of humanity for a long time and this makes it extremely difficult for individuals to escape from. It needn't be that way if we are consciously aware of how our own reality can be triggered into being by the reality of others, whether negatively or positively. The energies of the last Age, the Piscean Age, were characterised by the twin issues of poverty and victim consciousness. That time is now well and truly over. It is up to us to ensure that these lower states of consciousness are eradicated from our cellular memories and our behaviour patterns.

The choice is ours to make as to whether any purification process during frequency shifts is smooth or fraught with difficulties. It is difficult to shift through Karma or low frequency-clearing processes with ease, but it can be done, especially if the principles which govern the living ascension process are correctly understood. All the members of the working group can attest to this. Osiris stresses the fact that when we feel joy in our hearts as the predominant emotion we shift the easiest. Furthermore, if we keep the outcome of higher resonance in mind we will get through the releases with this more positive attitude.

Osiris enlightens us with further information about the release of Karma. He also gently introduces us to another of two of the Light Beings who work with humanity in support of the ascension processes. One of these Light Beings is Lady Portia and the other is Djwhal Khul, otherwise know of as the Ancient Tibetan. Osiris often brings this Light being through to lend us his supportive energy.

Osiris: Karma Release and Joy

"Beloved Ones, it is that I wish to bring forward the desire and intention to support all beings at this time in the bringing forward of the joy within the presence of being. It is the understanding that through that which takes place in the outer alignment, it is to bring forward the connection of the joy of moving forward through the experience in physicality, I bring forward this procedure. It is to understand as you move forward into the various experiences, it is to connect with the joyous experience of being in this position, and the understanding that you move forward through the celebration. It is always in this procedure, it is bringing forward the presence of many Beings to work with yourselves in moving forward continuously through this procedure.

"I bring forward message to each of yourselves on this day, it is the support and assistance of many Beings of Light to surround yourselves on this day in the continuation of procedure. There begins to be coming forward through coming two period of communication with Spirit the intensified position of communication. It is the Being that is coming forward with this great intensity - it is the Being that is Djwhal Khul, the position that is the Ancient Tibetan - to support all beings in the release of many aspect of that which has come to this position. It is to understand, Beloved Ones, on this day that I bring forward the presence of this Being to be within environment to assist and support through all pathway at this time of the release in many areas of that which takes place."

Q: Could we please have a message to support us at this time?
"It is through the connection of message that I have brought forward to each of yourselves - it is relevant to each of you, Beloved One. It is for the connection of the presence of Being to support you at this time, it is for each of you to communicate with the Ancient Tibetan at this time. In support of the releasing procedure taking place, it is greatly supportive at this time, Beloved One, to communicate with this Being."

Q: Osiris could you explain why Djwhal Khul is so supportive in these releasing procedures?
"It is merely supportive procedures that is known to this Being to assist with this, Beloved One, and it is of great importance to move forward through the releasing procedure in all areas of forgiving and in all areas of the movement forward of the desire and release of soul memory through the experience of

Karma - the release of cellular memory through the release of Karma and various aspect through the connections of physicality - in order to go forward through the completion. It is of great importance. There is the presence of Lady Portia to assist in this manner also, Beloved One."

Q: Is this why some of us are having flash-backs to previous lifetimes; is this the releasing of cellular memory?
"It is Beloved One, it is of great intensity at this time. Understanding as you move forward it is for this reason I brought forward the connectivity in the beginning to understand the joyous experience to take place at this time. As you move into the experience of the joy and laughter of the continuation through that which is felt within the heart, it is the ability to let go of all of the experience through the connection of the head, Beloved One. It is the understanding that through this procedure you have the ability to release extremely quickly. It is of great importance as you are moving into the heart-felt position of the joyous experience within your everyday environment in physicality, so there is the ability for this to take place in the experience without the various and many issue to come forward through this interconnection."

Q: Are you also saying that as we feel the emotion which is coming up for release from the cellular memory, we must not get too involved in thinking about what it could be or where it comes from, but that we should just feel it and let it go?
"It is to move into the feeling state - do not move into any form of the logistical experience of the head. It is to allow through the heart the feeling state of the heart."

Q: So there need be no attempt to understand it?
"It is to not understand it at all, merely to let it go entirely through the continuation of the joy felt with the communication of the feeling state of the heart centre. It is of great importance over this period to not question within the self. Many areas of the bringing forward of the negative ego that comes into the experience. There are many beings that move into the experience of the scepticism of connection with Spirit, many areas of the decisions in many direction to come forward. It is merely the negative ego that comes forward through the attack so to speak, and in terms of the presence of moving forward through the accessing of greater Light it is of great intensity that this comes forward. It is, therefore, to move into the feeling state of the heart centre to feel it from the heart - to move through the experience of joy."

Frequency Adjustments and Dimension Shifts

The significance of the 4th dimension is not just that it is the dimension which Earth is in right now, but it is also the crossover point from which the physical body expands into a state which is compatible with the living ascension realm of the 5th dimension. The highest level of the 4th dimension takes us to the rim of the funnel of the wormhole system: the entry point. When we approach this access point to the 5th dimension we begin to be able to experience the beginning stages of direct and open communication with the Godhead as our consciousness uplifts and our awareness expands. This happens momentarily at first and then develops into longer periods of connection. We often regard the results of this improved connectivity to be psychic. Naturally, the closer we are to the state of unconditional love of the consciousness of the Godhead, the easier all the processes are.

Accessing the inter-dimensional gateway begins with brief excursions up and down the energy of a wormhole system. This is our physical experience of the wormhole system. Although it is currently still very difficult for us to physically perceive as a gateway, this is how we begin to shift into and then back out of the 5th dimension and we adjust our physical, human frequencies accordingly. Generally, it takes some time to adjust to the faster vibration speeds of the 5th dimension and so the frequency integration process will take some time. Although there are many different understandings of the ascension process, the actual centre point of the 8, or of the middle of a wormhole system, may be regarded as the actual point where our consciousness shifts from one state to another, higher state. This is the Eye of Horus. Again, this is why passing through the 'Eye of Horus' was referred to so often by the Ancient Egyptians.

It is also interesting to note that the number 8 is considered to be the number of soul, as well as Osiris' own personal number. The figure-of-8 is a very important one Universally, because it is the actual pattern of energy movement throughout the Universe. This shape of infinity not only links us to the Universe of Light through our DNA structures of the same shape, but through the energy pathway systems as they spiral up through the portals, such as the Great Pyramid. The pattern of their movement upwards and downwards is in the same shape that we call the figure-of-8. This symbol, therefore, signifies creation - no matter which way up it is.

As a whole group, humans still resonate with a varying mix of the 3rd and 4th dimension frequencies - which is why these two dimensions of physicality are sometimes referred to in one group, as the 3rd/4th dimensions of physicality. It is important not to confuse the fact that although some 3rd dimension energies still exist as part of our reality experience, Earth as a *whole* is presently operating in the 4th dimension - and has been since the 1960s.

The complete changeover, by means of an integration process, from any one dimension to another and the total eradication of all associated behaviours which are derived from the consciousness of the lower dimension, takes time. The systematic progression of events, which leads to behaviour eradication or modification, also marks the progressive changeover to the next dimension. Therefore, only when we are fully within the 5th dimension can we claim to be truly free of 3rd dimension resonance. However, once resonating with the 5th dimension we are still susceptible to 4th dimension energies. If we do start resonating with the 4th dimension again we immediately become capable of resonating with 3rd dimension frequencies. This slip is often an insidious process which we approach silently and quietly, like a depression, or it may be felt as a rapid descent in resonance such as when we explode in a fit of temper, for example. Whichever version of lowered resonance is felt, it is wise to be aware of this potential shift into a lower frequency state. Once aware we can more easily apply the discipline of mind which ensures we catch ourselves and begin a simple resonance raising mantra. An effective example of this is one of Osiris': "*I'm love. I'm Light. I'm Peace. I am the master of ascension, in the presence of the Godhead at this time. And so it is.*"

Shifting into another, higher dimension is not done by all human beings all at once, although a lot of individuals amongst humanity are going through this process now. It is the more aware individual, such as the Light worker and any other person who lives and feels from the basis of unconditional love, who are the front-runners amongst the human population who assist with the following:
- Forging ahead on the Siriun energy pathway, breaking out of the confines of the lower dimensions so that others may follow if they choose to do so.
- Feeding their new higher frequency vibrations into the grid system of Earth, simply by walking the Earth, and thereby stimulating a higher resonance feedback system for everybody else.
- Clearing personal Karma, which automatically shifts the energy of the veil, because it reduces collective Karma.
- Thinking, feeling and behaving more positively. This impacts on the collective consciousness of humanity.

The powerful knock-on effects that a small group of people can have on many others is why the term '*en masse*' can be used to describe humanity's shift into higher frequency Light, and when the living ascension process is referred to.

Although it would be wonderful if the entirety of Earth and her inhabitants shifted back into the 5th dimension at this auspicious time, the reality is that 3rd dimensional Earth experiences will remain in existence for quite a while longer. This allows people to work their way up and down the various levels of the resonance ranges between the 3rd, 4th and 5th dimensions until such time as the upliftment of consciousness is at the point where it will support living ascension, individually and collectively.

For Osiris to have stated that the Earth has shifted into the 4th dimension means that sufficient individuals within humanity are living at this level of resonance to have effected this change. This is the case of our reality, even though many individuals are certainly still clinging to the old ways of the 3rd dimension, as is clearly evidenced by the low frequency behaviours of war, greed and disregard for the property or person of others. Furthermore, the fact that living ascension is now possible for us, suggest that we are within range of the 5th dimension - from the 4th dimension.

It is important to remember that it only requires a very small quantity of people to shift their conscious awareness to a higher frequency and to remember who they really are, in order to shift the entire energy field of an enormous area. Consequently, this energy adjustment supports the shift in consciousness, and therefore the experience of reality, of all the people living within that area, or within that resonance range. It is for this reason that Osiris states that 6 000 - 8 000 people are able to shift the consciousness of one billion people! In real terms that amounts to each person being able to positively influence between 125 000 - 166 000 people - just by working on themselves. The love, care and healing of the self is the greatest service we can perform for others. When noting the extent of our influence, we can determine that any form of martyrdom or self-attack will not only harm ourselves, but many others too.

It is very important to take note of the fact that the successful living ascension process means that we will be resonating with the higher frequencies of a different dimension of reality, and this reality state has a higher frequency than anything we have previously been exposed to.

In order to live comfortably in the higher frequency environment of an alternative dimension, the bulk of Earth Karma or low frequency connections with others will need to be cleared out of the body physically, spiritually and emotionally. This is true for the personal living ascension experience as well as for the shifted dimension experience of the whole of humanity. It takes enough individual human beings working on the processes of living ascension, to create sufficient critical mass to remove these low frequencies from the collective consciousness of humanity. The same holds true for the clearing and shifting of Earth as the two are deeply involved in a physical relationship. Ascended humans can only live on an ascended Earth which is clear from all the lower frequency vibrations that humans have been generating upon and into her.

Consider what the following actions and events have done to the Earth:
- Every explosion of war.
- Every nuclear test in the deserts or in the remote mountain regions.
- Every burial of nuclear waste.
- Every undersea explosion.
- Every negative thought, feeling or action every human being has had.

All of these release destructive energy into the environment, aside from the direct human impact they have. They have had a powerful, forceful consequence on Earth and it is a negative one. As she shifts at this time, all of these energies have to be released from her and, just as our own releases can be unpleasant, Earth's can be too.

Naturally, the processes of clearing out the low frequencies, which is done both by humans and by Earth itself, may be a little uncomfortable at times. However, once again it is important to stress the point that any clearing and purification which is done by significant numbers of people assists the clearing of many others within humanity, because the work of one person will positively affect many other people. Another way of understanding how few it takes to shift the whole of humanity is by considering what Osiris said about this where he stated that it takes the square root of 1% in numbers of people to change consciousness, and that this can change potential Earth calamities too. Therefore, although each person ultimately has to go through the purification processes one way or another, this is often stimulated by the conscious work of others.

Osiris spoke about the expected dates of some intense Earth changes (which we may refer to as calamities) in the 2013 communication which is in Chapter Four. He only gave us this information long after the working group had attempted to get actual dates from him a number of times. The communication below gives the clear message that what humanity does shifts the energy fields, through the collective consciousness, to such a degree that it changes the necessity of Earth performing these functions in her own way. Perhaps tsunami's like the one that struck the Samoan coastline on 29 September 2009 can be averted if all of those who read this book spread this information to as many people as possible. On the BBC News website after the event, it was reported that the Samoan Prime Minister Tuila'epe Sailele Malielegaoi spoke the following words: "*The winds have uttered their strength, Earth has spoken its grief and the wave has scattered its strength.*"

Osiris: The Square Root of 1% (of beings) Creates a Consciousness Shift

Q: With regards to the coming shift in the central position of the Age, there has been a lot of speculation about Earth changes, solar events, earthquakes, floods and all kinds of things. Are those catastrophes preventable, and if not, can you give us any indication, in terms of dates, as to when these events will occur?

"Beloved One, it is to understand, as you bring gatherings of beings together, so it is always through the connectivity of many beings together, that you have the ability to shift the consciousness and, within the collective of that which I have spoken, so you shift the collective consciousness and it begins to shift the energy fields and the ability to allow this to not take place, so to speak. There is great ability within humanity to do this, Beloved One. It is the understanding that it is through any one group, it is the square root, Beloved One, that is of 1% of beings, that there is an ability to create great shift."

Frequency and Evolution

The raising of conscious awareness and its resultant higher frequency states is the evolutionary process at work. Learning about our own individual progress towards higher frequency states informs us how it is that an entire species can evolve due to the efforts of the few. As human beings we can consciously evolve ourselves, our lives and our planet to higher and higher states. There is very little relevance to the concept of evolution if it is understood to be the so-called result of the natural selection of the fittest or random events, other than to the most insignificant degree. If this were the only manner in which life evolved, we, as humanity, would certainly not have made the progress we have made so far. This is clearly evidenced by the slow evolutionary pace of the rest of the Earth's primate populations. Osiris informed us that without that Siriun injection of Light, Earth life would be a vastly different experience today than it is.

Although the influence of consciousness on the evolution of a species is critical, it is also important to take note of the fact that there was this massive, Siriun injection of Light into the DNA of selected primate DNA about 300 000 - 400 000 years ago when our species was genetically engineered. We know from both Osiris and the ancient clay tablet texts that this came from outer planetary sources and it served its purpose in speeding up the enLightenment of the planet. The human species is the direct result of the re-direction of the DNA of a primate population. This was engineered by the higher consciousness of Sirius on our planet Earth, hundreds of thousands of years ago. This is the Hu portion of the name 'human' that Isis referred to, as previously discussed.

These statements are not the opinions of the authors. They are part of the rich and unusual history of our planet which very few people know much about, either because insufficient information has been publicised, accessible information has not been pursued by many people or information has been hidden or destroyed. Although this information may certainly be regarded as extremely bizarre, it is nevertheless contained on thousands and thousands of ancient clay tablets from around the world. Many different, independent translations from well-regarded archaeologists and other scholars can be easily sourced and read. An internet search for these texts will yield a lot of information.

Aside from the original Siriun interventions on specific primate DNA, which we may or may not accept as truth, yet, the evolution of a species is the direct result of the emotions, thoughts and behaviour - the consciousness - of enough members within that species who collectively hold a sufficiently high resonance, to create a shift. This is what effects change.

The vibrations of the emotions, thoughts and behaviour of individuals are what create the resonance field. Similarly, any human behaviour which is dominant becomes the collective consciousness simply because this is the nature of vibrational influence and control within a species. Change occurs within the whole species simply because *all* of the *individuals* within the species respond to each other energetically by means of harmonic resonance. This occurs due to the physical function of the responses to vibrations by the elements which make up our DNA. Therefore, each individual is able to energetically feel, respond to and shift with the new higher resonant frequencies that he or she is exposed to - whether internally or externally stimulated. It is thus that each individual within a species responds to changing frequencies in the environment, directly from the place within them which is instantly affected by subtle energy: the element-based structures of the DNA. This energetic response at the level of our genetic structure creates a positive knock-on effect of forwards movement which academia has termed 'evolution'.

On a more personal, or private level, it takes one single individual within a family to shift that entire group of people upwards into a higher frequency state of Light. Although it may initially seem impossibly difficult for one person to achieve this amount of change, the results are worthwhile when it is seen that the entire soul group of the extended family expands in conscious awareness and begins to live according to the principles of Light and love.

Before all the positive results are experienced some growing pains will be felt. When any one person in a family begins to shift, uplift his or her consciousness and change thoughts, emotions and behaviour, this can arouse extremely strong responses from other family members. That person is often criticised, mocked, physically attacked, ostracised or emotionally blackmailed by the family group. If this is seen for what it is, an upset energy system, then it is more easily tolerated. These responses from the family are designed to force that individual to remain true to the old, tried and trusted ways of the clan and not upset the energy applecart of the group. Often these actions are unconscious responses to the changing vibrations of the energy-shifting family member. Their strongest desire is to maintain their equilibrium at the known level.

The negative responses of family members may be regarded as unsurprising, because it is within the confines of the known, old ways, that each member of the family feels most comfortable. The human species seeks homeostasis, no matter how low the resonance is that the group feels balanced at. The aim of homeostasis is to ensure that the present equilibrium is maintained and any disruptive influence is resisted.

Knowing that the social organism of the human family unit will seek to re-balance itself to a known level, it is unsurprising that an individual may require a lot of courage, enormous strength of purpose, compassion and loads of unconditional love to withstand the onslaughts in the initial phases of change. Just as with all cleansing and purification procedures the processes of change within a family can be rather unpleasant to go through. The results of a happier, higher functioning family unit are always worth it though, and the powerful effect this potentially has within the context of the whole of humanity is inestimably valuable.

It is worthwhile bearing in mind that the soul group of a family on Earth extends to include both deceased and future, unborn family members. As such, the work of one human being incarnate on Earth, can positively affect every single life of every single member of that family, past, present and future - in terms of our current understanding of different lifetimes within the context of linear time.

The release of low resonance states within a soul group, by any member of that soul group, means that the Earth Karma which this low resonance state is responsible for, no matter whether it is held within the cellular memory or the soul memory, becomes literally non-existent. This happens because the work of one individual of a group ensures that the resonance of the entire group is raised to a higher frequency state. It is this higher resonance of shifted consciousness which precludes the Karmic experiences of the lower frequency states, for all.

This positive knock-on effect which the shifts to higher frequencies create is expressed genetically in future generations, physically and emotionally in the current generation *and* spiritually in past generations, across the whole group. These impacts are felt by all members of the soul group, to one degree or another. The

Chapter Twelve: FREQUENCY DETERMINES REALITY

low frequency, potentially traumatic Karmic experiences which current and successive generations might have gone through are thus nullified. This is the powerful effect which is potentially the result of the work of one individual within a family. Therefore, we are reminded that the individual worth of each human being can never be underestimated. Compressing linear time as we know it to Now Time, where all past, present and future events happen concurrently, helps to make sense of this.

Osiris discusses the effects of individuals going through the ascension process relative to the soul group, people in the working environment and the fact that individuals who are working on raising their consciousness through the processes of living ascension will affect others who come into contact with their energy field.

Osiris: Influential Energy Fields

Q: When we go through the ascension process personally, I understand that our soul group will go through the same process, but what about other people we come into contact with every day? Do we influence them in any way or assist them too?
"Beloved One, there is assistance to the connection with other beings, but it is to understand it is the acceleration of the feeling state of connectivity of your being, through the shift in consciousness. Therefore, there is the ability for each being to move forward into various questioning procedure. Various area of the desire to move forward into greater upliftment, and, therefore, it is similarly supportive."

Q: So it is beneficial for us as individuals to concentrate on our own procedures?
"It is Beloved One. You do have the ability to shift the consciousness of many, therefore, all beings coming forward to the connectivity of the energy field, Beloved One."

Q: To clarify - do you mean that when others come into connection with people who are shifting and raising their resonance they start to notice something and question what it is that is different?
"It is to question for their own capacity, Beloved One, it is perhaps this also, but it is various areas the desire to question further, in many direction to bring forward further knowledge."

Q: If we come into contact with the same person every single day, such as at work, the influence of our energy field on that person could be quite major?
"It is so, Beloved One, if it is you are working in same environment, Beloved One, it is a continuation."

It is because all human beings vibrate at different frequencies of Light, but still within the same resonance range, that it takes just a tiny amount of new, higher frequency vibration for a positive knock-on effect to be created, over a broad area. This is an encouraging effect of the reverberations that will be felt by shifting frequencies. Such is the nature of resonance. It is clearly demonstrated by the WordWeb definition of the word - 'Resonance: a vibration of large amplitude produced by a relatively small vibration near the same frequency of vibration as the natural frequency of the resonating system.' This definition implies that all human beings (the resonating system) have within them the natural ability to resonate with the high frequency vibrations of the Light of the Godhead.

All we have to do to 'wake up' our natural, high frequency vibration-sensitive systems within us and to resonate them into life again, is to have a small amount of the natural frequencies of the Light of Divinity sounding within and shining into our environment. We literally turn on more of the existing Light switches in our DNA. Our external environment is blessed with the valuable high frequency star-Light which is streaming into Earth. This resonates both within us and Earth and we continue to positively affect the vibrations of people and things around us. And, the wake-up call of vibration continues like a snowball effect of positive feedback across the whole planet. This is the wave of changing consciousness that we feel.

* * * * * * * * * * *

CHAPTER THIRTEEN

Power, Manipulation and Control

Banded together in an order, Brothers of Darkness, they through the ages, antagonists they to the children of men. Walked they always secret and hidden, found yet not found by the children of men. Forever they walked and worked in darkness, hiding from the light in the darkness of night. Silently and secretly use they their power, enslaving and binding the souls of men. Unseen they come and unseen they go, Man in his ignorance calls THEM from below."

(The Emerald Tablets of Thoth-The-Atlantean p31 - 32, pp6, 7)

Confused Realities

In the state of duality, which is the separated, physical 3rd or 4th dimension which we call our world, we become manipulable and controllable, because we confuse one portion of our reality (the physical realm) with the whole of our reality (the integrated physical and spiritual realms). Consequently we have little memory of just how powerful we truly are. Many people have an unconscious soul memory of living on Earth in a higher dimension and these memories of living here in a far more Blissful state than we currently able to do, often account for their unspeakable sadness and depression in this lifetime. Others have absolutely no conscious memory of the previous living state of ascension on Earth, such as during an Ancient Atlantean lifetime, because their souls only came into an individual state of being and began incarnating on Earth after the time of the Fall of humanity from the higher frequency state of physical existence. This can be the case even though they may have had many lifetimes on Earth as a human being.

For souls who began life as an individual consciousness on Earth, as opposed to on a higher dimension planet or star, any form of existence is a relatively recent occurrence in Universal terms. Regardless of their planet of first emanation, all souls begin existence in a state of Bliss. It is because Earth was resonating with the 3rd dimension frequencies for so long that many souls, old and new, had seemingly interminable experiences of suffering. Understandably, the processes involved with an Earth lifetime can be extremely difficult for any human being in either the 3rd or 4th dimension. This may be more so for souls whose planet of first inception is Earth, because there exists no natural soul memory of the 5th dimension experience on Earth and they only have the experience of living on Earth in its separated state to guide their physical experience. Alternatively, not knowing anything different, Earth existence may be experienced with pure joy.

All consciousness, or the soul presence which is the person, is always linked to its original soul state where it only knew itself as Divine and this suggests that young, new souls have a purer connectivity to the Godhead than some of the other older reincarnating souls, even though they are equally at risk of being corrupted by the energies of the lower dimensions. As a result young souls need not have a bad time here at all if the original, Divine soul state is tuned into while they are incarnate on Earth. Osiris has informed us that this is a frequent occurrence for many people who live an extremely simple life in poverty-stricken India.

If souls begin Earth life with no previous, Karma-laden lifetimes on Earth they have no previous soul memory to retrieve in the manner that more ancient, Atlantean souls would have access to, this could result in either one of two things:
- It could make the progress towards the state of living ascension all the more difficult, because 5th dimension existence is a completely unknown factor from the perspective of Earth and the lower dimension energies could negatively influence the pure Bliss of a new soul.
- Alternatively, some souls come to Earth for the pure and simple experience of an Earth life and happily pass through here without picking up Karma or feeling pain or suffering.

Just to potentially confuse matters further on Earth for souls incarnating into the lower dimensions, our super-sensory perception abilities have been shut down and we no longer consciously communicate telepathically, in the manner of souls and what Osiris has termed, "*The Ancient Atlantean form of communication.*" If we still consciously communicated telepathically, we would have no problem knowing the truth of the intentions of another person. We have become so used to being lied to, lying, misleading and being misled that we no longer know how to easily determine the truth of words which are spoken. Our human-best means of discernment has become listening to the tone in which others speak, watching their body language and trying to pick up on other non-verbal cues. We use these methods to determine the degree of truth their words carry. Too many human beings have become used to discounting the natural psychic skills we all have. Properly used, these non-verbal skills assist verbal communications. Fully developed telepathy obviates the need for verbal communication, because it incorporates all the existing senses into one huge super-sense.

Our reduced-skill communication systems have left us open to the confusion which powerfully gifted orators and actors who hold leadership positions prey on. Their verbal deception skills, ability to control their own non-verbal communications and use of emotive language surpass the discernment abilities of the general populace. Due to this, the minds of entire nations have frequently been held captive in the dark and people have been manipulated by their own fear.

Major contributors for the maintenance of humanity's confused sense of reality are:
- Nations of people are subjected to fear-creating public relations programmes, via the media, by the Masters of Spin on Earth.
- Deliberate manipulations by powerful institutions, such as government or religious, and the misinformation programmes they support, are designed to shut down the in-built, super-sensory skills of entire societies of human beings. Their aim is the enslavement of humanity, at one level or another.

Not consciously knowing better any more, vibrating at a less-than-optimal frequency and being trusting by nature, we have become easy prey to those who want control over us: the Brothers of Darkness. Worth considering is how millions of very special children have been doped up to the eyeballs with a powerful drug, ostensibly to help them concentrate better. Instead their senses are dulled and their spiritual connectivity is reduced. This makes them all the more controllable and far less individual and unique. They become automatons. In their dulled state they question less, rock the boat of the family, the classroom and society less and humanity loses the immense value of these unusual children's consciousness-shifting potential. There is a very small handful of children whose brain physiology genuinely requires the help of such a drug. Over-prescribed and over-used, drugs such as these lower a person's resonance and retard humanity's progress into higher frequency states.

Although so-called ADD (Attention Deficit Disorder) and ADHD (Attention Deficit Hyperactivity Disorder) issues are complex ones which often include developed behavioural problems, the obvious answers to children's concentration issues lie in the way they are treated, at home and at school. This includes what they eat, what their leisure activities are and where they live as much as how and what they are taught. Considering that the brain waves of these children typically swing between a dominance of overly active, anxiety-producing high beta states and under-active, day-dream producing theta (and delta) states - with very little alpha state brainwave activity in between - we may consider that somehow these super-sensitive children are alternatively being overly stimulated by their chaotic environment or bored to tears. That is an indictment of the society they live in.

It would serve us all well to re-look at the regimented systems that are both designed and enforced by parents and teachers alike and question whether or not these are in the child's best interests - especially with the understanding of the high frequency requirements of spiritualised physicality in mind. This is a natural, highly ordered state of being which is characterised by love (which children respond extremely well to), joy (which is the natural, playful mode of the child) and a lack of stress (which allows children to be calm and be peaceful).

Separately, Rudolph Steiner and Maria Montessori both came up with alternative education systems that are more supportive to the needs of the child. Many more creative child-rearing and education systems are needed, especially now. The shifted dimensional experience means that more babies of a much higher consciousness will be born from now on and they will need the support of *truly* child-orientated systems in the future.

When discussing the problem that people often don't know that they are able to move into a state of living ascension through the process of uplifting their state of consciousness, Thoth referred to his ancient written information, which we know of as the Emerald Tablets, in October 2008. He asked us to consider the feeling of truth within our hearts relative to our abilities. Knowing that Thoth intended his ancient texts to be used for the support of the ascension process of humanity is rather shocking news, because many people are quite unaware of the existence of these writings, let alone of the facts of living ascension in the present day. We can consider this against the backdrop of information about the creation of the time-clocks of Thoth and his teaching of linear time as we know it. We can appreciate that this time of the potential dimension shift was a known event, because the portal-opening processes (especially of the Great Pyramid) was timed to coincide with the super-alignment of outer-planetary bodies with Earth. It is now up to us, individually and collectively, to decide whether or not we want to take advantage of the shifted dimension opportunity, along with the processes of living ascension.

Thoth: Truth and Ability

"I've written vast - it is in the feeling of the truth within heart to ascend in support of many - to bring to idea the ability."

There are so many people who are not even aware that they are spiritual beings having a human experience and therefore, the probability of them moving into living ascension as a result of a personally shifted, uplifted state of consciousness is rather remote and too unpredictable for comfort. Knowing this, it then becomes all the more important for those Light workers who are aware of the process to shift themselves higher into the Light and thus positively affect the whole of humanity - this is regardless of the terminology which is used to describe a shift into a higher frequency state of consciousness, or who the Light workers are.

We all do this work on behalf of others when we do it for ourselves, because whatever we do individually affects the collective consciousness of humanity and this in turn determines the circumstances of the lives of all human beings, albeit largely in an unconscious way for most people. It would serve humanity well if more people began to speak up and share their new knowledge and uplifting experiences with others so that the new spiritual consciousness may be openly discussed and understood, regardless of the fact that they may initially invite criticism and ridicule in the process. Any criticism of this type of information will not last forever and in due course not only will the persistent detractors go their own way anyway, but more people will start to resonate with the new higher frequencies of Light on Earth. Proponents of the new knowledge will then be vindicated by the joy of higher resonance in the surroundings. This will naturally support the release of more and more information from all quarters.

Relatively small numbers of people are needed to fuse the two worlds of separated physicality and spirituality back together again during the massively powerful process of moving through the wormhole system. This is the reintegration of the energies which is a transmutation process. To this end, we are fortunate to be able to hear the wisdom and accept the help of the Light Beings in order to shift more consciously and easily in this direction - at this time of our greatest ascension opportunity as we approach the central position of the Age of Aquarius.

Control, Domination and Ascension
Controlling and maintaining control over humans in the 3rd or the 4th dimension is important to some people, governments or institutions, because this prevents those they control from claiming their own power, being free from limitation and moving into an ascended state. Aside from the more obvious issue of large-scale controls by governments or large institutions, many individuals have a desperate need to control others on a personal level, because this helps to assuage their own fears, no matter how briefly. Control has many faces, from aggressive action to subtle kindness. In order to identify these we may consider that the actions of others that make people feel frightened, trapped, worthless, unsettled, beholden or unhappy at any level may be identified as the actions of control. Underlying all acts of control is fear of one kind or another. If we fear the legitimate power of another person then we cannot truly be powerful ourselves. Power over another is an illusion.

The maintenance of power and control over vast numbers of people means the following:
- People will not realise that they are inherently powerful and that this is their birthright.
- People will not know that it is possible to ascend-in-the-physical and to attain enLightenment in this lifetime.
- People they will not know what the mechanisms are which enable the shifted dimensional experience, in a state of living ascension, if it ever even dawns on them that it is possible.
- Vast numbers of people stay on the Wheel of Karma, reincarnating into lifetime after lifetime of frustrating lessons, suffering unnecessarily.

This perpetuates the continued illusion of separated dimensions. The existence on the various treadmills of human life is perceived as the only reality. It keeps people, whether individually or collectively, bound to a system or a person. In the blinded reality of the 3rd and 4th dimensions the truth of our Divinity is hidden thus, as is the extent of our personal power. This makes humanity easy to subjugate. Too many people are enslaved by the systems that are supposed to support them.

This means humans will not only continue to live their lives from the perspective of a continual cycle of suppression where fear and relative unhappiness predominate, but it may also potentially result in them missing the living ascension boat time and time again, because the lower frequency state of fear cannot be part of a shifted dimension experience. Fortunately, the power points of the wormhole systems which link our world to the next, as well as the teachings thereof, will always exist for us to find. Even fear can drive us to change, when we have had enough of it and seek an alternative. However, not only is it easier to achieve the dimensional shift at certain times relative to astrological changes in the heavens, but it becomes all the more possible to do if we have a clear understanding that the option exists.

The movement through the inter-dimensional gateways is heightened due to the Earth's super-alignment with other stars and outer-planetary systems which already resonate with the higher dimensions. It is during these auspicious times, or midpoints of an Age, that humanity is naturally most able to move into a state of living ascension *en masse*, simply because we are being exposed to a stronger dose of consciousness-shifting frequencies.

Not knowing about this process or the possibility of moving through the gateways of a wormhole system would mean that many within the mass of humanity would not be in a position to realise that we can do this living ascension thing together. This group action of living ascension is important for both Earth and the outer-planetary bodies, because the positive high frequency vibrations that the correction of our detour into the dark creates reverberate across the Universe in ways beyond anything we can begin to imagine. The positive effects are first felt on our own planet, then further out in our immediate outer-planetary environment and they continue further afield within the Cosmic Universe.

The Importance of Earth's Ascension
Thoth has hinted at the importance of Earth moving into the state of living ascension and the impact this will have over the entire extent of our globe, when he communicated the following:

Thoth: Human Consciousness is Vast

"It is small planet, vast consciousness and power at this time to create great shift for many in planetary system."

Osiris enlarged on this further by informing us that there are planets, such as Mars and the Pleiades, and galaxies, such as the Andromeda Galaxy, within our immediate environment, relatively speaking, which will benefit enormously from our own shifts into higher states of consciousness. We will go into more detail on these concepts in a later publication.

Additionally, we can be appreciative that there are other planets, galaxies and star systems which are assisting Earth with her upwardly mobile progress through the dimensions at the moment - specifically the Sun, Nibiru, Venus, Orion and Sirius. As discussed, Osiris has also included Arcturus and Antares as friendly, high frequency supporters of Earth's ascension. Communication with some of the Light Beings begins from the 5th dimension states of existence within these star systems - in the step-down process from their own higher dimensions within the state of being of the Godhead. The planet Venus is most especially important to us now as it is this planet that the Light Beings use as a 5th dimension communication platform in order to be in contact with us. Time and again Osiris has stressed that this planet imbues the consciousness of unconditional love and this makes its energies perfectly suitable to support Earth at this time as we learn to think with our hearts. Lest we forget the importance of the Sun, we need just look at it daily and marvel at its constant supportive presence.

If all in the 3rd and 4th dimensions had to ascend-in-the-physical all at the same time, this portion of the Universal experience - that is the twisted, apparently separated physical reality - would cease to exist in the separated state, because it would be fully re-integrated within the 5th dimension. However, this is not likely to happen any time soon as there are still many souls who need the 3rd and the 4th dimension Earth experience to work from in order to release their low frequency connections and Karma which was generated from current of past life experiences. However, many people are working on ascending the 4th dimension to the 5th dimension. This will create a natural pull on the 3rd dimension. None of the work we do is in vain or can be seen in isolation. We all affect and influence each other.

Once resident in the beginning stages of open communication with the consciousness of the Godhead, in the living ascension state of reality, we would be highly unlikely to create such negative circumstances which led to the Fall of Atlantis and of Man again, because we take with us the valuable experiences we have gathered during our long years in the darkness *and* we remember the suffering too. These experiences are what we have to teach others in the outer-planetary system about. From a positive perspective, once we re-experience Bliss this alone is sufficient to persuade us not to lower our resonance again.

Furthermore, as Enlil shifts back towards the Light, as Osiris, Isis and Thoth informed us he has made the decision to do, this supports the eventual collapse of duality and the faster eradication of the lower frequency dimensions.

This is very relevant and very important. Wiser and more knowledgeable, we would not be at risk of creating or contributing to this level of reality again in a hurry. The 3rd and 4th dimensions are the reality levels which, due to their separation down the wormhole - away from the realms of Divine Intelligence - are dominated by the dense, low frequencies which resonate with issues such as fear, power needs and ego struggles. It is only here that dark behaviours and negative emotions can be supported and meet with such a large degree of success. This is supported by the illusion of duality which the separation of our spiritual selves from our physical selves has led to. It is only in the dimensions of duality, where the divide between Divine consciousness and physicality is so vast, that we feel so separated from communication within the experience of the existence of the Godhead and that human beings could think that this is all there is to life, to existence.

As humanity moves along the Pathway of Return back to the state of non-separation, individuals are awakening to a new reality and realising that there is more to life than we previously thought there was. When we enter the astrological time of the midpoint where the heightened energies provide for the fresh possibilities of living ascension, while the possibilities of ascension-at-death at any other time are maintained, a natural paring of the number of souls from the lower dimensions occurs. It is these souls who would otherwise be blindly available for the repeat cycle of Earth experiences in the 3rd and 4th dimensions.

Once we move on as souls in an ascended state we will very rarely come back to 4th dimension Earth, unless by choice. Some do come back in service to humanity, for example. If we do come back in service from an ascended state of consciousness, we come back to Earth with an open, higher conscious awareness of who we really are. As a result we are unlikely to incur Earth Karma in the process.

As more people learn about and choose the option of living ascension and shift dimension, those who remain in the 3rd or the 4th dimensions see what appears to be people 'leaving' the planet in their droves. They do leave the dimension, but not the planet. This is a difficult idea for those in the 3rd or the 4th dimension to comprehend, because the resonance of the lower dimensions does not support the expanded awareness that would allow for this full understanding. If everybody had a sufficiently uplifted consciousness everybody would exit the lower dimensions, never to return. This is the shift into another dimension. People do this when their Karma-clearing, reincarnation cycles in the 3rd or 4th dimensions, on the Wheel of Karma, are complete. In the process, the time when the 3rd and 4th dimensions of separated physicality disappear completely, begins to loom closer. This event is the vanquishing of the dark.

Even though this eventuality is very far off in human linear year terms, as we get closer to more of Earth consciousness reincorporating with the realms of Oneness, the Brothers of Darkness feel the shifting vibrations too. With this they know the proverbial writing is on the wall and that their time of Earth domination is almost over. Panic at the thought of the potential loss of power grips them already and they have started to thrash and kick like a dying horse. This creates its own brand of chaos. They wreak havoc in financial markets, for example, to manipulate and fan the flames of the fear to which mankind so readily responds.

Subsequently, as the vibrations continue to shift to higher frequencies - regardless of their best efforts and vicious machinations - they become increasingly more desperate and start to stimulate even more fear. This they do by creating further disruption and then stepping forward as the 'rescuer' only to put stricter and stricter control measures into place. The enLightened and outraged American public, for example, call this the removal of their civil liberties.

The global banking and stock market disasters which occurred in the latter part of 2008 are perfect examples of this attempt to gain greater control over the many by the few. Bully-boy games are played behind the scenes to manipulate the bankruptcy of smaller companies. Thus the scene is set for bigger companies, including the powers of state, to come to the 'rescue'. The goal is to gain further control over all financial sectors and the price people pay for this is the devastation of their lives.

Osiris is strong in his comments about these occurrences lest we are lulled into complacency or are tempted to respond with fear. He has repeatedly asked us to remember that there is a huge amount of fear currently being stimulated in the collective consciousness of humanity - by the effects of manipulated events - and we are all susceptible to this. Recently, these have proven to be ruinous of livelihood, capital reserves and property values. The stress this puts us under makes us feel tired, listless, fearful and insecure. These feelings stimulate the lower chakras and maintain a lowered resonance. Osiris reminds us time and again to stand strong against the feelings this manipulated insecurity will stimulate within us so that we do not add to the problem by feeding additional low frequency fear vibrations into the resonance system of Earth. It would be beneficial if we could try and support those people who lose their livelihood as a result of these disasters by helping them to shift from fear and despair and find their own Pathway of Light. As hard as it may be, this is the perfect time to remember to, "*Stand in your Light, Beloved Ones.*"

Standing Firm in the Face of Trouble
In answer to a question about people who rob and steal, or who otherwise try and create disturbance in other criminally abusive ways, Osiris stresses the importance of maintaining the balance within ourselves and the resonance of the 5th dimension. When we vibrate at these high frequencies of Light, no harm can come to us, because we transcend the world of duality, even if it is momentarily.

In this world reality we currently live in, duality exists because of the separation of physicality and spirituality. It results in our subsequent separation from the unity of the realms of the Godhead. The physical realms of the 3rd and the 4th dimensions echo the experiences of only one pole at a time, *as* stark reality. These one-sided vibrations are what man inadvertently started resonating with when the energy of the Whole split apart into the two energies of physicality and spirituality. When we understand this and re-integrate the two parts of ourselves in the process of living ascension, we will live the true reality of Illumination - where there is no Light versus dark. In that 5th dimension resonance state, there are none of the 'good guys' or the 'bad guys' of our 3rd or 4th dimension linear time reality. There is merely existence, in varying degrees of Bliss.

Chapter Thirteen: POWER, MANIPULATION AND CONTROL

Osiris: Disturbance and Shifting this Frequency

Q: The subject I require clarity on is about people who create disturbance with deliberate intent, such as those who rob our homes and whether they are planned or opportunistic events.
"Beloved One, you wish to understand if it is for the desire and intent of beings to come forward in this manner, Beloved One?"

Q: That's correct (*this person had an armed robbery at his house and wanted to know if this event was likely to be repeated*).
"It is to understand, at this time it is not so, Beloved One. There is to understand, Beloved One, through the connection of beings coming forward in this manner it is, as it has been stated, opportunistic. For many coming forward to see the experience that is shown, and open to each being, to go forward in this manner to take from another, or to move into the experience of creating great fear and disturbance to others.

"It is in this manner you do have the ability always to shift the connectivities that are in the environment, as it is moving in your surroundings in all direction. It is to understand it is not only in this environment into which you reside, it is across the planet at this time. Many, many beings moving into the desire to take from one another and to move into the control of others and to take from beings that is unsupportive for individuals. There are countries that choose to take from individual beings as they grow too large.

"It is in many respect, in many different direction this takes place, but it is to understand you have the ability, in the moving forward through the experience of 5th dimensional connections, it is to allow yourselves to know and understand there is great possibility to hold your resonance, to the extent to eliminate this. To move forward through the connection as it is, that it does come forward, on any form of occasion so it is to dissipate the energy to the extent it is no harm to you. And in this manner so it takes place on many occasion,, through the presence of individual beings such as yourselves, working in this manner.

"It is to understand, Beloved Ones, that you hold your resonance - shifting the frequency on regular occasion and continuing to hold this resonance for lengthy and lengthier period - so it begins to take place to greater extent, in the moving forward through the entirety of the 5th dimensional experience. There is

361

understanding, of no Light and dark, Beloved Ones, of no areas of the beings that have, and the beings that do not. It is in a state of greater Bliss, through the connection of the understanding of the elimination of duality, as it has been stated on earlier occasion. It is this that is created by man, the duality. It is not the experience of the planet. It has been brought forward by individual beings, to create this and, therefore, it is to understand as you have discussed in the connectivity of linear time frame, so it is as Light and dark, is not existing."

Man imposes his own sense of duality onto the planet of Light, which is Earth. As we shift and uplift our consciousness we change our perspective and experience more of what already exists all around us - the higher dimensions. There is no need to have food shortages on this plentiful and abundant planet, especially considering how many intelligent agriculturists, crop scientists and innovative technologists there are, but we do have them. Africa is particularly at risk from the manipulators of power who artfully play the roles of both destroyer and rescuer, no matter whether these people come from the East or the West. The prize is gaining access to land which has abundant mineral resources, rich farming soil and an extensive and needy labour force. They prey on populations which have been neatly reduced to manageable proportions by manipulated wars, food shortages and man-made disease.

These subtle crimes against humanity and Earth merely cause more low frequency vibrations to settle and lodge into the globe, thus contributing to the entrenchment of the divide, which each individual person ultimately has to bridge in order to get back to the state of being of the Godhead. The horrors of war and the political upheavals which are seemingly far away from us, personally impact on each one of us deeply. If more people were conscious of this we would take a keener interest in what goes on all over the world and ensure we all act in accordance with the fact that we are all responsible and accountable to everybody else for what we do individually. It is the human-created low frequency vibrations which rumble and heave as the Earth quakes, volcanoes erupt, cyclones rip and tsunamis devastate when the vibrations from the shifting consciousness of the planet and outer-planetary alignments are sufficiently high enough to shake them up and dislodge them. This happens more and more as we make progress towards higher frequencies of Light. Earth cleanses herself and individual human beings pay the price relative to how many people are working together to cleanse and purify themselves, or not. The more people who clear and release personally, the less catastrophic the Earth-cleansing events are.

The damage to our planet which the excessive use of fossil fuels has caused, and

Chapter Thirteen: POWER, MANIPULATION AND CONTROL

the results of this which contribute to what we call Nibiru-stimulated climate change, have become compounding problems for humanity to deal with at this time of the shift. It is interesting to know that this same problem existed in Ancient Egypt too. Surprisingly, the excessive, climate-damaging use of fossil fuels is a repeat pattern on Earth, just as the opportunity for human consciousness to shift higher is. With regard to climate change history repeats itself in the following manner:

- Nibiru is once again approaching Earth and influencing our planet with her high frequency energy. We are still relatively ill-equipped, in the 4th dimension, to deal with that energy and so it feels like a giant, unsettling pull on our magnetic field and this causes upsets on our planet and within us. We are once more being stimulated to change and it is this shift that will ensure we do not respond negatively to Nibiru drawing even closer in the future. When we are in the alternative reality of the 5th dimension, our energy will be fully compatible with Nibiru's and her arrival in the skies will be cause for celebration.
- The most significant contributor to carbon dioxide production, which is one of the gases which is gathering in our atmosphere and is the low frequency pollutant which is implicated in rapid climate change, is electricity generation because so much of it depends on fossil fuels to power up the electricity generation systems.

We consume power excessively. When we stand more firmly and more completely within our own personal power, this externalisation of our power needs (which are revealed as external power consumption) which feeds us within will naturally begin to dissipate. As the world once more shifts away from duality, weather patterns will stabilise and there will be less extreme seasonal fluctuations. A balanced and moderate climate will prevail. This means we will have less need for electricity-generated warmth. Essentially, there will be no shift between day and night, and all will be Light. Obviously then our power needs for light will be obviated. As we learn to appreciate the high frequency nature of the fruits of the Earth as our food, our power consumption in food manufacture, preparation and storage will be vastly reduced. When we easily trans-locate ourselves from one place to the next, there will be no need for vehicles either!

Interestingly enough, a lot of research has been done by many different organisations around the world which detail the issues of our changing world. It is well worthwhile looking up more details if this is an area of interest. The ideal is to find well researched information which plumps out what Osiris has told us about our changing climate, although most research makes no provision for influences which are external to the planet. James Hurtak's organisation, The Academy For Future Science (AFFS), have collated a lot of interesting Earth science research about this subject.

Considering what we can do to mitigate the effects of changes on Earth, it would serve us all well to act a lot faster than we are currently doing in order to prevent the Northern Hemisphere from going through a great freeze and the Southern Hemisphere from turning into a large rain forest region. Balanced energy between the two hemispheres of Earth is urgently required. This requires responsible physical action as well as a shift in consciousness for humanity.

We are all affected by what everybody else is doing, thinking and feeling on Earth. It is for this reason that no person on Earth may turn a blind eye to what others are doing. Entire cities and countries will pay the price as Earth's climate changes and as she cleanses herself, because the two processes go hand in hand. This is especially so in the time leading up to the midpoint of the Age of Aquarius in 2012, and even more so in the first year of high frequency energies in 2013, as has already been discussed. The coastlines of island nations have already been severely affected by rising waters and the expanse of beaches the world over have been markedly reduced. Yet, through all of this many people choose not to take note of what is happening - the educated and uneducated alike. When Osiris discusses these issues and is asked questions about when we can expect to see obvious changes that indicate the shifts, he replies that they are already there, but that people choose not to notice them, either because it is inconvenient to do so or because they are frightened. He has specifically mentioned the visible erosion of beaches the world over.

    We have seen enormous destruction on Earth in recent years as some ultra-low frequency areas have had their vibrations cleansed and rectified through the processes of flooding, immense winds and earthquakes. Existing undersea fissures in the Earth's crust, volcanically active zones and hurricane or tornado prone areas are particularly at risk as these places provide already weakened pressure points which the Earth uses to release its pent-up negative energy. However, living the high probability potential of large-scale damage and destruction need not be the case if every single human being starts to raise the frequency of his own thoughts, actions and emotions little by little, on a daily basis. We can curb fear of anything by repeating positive affirmations of happy, loving things to ourselves, by forcing ourselves to laugh until we feel the joy and by keeping in mind that we are the masters of our own destiny. We can do anything or change anything. This understanding will help to gently shift the lower frequencies in the collective consciousness of humanity to higher frequencies and prevent or reduce the severity of calamitous Earth shifts.

    Knowing this, the issues of Earth shifts and climate change then move into the realm of our own personal, emotional and practical responsibility and we realise the ability we have in mitigating the intensity of them. This is especially important as we approach the time of the most intense energy which will be beaming into Earth at the central point of the Age of Aquarius: the year 2012.

The new, higher frequency energy that Earth will continue to be exposed to in the immediate post-2012 years necessitates the need for a very much purer planet which resonates higher. This will ensure that the new, incoming Light that we will then respond to does not create upsetting reverberations. A cleansed Earth and an uplifted human consciousness go hand in hand and ensure that both the globe and humanity are able to tolerate the new, higher frequency energies.

Failing adequate, regular and relatively gentle purification and cleansing of our Earth pre-2012, the Earth catastrophes from purification releases may be of mammoth proportions post-2012. Exposed to the outer-planetary high frequency conditions at that time, Earth will release and cleanse herself more rapidly than ever before. 2013 is the year of our final examinations. That is when we finally 'pass' or we 'fail' - given that no madman has detonated nuclear warheads before then.

Although the midpoint energies will start to ease off in the post-2012 years in terms of the natural waning of the Age, the shifted dimension experience that the intense energies of shifting human consciousness which the lead up to 2012 has created, means that the Earth and humanity will be existing at a higher frequency consciousness than before that time period. This means that the resonance of Earth will be naturally higher.

Additionally, the planet Nibiru is continuing on its long elliptical orbit around the Sun, moving closer towards Earth and crossing our own orbit around the Sun at right angles, in the process. This means that Earth will be strongly influenced by the gravitational field of Nibiru and the proximity of her higher frequency energies. This influence alone is sufficient to create frequency upsets on our globe and it therefore behoves us to ensure we can tolerate these higher frequencies of Light in the very near future. We need to shift and change so that we raise our resonance. Energy compatibility with Nibiru prevents Earth wobbles.

Whichever way we look at things, all of these factors play an important part in the processes which are involved in the shifting of the dimension of Earth in the present day, on our Pathway of Return. All human beings and the planet respond to the changing frequencies that abound, daily.

Earth Shifts, Humans Shift
As humanity and Earth begin to shift to higher frequencies, the transitions in and out of the dimensions through a wormhole system may initially make us feel a little odd, but soon we will be sufficiently acclimatised to the new, higher frequencies

of Light and we will be permanently able to live our physical lives easily within the new level of the 5th dimension. At this point it could be said that we will have shifted naturally, totally and completely into the new dimension and we will vibrate constantly at a higher frequency. When this happens we will naturally be resonating more with the higher frequencies of the Godhead than with the dense, lower frequencies of the 3rd or 4th dimensions of separated physicality.

The 5th dimension then becomes our newly constructed, permanent version of unified, spiritualised physical reality and we will no longer experience the adjustment peculiarities which go with the early stages of splitting in and out of different 'realities.' Once Earth and humans are in the 5th dimension we will no longer experience our physical self as separate from our spiritual self. Our reality will have shifted and expanded. It will have morphed into something new, along with us. Progress to even greater states of enLightenment after this is far easier than we currently realise.

After 2012 the Earth will also have gone through her own potentially uncomfortable chakra clearing procedures along with human beings, because we are inextricably linked together in our physical experience here. It is these shifts which the physical body of Earth will make in response to higher frequency, outer-planetary Light body alignments and accommodate the changing consciousness of humanity during the living ascension process. If the concurrent shifts of Earth and humanity did not happen then the concept of living ascension would be a misnomer. We, as human beings made of combinations of elements and mineral Earth-stuff, move with our Earth in the living (as opposed to dying) ascension process on the Pathway of Return, because we are associated entities. Human consciousness contains Earth consciousness, and vice-versa. Both are Light of a specific form.

Knowing that the super-alignments of the various outer-planetary bodies with Earth are creating a powerful gravitational pull on the planet, we can acknowledge that there will continue to be adjustments for a while to come and that the severity of these will be felt relative to the low or high frequencies that Earth and humanity are resonating with. Essentially, any low frequency resonating systems will be extremely uncomfortable under high frequency conditions.

If we want the Earth shifts and adjustments over the next few years to be relatively smooth rather than ones which are characterised by massive calamities, then it follows that individual human beings should ideally do their own individual, consciousness-shifting work, as often as possible. If many more people consistently do a little bit more than before we can achieve the following:
- Make our planet a better one, from all perspectives.
- Improve our own and our neighbours' awareness of themselves as a spiritual,

soul presence who are having an Earth experience and act in accordance with this.
- Shift negative thoughts, emotions and behaviours to a more positive place so that the likelihood of Earth and humanity shifting more easily in the pre- and post-2012 years is far more likely.

It is in everybody's best interests to ensure that this happens. Firstly, to ensure a smooth dimension transition for ourselves by limiting our own physical and emotional trauma through the process and, secondly, to facilitate the easy movement of more people and more of Earth into the living state of ascension, into higher states of Light, towards Oneness. This is the, "*Passing of dimension*," as the Light Beings call it. Refer to Chapter Four for practical steps to achieve this.

The Physical Ascension Process
The living ascension process is just that: a process. Human beings ideally need to become more acclimatised to the higher frequencies of unconditional love gently and consistently, and this is a process. To more easily adjust to the changing frequencies it may serve us well to know what this means in our day to day lives. As we physically and emotionally begin to expand into the reality of these new vibratory states, we may experience some rather strange physical symptoms. Although we would typically seek medical help if these symptoms cropped up previously, this is not necessarily needed at this stage. Some of the dimension-shifting symptoms include the following:
- Light-headedness.
- Vision disturbances of all kinds.
- Hearing disturbances such as an electrical-type, high frequency buzzing in the ears which is commonly misdiagnosed as tinnitus.
- Momentary dullness of hearing, or even complete deafness.
- Spaciness.
- A sense of 'splitting' in and out of reality.
- Emotional instability or irritability.
- Exhaustion or high energy.
- Appetite changes.
- Swings between fear and elation.

If we didn't know about the dimensional shift and its typical, but transient, 'symptoms' we could become very fearful about our own sanity and health. These reality-shifting symptoms are in addition to what may be felt as the potentially powerful detoxification reactions of the human body. Physical clearing and detoxification processes are part of the procedures of clearing, re-energising and purification of the physical and spiritual parts of ourselves. Often, the healing processes which release low frequency vibrations from our bodies can be difficult to do, considering that the idea that pain and suffering as a necessary part of progress is so well encoded within our human cellular memory. Furthermore, this negative attitude to change is constantly stimulated by our resonance with the collective consciousness of humanity.

The quickest way to resolve the disturbances which are typical of a dimension shift is to do some grounding exercises. When this is done, the new, higher frequencies are automatically grounded firmly into our physical reality and become the new level of functioning. In this manner we imperceptibly shift upwards, with the minimal amount of fuss. The standard advice when going through a detoxification process also applies: drink more water, rest more and do not expose yourself to harsh environments or people. Following this simple advice helps the entire system to re-balance itself at a higher level.

During the dimensional shift we begin with a process of getting used to the higher frequencies of the 5th dimension and then we gradually shift into the full experience of this reality, until there is no more backwards and forwards movement between the higher and lower dimensions. Once we have gone through many of the adjustment and cleansing processes of the initial phase and the 5th dimension of reality is real to us, we do the following to maintain our higher frequency status:

- We concentrate on maintaining those higher dimension life experiences all the time, primarily by operating from the basis of unconditional love for all.
- We take care not to slip backwards into the lower dimension, negative-ego reality experiences again, regardless of the occasional human tendency to respond to negative emotions or events around us.

This is how we deliberately move deeper into the full experience of the total 5th dimension reality. Essentially, life does not *suddenly* change for the better from one day to the next, but the daily experiences of living do become more pleasant, detoxification and Karma-clearing processes notwithstanding.

Aside from active consciousness upliftment work which each person may do individually, it is possible to assist the shift to higher frequency states by using products which hold a high resonance. Visit the website www.stargateway.co.za or www.phoenixhealth.co.za or email info@phoenixhealth.co.za for some information on natural, mineral, frequency-based products which assist with gently shifting the vibrations of the body so that it is stimulated to heal itself by balancing itself. These types of products assist the body to shift itself back into a state of balance and optimise its own functions. Imbalances result in pain, illness and ailments - which all hamper spiritual progress towards enLightenment. Physical and emotional balance assist with the enLightenment procedures of living ascension.

Osiris provides us with encouragement when he discusses how we let go of whatever doesn't serve us any longer, through our connection to great Light.

Osiris: Letting go of Past Issues

"Many of yourselves in the experience of physical form at this time, moving forward through great advancement. Through great advancement of understandings, that you begin to shift and let go of many experience no longer to serve, it is spoken of on many occasion, Beloved Ones. It is at this time you relinquish entirely through the expansiveness of the dimension shift, into the pathway through the connection of great Light, Beloved Ones."

There is an actual shifting of frequency that we experience as we move between the 4th and the 5th dimensions, because we are resonating with the full range of frequencies within the wormhole as well as on either side of it. These shifts in frequency have a direct impact on the physical body. It is because of this that we feel physical and emotional changes. Ideally, once identified and as we experience them, any altered dimension experiences should be consciously grounded and brought to Earth, because this is an essential part of the living ascension process. It is the transmutation of energy - from one state to another.

The process of grounding the 5th dimension experiences into our daily lives denotes the 'descent' of more higher frequency Light to Earth. This in turn assists with the 'ascent' of the physical body into the higher frequency realms, without losing physical life in the process.

The Playground Shrinks, the Income Stream Dries up

Once there are no more spiritual souls willing or needing to inhabit the planet as physical human beings in the 3rd or the 4th dimensions and once the last of us have moved through the Karma clearing, or frequency-raising, processes on Earth, what little will be left of these lower dimensions of separated physicality become rather a dull and lonely place to inhabit. Of course, we acknowledge that in a linear time sense, it may certainly take quite some time for Earth to reach that point, if she ever does. In consideration of maintaining this dimension is the fact that Earth is a great place of learning and experience for souls and some incarnating souls require more time in the separated states of physicality than others do.

Nevertheless, once Earth's inhabitants have become significantly diminished in volume, there would be very little reason for the Brothers of Darkness to stay here either - not enough people left to make significant money from or feel powerful over, reduces their interest in them. However, at that point the Brothers of Darkness will have a serious problem, because they no longer know how to ascend-in-the-physical, even if they wanted to. Their natural ascension would be unlikely, because they would still be caught up in their ego issues and the desire for power and control. However, by the same token, this might be the turning point for Beings of the Dark as they look around and begin to realise what has happened. The only way forwards then is towards the Light. The alternative is 'nothingness'.

Ascension implies that the vibrations of the high frequency of Light are dominant. Where there is Light there cannot be darkness and, therefore, where there is a predominance of Light there cannot be control or power issues. Light is Love. This in itself indicates to us that any system of worship or governance, whether ancient or 'New Age', which is based on an hierarchical system of power, has to be incorrect. In the realms of Light no power or control is ever exerted by any one being over any other being, simply because this behaviour would be contrary to the very existence of the high resonance states of Light.

> The highest resonance of Light is felt as the Bliss of Perfect Balance and this itself describes the Divine Order of the Cosmos.

As more and more of the physical planet of Earth expresses itself in the ascended state of being there will, literally, be less and less physical Earth populated by lower dimension humans. As we ascend-in-the-physical, then the actual, physical portions of our planet respond in kind, because the two entities are interlinked as crystalline, mineral structures which resonate harmonically with one another. We may view Earth as a contaminated body of Light which has become this way due to the dominant consciousness upon her: humans. As humans uplift their consciousness, Earth is able to express more of her Light too.

Our personal living ascension has to include the process of the ascension of the entire physical planet and this is happening on an on-going basis. When we see the up-coming Earth shifts which create the actual loss of physical portions of our Earth, we may understand this to mean that these portions have shifted into another dimension, or frequency zone. Many of the` landmasses of the Atlantean Era are a case in point.

In a dimension shift, the shifted dimensional experience can be to another, higher dimension of the Universal System, back into the 3rd dimension, or it can be to a state of 'nothingness.' Presumably, if we notice that Earth has changed, then we ourselves can be certain we have shifted higher - rather than disappeared into 'nothingness'. We cannot be in the void of 'nothingness' and still be conscious. It is a very real eventuality that some areas which disappear from our sight in Earth calamities during the dimension shifting process may physically cease to exist. This happens if the energy of that area has devolved to such a low resonant frequency state that there is no lower dimension for it to devolve to, to shift into. This causes its disintegration into the void of 'nothingness.'

Therefore, whether these portions of Earth have shifted into the 3rd or the 5th dimension depends on the Karmic issues, or resonance states, of that region and the humans who inhabit it. Human beings are responsible for what happens to the Earth.

The New Earth
As and when the Earth changes happen over the next few years, as well as when we personally respond to the higher resonance that supports living ascension, it is important to realise that life as we know it will be pretty much the same as far as basic physicality is concerned: the grass will still exist beneath our feet and the birds will continue to sing. However, life will be more pleasant in every respect. The buildings and structures of the 3rd and 4th dimension Earth will still be fully in place, but the humans who inhabit them will have a vastly different consciousness and because of this the use and possible appearance of those structures may be different too.

If we consider that Now Time (or No Time) is a part of the higher dimension experience where there is no delineation of past, present or future, we can appreciate the fact that when all time is current, in the present moment, we can experience the magnificence of the ancient temples as they were in ancient times. They were all extremely grand and beautiful. In Now Time they still are.

It is because we link the spiritual with the physical aspects of being that 5th dimension existence enables us to be able to see and feel the physical world around us as a place of great peace and beauty and consider it to be normal, while in a spiritual state. This perception of reality is a developed one which the vantage point of a heightened state of awareness affords us with when our thoughts, emotions and actions are in line with unconditional love. We need not necessarily be consciously aware that we have physically shifted dimension or that others have either. Ultimately, the reality effects of a shifted dimension create a completely different life experience, after the cleansing processes which precede this shift. Some of the more pleasant reasons for wanting to live in a higher dimension of reality are the following:

- We will realise that we are generally happier and more content, and so are the people around us.
- Our corporate institutions, schools and state systems are obviously based on the rules of fair play and compassion for all. Those that are not, cease to exist.
- The issues of crime in our local areas recede and disappear.

- The rapid resolution of issues which lead to wars begins, and war is no longer considered to be an option.
- Government leaders are truly considerate of the needs of the people and serve them, instead of advocating power or following selfish acquisition agendas.
- Our health care programmes and eating habits are holistically orientated.
- Our food excludes toxic, low frequency additives.
- Our immune systems are stronger and we easily heal ourselves if we do get ill or hurt.
- Spirituality, as opposed to religious dogma, is important in people's lives.
- Our psychic skills enhance communication, understanding and ease of relating to one another.
- Our improved manifestation abilities increase our level of pleasure and joy on Earth. This reduces our dependency and reliance on anybody else, institution or individual.
- Animals are at peace with each other and with humans.
- There is respect for all forms of life and an understanding of the different forms of consciousness which make up our world and our Universe.

With plenty of everything available for everybody and with a pervading sense of peace on Earth, we can get back to concentrating on our original reason for existence - increasing our state of enLightenment on a beautiful and abundant planet. In the dimension shifting process, the issue is one of moving through the wormhole and literally collapsing the lower frequency states, in the process of their reintegration with the higher frequency states. When this happens everything harmonises with and into the Light. Once this has occurred, our perspective naturally changes and we are more aware of that which is Divinely Intelligent than of that which is not. Those who choose to continue to resonate with more of the lower frequencies will maintain their life reality at the 'bottom' of the wormhole. This continues until such time as the choice is made to raise the resonance sufficiently so as to move through the gateway. With the shifting processes continuing and the higher frequency states settling into reality, humanity continues to move away from the illusion of separation - where polar opposites of reality exist - and into the Light, where the Oneness of Being is Supreme.

A distinction between the two options of continued and discontinued human life has to be made, no matter which dimension life is experienced in. Osiris has advised that one way of determining what has happened after significant Earth shifts or events, is to look for bodies. If dead bodies are found, obviously we know physical death did occur. Those souls will move back into Spirit and return - either into the lower dimensions on the Wheel of Karma, or into a higher dimension, with a stronger soul presence - once the planet has shifted. However, if bodies are not recovered, no matter whether they are presumed lost at sea or blown to smithereens, then we can safely assume these people have probably shifted into a different dimension of reality - whether upwards into higher frequency realms or downwards into 'nothingness is dependent on their own Light. As peculiar as this notion may seem to us at first, further consideration of it allows our understanding to develop. Frequently large groups of seemingly unconnected people die together in a disaster for the express purpose of highlighting the issues at this time. By doing this they assist the rest of humanity to ask the right questions, pertaining to their existence and reason for living, which will help them to shift. Once again, the right question to ask after a disaster is, "Where are the bodies?" If there are none to be found, rest assured that your loved ones are most probably alive and well and living in ascension.

A catastrophe is always an opportunity for a dimension shift for some people, regardless of the fact that we presently have the opportunity to shift physically into ascension. For some people, this rapid change in dimension at the time of a calamity can result in the same effect we are trying to achieve by systematically training ourselves to move through the wormhole system in the living ascension process. However, for most of us, a dimension shift will not involve a catastrophic procedure such as a plane crash.

Another option to consider is that at this time of heightened energies on Earth, many people choose to physically die and leave the planet. They do this so that they may come back to Earth at a later period. When Earth is once again resonating at a higher frequency of Light souls can reincarnate with greater amounts of their own soul-Light of the Higher Self within the human body. This is one of the reasons why it has been noted that so many young people appear to have been dying recently.

As a result of all of these processes, as more of Earth becomes Lighter along with its ascending humans, the remaining bits which may still hold a lower resonance, and are therefore able to be inhabited by the Brothers of Darkness, become smaller. The world literally shrinks as a 3rd or 4th dimension inhabitable space - at least in its separated, physical state it does.

The Great Divide
Once they have spent a long time in the dark, the low resonance of the Brothers of Darkness means they lack sufficient Light energy to maintain high quality human life. This Light energy can only be provided by the high frequencies of Light and they usually 'steal' it from others in the surrounds. The divide between the physical and spiritual realms can become so vast so as to appear insurmountable as well as being insurmountable. Bear in mind that the Princes of the Dark use the higher

frequencies of Light from other people to support them physically on Earth. They can only benefit from this energy as long as these higher frequency people are all alive and inhabiting the same space as them in the 3rd and 4th dimensions. When we consider the reality of life experiences relative to resonance, the issues of higher and lower resonating people creates a definite distinction between 'them' and 'us.'

It is people with a higher resonant frequency that the beings of the Dark literally feed off energetically. This is because their low energy systems have to be supported by these higher frequency vibrations. Those people who resonate with higher frequencies stimulate the grid system and the Earth with the minimum amount of life-giving high frequencies which the Dark Brothers also need in order to exist healthily on Earth. They have to rely on others to do this as they do not have sufficient high frequency vibrations of their own soul-Light shining forth or resident within them on Earth to enable them to maintain sufficiently good health of their physical bodies on their own. Without this higher frequency Light to feed off and stimulate a resonance effect within their own element and mineral-structured bodies and Earth, low resonance human beings tend to get very sick, very quickly.

Once people who resonate with higher frequencies leave the lower dimensions, the playing field of the physical dimensions thus dramatically reduces in size and frequency. With their unsuspecting playmates all gone, not much fun will be left to be had in the separated states of physical reality for the Dwellers of the Dark!

Maintaining their physical bodies without sufficient stimulating higher frequency vibrations feeding them, positively stimulating the dimensional grid or resonating with Earth, will be a very serious problem for them. We can only imagine the in-fighting that will emerge when the only people they have left to play with are themselves and their low frequency behaviour becomes even lower. The only energies left for these people to feed off would be those insufficient vibrations of lower frequency of Light of themselves and the vibrations of the low frequency portion of Earth which they still utilise! Unless they too shift, they will develop life-threatening diseases and die, because the dense solidity of their bodies will not create sufficient high frequency vibrations to sustain physical life. This is a horrible thought for those Brothers of Darkness whose goal is power and control over others. They are fully aware that they need the higher energy of other humans who are able to keep the energy system, as well as their systems, of the Earth sufficiently intact, in order to survive. Considering that the external world is an expression of the inner world of the human being, when the systems of the outer world collapse, we know that the inner ones will too. The only way to prevent this collapse within is to ensure that the inner systems of the self change to function at a higher frequency.

Aside from the obvious desire for domination and control, it is precisely in order to avoid this devastating eventuality for themselves that they desperately try to manipulate human beings in order to maintain control. The Brothers of Darkness need as many people as possible to be stuck on the Wheel of karma and reincarnating time and time again onto Earth in the 3rd and 4th dimensions of separated physicality. They need workers to run and utilise their systems and institutions of control. It is only in the separated state of reality that human beings are blind to their own natural power. For these manipulators, it is more preferable that humanity continues to resonate with 3rd dimension reality, where human beings are highly susceptible to and malleable by fear. However, there can only be successful Lord and Master 'vibration thieves' if there are willing participants in the game.

When the bulk of humanity has reclaimed their power and are no longer predisposed to responding to the manipulations which are designed to deliver power and control into the hands of the few, there will be insufficient unenlightened people left for the Brothers of Darkness to draw energy from or to use as slaves in the system. The higher frequency human being naturally resists the efforts of those who attempt to rob him or her of energy.

Furthermore, there will be an inadequate supply of people to do their bidding or to keep their low energy systems running smoothly. At that point, if these Brothers of Darkness do not uplift themselves and shift their resonance higher towards the Light, their own energy will devolve still further. It is in this manner that these individuals unavoidably approach the potential for disintegration into 'nothingness', of the body and the soul - or turn around completely and work towards their redemption. It is likely that they know this at some level of their consciousness and so we can understand, although not condone, their almost insane, desperate quest for Earthly power and pleasures. This, along with the desire for power and control, is practically all the comfort they have. Due to their need for the energy of other people to sustain their systems and their desire to manipulate everything that humanity can hold near and dear, they need to ensure that the minds of the majority of people remain enslaved.

The upliftment of consciousness at the individual, personal level is the sure antidote to the feelings of enslavement, confusion and fear which bind humanity to the lower dimensions and the manoeuvrings of the Brothers of Darkness.

* * * * * * * * * * *

CHAPTER FOURTEEN

Issues and Antidotes

"Ye are a Sun of the Great Light. Remember and ye shall be free.Stay not thou in the shadows. Spring forth from the darkness of night.Light, let thy Soul be, O Sun-Born, filled with glory of Light, freed from the bonds of the darkness, a Soul that is One with the Light."

(The Emerald Tablets of Thoth-The-Atlantean p52, pp1)

Multi-National Power and Control

The converse of the upliftment of consciousness for human beings is the creation of emotional anxiety and other issues. This is often where many of the multi-national corporations of the world come into play when they or their products and services are used for the subversive control of humanity. There are corporations which are dominated by a few individuals who have enormous ego needs which can only be fed by the power and control over vast numbers of people. No matter what the mode of control is, the end result is always the same: power. When this is the case, these needs and the reach of these governmental, institutional or corporate powerhouses, surpass all borders of all nations. It is for this reason that some corporations are often able to grow so substantially and so quickly on a global scale. This is most especially noticeable when supplying the needs of war significantly boosts their coffers. It has been said before that the war machine is a self-propagating income-generator at many levels of a society.

Those who are truly in charge of these corporations, far from the public eye, care little for the lives of their many employees other than what is required to maintain a certain face in the media or other public forums. There will always be well-controlled puppets in place to do the bidding of the highest level controllers, even though these highly paid marionettes generally don't realise just how they are being used. This is most especially so if their own egos are sufficiently stroked, in the correct manner, in order to maintain their behaviour. Often lauded as 'Captains of Industry' their egos are supplied with ample means to feed and satisfy innumerable human vices: greed, money, sex, access to the high life in the fast lane, special favours and power. Their many minions are kept similarly enslaved to the system, their reward relative to the level they have risen to in the hierarchy. As in-house supporters of their own game they pat each other on the back, lauding each other as they rise through the corporation. Conversely, there are many Light workers in place in these organisations, at every level, and they help inestimably with mitigating the damage that others do.

Anybody within these types of corporations, especially if they are employed at a high level of management, who does not toe the 'party line', will be axed with impunity. Fabricated stories will appear in the media, often under the guise of an 'anonymous source' whose theories will all too readily support and white-wash the otherwise suspicious moves from on high. The puppet-masters know who they are and they are fully aware that they are rampantly power-hungry. They relish in their conquests and take great pleasure in winning at all costs. The true heads of these organisations often have little need for public recognition and tend to shy away from the limelight. Their pleasure is not of the back-slapping variety, it is Earthly dominion. Very seldom do the public get to know where the true power sits. Power is critical because control and domination on Earth is the aim. This may sound a bit strong to some people, but this 'game' has been played over and over again, century after long century, in the lower dimensional reality of Earth. It is what keeps Earth and her inhabitants stuck on the Wheel of Karma.

These facts are not hidden amongst the true power-mongers and they strategise accordingly, but they hide these schemes behind closed, corporate, institution or government doors and they present themselves to the world with an altogether more pleasant, acceptable and amiable public face. Nevertheless, although the puppet-masters are highly intelligent people they are not spiritually far-sighted enough to understand that the results of their ill-gotten global power and control are short-lived at best within the space-time of the Cosmic Universe.

It is necessary for us, as the average man-in-the-street, to be aware of this because, at very worst, the behaviour of the few can lead to the complete obliteration of the planet Earth. It almost happened before in Atlantean times with the combined forces of the detonation of nuclear warheads, the pole shift and climate disaster. In the lower dimensions of blinded reality we always remain at risk of it happening again. It is absolutely essential that we uplift our consciousness and expand our awareness.

In this excerpt from the 26 March 2009 meditation (the entire transcript and an mp3 are available on the website www.stargateway.co.za), Osiris spoke about the destructive forces at work which are used for the purposes of control of humanity. He also reminds us of our connection to the greater state of soul, to the Monad. He mentions the annual celebration of Wesak - which lasts from the full moon May until the next full moon. The energy of Wesak builds and then wanes for about a week on either side of this period, so all in all the high intensity of the Wesak period energy may be regarded as lasting six weeks. At this time, the outer-planetary Light Beings come to Earth in their droves. Osiris describes this best in the following communication - as well as their reason for coming to Earth. Just as he does prior to any meditation, Osiris reminds us to create the form of the star tetrahedron of the Merkabah Vehicle of Light around us as a supportive energy field. This high frequency energy field helps us to connect to higher frequencies of Light.

Osiris: Release of Difficulty

"Greetings Beloved Ones, I am Osiris, come forward on this day from Spirit to be with you, greetings. It is on this day that I wish to take you forward through visualisation - it is procedure of moving forward through ascension process once more. It is the understanding that I take you forward through the deep connectivity of the movement forward through the pathway that is the ensuing path of enLightenment, the pathway forward through the connectivity to the Godhead. The understanding that through the procedure as you move forward in the many directions of the understanding of ascension, so it is the procedure to go forward.

"I bring forward in the interconnection at this time - it is for each of you to move into the understanding that as many of you move forward through the environment of the rough experience at this time, many areas of darkness and the bringing forward of the many areas of the understanding of difficulty and destruction in various areas such as this - it is the understanding for yourselves to hold your Light and move and transcend this position within the environment, to move forward into the interconnectedness with your Divinity. From this perspective know and understand that through many manipulation taking place throughout the world experience at this time, to bring all beings into the controlled environment. To understand of that which is to be guided forward through many aspect of that which no longer serves you as Light Beings and beings working through the ascension procedure.

"It is I wish to support you on this day to take you to the experience of connection - it is in the position of the environment that begins to prepare for the period of Wesak. It is the understanding of the connection of the area to Ancient Tibet. It is I wish to take you forward into the connection; it is within the etheric with Beings of Light to go forward with yourselves in the understanding of the pathway of ascension. It is as you find yourselves in the reconnectivity to the Monad - the understanding of bringing forward all that is to be desired through the experience at this time to move forward into the accelerated procedure. It is that I support you for many days to come over this period, in the support and assistance of the holding and working with your energy from a soul perspective - from the communication of Spirit in the out of body experience in the sleep state.

"It is to understand that I take you forward through this procedure at this time as you begin to move into the visualisation position. I wish to connect with yourselves on this day through the Merkabah - that is through the understanding of the formation. It is a Vehicle of Light surrounding and supporting you - it is on this day to work with the connectivity of the pyramidal of tetrahedron procedure of sacred geometric shape - to begin to feel the formation taking place surrounding yourself. It is for reason to bring forward this particular shape of the environmental experience of great Light of support of energy and frequency to support yourself in this way forward, as we work with specific procedure in order to allow for the movement forward through dimensional shift."

The Light Beings gather in the valley of Wesak in Tibet. There they celebrate the progress of Earth and humanity and support us with their energy. As the Planetary Logos, Lord Buddha presides over these celebrations.

Osiris: Wesak Beings

"It is all beings at this time coming forward through the support and assistance of the almost return to Earth through the dimensional shift - in order to experience the communication to support many in humanity, to allow for the procedure to follow forward that has begun from intention of each individual being in physicality."

Without the energising Light which is generated by the mass of humanity, low resonance, manipulative corporate life just cannot be maintained with any degree of order for very long - especially in what has become our rapidly-paced, fast-changing world. This is more so the case if we bear in mind that although slow, low speed vibrations are not easily prone to change and are not highly adaptable, they will be influenced and upset by the high speed vibrations of shifting consciousness.

It is because of this that those power hungry corporate systems which have a low resonance will ultimately crumble under the dense weight of their own low frequencies, as they are upset by the new higher frequencies on Earth. Whether their markets fail, their systems collapse, their people mutiny in their droves, or whatever other effect the high frequency vibrations may have on the low frequency system, the sheer slow bulkiness of their dense mass will be exactly what causes these systems to auto-destruct. When they tumble it is usually spectacularly fast. Similarly, any low frequency generating structure will collapse in due course. This has to be the case, because of the higher frequencies of Light which are beaming into our planet and which the uplifting consciousness of humanity is creating. Although people do not always regard these collapses as positive experiences, Osiris suggests that we trust that this is part of the cleansing of our planet and our lives. The shifting of structures to allow for greater Light is mentioned in this extract from the meditation of the 26 March 2009 (the entire transcript and an mp3 are available on the website www.stargateway.co.za).

The end result of life in the true fast lane of a higher dimension will be infinitely more satisfying than anything we have known to date. Considering that we are learning to be master-manifesters of everything we need, soon our material security issues will be a thing of the past. Once we are all able to manifest what we need, the structures of our societies have to change, the work we need to do changes and our needs change. When we want for nothing we become very difficult to manipulate. When we can easily fulfil all of our own needs, nothing is out of our reach and we have no need to strive after the trophies of others.

Osiris: Structures Shift

"As you begin to go through in physicality many experience of many areas of past discussion of connection of various pathways shifting, many areas of the structural system beginning to shift and change into the experience of greater Light, it is not always felt in the position of greater Light at this time, but it is movement - know and trust in the formation of Spirit and takes in the form to create shifts and cleansing."

As the rest of the planet moves more quickly into living ascension, even the lower ranges of the 3rd dimension will not be able to easily support continued low frequency vibrations, because the magnetic-like pull towards higher states of Light will make it difficult to comfortably maintain the lower resonance. As a result, portions of the Earth which can be inhabited by the people of darkness, or anybody who chooses low frequency thoughts, emotions and behaviours, will ultimately cease to exist as a low frequency reality. More of Earth and her resources become available to those who choose to raise their consciousness.

If people resist the change to higher frequencies and choose to shift their vibrations to frequency states which are lower than the 3rd dimension frequencies, they will take some time to completely devolve their soul energy. The ultimate state of soul dissolution is called 'nothingness,' and some souls will dissolve. How long this takes is dependent on the degree of resident Light within. If dissolution happens, the energy of these individuals returns to the disordered background noise of non-differentiated 'nothingness': the so-called random dots and squiggles of elemental energy in the void. This result is antagonistic to what we intend for ourselves as souls: to return Home to the highly ordered, specialised state of high frequency Universal Light - via the pathway of the Higher Self, the Over Self and the Monad - within the collective of the state of being of the Godhead.

Osiris speaks of shifting ourselves so that we connect to the feelings of love within the heart, because it is from this basis of love that we make the totality of the great soul experience of the Monad real on Earth, in physicality. As we reconnect to the greater state of ourselves, dimension by dimension or when in a meditation, we remember our original intention for wanting to come into physicality in the first place. When we reconnect to this memory, we more easily work in accordance with it - as it is the true pathway of soul, our soul purpose.

Osiris: Soul Intention through the Heart

"There is the connectivity which is Sanat Kumara to bring forward deep understanding within the heart centre as you begin to open further - it is opening further into the feeling state of deep connectivity at this time of moving forward through intention of connectivity of that which has begun from the Monadic beginning of your experience of physicality. It is in the understanding of moving into the connection of all that has taken place from soul perspective, it is from soul memory, so it is in the understanding of the full expansiveness of this you have the ability at this time to move into the intention that has been set prior to the moving forward into this whole experience from the Monad.

"I bring forward many blessings and support you in much love. Feel the surrounding energies of Spirit in your heart. I bless you in love."

The interesting thing to note with regard to any large system, such as a government or corporation which is used for the purposes of control and the manipulation of power is that in the presence of the naturally increasing Light of many of its members, the dark itself becomes more obvious too. The possibilities of a shadowy existence are becoming less probable due to the intensity of this time of shifting consciousness and increased Light. This is because as we move into the central position of the Age of Aquarius the intensified Light, which is streaming into the planet, stimulates more and more people to realise that they have to choose their path. This effectively amounts to choosing a side.

The increased illumination of high frequencies of Light causes a noticeable sharpening of the division between the Light and the dark, with less indecisive, shadow-space in between. The intense duality of polar opposites is starkly clarified. This creates the opportunity for an obvious choice, one way or another. Everything and everybody can more easily become enLightened and transformed into Oneness.

With this rapid polarisation, the actions and reactions of people on both sides of the divide intensify and, just as intense Light shines forth more brightly and Illuminates, so the existence of intense darkness must behave true to type too: it must retract onto itself. As a result we can expect to see the Brothers of Darkness band together more strongly. This retraction creates an intensity which makes the actionable space of the darkness both smaller and more viciously obvious.

In this way many people easily begin to notice, and reject, the Path of Darkness as it deepens in intensity. This is contrasted against the incoming outer-planetary Light and the response to the growing Light of vast numbers of the wave of rapidly enLightening people. This obvious shift in intensity causes further, rapid polarisation of the dual forces of Light and dark as more people suddenly realise they have a clear opportunity to change their lives. This marks the decision as to whether or not to choose the Light. If they do, this naturally means they will withdraw their energy and support from the darkness.

In this manner the darkness of humanity, whether in personal, religious, government or corporate guise is exposed quickly. This is how and why many of the old structures of control and manipulation will crumble and fall. They will be replaced with new structures which have a greater Light energy, are compatible with 5th dimension energies and serve us all into the future.

Bullies and Victims
Regardless of how large and powerful the bands of the Brothers of Darkness are, we all know that a bully is only powerful relative to the weakness of his victim. Once the enslavement of the minds and emotions of the victims-of-old of the 3rd or the 4th dimensions is halted, vast numbers of people will have awoken and

reclaimed their power of Light. The bully's sport will be over. Advancement and empowerment, along with the mass awakening of humanity is happening right now and the process is rapidly gathering speed. No longer a gentle swell, the big wave of changing consciousness is carrying us all along on it.

One has hope that the bullies and manipulators of old will also learn to ascend from the 3rd and the 4th dimensions of physicality, as they too are a part of the original Whole of Creation. The uplifting consciousness of humanity supports this possibility. Just as we positively affect people whom we love, we also affect many others whom we don't know at all and this includes those who resonate at very low frequencies. A positive change in direction of the consciousness of Enlil was communicated to us in August 2009 by both Thoth and Isis. Considering this, we are bound to see many changes of heart amongst humanity within a very short period of time.

In the meantime we are still dealing with the hangover effects of the darkness of the past. The Brothers of Darkness, in all their modern guises, strive at all costs to ensure individuals feel enslaved to these physical dimensions and that people believe all the covert lies which are so cleverly fed into the social systems that influence all human lives. The Brothers of Darkness need as many people as possible to be fearful of everything: from their lives, their jobs, their finances, their health, their loved ones, and even the life hereafter. They stimulate this fear amongst the members of society in order to maintain the status quo of their power and dominion on Earth, no matter how transient this may be. In the final analysis, when individuals have reclaimed their personal power and realised the truth of their own Divinity, people will have found their voice and will no longer be susceptible to being manipulated. As this point, humanity as a whole will no longer need many of the structures which underpin our societies in the present day. With this in mind we may consider the following:

- That any religious institution preys on the individual's desire for the re-connection to his soul, creates fear of damnation for the purposes of control or to ensure a swollen membership, or in any way manipulates spiritual information, is a display of objectionable behaviour.
- That any corporate institution preys on the fears of individuals to create wealth through structures such as life or health insurance, crippling loans and mortgages in the guise of financial support, or the potential of being replaced by a cheaper or younger worker, is equally corrupt.
- The extent to which any government supports war in the name of God, security or liberty, prohibits or limits the open pursuit of spirituality by its people or in any way limits the joyful life experience of any individual, is an indication that they do not have the best interests of others at the core of their statutes, regardless of what they claim.

No matter where within the structures of society any of these offences against humanity originate, they all amount to the same thing and all of them are essentially contrary to the true pathway of Divinity. Divinity is all about living from the basis of love and compassion for all. It is the understanding and realisation of our own Divinity that protects us from the various forms of the abuse of power in the external world - no matter whether as perpetrators or victims. Isis has a particularly beautiful turn of phrase when she refers to our ability to shift to higher states of the Light of our Divinity.

Isis: Take Flight

"Take forward holding the physical self, the ability at this time: let go and take flight, feel your strength, feel your might, feel your Divinity of Light, the presence of Godhead within each one.

"Beloved Beings of Light, I bring forward great love to yourselves on this day, to surround each one in the Wings of Light. I bring forward great love and bless you on this day, Beloved Beings of Light."

Most important in any programme of manipulation and control is that the Brothers of Darkness seek to cut us off from our Light and to hide the truth of our natural Divinity from us. To serve their best interests, these manoeuvrings have to be prevalent in society so that human beings inadvertently keep themselves within the Karmic cycle, or low resonance state, of reincarnation.

This reincarnation cycle is known of as the Astrological Wheel of Life or the Wheel of Karma. Our cycle of birth and re-birth at specific times in the Astrological calendar energetically governs the resonance of the human body and life due to the specific combination of the energies of the attending planets and stars at the point of birth. This timing of birth is dictated by the resonance of the soul and, therefore, the necessary experiences and lessons which are typical of the ever-returning cycle of lifetimes in the 3rd or the 4th dimensions of physicality. In this way we create repeat opportunities for ourselves to raise our resonance in each successive lifetime. With limited perceptual abilities in the lower dimensions, this is often a hit-and-miss affair.

Interestingly enough, knowledge about the importance of Karma, the astrological cycles and the role they play in reincarnation is exactly what many religions have removed from their teachings. No matter how abhorrent the idea may seem, it may be a good idea to question whether or not the religious doctrines we subscribe to support the role of manipulated teachings, no matter whether these controls are overtly or covertly presented or whether they support the development and growth of the personal power of the individual

The on-going programme of creating myths and then repeating them regularly and teaching them as truth, ensures that myth becomes reality in the minds of many, no matter who began that myth or what it is comprised of. Many of the creation stories are myths and have no bearing whatsoever on the actual truth of creation. Repeating something often enough does not make it true. Generation upon generation of people have been successfully brainwashed in this manner. Many of the original spiritual reasons for most of the dogma and doctrines of our currently practiced religions have vanished over time and most of the ancient knowledge has been lost, destroyed or discarded. All we are left with is the modern understanding of an ancient, apparent 'reality.'

If all of the structures and teachings of religion are examined by us learning to think with the heart, then we may more easily discern whether or not they are relevant or necessary in our lives today. The determining factor for religious or spiritual relevance has to encompass the following points:
- Whether or not they are based on the principle of unconditional love and compassion for all.
- Whether or not they help us to re-claim the fullness of our Divine Intelligence and encourage us to shine as Divine Beings of Light ourselves.

Some Eastern religions have a much more circumspect approach to life and death than Western ones do, specifically because they have a working understanding of reincarnation, Karma and the cycle of lifetimes on Earth.

We would do well to consider the rich information which has been uncovered at so many of the ancient sacred sites around the world, including reading the various translations of the clay tablets. There are numerous scholarly works which detail these. This would help plump out our understanding of the cycles of Earth. With this ancient physical proof we could easily piece together the real story of our history on Earth and the real history of all religions and spiritual practices. By doing this we would go back to the beginnings of the Osirian teachings. Most people would be astounded to learn that the Holy Trinity came back to Earth in Ancient Egyptian times to teach humanity about the Pathway of Light. Many of our most fondly-held religious stories, such as Moses in the Bulrushes or the Exodus, are an account of real events which were experienced by real physical beings on Earth. This may sound like blasphemy to some and be highly amusing to others, but we are at the time in our Cosmic lives where nothing can be spared in the pursuit of Truth. There can be no sacred cows, anywhere. The journey of discovery in search of the historical truth is a very exciting and Illuminating one.

There is no doubt that people have powerful spiritual experiences within any and every religion, but these Divine experiences are in danger of being clouded over, distorted or hampered by the laws, stories and controls of man which govern these institutions.

A good balance to the disturbing facts about the manipulative misinformation that we read about is to read the following meditation which Osiris led in March 2008. The heading suggests the entire subject matter: fearless compassion. These two words encompass the vastness of non-judgement, compassion, tolerance and understanding. Cultivating those qualities within us immediately connects us to the highest frequency of Light. Osiris brings in the supportive energy of various other Light Beings to support the procedures, such as the Hindu Goddess Lakshmi, Lord Matreya and Lord Buddha. This visualisation is held in the etheric space in the spiritually powerful area of Mount Kailash in North Western Tibet. Here we see how we can create another style of a Light Vehicle around us, the Lotus Flower.

Osiris: Fearless Compassion

"Greetings Beloved Ones, I am Osiris, come forward on this day from Spirit, to be with you. As I communicate with you from Spirit on this day, Beloved Ones, it is on this day I wish to take you forward, is through visualisation, connectivity with Beings of Light. I wish to take you forward through the deep understanding of the connection of the pathway of many Beings of Light: the communication with Lord Buddha, the presence of being which is Lakshmi, the presence of being which is the Lord Matreya.

"I bring forward in my presence to work with you, to allow for yourselves to move through a deep understanding of that which is fearless compassion. It is the understanding of the many teachings of the Beings of Light to bring forward over lengthy period, and therefore it is at this time for yourselves to be in the full understanding of the service path in the state of living ascension. It is, Beloved Ones, for yourselves - as you begin to bring forward into the connectivity of that which takes place in the understanding of the movement forward in the ascension state of being in the physical - so it is to allow for the understanding of all that takes place within the environment of physicality, of all that takes place within the Earth experience at this time.

"It is, Beloved Ones, as we take you forward into a connectivity, each being coming forward to be in the collective energy. It is each being in their own presence coming forward for the continuation of an intention. As you move forward with the understanding of this state of fearless compassion, all areas of the continuation of service to humanity throughout the experience of many, many lifetimes, it is in the state of deep tolerance of Spirit, deep understanding and compassion, the ability to transcend all from the perspective of judgement, to transcend all from the experience of loyalty through the connectivity of Spirit and with Earth.

"So it is on this day that I take you into an experience within the etheric - the connectivity of the area and environment of ancient Tibet, the connection of Mount Kailash. It is the understanding to support you further in the understanding of that which takes place across the planetary system at this time, to take you into the experience of the etheric. We have worked in the connectivity of the Earthly experience, so it is the understanding as you find yourself above in the etheric ascension seat - it is the connectivity of Lord Buddha - it is to understand that through this pathway you are in a central position once more of that which has taken place in Ancient Egypt, it is within pyramid.

"And so it is in this particular state of frequency you have the ability to know and understand, through this central position, to connect with that which takes place to that which is below and to the central position of moving forward through the dimensional experience. So it is greatly supported for each of yourselves on this day, in the full understanding of the expansiveness of the living state of ascension. There is that I work with each of yourselves in the coming period through this interconnection. So it is that all beings that I bring forward to yourselves on this day continue to work with you in the upliftment of your state of being to follow forward in all areas of the service to humanity.

"As you move into the connective procedure of the feeling state of Vehicle of Light, it is to begin to feel the letting go of physical form. As you feel yourself in the experience of Light Vehicle surrounding you, to feel the energy field surrounding you, allow for yourselves to let go entirely. It is in the movement into the connection with Spirit - allow for it to be a gentle movement, gentle experience of the moving forward into the connection with your Light. It is to be in the feeling state of communing with Spirit at this time, to feel the presence of being to support you on the way forward.

"Allow for the physical form to remain. The consciousness leaves the physical form, allowing yourself to let go in a state of pure trust and being in a state of great Light and communication with Spirit. Allow for the connectivity to take place, moving gently and slowly into the experience of the etheric. It is above the mountain area. It is the understanding of the movement forward through this position, the central position, it is the opening of heart centre, the connectivity of that which takes place, the bringing forward of the opening of the crown centre, of the position on the planet.

"So it is as you move into the experience, to be in the feeling state of feet on the ground, but it is to feel it in the etheric. Know and understand that in this particular position it is of central position. And as you begin to find yourself in the standing position, perhaps not the entirety of the feeling state of physicality, but it is the feeling of the ability to see before you Lord Buddha, it is to the left. You have the ability to communicate, to see the vibratory energy of the Lord Matreya, it is to the right. The presence of the lady Quan Yin, it is to the side of this Being of Light, the presence of Lakshmi, and so it is, my own presence is in central position, between the feminine and masculine energy.

"As you feel the interconnection, it is within central position to begin to feel the energy field, the communication. At this time you begin to feel the formation of the lotus flower of the state of consciousness of communication of the Godhead, feel yourself in the position of the Light Vehicle - the formation of vast petal of consciousness. Feel within the experience of the beginnings as we find ourselves within the central position of the core of consciousness. As you begin to feel the unfoldment, each movement outward from central position is the presence of great intensity of Light - communication of the Godhead - supportive of bringing forward through Lord Buddha, the ability to feel the communication and connectivity of that which is to be brought forward from Spirit in connectivity to the Godhead to Earth, through Lord Matreya.

"It is through your presence the ability already to bring forward, through physicality, the understanding of unfoldment through communication of the connectivity of Beings of Light from Spirit. It is from the understanding of yourself, the presence of Lord Matreya, the ability to go forward in a continuation of experience, the blended procedure of that which takes place above to that which takes place below, the upliftment of the state of consciousness in many direction through this communication.

"As you begin to feel yourself moving into the silent state of being, to begin to feel the unfoldment of the Light energy surrounding you, opening and moving in a gentle procedure - at all times lifting and raising vibratory energy. From central position you see it in form of connectivity of pyramid of Light to Earth, pyramid of Light to Spirit. Feel the expansion of being as you begin to open further and further. It is in connectivity on this day in the presence of the Venusian energy: as you begin to feel the experience of connectivity of this energy of Light of the Godhead. Feel it moving through your being, coming forward into the experience of the unfoldment further. It is of Light type of consciousness, allowing it to move in a continual opening.

"It is at this time you begin to feel this taking place in the outer experience and in your own heart centre - feeling state of the unfoldment further of that which takes place within to that which takes place in the outer experience - through central position of the feeling state without form. At this time you begin to feel yourself as only heart. Movement into the feeling state of ascension together - it is the experience of pure compassion, the understanding of that which is fearless compassion, of great Light of Spirit.

"All low energy dissipates; all ego state dissipates entirely, into the state of unconditional love. Support of the feeling state of energy fields coming forward, surrounding you with the energy. We move two into experience of Godhead and bringing forward support of Venusian energy. As it unfolds further in the area of the heart centre, allow for the state of unconditional love to unfold further in the silent state of your being, the recreation of your Divinity and the great Light of Spirit. Feel yourself in the unfoldment of pure energy, moving into the frequency of great Light, through the dimensional experience of connectivity, moving into the feeling state of the vibratory energy surrounding you - it is of the movement forward into the experience of dimension of the Godhead, into connectivity. Drift into the experience of deep resonance with Spirit.

"Within the feeling state of deep connection, allow for further unfoldment - the expansion of heart centre, allow for opening of crown centre - to bring forward into central position the Light of the Godhead to be in the expansiveness of the return, to be in the feeling state of great Bliss: State of return to Oneness - expansiveness of the understanding. Feel the blending taking place, interconnection of all beings from position of deep connectivity of great Light, allowing to move into drifting movement, gently shift dimensional experience and understanding of the feeling state of deep compassion.

"Allow yourself to find the movement into the feeling state of the etheric once more. Come together in the experience of the blessings coming forward from the Godhead, through the experience of the interconnectivity of the Buddha and the environment of the surroundings - so it is each being moving through the deep upliftment of communication. Feel the heart centre: shift taking place of all that is, of the understanding on the return to physicality to support and uplift humanity in service of intention - service of much love and compassion, service of great love, service of great Light.

"You feel yourself beginning to move within the feeling state of Light Vehicle having opened the state of consciousness - allow for the formation to come forward. It is in the collective, we move within the experience of Light Vehicle to gently return to the physical state of being. There is a gentle movement. Allow for the feeling state of reconnection with physicality, in the heart centre to feel expansiveness, to feel the return in this central position.

"Begin gently to feel the reconnection to physicality, moving downward from heart centre and upward from heart centre till it is in the feeling state of return to physical form. It is the feeling of great love and compassion for the self, to feel within the environment the connectivity of beings in the surroundings to continue to support you. The presence to be felt.

"So it is, on this day I support you in the continuation to take you forward on further occasion into the out of body experience, further into this state of connectedness. I support you at all times, through the moving forward in the upliftment of your pathway, holding of your Divinity and your Light - opening further of the ability, communication with Spirit the support of humanity. Bless you in much love on this day. With love, I am Osiris."

In the previous communication it was clear that the Light Beings were working on the opening of the new Crown Chakra on Earth: Mount Kailash. The Crown Chakra of Earth used to be in the United States of America. Noteworthy is the fact that as human beings work with the principles of fearless compassion within their hearts, this energy supports the unfoldment of unconditional love and the subsequent dissipation of all low energy states.

It is worthwhile considering the importance of the sacred sites of the world with regard to their portal energy, especially Mount Kailash, as we see in the following excerpt from a March 2008 meditation. When any one of the power points of the sacred sites is stimulated, it activates all of the other sacred sites around the world, through the energy grid system of Earth.

Osiris: Mount Kailash

"Allow for yourself to move into the connection - it is of the feeling sate of the Vehicle of Light to surround you, to work with you and hold you in the presence of great Light of Spirit. To find yourselves moving, as you let go, to the experience of the position of the Mount Kailash. It is the understanding that you find yourself in the position of mountain in the area of Ancient Tibet, the holy mountain. The understanding of this position, which is greatly supportive for the shift of consciousness for many Beings of Light - the shift of consciousness to allow for yourselves to be in the feeling state of deep connection with the Godhead.

"The understanding of this position, if you visualise it, merely to see it as mountain. It is to be at the position it is greatly supportive for the accessing of various Great Beings to come forward to be in the portal of energy to communicate and to assist all beings in humanity at this time. Allow for yourselves to move into the feeling state of the connection of this area and environment. As I see, there is to be in the position of standing, as you feel yourself moving into this state of being in various feeling state, I come forward to support you through the feeling state. As you follow it is, Beloved Ones, allow for yourselves to let go entirely and the gentle procedure, through the Light Vehicle, into the position of connectivity with the particular Mountain of Light, Beloved Ones."

The Lucrative Business of War

Just by looking at one aspect of the power-orientated and self-serving practices which have been created on Earth, we see that the war machine itself is very lucrative. The revenue streams of the associated 'businesses' which support war should not be underestimated. In this 'business' most of the very big money which is globally available, whether for war or for 'development' purposes in poorer countries, is continually recycled back into the hands of the very few. This is often done via the suppliers to the projects or through the creation of what becomes crippling debt that is created as a result of over-optimistic revenue projections from the developments. Some call the band of elite beneficiaries of these types of manipulated world chaos the Illuminati, others call them the Luciferian Brotherhood or the Elite. Whatever they are named, these groups of people are real and they do exist. They are devoid of the feeling of love in their hearts. These are the Brothers of Darkness on Earth. There is no such thing as a conspiracy *theory*. It is a fact. Conspiracy exists.

These people, as well as many other non-influential, low vibration people, are the human continuations of the souls of the Brothers of Darkness from Atlantean times and before. At the top echelons of their structures, they work stealthily and quietly and they persist with their low resonance behaviour on Earth. They have many puppets and many stages. To understand this band of individuals for what they are, we need to flush out and expose the motives behind the purported reasons given for war, for example, or the story behind any unkind or cruel actions, such as police brutality - regardless of how they are justified. At their core, these groups of individuals are neither nationally nor religiously bound, but they use the emotive issues surrounding these notions to incite violence and foment war, all to further their cause: the maintenance of power and control on Earth. When these power structures become unbalanced, in-fighting begins in the lower levels and may become uncontrollable. Their vicious attacks on each other then spill over to the rest of humanity.

We would be naïve to underestimate the power and cunning of these people. In their many guises, whether human or otherwise, they have been fighting it out with the Light Beings for aeons, on Earth and elsewhere. As Osiris once said to me, "*It is the War of the Stars, Beloved One.*"

The withholding or misappropriation of information didn't only occur in the bygone years of the Dark Ages, or in the, "*Ancient of days*," to use Isis' term of reference for these antediluvian times. Information manipulations continue even today in our modern societies and highly developed nations, in the same self-serving manner as they always have done. Often one of the nonsense-justifications given by the governors of humanity for withholding information is for the prevention of mass hysteria and fear. The fact of the matter is that withholding important information can never be regarded as an act of love. It is unfortunate that there has been such a dominant, all-controlling vice-grip on information for so long.

Our intentions, coupled with the energy impacts of Earth's alignments with the powerful outer-planetary bodies in the approach to 2012, have increased the resonant frequencies of ourselves and of our Earth. This, in turn, has stimulated humanity's desire to request contact with, and communication from, the Light Beings and thus make it possible for them to chat to us and to help us round out our understanding of what *has* happened, what *is* happening, and what *will* happen. This is all part of the process of us moving into the energetically powerful central position of the Age of Aquarius. We need to raise our awareness and uplift our consciousness if we are to cope with the higher frequencies of Light which will abound post-2012.

The Beings of Light will only ever make contact with us if we request them to do so, similar to the manner in which souls reincarnating on Earth will only ever do so at the permission of their human parents. Permission may be consciously or subconsciously communicated.

Worship of Gods
Just as Osiris has discussed with us, we know that the deification of any being, god-like or otherwise, was never intended by any representative of the Godhead, whether on Earth or anywhere else. The fact that this worship-based practice of acknowledging Beings of the Godhead has occurred, that there has been war on Earth between the Light and the dark and that currency or power of one form or another is typically involved in the process, is clear evidence that there have been powerful manipulations at play in religious institutions for a long time.

Aside from displaying respectful behaviour towards others, the fact that we bow and scrape, speak in hushed tones or avert our eyes in deference to anybody at all, whether living or dead, affirms the fact that we believe we are personally less than some other being. Considering that we are all Divine in our own right, this behaviour indicates our loss of power and is tantamount to the sale of our souls to the Brothers of Darkness. This is a strong departure from the respectful manner with which we approach a being - whether Light Being or human being - from the basis of love.

The modern so-called New Age movements are no less guilty of engendering this type of worship-based behaviour than the more traditional religions often are. Wherever there is an hierarchical structure in place in which beings are arranged in such a way as to indicate that they have greater or lesser power or that they are to be revered or worshiped, we many reasonably begin to question who or what is guiding this system. Control and power are often integral parts of these systems.

The spiritual function of a being, no matter whether it is on Earth or elsewhere in the Universe, is relative to the resonance of that individual. The higher the resonance the greater the abilities of that being will be. This ability-based function should not be confused with a power-based pecking order.

Furthermore, we could begin to think about the role that our currently limited, human consciousness plays in maintaining our sense of self in a separated state which is apparently outside of the state of being of the Godhead. This polarisation of ourselves into a 'them' and 'us' (whether of god-like or of hu-man status) is what chokes our ability to experience the Oneness of Being, within the greater state of the consciousness of the Oneness of the Godhead. We are, after all, all parts of the One, in a holographic way. The very fact that the prefix 'Hu' is part of the name 'hu-man' is because we, as Earth-man carry the God-essence of Hu within us. The inclusion of these two letters in the name of 'human' assures us of the innate fact of our Divinity, although few people are aware of this fact.

Ultimately, there is no difference in the Divinity between any beings anywhere in the Universe - aside from each individual's realisation of him or herself as Divine - because together, we are all One. The difference in our understandings about our Divinity comes into play relative only to our resonance and who, what or where we then perceive ourselves to be. The concept of our own intrinsic Divinity, which we are in the process of realising, is often very difficult for us to get our heads around. This is because we are so used to operating and thinking in the lower frequency states of separated physicality, where our state of conscious awareness is as limited as our reality. Hence, there exists the certain and explicit necessity to uplift our consciousness in order to resonate with higher frequencies. Then, we will perceive it all. This gives us an inkling of the meaning of omniscience and omnipresence.

> In order to be in existence God (the Oneness of Being, Divine Source of the Godhead) does not require to be acknowledged - any more than the existence of you or I requires acknowledgement. God is. I am.

Perhaps we may consider that in order to love us, 'God' or any of the God-realised Beings of Light, does not require humility, obedience and obsequiousness from his 'offspring', any more than you or I require this in order to love ourselves or our own children. Dictators and tyrants require various types of conformity, submission and deference in order to maintain their power.

The true, loving representatives of the Godhead, whom we call the Light Beings from our Earthly vantage point, are privy to the endless and complete information of the Universe and they impart this knowledge to us when we request them to do so. The purpose of this is so that we can know that all parts of the Self are Divine, no matter how scattered or small they appear to be, and so that we can re-live the Oneness of Being within the state of being of the Godhead.

The Light Beings help us with our upliftment by stimulating our consciousness with higher frequency vibrations so that we can become more aware of the following:
- Self-empowerment through knowledge.
- New information which develops personal responsibility and skills.
- Feeling unconditional love and thinking from the heart.

Osiris has delivered weekly, channelled meditations to us and many of them relate to healing ourselves so that we can move into, "*The feeling state of the heart, of unconditional love.*" Visit the website www.stargateway.co.za to download these powerful meditations and their transcripts. Hearing the sound vibration alone can assist enormously with shifting the vibrations of the entire being higher into the Light.

We are a part of the Godhead. In fact, we make a grave mistake in even referring to any technologically advanced or highly capable being as a 'god' being, purely because of the misconceptions and misdirection of worship which this tends to stimulate in human beings. We have been brainwashed into slavishly following the processes of worship for so long. These systems of reverence, adoration or adulation are all too often intended to prove or display adoration for a deity. 'Prove to who?' we could reasonably ask ourselves. The answer in all likelihood will be, 'To others like us'. There is no God who requires this adulation any more than there is a God who punishes us.

We could, ideally, employ a completely different reference system until we understand the difference between the Divine state of being of the Godhead and its Divine representatives, as opposed to other beings from other places, or states of consciousness, who are not necessarily any more God-realised than we are, but who have powerful technologies which are different to our own. Although all are emanations out from the Divine Source, they only behave in a Divine manner relative to the state of their consciousness. The upliftment of consciousness therefore is directly related to the realisation of Divinity.

We may regard the Light Beings who guide us as highly experienced, highly competent Light workers who have passed through this school of Earth, as well as many others both like it and unlike it. Earth is one of those schools which human beings are still trying to graduate from. As such we have a lot to learn from the Light Beings. This does not mean that we should ever imagine that it is required that we kow-tow to them or deify them, but it does mean we might consider what it is they have to say to us. They have a higher vantage point than we do, relative to their resonance with higher frequency Light. Consequently, they have more of the big picture available to them to work with than we currently do, until we too uplift our consciousness. Regardless of this, during the course of the communications from the Light Beings of the Godhead there can be no coercion, because the free will of the individual is supreme. It is always our own choice to decide what to do and how we want to live our lives, on Earth and elsewhere.

The Wisdom of the Universe is maintained always
Questioning what agendas are being served in the pursuit of power of any kind

could be a source of enLightenment. The story of Adam and Eve is a case in point. Most people would be horrified if they learnt the truth behind the creation of man on Earth, as is so ably told in the translations and discussions of the Sumerian clay tablets such as in the books by Zecharia Sitchin and Alan F. Alford. Once we research this subject further, perplexing questions have to arise as to just who or what is behind all the mistranslation and misinformation which we have based our religious faith and our spiritual questing upon.

Many people are horrified by the idea that the spiritual progress of humanity may have been hijacked by power-hungry individuals, human or otherwise, even if only for a short period of time. It is sad that so many souls have had to endure so many difficult lifetimes on Earth in search of the truth, sometimes incurring horrible Karma along the way. We can free ourselves of our own Karma and all low resonance states and connections to others. We can release ourselves from the obligation to connect with others in difficult human relationships which help them release their Karma, by shifting the state of our conscious awareness higher. In this way we no longer resonate with any issues of the human ego. This is the upliftment of consciousness.

The release of Karma is both the end result and the originator of the process of uplifting our consciousness. Karma release is rapidly achieved through the processes of re-feeling and acknowledging the emotion behind all of our issues. This is because the resonance of any frequency is always held within the consciousness as a feeling. By being conscious of feeling an emotion as it arises, acknowledging it and then letting it go, we more easily shift into the higher frequency experiences, including living ascension. The alternative to the upliftment of our consciousness is to maintain the dullness of our minds, and continue on the repetitive cycle in which we come back to 3rd or 4th dimension Earth, lifetime after lifetime - often suffering horribly in the process - because we retain low frequency resonances which create low frequency experiences of reality.

Discerning Wisdom from Misinformation
For the Brothers of Darkness power is achieved practically, by the means of mass control over as many aspects of our lives as they can garner. This they easily do by alternatively instilling fear into human beings or rewarding individuals richly when their bidding is done. Unfortunately, the generalised fears of humanity are part of our collective consciousness and we are therefore all at risk of falling foul of fear and being stimulated by its energy. This remains the case as long as we still resonate with the 3rd or the 4th dimensions. We avoid this by shifting to the 5th dimension and progressively learning to resonate higher and higher.

We maintain the energy of the collective consciousness of humanity by means of an unspoken consensus. Although it is generally not considered consciously, this is a consensus in the true sense of the word, inasmuch as there are many opinions, emotions and behaviours which are collectively subscribed to by the majority of humanity. The only way we can change this collective consciousness is to change our individual consciousness - and therefore the resultant group consensus - of sufficient within humanity to make a difference in that collective. A groundswell of changing opinion can begin with a little bit of knowledge and information and we can undo the damage in the exact same way as it was created.

Nothing has changed in the annals of time and we easily see this when we reference various religious texts that give us the angry vengeful god of divine retribution who metes out punishment, or the rewarding, benevolent god who dispenses riches and gifts. These references to a 'God' who is both manipulative and power-hungry have nothing to do with the true state of the Godhead, which is the Bliss-state of unconditional love. These are stories which tell us about a god-being who dispenses favours relative to judgement. Judgement is an all-too-human, lower dimension trait. It is only beings in the separated state of existence who judge others. Most human beings currently fall into this category. There is no place or need for judgement in the all enveloping love-consciousness of the Godhead. Stripped of their personal power and suffering in their blinded state of reality, it is no wonder that misinformed human beings have sought to appease the gods in each era - no matter whether by offerings, prayers or obedience.

The Beings of the Godhead do not judge. In the state of Oneness, the concept of judgement is both impossible and nonsensical. In this regard, re-reading the excerpt from Osiris' opening dissertation (repeated below) that discusses the concept of spiritual self-responsibility, the so-called god-beings and the non-existence of a God that judges may prove useful. Re-reading the meditation in which Osiris discusses the concept of fearless compassion is especially helpful in understanding the principles which are important for us to instil into our hearts and minds if we are to live from the basis of unconditional love.

Osiris: No God Judges

"It is the understanding, it is at this time, it is relevant for all beings to know and understand that if it is they do not take responsibility for the self, in their own understanding and in the uncovering of their own information and guidance for the future. The understanding that there is the connectivity of the Godhead to support all in the state of deep love and support and assistance for each being to go forward.

"So it is much begins to become uncovered, much begins to move forward in a state of great upliftment and the bringing forward of great peace.

"There is in all areas of connectivity with others and the intolerance of the support of one another, the lack of compassion in connection with one another, it is from the percentage, it is always in connection with that which is the disbelief with one religion or another and the bringing forward the shedding of blood in order to worship your god. It is the understanding I bring forward at this time, there is no God that judges in this manner.

"There have been brought forward at a period prior to the understanding of many, the existence of the god-being as they have become human being, it is through the connectivity of that which is understood as god-man and therefore it is far from this.

"So it is that many, many information comes forward, but it is to know and understand there is no judgement from Spirit. There is only love to support those if it is they have done wrong to move and assist in the return to the state of rightness, to the state of love."

If we use the concept of unconditional love as a handy yardstick at all times we will more easily be able to assess the words and behaviours of ourselves and others for truth, whether current or ancient. War, pain, suffering and vengeance have nothing to do with love. The state of being of the Godhead is love. In the state of Oneness, no part of it can hurt another part, any more than a normal, sane human being would willingly and deliberately hurt himself. In the state of Being of the Godhead, all parts are connected because they are One.

Conversely, those purveyors of the human conditions of suffering are both the creators of world destruction and the self-proclaimed fixers of it too, although we rarely realise, hear about or even see this two-faced behaviour of theirs. This manipulation has been going on for century after long century on Earth. These individuals of darkness work together as a group, reaching across international borders and assuming whatever role is required to maintain their own sick balance of power.

Once we are insecure from all the manufactured disturbances of world peace we, as the mass of humanity, come running for cover. They, the war-and-peace-manipulating Brothers of Darkness, offer solutions for our on-going 'protection' and 'security' and then they ever-so-willingly supply it, at a price. As we heave a heartfelt sigh of relief, little do we realise that the ultimate price we pay is the surrender of the knowledge and experience of our Divinity and our natural living ascension abilities. This is our power.

It is the use of our high frequency living ascension abilities which allow for the collapse of duality and results in the removal of the experience of polar opposites as the Earthly living experience. This means the following:
- We will be sufficiently conscious once more and able to make rapid progress towards enLightenment.
- We will be able to reclaim our personal power and make progress on the Pathway of Return.
- We will consciously move forwards throughout the higher dimensions of the Universe, according to our individual free will and without the risks we ran in Ancient Atlantean times when we were too inexperienced to realise the full import of the dire consequences of low energy behaviour.

Fortunately for us there are many inbuilt truths in the ancient religious texts which are still accessible to us. Unfortunately, the stories the correct translations which the less popular texts tell are seldom taken much notice of, as they are now so foreign to us that we cannot easily relate to their meaning. It is always a good idea to familiarise ourselves with more than the popular texts about the ancient stories which detail our history. The fact that we are currently incapable of placing them within the correct paradigm is not a good enough reason for us to not find these correct translations and begin to work with them, any more than we can ignore the massive temples and pyramids which were constructed so long ago. The extensive works of many scholars and authors provide easy access to some accurate translations and discussions of ancient texts. The internet provides access to immediate information about this subject.

Manipulations Continue
We are so busy marching to the beat of the drum of the false 'values' of the manufactured societies of the Brothers of Darkness that we think we are having fun. We have forgotten to listen to our own sweet song, the song of soul.

Osiris describes the importance of maintaining the frequency of love within ourselves in this extract from a March 2008 meditation.

Osiris: The Frequency of Love Within

"So it is in the bringing forward of your being in the offering of your Light and Divinity, so it is in the receiving procedure that you begin to feel it, moving forward through your being - the unfoldment of knowledge of Akasha, the understanding of bringing forward of all that is known from soul perspective. It is to move forward with the ability to that which is relative to your progress at this time, to the understanding of that which is to be felt by your being, the ability and maintaining of frequency, the ability of maintaining the state of the feeling of great love within.

"Move forward, Beloved Ones, in the owning of your Divinity further, and further the understanding to hold yourselves in this Light. In much love, I am Osiris, I guide and support and bless you on this day. I greet and bless you, Beloved Ones."

We have horrific information incessantly beamed into our brains through the ever-blinking media. Very few of these images or this information which we allow into our conscious and subconscious minds has anything to do with unconditional love. This stream of poorly constructed information, or misinformation, instils into us everything from fear to über-patriotism which stimulates us to go to war against each other. This is hardly surprising because this form of social engineering is usually designed either to create desire or to put fear of anything, everything and everybody into us. The purpose behind most fear is to ensure we keep the machine of finance going and this financial machine feeds ideological-based wars. Wars destabilise people and threaten their existence at the most basic level and this is the perfect background to ensure that the processes of self actualisation are so far from the minds of humanity so as to be almost non-existent.

The sophisticated finance machine is the most powerful vehicle of control in modern times. It is because it stimulates fear, greed, insecurity and war that this control system is the means to a low resonance end for many people. Consider the following:
- We buy insurance, earn money at a frenetic pace and stash it in the banks which have been established to control our money and, therefore, us. Daily, we unconsciously subscribe to numerous systems of financial control, supporting the system which controls us with fear and paying its fees too.
- Just to sweeten the bitter pill of our fearful lives, we are all but finished off with large, unhealthy doses of 'fun' foods and tasty snacks to fill the yawning holes

in the pits of our stomachs. It's a pity we don't realise this is anxiety which only love can ease.
- Kindly, we are 'saved' from our illnesses by toxic medicines. These palliatives do nothing to salve our sad souls. What a pity we don't realise the illnesses and injury are symptoms of both a lack of love and dominant, low frequency vibrations.
- To top it all, we chase after fun, fun, fun in its many advertised guises to take our minds off our sorry, empty lives. Sadly, we don't realise that this is our yearning for spirituality and the reconnection to the Divine, non-physical parts of ourselves.

Essentially, most of the individuals amongst the mass of humanity are controlled by societal means which ensure that everything they take in through their senses keeps them on their work-a-day treadmill, entrenched in the habits of their fear-driven lives and far away from accessing their spirituality.

So what happens to those who don't Ascend-in-the-Physical now?
They stay on as normal, living in their 3rd or the 4th dimensions of separated physicality. Living ascension at this time is not a guaranteed process for all human beings, but it is certainly possible for all, and many people will achieve this. The choice to follow this Pathway of Return is an individual one. As more and more people - normal, simple, everyday people like you and I - become aware of information such as is contained in this book, the upliftment of consciousness which is necessary for the living ascension process becomes easier to do and more widely practiced. This results in a more highly ordered state of consciousness. Order replaces the haphazard processes of blindly trying to attain a high enough frequency so as to be compatible with the ascension-dimension of the 5th dimension of spiritualised physical reality.

The upliftment of consciousness results in a new awareness, regardless of how this begins.

This book is only one of the means of developing awareness about the processes for the upliftment of consciousness. There are many more, simple, everyday ways of doing this, such as the following:
- Eating as much raw food as possible.
- Ensuring no toxic chemicals enter our bodies.
- Getting sufficient rest and leisure time.
- Resolving toxic relationships at home and at work.
- Acknowledging, feeling and releasing old issues.
- Taking note of how others mirror our own issues.

- Meditating daily.
- Clearing our auras.
- Energising and re-aligning our chakras.
- Setting the intention to change.
- Setting the intention to shift into living ascension.
- Setting the intention to manifest what we want.
- Taking active steps to heal old wounds, emotionally and physically.
- Loving ourselves unconditionally, in each moment.
- Loving others unconditionally.
- Practicing fearless compassion: non-judgement, compassion, tolerance and understanding.

These simple, but practical points are easy-to-implement ways to raise resonance. As the speed of our vibrations change, our consciousness shifts and we become more aware. It is the new awareness of our changing world which raises the resonance of each individual further, uplifting them closer to the higher frequencies of Light. This stimulates more conscious intentions to shift further and people start clearing out the things, patterns and people in their lives that no longer serve them. Although innumerable practices, both simple and complex, may be used to begin the shift in energy which will result in the shift in consciousness of a person, ultimately, it is the *conscious awareness* of each person about himself as an integral part of the Divine, which will determine his or her resonance state. Resonance determines the ability to ascend-in-the-physical. It is this, which is unconditional love in action, which ultimately allows for the experience of the 5th dimension as our permanent reality. This alternative realm of reality is accessed through a frequency gateway in a wormhole system which we can only move through when we raise our resonance. All the dimension shifting possibilities and processes are the natural and simple response of each person when we harmonically resonate with higher frequencies of Light. The gateways to other realms resonate with high frequencies. The key to this gateway is our uplifted, raised-resonance consciousness.

Intention is where the process of living ascension begins.
EnLightenment is the result.

The concept that intention is the first stage of enLightenment and a shifted dimension life does not necessarily imply that each person has to know the term 'living ascension' in order to do this, but it is essential for people to have the desire to know more, to seek more information and to live more fully within the boundless state of unconditional love, in order to shift consciousness higher. This is the reason there is such an enormous hunger amongst humanity for information from Spirit right now.

Feeling unconditional love is the starting point from where we access the frequencies of living ascension. Using this mode of living as a yardstick we can easily appreciate that no amount of intellectual understanding about the concept will allow us to shift dimension. We have to live, feel and think unconditional love to change our resonance.

The information which is contained in this book is designed to satisfy some of that spiritual searching and hunger. The Light Beings provide us with a broader knowledge base which may provide answers to many of our questions about life and spirituality. More information from Isis, Thoth, Horus and Enki about the processes of living ascension, as well as unknown information about the arrival on Earth of the god-beings and the nature of the Universe, will be available shortly as follow-on publications. They will support the further advancement of the upliftment of human consciousness. There is vast information and knowledge, both simple and complex, which the Light Beings are imparting to us and this follows on from the information which is contained in this book. Visit the website www.stargateway.co.za to download meditations mp3s, transcripts, new course material and other information which will help with the processes of shifting into an alternative reality.

Although it is not always easy for Spirit to communicate with us 'down' here on Earth, it becomes easier and easier for the Light Beings to do as humanity consistently moves higher within the 4th dimension. Once we are in the 4th dimension we can harmonically resonate with the 5th dimension. As we tune ourselves up and raise our resonance we become consistently more capable of communicating with the higher levels within the 5th dimension, until we find ourselves constantly experiencing that reality.

When we are resonating with higher frequencies of Light we are far more approachable by the Light Beings, who themselves step down their Light from the state of Oneness in its completeness when they communicate with us. This they do so as to operate and vibrate at speeds which we are physically capable of perceiving, which are within our range. It is this process which allows for the communication between us and the Light Beings through the process of harmonic resonance octave, or dimension, by octave. Harmonic resonance is the process of us being able to resonate with the resonance field, or octave, above and below our own.

We can only begin to resonate with the 5th dimension once we are in the bridging zone of the 4th dimension. When humanity is there, which we presently are, we can hop backwards and forwards between these two dimensions. Once contact with the Light Beings begins this makes our progress higher into the 5th dimension easier and faster thereafter, because they mentor us through the processes of living ascension and stimulate our vibrations to resonate with higher frequencies. It is interesting to note that Osiris said all people who are exposed to the communications of the Light Beings will be positively affected by them, regardless of whether they just hold the book, hear the words or read them. It does not even matter if the communications are properly understood. The vibrations they contain create a shift.

Those human beings who choose to take note of what is happening in our world presently are those individuals who will most easily move along the pathway of living ascension into the 5th dimension, whether they use this terminology or not. We are all being influenced by the following:
- The alignment of our Earth with high frequency, supportive planets and stars as all change position within the galaxy.
- The alignment of Earth with the energy intense position of the centre of the galaxy.
- The frequency and positional shifts of the galaxy within the context of the Universe.
- The energetic changes of Earth as we approach the central position of the Age of Aquarius.
- The gravitational influence of Nibiru as this planet comes closer towards Earth.
- The shifting consciousness within the collective of humanity themselves as we are exposed to higher frequencies at this point on our Pathway of Return.

There will be people who resist or ignore the information offered to them by Spirit no matter whether this is consciously or unconsciously communicated. This they will do irrespective of how the information is delivered. It is important to note that resisting the influences of the higher frequencies of the Light is tantamount to resisting the influence of the unconditional love of the Godhead.

If unconditional love and compassion for all is not present in our lives, our work or our countries, we cannot be in synch with the consciousness of the Godhead/God. As long as this continues to be the case people will continue to resonate with the 3rd or the 4th dimension of separated physicality. This is where individual choice is important in determining our personal reality.

Aside from the importance of our own personal ascension, it is by choosing to work with the high frequency Light energy of the Godhead that we each help to create the uplifting energy which supports the frequency shift for many others amongst the mass of humanity on Earth. Everything that each person does for him or herself, directly impacts on all other people.

As we make progress on the Pathway of Return the realities of the different dimensions, and therefore our sense of the different options of experience, will appear to split away from each other in the exact same way as the reality of the Atlanteans did 34 000 years ago. This time though, the shift will be back upwards to higher frequency states, rather than downwards into a lower frequency, fallen state. This is the transmutation process.

Part of this process of shifting upwards in frequency involves a gentle and slow morphing as we transform the matter of lower frequency states, and other parts of the process may be rather catastrophic or eventful. We will experience varying degrees of catastrophe, during the more intense Earth shifts, as well as discomfort when we are detoxifying ourselves physically or spiritually.

The degree of discomfort we experience, individually or collectively, during any kind of a dimension shift is directly related to the following:
- Whether or not we are living in accordance with our intentions.
- How much low frequency matter we have to clear out of the system, whether of the Earth or the personal self.
- How much high frequency vibration we are exposed to and stimulated with.
- How fast we go through these purification processes.
- The supportive mechanisms we employ to assist us through the changes.
- Whether or not we resist the process.

Essentially, each individual determines the speed of their own transformation processes.

Dimension Differences
It is often very difficult for us to appreciate many of the facts involved in a dimensional shift, because we are not vibrating at the frequency which allows us to perceive much beyond our current reality. For example, many of the ex-Atlanteans, as 5th dimension dwellers, still exist in their own space-time. We have not been able to perceive them since the Fall of Atlantis and of Man, because of the extremely disparate frequencies of the different dimensions. In this same way Venus is inhabited in the 5th dimension and parts of it exist in higher dimensions as well. It is for the same reason of our under-developed resonance that we are not yet able to perceive life on that planet either.

As we move fully into the 5th dimension again, we will once more begin to become aware of more highly advanced physical beings that inhabit our world, as well those who exist on other planets and stars. Our new world experience of living ascension will be a very different one to the one we currently experience as real.

The experiences of our new Earth will not be a shock to us in the new dimension, because we gradually move, or morph, into this experience of our new, integrated reality. Although things around us will generally look very familiar to us, there will be many subtle differences. Once we are through the relative war zone of the necessary purification processes life will be nicer and more pleasant all around.

If individual people choose not to uplift their consciousness so as to access the new, higher dimension reality space, there would be no experience of the 5th dimension to discuss. Then, as always, the current reality remains the only reality. Whether or not humanity can, could or will cope with the new experiences in the higher dimensions then becomes a moot point. No person would have the expanded experiences of an alternative dimension unless he or she had developed the capability of resonating with the higher frequencies which make up the new reality and allow it to be experienced as real.

Whatever happens to our personal sense of reality - whether back at the point of the Fall of Atlantis and of Man, or now at the high point of the Pathway of Return in the years surrounding 2012 - each dimension resonates with different frequencies of Light. Therefore, these different vibration speeds are what ensure that people who inhabit the various dimensions will continue to be unaware of the others even being in existence, exactly as is the case right now.

In both instances of the 4th dimension and the 5th dimension frequencies, both versions of reality will continue to include physical Earth experiences, just as they do presently. This sense of the other not being there, yet at the same time still being very much part of Earth, is because all frequencies are inter-twined in and amongst each other as one. They only appear separate or non-existent because they are perceived as different. Perceptual ability is different for each individual and is directly related to resonance.

Considering that our current reality is all we experience as real, this is what is relevant to us. The motivation to explore the possibility of shifting into an alternative dimension would be to access the greater, expanded life experiences that a higher dimension can provide. These altered dimension experiences are the ones that many people get fleeting glimpses of in their dreams or in psychic states of altered consciousness. Aside from this, the current reality remains the only reality, at all times. Reality changes when we change. Therefore, whatever we call reality is actually a transitory experience. This is true at all times. Reality is continuous, but we experience it as changing, because that is the nature of consciousness moving through the different states of being - throughout the dimensions.

This gives us a glimpse of what it means to live in an 'illusory' reality where there is an apparent separation of states. In the dog whistle example, which is discussed under the heading 'Perceptions' in the 'Definition of Terms' section at the end of the book, we are provided with a very clear view of what something being there for one being and not there for the other looks like. Even though both these two beings (dog and human) are clearly in the same place on Earth, at the same time, only one of them can hear the sound.

Therefore, it is because the whole of Earth will not ascend at this time that the nature of duality will be maintained. It will be business as usual for the still-separated-reality human beings who dwell in the 3rd or 4th dimensions in the purely physical world. This will be no more strange for them than it is for us today, because this is exactly what life feels like for all of us right now in the 4th dimension. As Earth and her inhabitants adjust to shifted dimension experiences once more things will change for those people whose consciousness expands and uplifts. Once settled into the 5th dimension reality experience, life continues at the level of the new normal and what were previously felt as peculiar dimension shifting wobbles will disappear. We adjust as we progress.

Regardless of the fact that some of Earth and her inhabitants will shift into the 5th dimension, the states of separated, 3rd and 4th dimension physical reality will continue for as long as the sense of an either/or split of reality is experienced as the only reality. This is the perception of the dual, but separated existences of the physical and spiritual states of being within the consciousness of human beings. If they were not separated in our hearts and minds, we would not have to die in order to get to the 'other side'. Different perceptions occur by virtue of the level of awareness of the human being and it is this which sets up the resonance of that person so that the individual is able to perceive certain frequencies as substantially real.

Continuous Reality
The state of reality which is perceived by any individual always remains continuous until such time as the consciousness of that person uplifts. It is at that point that the person begins to be aware of possible alternative states of existence. This is when our world starts to look a bit odd and we may feel out of sorts for a while, but overall reality remains continuous. These changes enable the on-going expansion of awareness and the perception of different options of reality. The potential exists for us to access all the dimensions all the way up to the full expanse of the Godhead within the 49th/50th dimensions, but we can only begin to do this once we have accessed the 5th dimension. Even within the highest dimension possible in this Universe, the consciousness-expansion opportunities continue, because consciousness is never static.

When our perceptual ability shifts our reality, which we always perceive as authentic and solidly real, reality may have moments of weirdness to it until we integrate the new frequencies within the context of our daily lives. That is the grounding process. This is how we adjust to and develop our continuous reality. Simply put, this means that when our brains are operating at a higher level in the areas which govern our sensory and extra-sensory perception, we will then see, hear and feel much more of what already exists around us. We will then perceive more things as relevant and real.

> As we change the experience within, the entire outer
> experience of our reality shifts and is affected too.

The description in the preceding paragraph about the changing nature of perception occurs because we function relative to resonance. This resonance function is relevant for individuals and for the group human experience in the collective, at every level of reality. The nature of consciousness, of all kinds, is determined by resonance.

The outer world of an individual is *always* a reflection of the inner world inasmuch as people will only perceive what they are personally and physically able to perceive. The fact that many people perceive the same thing at the same time means that they are all operating within the same resonance range and that they agree on the nature and meaning of this reality, as a group. As any one individual changes within that group, the reverberations of that change will be felt across the extent of the entire group. When more individuals change, the reverberations will be stronger for all.

The idea of an external reality that can change as our perceptual abilities within change is a very important concept to assimilate within us as human beings, because people are generally unused to this concept of being personally responsible and able to change their outer world - with a thought or a feeling. It begins to make more sense when viewed from the perspective of popular psychology dictates such as, "The power of positive thinking," or, "You are what you think you are." It is only once we go within and shift our consciousness from a personal basis that we will be able to truly expand our experience of reality. These experiences can extend to reaches which are beyond the current dimension which the logical mind presently deals with.

> Consciousness creates form.

The logical mind orders and regulates our experience of physical reality and so it plays a necessary role in our lives. However, when our left-brain intellectual ability is dominant it is so limiting that it becomes the jailor of our soul in the hell-hole of the lower dimensions, down at the bottom of the wormhole. This is because in its current state the left brain functions are rather limited - to an estimated and oft-repeated maximum of 10% of our abilities.

Although the existing functions of the logical left brain are important for creating order in our daily lives, as we expand our consciousness and uplift our awareness we utilise more high frequency, right-brain abilities. We are then able to blend the two brain functions and the reality experiences they govern into one new reality. This is how brain functions assist us to shift to higher and higher frequency states, or realms. When we are functioning with super-psychic abilities we have little use for pure logic, because the creative aspects of consciousness far exceed the power of logic. Then, the quintessential logic of Divine Order prevails.

As we expand our consciousness and uplift our awareness we utilise more high frequency, right-brain abilities and we are then able to blend the two experiences of the 4th and the 5th dimensions into one new, expanded reality. Presently, duality is expressed in the two separated brain functions as well. When these functions are balanced they provide us with the ability to perceive a blended reality. We will fly free, soaring to great heights as the glorious spiritualised physical Beings of Light, Colour and Form that we really are.

The Wisdom of the Universe, when it is expressed in the Divine Intelligence of all individual souls, outstrips the domain or control of anything or anybody on Earth at any time. If we come to the conclusion that we have been misled by others who clearly do not have our best interests at heart, then we have to look elsewhere for some answers to fulfil our desire for spiritual connection with the Divine, and our reconnection to Oneness. The answers are always found within us.

Within the scope of operating from the basis of Divine Intelligence, which is underscored by love, we are capable of any type of manifestation in our inner or outer worlds because we release the feeling of separation, even if it is only momentarily. The result of this is the shifted dimension experience and the natural awakening of what Osiris terms our abilities of, "*Creation or co-creation.*"

Osiris: Divine Intelligence and Manifestation

"Beloved Ones, in the silent state of love, we blend together. The Divine Wisdom to come forward to support all pathway through the release in all areas, of the understanding of separation, of duality - be it for momentarily the feeling-state. So it is to continue forward, the allowing and the acceptance of the self to the moving forward though the dimensional experience, abilities in all areas of manifestation, of creation or co-creation."

The connection to Divinity is where it has always been: physically within us, in our DNA, because we are Divine Beings of Light. We cannot really be robbed of this connection and it cannot truly be hidden from us. For us to remember this and to live its truth, all that is required is for us to still our fearful, argumentative, logical, negative ego-enslaved minds. Then we can hear the perfect order of the subtle language of the Sound and the Light of the state of being of the Godhead. This language is unconditional love and it's frequency is all around us, all of the time. Listen and you will hear it. It is the voice in your head, the feeling in your heart, the words that jump into your mind, the insistent inner voice and your unconscious acts of kindness. We are reminded of this by seemingly inexplicable coincidences or the words of a song. All of this shows us that a different pathway exists and is real. Follow your heart.

The secret to reconnecting with our Divinity is to go within and expand our awareness by working from the basis of the high frequency state of unconditional love. Accessing meaningful spirituality is a lot simpler and a lot more accessible than most people think it is, cheaper too! Just go within and *listen*.

Osiris' next communication expresses the deep gratitude that is felt from Spirit for the opportunity to work with us. He acknowledges the development of our own expanded state of being and he assures us of the great love and blessings of Spirit that surround us at all times.

Osiris: Love and Gratitude from Spirit

"It is through the blending together of the experience of deeper acknowledgement, of the presence of experience in existence of the connectivity with Spirit. It is the understanding for the continuation of pathway of the living state of ascension, of the continuation of the work that you do together, so it is to support in the procedure going forward in the acknowledgement of all that has gone before, and all that begins to open to yourselves in the expansiveness of your being, the expansiveness of your understanding of connectivity of the presence of Spirit. Of the presence of the surrounding energies that take place, to be with yourselves in connectivity in unconditional love always to support you. Always to work with you, always to be in the experience of great Bliss and joy together, and the opportunity that it is for Spirit to communicate in this manner with great joy and supportive and continued communication.

"So it is with great gratitude always from Spirit, to over light your presence and communicate in this manner. So it is, Beloved Ones, for each of yourselves to move into the connectivity at this time with Spirit, to feel the blessing I wish to bestow upon your being, to work with you, to feel the presence within your heart.

"So it is that you are truly blessed, Beloved Ones, the ability in working in continuation through the discernment with Spirit, the discernment on your pathway of the connection to the Light presence, to the ability to feel the resonance and communication of the field of Light, of the Vehicle of Light. Moving forward into the understanding and owning of your Divinity, the owning of your presence of great Light."

"Think not that man is Earth-born, though come from the Earth he may be. Man is a light-born spirit. But, without knowing, he can never be free. Darkness surrounds the light-born, Darkness fetters the soul. Only the one who is seeking may ever hope to be free."

(The Emerald Tablets of Thoth-the-Atlantean p51, pp6)

* * * * * * * * * * *

CHAPTER FIFTEEN

Closing Messages

"Unto thee, O man, have I given my knowledge. Unto thee have I given my Light. Hear ye now and receive my wisdom brought from space planes above and beyond. Not as man am I for free have I become of dimensions and planes. In each, take I on a new body. In each, I change in my form. Know I now that the formless is all there is in form."

(The Emerald Tablets of Thoth-The-Atlantean p43; pp1,2)

The 11.11.11 Meditation
Please note that due to the fluctuating frequencies of the high frequency communications by the Light Beings, the recording quality can vary. This is not only dependent on who is present during the recording, but on various other variables as well. Every effort is made to provide as good a copy as possible - both on the CDs and on the website.

Osiris' special channelled meditation of 11 November 2009 is referred to as the 11.11.11 meditation. People all over the world recognised the significance of this unusual configuration of numbers and many of us were joined in meditation on this day as a result. We were joined in this glorious celebration by the many Ascended Beings of Light in Spirit as they surround us to support us and our planet during the time of the shift of dimension, on our living ascension pathway towards enLightenment.

As usual, Osiris led the channelled meditation on that day and he hosted four other Light Beings during the communication. We are privileged to receive information and messages of support from not only him, but from the Goddess Isis, Thoth, Sanat Kumara and Quan Yin as well.

It is time for humanity to return to the state of Oneness, through the feeling of love within. Osiris speaks extensively about this. The presence of Light - both of the Light Beings and through the energy field of the Merkabah Vehicle of Light - supports this.

Isis speaks about the reconnection of the feminine energy, in pursuit of the Oneness of Being of the Godhead, through the pathway of the Monad which is our state of wholeness. In the guise of the Ancient Egyptian being, Jsat,, she explains that the etheric platform (Rostau) begins to activate, above the energised capstone of the Great Pyramid.

Thoth introduces us to the concept of the pathway of Orion and the supportive Light from that star system of Light through the Sword of Orion. Exciting news from this great Light Being assures us that the information in the Akasha beings to unfold to us as we shift dimension and hold more Light within ourselves. This means that the as yet undisclosed thirteenth Tablet of Thoth (there are twelve in the Emerald Tablets) begins to download into our consciousness. All of these consciousness shifts are possible due to the physical shifts of our DNA.

When introducing Quan Yin to us, Osiris confirms once more that this Being of Light has made the sacrifice to always be available to human beings on Earth, "*To support all in humanity until it is they reach the pathway of enLightenment further.*" We are assured that we are always welcome to connect with Quan Yin and request her support. She offers us her help with joy.

Quan Yin herself states that there are more of us than expected who are going to complete our present cycle on Earth and shift dimension. Furthermore, we are heartened to hear that, "*They have moved beyond dimension of 5.*"

Thoth returns to tell us that ancient knowledge comes to Earth once more and the truth begins to unfold. He confirms the presence of the Nibiru-ite Light Being, Anu, as well as the approach of Nibiru: the Planet of the Crossing - all in the presence of the Dweller. The Dweller may be understood to be the Godhead presence on Earth who dwells in the Halls of Amenti, within the temple complex of the Great Pyramid. We can access this greatness when we raise our resonance in order to be able to tolerate and perceive the secrets that the Great Pyramid holds. Thoth points out that ascension is all about operating from the heart centre when he says, "*Ascension allows for yourselves to be felt, always in your heart.*"

Osiris: 11.11.11 Meditation with Isis, Thoth, Sanat Kumara and Quan Yin

"Greetings to you Beloved Ones, I come forward from Spirit on this day Beloved Ones, to bring many blessings to yourselves. I come forward on this day to support and assist the procedure of moving forward, through visualisation.

"It is on this day, Beloved Ones, that I work with yourselves in connection firstly, to bring forward the presence of Beings of Light to surround you. I bring forward the presence of Beings of Light in a continuation of support and assistance - the surrounding energies of the presence of the Beings, from the energy in the connectivity of the Godhead, to support you.

"It is on this day, Beloved Ones as I work with you, it is to take you forward through a procedure. It is on this day the connectivities and alignment with Spirit - so it is I come forward through the presence of alignment with Orion, through the connectivity of the Great Pyramid.

"The understanding through this procedure that you connect in the etheric and from this perspective so you have the ability to move forward through an acceleration - through the pathway of the living state of ascension.

"It is through this procedure on this day, Beloved Ones, you have the ability to access - having moved forward through various procedures of repetition of patterns that have come forward for yourselves - to move through the growth and the experience, of advancement through physicality.

"For many of yourselves, through the pathways of Light, you begin to feel the moving forward and the emanating presence of great Light to come forward into the experience of your Being. It is all beings in humanity that have the ability at this time to move forward through the pathway of Light.

"The ability to extend beyond the understandings of all period - having been in physicality over many, many lifetimes, many experiences of continuation upon an area of repetition - through the experience, Beloved Ones, of an energy field and a vibratory resonance of being and the ability at this time to return to the connectivities of the great state of Oneness, through the perspective of communion with the Godhead. It is into the understanding of reconnection of the Godhead within the self and the communication with the presence of great Light.

"It is on this day Beloved Ones that I work with yourselves to prepare. In order to understand the pathways you begin to form, surrounding the self, the Merkabah. The experience of star tetrahedron that begins to form, in the sacred geometry surrounding your physical body. And as you begin this procedure so it is I take you forward through the connectivity of the etheric - it is above the ancient Pyramid.

"It is in this position, Beloved Ones, that there are many beings upon the planet at this time that find themselves in connection through the pathway of Light. It is many beings with the choice and intent, having moved forward through the various and many area of clearing to this point. So it is the ability to advance through the perspective.

"The understanding that as you move through these procedures - the abilities that as you begin to acknowledge, to see and to feel, the desire and intent in creation and manifestation - is as it is you see it, so it is. From this perspective it is to understand the intensified energy that comes forward, through the resonance that is felt within the self and the ability to go forward on the pathway of Light, begins to unfold further and further into the Light of the Godhead.

"Beloved Ones, it is the beginning procedures to allow for yourselves to form the vehicle of Light to surround you. As you do this so it is the ability to feel the shift of resonance, as you let go of all anxiety within the physical body; to let go of all that takes place within your physicality.

"So it is you continue forward and as you move forward, so it is I bring forward many Beings of Light to surround and work with you and to bless you on this day and to work in a continuation of communication. At the presence of the request to come forward, so it is they do.

"In this manner, Beloved Ones, so it is you work on this day to begin the procedures. To allow yourselves to move into the silence - to move into the connectedness within the self, to feel the presence of the heart within, to feel the presence in the heart of great Love that I bring forward to touch your heart.

"In the connectivities of great Light you begin to feel the resonance beginning to shift; the resonance of the surrounding presence of great Light begins to take place. Allow your physical form to let go entirely into the experience of the peaceful state, the presence of meditative state - to allow yourselves to go through the feeling state of great vulnerability within the heart centre, moving forward through a state of pure bliss, into the connectivity with Spirit.

"It is at this time, Beloved Ones, that we begin the procedure. Begin to feel the formation as it extends outward through the auric field - the formation of great Light, the energy of connectivity with Spirit. Allowing yourselves to move through the peace, through the Light and to let go into the experience of a shift of consciousness.

"Allowing yourselves to let go entirely. The feeling state within your heart to let go, Beloved Ones, allowing yourselves to find the peace and understanding within the self that you begin to embark on an activation, an initiation through the pathway of Light, that you begin to open yourselves to the energy centre of the ascension procedures.

"To allow for the continuation - to walk the pathway in physicality - in the ascended state of being, Divine Beings of Light. Begin to feel the presence of moving forward, letting go into the experience, drifting and continuing forward.

"It is to find yourselves to move as you shift through the consciousness within your form. It is the spinal pathway of the physical form that you shift consciousness, through the connectivity, as felt in the understanding of the connection to the position of the Great Pyramid.

"So it is, Beloved Ones, that a communication to come forward through the understanding that I bring forward the presence of Thoth. It is to begin the procedure, to come forward into my presence Beloved Ones, as I support you to come into the etheric, to connect with great Light, to feel the presence of my Being.

"It is to support yourselves to go forward - it is through a slight cleansing procedure - and as you begin to feel, as you stand before the presence of many Beings in the surroundings. There are many Beings that come forward at this time: beings of Ascension, beings with intent, through connection from humanity, to move forward in their Light, to connect in this manner, and as you move through the pathway, it is a pathway of Light. There is the feeling state of moving forward, through the deep cleansing from the physical state, through the connection, to dimension.

"It is supportive for yourselves - begin to feel the pathway that is lit by the presence of the experience of Angelic Beings. Through the connection it is as you see it as a pathway of Light of all Beings being present. Allow yourselves to walk the pathway, to come to position.

"So it is on this day, Beloved Ones, that you are taken through the experience of a connectivity through dimensional state of the Godhead - the experience of connectivity to go forward through the pathway of ascension within the feeling state of your form - to allow yourself through the shift of consciousness, for it to take place.

"In the feeling state of re-connection to your Divinity, to your Light and through the Presence, you begin to feel the communication as it enters your being. The understanding of the entirety of the shift of consciousness of humanity begins to be felt. The ability from this position to create the shift of many, many beings throughout humanity takes place, as the soul presence of many, many beings, to be in position.

"So it is, Beloved Ones, for yourselves to feel a connectivity as you feel yourselves having been cleansed, through the experience, to walk the pathway further. It is to find yourselves in the silence, in the peace of connectivity with the great Beings of Light serving the planet at this time, serving all beings upon the planet at this time.

"So it is, Beloved Ones, that you come forward into a communication with the presence of the Goddess Being. As we come forward in the pure balance of the masculine-feminine energy together, the presence of the Goddess Being that is Isis. So it is to come forward to bring into the balance of the experience: the feminine.

"So it is with many blessings that I return to support the pathway further, your ability to communicate with the presence of the Goddess Being. With great love I serve you on this day, Beloved Ones."

Jsat (*Isis*)

"I greet you Beloved Beings of Light, I am Jsat. I come forward on this day in the feminine to support and hold your presence in the heart, to bring forward through the Divine feminine, the activation. The understanding of all period in humanity, at this time the ability to advance, through the activation of the feminine, in all areas of spirituality, of the bringing forward of the great balance on Earth.

"So it is at this time - through the presence of the great Light of Spirit, Beloved Osiris, the presence of my Being - that we move forward as One, through the connectivity of great Light to the presence, further dimensional experience, that we move, in Love.

"As you move through the connection in great Light begin to feel, Beloved Beings of Light, the expansion of consciousness, placed through purification of the soul presence. The coming forward of the connectivity, of the Monadic Being to the self, the presence of Light to enter once more, to feel the self as the whole, begins to take place.

"Allow yourselves to know and understand that as the Earth begins to go forward through dimensional experience of shift, your ability to hold your Light further; to bring forward through compassion and Love to all. There begins to take place the procedures of consciousness that begin to shift as you feel in your heart the vibratory energy that moves through the connectedness of Spirit.

"We move to the Hallway, of the communication of the many Beings of Light at this time. So it is Beloved Beings of Light, I am Jsat and I serve you on this day, to continue. As we stand at each side of yourselves, to go forward through pathway of Light, to enter the Hallway, the connection in the etheric. It is the understanding of platform - it is above capstone that begins to accelerate - through the illumination of consciousness and Light - that begins to take place.

"I do support you, Beloved Beings of Light, on this day in Love, in Light and in blessings. We walk together at this time as you visualise and see the pathway of Light before you, to enter the Hall of the Presence of the Godhead, to allow for the shift to take place.

"I bless you, Beloved Beings of Light, on this day. I am Jsat."

Thoth

"I greet you. I am Thoth to come forward, the presence of Light to support. The presence of mankind begins to move through the Hallway of Light. You are supported, Beloved Children of Light. We move together. Begin to acknowledge, through passage of Rostau (*etheric platform of Light*), to this consciousness of man may unfold. Never to be felt at this time - through the passing forward of time and space you begin to shift, through time and space we begin to move, as we hold together, beings of mankind to continue.

"I come forward through the presence and alignment of Orion. I come through the understanding (*of*) Thothmus (...), through the pathway. Sword of Orion begins to open. The Passage of the Lion we begin to live; that has brought forward the understanding of the ancient Temple that we have come forward from the Ancient Atlantean period to build.

"Through the presence of creation from this position, allow yourselves to begin the procedure of teleportation, through the experience of Light and consciousness, as we move together as One.

"Beloved Children of Light, you are supported through the feeling of the physical form, the ability at this time begins to come through your experience. The shift of DNA that begins, in opening your understanding of all knowledge to filter through, the beginnings of communication, the word unfold.

"For yourselves to bring the recollection of old - from ancient period to this - the understandings at this point. The energy fields support all Beings of Light to come forward once more, to follow the pathway through this Hall of Light.

"Your understandings of Halls of Amenti begins to unfold. Tablet of Light in Akashic form comes through the energy field to yourselves. In the presence of Light we move continuously, allowing yourselves to follow forward.

"I am Thoth that comes forward in Love, to bring through your consciousness communication that follows. Always through mankind to understand their pathway of Divinity unfolds once more. The ability through resonance as it begins to shift, so we move always on the path of Light.

"You are blessed on this day, Beloved Children of Light."

Osiris

"Beloved Ones, it is a connection further for yourselves to continue. There begins to be the formation - the Star tetrahedron to surround yourselves and it is all beings in this position. Begin to feel through the consciousness, allowing each position of the physical form, that you feel the procedures of alignment taking place.

"The activation within the experience of energy centre of the head, the ascension chakra, begins to open further. As you move through the understanding of the opening of connection in this way so it is allow yourselves, Beloved Ones, to feel the connectivity of many Beings of Ascension to come forward.

"It is as you shift the state of consciousness so it becomes clearer and clearer: the expansiveness of many Beings of Light, allowing yourselves to come into communication. As each Being of Ascension moves forward through a pathway of shift each Being in Ascension begins to take place through the pathway of movement.

"As you begin to find yourselves in a connectivity so it is we move forward - through the connection through Spirit, through space and time, through the experience of movement - of the understandings of all that has been brought forward.

"From the Temple of Osiris, the understanding through the connectivity of the ancient Pyramid to the understanding of how it has come forward, from the presence of Atlantis, though the experience of alignment, to support all in the planetary system to go forward, through great shift.

"The experience at this time and the connectivity through the position - it is in the alignment with the ability to teleportate, through the experience of Light. You begin to feel the presence at this time, lifting and moving into the connectedness with Spirit. Moving through dimension after dimension, through the presence of Beings, as we move as One, through the experience of many.

"I take you forward into a connectivity of a dimension of the Godhead - to begin to feel the presence of an area of great Light that begins to filter through your being. Begin to feel yourself in form. It might not be physical form. It is in the energy field of Light of the Godhead. You feel yourself letting go further into the connectedness, allowing the procedure to take place, letting go entirely.

"Beloved Ones, as you begin to enter through the experience of dimensional state so it is the presence of the connectivity of the Beings of Light, the presence of Sanat Kumara, to be in the connectivities of Light. Begin to feel the presence in great Love to come forward.

"The presence of the Beings of Ascension to support Being to come forward to communicate. The over lighting presence through dimension begins to be felt, allowing yourselves to let go further. These vast area of many Beings of Ascension moving forward through procedure, allowing the communication to come forward. Find yourselves in the energy field of Bliss."

Sanat Kumara

"I come to you, Beloved Beings of Light, come to you Beloved Beings of Light. I am Sanat Kumara, to offer to yourselves the Bliss and joy of presence of God to feel. Your intent of understanding the pathway of Oneness, the pathway of Light - that does offer through the field of your being, field of intelligence of super-luminal Light, of the presence going forward - begins to take place.

"As you come forward in your Divinity that opens to the presence of Light, I offer to you great love to be felt. The presence of planetary system unfolds; communications of Light Universal positions - language of Light - filters through your being.

"Beloved Divine Beings of Light, you are offered to support Angelic presence, the communication that comes through yourselves. Always in love, I bless you."

Osiris

"It is for yourselves, Beloved Ones, to feel the presence further. We begin to be surrounded - it is all Beings of Ascension begin to move on a pathway forward. As you begin to feel the movement, as you begin to walk the pathway - it might be in the feeling state of a form, it might be merely through an energy field of consciousness.

"All moving together, it is vast energy of many, many Beings of Light together. Each of yourselves in a connectivity to the Monadic presence of your being, that you feel the reconnection to your Light. You feel the reconnection to your Divinity.

"You have the ability at this time to acknowledge and to see ahead in all direction, of that which is intended through your pathway of Light on Earth. The ability to awaken all beings on Earth begins to take place. The ability through the reconnection to your Ancient Atlantean presence, the presence on Earth of ancient period prior to this, you begin to feel the reconnection and you begin to feel the owning of your Light further and further.

"The understanding of all that has taken place, from many lifetime upon lifetime, after the experience into the presence of great Light, once more you return. Through the pathway of connection you begin to feel the expansiveness, through connectivity to the Godhead.

"Allow yourselves on the pathway, many beings to follow. Your support and assistance at this time allows for all beings upon the planet to shift through the communication of their soul presence, the intent is there. So it is, Beloved Ones, that we move as One through this pathway of Light.

"Begin to feel yourselves - it is experience not ever in the connectivities of the presence of Spirit to take place. Allow yourselves to continue through the pathway, further and further. Begin to feel in your heart as it opens, the understandings of all experience that begins to unfold. The connectivities to the Akashic Record begin to filter through your being.

"Further and further you feel yourselves through the pathway of Light, the continuation takes place. Beloved Beings of Light, Beloved Presence of Divinity, as you unfold the balance of all, as we begin to feel the presence of understanding in the heart, the Sophia begins to emerge, the presence of Light begins to be felt.

"Allow yourselves, Beloved Beings of Light, always to begin the procedures further. Continue. Let go always of fear. There is no fear in existence. You move from the understanding of that which is above to below, the experience of connection that in this state, there is no above and below.

"Through the connection of Light in this position there begins to unfold the Divinity of the presence of the Godhead within. Allow yourselves on this pathway to continue. Allow yourselves to feel at this time, as we move as One, there begins to be felt all knowledge of your existence begins to come forward.

"The presence once more, as you begin to feel many Beings of Light, I bring forward once more the presence of Being that has chosen to continue on Earth. For all beings to continue through the pathway until it is they reach the pathway of enLightenment. Being that has offered the continuation of support - always to be supported and assisted in the knowledge that this sacrifice has been made in this manner - to support all in humanity until it is they reach the pathway of enLightenment further.

"I bring forward the presence of the Goddess Being that is Quan Yin to communicate, to support yourselves in holding of your Light. There is an ability always to communicate with the presence of Being of Light; to support and come forward at will, always with great joy, Beloved Beings of Light."

Quan Yin

"I greet you, Beloved Ones, I am Quan Yin. I come to assist planetary system of Light, to support each of yourselves. They have moved beyond dimension of 5, we move to experience through the pathway, which brings great joy to yourself, as I teach many to move in this way.

"There begins to be felt all abilities within, for yourselves each and one, to complete. There have been many more than ever expect. Beloved Presence of Beings of Light, continue to work to support the planet, to hold the position of Light - we work as One. I support yourselves in unconditional Love.

"Beloved Beings of Light, I am Quan Yin. I bless you on this day."

Thoth

"And so the pathway continues. We move through the consciousness. I am Thoth once more. We move through the consciousness further, begins your understanding to continue. All exercise to be acknowledged, Beloved Osiris to support yourselves.

"You move once more; Dweller to communicate, the presence of Anu is felt surrounding, the planet of crossing begins to be felt. Once more we move through the Light, to bring to Earth greater knowledge for all. Many areas of understandings of old begin to bring truth to the Earth.

"At this time I come forward, in presence once more from ancient period, to reconnect with yourselves to work to support to unfold the knowledge. The truth begins to be felt by all.

"You are blessed on this day, Beloved Children of Light, to follow forward. This is requested, the pathway of (...) we move as One. The consciousness of Rostau (*etheric platform of Light*), the opening of the energy centre begins. Ascension allows for yourselves to be felt, always in your heart.

"As you move, Beloved Children of Light, you feel the connection of the Godhead at this time. Move into the state of peace once more.

"I bless you on this day, Children of Light."

Osiris

"Beloved Ones, it is to let go to allow yourselves to go into the silence, to let go into the peace of communication, to feel it in your heart. To feel the entirety of humanity as it is felt through the presence of the Godhead: in unconditional Love for all.

"The judgement of all begins to fall away in its entirety as you move forward on your pathway on a connection in service to humanity. Allow yourselves to feel the presence surrounding the entirety of the planet.

"The connection through the presence of Orion at this time - you feel the shift of movement throughout the system of communication - that, as it begins to come forward, the connection of planets that support once more.

"Begin to feel yourselves in a state of peace and Light. Begin to feel the presence Beloved Ones, surrounding you. There begin to be felt, through the silence, the communication of Elohim; the connection of Angelic Beings. There is the presence of all Beings of Angelic form to surround in great unison of Light. Allow themselves to be felt, as they support your pathway, to bring into your experience your physical life of all that you desire through manifestation, to support the entirety of Earth.

"So you are blessed as we begin to raise the consciousness of Earth. Allow yourselves in this position, through the etheric, to feel the raising of the consciousness of the planetary system. Allow yourselves to feel it in your hearts, to feel it in your consciousness.

"As you support, as you move forward in your own experience of Love within the self, as it begins to allow for all to continue further, feel it in the silence for short period Beloved Ones. As all go forward through further connection.

"Beloved Ones, you have the ability at this time to begin to see surrounding the entirety of Earth - all animal beings, all beings of humankind - connecting with the understandings of themselves as part of the Godhead, part of the experience of creation.

"Allow yourselves to feel the presence of the raising of consciousness of all. The Earth begins to shift at this time. The Light is felt. So, through the communication, connectivity of the Sun as it begins to be enhanced in its energy field supporting the planet in greater capacity, so it begins to be felt, the entirety the surroundings of the Earth.

"Begin to move into the healing state. The presence of Light of all Beings supporting the procedures to take place. The presence begins to form - of all Arcturian beings, the presence of beings of Antares - begins to be moving into connectivities. There are various and many Beings of Light, to surround the planet at this time. Begin to feel the experience of all, Beloved Ones.

"Allow yourselves to feel the energised experience of communication of Beings of Light - to assist the planetary system at this time. The presence of Beings, the connection to Andromeda - allow the experience of Beings to form and circular movement further they begin to enter though the field of Light communication.

"Allow yourselves, as it begins to allow for all areas of darkness to fall, the experience of communication continues. As we move through the understanding of the intent of the continuation of life upon Earth - in peace and in Love for many an experience of many linear year - allow yourselves to feel the pathway that it begins to open, through the path of consciousness and Light.

"Allow yourselves, Beloved Ones, to begin to feel the celebration of all Beings of Light at this time, to open their hearts. As you are filled with Love, allow yourselves to move into the connectedness of the presence of unconditional Love that is surrounding the entirety of the planet.

"Beloved Ones, begin to feel the ability to move through reconnection once more to the physical form. Prior to doing this, allow the feeling state of a formation of Vehicle of Light to surround your physical body and begin to feel the experience: to not descend, but to feel the experience of reconnection in Light. To feel the connection in ascended procedures to re-enter the form. Feel the connection, through the heart.

"All that begins to be felt in the continuation of communication - comes forward in Love, comes forward in the compassion and tolerance of all - the surrounding energies of many in humanity that begins to be felt. Allow yourselves in the acknowledgement as you feel it, Beloved Beings of Light. Feel yourselves as we blend as One - all Beings of Ascension that communicate, all blending together at this time in Light - allowing for yourselves to feel in your heart the continuation of connection of the Godhead.

"The understanding that it is in your Light that you are in yourself the Divinity in the presence of One. Own, in the understandings as you bring forth Love, the connection of accountability within. The Presence of the Godhead exists and continues forward in the openings of greater Light, for you all.

"You are blessed in this, Beloved Beings of Light, to continue forward, always on your pathway in Love. In Love we bless you, with gratitude from Spirit to communicate on this day, and to continue forward - it is for 7 day period in peace and Bliss - to find yourselves to feel it in this state, Beloved Beings of Light, to continue forward in this way.

"Beloved Ones, I bless you on this day in great Love from Spirit. I bless you on this day from all the Beings of Light through the connectivity of dimension of the Godhead to over light and support you further. And so it is with many blessings, I greet you.

"I am Osiris: connectivity of the Goddess Jsat, Beloved Thoth, Beloved Sanat Kumara and the Beloved Goddess Quan Yin. So it is we come together to support and serve further as a continuation over these days ahead, to support and assist you to unfold your Light and to live on the pathway of ascension.

"We bless you."

The Closing Communication
The following, short final communication from Osiris was recorded on the 11 November 2009 (11.11.11). It is recorded on the accompanying CD, along with the channelled meditation of the same day. In this final message we are assured that the communications from Spirit which are contained within the book begin the process of the upliftment of consciousness and that the communications are over lit by the highest frequency Light of Being possible: that of the Godhead. We are blessed with the Divine love of Spirit and are assured of the continued love, blessings and support from those in Spirit on our pathway of living ascension towards enLightenment.

Osiris: Closing Communication from Spirit

"I bring forward greetings from Spirit. I bring forward greetings of the communication in the presence of Osiris, the communication of the over lighting presence of the Godhead to support all beings - having moved forward through the experience of communication, of moving forward through the reading matter of connectivity from Spirit.

Chapter Fifteen: CLOSING MESSAGES

"It is to understand for all beings that go forward through a shift of consciousness pertaining to the experience of communication of great Light to support and assist all beings, to bring in the understandings within the selves, to move forward through the understanding that the shift taking place within the being begins to take place. The communications begin to come forward with far greater capacity within the self.

"This shift taking place through all of humanity at this time. It is greatly supportive for all beings to be in the cognisant nature of the understanding of that which *does* take place within the surroundings. On many occasion, through the entirety of physicality, there have been many areas of suppression of the physical self and various aspects to create the dullness of being - in order to go forward without knowledge of that which takes place in the surroundings. So, it is from this publication, the intent to bring it about through the Light of communication from Spirit to the beings upon Earth, in the Divinity of themselves to awaken.

"In this manner, so it is of deep intent of Spirit to communicate, to bring forward the upliftment of the state of consciousness. In the state of consciousness that begins the procedures of upliftment, having read first sentence of communication of publication, so it has served you well, Beloved Ones. It has served you well in order to continue forward always on the pathway of Light and the pathway of understanding - that you are beings of Divine Light, that you are beings that have come forward into the connectivity of Earth through the aspect of understanding of that which is hu-man: the god-man being to the presence of humanity. And so it is within each of your own selves the pathway of Light begins. The journey of the passage of awareness begins to awaken within your being and within your heart: to be in a state of unconditional love for all that exists, and the understanding that the presence of all beings upon the Earth are One.

"I bring this forward, through the blessings of the Divine Light of Spirit to support always all in humanity at all period of time frame of that which has been and that which is always to come. The presence of Divine love from Spirit, the blessings to support your journey and pathway. It is with blessings, with great love from Spirit.

"Greetings and blessings. We come forward through the communication of the over Lighting presence of the Godhead. I am Osiris. Blessings to you."

* * * * * * * * * * *

CHAPTER SIXTEEN

Postscript, Definitions, Bibliography and Recommended Reading

"Thou, O man, art thy brothers helper. Let him not lie in the bondage of night."

(The Emerald Tablets of Thoth-The-Atlantean p35, pp3)

Postscript
Earth History in a Nutshell - the Atlantean Era onwards to the Modern Era
- Life on 5th dimensional Earth degenerated over a long period of time for human beings - from when they were created, about 300 000 - 400 000 years ago, until the end of the Atlantean Era, about 34 000 years ago. Aside from creating human beings, the Siriun immortals created the god-men from Nibiru - these were the Annunaki or the Nephilim and they were all originally Light workers, but this changed as time went by.
- About 300 000 years ago one of the original god-beings of Light, Enlil, fell into a state of darkness. With this he established the potential for all others to do so too. This was the beginning of duality on Earth. This meant that others could choose to follow his example until there were sufficient in number to cause the Fall of Atlantis and of Man.
- Towards the end of the Atlantean Era, after a long time on the downward slope towards full duality, the vibrations of Earth and her inhabitants eventually became sufficiently low so that the approach of higher frequency Nibiru in her usual 3 600 year orbit around the Sun, upset the energies of Earth so much that this outer-planetary event further increased disruptions on Earth. This destabilisation created climate change and societal upset to such an extent that nuclear warheads were exploded by the beings of darkness, led by one of the original immortals: the 'Fallen Angel' Enlil (Lucifer or Satankhare).
- The Great Deluge and a pole shift ensued. Earth life was almost completely obliterated for the second time (the end of the Dinosaur Era was the first time).

The outer-planetary visitors either perished along with other Earth inhabitants or left Earth, and the small number of humans who survived carried on as best they could.
- It is important to note that a dimension shift of the Earth of any kind, at any time, is such a massive event that it requires a lot of energy for it to take place. A cohesive whole of energy, such as that of a particular dimension, does not easily split apart, because its attractive forces act like glue which keeps its bits together. If this were not the case we would not see an apple as a single unit, for example, but as lots of tiny apple molecules.
- To appreciate a dimension shift within the context of how much energy is needed for it to cleave in two, we just need to remember that it was nuclear explosions that achieved this at the end of the Atlantean Era, but only because the lower frequencies of duality had become rampant by this time. An atomic bomb blast-like amount of energy is the amount of energy effort that is required for a dimension shift to occur. If a dimension shift occurs (up or down), we can be sure that there will be (or has been) a massive event, or series of events, that will (or has) create (created) this. Those events can be violent Earth cleansings such as volcanic eruptions, earthquakes and tsunamis as she either rids herself of lower frequencies vibrations or is disturbed by them, or it can be a massive man-made event such as a nuclear explosion or a series of smaller nuclear explosions.
- The alternative to the disruptions of a difficult dimension shift occurs if sufficient numbers of people all raise their resonance at the same time. The thoughts, feelings and actions of numerous positive Light workers who are all working to shift consciousness can create sufficient energy to achieve a gentler dimension shift - by easing us through into the next dimension as if on a wave. That is the importance of as many people as possible working with higher frequencies of Light all at the same time. It is in this way that we can avoid difficulties in our ascension programme.
- The possibility of a massive Earth event is always stimulated by the arrival of Nibiru in our outer-planetary neighbourhood, because her high frequency energy disturbs the lower frequency energy of Earth. The easiest way to withstand this is to raise our resonance. This circumvents the occurrence of difficult natural disasters and people behaving badly.
- The energy around and within Earth may be further enhanced by other planets and stars shifting and moving into their various places in the heavens - such as Orion coming into alignment with the Great Pyramid on the 11 November 2009. When a specific arrangement of planets and stars occurs, which we have termed a super-alignment, this creates a spiralling energy pathway between them - a pattern which includes Earth. This energy moves in a figure-of-8-type manner. It is for this reason that at these times, the potential for movement between these

planets and stars, in the various different dimensions, is the most profound. This is why it is most likely that we will achieve a dimensional shift at this time of planetary and stellar super-alignments, which includes our alignment with the centre of our galaxy.
- The nuclear warhead explosions at the end of the Atlantean Era were so massive that they literally split the energy of 5th dimensional Earth in two. Those people and parts of Earth which resonated with the higher 5th dimensional energies stayed in the 5th dimensional space - and remained largely unaffected by the explosion, other than the fact that their physical bodies were destroyed. Those which resonated lower than this shifted instantly into the 3rd dimension and their life experiences degenerated accordingly - including the loss of memory (descent of the veil) about most of the higher frequency experiences.
- The 4th dimension - the Astral Plane - did not exist as a physical place at that time. When human consciousness uplifted sufficiently, which it did over a long period of time, it evolved from the 3rd dimension. In this way the 4th dimension was grounded on Earth and became the physical link between the 3rd dimension of pure physicality and the 5th dimension of spirituality. Most of Earth and her inhabitants are now in the 4th dimension, with some existing in the 5th.
- Eventually, around 2037/67BC, the Earth had recovered sufficiently from the Atlantean Era damage and the god-beings began to arrive on Earth again in Ancient Egypt - although many of them had arrived prior to this in other areas across the globe, as is evidenced in many of the older world religions. This was a time of peace on Earth. They roamed the planet, teaching and helping human beings. They generally used the planet Nibiru to get to Earth, via the inter-planetary energy-highway (sometimes linked up to the super-alignment of other planets and stars and at other times not), because this planet's orbit brings it close by on a regular (every 3 600 years) basis. The Pleiades were also an easy hop to Earth.
- A lot of this information began to be recorded on ancient clay tablets (Sumerian, for example) all over the world and modern man has found thousands of those at numerous different sites. We can use this physical information as part of the evidence of our history from that time as well as about the pre-Fall Era. This information is not mythical. It is an account of actual happenings.
- We cannot dismiss some of those ancient clay tablet texts as myths (about our outer-planetary ancestors) and accept other ones (such as harvest or bread delivery records) as fact just because we don't currently have a broad enough frame of reference about our place in the Universe to allow us to accept the more unusual actualities. No matter how difficult it may be, we need to expand our perception to include accepting what happened, historically, rather than to reduce our understanding and delude ourselves - relative to our lower dimension skills and

perceptual abilities. We might begin to question how best to reclaim the skills of those days when Earthlings were clearly extremely advanced in many ways, instead of trying to box that greatness into our current, small-world version of reality.
- Shortly after their re-arrival on Earth, the Nibiru-ites introduced a system of Kingship, by means of the rule of the god-being Pharaohs. This was done to help the people of Earth progress more rapidly. The priesthood were installed as an interface between the god-beings and the people, because the god-beings were very different from the local, human species - as is evidenced by temple reliefs of what the various god-beings looked like. The priesthood assisted by liaising between the two groups. A long period of peace ensued, until those of the dark began to interfere with the enLightenment programme of Earth once more. Human society degenerated again - as is seen by the fact that wars began in previously peaceful cultures - as the currency of the priesthood, in the guise of all matters of power and control, developed.
- The priesthood took control of the Cult of Amun (a being from Nibiru: the 'father' of Enki and Enlil) and vied with the Pharaohs for power. In every instance they tried to install their own people into power, preferably as the Pharaoh. The Wars of Light and dark began in earnest in Egypt.
- In 2037/67BC the outer-planetary arrangements were such that the line up of high frequency stars and planets relative to Earth was such that it created an information super-highway of high frequency energy. As this energy moved backwards and forwards within all in its pathway, in the classic figure-of-8 manner, this meant that Earth and her inhabitants would be energetically shaken up. The result of this disturbance is always determined by each individual's own resonance and choices. This heavenly sequence of events always provides the opportunity for Earthlings to choose to re-ascend to life in the 5th dimension by clearing out low frequency vibrations from themselves (emotionally, physically and spiritually) and the Earth. This results in a shift in resonance to such a degree that humans and Earth can tolerate the higher frequency energies and feel their benefit. For us this benefit is a potential dimension shift upwards as consciousness uplifts. The approach of Nibiru always signifies upheaval on 3rd or 4th dimension Earth.
- From the modern world, especially from a Western or Middle-Eastern perspective, we always look to Ancient Egypt as the (post-Atlantean Era Fall) beginning, because it was against the backdrop of this political climate that our current world religions developed. All the political and religious truth and all the distortions and misinformation that we live with today, had their beginnings then. If we can sift through the mess of things and get to the truth of what living a spiritualised, physical existence on Earth was supposed to be about, then we will have waded

through the muck of power, control and greed that have dominated ever since. Therein lies our freedom - physically and spiritually - in the present dimension, as well as in all other dimensions of the Universe.
- In order for Light to triumph in Ancient Egypt, the priesthood had to be stripped of their power and the people taught the truth about their spiritual connections to the Godhead and how to re-ascend to the 5th dimension. Hence, we see the arrival of many of the god-beings into that area, including the Pharaoh Akhenaten. He was an extension of the consciousness of the great Light Being, Osiris. His purpose was to shift the consciousness of the people quickly and effectively - away from worship-based, self-serving practices and back into accessing the power within, towards the Godhead.
- Akhenaten effected widespread, massive change within a very short period of time. Nevertheless, eventually galloping darkness gathered more ground and humanity lost the 2037/67BC opportunity for living ascension *en masse* and life on Earth again degenerated further, into wars and further strife. The information super-highway opportunity passed us by, under-utilised.
- The end of the Egyptian Era in 30BC marked the end of the Age of Enlightenment on Earth, although many of the Light Beings remained here for a long time after that and continued to reincarnate as different physical beings over time. They have persisted with various forms of assistance.
- The overall darkness on Earth continued for a long time, going up and down, vying for position with the Light - throughout the trauma of the Middle Ages and the people's revolt of the French Revolution (and other wars), and into the Industrial Revolution - until it culminated in the extreme darkness of World War II (1939 - 1945). Most Northern Hemisphere countries and some Southern Hemisphere countries that were British colonies (South Africa, New Zealand and Australia) were involved in that war, on one side or another. The Allies opposed the Axis countries.
- World War II was an extremely important turning point in our history since the Fall of Atlantis and of Man, over 34 000 years ago, because, once more, nuclear warheads were exploded on Earth. Although we all know about the physical damage they caused, most people are unaware of the energetic impact of those events which almost completely destroyed the two Japanese port cities of Hiroshima (6 August 1945) and Nagasaki (9 August 1945).
- It was these events which created a sharp and profound physical polarisation of energy which heightened awareness of what was going on. This ultimately led to the split of Earth's dimensions once more - in the 1960s. Although less noticeable this time around, it was this nuclear fission energy which began the split the 3rd dimension energies and created the obvious distinction between the thinking of different people. This shift in consciousness ultimately formed the new, 4th

dimension within the physical energy place of Earth. The nuclear explosions were unusual events. They effectively created an even more stark division between those people who like to persist with war and the creation of more suffering on Earth for the purposes of power and control, and those who would ultimately begin resonating with the 5th dimension energies of this present time, as we approach 2012: the central position of the Age of Aquarius.

- The 'Flower Power' counterculture of the Sixties was the most obvious show of the cohesive, 4th dimension energies and it came to the fore as a youth movement at the beginning of the spiritually important, 100 year period of the midpoint of the Age of Aquarius. There is no such thing as a coincidence.
- Now that we are almost in the dead-centre of the Age of Aquarius, we are faced with the Earth reality that the bulk of humanity has uplifted their consciousness sufficiently so as to exist within the reality space of the 4th dimension. However, the potential for the energy of Earth to spread across the three different dimensions (3rd, 4th *and* 5th) as it is doing now, means that any significant disruption of Earth's energies will create a rapid polarisation once more - because the 'glue' of the cohesive forces between the dimensions is less strong when spread out than when well defined as one dimension. The good news is that this also means that a dimension shift can be more easily achieved, with less effort.
- Within the 4th dimension there are people who resonate more with the 5th dimension energies and there are those who resonate more with the 3rd dimension energies. The difference between being able to inhabit either of the two dimensions on either side of the 4th dimension is relative to how much Earth Karma has been released from each individual: less than 51% means they will resonate with 3rd dimension energies, and more than 51% means they will resonate with 5th dimension energies.
- The 4th dimension of reality, where we are now, is the energy watershed. As we approach the midpoint of the Age *and* its accompanying dimension shifting, or catastrophe potentials, we are faced with the issue of whether or not we will go forwards into the main river of consciousness (5th dimension) or take a left turn (3rd dimension), back into the backwards-looping tributary once more. The choice is ours. The result is based on our intentions. The time for the split is now.
- If, or when, we face another massive Earth catastrophe, no matter whether caused by natural disasters or man-made nuclear disaster (and the chances of this are extremely high due to ongoing war plots and plans), then the energies of Earth will be split apart once more. This means that we will either shift upwards, into the 5th dimension if we are on the 'right' side of the 51% Karma-clear split whilst living in the 4th dimension, or it means we will go 'down' to the 3rd dimension if we are on the 'wrong' side of the 4th dimension, 51% Karma-clear split. Those who resonate with frequencies at the lowest levels of the 3rd dimension will shift

into the void of 'nothingness'.
- After this, a new cycle of the upliftment of the consciousness of humanity who exist within the reality state of 3rd dimension Earth will begin again, just as it has done in the past. An extensive period of peace will reign on Earth.
- The re-cycling of those in the lower dimensions will continue, with new ascension and upliftment opportunities presenting themselves as the planets and stars continue to align and shift, until such time as the entire population of Earth has shifted and the existence of the lower dimensions are no longer necessary for experience and learning.
- The uplifted, 5th dimension individuals will continue with their lives, potentially all over the Universe, free from the limitations of 3rd or 4th dimension Earth energies, at last.

This is our reality as it is now. We are faced with choices, important choices. More information and a greater awareness assist us to make those choices.

We can help to control what happens in the world by feeling love towards everybody, including our adversaries, because this raises the resonance of every human being due to the positive knock-on effects of the high frequency energies of unconditional love.

Please refer to 'Information for Pro-Active Light Workers' in Chapter Four for positive steps we can all take steps to help shift the planet and her inhabitants, with love.

We can protect ourselves with a high frequency field of Light which is called a Merkabah Vehicle of Light, because this maintains our resonance in a raised state - no matter what happens around us. Within this 'vehicle', or field of energy, we 'travel' to, or access, the higher dimensions, regardless of the Earth events that may unfold around us.

The most important decision we all face right now is voiced by Isis in the following communication.

Isis: Do you continue Forward or do you Return?

"It is, Beloved Beings of Light, it is for yourselves to not go forward in a continuation of the feeling state of darkness and doom. It is not to bring forward

Chapter Sixteen: POSTSCRIPT, DEFINITIONS, BIBLIOGRAPHY AND RECOMMENDED READING

in this manner, Beloved Beings of Light. It is to bring forward to support the upliftment. You have the ability. You have seen it before, to create great shift in environment, and so it is once more for yourselves to connect to work with this. To feel the presence of Light that shifts, to feel a Love within your heart as you begin to communicate with all in existence, to feel the experience of communication of the Angelic Realms, the communication of all Beings in Ascension, to do same at this time: to come together as One. To work in this way it is supportive, Beloved Beings of Light.

"There have been yourselves, perhaps not all, it is to understand the feeling has been, there have been yourselves that have gone forward to question in which direction do you move. There is the knowledge within the self that goes to return for many lifetimes that have been spent in connection. In European lifetimes, the presence of religions, it has not been of darkness, but it is to understand it is there, the remnant of this is always there. Therefore there has been the question by many of yourselves: **"Do you continue forward with that which you are taught at this time, or do you return. You resonate with this, Beloved Beings of Light?"**

Paragraph Definitions of Commonly used Terms
The following concepts and terms are discussed briefly and may be regarded as a broad overview of the concepts in the book. An A - Z glossary of terms, bibliography and recommended reading list are placed at the end of this chapter.

A
Age of Aquarius - refer to 'The Mayan Calendar, 2012 and the Age of Aquarius'

Alignments of Planets and Stars with Earth
The alignments of numerous other planets and stars in the outer-planetary environment of Earth are contributing to the energy intensity of the midpoint of this central position of the Age. Interestingly enough, they are in exactly the same position as they were in 2037 BC. It was at that ancient time that the returning god-beings of Ancient Egypt worked intensely with Earth and her inhabitants to assist them to return to a greater state of Light. Civilisations on Earth had begun a significant degeneration into war and pillage orientated behaviours. A massive injection of Light into the Earthly situation - by the god-beings - was designed to help shift this energy and slow the degeneration into further darkness.

The super-alignment of these high frequency, outer-planetary light bodies means that the energies which surround Earth in the present day are as conducive to similarly profound spiritual experiences as they were during Ancient Egyptian times. The difference in the outcome of the same opportunities we have now as were available then, is the relative difference of the energies of this Age versus that Age - and the influence of the expanded consciousness of humanity. These factors have already allowed us to shift from the 3rd dimension frequencies of conscious reality to the 4th dimension of reality.

Ancient Egypt
The era we call the Ancient Egyptian Era spanned from the end of the time of the Ancient Sumerians to around 30 BC - when Cleopatra VII, the last of the reigning Ptolemies, died. What is significant about the whole area of Egypt and the time of the Ancient Egyptian Era, in terms of the Light Beings, is the fact that many of them returned to Earth (a long time after they originally left Earth during the Atlantean Era disaster) to help humanity in the Ancient Sumerian and Ancient Egyptian times after an extended period of absence. They left Earth at the time which is often referred to as the Great Deluge or the end of the Atlantean Era.

The denser energy state which Earth physically shifted to after the Fall at the end of the Atlantean Era, meant that any soul incarnating on Earth post-Atlantis would be subject to the denser energies of this lowered frequency reality. This means they would struggle to remember themselves as a Divine soul presence within a human being and they would perceive 3rd or 4th dimension reality as the known state of being. In this post-Atlantis state of reality, it became difficult for Earthlings to know how to bridge the divide and reclaim a higher frequency, living state without some powerful guidance from more knowledgeable beings.

While suffering the illusion of separation in the dimensions below the 5th, Earthlings would be at risk of falling prey to unscrupulous operators amongst themselves, because they were bereft of the understanding about the higher dimensions and the nature of their soul presence. It was against this backdrop that human power games developed, in the guise of priestly misdemeanours. Many of the Light Beings re-entered the realm of Earth in the area of Egypt, although a lot of them had been there since Ancient Sumerian times. The aim of their arrival on Earth once more was to assist human beings in their journey towards enLightenment.

Ascension Pathway - refer to 'Karma and the Ascension Pathway'

Atlantis
Although there is a lot of information available about the great, lost civilisation of Atlantis referred to in this book, it is often deemed to be a mythical one by many

people. Our information from the Light Beings is that this civilisation was far from a fantastical notion about lost people or sunken lands. Furthermore, the Light Beings, Osiris and Isis have informed us that there were even greater civilisations on Earth that preceded the time of Atlantis. As we explore this from our current perspective in the 4th dimension we are often incredulous of the results of our searches. As we sit on the brink of re-entering the 5th dimension, the Atlantean Era may be understood as the last period before the whole of Earth and her inhabitants dropped from the 5th dimension into the lowered frequency state of existence. It is this event that is referred to as 'the Fall' in many religious texts. The actual event that created the dimension shift of the Fall was an Atlantean Era nuclear explosion, but the problems had started long before that with the development of duality.

Regardless of how far-fetched this may sound, there are some scholars who consider they can prove that there *was* some form of nuclear explosion in the Middle East a long time ago. These conclusions have been arrived at by examining the physical evidence which has been left behind that can still be seen today. Zecharia Sitchin refers to this in some of his books. Travelling through the Namibian deserts and seeing the little 'fairy circles' where no plant life can exist, it is clear that this area also suffered the same nuclear fate.

Inasmuch as there was a forced shift at that time which split the single dimension of integrated spiritualised physicality into the spiritual and the physical dimensions, it may certainly be considered that this may be viewed as a fall from the grace of higher frequency existence. Humanity lost the *living* experience of resonating with the higher dimensions - the dimensions of spiritual knowledge and experience where our soul presence comes from.

Physically, this final Atlantean Era dimension drop created the illusion which is the separation of our physical and spiritual realities. Transcendence of the lower dimension energies of the 3rd dimension (and the experiences that resonance at this frequency fosters) has, ever since then, been the challenge - for all human beings. That we have managed to shift consciousness to resonate with the 4th dimension is proof that humanity has made tremendous progress.

The *transmutation* (transformation) of Earth and her inhabitants from the lower frequency state (of the 3rd dimension via the 4th dimension) back into the higher frequency state (of the 5th dimension) is the reason behind the living ascension processes. It is this progression forwards that is understood to be the Pathway of Return which the Light Beings refer to. The 'return' is, initially, the return to the 5th dimension mode of existence that was the natural way of life in Atlantean times. After this the Return continues back up the dimension ladder of existence until we attain Oneness of Being with all existence.

C

Cleansing and Purification

Considering that the main spiritual thrust as we approach the year 2012 is the issue of shifting dimension from the 4th to the 5th dimension, it is understandable that the challenges we face now in our lives as well as on our planet, will be directly related to this. The important events surrounding any dimension shift upwards towards higher frequency Light will be the issues of cleansing and purification - so that we can tolerate the higher energy fields. It is because we intend to shift our physical body to resonate higher that this means there will be physical processes in the shift from lower frequency states. The frequency shifts create changes (which may be likened to a detoxification) in the energy of the physical human body as well as in the physical body of Earth, because both are vibration sensitive bodies. Hence, the numerous emotional and physical changes which people are noticing, the enormity of the Earth shifts and changes (climate, plate tectonics, eruptions etc) which we face in our present day, the potential these shifts have to generate fear amongst humanity and the social reorganisation, no matter whether corporate, religious or politically orientated, which is the result of humanity's greater state of conscious awareness, all play an important part in any discussion about the living ascension processes.

Climate Change - refer to 'Great Deluge, Pole Shift, Climate Change and Nibiru'

Collective Consciousness and Siriuns

We are told by Osiris that many of the Light Beings came into physical life on Earth in ancient times as a collective consciousness of a number of souls - often as the Pharaohs. This means that a number of souls inhabited the same body at the same time, in order to give that one individual more power. It was the many great men and women of the ancient world who were 'made up of' these collectives. Even in more modern times we have seen this phenomenon - the consciousness of one of the great Indians, Mahatma Ghandi, was a collective of no less than three souls. Strange as this may seem to us now from our unschooled perspective, this is nevertheless very interesting information to consider. It may also help to explain some of the anomalies of the ancient world as well as the profound changes some modern leaders are able to make.

Even more unusual to consider is the Osiris-confirmed information that some of the Pharaohs were pure Siriun Beings inasmuch as they arrived on Earth from the star system of Sirius - and took up a physical, human-like body. These were the true god-beings. This is important because Sirius is one of the star systems which has a very high frequency vibration and the Beings of Light who arrive on Earth from there are extremely powerful spiritual beings. The Pharaoh Akhenaten, his Queen Nefertiti and their son Tutankhamun are a case in point. Perhaps this information about their star origins may help to solve the riddle of their unusual appearance. The reign of this Pharaoh was fraught with immense difficulties because of the political upheaval the family caused when they stripped the manipulative priesthood of their authority, introduced a monotheistic religion which concentrated the idea of Divinity on a force emanating from the Sun rather than on individual god-beings and started teaching the genuine principles of Divinity on Earth once more. Light returned to Earth and the changes it brought were not always popular.

The actions of this family are an example of the attempts by the Light Beings to help Earth and her inhabitants to understand the principles of Divinity once more, without the corruptive influence of human beings. When we look at how prevalent wars were prior to their reign, or the manner in which the temples of this couple were defiled, defaced and destroyed after their reign, we see a clear example of how powerful the forces of darkness on Earth were at that time. The war of the Light and the dark on Earth has waged almost since time immemorial. It continues today.

Therefore, the reference to Ancient Egypt and the god-beings who worked with the Light are relevant to us today inasmuch as the Light Beings who communicate with us are none other than the ascended soul presence of some of those powerful individuals who attempted to help Earth recover to a higher frequency state at that time.

Communication with the Godhead

Resonance with the spiritual worlds (where we can be in open communication with the Godhead) begins when we are within range of the 5th dimension. Practically, this means that once our vibrations are within range of the vibrations of the 5th dimension we can begin to perceive it as our reality. This is exactly what is happening now, from the perspective of the 4th dimension - as evidenced by the widespread spiritual awakening amongst humanity. If we stay within range of higher frequencies for long enough we will start getting caught up with them in the process of entrainment. This is the positive influence of being exposed to higher resonance.

The aim of raising our resonance is to be in open communication with Divine Source once again. Our currently underdeveloped, or restricted, perceptual abilities and the lower resonance which this creates, maintains our sense of separation. However, although we experience it as real, our separation from the Godhead is not true, inasmuch as we still have a connection to the higher frequency states. The sense of separation is a trick of our perception - hence the reason the term 'illusion' is used when referring to physical reality in the 3rd or 4th dimensions. It is as if all beings are all in the same 'room' of the Universe, but human beings have been magnetically drawn to congregate in one corner and turned their backs on the rest of the room as they moved in that direction. They can't see anybody else other than themselves in the corner and so they believe that they are alone.

Therefore, it is *because* human beings are resonating with the 4th dimension of existence (in their own little 'corner' of the Universe) that we perceive the high frequency Light of Divinity, of the God state, to be far beyond our human reach, and in realms far removed from us. The Light Beings help to make us consciously aware that the planet and all of humanity are currently able to resonate with higher frequency Light that will reactivate our perceptual abilities. In this way we will begin to perceive other, higher states of existence - the realms of the Godhead. This we can now do, whilst in the 'living state,' as we go through the processes of living ascension. This shifted dimension experience is achieved by means of our deliberate actions to change our physical frequencies - so that we resonate higher. Whether or not we do this, is our personal choice.

Both the tireless energy support work they do for the planet and the communications that the Light Beings have with humanity help to remind us that when we live in a state of unconditional love we make love the manifest, Earth experience. This consciousness uplifting, Divine emotion allows us to shift into the state of spiritualised physicality of living ascension on Earth. The importance of this shifted dimension reality is that we then live with true spiritual awareness and are able to be in open communication with Divine Source. This denotes a human being with conscious soul presence. It is because of this that we are then more easily able to work towards God-realisation and the re-attainment of the Oneness of Being - right up to and within the dimensions of the Godhead.

D
Divinity and Frequency

If we refer to that which is Divine as the brightest form of any possible Light, then we may consider that the highest frequency of a vibration anywhere in the Universe is Divinity itself. With this understanding we can certainly appreciate that our quest for God-realisation from the perspective of Earth has to include the shifting of the vibrations of our physical human self into a higher frequency state - towards Light. How we shift our vibrations is relative to our understanding of the processes involved, as well as the knowledge that it *is* humanly possible to do so.

Mostly, we are not aware of the fact that the shifted vibrational experience is both achievable from the human perspective and well within the reach of everyman. The information in this book seeks to redress some of the lack of clarity on the potential we all have for the higher frequency experiences of the non-material world - and most importantly - an understanding that we can do this whilst we are still physically, humanly alive and conscious. This endpoint is what has been termed 'living ascension' by the Light Beings.

The high frequency communications with the Beings of Light are intended to help human beings on Earth shift their entire living experience to the higher level of *spiritualised* physicality. Physically this means that the particles of our human bodies will begin to vibrate at faster speeds than before. When this happens it may be said that we will then physically be functioning at a higher frequency than before. If we continue to train the solid, physical particles of our human bodies to be able to tolerate, resonate with, higher and higher frequencies, we will ultimately be able to perceive the non-material realms in their totality - from the perspective of our human lives. This is the direct opposite of spiritual awareness which is gained only when we die and our souls naturally shift back into the non-material realms. Naturally, it will take time and practice before we develop the necessary skill and proficiency for accessing the high frequency, spiritual realms from the human state.

Duality - Separated Reality
The resonance of the 4th dimension experience of *physical* reality, for example, is created by vibrations which move at specific speeds. These are different to the speeds of the 5th dimension vibrations of *spirituality* - although the two groups of vibrations are so close to each other (within range) that they have an influence on each other. They exist concurrently as two different and opposite states of energy at the same time. The physical world is understood to be a separated reality, because it is separated from the rest of the spiritual existence of the Universe. The separation of the one realm (Unity) into two, created our current reality (Duality), inasmuch as that which was previously *unified* (spirituality and physicality) is now *split*.

When we resonate with the lower frequency states (of the 3rd or the 4th dimensions), it is these vibrations which form the specific physical living experiences *and* create the illusion that this realm (where there is separation from Oneness) is the only thing that is real. Duality implies a split into two portions. The concept of a *split* signifies that the twin states of being came from the *one* origin. To live in duality means that we have separated our Oneness of being into two. These are the polar opposite states of spirituality and physicality. On Earth, this split experience is known and felt as our reality, because that is what it is. The mistake some of us make is to believe that this reality is all there is, because that's what it feels like.

Duality - refer to 'Resistance, Duality and Illusion'

E
Expansion of Consciousness
It is the learned ability to vibrate at higher frequencies that is part and parcel of the expansion of our consciousness, because higher states of knowledge naturally

resonate higher than lower states of knowledge do. Resonance may be defined as the reverberation which is created by the vibrations which are sounded in any environment - whether in a body or anywhere in the Universe. Knowledge is prized the world over and this is not surprising because knowledge often equates to power. The knowledge-based expansion of consciousness is what begins the 'upliftment' of consciousness. Attaining any greater state of being, or higher resonance, may be considered to be an uplifting experience.

F
Frequency: see 'Divinity and Frequency'

G
Gateways - refer to 'Star Consciousness, Stargates and Gateways'

God and Science
Many people consider joining scientific and spiritual principles to be unorthodox. Some would go so far as to call it heresy - either scientific or religious. Outrage is often expressed about this issue, but we, the authors, acknowledge the discussions of the Light Beings when they link science and God. That which science studies are the results of the handiwork of Creative Divinity, and that which science takes pride in explaining according to the man-made laws of physics (mathematics or the like) is nothing less than the brilliant observations, by man, of the Laws of the Universe - in place and functioning on Earth.

True scientific brilliance always results when the principles of Divinity are acknowledged and utilised. Bear this idea in mind when reading the book - even if this is regarded as the viewpoint of the authors.

Godhead - refer to 'Communication with the Godhead'

Great Deluge, Pole Shift, Climate Change and Nibiru
At the end of the Atlantean Era there were serious problems on Earth. These issues existed within the degenerated consciousness of her inhabitants as well as in the physical environment. To place this within the relevant context we may consider that the people who made up Atlantean Era societies were not very different to the people who make up our present day ones - and this is aside from the fact that they were inhabiting a higher dimension than we are presently.

There existed a mix of good and bad influences with a predominance of selfish, greedy behaviour - just as we see around us today. The gradual degeneration of the greatness of Atlantean society took a long time to achieve and the resultant lowered resonance is what eventually set the scene for climate change, the war that led to the detonation of the nuclear warhead;- the Great Deluge; - and the pole shift of that time. The compounded effects of these disasters were made possible on Earth because of the manner in which her inhabitants behaved. The consciousness of Earth's inhabitants set up the appropriate resonance for the occurrence of disaster and calamities of all kinds. There is no such thing as a natural disaster which is divorced from the consciousness of humanity. Because of the Law of Resonance, the one creates the other. Nevertheless, the natural disasters of that time would not necessarily have created a dimension shift. The nuclear explosion achieved that. The approach of Nibiru in her usual 3 600 year orbit around the Sun meant that her strong gravitational pull on Earth would have its usual effect. If the consciousness of Earthlings was such that it could tolerate these high frequency stimulations, then would be no catastrophic events. The degeneration of Atlantean society meant that this most definitely was not the case. Therefore, the effect of Nibiru further destabilised Earth and all upon her. This event is always an opportunity to release and cleanse and shift into a higher state of consciousness, but this obviously did not happen. The massive Earth disasters which ultimately resulted in complete disaster as we dropped downwards in dimension are proof of this.

Due to the knock-on effect of resonance, Earth's climatic conditions, no less than the shifts of her poles, are determined by the consciousness of the entire planet. Towards the end of the Atlantean Era a contributing destabilising influence came in the guise of an approaching planet called Nibiru. The path of her long elliptical orbit around the Sun bisected that of Earth's orbit at right angles. She was known as the 'Planet of the crossing' as a result. The strong gravitational pull that Nibiru's presence nearby Earth exerted on us was considered to be difficult at the best of times, but intolerable when in a lowered frequency state. Atlantean consciousness had degenerated sufficiently to feel the powerful effects of Nibiru's approach as negative. The approach every 3 600 years of an otherwise distant, high frequency planet may be seen as the precipitating crisis for Earth calamities at that time - just as it is today - when we are in a lowered state of consciousness.

Other than from references to it in the Ancient Sumerian texts, many people don't know about the existence of the planet Nibiru. The Light Beings have confirmed that we will gather more astronomical knowledge of Nibiru within a short period of time when she reappears within closer range of Earth. Today we are in the 4th dimension frequency state of existence and the approach of Nibiru is once again creating a disturbance in our gravitational field. Although the frequencies of each planet are so vastly different, Earth (in the 4th dimension) and Nibiru (in the 5th dimension) are still within range of each other. As such they resonate with each other.

The potential for Earth catastrophes notwithstanding, our modern day may be considered an auspicious time to be living in, because we are currently on an *upward* trend with regard to consciousness. This is the complete opposite to the time of the Atlantean Era disasters which resulted in a dramatic drop in the energy of the entire planet - and all of Earth continued existence in the 3rd rather than the 5th dimension.

We have gone through the dark times of the 3rd dimension and have emerged into the higher vibrational experience of the 4th dimension existence on Earth. If we continue this positive trend we can utilise the stimulating energies of approaching Nibiru to help us shift rapidly back into the 5th dimension. The reverse option is that we deny these outer-planetary influences, resist the natural changes of resonance and make our lives more difficult. When we are aware of the many outer-planetary influences and the processes that accompany a change in dimension, we can not only improve our own living experience, but we can also help to mitigate the present day effects of climate change, a potential pole shift and avert nuclear war on Earth. All of this will ensure we continue living on Earth in a calm and happy state, instead of having to go through catastrophes, or even complete obliteration, if these eventualities are played out to their fullest extent.

I
Illusion - refer to 'Resistance, Duality and Illusion'

K
Karma and the Ascension Pathway
It stands to reason that the pathway towards the greater Light of the 5th dimension has to include the eradication of Karma, because that which we refer to as Karma are the issues of the ego - no matter which lifetime they were created in. Karma may be defined in terms of the low frequency resonance which is created when we create hurt for another or for ourselves. The determination of how much Karma we create for ourselves when we do harm to others is relative to the dimension that we exist within. The higher the dimensional experience, the more knowledge we have and the more responsibility we bear towards ourselves and others. In this manner we are more accountable for our actions the higher we progress spiritually.

It is worth bearing in mind that when we gain deeper insight into the processes of living ascension and choose to move forwards on this shifted dimension pathway, we also become more responsible and accountable than the person who is oblivious to these facts. Accountability is relative to 'no man is an island' and the fact that everything we do has an impact on those around us. The impacts of our actions are not limited to our nearest and dearest and they have far-reaching effects throughout humanity, because of the never-ending knock-on effects of the energy of our actions. As we develop higher levels of knowledge we become more accountable in terms of those who are in our direct sphere of influence, and that is everybody. Our responsibility to always act in accordance with that which is in line with the highest order of all souls concerned should be uppermost in our minds. This is the soul-sensible thing to do.

Ego issues (which create Karma) belong in the Light/Dark of duality, not in the Light of living ascension. Shifting ourselves so that we do not resonate with issues of the ego in our bodies, minds and our souls is best done when we are consciously aware of what we are doing. Conscious change makes the process all the more understandable and bearable, because shifting from something means first confronting it and acknowledging its existence before letting it go and moving on. This may not be a pleasant process when it involves clearing Karma, but is it necessary if we want to shift from the experiences of duality.

In terms of Karma release or Karma gathering when we are on the pathway of living ascension, the idea is to release Karma so as to be able to live in the Light - rather than to remain fixed in the Light/Dark. We will naturally take *great* care not to incur further Karma along the way - because this would be both counterproductive and highly destructive. Were we to do this we would continue to go around in circles instead of going forwards. Treading a perpetual circle which is maintained by the repeat performances of our lives which so many of us tend towards, creates a deep groove which is very difficult to shift out of.

L
Living Ascension
Living ascension gives human beings, who are currently living within 4th dimension Earth reality, the opportunity to experience the spiritual dimensions, beginning with the 5th dimension, without having to die first. This involves the shifted dimension experience and is achieved by means of raising our resonance - so that we can perceive the dimensions of Spirit. Being able to function at the level where we are 100% spiritually aware while 100% physically alive at the same time is the challenge of living ascension. It is also the end result of this process.

Although it is a new concept to many people in the present day, the idea of living ascension has been around for many centuries. Many ancient spiritual teachings - which many call myths - centred around this concept of being able to physically live in the after life. This is why there were burial practices that included the internment of the most important worldly goods with the dearly departed - from chariots, to gold and horses.

The ability to choose between living ascension (physically living in the world of Spirit) and the human guarantee of dying ascension (soul movement upwards into the non-material dimensions) is determined by the degree to which the individual is Karma-free. The term *living* ascension presumes that the human being has worked off sufficient of the low frequency clutter of the body and the soul, that is commonly called Karma, which he or she resonates with, *while still humanly alive*. It is this process which creates the ability for individuals to physically, humanly resonate with the Heavenly realms of Spirit. This also ensures that the soul is not obliged to reincarnate in human form again in order to work off Karma. *Dying* ascension relates to the natural movement upwards of a soul as it separates from the body at the time of physical death - even if that soul still resonates with Earth Karma. Progress through to either the higher frequency states of Light or reincarnation back to Earth to work off Karma, are the two different results of ascension. Whether this is in a pure Spirit form or in physical form depends on the choice of living or dying ascension, for each individual.

Relative to ascension, the term Ascended Master denotes a being who has acquired the master vibration and has released all Earth Karma, or low resonance vibrations from his soul, and is either living on Earth or has moved completely into a higher vibration, different dimension, Karma-free. This individual will then live on Earth in the physical state of ascension or elsewhere in the non-material state of ascension, as the Light Beings do, depending on the processes that were undertaken by that individual soul presence. Until now ascension of any kind has been mostly done after physical death.

M
The Mayan Calendar, 2012 and the Age of Aquarius
The importance of 2012, relative to the Mayan Calendar, has gained widespread attention. Many books, movies and discussions are available on the subject and people generally want to know more about it. Aside from what has already been written and what is generally understood, it may help the reader to focus on the spiritual reason behind this date and the astrological Age within which it appears.

Each astrological Age, as denoted by the precessional movements of the various planets relative to Earth, lasts for a long time - a couple of thousand years. The energies of the Age build up and then wane over this entire period, with the declining energies of the previous Age overlapping the incoming energies of the new one. This transition takes place over a significant period of time.

The Light Being, Osiris, has informed us that it is the midpoint of each Age which is critically important from a spiritual perspective. Osiris refers to the specific period surrounding the midpoint as the, *"Central position of the Age."* This entire period which equally precedes and is after the midpoint, lasts for 100 years. It is during this 100 year period that the energies which are created by the specific alignments of the outer-planetary bodies relative to Earth are not only at their clearest, but also at their most profound - with no overlapping energies from the previous *or* the coming Age. It is these very pure, high frequency energies which are the root cause behind the fact that the issues of the Age will be heightened at the midpoint. The midpoint of the Age of Aquarius is the year 2012. Therefore, we can appreciate that the lessons that Earth and humanity are undergoing on their journey towards higher frequency states will be intensified at this time.

The Mayan Calendar is an ancient, sacred calendar which pinpoints the various shifts in the consciousness of humanity. It has provided a timeline of the historical and biological changes on Earth. The wave pattern that the developing consciousness which we call humanity has followed is recorded in the Mayan Calendar. The existence of this calendar and the concurrent developments on Earth prove that there is a schedule for humanity - one which was already known aeons ago. Thoth created this calendar as his record of the times when significant Earth events would occur - most specifically, the dimensional shift in 2012. This shows us that Divine Intelligence not only exists, but it is relevant for us on Earth today - just as it has been throughout our history. That fact should not surprise us, but it informs us that there is a lot for us to learn and to rediscover.

Therefore, the interesting thing about this calendar is the fact that it may be regarded as a tool of prophesy - it was stated many thousands of years ago that humanity would reach this point in time when consciousness would shift radically, just as it is happening now. We are right on schedule! It is this awakening of consciousness, which is shifting in accordance with the energy systems of the time clocks of Thoth, which will allow us to end the old ways of the illusion of separated reality which is created by resonance with the 3rd and 4th dimensions - and enable us to perceive the pathway of re-unification with the spiritual realms.

The time-clocks of Thoth are the Earthly time-keeping energy systems which link us up to the Cosmos. We cannot ignore the physically obvious fact that the massive structures that house their energy, align with certain planets and stars at certain times, including a sunrise and sunset. Orion is particularly important in this regard. As part of the massive structures themselves, the time-clocks were activated energetically in some of the power-point situated portals on Earth - such as the Great Pyramid. These portals were encoded to allow for their energy gateways to be opened, supported by Thoth, when the super-alignment of certain planets and stars came in position, relative to Earth, in the way they will be in 2012.

This period in time is truly the end-time of separation - if that is what we want it to be. Human beings no longer need to feel removed from the realms of Spirit, because we have the opportunity for easy spiritual access. As we shift ourselves to be able to recognise our soul presence, we begin to raise our resonance and we begin to move back towards Oneness. We can appreciate why this time, in this Age, is referred to as the Point of Return by the Light Beings. We can choose to un-polarise our reality and move towards the centre so that our spirit self is one with our physical self once more.

N
Nibiru - refer to 'Great Deluge, Pole shift, Climate Change and Nibiru'

Non-linear Dimensions
Although the non-material worlds are not really arranged in a linear fashion, our limited human understanding does not yet easily allow for the full comprehension of these realms other than with reference to their prescribed numerical values. It is for this reason that the Light Beings have discussed the higher frequency levels as being arranged in that linear-like fashion. They have informed us that Earth is currently in the 4th dimension of reality. This means that we are vibrationally capable of having experiences of living relative to solid physicality. They have also informed us that the 5th dimension is the next frequency band above us and it is the first *non-material* realm of existence. Earth and humanity are in the process of transmuting to a higher level of consciousness - which is the 5th dimension. Regardless of the fact that we use linear descriptions of the dimensions it should be borne in mind that all the dimensions actually exist in the same place, at the same time, within the Universe, separated and demarcated only by the nature of the different frequency states.

Interestingly, it is in the 5th dimension that we have an option to exist as physical beings if we *physically* shift our vibrations sufficiently so as to resonate with that higher frequency. We do this from our state of our current resonance with the 4th dimension. It is within the 5th dimension that conscious existence, whether in material or non-material form, is in open contact with the Divine communications of the Godhead. There are a total of 50 dimensions in the Universe. The Light Beings state that the dimensions of the Godhead are at the level of the 49th/50th dimensions and that we can make progress throughout all of these dimensions.

The fact that our resonance is within range of the 5th dimension is an extremely important piece of information, because it informs us of the fact that there is a frequency divide which we have to cross - from the 4th dimension - in order to experience 5th dimension existence. This divide is generally referred to as the energy 'veil' which separates the physical world from the spirit worlds. The means with which we cross this divide from the position of 4th dimension, physical Earth-living human beings, is by uplifting our consciousness so that we can physically vibrate with the higher frequencies. This is referred to as the transmutation of our energy. This is the way we expand our awareness and perceive greater knowledge and information which exists in the higher dimensions of the Universe. Another means with which we may cross this divide to the other side is by dying, because that is when the naturally high frequency, non-material soul presence separates from the lower frequency, material body.

P
The Pathway of Return - the Shifted Dimension Experience
It is helpful to read Osiris' own words about how the Earth and humanity are returning to the higher dimension experience of expanded spirituality. He tells us how it is that we are back at the point of a dimensional shift. This time however, as we approach the spiritually important time of 2012, the shift is *upwards* in frequency - back to the 5th dimension, instead of *downwards* to the lower resonance of the 3rd dimension which occurred at the end of the Atlantean Era. It is in support of this dimension shift that the Light Beings communicate with humanity at this time.

Perception
The love and support of the Light Beings extends towards us from the altered frequency realms of Spirit in the form of psychic understandings and the channelled communications in this book. They have given us information that the frequency level they communicate with us from resonates with the 5th dimension (Earth and humans are currently in the 4th dimension) and that their high frequency Light communications are often beamed to us from nearby in our solar system: from the planet Venus. Although they themselves are fully God-realised Beings of Light from the highest dimension of the Universe, they frequently use Venus, in the 5th dimension, as a communication platform because of its proximity to Earth - vibrationally and physically. From this information we begin to glean that, in the Universal sense, the material and non-material worlds are not as divorced from each other as we may originally have thought them to be.

It may be questioned why it is that astronomers are not aware of the existence of the Light Beings on Venus, if this is where they are? The reason for this is simple - human beings have to be physically vibrating at a high enough frequency in order to resonate with higher frequency states of existence elsewhere in the Universe. Failing this, we will not be able to see or hear them.

It is our ability to perceive different frequencies which will determine whether or not we are aware of them in manifest reality - in the exact same way that a dog is able to hear the pitch of a dog whistle and humans are not. That dog whistle sound is very much in existence right where we are and the dog responds to it, but we cannot hear it. Likewise, the Light Beings are in existence on Venus, but we cannot see them. Raising resonance is what will enable human perception of other, higher states of being.

Therefore, it may be stated that there are humans with different perceptual abilities - and these are based on individual vibration frequencies. This is generally why people are referred to as psychic or not. Considering that psychic skills are developed, frequency dependent abilities it may be considered that all human beings are potentially *infinitely* psychic.

Polarisation
The movement towards one or other of any two states, within any context, is polarisation. This movement implies that a choice is made - regardless of direction. Polarisation restricts movement in the direction of the vibration. It is this restriction which is both the result of the separation while also maintaining it. This is why we have a non-unity state of consciousness in the realm of duality. The result of this is that we have a sense of ourselves versus the other, of this and that, of black and white, or of right and wrong. In the state of Oneness, none of these comparative states (or restrictions) exist. When we resonate with the realms of the Godhead, limits no longer exist and we experience freedom. This is Bliss.

In the 3rd and/or 4th dimensions, or energy fields, the determinant of how great the divide is between the two separated states of being, namely, physical and spiritual, is how radically different our physical lives are from our spiritual lives - how polarised we are. The extent of our polarisation determines the degree of our restriction (as physical human beings) into the spiritual realms, because it determines our resonance. In order to perceive something as real we have to be within *range* of its vibrations. This enables us to resonate with something different to ourselves.

Pole Shift - refer to 'Great Deluge, Pole Shift, Climate Change and Nibiru'

Psychic Perception
There are many different ways of perceiving the Light Beings from the perspective of the material world, but only once we have shifted the speed of our own vibrations to be within the range of their frequency. The so-called 'psychic skills' of clairvoyance (sight), clairaudience (hearing) and clairsentience (sensing) are pertinent in this regard. It makes no difference how it is that an individual human being shifts his or her frequency higher in order to perceive communications from the Light Beings. What is important is that these communications are understood for what they are. They are glimpses into another world, another reality state of being. In the higher frequency states of being, the nature of existence is more ordered and the awareness is expanded - this is referred to as Bliss.

As we gradually learn to trust our communications with the higher frequency realms, from the human perspective, we begin to get a foretaste of potential states of existence which are very different from our own. It is in this way that we gain knowledge and information beyond that which is currently available to us on physical Earth.

We never arrive at the end point of these expansionary processes because the expansion and development of consciousness is interminable in the Universal sense. This is because the more we learn the more we develop our awareness, and the more we do this, the more we learn. This positive knock-on effect is the reason for the continual expansion of both our own consciousness and the consciousness of the entire Universe.

R
Religion

Although the subject of religion, like politics, is best avoided because of its potential to create dissention and discontent, it is an integral part of our societies. As such religion has been and continues to be a significant composition of socialisation the world over - in both the primary (in the home) and secondary (outside of the home) sense.

Much of humanity's understanding of spiritual concepts is governed by some religion or another and therefore it is no wonder that the Light Beings do discuss religion. Part of the correction of the historical and spiritual misinformation that humanity has been exposed to for centuries, has to include the reconsideration of incorrect information. All religions may be open to criticism because their teachings have deviated from the purity of the teachings of the Divinity of unconditional love. If we use love as the acid test for Divine Truth we may more easily assess a teaching and all religions may be found wanting from this perspective - and so too may all of society's structures of law and morality.

Resistance, Duality and Illusion

The critical thing to understand in any discussion of living ascension is that it is a state of *Light*. In it there is no duality - no darkness. For the human being this means that there is no opposing force of the negative ego to pull the soul downwards. The problem with living in the world of duality (in the 3rd or the 4th dimensions) is that there are dual forces of the soul (subtle forces) and the ego/personality (overt, obvious forces) to contend with. These opposing forces within create a constant struggle until the lower energies of the ego are transmuted, or transformed, into the higher energies of the soul presence. This is when the person finds peace inside himself. This is when life stops being a place of suffering.

The ego resists the transformation processes that would prevent its dominance, because it (the ego-driven personality) fears that this means giving up on itself. It doesn't realise that transformation is actually an *evolution* of the personality-self to a higher state of function. As such, shifting from negative ego-bound thoughts, emotions and behaviour should not be seen as a *loss* of a part of the personality-self, but as a *growth* process for the whole self.

When we are operating predominantly from the ego state we are so distracted by the fun, pleasures, drama, pain and suffering that are our lives that we struggle to hear the gentle sounds and urgings of the soul. Finding and following the soul pathway is then difficult. The ego drives will always have the tendency to drown out the sweet sounds of soul presence.

For people, the problem with shifting from an ego state (where negative emotions and extremes of human pain *and* pleasure are felt) into the soul state is that so many things in the world of ego are indeed fun and pleasurable. These are perceived as comforts and as such it is rare for a person to want to give them up - until and unless that person starts to get an inkling of the far greater comforts and pleasures when they are transformed with the energy of the other side, in the Light. Alternatively, the human suffering that ego can create often provides the necessary spur to change.

Many people go into resistance when they start on their spiritual journey. In fact *everybody* will have some or other form of resistance at some point along the way. This is confusing and seemingly contradicts the desire to progress spiritually, but there are very good reasons why this happens. The rationale behind any form of resistance in the pathway forwards can be endless. The most common reasons are because of the following:
- We do not truly understand exactly what it is we are working towards on the other side of duality - transformed ego.
- We are so entranced by the pleasures of the ego world (having fun - no matter whether 'good' fun or 'bad' fun - that we believe it will provide for all our needs.
- We fear our ability to cope with the processes and demands of the new pathway - because we do not perceive we are strong or worthy enough.
- We fear, or feel, the loss of the comforts of the old way of life and so we cling to them - because we have not yet grasped or settled into the new comforts, on the new pathway.

Perceptions are the trap of the illusion. The illusion in this instance is the feeling that human comfort (and therefore peace of mind) can only be achieved in the 'real' world that we currently know. The true reality is that our current state of consciousness is the limiting factor to what we perceive as real.

In order to change this limited perception and live the experience of Light (where the soul desires and experiences of living are dominant) rather than of Light/Dark (where we constantly struggle between our soul desires and our ego

needs), human beings have a clear pathway to follow. These involve the following choices:
- Recognising the fact that the Light/Dark existence of duality is very real - in the 3rd and the 4th dimensions.
- Acknowledging that there *is* another option, which is Light, beginning with the 5th dimension.
- Choosing the pathway of Light - from where we are now.

Choosing the Light involves recognising that we do have an option in *each instance* of our thoughts, emotions and behaviours. When the pathway of Light is chosen, the world of duality automatically and effortlessly begins to collapse behind us. In this way we naturally and easily transform the difficult illusion of duality into pure oneness of being. Suffering fades and joy emerges.

S

Science - refer to 'God and Science'

Siriuns - refer to 'Collective Consciousness and Siriuns'

Star Alignments
There is frequent reference throughout the book to the importance of the particular alignments of the stars and the planets relative to Earth at the moment. The reason for this is very simple: the arrangement of the outer-planetary bodies in the skies is *exactly* the same in the present day as it was in the corresponding time of 2037 BC. That time was when the god-beings lived on Earth in Ancient Egypt.

This means that the energies surrounding our planet are supportive for powerful, high frequency outer-planetary helpers to get involved with Earth. The fact that our present time is a repeat, astronomically speaking, is significant, because Earth and human consciousness is resonating within a higher frequency bandwidth than it was in the 2037 BC times. *Then* humanity was resonating within the frequency bandwidth which corresponds to the 3rd dimension. *Now* we are resonating with the frequency bandwidth which corresponds to the 4th dimension. This means that we are currently harmonically capable of resonating with the higher frequency spiritual realm of the 5th dimension for the first time since the Atlantean Era Fall - which was a drop in frequency. We are within range of the Godhead once more.

    This is highly significant information because it relates directly to the heightened energy which enables us to achieve the spiritualised physical state of being which is called living ascension. We do this by shifting dimension. It is not surprising that the Light Beings often refer to the importance of the alignments of the outer planetary bodies considering that the higher frequency stimulation of Earth by these planets and stars are what will assist Earth and human consciousness to shift to a higher level. This is like receiving a Divine turbo-boost from the heavens.

Creating awareness about these alignments, the existence of the high frequency consciousness of some of the outer-planetary bodies, how this consciousness relates to the Light beings and how this all influences human consciousness on Earth, is a very important part of our own spiritual development.

As with all the concepts in this book, the reader is requested to consider the nature of the opportunities and the information which are presented in order to personally discern whether or not they resonate with his or her pathway towards enLightenment - no matter how bizarre the concept may sound initially.

Star Consciousness, Stargates and Gateways
The Light Beings speak of the high frequency stars and planets in the Universe and stargates, or gateways, which are the access points to the higher frequency dimensions. They refer to some of the high frequency star systems as places which are part of the collective consciousness of the Godhead; - from where the high frequency Light of all the greater collective of non-material soul presences emanated from and which are the existence state we all call Home, because high frequency star consciousness is what we refer to as the state of Bliss.

Bliss can be equated to Nirvana, but Bliss and Heaven should not be confused. According to the Light Beings, the place which the ancient texts referred to as Heaven is an actual star: Antares. In the Ancient Sumerian texts, the higher dimension planet of Nibiru is identified as the planet from which the god-beings came to Earth and it was them who referred to the star of Light as Heaven. By imagining the impact by the arrival of these powerful and highly unusual visitors from the sky on human beings of that time, we can more easily understand why they referred to them as gods or lords. These facts of our ancient history, including the rich details of our outer-planetary visitors, have become somewhat confused over time - as is evidenced in many of the religious texts which are in use today. Although these may be a difficult concepts for modern human beings to accept, this is mainly because we have had little or no exposure to this model of Heaven. These facts may be explored by reading the translations of the Ancient Sumerian Clay Tablets.

Our physical ability to experience the existence of other, high frequency beings who exist in the same Universe as we do, but within a different bandwidth or realm of experience, has to positively correlate with the frequency which we currently resonate with. Theoretically, we can accept that from a harmonic resonance perspective, it *is* possible that we are not yet perceptually able to distinguish the ultra-high frequency states of the various different dimensions - let alone of the one just above us.

We therefore suggest that the reader once again maintains an open mind about this concept. The subject promises to become very interesting from many different perspectives.

Stargates - refer to 'Star Consciousness, Stargates and Gateways'

T
Truth as a Concept
The accuracy, or the facts, of a statement is considered to be the measure of its truth. However, the notion of truth has been misappropriated so often by individuals and groups that people tend to be rather sceptical about any claim to truth. Due to being misled by unscrupulous individuals, our ability to discern truth has become clouded with past disappointments and disillusionment. The legitimacy of claims of truth has been questioned. This is typified by the following comment from a friendly editor, "Personally, I am always scared of people who claim to have 'truth.' There have been just too many Messiahs. As a 'mere mortal' I still like the idea of people who say, 'the truth as I know it.' "It is from this perspective, therefore, that we request the reader views the information contained within this book.

We attempt to explain who the Light Beings are and why they are representatives of Divine Knowledge, but this may be regarded as the point of view of the authors, or the truth as we know it, until such time as the reader is able to discern whether or not the truth as we know it resonates with the truth as she/he knows it - or the truth within. To this end we suggest that readers approach the information within this book with an open mind, knowing that a lot of the information it holds requires a different mindset in order to be read or digested.

To the sceptic we suggest that judgement of the contents of this book is genuinely withheld until further information is gathered. It is only then that an informed, personal decision can be made about the information which it is presented.

2037BC
The year 2037 BC actually relates to a true-time of 2067 BC from where we stand now. This is because the yearly count backwards in time is referenced against our current linear year system of the Gregorian Calendar and the terms AD (*anno Domini*) and BC (before Christ), which is relative to the year that Christ was supposedly born. The true-time end of the Egyptian Era was in 30 BC and it is this date that the Light Beings use as the beginning of so-called post-Light Being Era on Earth. Therefore, we add or subtract these 30 years to the 2037 years Osiris

refers to now - cautioned to do so by both him and Thoth, in communications which date back to 2007. Therefore, we use the term 2037/67BC throughout the book.

U
Unconditional Love
This is a pivotal concept in the process of achieving God-realisation as it naturally implies that individuals who live with this feeling are only thinking, feeling and acting from the basis of compassion and love for all, including the self, and as if the other is the self. Unconditional love creates natural boundaries between people. It is when there is a natural and deep respect for the other that boundaries do not have to be imposed or stipulated. Unconditional love ensures that no act or attitude of abuse is possible. From this we can deduce that if we are acting in unconditional love and being treated in the same manner by others, no *placement* of protective boundaries or limiting conditions is necessary. Merely by observing the type and style of most of the personal and business relationships which many human beings are involved in, it is clear that humanity is still very far off from operating from the basis of this ideal state of love. Boundaries (including rules and regulations) are very important for most people to have in place as a result. Laws are not the remedy or the preventative of chaos, unconditional love is.

Short Definitions
The author's definitions and notes are marked by an asterisk (*) and all other definitions come from WordWeb. The definitions which are listed in this chapter, no matter where they come from, are included in order to help provide a quick, concise overview of a subject, place or person. Some of the inclusions in this section will not necessarily pertain to a particular book, but they may appear elsewhere in the various publications from the authors. Regardless of where they appear, these definitions serve to enhance the understanding of the terms which may be used.

Numerical
21 December: * The predicted end of the Mayan Calendar in the year 2012.
22 December: * Akhenaten's birthday;- the day in 2012 when the presence of Nibiru will be indisputably known.
2012: * The midpoint of the 100 year period at the centre of the Age of Aquarius. The 100 year period has significant spiritual relevance due to the heightened energies of Light which are available to Earth at that time, as with any midpoint of an Age. This is caused by the super-alignment of certain planets and stars relative to Earth. The lead-up to 2012 is a powerful period of cleansings for Earth and her inhabitants in order to tolerate the higher frequencies of Light post 2012. 2012 is the year of completion of our time in the dark, relative to the Fall and the alignment of the

time-clock structures of Thoth with outer-planetary bodies.

2013: * The first year of the higher frequencies of Light, after the cleansing period leading up to 2012. The likelihood of tsunamis, tidal waves, volcanic eruptions and earthquakes increases in this year if Earth cleansings prior to 2012 were incomplete or insufficient - allows Earth and Earthlings to tolerate even higher frequencies of Light in following years.

352: * The number of possible initiations, or knowledge jumps, in the Universe which will take us to the state of being of the Godhead. They consist of major and minor ones.

3rd Dimension: * The lowered resonance state to which Earth 'fell' to when it dropped from the 5th dimension at the end of the Atlantean Era. The reality state where there is an apparent separation of the material and non-material states of being, because we are 'out of contact' with the spiritual dimensions which begin with the 5th.

34 000: * Approximately how long ago, in years, that Atlantean society's war between the Light and the dark created the drop in dimension - from the 5th to the 3rd, for the whole of the planet Earth - when nuclear warheads were exploded, the poles shifted and a Great Deluge ensued.

4 or 5: * The initiation level which some people on Earth have recently managed to achieve. In the past this often took people 50 lifetimes to achieve.

7th Dimension: The dimension which is relatively easy for us to access, once we have progressed through to the 5th dimension in living ascension. Note: the dimensions have a non-linear 'arrangement' but are denoted in numerical form by the Light Beings purely for the purposes of understanding and explanation.

49th Dimension: * The level of the state of being of the Godhead;- linked so closely to the 50th dimension that they are usually termed as one;- may be understood as the inner zone of a single balloon membrane.

4th Dimension: * The resonant frequency state which Earth is in currently and which Earth recovered to after a long time in the 3rd dimension state of resonance.

50th Dimension: * The final level of the state of being of the Godhead;- linked so closely to the 49th dimension that they are usually termed as one;- may be understood as the outer zone of a single balloon membrane.

5th Dimension: * The resonance state, determined by vibration speed, which Earth is in the process of evolving into currently;- the resonance state which Earth was in before the end of the Atlantean Era, the first dimension which is in the beginning stages of being in open communication with the state of being of the Godhead;- the dimension of spiritualised physicality where duality does not exist.

Chapter Sixteen: POSTSCRIPT, DEFINITIONS, BIBLIOGRAPHY AND RECOMMENDED READING

Alphabetical

A

Activation: * The energy-shifting processes that prepare us for major initiations;- they may also be known of as mini-initiations. All in all there are a combination 352 activations and initiations for human beings to go through before ascension.

Akhenaten: Early ruler of Egypt who rejected the old gods and replaced them with sun worship (died in 1358 BC). * First of the four Amarna Kings of the 18th dynasty. Father of Tutankhamun;- husband of Nefertiti;- his name was originally Amenhotep IV, known of as the son of Amenhotep III, although Osiris informs us they were one and the same consciousness. He broke the political stronghold which the powerful priesthood had over the spiritual practices at that time an made himself a lot of enemies as a result - even to the extent that he and the other three Amarna Kings were left of the otherwise complete list of Kings on the wall of the Temple of Seti I in Abydos, Egypt. He was an aspect of Osiris.

Akkadian: An ancient branch of the Semitic languages.

Alignment: (astronomy) apparent meeting or passing of two or more celestial bodies in the same degree of the zodiac.

Amen/Amun: A primeval Egyptian personification of air and breath;- worshipped especially at Thebes. * From the planet Nibiru.

Amenhotep IV: Early ruler of Egypt who rejected the old gods and replaced them with sun worship (died in 1358 BC). * A.k.a. Akhenaten.

Amplitude: (physics) the maximum displacement of a periodic wave.

Andromeda: A constellation in the northern hemisphere between Cassiopeia and Pegasus, contains the Andromeda Galaxy. * Earth serves as a good example to the inhabitants of this galaxy as to why it is not a good idea to continue on a low frequency pathway.

Angel: * A Being of Light. Early humans referred to the outer-planetary visitors who came here, as angels.

Annunaki: * The god-man inhabitants of Earth, originally from. Osiris refers to them as the Nephilim.

Antares: The brightest star in Scorpius. * The place which was referred to as Heaven by the ancients.

Anu: Babylonian god of the sky;- one of the supreme triad including Bel and Ea. * Nibiru-based 'father' of Enki and Enlil.

Apsu: Father of the gods and consort of Tiamat (Babylonian).

Archangel: * A Great Being of Light who has not incarnated on Earth before, yet assists Earth with Light energy, e.g. Michael.

Arcturus: The 4th brightest star and the brightest star in the constellation Boötes, 36 light-years from Earth. * Earth is being assisted by the high frequency Light Beings from this star system with the dimension shift and our living ascension process.

Ascended Master: * An individual who once lived on Earth and achieved ascension;- some come back to Earth regularly to help humans make progress into the Light.

Ascension: A movement upward. * Involves transmutation from one state to another.

Assyria: An ancient kingdom in northern Mesopotamia which is in present-day Iraq.

Assyrian: An extinct language of the Assyrians regarded as a dialect of Akkadian.

Asteroid Belt: The region of interplanetary space between Mars and Jupiter where most asteroids are found. * Shattered portions of the larger planet that Earth was originally a part of.

Astrology: A pseudoscience claiming divination by the positions of the planets and sun and moon. * An important science of the heavens which the ancients used to plot the movement of celestial bodies, relative to Earth. They knew that the different energies influenced the Earth differently and planned their lives accordingly. Only in relatively modern times was this shunned as 'pseudo'.

Astronomy: The branch of physics that studies celestial bodies and the universe as a whole.

Aten: The sun (or solar disc) which was the deity of a monotheistic cult under the Pharaoh Akhenaten. * The representation of the originating energy of Divinity for people on Earth, used as such because people had become used to worshipping something.

Atenism: * This was the first religion in the world. It incorporated the original Osirian teachings about Divinity, Love, Light and Truth. Atenism was formed to replace the dismantled Cult of Amun because those teachings, although they were originally based on truth, had been so badly distorted by the priesthood in their pursuit of Earthly power that they no longer served humanity in the pursuit of truth.

Atlantis: * Refers to a period of time which stretches back many hundreds of thousands of years. It was a time which was characterised both by great Light on Earth, under the stewardship of the god-like beings or Angels, and by the encroaching darkness of the fallen Angels. After the society has collapsed to a low enough point and against the principles of Light, Atlantean society's leaders detonated nuclear warheads which created devastation. This occurred alongside issues of the Nibiru-created pulls on the magnetic field of the planet and resulted in climate change and a pole shift which created floods, earthquakes, undersea volcanoes and the obliteration of almost all life on Earth, about 34 000 years ago. Santorini Island in Greece is one of the few remaining remnants of the great landmass of that civilisation.

Ay (also Aye): * the vizier, or military advisor, of Pharaoh Akhenaten. He was the last of the four Amarna Kings. He was instrumental in managing the successful escape of the royal family of Tutankhamun to India when it became too dangerous for this powerful family to remain in Egypt. He was involved in ensuring the correct documentation was contained in the tomb which was labelled as being that of Tutankhamun and placing a stand-in in the sarcophagus. Humanity were supposed to find that information which related to our beginnings, Earth history, spirituality and our connection to the stars many thousands of years later.

Atom: (physics and chemistry) the smallest component of an element having the chemical properties of the element.

Aura: * The field of light, or the light body, which surrounds the human body, created and influenced by the energy and alignment of the chakras.

B

Babylon: The chief city of ancient Mesopotamia and capital of the ancient kingdom of Babylonia.

Babylonian: The ideographic and syllabic writing system in which the ancient Babylonian language was written.

Betelgeuse: The second brightest star in Orion.

Black Hole: A region of space resulting from the collapse of a star, extremely high gravitational field. * The intense, energy area which is created when an energy form either devolves back into the void or emerges from it.

Bliss: * A state of extreme happiness, the feeling when in open communication with the Godhead.

Blue-print: * The original plan, shape and state of our souls when we emanated out of the collective consciousness of the Godhead into the Monad state of being - hence 'Monadic Blueprint'.

Brothers of Darkness: * This is a collective term which is used to describe beings, whether current human beings, or ancient god-beings, whose resonant frequencies caused, firstly, duality, secondly, the Fall of Atlantis and Man and, thirdly, perpetuated the fallen state of existence for humans incarnating into the 3rd dimension of separated physicality for thousands and thousands of years. Any behaviour, by any person which is not in the light may be termed as belonging to the Brothers of Darkness. See 'Dark Brother.'

Buddha: * The Light Being who Osiris calls the 'Planetary Logos';- over lights the Earth and humanity and supports our shifting consciousness to a higher level.

C

Canis Major: A constellation southeast of Orion, which contains Sirius.

Capstone: * The tip of the Great Pyramid that used to glow with tremendous Light;- the conduit through which outer-planetary Light streams into the planet;- the more it glows, the more Light we can receive into Earth.

Cell: (biology) The basic structural and functional unit of all organisms;- they may exist as independent units of life (as in monads) or may form colonies or tissues as in higher plants and animals.

Cellular memory: * The vibrations within our cells create a specific holding pattern of that cell - its cellular memory. It is from this vibration-created holding pattern that our cells reproduce each day. When we change that vibration we change the expression of the cell. Great healing and bodily change results.

Chakra: * The series of energy centres which are arranged along the central meridian of the body;- considered to be 7 major ones in total, but Osiris has encouraged the awareness and energising of a further 5 above the head and the transformation of the energy of the lower 3 so that we become heart-based.

Christ Consciousness: * The consciousness of the Godhead as expressed through the original Christed Being (Tutankhamun) and that of all others that followed on with that particular consciousness from that point onwards.

Crystal: A solid formed by the solidification of a chemical and having a highly regular atomic structure. * Crystals assist with intensifying all forms of Light and are used for healing and manifestation.

Crystalline: Transmitting light;- able to be seen through with clarity.

Cygnus: A constellation in the northern hemisphere between Pegasus and Draco in the Milky Way;- contains a black hole.

D

Dark Brother: * This is Enlil, who was originally a great Light Being when he arrived on Earth from Nibiru. He fell into a low frequency state of darkness in the very early days on Earth. He was the 'brother' of Enki (the Siriun Being of Light who was working on creation and the enLightenment of the planet Earth right from the beginning). Aspects of the original soul of Enlil regularly reincarnate on Earth for the opportunity to recover their lost Light, just as other souls do. Some portions of this original Enlil soul have recovered their Light, but many have not. Those who have not and who are incarnate on Earth, continue to perpetuate the state of darkness on Earth. As of August 2009, we were informed by Isis and Thoth that Enlil is working his way back to the Light, through redemption of the physical self.

Darkness: 1. Absence of light or illumination. 2. An un-illuminated area, "he moved off into the darkness". 3. Absence of moral or spiritual values, "the powers of darkness". 4. An unenlightened state, "his lectures dispelled the darkness". * Where high frequency Light is absent;- a state of being awaiting Illumination into the Light.

Dark night of the soul: * The experience of plunging into the depths of despair during a clearing or healing process;- precedes balance;- the opposite extreme of bliss.

Dark side of the Moon: * The 'other side' of the moon which, from Earth's perspective, is never illuminated by the Sun.

Deity: * A god-being by another name.
Dimension: A construct whereby objects or individuals can be distinguished. * A specific realm of existence for consciousness, ranging from the 3rd to the 50th dimension, may be physical or non-physical. Delineated by the harmonics of an octave, or frequencies.
Detonate: Cause to burst with a violent release of energy.
Divine: Emanating from God. * That high frequency Light which is contained within all human beings, within the DNA.
DNA: (biochemistry) a long linear polymer found in the nucleus of a cell and formed from nucleotides and shaped like a double helix;- associated with the transmission of genetic information;- "DNA is the king of molecules." * Our DNA contains the structures which resonate with the high frequencies of the Light of God-consciousness;- our inherent Divinity lies within our DNA structures;- the physical structures that contain the Hu-essence. We are presently changing our DNA in a rapid evolution process.

E
Ea: the Babylonian god of wisdom;- counterpart of the Sumerian Enki;- as one of the supreme triad including Anu and Bel he was assigned control of the watery element. * Usually known of as Enki or Enki Ptah.
Earth: The 3rd planet from the Sun;- the planet we live on. * A body of Light which was originally a part of a much larger entity.
Ecliptic: The great circle representing the apparent annual path of the Sun;- the plane of the Earth's orbit around the Sun;- makes an angle of about 23 degrees with the equator.
El-Menia: * small town in Upper Egypt, close to Akhenaten's ancient city of el-Amarna.
Electricity: A physical phenomenon associated with stationary or moving electrons and protons.
Electromagnetic: Pertaining to or exhibiting magnetism produced by electric charge in motion.
Elements: Any of the more than 100 known substances (of which 92 occur naturally) that cannot be separated into simpler substances and that singly or in combination constitute all matter.
Enki: Water god and god of wisdom, counterpart of the Akkadian Ea.* He was a Siriun who arrived on Earth millions of years ago, as the first being on Earth, for the purposes of the further enLightenment of the planet, via the planet Nibiru;- an emissary of Light from the Godhead;- he was known as Enki Ptah when he returned to Earth in Ancient Egyptian times;- he was the creator god who originally genetically engineered god-men and the human species - who were originally intended for use

in the gold mines of Earth.

Enlil: God of the air and king of the Sumerian gods. * So-called "brother' of Enki who was supposed to participate in the enLightenment and upliftment programme on Earth, but fell from grace towards the end of ancient Lemurian times due to his desire to have power on Earth and his resultant inappropriate genetic experimentation. In Atlantean times known as Satankhare, or who moderns call the fallen Angel Lucifer.

Enlightenment: * The search for, or the attainment of, a great state of Light which incorporates open communication with, and conscious links to, the Godhead. Characterised by more parts of our Divine DNA being 'switched on'.

Entity: * A 'thing' of a specific, non-Earthly energy which attaches to a human being through a hole in the aura;- discarnate energy which seeks the incarnate experience through human beings;- seeks 'good' hosts who have lowered their vibrations to a low frequency due to poor lifestyle choices (drug or alcohol abuse for example).

Evolution: (biology) the sequence of events involved in the evolutionary development of a species or taxonomic group of organisms. * The process which the human species is always engaged in all the time. At this time in Earth's history we are currently in the process of the most rapid change to another state - characterised by more Light within our DNA and different abilities, such as better immune systems and highly developed psychic skills.

Extra-terrestrials: * Outer-planetary visitors who come to our planet for the purpose of growth, information and experience;- they are not all benign and may be dangerous for us to deal with;- many of them just want to learn and observe;- they come to Earth in physical space vehicles, as opposed to Light Vehicles;- they begin to follow their own Light relative to the amount of emotion they feel in their hearts;- very different to the ultra-terrestrials of the Godhead consciousness.

Eye of Horus: * The name for the gateway of consciousness as we pass from a lower dimension to a higher one. The consciousness ascends, through this gateway, to a higher dimension from physical Earth.

F

Faerie/Fairy (devic energy): * The consciousness of human beings who came to Earth from the Pleiades;- playful, impish, childlike energy.

Fall: * The shifted dimension downwards, from the 5th to the 3rd dimension, which was the result of the dramatic drop in frequency which the events of the nuclear war caused, approximately 34 000 years ago at the end of the Atlantean Era.

Flower of Life: * The ancient pattern discovered on the walls of the Seti I Temple in Abydos, Egypt;- a sacred geometrical shape which depicts creation out of the state if consciousness of the Godhead.

Frequency: the number of occurrences within a given time period.

Funnel: * The physical shape of the wormhole at both ends;- a conical shape which has a wide end and a narrow end which are connected at the narrow ends;- used as a access channel between the two open ended funnels;- a wormhole system.

G

Gas giants: any of the four outermost planets in the solar system, much larger than Earth and gaseous in nature (like Jupiter).

god: any supernatural being worshipped as controlling some part of the world or some aspect of life or who is the personification of a force.* What the powerful Ancient Egyptian Beings of Light became know of when they lived on Earth (female = goddess).

God: the supernatural being conceived as the perfect and omnipotent and omniscient originator and ruler of the Universe;- the object of worship in monotheistic religions. * Human beings have come to believe that there is only one God, a being. The truth is that God-realisation is a state of being, a consciousness of brilliant, super-luminal Light. This highly ordered state of Light is super-luminal. It is the Source. It is Divine.

Gravitational field: a field of force surrounding a body of finite mass.

Great Deluge: 1. A heavy rain. 2. The rising of a body of water and its overflowing onto normally dry land. * The great flooding of water which occurred at the time of the Atlantean Era nuclear explosion about 34 000 years ago;- concurrent with the pole shift and nuclear explosions of that time too. It resulted in the flooding and destruction of most of the landmass which was known of and inhabited at the time of Atlantis. Most of life on Earth was obliterated at a result.

H

Heaven: any place of complete bliss and delight and peace. * The name given to the star Antares, and to no other star.

Helios: ancient god of the Sun;- drove his chariot across the sky each day;- identified with Roman Sol. * Supportive Light Being of the Sun.

Hermes: (Greek mythology) messenger and herald of the gods;- god of commerce and cunning and invention and theft;- identified with Roman Mercury. * Thoth.

Higher Self: * The next intensity, or integration, level - upwards from the 4th dimension - for soul;- perceivable in the raised resonance state of the 5th dimension;- the state of reintegrated being which is below the Overself - which itself is below the Monad level of being.

Horus: Egyptian solar god with the head of a falcon, the son of Osiris and Isis. * One of the true Trinity - Osiris, Isis and Horus - which emanated out from the creator-god Enki Ptah..

Hu: * The god-essence, portion of the hu-man being, of outer-planetary origin.

Human Beings: * The members of the species, Homo sapiens, to which men and women belong;- were genetically engineered to be part god-being and part primate, by virtue of their DNA.

I

Immortals: * The name of the god-beings in Ancient Greece.
Incarnation: * The embodiment of the soul in a human body on Earth.
Initiation: * A knowledge jump or movement up from one level to another.
Intention: * Goal;- purpose;- or objective.
Iron: a heavy ductile magnetic metallic element, is silver-white in pure form but readily rusts, used in construction and tools and armament, plays a role in the transport of oxygen by the blood.
Isis: Egyptian goddess of fertility, daughter of Geb, sister and wife of Osiris. * One of the Trinity - which includes Osiris, Isis and Horus.
Issa: * Tutankhamun was known by this name in India after he left Egypt;- the name commonly ascribed to the being Jesus.

J

Jesus: * The individual who became known of in Biblical stories as Jesus was John the Baptist, a devout follower of the teachings of Christ. The true miracle-maker we call Christ was Tutankhamun, 'son' of Akhenaten and Nefertiti.
John the Baptist: * A Gnostic who was a proponent of pre-Catholic Christianity;- the man whose life was used to create the character of Jesus;- often known by his soul name of Sananda;- took one more lifetime after his documented one to achieve ascension.
Jupiter: the largest planet and the 5th from the sun, has many satellites and is one of the brightest objects in the night sky.

K

Karma: * The 'hangover' lessons from various past lifetimes which are lodged in our soul, or consciousness, as a low frequency vibration, and which become part of our cellular memory when our soul moves into a human body at the point of birth or that we gather in our current lifetime. This is the low resonance which we try to clear out of our consciousness/spiritual bodies and physical bodies in order to raise our vibration and achieve living ascension. Being clear of Karma means not having to enter the reincarnation cycle of human life on Earth, unless by choice, in future.
Khem: * The name which Ancient Egypt was know by in ancient times, so-named by some of the god-beings who arrived there and who were known of as the Zem (they originally came from another galaxy to Earth, according to Isis). More of this information will be available in future publications.

L

Lakshmi: Hindu goddess of fortune and prosperity. * One of the Light Beings supporting Earth at this time of the Return.

Lemuria: * Refers to an Era which ended around 300 000 years ago, but ran concurrently with the Atlantean Era for a while. It was a time when Enlil created a lot of darkness on Earth and formally became known of as the Brother of Darkness. Lemuria was Enlil's domain.

Light: 1. A divine presence believed by Quakers to enlighten and guide the soul. 2. (physics) electromagnetic radiation that can produce a visual sensation. * The nature of all things, including the Godhead and human beings.

Light worker: * A person who works to further the information and knowledge of the Godhead, in Light.

Living Ascension: * The process which allows physical beings, such as human beings, to shift dimension (from the 4th to the 5th) in the process of reincorporating with the spiritual worlds. It is a process of spiritualised physicality where existence is characterised by a raised resonance. This allows for a higher dimension experience. The movement upwards of the physical body into a higher resonant frequency without having to physically die to achieve this, reunification of the physical and spiritual states of being, in the 5th dimension, the 'Return' to the state of consciousness of the Atlanteans.

Logos: * A Logos is a Light Being who chooses to support a planet or a star, with their over lighting energy, as part of their pathway of service.

M

Magic: Any art that invokes supernatural powers. * Synonymous with the word 'miracle', a function of high frequency Light. We use the magic of the Light for manifestation because all life comes from Light of one frequency or another.

Manifestation: * The materialisation of that which is visualised and desired, through the process of holding oneself in the high resonance state of unconditional love, when unstressed and unattached to the outcome. Un-attachment is critical in manifestation, but conversely when we know that we can manifest anything we desire, at any time, we will not be attached to anything we have. This gentle are is the cure-all to all the evils of society, including theft.

Magnetic: Having the properties of a magnet, i.e. of attracting iron or steel.

Marduk: The chief Babylonian god, his consort was Sarpanitu.* He was also know of as Ra, 'great grandson' of Amun. The most important thing about this Ancient Egyptian god-being is that when he came to Earth he was from the planetary consciousness of the planet Nibiru. As this he was known of as Marduk. He was not always aligned with the Light.

Mars: A small reddish planet that is the 4th from the sun and is periodically visible to the naked eye, minerals rich in iron cover its surface and are responsible for its characteristic colour. * A truly dead planet, made that way by the misbehaviour of its inhabitants in very ancient times. Osiris has warned us not to continue on the pathway which could create this status for Earth - nuclear war.

Meditation: * A state of consciousness when the person has stilled the mind;- moving past and through the confines of the human mind into another state of consciousness where time and thought do not exist, but everything is known or felt;- an altered state of consciousness.

Mercury: The smallest planet and the nearest to the sun.

Minerals: Solid homogeneous inorganic substances occurring in nature having a definite chemical composition.

Monad: 1. (chemistry) an atom having a valence of one. 2. A singular metaphysical entity from which material properties are said to derive. * The individualised state of being which emanates out of the Godhead into existence on a particular planet or star;- the Oneness of Being from where our souls emanate; is the blueprint of our Divine selves. We strive to reintegrate first with our Higher Self, then the Overself and then the Monad.

Moses: (Old Testament) the Hebrew prophet who led the Israelites from Egypt across the Red sea on a journey known as the Exodus, Moses received the Ten Commandments from God on Mount Sinai. * According to Osiris, Moses is none other than the Pharaoh Akhenaten - see the Osman book for more details.

N

Nebula: An immense cloud of gas (mainly hydrogen) and dust in interstellar space.

Nefertiti: Queen of Egypt and wife of Akhenaten (14th century BC). * An aspect of Isis.

Neptune: A giant planet with a ring of ice particles, the 8th planet from the sun it is the most remote of the gas giants.

Nibiru: * The planet which has a very long elliptical orbit around the Earth that takes some 3 600 (known of as a shar) years to complete. The Siriun Light Beings first worked on the advancement of this planet, in the 5th dimension, before they came to Earth from there in the most ancient of Earth times as well as at the time of Ancient Egypt. This is the planet which has a profound influence on the energies of Earth at the moment and it will come into full sight in the year 2047. Its powerful gravitational pull is already exerting an influence on Earth and her magnetic field which is responsible for creating some of the 'upsets' and cleansings in the lead up to 2012.

Nirvana: Any place of complete Bliss and delight and peace, (Hinduism and Buddhism) the beatitude that transcends the cycle of reincarnation, characterized by the extinction of desire and suffering and individual consciousness.

Non-physical: lacking substance or reality, incapable of being touched or seen.
Nothingness: * The disordered, undifferentiated 'place' of low frequencies of Light and Sound which resonate with frequencies which are lower than those of the 3rd dimension. It is a state of non-individual, non-conscious existence which is separated from the Universe by virtue of the difference in potential between high resonance of the Universe and its own low resonance. A state of non-individuality which individual souls may disintegrate into if their resonance with Light drops too low.
Nuclear fission: A nuclear reaction in which a massive nucleus splits into smaller nuclei with the simultaneous release of energy. * Such as happened at the time of the Fall.
Nuclear fusion: A nuclear reaction in which nuclei combine to form more massive nuclei with the simultaneous release of energy. * As happened at the time of the 'Big Bang' event of the creation of the Universe.
Nucleotides: A phosphoric ester of a nucleoside, the basic structural unit of nucleic acids (DNA or RNA).

O
Orion: A constellation on the equator east of Taurus, contains Betelgeuse and Rigel. * Planet of Osiris;- aligns with the Great Pyramid on 11.11.11.
Osiris: Egyptian god of the underworld and judge of the dead, husband and sister of Isis, father of Horus. * One of the Trinity - which includes Osiris, Isis and Horus.
Overself: * The next intensity level of soul, above the Higher Self, below the Monad, in the 5th dimension.

P
Pathway of Light: * The pathway of the Godhead consciousness;- high frequency pathway;- the pathway towards enlightenment.
Pathway of Return: * The pathway of expansion and upliftment which consciousness, or soul, follows to reclaim the former 5th dimension (or Atlantean) pre-Fall glory. We return to the point of our departure from the Light.
Pathway of Sirius: * The pathway we follow, from Earth, to reclaim our Monadic Oneness of Being, the pathway the star system of Sirius took to reclaim its own Light long, long ago.
Pegasus: Contains the Andromeda galaxy.
Physical: Involving the body as distinguished from the mind or spirit
Physics: The science of matter and energy and their interactions.
Planet: (astronomy) any of the nine large celestial bodies in the solar system that revolve around the sun and shine by reflected light, Mercury, Venus, Earth, Mars, Jupiter, Saturn, Uranus, Neptune, and Pluto in order of their proximity to the sun, viewed from the constellation Hercules, all the planets rotate around the sun in a

counter clockwise direction. * The Light Beings state that all planets are actually stars.

Pleiades: A star cluster in the constellation Taurus. * The star system which many human beings have passed through on their cosmic travels to and from Earth, specifically via Peru as the Ancient Mayans;- the star system from whence many of the new children will come through to get to Earth. This is the star system of the devic (fairy, or elemental) energy and it is one of the star clusters which is nearest to Earth.

Pluto: A small planet and the farthest known planet from the sun, has the most elliptical orbit of all the planets.

Portals (of Light): * High frequency places on Earth which are highly energised areas of Light. When we are in these areas they will naturally stimulate us to vibrate at higher frequencies. They can be used for outer-planetary communication and connection and for a dimension-shifting experience. Outer-planetary high frequency Light beams into Earth through these portals and the Light Beings use them for easy communication.

Psychic abilities: * Super-sensory abilities which develop as individuals raise their resonance:- typically clairaudience (psychic hearing), clairsentience (psychic sensing) and clairvoyance (psychic sight).

R

Radiation: The spontaneous emission of a stream of particles or electromagnetic rays in nuclear decay.

Radio: An electronic receiver that detects and demodulates and amplifies transmitted signals, and, a communication system based on broadcasting electromagnetic waves.

Reptilian: * An individual who looks like a human being, but has more lower frequencies than higher frequencies activated, which activates more of the 'reptilian brain' within the mid-brain. This energy and terminology is characteristic of those who do not feel any emotion whatsoever and who are desirous of war. These individuals may include outer-planetary entity-infested human beings. Emotions of love reverse and shift this condition.

Resistor: An electrical device that resists the flow of electrical current.

Re-incarnation: * The re-birth or re-embodiment of the soul into another human body;- a new life time.

Resonance: A vibration of large amplitude produced by a relatively small vibration near the same frequency of vibration as the natural frequency of the resonating system.

Rigel: The brightest star in Orion.

Rostau: * "*It is the etheric field of consciousness and light*," according to Thoth;- type of energy platform, in the etheric;- when Orion lines up with the Great

Pyramid, then whatever is held in the etheric, that which holds the architectural energy of whatever it is that is required to be created on Earth (such as the Great Pyramid or mankind) is easily filtered through into the consciousness of those on Earth via this platform of energy;- the use of etheric energy formations that come from other star systems explains the formation of great structures and the miraculous on Earth.

S
Sananda: * The soul name of John the Baptist.
Sanat Kumara: * The Light Being of Venus who is assisting us with shifting ourselves into the state of unconditional love so that our own vibration speed can be high enough to resonate with the open consciousness of the Godhead. The colour associated with this Light Being and this planet is magenta.
Saturn: A giant planet that is surrounded by three planar concentric rings of ice particles, the 6th planet from the sun.
Serapis: Osiris was known of by this name in Ancient Greece, although it was usually spelt 'Sarapis';- Osiris originally spoke to the working group under this name, until they were aligned with a higher frequency energy of Osiris.
Sirius: The brightest star in the sky, in Canis Major. * Star system of the Monad of many human beings. This is Home for many of us as well as the home of Isis and many of the god-beings who came to progress Earth's enLightenment.
Smenkhare: * Brother of Pharaoh Akhenaten. Biblically he was known of as Aaron. One of the four Amarna kings of Egypt.
Solar system: The sun with the celestial bodies that revolve around it in its gravitational field.
Soul: The immaterial part of a person, the actuating cause of an individual life. * The Light presence of consciousness, incarnate within a human body. The 'I' that I know myself to be.
Soul-group: * The group of people who all belong to the same, original Monad;- usually all the members of your family and some close friends belong to this group.
Soul-mate: * A particularly close member of the soul group;- there are many levels of soul mates, from all the levels between where we are now and the Monad presence;- ultimately all human beings are all soul mates because we all emanated out from the Godhead consciousness
Sound: The audible part of a transmitted signal.
Spiritual: Concerned with or affecting the spirit or soul, and, lacking material body or form or substance. * Currently unseen by us because we are in the lower dimensions. Once we transcend these and resonate with the 5th dimension, we easily see the form and substance of that dimension.
Spirit guide: * A being who is in the non-material state of Spirit who offers his/her

services as a guide to a human being on Earth;- many different levels of a spirit guide, from our dearly departed relatives to the highest level of all of the Light Beings;- they resonate with the various different dimensions, depending on the state of their own Light;- we ideally want to work with the highest state of consciousness possible in order to be assured of the best guidance and information.

Star: (astronomy) a celestial body of hot gases that radiates energy derived from thermonuclear reactions in the interior. * The origin of life and of Light and or o urselves, as human beings. The Light Beings come from the stars.

Star tetraheden: : * The sacred geometric shape of Light;- looks like a Star of David, or Solomon's Seal, in one plane;- a multi-faceted set of two inter-locking, opposite-orientated pyramids;- a protective shield of Light;- a handy high frequency space we put around ourselves daily to assist with communication with the Light Beings.

Sumerian: Of or relating to ancient Sumer or its inhabitants

Sun: A typical star that is the source of light and heat for the planets in the solar system. * The supportive Light Body for Earth, physically and spiritually.

Super-Alignment: * Refers to the unusual alignment of a significant number of high frequency planets and stars with Earth;- the energy of each planet and star in the super-alignment with Earth compounds in connectivity to the other ones.

Super-Luminal Light: * Extremely high frequency Light that human beings are not yet able to perceive;- the nature of the Light of the Godhead beings.

T

Tel el-Amarna: * The place where the Pharaoh Akhenaten lived and set up as his capital in place of Thebes - hence the name 'Amarna Kings'. His reign was followed by the remaining four Amarna Kings - Tutankhamun, Smenkhare, Aye and Horemheb. The 18th dynasty kings of Ancient Egypt ended with the reign of Horemheb.

The Godhead: * The unified state of consciousness of the Oneness of All Being which is the collective of all so-called God-realised beings that is characterised by the consciousness of unconditional love and Bliss. The dimension of the Godhead is understood to be in the 49th and/or 50th dimensions. This is the level we seek to resonate with.

Thebes: An ancient Egyptian city on the Nile River that flourished from the 22nd century BC to the 18th century BC, today the archaeological remains include many splendid temples and tombs. * Modern day Luxor.

Thoth: Egyptian deity with the head of an ibis, god of wisdom and learning and the arts, scribe of the gods. * Wisdom teacher and scribe of spiritual wisdom. build the pyramids in Atlantean times, linked these up with the energy-based time-clock system so that in the future human consciousness could keep pace and be ready for the time of ascension and the end of our time in the lower dimensions, which is

2012. He wrote many tablets and manuscripts, some of which we are still to rediscover, including the vibrationally powerful 'The Emerald Tablets of Thoth'.

Tiamat: * This is the name of the larger planet which Earth was originally a part of, before an outer planetary collision broke her into many piece - some small and some large.

Transmutation: An act that changes the form or character or substance of something. *The act of the shift of energy from one form to another, such as from the lower 4th dimension energies into the higher state of the 5th dimension energies. This is achieved by shifting of the lower energies into the higher energy of the feeling in the heart.

Tutankhamun: Pharaoh of Egypt around 1358 BC, his tomb was discovered almost intact by Howard Carter in 1922. * He was the son of the Pharaoh Akhenaten and Queen Nefertiti, according to Osiris, and this information was found in the so-called tomb of Tutankhamun when it was opened early in the 20th century. Hence the poor survival rate of those who were involved in this tomb-opening! This information was given to the American government by the Egyptian government and it has since been hidden away in the Vatican vaults. It is vastly important documentation for the entire world as it details, as ancient papyri documents, information about the outer-planetary god-beings, their connection to Divinity, who Christ really was, and what we are doing on Earth. The information in these papyri potentially disarms the power of most world religions and most powerful world governments. As a result many of these institutions have a vested interest in ensuring that they stay hidden. The author Ahmed Osman details some of this information in his book 'Jesus in the House of the Pharaohs.' This Egyptian King was an aspect of Horus. He was the true Christ.

U

Ultra-terrestrials: * These are visitors to our planet who come from the heart of the Godhead;- who work through their hearts;- work with humanity to assist them to unlock their Light so that they can move forwards on the pathway of Light and love;- such as the Light Beings who communicate with us in this book;- they are very different to extra-terrestrials;- they travel in vehicles of Light.

Universe: Everything that exists anywhere in this system (also Cosmos).

Uranus: A giant planet with a ring of ice particles, the 7th planet from the Sun has a blue-green colour and many satellites.

V

Veil: * The so-called resonance-related division between the 4th and the 5th dimensions that creates the apparent illusion that while in physicality we are disconnected from the realms of the Godhead, or the spiritual dimensions. It is this division we transcend in the living ascension process.

Venus: The second nearest planet to the sun, visible from Earth as an early 'morning star' or an 'evening star'. * The place from where the Light Being Sanat Kumara is supporting us with the 5th dimension communications with the other Light Beings, during our living ascension processes. It is a planet of unconditional love which resonates with the colour magenta.

Vibration: (physics) a regular periodic variation in value about a mean.

Visualisation: * A meditation.

Void: * The place of random, undifferentiated, non-conscious energy, outside of the Universe, which is the place of origin of creation - which is usually a random event.

Vortex: 1. The shape of something rotating rapidly. 2. A powerful circular current of water (usually the result of conflicting tides). * The shape which is created by the incoming and outgoing spiralling energies through the hourglass shape, or the figure-of-8 shape, of the wormhole system.

W

Warhead: The front part of a guided missile or rocket or torpedo that carries the nuclear or explosive charge or the chemical or biological agents

Wave: (physics) a movement up and down or back and forth.

Wormhole: * A theoretical concept of science which apparently describes the linking system between different dimensions;- a linking system between dimensions;- an extended portion of the one low frequency dimension with another, higher resonant frequency dimension at the other end, connected by a common area or 'thread';- is shaped like an hourglass with open-ended funnels;- the energy system we use in the 4th dimension to access the higher dimensions.

Z

Zodiac: A belt-shaped region in the heavens on either side to the ecliptic, divided into 12 constellations, or signs, for astrological purposes. * As we progress and trace our pathway back towards the time of the Fall at the end of the Atlantean Ear, we effectively go 'backwards' through the Zodiac, back to the point of our departure. This is the movement of our Return.

Bibliography (Books, CDs and DVDs) & Recommended Reading

The authors, books, CDs or DVDs which are mentioned are not reference books for the authors, because the information in this book is of a channelled-from-Spirit nature. However, these publications are pertinent, because many different people have researched and written about some of the subjects mentioned by the Light Beings. Therefore, they provide valuable peripheral information about many of the subjects which we have brought up or discussed in this book. It is always helpful to do further research about many of the subjects which we can only touch on in this publication. Good examples of areas for additional research are the translations and discussions of the clay tablets by the author Zecharia Sitchin. The work of this author is particularly important in terms of his extensive modern documentation of the historical evidence about the outer-planetary beings that lived on Earth in very ancient times, where they came from and what they were doing here. Although there is an enormous amount of this information available, not many people are aware of it.

Therefore, as with all books, if the subject matter resonates with you then you will read it with interest. It is also interesting to take note of the fact that a lot of the information in this book can actually be verified by checking other sources. Osiris' communications provide us with a handy reference check with which we can establish greater truth about our Earth history and he provides us with handy hints about where to look for some of the information.

Sadly, some of the most important documents which would give us all the information we could wish for and which details our Earth history and our origins as souls, are hidden away in various vaults around the world. These documents have been deliberately kept from the eyes of humanity, but their contents are being released in other formats by the Light Beings regardless of this. It is with interest therefore, to see the wonderful spiritual information in some of the listed publications. Ultimately, it does not matter how spiritual truth is delivered and it is true to say that whether people consider themselves to be highly intuitive, switched on, a meticulous researcher and scholar or a conscious channel for Spirit is irrelevant. Only the essence of truth is relevant. Truth is felt, not necessarily intellectually understood.

The books or DVDs of the authors listed below contain extensive and impressive bibliographies and recommended reading lists. Should any particular subject matter be of interest to the reader, it is recommended that these lists are looked into and that the website of the particular author is visited for more information.

Books
B
Bach, Richard:	One
Bays, Brandon:	The Journey
Braden, Gregg:	The God Code
	Fractual Time
Byrne, Rhonda:	The Secret (Book and DVD)

C
Chopra, Deepak:	Ageless Body, Timeless Mind

D
Doreal, Dr:	The Emerald Tablets of Thoth-the-Atlantean

G
Gardner, Laurence:	Ancient Secrets of the Lost Ark

H
Hawkin, David R:	Power vs. Force
Hawkings, Stephen:	The Universe in a Nutshell
Louise L Hay:	You Can Heal Your Life

M
MacTaggart, Lynne:	The Field
	The Intention Experiment
Melchizedek, Drunvalo:	The Ancient Secrets of the Flower of Life: Vol.1
Mishlove, Jeffrey:	The Holographic Brain with Karl Pribram, MA, Ph.D

O
Osman, Ahmed:	Jesus in the House of the Pharaohs

P
Perkins, John:	Confessions of an Economic Hitman
Phillips, Graham:	Act of God
Pribam, Karl:	Brain and Mathematics

S
Schwartz, Gary:	The G.O.D Experiments

Sitchin, Zecharia:	Earth Chronicles
	Genesis Revisited
	The Lost Book of Enki
	The Wars of Gods and Men (and others)
Smith, Jeffrey M.:	Seeds of Deception
Solomon, Jane & Grant:	Harry Oldfield's Invisible Universe
Spalding, Baird T:	The Life and Teachings of the Masters of the Far East

T

Temple, Robert:	The Sirius Mystery
Tiller, William:	Conscious Acts of Creation: The Emergence of a New Physics

Z

Zukav, Gary:	The Seat of the Soul

CDs

Braden, Gregg and Goldman, Jonathan:	The Divine Name of God - Sounds of the God Code (CD)

DVDs

Byrne, Rhonda:	The Secret
Fricke, Ron:	Baraka (non-narrative movie)
Zeitgeist	Zeitgeist: The Movie
	Zeitgeist: Addendum

Websites of Interest

www.affs.org	- future science information
www.ahmedosman.com	- historical information
www.ancientwisdom.co.za	- publisher's website
www.phoenixhealth.co.za	- vibration enhancing products
www.sitchin.com	- clay tablets information
www.stargateway.co.za	- channelled meditations, courses
www.wordweb.co.uk	- online dictionary
www.wikipedia.org/wiki/Enki	- information about Enki
www.youtube.com	- Zecharia Sitchin video interviews
www.zeitgeistmovie.com	- information

End of Book One

Forthcoming books communicating knowledge and
information from the Light Beings:

Living Ascension: Lessons from Osiris
Balancing Masculine and Feminine Energies: Lessons from Isis
Choose Your Pathway: Lessons from Isis
Information, Communications and Lessons
from Thoth, Horus and Enki

Please check our websites regularly.
The new information will be uploaded and
made available in both e-book and hard copy formats
as soon as they are completed.

Visit
**www.stargateway.co.za or www.ancientwisdom.co.za
email: info@ancientwisdom.co.**

Made in the USA
Monee, IL
01 February 2022